Pats On the Head for HARE OF THE DOG:

"It certainly deserves a place on every Hasher's bookshelf." – *Gordon 'Prof' Williams, UK Hashtorian, Bicester H3.*

"Brilliant!!! So evocative I can only read a few pages at a time."
– *Richard 'Gunga Dick' Murphy, ex-Singapore H3 (mid-60's), Barnes H3 (possibly the world's first American Hasher).*

"An excellent job well done. Your best yet." – *Bill Panton, KL H3 since 1958, founder Washington DC H3.*

"The best one I've seen so far. Bravo!" – *Likk'mm, Generic Swiss Hasher.*

"Well done – Magic above will be pleased there is someone to carry on his work." – *Chee Bye, Malaysia, InterHash Survivor since '78.*

"Most entertaining. A handsome looking book, bringing back very many happy memories of Hashmen I had long forgotten." – *Harry Howell, KL H3 '58, Sydney H3.*

"Great read – I haven't put the bloody thing down for a couple of days."
– *Pissoles, African/European/Kiwi Hasher at large.*

"Great bathroom reading." – *Fungus Amungus, USA.*

"A great achievement." – *Brian 'The Gent' Orton, founding member Durban H3, South Africa.*

"Fantastic. Incredible." – *Honkers, Hobart H5, Australia.*

"Love it!" – *Shoe, Florida, USA.*

"Overachieving bastards!!! Congrats." – *Cum Artist, USA.*

"A great talent for picking hot subjects!" – *Nury Vittachi, Far Eastern Economic Review, Author.*

For more reviews see www.hash-onon.com

HARE OF THE DOG

**History, Humour and Hell-raising
from the
Hash House Harriers**

Compiled and edited by
Stu 'The Colonel' Lloyd

Barking Mad Press
Purveyors of low-brow literature to the gentry since late last century.

Boring stuff about the publishers …

Limited Edition: only 1,800,000 copies lovingly handcrafted by virgin typesetters and bookbinders in the misty highlands of Malaysia.

This book is number **000,001**

Available in paperback or double-ply perforated roll. Printed on 100% recyclable paper.

Published by Captions of Industry Pty Ltd
PO Box 350
Pymble, 2073
Sydney, Australia.

Email: Captions@bigpond.net.au
Website: www.hardshipposting.com

Legal advisers: Goh, Fook, Youssef and Partners, Kuala Lumpur.
Senior partners: Soh Su Mee, Eu Wang Kah.

Lloyd, Stuart, 1962– .
Hare of the Dog : history, humour and hell-raising from the
Hash House Harriers.

ISBN 0 9578332 1 0.

1. Hash House Harriers – History. 2. Hash House Harriers –
Anecdotes. 3. Hare and Hounds – History. 4. Hare and
Hounds – Social aspects. I. Title.

796.428

Brilliant cover concept: Stu Lloyd. Designed by Said Studios, Sydney.
Typeset by Asset Typesetting Pty Ltd, Moruya.

Printed in Australia
10 9 8 7 6 5 4 3 2 1

Endangered species and human brain cells by the million were harmed in the making of this book. Stiff shit. Anyway, why are you reading this? Get a life, Half Mind!

"Growing old is inevitable. Growing up is optional."
ANON.

"I do not wish to belong to any club that will have me as a member."
GROUCHO MARX.

"Son, when you're participating in sports events, it's not whether you win or lose... it's how drunk you get."
HOMER SIMPSON.

A Little Dog-Eared: The Contents.

Author's Preface.

'Is it about drugs?' was the first question people asked when I told them I was working on a book about the Hash. The answer is a resounding No. (So, Mr Singapore censor, sir, put down your scissors and approve us for distribution please.) But it did make me realise that the Hash is still something of a best-kept secret – within the Hashing world, people live and die for this passionate pursuit, blowing their horns in joyful exuberance. Yet to the outside world, surprisingly, we remain an enigma or simply don't exist, despite our often raucous presence and an increasing amount of media exposure.

Instead, Hash is a noun, a verb, and adjective … a word loaded with meaning, and which has given so much meaning, to the fleet of foot as well as the flat of foot. Are we r*nners who drink, or drinkers who r*n? Absolutely!

And that is just part of the paradox that is the Hash. As Toothprick wrote in the Sydney Hash House Harriers 1983 year book: "Hashing to me is the irreconcilable conflict between opposites: the r*nning and the drinking, the pain and the pleasure, the thirst and the bucket, the athlete versus the non-athlete, the yinning and the yanging, the giving and the getting, the action and the inaction, the something and the nothing." Furthermore, we are a club that has no official sporting ground, no spectators, no prizes, and no winners (although, admittedly a lot of losers!). There is no high-water mark in Hashing. Even describing the action itself is deemed blasphemous, so vulgar words like r*n, r*nner, and r*nning have been censored to avoid offence.

The easy part of doing this book was flying around the world, enjoying the company and hospitality of some of the finest people you'd hope to meet. The Hash has in its ranks scientists from the Antarctica, porn stars in LA, mining engineers in the outback, astronauts, prison warders, the odd person with letters after their name having had afternoon tea with the Queen, retired military colonels and brigadiers in England, housewives, and active marines about to go and fight the War Against Terror. But somehow they are all the same. There are no strangers in our club – just Hashers you haven't met.

The hard part was separating pure hearsay, conjecture and rumour from hard historical fact. For instance, I can't for the life of me remember the name of the Harriette who took me to my first Hash in Hong Kong in 1987. Nor which Hash kennel it was. Yet others have been able to recall events more than 40, 50 or 60 years ago with precision. Actions and deeds are related as I remember them, or as the people themselves told me in tape-recorded interviews. Some conversations and anecdotes are as close as I can recall them – bearing in mind you might have been pissed when you told me, and I was probably pissed when I was transcribing it. But, hopefully, the essence and detail is captured accurately. If you think you've been misquoted, you were just more pissed than you thought. If you can't remember talking to me at all, you really must ease back on the grog.

Exhaustive? No. Exhausting? Definitely. Through exacting research (usually in a pub) and corroboration of events (ditto), the facts were ultimately identified and established. The wheat was separated from the chaff. And, once the facts had been discarded, we were on our way!

When one piece of the jigsaw fell into place, I was in awe of the much-clichéd global village we have become. Trying to piece together the Hashtory of Africa, I followed up on a casual comment made by a Kiwi Hasher living in Vanuatu who had Hashed in Brunei in the mid-Sixties with someone who then moved to Kenya. A Dutchman in Kenya put me in touch with a Brit back in England who could remember the face but not the name. The two came together, and Hashtory was literally made.

My interest in Hashtory comes out of my love for colonial history. Certainly the Hash started as a British expatriate bachelor pursuit, a tag it has now outstripped in many places around the world. However, the free-spirited, iconoclastic and often irreverent essence of the expatriates who created it lives on, even as the expatriate himself has invariably moved off. I wasn't so much interested in the fact that a Hash kennel started in a certain city on a certain date, as much as *why* those people were there. What economic, political, and social factors led them to these often remote outposts in the first place. For the spread of Hashing reads like no logical corporate 'pins on the map' expansion – while multinational corporations typically start with London, New York, and Tokyo, Hashdom is made up of Benghazi, San Jose, and Zagreb. It's been an incredible geography lesson for me, and I've got a confession to make: Before I started this book, I thought Burkina Faso was an Italian racing driver!

The who, the what, the where, the when and the why have all been dealt with. However, some caveats: Where, when and what are occasionally intact and partially accurate. Who is occasionally lacking or clouded by jumped-up claims of wannabes who might've been on the same continent at the time. The why, of course, we'll never really know. But when you piece the Hash together, it makes sense of the world's own story. A global barometer. A microcosm in which many believe they've found a recipe for integration, tolerance and world peace. Doubly poignant since the events of September 11.

Though some feel that Hashing might be a one-generation event, in an age of stifling political correctness, temperance and sexual restraint, the Hash is still spreading like an, ahem, nasty virus over the internet. But like the WWW, nobody owns the HHH. The thousands of active kennels in 135 countries, with a 'best guess' of about 200,000 Hashers worldwide, is ultimately a headless chicken. And, as any self-respecting Hasher will tell you, there are no rules in the Hash … but there are violations of tradition. So are we anti-establishment or have we become the establishment? Who gives a shit!

The Hash has done many wondrous deeds for charity and community over the years – perhaps as atonement for its transgressions – so in that spirit, I will be donating my standard writer's royalties from this book to an underprivileged children's charity in Goa and the Hash Heritage Foundation in Malaysia. I'm pleased to say that John 'Honkers' Ellsmore and Randall 'Nut 'n' Honey' Salisbury – in their roles as sub-editor and cartoonist, respectively – also entered willingly into this spirit and provided their professionalism gratis in lieu of a donation to these causes.

I humbly submit this work not as an expert, rather, as a fan. For how can one deal in certainty in something so fluidly amorphic as the Hash.

I hope I have captured the full spectrum of Hashing in the new millennium, and give you a lot of memories and laughs in the process. If not, you'll be pleased to know that – somewhere around the world – I'll probably be getting a Down Down for my sins.

ON! ON!

Stu 'The Colonel' Lloyd.
Sydney H3.

Foreword.

This initiative of Stu Lloyd in chronicling some of the myriad activities and antics of Hash chapters from around the world is highly laudable. He has assiduously mined the written records and dredged some of the best tales and anecdotes from the vast literary pool of Hashdom, previously only available to members of individual Hashes through their weekly newsletters or periodic celebratory magazines. Much of this material deserves to be made available to a wider readership, including members of the non-Hashing public who may be intrigued enough to wish to learn more about our esoteric pastime and join in the fun. Perhaps a few may be encouraged to search out a chapter in their own neighbourhood, or maybe even start a new Hash with a few like-minded friends. There are presently about 1,700 Hash chapters, or kennels, around the world, on every continent, even including Antarctica. All Hashes are basically the same, but each is different to a lesser or greater degree from all others, depending on how they interpret the general 'rules' to suit their own tastes or local circumstances. Each has its own way of doing things, and part of the mystique of Hashing lies in experiencing those differences. In the year 2001 after the passage of many miles and countless tipples, the Mother Hash chapter in Kuala Lumpur reached its 3,000th r*n. As one of the oldest of extant Hashmen, who first ran with the original Hash way back in 1954, and who still r*ns regularly with them as well as with other Hash chapters in the course of frequent circumnavigations of the globe, it has been my privilege and pleasure to witness the growing popularity and steady expansion of the Hash House Harrier movement to all corners of the earth over the past several decades. I continue to be amazed at the manner in which the simple and ancient ritual of hare and hound-style foot chasing followed by good-humoured socialising with appropriate refreshments, has exerted its spell over exercise-hungry, fun-loving zealots of all races and in all climes. A new-age cult for the modern man and woman! The spread of Hashing around the world is an interesting social phenomenon. By 1967 a virtual Hashing Diaspora was under way – mainly around the southern confines of the South China Sea, including the Malayan peninsula, Brunei, Sarawak, and Sabah, then known as British North Borneo – and continued for about 10 years, with pioneer Hashers starting new Hashes all over the world. Later still, these outposts of Hashdom established during the Diaspora took up the r*nning by spawning new Hashes in their areas of influence, leading to the virtual colonisation of the world by the Hash movement, a process that continues to this day.

In 1998 a small number of long-time Hash enthusiasts in Malaysia formed the non-profit Hash Heritage Foundation, charged with a mission to enhance the pursuit of Hashing in the interests of Hashers worldwide, and to preserve the traditions and history of Hash. The most important long-term objective is to build a replica of the original Hash House at an appropriate site in Kuala Lumpur that could be a suitable club-style headquarters for all Hash persons. It would also be a repository for the preservation of the more important archival records and memorabilia of Hashing, with permanent exhibition space.

An important current objective of the Foundation is the compilation of a genealogy of Hashing that attempts to trace the descent of all existing and past Hash kennels from the original Hash House Harriers, Kuala Lumpur. For this purpose we have adapted a human genealogical software program, by substituting the date of the first r*n of each Hash for the date of birth; designating the person (male or female) who did the most to get the Hash up and r*nning as the Founding Father; and declaring the Hash that the Founding Father ran with on a regular basis immediately prior to begetting his/her new Hash as the Hash Mother of that Hash.

We have also introduced a new category of Midwives, to honour those other inaugural members who assisted the Founding Father in any substantial manner up to the conclusion of the first r*n. The resulting computer-generated genealogical table provides a fascinating picture of the relationship between Hashes and of how Hashing spread around the world. It also affords a unique unifying feature for the Hash movement as a whole. Meanwhile, the collection of important records and memorabilia proceeds apace. A considerable fillip was given to this task when the Foundation received a large consignment of files and papers from the estate of the late Tim 'Magic' Hughes, formerly of the Bangkok H3, who died early in 1998 and who single-handedly took upon himself the role of publisher of Hash magazines and international Hash chapter directories from the mid-Eighties through the late Nineties. Other Hash persons continue to make valuable contributions to the archives, and on the basis of these gifts the Foundation has been able to mount exhibitions of Hash memorabilia at the Kuala Lumpur and Hobart InterHashes in 1998 and 2000 respectively, and the Goa InterHash 2002. The Foundation has also accumulated a unique library of Hash literature, containing more than 470 volumes of celebratory magazines, directories and songbooks. If you wish to know more about the history and genealogy of the Hash check in to the Hash Heritage Foundation website www.hashheritage.com

William 'Tumbling Bill' Panton, Kuala Lumpur.

Thanks for nothing.

I could've done this whole thing on my own. Easily. On my head. But as usual, there were all the freeloaders that just wanted to get their snout in the trough, and jump on the bandwagon, well, anything really to get in the way or get a gratuitous mention. Their assistance, in whatever form, is much depreciated.

So here are the offenders who gave me lifts, a couch or bed for the night, bought me a beer, poured out their hearts, retrieved old photos or dumped dusty archival boxes on my doorstep thus aggravating my hayfever:
Adrian and Annie Barrett; Amnesia; Andrew Kefford; Baldrick2Dogs; Bill Panton; Briggs & Stratton; Bunny; Bunter; Bushranger; Bum Crack; Camel & Carguard; Chopper; Chris Destrieux; Clementine; Clepto; David Scourse; Dags; Des Pearson; Digit; Dinosaur Don and Melodrama; Flying Booger; Francis Arnold; Fuch; G String; God's Father and Joan Whitaker; Goody Two Shoes; Gunga Dick; Hammer; Honkers; Hops; Horst Whippern; Huggy Bear; Iron Balls; John Duncan; John Kennedy; John O'Rourke; John Ward-Turner; Likk'mm; Man In Black; Mike Miall; Neptunus; Old Wares; Polly; Prof; Ralph Wadsworth; Ray Thornton; Rhonda; Renee Lim; Richard McAllister; Robbercop; Running Joke; Phil and Jane Riddell; Slabeye; Stick the Tongue In; Teazemaid; Ted Quirk; The Grocer; The Lord; The Vicar; The Wolf; TNT; Trembles; Wanda.

These people referred me to others who knew a lot more than they did, or helped me track down lost and elusive souls:
Aarfabithore; Big Bird; Big Poo; Bina Bottomless; Blowfish; Blowjob; Bob Bell; Brown Underpants; Bushranger; Captain Marvel; Chapa Chatty; Chee Bye; Cock of the North; Coppertone Bone; Cuming Mutha; Dayak; Deep Throat; Denis Bouclin; DuckJob; Electrocuted; Hags; Hash Willie; Iron Maiden; Jetstream; Jim Stites; John and Robin Ewing; Kiddy Licker; Likk'mm; LubriKate; Maaandi; Mad Cow; Major Monkey Spanker; Mak Mak; Mastikator; Merkle; Milestone; Mitey Byte; Moana; MoneyPenny; Monique; Nuisance; On The Rocks; Ott; Patrick Coyle; Pete the Pilot; Phantom; Pinky; Plastered; Plunder; PMW; Polly; Preparation H; Quickie; Rambino; Red Snapper; Rompy; Rottweiler; Roy Frylink; Sabun; See More Buns; Sir John Howe; Snappy Tom; Steve Chapman; Stool Sample; Swamp Thing; Sweetie; Tattoo; The Wolf; Tom Witzke; Tonedeaf; Tony Jones; Treefeller; Underwear; Vaseline Thighs; Volva; W.E.N.D.Y.; Wacko; Warbler; Wigless.

These wankers contributed stuff – either verbally around a keg of beer somewhere or by email (around a keg of beer somewhere) – and are listed by their current continent of residence not by locale of anecdotes contributed.
USA and The Americas
1/4 Barrel; 2 Angry Inches; 8 Yellow Snow; A Joy To His Mother; African Queen; Alias; All Head and No Shaft; Amazon.cum; An How's Her Bush; Async;

Atame; Backdoor Dwarf; Battery Operated Buddy; Bermuda Short; Big Gulp; Birdman; Blowjob; Burnt Sox; Cannabis Licked Her; Captain Titanic; Captain Zero; Chapa Chatty; Chemical Mike; Chemical Whorefare; Chile; Cock Pit; Cockpit; Coppertone Bone; Cox Stroker; Crash and Burn; Cuntinental Divide; Dark Tanyon; Debriefed; Deep Doo Doo; Dick Long and Prosper; Dick the Boy Wonder; Dr Spock; Dreary the Hugging Man; Driving Miss Daisy; Duckjob; Ear of the Sperm; Elephant Dick; Face Plant Puke Princess; Fag; Finger Lickin' Good; For Sale or Rent; Forest Gulp; Francis Arnold; Free Meat; Fried Green Tits; Garfield; Glow Worm; Golden Eagle; Grandslammer; Grapes of Wrath; Grease Monkey; Groper; Hamburger Helper; Hammer; Hasher Humper; Head Nurse; Hedges; High Beams; Himalaya; Hung Like a Gerbil; Hops; Hostitute; Human Resources; I B Dick; I Blow Silver; Ian Cumming; Inuendo; Papa Smurf; Jerry's Kid; Keith Kanaga; King Shit; Kojak and Lollipop; Konkorde; Lady in Red; LCB; Leisure Suit Larry; Long and Hard; Martha Fucking Stewart Anal-Lytical; Mellow Foreskin Cheese; Mistress Viagra; Mummy Rearest; Mother Inferior; Mr Jackson; Narcolepsy; Nutless Sac; On the Rocks; Ouipee; Parrot Head; Pearl Necklace; Pillsbury Blow Boy; Polly Wanna Cocker; Prego; Preparation H; Pussy Gourmet; Ralph Wadsworth; Ranger Dick; Rompy; Rosie Lickety Split; Running Bare; Screwed Up; See More Buns; Sex Addict; She Mussel Bitch; Shiggy Bob; Sin Bad; SmegmaBalls; Stick Your Finger in It; Stool Sample; Struck from Behind; Sympathy Fuck; Tampon Drizzle; The Decorated Asshole; The Famous Explorer; The Great Kahuna; Upchuck; Wacko; Wet and Dry; Wet Toe Job; Wipe Her Ass; Womb With a View; Wurz; Yanksit.

United Kingdom:
Amnesia; Annual Fisting; Barcode; Barmitzvah; Blow; BOF; Boggers; Bounder; Bunter; Chopper; Cocksure; Commercial Whale; Crackin' Pussy; David Scourse; Deadeye Duck; Digby's Dad; Dizzy; Dragonarse; Edna the Inebriate Woman; Eric The Viking; Fanny Rat; Fat Bastard; Fevvers; Floater; Fu Man Chu; GBH; Groin Biter; Gromit; Gunga Dick; Half-a-Fuck; Half Pint; Hi De Hi; Hughie Blaaaaaaargh; Jailbird; Jetstream; John Ward-Turner; Juggling Banana; Jumper; Khaw Fucker; Kipper; Le Voisin; Leatherback; Lesley – the vicar; Lifeboats; Living Bra; Looberty; Low Profile; Marxist; Megavirgin; Mother Brown; Mountain Rescue; Mr Minty; Nigel Cross; Nookie; Olymprick; Paella; Pampers; Pete the Pilot; PMW; Polly; Pork Torpedo & Horny; Prof; Pure Genius; Radar; Rapunzel; Ray Thornton; Redlight; Revolta; Right Hand; Robocop; Ryde; Sergio; Sex Reject; Shagger; Shiddy; Shit for Brains; Spanish Fly; Speed Bump; Spoons; Squits; Stick the Tongue In; Swollen Member; Tampon; Teepee; The Brewer; The Penguin; To Lose Le Trek; Treefeller; Vicar

Africa/Middle East:
Baldrick 2 Dogs; Balloon Balls; Beerhound; Bwana; Byclops; Camel; Deceased; Diable; Dinosaur Don; Dog and a Half; Electrocuted; Friki da Priki; Flasher; Gandhi; Garfield; Gin Bin; Gumby; Haji Babi; Head Butt; Helicopter Coming; Huggy Bear; Klippies; Luft Schwein; Mad Cow; Mamma Hen; Milestone; Miss Maggots; Nuisance; Paul Stock; Pissoles; Ra; Rambo;

Schwarzkopf; Shark Shift; Sir Clugs; Stoker; The Gent; Timberdick; Tinkerbell; Tulip Eater; Uranus; Welsh Git

Europe/Scandinavia:

18 Inches; Absolutely Pathetic; Big Balls; Big Mac; Blimey; Bloody Dick; Bloody Hanoi; Blow My Bagpipe; Bold Fokker; BoneUs; Bouncing Czech; Brian Gray; Bumboy; Caroline Bright; Clueless; Dancing Queen; Dirty Old Man; Doggy Style; Drunk and Desperate; Easy Rider; Efes; Effin Thong; Flasher; Flying Chicken; G String; Gagarin; Gigolo; Guerilla Groupie; Haggissimo; Higgins; Horny Goat Weed; Hot Dog; Ice Hole; Iceman; John Jackson; Loping Scrotum; Major Monkey Spanker; Mak Yak; Man in Black; Mastikator; No Mercy Master; Overdrive; Pippi Wrongstockings; Rug Burns; Screw My Bike; Sharkfin; Smurf; SpermAid; Standing Ovation; Strawberry Foreskin; The Vicar; The Wolf; Tom McSherry; Tonedeaf; Two Holes; Viagra; Viking Puker; Vodkasplite; Wimpy Limpy.

Australia/NZ/Oceania:

Big Legs; Birdman; Blip; Boomer; Bushranger; Cabbage Patch; Cans; Chuckley; Copteaser; Corporal Punishment; Corrigan; Cream Puff; Chastity Belt; Crystal Balls; Cuddles; Dagy; Dammit; Darwin; Deep Throat; Dreaded Fog; Dyke; Easy Rider; Effigy Snoz; Ferret; Figjam; Flatbitz; French Connection; Fresh Fanny; Fussy Not Desperate; Geestring; God Knows; God's Father; Greasy; Grewsome; Gypsy Rose Lee; Hanoi Bill; Honkers; Hugo; Innerspring; Jed; Jock in a Box; John O'Rourke; Jrgee; Kava Queen; Kiwi; Lead Balls; Leonardo; Likka; Lofty; Longhorn; Lovechild; Max Collins; Menstrual; Mikan Bush; Mixo; Moana & Lisa; Moishe; Oggie; Old Wares; One Hung Low; Paul McDonnell; Phantom; Physio; Pilko; Plunder; Pockets; Postie; Puff; Pussy; Rhonda; Rodney Rude; Roobarb; Scandal; Screwtom Squasher; Sex; Sheepshead; Shortplanks; Sir John; Sirloin; Sniffer; Souvenir; Spawn of Satan; Super; The Flange; The Lord; Thrill Furkhand; Tombstone; Toyboy; Treadmill; Van Der Who?; Virginus Illigitimus; Volva; W.E.N.D.Y; Wally Kanga; Wigless; Wontok; Yo Adrian.

Asia

Aritono; Bambang; Bentone; Bill Panton; Bird Fucker; Blue Lugs; Bo Bo; BOF; Boney; Brian Columbus; Bushwhacker; Cap'n Squall; Chaztitty; Clit Face; Cocksucker; Creeping Jesus; Dances With Dogs; Diamond Cutter; Dick the Prick; Digit; Doggy Dave; Dubai; Fuck Off; Fukawe; Father; Gympy; Hazukashii; Horst Whippern; Itchy Scratchy; James Naingolan; Jean Tan; John CN Yap; John Duncan; John Hogan; Jollygreenknob; Lifa; Louis The Lip; Maid Marion; Mak Mak; Mr Bean; Nasiturd; Neil Thomason; Paddy O'Kane; Perpetual Poofter; Pigeon Leg; Prosperous Chicken; Railjerker; Ratchucker; Richard Jones; Sand in My Crack; Saput; Sex; Slippery Beaver; Snow White; Stainless; Stainless; Stick Insect; Sweaty Pie; Target; Teacher; TNT; Two Lips; Uncle Kueh; Walrus; Where the Fuck's Me Keys?; Young Andrew.

Without their input there would, simply, be no book. So now you know who to blame.

The Cradle of Uncivilisation.

Hashing in Asia.

A dog's breakfast.

It was only after his fourth gin and tonic that the stockbroker managed a rather dry nod of 'good morning' to those around him. Slightly greying and smartly dressed in white *tutup* jacket, he sat alone at a long table in the decaying Empire Hotel dining room. He waited impatiently. So he had another gin and tonic. Then another. Then another. Seven in all. A Chinese waiter, dressed in snappy white attire, had seen it all before and finally brought the man's porridge.

The serious drinking would have to wait. After all, the stockbroker had a busy day in front of him.

It was early 1938 and Malaya was again prosperous and expanding because good prices for rubber were being fetched, and new bodies were being shipped in to feed the boom. Wide-eyed John Kennedy, a fresh-faced 22-year-old, was one of them. He had just got off the boat from England for his assignment as assistant manager for Malayan Fertilisers Limited, responsible for peddling their range of chemicals and fertilisers to plantations throughout the country.

He had checked into the Empire – which was oldish and certainly in need of fresh décor – and straight onto the real-life set of this Somerset Maugham, Joseph Conrad and Noel Coward co-production. Mad dogs and Englishmen indeed. Although perhaps the dogs would've won a sanity contest. Maugham gave us our public image of the British in the Far East as a 'fast, hard-drinking, socially and morally second-rate set'.[(107)] "A first rate country for second rate people," is how Maugham himself described it.

But contrary to Maugham's summary judgement, Civil Servants assigned to the Far East were upper class fellows, hand picked from the best public schools and top universities, namely Oxford and Cambridge. Not that they were all from the same mould. It was often said that Cambridge men walked into a room as though they owned it. Oxford men walked into a room as though they didn't give a damn who owned it.

Then there were those for whom no mould ever existed. The true colonial eccentrics, be they residents in the provinces, judges, or police officers. Cheap liquor no doubt fuelled a lot of their antics. A bottle of Dewars whisky – which was cheaper than Tiger Beer – cost about $3, and gin half that. Whisky was drunk as a long drink with water – "not very strong, but you drank a fair number of them," says Kennedy. Many of the drinking traditions and quirky behaviours – such as a bottle of gin on the table with the coffee – were borrowed from the Raj in Calcutta.

Mind you, the locals were holding up their end quite admirably as well. The Sultan of Johor, a well-known carouser, was banned from Singapore in 1938 for 'stealing' a doctor's Scottish wife from Singapore. But usually he would patrol the streets in his official car looking for the prettiest ladies then whisk them back home over the Causeway for a frolic in his Bukit Serene love nest. Dancing girls from Singapore's buzzing Happy World were a particular delicacy.

These were heady times alright. Dances would be held in Kuala Lumpur most weekends, and not cease till the roosters crowed the new day in. Flat Foot Floogie with a Floy Floy or Glen Miller tunes like In the Mood would raise the rafters. Afterwards, groups of friends might head into town to enjoy satays at the late night stalls. But these young expats with hormones raging through their bodies had an excuse for going hard at it in the tropics. The few ladies to be seen here were usually daughters of high-ranking officers or seniors, but were horribly outnumbered. Some report as few as two single and unattached English women in the whole of Kuala Lumpur.

Strong restrictions were placed on marriage on their first tour, considered to be a five-year period. No entitlements for their spouse would be forthcoming. Also, fraternising with the local women-folk was frowned on; young rubber planters often shacked up with local girls for convenience, but for the young professionals in the city such a relationship uncovered could mean the end of your contract.

So, rather than take matters into their own hand, discreet visits to prostitutes were the order of the day. "Batu Road was where the little knocking shops were," recalls Kennedy. "People used to go there quite often after a night at the club or on a Saturday night they'd go there, have a meal socially, then there'd be girls … and the girls upstairs if you were interested. A lot of them were r*n by Japanese. Some of them were supposed to be Japanese spies, the ladies. Thais used to come down. Mainly Chinese, very few Malays."

There were about half a dozen bars in this stretch, with Mary's Bar being a particular favourite. "They weren't very grand," says Kennedy, "with usually a big advertisement for Asahi beer, the Japanese beer, up on the wall." The Coliseum on Batu Road was probably the best known of the restaurants and bars. An institution.

"Then of course there were The Eastern and Bukit Bintang where you had taxi dancers," he says, referring to the practice of buying a book of dance tickets to go with the girls of your choice.

Then on Sundays, they'd wake up late and do it all over again. Late morning they'd front up and get stuck into the Tigers and gin and tonics, then around two o'clock curry tiffin lunch would be served. Occasionally a visit to the cinema, where a movie such as Pygmalion or Bob Hope's The Road to Rio might be showing at the spanking new $200,000 Pavilion cinema at the corner of Pudu Road and Bukit Bintang Road downtown. Or they retired for a nap, when they might have read a few pages of that new book by Tolkien, The Hobbit.

In case you thought they were just here on an end of season rugby tour, we need to understand why the Brits were here at all, let alone in such numbers. In 1938, there were 30,000 of these worthies in Malaya, mostly in Kuala Lumpur itself.

The British first appointed an Adviser to Malaya in 1874 at the request of the Sultan to help sort out some in-fighting on some national domestic issues. At that time, coffee was the chief crop. Rubber was introduced a few years later, although it wasn't as popular as coffee, but as global coffee prices fell, estates switched to rubber, aided by the British government providing loans to planters establishing estates.

Large firms such as Harrison's and Guthrie's opened offices in Kuala Lumpur in the first decade of the 1900s. General administrators were required for the expanding colony and its attendant government service. Soon, additional engineers, doctors, police and technical advisers were required. Even newspaper editors and journalists.

The Malay Mail reported that Douglas 'Wrong Way' Corrigan had defied orders intentionally and made a solo trans-Atlantic flight from the United States in a tiny wooden bi-plane, landing in Ireland twenty-eight hours later. Across the oceans, England had just beaten Australia in the fifth cricket Test at the Oval, handing out the largest defeat – which stands to this day – of an innings and 579 r*ns. Importantly to those involved with rubber, Franklin Deleanor Roosevelt backed an US$8 million transcontinental highway system in the United States, which meant more cars and therefore more rubber needed for their low-pressure tyres, and more jobs for rubber workers.

Dunlop, Guthrie's, Hongkong and Shanghai Bank, Boustead's and Asiatic Petroleum were among the largest employers. They were hiring again, after the Great Depression of 1929 which saw about half of all planters shown the back door to Blighty.

Kennedy walked across to the Harrison Barker building. It was a good three or four storeys tall. The only other building of the same height at the time was the Majestic Hotel near the pink-and-white striped railway station. Model T Fords, Morrises, MGs, and the occasional Ford Prefect puttered along the streets of Kuala Lumpur. Overhead, he watched the odd Tiger Moth plane buzz across the blue sky.

In the Harrison Crossfield Rubber Agency, which owned the building that Malayan Fertilisers tenanted in, Kennedy met a bespectacled auditor in the Estates Department, Cecil Lee by name. They talked about the Empire Hotel, one of only three European hotels in the town. 23-year-old Lee spent his first night in 1934 there and found it "rather a comedown" with its *jamban* thunderbox sanitation and "a generally depressing ambience,"[107] but he loved KL, calling it a "fascinating little colonial town".[101] He was presently residing at the Selangor Club Chambers. They struck up a friendship, Kennedy recalling he was "around 5'10", a witty and charming fellow with great literary taste."

A five-and-a-half-day working week was the norm, including until lunch time on Saturdays. "We were being paid reasonably well … compared to the sort of money you could get in England," remembers Kennedy. "There was no income tax. We were living in clover." Halcyon and idyllic is how Cecil Lee described it.

In the Colonial Service, a starting salary of about $250 Malayan – equal to about £30 then – could be expected, and up to $400 in the Malayan Civil Service (who were unofficially referred to as 'The Heaven Born'). Who you worked for and the nature of your job was – in typical British style – the key.

But Brits, unlike other colonial masters, preferred to get the workday over and done with so they could use the remaining daylight for recreation. Or more gin and tonics. Kuala Lumpur had the perfect climate to afford this, with a thunderstorm most days around three or four o'clock, which knocked the temperature down suitably before they headed out from work at five. In the tropics – being close to the equator – twilight is uniformly short and fast throughout the year.

Many, including High Commissioners assigned to Malaya, held a 'Blue' in some sport, often rugby. Membership of the right rugby club, such as Harlequins, was also a plus, and quite often a pivotal question in the recruitment interview. Norman Cleaveland, a rugby player at that time said: "Whilst it was taken seriously, rugby training generally consisted in not going on the field under the influence."[(107)]

Every healthy Englishman would participate in clubs and sporting groups, which often formed the centre of social life for planters, "who would think nothing of trekking miles to the nearest club for the monthly dance or to sip a *stengah* or gin *pahit* in the falling dusk. Other attractions included billiards, snooker and the rare chance of meeting someone new."[(95)]

In Kuala Lumpur, there were three clubs to chose from, depending on your station: The Lake Club for seniors, Golf Club dominated by the Scots, and The Selangor Club which was regarded as egalitarian as juniors and seniors would mix there, and even the occasional local – were he "wealthy enough or of a certain class or standing".

Kennedy was a keen rugby player and signed up with the Selangor Club to play straight away, making friends with Eric Galvin, a journalist with the Malay Mail. Very few called The Selangor Club by its real name. It was known as The Spotted Dog, or simply The Dog.

Some say the term came from the club's relaxed 'mixed' racial policy which was somewhat against the prevailing sentiment of the times. This was perhaps best summed up by Colonel Jack Foster who built a retreat in the Cameron Highlands called the Lakehouse. It was r*n by his Chinese mistress, but had a sign out the front that simply read: 'NO DOGS, NO WOMEN, NO ASIANS.'

"One thing about Malaya was that it wasn't anything like the same sort of racial barriers that you got in India, it was more egalitarian," says Kennedy who developed some good friendships with the few local Malays in his team. "Much more mingling."

But the story which most go along with was that the club was so named after the wife of the Chief of Police – Captain Syres – who used to keep her two dalmatians tethered to her coach while she picnicked outside on the *padang* when the *atap*-roofed club was being built in 1885.

One advantage of belonging to The Selangor Club was that members could sit on the open verandahs and read newspapers which had been shipped in from Britain. They were weeks old, but kept the expatriates in touch.

Interesting snippets of news around this time were that the first nylon toothbrushes were being marketed in the US, and a patent for a product called Teflon was taken out [Interesting to whom? –ed.]. And the prestigious Time Magazine 'Man of the Year' award had just been bestowed on an Austrian man with a bad haircut and funny Charlie Chaplin-esque moustache. Adolf someone or another. It was that kind of a year.

Behind the gleaming white tudor-style Selangor Club building, joined by a walkway, stood the residential chambers. A two-storey building, it had large arched windows along the ground floor and a balcony that ran right around the upper level. The Selangor Club Chambers, too, had a nickname The Hash House, named for its reputedly indifferent food. The chambers, according to Curly Lee (Cecil's older brother), "sheltered from storm the humbler and younger members of the expatriate community, plus a few older oddities,"[93] such as married gents and senior officers inevitably separated from their spouses while on civil service abroad. The Chambers had a pub and mess hall downstairs, with about 16 or 18 rooms upstairs.

"Downstairs, it provided breakfast for people who lived in the club chambers. They did lunches and breakfast for people who were in there. The chambers were like little apartments with their own bathroom, if I remember rightly," says Kennedy. "They were much sought after and quite expensive, that's why I moved elsewhere."

'Elsewhere' was often living out with planters. "If there was a spare part of the bungalow we went in and shared with them," he says.

Kennedy doesn't remember the Hash House crowd as being particularly lively, behaviour perhaps moderated by some of the more staid older tenants who felt the social protocols of the time should be upheld. But the carefree bachelors lowered the standards where they could. Cecil Lee found the heat stifling and monotonous, not invigorating at all. He took to wearing a sarong to dinner for a while, until some of the more senior residents prevailed upon him and others to dress a little more decently – if impractically.

Societal dress codes were rather starchy. If you went out for a dinner in mixed company, a stiff collar and jacket were the expected minimum levels. In the office, ties were a must but jackets optional. The best offices were just installing air conditioning, but usually only for the boss's office. Others made do with swirling ceiling fans and rolling up their sleeves. And you could spot the new boys in town. They were the ones sporting the radiant white solar *topees* to keep the blazing tropical sun off their heads. Generally, anyone who'd been here a little while went without.

Once they'd acclimatised to the initially oppressive heat, many spent Sundays bush-walking in the jungles which abutted the town, or driving to Port Dickson for picnics. The more adventurous duo of Cecil Lee and John Kennedy enjoyed rafting trips. On one occasion in Negri Sembilan, they took their rubber dinghy down a river and pulled over into a little ravine surrounded by high cliffs as they were getting hungry. "We got out on this little sandy spot and ate some sandwiches and saw these tiger paw marks," says Kennedy. "So we ate our sandwiches rather quickly and got back in our dinghy."

While Lee recalls the time with great fondness and many memories of happiness, he states that overall "life went by placidly and monotonously"[101] in those years of colonial calm.

Although he'd moved out, Kennedy was part of a group that met regularly for lunch at the Selangor Club Chambers, as it was just a short walk across from their offices. At that table downstairs in the simply, almost sparsely, decorated restaurant sat an assortment of young gentlemen: Torch Bennett – so called because of his mass of flaming red hair, Cecil Lee, Harry Doig, Eric Galvin, John Barratt, and Humphrey Brook. Perhaps John Haskins from time to time. The lunches were jovial affairs, with Lee's amusing stories and "excellent imitations" providing many laughs. They often dived into English fare such as cold ham or beef and salads. To beat the heat of the day, thirsts were slaked with *ayer limau*, lime and water. Beer was rarely drunk at lunchtime by this group.

A dark-haired chap called Gispert started joining these lunch sessions around October 1938. Kennedy describes him as "quietish, good-looking." Gispert, at 35 years of age, was the mentor of young Bennett when they worked for the same firm together in Singapore, before being posted to Kuala Lumpur. Like Cecil Lee, he was a member of that notoriously wild and crazy profession – chartered accountants!

G, as Albert Stephen Gispert was known, stayed at the Selangor Chambers, too. The gossip mill worked overtime: In Singapore a year or so earlier, G's dalliances with a married woman had resulted in a child. He reportedly had to pay £200 to the unfortunately named Nobby Land, an old Malaya hand, to placate him. So here he was, a respectable and highly qualified chartered accountant, with a pregnant woman as his prospective bride who was still not divorced from her husband. The child came first, the wedding later.

Talk at lunch turned to Hare and Hounds, the game that many of them had been exposed to and enjoyed as public schoolboys in England. G also talked of the fun he'd had with harrier clubs. Horse Thompson – an office colleague of Gispert with a rather equine face – had r*n paper chases in 1932 when based in Johor Bahru. He then moved to Malacca and started another club there, the Springgit Harriers, a year or so later. Gispert would occasionally pass through on work matters and Horse would invite him to join the r*n.

"As a matter of fact, we started the Hash in Johor Bahru in 1932," said Horse Thompson.[76] "Then we started another one in Malacca a year or two later and, thereafter, we started r*nning in Taiping." They were mixed groups. Even dogs occasionally ran on these paper trails. They used to r*n on Sundays, followed by a curry tiffin lunch.

These clubs all became progressively extinct sometime around 1934 [Doesn't sound very progressive to me –ed.]. However, some reports had G taking Torch Bennett on a harrier r*n when on an outstation audit in Malacca in the first few months of 1938.

The lunch group – starved for entertainment and recreation in the absence of TV and women – talked of starting something similar in Kuala Lumpur. Kennedy acknowledges that the r*nning group started shortly after G arrived. "Although he puts the ... kudos on G, I think Cecil probably was really the one that got the thing going," says Kennedy. Thompson called the expansion into Kuala Lumpur "a natural progression". Bennett went on to say: "This was the seed which sprouted into [The Hash House Harriers] when G finally came to KL. The only difference was that the Springgits had female r*nners and we were chauvinistic pigs in those days."

And so, one balmy [Or is that 'barmy'? –ed.] evening in late 1938, Gispert and his gang of accountants, solicitors, auditors and fertiliser salesmen – wearing ankle boots or tennis plimsolls, some with baggy and long khaki pants or rugby pants – gathered for their first trail. "It was nearly all young people in their twenties," recalls Kennedy who was the youngest of the bunch. Only Doig and Thompson, both around 30 that year, were anywhere near G's age. "And there were probably only about 10 or 15 of us that started off. And we were merely started from the seven or eight that used to have lunch." He remembers the group as "not that athletic" because the 'serious ones' used to play rugby and cricket instead of the Hash "and there weren't that many that did both."

"Galvin was useful because he had access to the Malay Mail and could bring spare copies which were chopped up into the trail," Kennedy says. The hounds followed the four inch by four inch squares strewn by the fleeing hares, probably laid in the tin tailing areas around Ampang Road. As they found paper, calls in plummy English tones of 'On!' were made. False trails were included, but no checks or arrows to guide them through the sandy stretches, Chinese squatter holdings and low vegetation.

Then it was back to The Spotted Dog for beer, beer and more beer. "It wasn't nearly as strenuous as playing a hard-fought rugby match!" says Kennedy [Presumably referring to the r*nning and not the drinking –ed.]. "It was just thought of as getting a bit of exercise. One has about an hour and a half after the office until it gets dark and just getting a little bit of exercise in there."

"Gispert was not an athlete," recalled Cecil Lee[28], "and stress was laid as much on the subsequent refreshment, etc as the pure and austere r*nning. It was non-competitive and abounded in slow packs."

After the first r*n, it was decided to do a trail each week. Monday evenings were declared Hash night. That way they could work the Sunday excess out of their systems and get right to work on Tuesday's hangover instead. The name was chosen at a lunch at The Hash House after one or two r*ns had been successfully completed. "Then Cecil and G suggested we give it an official name," says Kennedy. The Hash House Harriers. "That was the only name put forward and it was adopted as being a good name."

Irreverence and self-deprecation were there right from the start. "Calling it the Hash House Harriers was already a self-deprecatory term, I mean playing it down a bit," says Kennedy. "You think of a Hash House Harrier as dogs going round making their living picking up scraps from the back of kitchens and things like that. It's a derogatory term deliberately picked by someone with a sense of humour like Cecil Lee." So exactly who came up with the name Hash House Harriers? "I thought it was Cecil," says Kennedy. "It was either Cecil or Gispert."

"The name of this chapter ... has only helped it to expand faster," said Horse Thompson.[76]

"So the Hash House Harriers was not a completely new idea, but was a completely new show with a novel name,"[60] said John Duncan, long-time KL resident and Hashtorian.

And so the weekly trails took shape, the hares usually selecting the Ampang Rd area which, apart from tin tailings, also had market gardens. "The area was criss-crossed by little drainage ditches with flimsy plank bridges here and there,"[123] said Kennedy. "I remember one of them breaking during a r*n and decanting a group of Hashers into two or three feet of muddy water! Generally we didn't go to the jungle much at all – it was nearly all on these old tin tailings and things like that, which were quite pleasant areas. Chinese market gardens were there – we used to cause quite a stir sometimes ... Chinese children would come out and look at the sight of these hairy-legged people r*nning. There were paths; a whole lot of waterways with little bridges. Basically there was a good deal of *lalang* (long grass) about the place. But usually the places where we went were little paths that had been used by the Chinese or the Chinese children going to school and we tended to work along these paths."

Suburbs r*n included Old Klang Rd, Ampang Rd and Kenny Hills, close to the growing city itself as there was no time to get further afield. The pack size grew to about 15 to 20 on average – with names such as Colin Symington, Charles Durant, Eric Galvin, Harry Doig, Morris Edgar and Rupert Mackie regularly on trail. Most of these were professionals working in the Colonial Government Service, or in the private sector trading houses with Lee and Gispert. Many were irregulars and visitors from outside Kuala Lumpur by virtue of the nature of their jobs, including Rupert Mackie's younger brother, Gus, who was in the British military and garrisoned on the peninsula. "Occasionally if people hadn't r*n they'd r*n in long trousers," recalls Kennedy.

Arthur Westrop, Kennedy's teetotalling boss, who had been very involved with previous harrier groups in Malaya also eventually joined the fray. Horse Thompson – the champion of the earlier harrier groups – was conspicuously absent at this stage. He was on leave, usually a lengthy spell in those days considering the lack of rapid transport options. If you went all the way back to England on home leave, you'd want to spend several months there. "I don't think Horse was really one of the progenitors of the thing," says Kennedy. "I don't remember him r*nning ... right at the beginning. I think he probably got more involved in it later on. I don't recall him as part of the original group that got it going. He was the only older one. He was the boss of Malayan Telecommunications (sic) ... he was quite young to be in that position. He didn't drink all that much but was very pleasant when drinking was being done. He certainly spent quite a lot of his time exploring the nightlife of KL. He blossomed out." Horse was unmarried.

Kennedy concedes that generally speaking a "fair amount" of beer consumption went with the lifestyle. "We didn't take any drinks to the r*n itself," he recalls. "Most of the head offices of the rubber estates were (in KL) and planters would come in and various other people and a number of public servants reporting back," says Kennedy of the transient nature of the expat population. "And quite often people who were just coming in for a short time would come along on those r*ns ... so it was all very informal in that respect. Anyone who turned up contributed a Malay dollar just to cover the expenses. We often used to decide from the previous r*n where the next week was, and who the hares were going to be," says Kennedy who hared only once, with Harry Doig.

Kennedy doesn't remember any singing. "I don't think there was anything particularly extreme about it to begin with," he says. "People went out and ran and ran. The stripping off and that sort of thing I think evolved later on. It was really considered a means of getting a little bit of light-hearted non-competitive exercise. An antidote to rugby or cricket, to *organised* sport."

In 1939, the Malay Mail broke news of the Yankee Clipper landing in London, completing the first passenger flight over the Atlantic. Nylon stockings also made their debut, sending pulses racing among the bachelor folk in the chambers. Meanwhile the few single women were cooing over Clark Gable in Gone With the Wind. Closer to home, Somerset Maughman's book The Letter – about the murder of a Malayan rubber planter – was made into a movie with Bette Davis and brought in the crowds. Maugham had based the book on a scandalous real-life incident well known to the expats ... a tin mining consultant, who lived around Puchong, was involved with the wife of the acting head master of the Victoria Institute, who lived in a house on the Kelang River behind what is now the High Street Police Station. They lapped it up. Duke Ellington tunes livened up the regular dance parties, and the radio played new songs like You Are My Sunshine and Somewhere Over the Rainbow.

A young gent, Frank Woodward by name, arrived in KL in February 1939 and wasted no time getting on trail with the Hash as much as possible. "Curiously enough, I cannot recall G Gispert," he said. "I can only assume that he must have returned to Malacca or Singapore before I arrived."[76] Woodward went on to write his own tome, The Origins of the Hash House Harriers [If I'd known that, we could've just copied it and gone to lunch –ed.].

Torch Bennett's name was also conspicuously absent because he was on home leave for eight months. He returned to KL to find the Hash House Harriers up and r*nning, albeit a bit chaotically. OK, it was a shambles. Being the organised person he was, he offered to take over the secretaryship from G and knocked some semblance of structure and order into this rabble. R*ns needed to be numbered, he felt, and a circular advising of r*n locations. If funds were collected, they should have a bank account. The 'members' were owed accountability of the ins and outs. G happily handed over the job, in what has now become a Hash tradition – delegation and washing the hands of anything remotely resembling responsibility! Horse

Thompson – the world's first Short Cutting Bastard by all accounts – and Cecil Lee were the first Joint Masters.

"The early days were all very informal and I think only became better organised when Torchy Bennett returned from leave," says Kennedy.

War and Piss.
Then, showing an alarming lack of priorities, the Hash was changed to Friday nights as the distant rumblings about a war in Europe got people to sign up with the rag-tag Selangor Volunteers outfit. The Federated Malay States Selangor Volunteers, to use its full and fancy name, had drills and training on Monday nights, Hash night. "Pretty well everybody was a member of the Volunteers," Kennedy says. Cecil Lee found himself in an armoured unit, under a ridiculous senior officer. Naturally, this gent found himself the subject of one of Cecil's famous imitations in very short order.

Horse Thompson was supposedly one of the top brass in the telecommunications area, but was strangely fluent in the Hokkien Chinese dialect. Some – like John Duncan – are convinced he was some sort of espionage operative, believing it unusual for a highly qualified colonial civil servant to be "wandering around with a screwdriver fixing phones" as it had been colourfully described to him by an old friend of Horse's.

As the war crept closer, extra evenings of training were added, and also began to take up weekends. But still, their daily jobs – exciting as they must have been for the auditors – could not be overlooked.

"Of the many memories of r*ns before the war," said Cecil Lee, "I recall that it was a Friday night in September 1939 at Klang Gates we had the news that Poland was invaded and wondered how long we would continue our weekly sport."[78]

Life went on as usual, albeit with a sharp increase in the cost of living. "The cost of living was quite high," Kennedy concedes, adding that he hardly saved any money at all in his tenure in Malaya. "I spent quite a lot of my money on learning to fly Tiger Moths in the local Aero Club. I think it cost about eight Malayan dollars an hour to hire an aeroplane," he says, noting that it would have cost double were it not subsidised by the FMS Volunteers.

At this point, several families started packing up – the children and womenfolk at least – and heading back to England. One of these was a young lass called Marjorie whose father was the influential Director of Forestry in Malaya. Through a mutual friend, Kennedy was invited to a farewell party for their family who were leaving to return to the UK. They got on famously. However, declaration of war in Europe postponed their departure and Kennedy and Marjorie struck up a courtship.

1940 dawned and the Hash continued doing what it knew best – r*nning and drinking. In January, an athletic fellow in forestry named John Wyatt-Smith ran his first r*n. He was often a Front R*nning Bastard along with his striped bull terrier, *Belong*.

"Possibly beer and shandies at the end of the r*n became part of the program around April or May of 1940," recalls Kennedy who at that point used to drive a "very old" Alvis to the r*ns. Sometimes he'd go with a friend in an MG. For some reason, the shandies – known as the Hash Brew – were made from ginger beer, not lemonade.

It was the job of the hares to supply drinks, which were purchased from the Fraser & Neave warehouse, then in Campbell Rd. With the small pack size, all that was needed for on-site refreshments were two dozen large bottles of Tiger Beer and F&N ginger beer. A galvanized iron washtub, carted around in the boot of the hare's car, was filled with crushed ice to keep the drinks cool. Large enamel mugs, also the communal property of the Hash, were used by the r*nners. Incredibly by today's standards, a couple of tins of cigarettes also had to be on the hare's shopping list.

Most r*ns were what are now called 'A to A'. That is, the end of the r*n was back at the place where it had set out from. Savvy short-cutters such as Horse Thompson and others would always be back at the beer first, much to the chagrin of the other try-hards [Seems like some things don't change! –ed.]. Horse, a short-cutter even when it came to oral expression, recalled that the aims of the Hash at this point were "to get as pissed as possible in as many Chinese suburbs of Kuala Lumpur as could be managed."[76]

To solve this, it was decided that 'A to B' r*ns would be introduced, with the end point of the r*n being unknown to the hounds. This presented a logistical nightmare of epic proportions as in those days most people drove their cars to the r*ns, or – more usually – had their syces drive them there. This meant that the hares' drivers had to wait for the hounds' drivers, and once the pack had set off, the hares' drivers would lead the others to the mystery end point where the beer would be served. On the first 'A to B' r*n, unsuspecting hounds (probably including Horse Thompson) headed back to the start to find – dadaaaaaa!! – an empty car park and no beer.

Everyone's problems were solved when Thompson was allowed to leave Malaya before the outbreak of hostilities on the peninsula. He joined the RAF, who posted him to Hong Kong.

Kennedy had stopped Hashing a few months earlier as he'd become engaged to be married to Marjorie. He spent more time with his fiancee playing tennis or bush-walking instead. His wife-to-be left Malaya a few months before he did, so he rejoined the group again. He later heard she was on a ship in the English Channel the day of the Dunkirk evacuation.

On his rejoining, Kennedy noticed some differences. "It had grown a lot," he says, indicating that the pack was more in the order of 30 - 40 Hashers strong, including his boss Westrop, Colin Symington from the Forestry Research Institute at Kepong, and M.C. Hay. "And there were quite a lot of older people."

These older, and presumably more experienced, individuals were ironically not allowed to return to Britain to sign up and serve in the forces. They were deemed far more valuable keeping the primary industries going in the colonies – because Britain and her allies would be needing a lot of tin and rubber to keep their war machinery in the air, on the roads, or afloat.

Sadly at this time, Harry Doig crashed a plane out in the jungle, and Kennedy and others were sent off in a vain search for the wreckage. Then Kennedy, who managed "under 20 r*ns altogether" left for England in July 1940 on special dispensation to join the RAF. All those flying lessons had paid off.

In December, another English rubber industry type, Llew Davidson, was 'on' for the first time. Eric Galvin, the newspaper man, availed himself of the opportunity to use a column in the Malay Mail paper to announce the starting point of the r*n each week to the growing numbers of Hashers.

In 1941 British Hashmen scratched their heads at the adulation of some Yank called Joe Dimaggio who would go on to set a record of hitting safely in 56 consecutive games that year. It sounded good, but it wasn't cricket. Torch Bennett and M.C. Hay – head of the Tin Department in Malaya – were appointed Joint Masters.

There were reports around this time of the Hash r*nning 'against' other athletic clubs. One example was Dr. John Reid's recollection that they ran against a local Indian athletic club and got beaten home soundly by the younger, more athletic Indians.

Around September of 1941, r*n #100 was celebrated. And celebrated with gusto. It so happened it was on the same night as The Selangor Club's AGM, in which the formally attired attendees were sitting around like stuffed shirts. This was too good an opportunity for the Hash to pass up on, and – having seconded every toilet roll they could lay their hands on – the Hashers stormed down the aisles mummifying the unsuspecting AGM guests.

Indeed the Hashers were seen as a very eccentric group around The Spotted Dog. Datuk Sir Jameson Ffitch Heyes recalled: "Hashers were, it must be said, very much outcasts of society … due to their bizarre behaviour."[48] But John Duncan believes they were not outcasts *per se*, just not welcome in their dirty Hashing gear on r*n nights. "What people used to do if they lived out of town," explains John Kennedy, "they might even just bring in their r*nning gear and strip off their office things and whatever they were wearing and then perhaps go back to the club and take a suitcase or something like that, and have a shower, and go out for a meal, rather than going home first." In any case, it gave them a great excuse to head off – after a shower or clean-up – to Batu Road. Here Mohammed Pitchay's laid on a good curry, according to John Wyatt-Smith, and thereafter Rupert Mackie was often heard to call the On On straight to the girlie bars in Batu Road.

"It was accepted as an eccentricity," says Kennedy of reactions by expatriates and local villagers alike. "They were fun days. The locals used to call us *Orang Gila* which meant madmen," said Cecil Lee.[23]

Japan's Premier Tojo aimed a blunt message to America and England about their 'exploitation of Asiatic peoples', adding that they must be 'purged with avengeance'. But America were doing a good job of exploiting their *own* people with police using teargas and clubs to disperse a strike by the United Rubber Workers of America Union in Akron, Ohio. Goodyear Tyres agreed to the new 'fair labour standard' of 40 cents an hour and a maximum 44 hour week [I can only *dream* of those conditions –ed.]. The Model T Ford had sold 15 million units, almost single-handedly creating a world on rubber wheels.

But the Hash kept flourishing. "We didn't know the extent of the danger or how near it was,"[107] said Cecil Lee indicating that it was ignorance of the growing storm ahead, rather than complacency. And on and on they ran in growing numbers. Then Gispert took leave in Australia. They soldiered on, Cecil Lee finding the dual duties "quite burdensome, and for some the outbreak came almost as a relief – for a short while,"[101] he noted.

On December 2, the Volunteers were mobilised following an erroneous report that Japan had attacked Malaya. Any expatriate under the age of 41 had to leave his office and join up full time with his respective military unit. Cecil Lee was with his Armoured Car unit when news of Pearl Harbour crackled over the wireless.

The Japanese invaded Malaya on December 8 1941, with the last Hash r*n #117 held a week later on December 12. A month after the Japanese landed, the expatriate wives and children were hurriedly evacuated from KL as Yamashita's army proceeded down the peninsula in a withering onslaught. On January 10, all European officials and residents had to leave KL, with a ban on people returning to the Malayan peninsula put in place. The defiant Gispert found a way around it in order to answer the call of his adopted country. He signed up with the Argyll Regiment and – being a true Hasher – wasn't too concerned with rank and even forwent a 'pip' in order to sign up for action.

Meanwhile, Hong Kong had fallen to the Japanese. Horse Thompson was interned but managed to escape. Joining some Chinese guerrillas, they tried to make their way to Chung King [Is this anything like Burger King? –ed] and walked into an ambush. Horse copped a bullet in the neck and, uncharacteristically, the Japanese had him transported back to the camp in Hong Kong where he was nursed back to health. It left him with the distinctive cant to his head thereafter.

During the chaotic and frenetic retreat by the Allies down from Malaya to Singapore Island, Cecil Lee and Torch Bennett were serving together in an Armoured Car division. When they reached Johor, the Argylls were coincidentally digging in for a last stand to defend Singapore. A bombing raid by 25 Japanese bombers sent everyone scurrying desperately for the nearest foxhole. And who should jump in next to Lee and Bennett? Their long-lost Hashing fellow, Mortar Officer Gispert. On In! The raid over, they exchanged farewells and moved on.

The Argylls held the defensive ring and were the last out of Malaya, crossing the Causeway into Singapore on January 31. Gispert was killed by the Japanese while asleep in the early hours of February 11, near Dairy Farm Road, in Bukit Timah, Singapore. His body was never recovered. G is remembered by his friend Lee as having had "a great sense of fun and humour but underneath noble instincts". Cecil Lee often modestly credited G with being 'the real founder' of the Hash House Harriers.

Within days, the unthinkable happened. Fortress Singapore, the defensive jewel of the peninsula, had fallen. M.C. Hay, along with fellow Hasher E.A. Ross, obtained permission to escape, and did so successfully albeit controversially with Lieutenant General Gordon Bennett – Commander of the Australian Forces no less – on board their little boat. Rupert Mackie was captured in Johor Bahru, and Cecil Lee and Llew Davidson were also captured and interned in Singapore's notorious Changi Prison. They were then sent to work on the notorious Siam-Burma railway in inhumane conditions that killed about 40 percent of all internees. Frank Woodward was interned in Kuala Lumpur's Pudu Jail and Thailand, and was saved from going up to Burma in the nick of time by the happy news of the war ending.

Up and r*nning, again.

Post-war, Britain had to re-establish a semblance of normality to the Malayan colony, although there was a realisation that the curtain had fallen on the colonial empire – the mighty Raj. The show was over.

Basics such as water supplies and electricity were paramount [Beer? –ed.]. So expatriates – including M.C. Hay and E.A. Ross – were shipped back to restore the services. Then services such as banking, finance, law and accounting needed to be turned back on. It was Cecil Lee who first returned after the war in 1946 to pick up the pieces and revive the Hash. However, he attributes the resuscitation of the Hash after the war "principally to Torch Bennett". Phillip Wickens and Dr John Reid are also credited with being stalwarts.

"We started by a small r*n in reduced circumstances around the racecourse," said Lee[28], adding "then the horses weren't much better." The Hash had amazingly lost only one of their number – Gispert – killed in action, and another in a prisoner-of-war camp. Others had simply moved on and not returned to Malaya.

Monday nights, no longer taken up by military manoeuvres and im-personations of silly officers, were reclaimed as Hashing night. Torch Bennett did some detective work and found out they still had some funds in credit at the bank. Alas, the tin bath and enamel mugs had been lost or destroyed or stolen somewhere in the intervening war [Unacceptable Hash behaviour by the Japanese Imperial Army! –ed.]. So he lodged a War Damage Claim for the bath and the mugs plus two old bags. Much to his surprise, this was honoured and full compensation made. The Hash was back in business, but life was different. Times were harder. Perish the thought, but income tax was now applied. Many had no servants and had to cook for themselves. Many of the footloose and fancy-free bachelors of the pre-war era – including Cecil Lee – returned as married men. Many expats could no longer afford cars, let alone drivers, as they had before the war. This meant that 'A to B' r*ns were no longer practical, so it was back to shortcutters' paradise … 'A to A'. And they started with r*n #1 again.

But just as life seemed to be getting back to normal in June 1948 – with tin and rubber booming – Arthur Walker, manager of a large rubber plantation, was shot. That very same day three planters near Sungei Siput were murdered simultaneously. This signalled the start of the Malayan Emergency, a polite euphemism for a long and bloody war by Chinese-backed communists against the British and their Malayan allies – contemptuously known as 'The R*nning Dogs'. It was an ironic situation – the Communists fighting for independence which the British wanted to give them.

Cecil Lee went on home leave to England and bumped into John Kennedy at this time. Kennedy had ended up in RAF Training Command for most of the war as an instructor. Latterly he was assigned to Coastal Command, trying to spot and destroy German U-boats. Lee told him of Gispert's demise. For his part, Kennedy says Lee struck him as much the same person he knew, despite the atrocities of his lengthy internment. Kennedy believes Cecil Lee modestly deflected a lot of the credit to G. "Well I think it's because Gispert was killed, you see," says Kennedy. "But I think that Cecil probably was the … it was a joint thing between them. They were the two," he finally resolves, although he always references Lee first and mentions Gispert as an afterthought. Kennedy left to resettle in Tasmania, Australia shortly afterwards.

In 1949 Torch Bennett handed the secretary's baton on to Don Kennedy. While life in KL itself was not immediately and noticeably effected [By the emergency, not the change of On Sec –ed.] there were signs that things had changed. Police, even those on traffic duty, now wore side-arms. Hashers enjoying a beer or sizzling steak in downtown haunts such as The Coliseum could see those from further out of the city, such as rubber planters, checking in their revolvers or rifles at the door or stacking them on the mahogany bar before getting stuck into a few hard-earned beers and curry puffs. At The Spotted Dog, cricket and tennis matches went on as usual. Spectators watched from the verandah, *stengahs* glued permanently in one hand. Most felt it would be a brief skirmish and be done with in a matter of weeks. In fact it was to last the next 12 years.

R*n sheets made a humble reappearance – mainly because the Malay Mail no longer posted the Hash's r*n notices – usually being no more than a circular which was "just a flimsy slip of paper with the most basic directions to the next week's r*n," according to John Duncan. By 1951, 40,000 British and Colonial troops had been brought into Malaya to fight alongside the Malay police. 25,000 of these were Royal Navy and RAF personnel. While a few may have r*n with the Hash in KL, more importantly many officers were exposed to the Hashing concept – as they would sometimes drink at The Spotted Dog in transit through KL.

Up to the north, hundreds of thousands men were fighting against communism, driving up rubber prices in the meantime and creating good economic times for rubber firms. A young fresh-faced lad named Bill Panton was invited to the Hash one day in 1954 by Hashing colleagues in the Agricultural Department. He ran and somewhat enjoyed it. "But I said 'to hell with this I'll join you when I really need to'," says Panton, "'which will be when I become chair-bound and start putting on a bit of weight'."

"I wasn't interested because I was already exerting myself, and I was thin as a rake eating rather poorly on two-week jungle trips and things like that, sweating away, so I was super fit, almost r*nning myself down frankly. And Hashing just wasn't on my agenda." It would be another four years before he ran the Hash again.

He often stayed at the chambers when stationed in Kuala Lumpur. The partitions in the rooms were rather thin wood which didn't go all the way to the ceiling, Panton remembers. Hence nefarious noises would resonate through the chambers to collective mirth or envy of the others. In the morning, the tenants – a number of whom were also Hashers – had their breakfast downstairs and often awaited the arrival of a 'noisy' couple as they came downstairs, greeting them with a loud cheer and a round of applause.

Slowly, the effects of the war began to show on the streets of KL. Few shops dared to open all hours like they usually did. Now sundown signalled shutters down for many. At the Coliseum, 'the place looked like an arsenal till five o'clock – and like a morgue by half past' as planters took their guns and headed home before dark. In 1955, a turning point in the war was achieved, and a new air of optimism washed through the capital. Once more little signs of normality – like a bunch of planters singing around the Coliseum Bar until midnight – returned. By the end of 1956 the Communists had been cleared from more than half the country.

The Hash was still having fun. They would have the occasional Chinese dinner thrash and it wouldn't be unusual to see Dr Reid – having staged a remarkable Tiger Beer inspired recovery after a hard r*n – singing his famous rendition of One Fish Ball, a localised version of the better-known ditty, One Meat Ball. British eccentricity "that so often seemed to thrive in the Empire", according to intrepid travel writer Noel Barber[121] was still evident at these times leading up to the Malayanisation of the peninsula. But the r*ns were becoming invariably longer and harder, establishing a robust physical culture. Few were the r*ns that lasted less than an hour and a half. Hashers like Dr John Reid gave up Hashing when he was 35 as he was consistently the last home. Few Hashed past 40 any more.

Malaya finally gained sovereign independence in September 1957. Freshly-arrived Englishman David Scourse – working for a subsidiary of Harrison and Crossfield – ran his first trail, along with the standard Hash pack of around 20 others. Cecil Lee by now was 46, a lofty Director of the Harrison's Group, and found Hashing a bit hard going. His dog, Tribly, was also ageing and got lost frequently on trail. "Being a very junior employee in the company, I usually ended up looking for it," says Scourse. "It was decided in the end that the dog was trying to lose Cecil!"

Lee hung up his boots and moved on to Sandakan in Borneo for four years before returning briefly to KL then retiring to Surrey in England in 1961. He took an active interest in military history and wrote several books on this subject.

Incidentally, the Hash could hardly be accused of littering with their paper trails – in the course of the war over 525 million leaflets had been dropped over the jungles of Malaya, propagandising the anti-communist message. In June

1958, a young British fellow who worked with Boustead's signed up. Harry Howell was his name. Torch Bennett retired at this stage and left Malaya with his wife, heading for South Africa [That's a long way to go to avoid Harry –ed.]. A couple of months later in August, that young fellow Panton showed up again, in an old button shirt, and a pair of old khaki shorts. He now had a job which kept him in a chair most of the day, not out in the field. Keeping to his word, he rejoined the Hash.

"We used to use either normal gym shoes or in my case – and many others – we used to use Fook Yong jungle boots," remembers Panton. "Little canvas boots that go up to the ankle and they have a sewn-up tongue so that leeches can't get in between the tongue through the eyeholes of the laces." Fook Yong was a canvas boot maker with a shop in downtown KL. "And then when we were in the jungle we wore *puttees,* the old army style things. They gave you decent protection for your ankles and at least prevented the leeches from getting into your feet. Gym shoes didn't last very long of course with the tough treatment they got on a r*n in the Malaysian forest."

Gruelling r*n over, they'd get into the refreshments. "We'd just have a shandy or two – and then we'd split a large beer and then it would be time to go home," remembers Panton. "Many of us were married, some of us were bachelors in bachelor messes, and there was a meal waiting for us. So we didn't go carousing around the town. It's not that we were constricted quite frankly, it's just that it wasn't the proper thing to do in Colonial Service circumstances."

However, despite the enthusiasm of r*nners such as Cumming, Panton, Llew Davidson, Arthur Broom, John Duncan (who had been introduced by his workmate, Howell, with whom he billeted), Mark Olver, Ralph Wadsworth and David Scourse, the pack sizes were dwindling from a couple of dozen down to a dozen. "It got down to seven at one stage," says Panton, "after everyone took their bags of gold and went home" in the post-*Merdeka* (Independence) period.

With Colonial Servants returned to the UK, work permits were required for any expatriate staff now brought in. Scourse became On Sec in 1959, and – having set a r*n for only seven persons the year before – embarked on a recruitment drive. "We had a major drive to recruit new members from commercial companies whose staff would be longer term," says Scourse. Among these were Linatex (for whom he worked), Shell and the Rubber Research Institute. It obviously wasn't very selective, as Ian Cumming [Yes, that's his *real* family name – ed.] was roped by Scourse "into this unknown group of upright citizens behaving in a bizarre manner". It seems that it was a quiet time for the Hash. "It may have been a temporary lull in singing activity," says songmeister Cumming. "It did not occur to me to attempt to introduce rugby songs into their lifestyle." But the Hash cobbled together enough for a rugby team for occasional matches against The Dog. A pint of beer at half-time was the Hasher's preferred refreshment.

Then the On Sec in KL had a new problem – how to inform 25 Hashers by mail of the starting point of the next Hash in less than six days time. Typing seven times with two carbons was the standard. Brevity was its own incentive, particularly when the hare frequently ate into the lead-time by failing to carry out a recce until the preceding Wednesday or Thursday. One day the On Sec apparently lost his cool and added an announcement to the circular: "Somebody has stolen the Hash enamel beer jug. It was obviously mistaken for a specimen container. We diagnose the vandal's problem; with a specimen so large he has a severe case of Galloping Australian Bladder-Blight. Please be on the lookout." With this frivolous outburst, a new life – indeed a whole new dimension – was given to the humble circular. Cumming left Kuala Lumpur and moved down to Singapore in 1961. The Hash gave him a mug for his troubles, and his wife Jane made a speech. "Said how much she would miss us all," recalls Scourse, "but was glad than Ian would be out of the bad influence of his Hash mates."

The Hash was in danger of falling away completely. The hardliners wanted it to remain true to its origins. Men only. No dogs. No women. No Asians. But in desperation – and with much resentment from some quarters – the Hash opened its membership to 'local' nationals for the first time. K.C. Chai was one of the earliest local members. The likes of Horse Thompson and John Kennedy insist that locals were always welcome from the start, it's just that they felt uncomfortable in sports events dominated by *mat sallehs* (foreigners). Slowly, locals dipped a toe in the water, but fortunately enough expressed an interest, and Hashing was saved from an ignominious ending. "The future of Hash was assured," says Scourse, who'd put in the most effort on the recruitment drive. Still, it remained a gentile preserve, whereby Hashers – now including the likes of Phil Riddell, Wes Carter and Horst Whippern – would often have a couple of shandies and beers after the r*n, have a shower and get changed (sometimes into shirt and tie!) for the On On dinner, often "an arse-burner" curry, according to Carter. But the spirit was still much the same, with a few beers being enjoyed and bawdy, often insulting songs being sung well into the night. A small group might have found its way to Kepong where the earthy Annie's Bar was a firm favourite, or else The Rex Bar, Tivoli, Kowloon Bar or Paramount in Batu Road, which soldiered on, with its busy shops at daytime and assorted massage parlours at night. An Anchor Beer could be had for $1.60 Malayan at that time.

In 1964, TV was introduced to the country. The following year the original Hash House Chambers were taken over by the local Water Board for offices.

In March 1966, at KL's 1,000th r*n, it was decided to add back those missing 117 r*ns from pre-war to the total. So r*n #1002 became 1119.

1968 saw Aussie diplomat Karl Henne head back down under, clutching his pewter mug of appreciation.

The first 'local' office bearer was Eddie Fong, Joint Master in 1971. In a sure signal that the Hash was really r*nning the country and dictating its destiny, Tunku Abdul Razak became the *country's* first local office bearer when he was elected Prime Minister of Malaysia that same year.

Werner Krebs – yes, that's his real name – left at this time to head to Switzerland. Peter Dominey left for Durban, South Africa. Jeremy Pigeon for Jakarta, Indonesia. Bill Panton left in 1972 to take up a posting in Washington,

DC. As the pack sizes grew, so logistics – getting beer to the r*n site – became more complicated. In the Seventies, drinks were brought in crates to the r*n site on a flatbed truck by the local supplier. And after the beer and the Down Downs, "the On Sec just announced the r*n site and that," says Alex Thomas.

The original Selangor Club Chambers – the sacred Hash House – was sadly demolished in 1974 to make way for the Jalan Kuching Highway overpass [And lovely it it is, too –ed.]. At this time, Bob Rooke, a Brit, headed for Little Rock, USA.

Panton believes the KL Hash is much the same as when it started even though there is an overwhelming majority of 'local' nationals and long-term Malaysian residents now in the chapter. Brian Columbus agrees: "The Hash remains the same where it matters most, in its enduring spirit and camaraderie. A blend of race and culture, of colour and creed, where mechanics mingle freely with managing directors, all together in a common endeavour – the Hash."[60] Mother Hash – as it's come to be known for its maternal role in the Hashing dynasty – didn't have circles as we know them today up until about 10 years ago. To this day, Hash names are generally not bestowed. There is no Grand Master. Just a simple paper trail laid, and Down Downs enjoyed after the r*n. The range of soft drinks available and introduction of isotonic drinks has made a slight difference – the sheer volume of fluids can no longer be crammed into an old washtub. Today's 'washtub' is an enclosed van with its own regular crew of two to lay out the drinks in preparation for the r*nners' return. Beer is strictly not served until 7:15pm, regardless of when the Front Running Bastards get in. Horse Thompson would turn in his curry gravy.

One recent visiting Hasher referred to their penchant for hard and fast r*ns as "macho Malaysian bullshit". Amazingly, in the Klang Valley of Selangor alone there are now 16 active Hash kennels. But long-term inmate and purist John Duncan says: "Mother is still the best, by a long way; what happens on other evenings masquerading as a Hash is frequently disgraceful, and you plan your attendance with care." Duncan easily holds the record for continuous membership of a single Hash, having r*n with Mother Hash from 1958 till present.

Kuala Lumpur today is a bustling metropolis, and home to the world's tallest building, the twin Petronas Towers. Across town, in stark contrast, The Selangor Club's white tudor-style buildings still overlook the green oasis of the Padang, where the sound of bat on ball still reverberates in the tropical sun, and the clink of ice being swirled in gin-and-tonics can be heard over the whirring ceiling fans.

A bridge not far enough.

After its initial formation, the Hash House Harriers remained unique to Kuala Lumpur for many, many years. This was possibly because Malaya had a less transient population of colonials and expatriates. Or more likely because Hashers – being the lazy ne'er-do-wells they are ... There were claims by Sandy Sanford, a long-time Singapore Hashman latterly of Perth, Australia, that a Hash r*n was laid from the Singapore Cricket Club through Chinatown in 1959. Whether this was a one-off event or not is unknown, and unfortunately Sanford passed away in 2001 so his claim cannot be substantiated [He could've at least returned our calls –ed.].

However, Scotsman Ian Cumming had moved down to Singapore Island in 1961. Singapore had become an important trans-shipment port for the peninsula, with the majority of rubber and tin being exported from here. Warehousing and distribution for imports was also centred here. Lee Kuan Yew, a young firebrand and ex-lawyer, was already in the majority with his party, and communism was deemed to be the real threat facing the island.

The city – its skyline dominated by the seven-storey Shell building – was reportedly ugly, with virtually no greenery in the city area. Hotels such as The Cockpit and even Raffles had seen better days. Singapore itself had that heady Asian aroma of sewage, food and sweaty bodies exotically blended. Orchard Road had a big canal r*nning alongside it, which "stank to high heaven". Still, it was a relatively free and easy lifestyle. You could cross Orchard Road quite casually without looking … the first of the little Japanese-made Suzuki bikes were seen on the roads, zipping between the more common Morris Oxfords and Austin Cambridges. Old Constellation planes flew overhead, landing just outside the town at Kallang Airport. Soon construction would start at the new Paya Lebar Airport.

Of course, expats could always seek refuge in the exclusive Tanglin Club, American Club or the Singapore Cricket Club for sports, recreation and the odd gin and tonic. There were two golf courses: The Singapore Club and The Bukit Course. The Japanese were moving into Singapore in droves behind their consumer goods: cameras and transistor radios. Golf was their status symbol and in Singapore they could play virtually for nothing. The courses became crowded almost overnight.

"My wife and I became aware of the eerie dearth of activity following weekends, and although she has denied it vehemently ever since, Jane was the first to suggest that what was lacking was the Hash," Cumming said on the birth of the Singapore Hash[93]. "I discussed this with the only other ex-KL Harrier I knew in Singapore, Chris Verity, and we both agreed that although the terrain on the island was totally lacking in Hashability, having almost no rubber plantations or tin tailings, it might be worth a try." Verity – a moustachioed 'Pompous with a capital P' Brit – had been Secretary and Joint Master of Mother Hash in the late Fifties.

Cumming then wrote to John Vincent, the On Sec of the KL Hash, indicating he was going to start up a Singapore Hash chapter and asking him what the relationship and reporting protocol of this offshoot should be. The response was short and to the point: "Do what the hell you like. Nothing to do with us. Let us know how you get on."

Inadvertently, the informal anti-establishment persona of the international Hashing world was set there and then. "Undoubtedly, the most significant step in the spreading of the Hash worldwide was Mother's inspired decision not to become involved in any form of control," says Cumming, calling Vincent an unsung hero. "The reasoning behind this decision is not important – it may have been sheer laziness, or lack of administrative ability, but it has become the cornerstone of our success leading to an awe-inspiring variety of operations and activities, and a wonder of mythical so-called traditions, some of which even the Mother Hash has retro-adopted."

So Cumming sent out a written invitation to others to join him for a "cross-country r*n" after which "the formation of a r*nning club" would be discussed.

Appropriately, Ken Kesey's book One Flew Over the Cuckoos Nest was released around the time that twelve Hashers-to-be fronted for the first r*n on February 19 1962. The trail started from Cumming's house near the Hollandse Club (now The Swiss Club) off leafy Adam Road. Among them was Harry Howell, who had changed jobs and moved down from Kuala Lumpur without missing a beat. One Monday he was r*nning with KL, the next week he ran on Singapore r*n #1.

"The r*n marked with paper strips took off northwards across Adam Road, following a monsoon drain long since built over, cut through the Chinese Cemetery and bush-whacked to Ulu Kalang," remembers Cumming. "The r*n-in skirted the Royal Singapore Golf Club and returned to Adam Road via Sime Road."

R*n over, they got stuck into the ginger beer shandies and Anchor Beer, and the Cummings whipped up a culinary feast of bangers and mash. Followed by more beer. "My recollection was that there was some singing, most likely Be I 'Ampshire Be I Buggery, I Be Up From Wareham, the Dogs Meeting, John Thomas Was a Footman Tall and The Lobster Song," says Cumming. "There was a unanimous decision to repeat the event."

Either Chris Verity or Tommy Voice set the next r*n, with Mike Miall and John Gastrell fronting for their first punishment. Cumming's car, a Ford Consul station wagon, was "just about the right size for several cases of Anchor and ginger beer, an ice tub, 30 or so tin mugs, three or so HHH signs and a can of cigarettes."

On one of the early r*ns, Ian Cumming remembers Chris Verity standing in the middle of a Singapore *kampong* (village) where there was a check, yelling out in his pukka accent, "Well, somebody ask the bloody villagers which way they went!" A Hasher in the grand colonial tradition if ever there was one. Others on early Singapore trails included Doug Smith, John O'Rourke, Mike Dudderidge, Colin Berwick, John Kingham, and Peter Flanagan, a fine mixture of Brits and Australians. A jet-fresh Royal Commando, Ray Thornton, parachuted in on r*n #10. Even Curly Lee (Cecil's shiny-headed brother) who lived in Johor Bahru then moved down to Singapore, was among them. Cumming and Voice were the first Joint Masters, Verity first Secretary.

As the standard dress code for business in those days was short white-sleeved shirts with ties, it was decided that a club tie for the Hash should be designed and produced. Green for the jungle was the preferred colour scheme, with silver for the HHH to represent the importance of tin. However, HHH – while nicely symmetrical and alliterative – seemed visually clumsy. Never short of an opinion, Colin Berwick suggested abbreviating that to H3. Not a bad idea, they thought. Thus H3 was adopted. Whether in connection to the tie or not, Berwick departed shortly after for Brunei. Incidentally, as any self-respecting physicist will tell you, H3 is Hydrogen 3 (or tritium) a key component in nuclear energy fusion [Wasted on this lot –ed.].

The Singapore Hash started in the traditional manner of KL. Male only. No names. No horn. After the r*n, the Hashers would stand around in small groups chatting, laughing, drinking before soon adjourning to the On On. And they always enjoyed good and rowdy On Ons, relishing the challenge to get local stall-keepers down to the lowest possible price for a bottle of beer – about $1.40 Singapore. Typically, in those days they could enjoy a couple of large Anchor beers plus a chapatti and curry gravy for S$4.00.

Under Ian Cumming's personal guidance they sang – loudly and often. "The Singapore startup, with extensive On On On activity, lent itself immediately to singing," he says. "While we could not boast a choir to lead us we had a wealth of solo singers and stand-up comedians. We had a repertoire of jokes and songs from a wonderful variety of sources," he says of the pack which grew to include New Zealanders, even Russians and central Europeans.

Cumming says many of these early neck-tie wearing Singapore Hashers "probably enhanced the anti-establishment nature of the Hash more than anyone else"[61]. He said he specifically took into account the behaviour of three individuals, John O'Rourke, Peter Flanagan and Harry Howell "all now or former Australians" when he said that. "They all displayed an ingenious disrespect for authority and pomposity that was refreshing and enlightening in a newly established ex-colonial environment." He talks fondly and in awe of their propensity to demolish the location of their AGM dinner until there were no locations left to stage the event. He also found their traditional farewell to a departing Hasher at the end of the On On On – "Wannanotherbeer? Pissoffthen!" particularly endearing.

Newsletters around this time often included letters from a fictitious Hashman, I.M. Lastin. "Lastin's attitude was typical of the characterisation we liked to publish of the idle, disrespectful selfish Hasher we all tried to emulate," says Cumming. "Remember, this was years before Jerry Seinfeld!"

But it wasn't all beer and skittles in Singapore. In July 1963, British prison officer Daniel Dutton was hacked to death and set on fire in a prison riot. In September 1963, the Federation of Malaysia was formed, which included Singapore. The national airline was renamed Malaysian Airways Limited. As it happened the Flying Club was a popular On On venue for the Hash. Thereafter, fully fuelled for take-off, they would indulge in other favourite past-times such as darts, and Red Cap [military guard] baiting. "We kept on getting pulled over by the Red Caps who didn't believe we weren't Army," remembers Howell.

In 1964, one Hasher's new Volvo was accidentally set alight by the Joint Master, and the assembled Hashers – altruistic to the last – helped douse the flames by emptying their Anchor-filled bladders on it.

At r*n # 170 a new – although at the age of 40 not young – Australian face appeared. Fred Whitaker, ready for action in his $1.50 Bata sandshoes and singlet. Fed up with trying to get a game on the crowded golf courses, he was invited by an architect friend to come "for a cross-country r*n". Thinking he had allowed himself enough time to get to the site, by the time he arrived in his Holden, he saw a pack of people disappearing over the hill. "I didn't know what it was all about, trails or anything like that," says Whitaker, "so I pulled up and dashed after them. Of course, being relatively unfit I was very soon lost. I didn't know where the hell I was, and about an hour later I was wondering around in a Chinese cemetery looking at the headstones – didn't know if I'd ever find home again – and a fellow walks up behind me and puts his hand on my shoulder and says 'Are you lost, too?' I looked around and it was Dr Clyde Lane."

"We'd come back to the bucket, drink at the bucket – there were no bottles – then we'd all go on to an On On which would be the nearest nosh place we could find and we'd stay there drinking Anchor. It was just a bloody riot that night … I'd never seen a better singing night in my time. They went till two in the morning. Derek Roy was the greatest rugby song singer of all time. You couldn't beat him, he was just unreal … he'd challenge anybody. He knew more verses, more songs, he was bloody marvellous. I was captured there and then."

Other faces in the crowd were Chris Eastgate, Jim Corsey, Paddy Bye, Jim Ambler and Don Madden. "There were a lot of younger single blokes," remembers Whitaker, "but the married blokes were getting up to my age in their 30s. I would've been probably the oldest there."

Whitaker's second r*n proved to be equally enjoyable, in retrospect. "We went out on Bukit Timah Hill," he says, "and still with no real knowledge of Hashing I get out on the track and take the wrong turning and I end up in pitch black in the jungle. There were still tigers at the time. So I'm wandering about in the black when out of the darkness come these great shapes … I nearly died of fright. Turns out to be these cows. There's only half a dozen cows in the whole of the East let alone in the middle of the jungle. I didn't know, but behind Bukit Timah Hill was a dairy, and they're finding their way home. I was out there till 10 o'clock at night."

While the official advent of Dirt Road Hash was some way down the track, Singapore H3 held a 'Massage Parlour Series' in neighbouring Johore Bahru in 1964 – a series of four r*ns that saw the Hash impose itself on establishments such as Tokyo Nights, New Scientific, Curly's Joss House and Tokyo By Night across the Causeway from Singapore Island. One night at Tokyo Nights was especially memorable for all involved. A certain Hasher was 'otherwise occupied' [You mean shagging his brains out? –ed] in one of the rooms, and eight voyeuristic Hashers were peering over the top of the partition. The wall collapsed, the lot of them landing on top of the prone Hasher in fits of snorts and giggles among the dust and debris.

On Singapore island itself, the delightfully seedy and sexually ambiguous Bugis Street with its colourful transvestite denizens was in full swing. However, the Hash didn't do too much consorting with them or the local femme fatales in the bars. "We were too interested in the piss I think," says Whitaker. In the absence of any pubs, mostly they'd go to places like the Bukit Timah bar and 'coffee-shop' stalls. "Some of the places had a few girlie bars but we didn't frequent them too much, only because we were after nosh. Cheap nosh and cheap beer." Local *nasi padang* style meals were a favourite.

On Tuesdays, whoever was available would front for the editorial meeting to put out the week's circular. This was invariably held at The Eyes and Piles – an Indian restaurant in a row of shop-houses down near Hill Street – nicknamed thus as it was between an ophthalmologist's shop with jars of eyes on one side and a construction business with steel piles on the other. "The lunch was open house, but generally John Gastrell, wordsmith, and John O'Rourke and I were there," says Cumming, "and ideas bandied about, graphics improvised or described, the whole mess being dumped on my office manager's desk. She promptly vetted the entire document to avoid violation of anti-government propaganda legislation and a personal dislike of four-letter words, typed up the copy, ran it off and had it in the mail. The material was very topical, involving many members of the pack, solacing the damaged and deflating the highly self-esteemed. All on one side of a single sheet."

"That was always a good piss-up on a Tuesday afternoon," remembers Whitaker, who availed himself of down time between regional projects when he could. "That was more important than the Hash." It was at one such session that someone came up to Whitaker. "By the way, that American came up to me last night – what's his name, Murphy? – and said 'It's a very strange club this … very strange people … I've been here three times and I haven't been introduced'." So they decided that the next time Dick Murphy – a visiting geologist for Esso and possibly the first American Hasher – was going on a r*n they'd arrange to have him picked up under the guise of it being a very distant venue and difficult to find. Sure enough, the next week they told Murphy they'd pick him up from the Goodwood Park Hotel where he was staying, and turned up in a convertible Rolls-Royce, complete with the Union Jack and the Stars and Stripes flags crossed on the front, plus a syce dressed in full driver's regalia (actually an airline captain's cap). John Gastrell sat regally in the back seat with Murphy. And when they got to the venue, they had a tape playing 'Land of Hope and Glory' and a great big banner which read: 'SINGAPORE HASH WELCOMES DICK MURPHY!' Others wore rosettes saying 'Murphy For President' and so on. "He just about collapsed," remembers Whitaker. "I reckon he's the only bloke that's ever been introduced on the Hash among all the thousands who have r*n."

"There's an important point about the spirit of Hashing here," said Murphy. "When the Hash encountered a loose cannon, which I certainly was in the 1960s, they rewarded outrageous behaviour by making you a Hash official. I was the first American Hash official anywhere. The idea was that they made the current Asshole a Joint Master – providing they saw some potential merit – wherein he grew in office and in Hashdom. It always worked."

Cumming liked the American Hashers as they "knew the more obscene ditties" such as I Love My Girl . . . In the mid Sixties, Torch Bennett joined one of their On Ons, even correcting Cumming's rafter-raising version of the Alphabet Song. "We had I and N completely screwed up," says Cumming. "Believe me, that's about as deep as anyone gets in the mire of dirty songs."

Singapore H3 Hashers often found their way to KL for business and a r*n with Mother Hash. Possibly as a result of those visits, on August 9 1965 Singapore exited from Malaysia, becoming an independent republic. Lee Kuan Yew was installed as Singapore's first Prime Minister, a post he would hold for 31 years. David Marshall was named Singapore's first Chief Minister. A new nation-building blueprint was put in place. Amid the confusion and uncertainty of independence, only nine Hashers (including the hares) fronted for the r*n that day. Ironically it was held in Johore, Malaysia. Thereafter, Johore r*ns became difficult because of the new immigration point passport requirements and the delays they caused.

Though it was hardly any compensation a Scotsman, Gordon Benton, was brought along to the Hash one night. "It was John Gastrell who got me started," he says. "I don't recall that the first r*n was anything other than painful, but things improved I suppose as the r*ns accumulated."

Plenty was going on at this time in a society trying to find itself and forge a new identity. Murders, kidnapping and gangster behaviour proliferated.

In 1966, with membership growing and names like Harrison joining the ranks, logistics became an issue. It had been relatively easy until now for the hares to lay on beer, ginger beer, ice and – like KL in the old days – cigarettes, supplied free of charge by contacts at the tobacco company. But now they had to sign up the local brewery to provide and transport the drinks for the growing numbers.

Perhaps because Peter Flanagan was a pilot for Malaysia-Singapore Airlines, the Singapore Hashers decided to go to KL by train instead when they were invited in March 1966 to go up and celebrate Mother Hash's 1,000th r*n. About 24 Hashers had drunk the train dry by the time they reached Kluang, about a quarter the way there, and sent out teams to buy up all the beer they could from provision stores at every stop the train made thereafter. They arrived in splendid form for the event, and received a 'certificate of survival' in the circular that followed. "We didn't consider it to be anything special, just an excuse to cause trouble at The Dog – in which case it could be considered a success," said Cumming. Friendly rivalry with the more 'pukka' KL kennel was never far from the surface.

At the end of 1966 Ian Cumming departed for New York. He had started the Singapore Hash, one of the most influential Hash chapters in the world. And with it, an undeniable disdain for bureaucracy and formalities. So short were their AGMs, that each year they tried to make it even shorter. Apart from On Sec, all officers were rotated annually, and many formalities dispensed with. "The whole thing would happen 'You've got the job' sort of thing, that was it," remembers Whitaker. "About three seconds – bang, bang, bang. A very democratic show." At their AGM in 1970, they got through the formalities in one minute and 25 seconds. This was bested in 1978 with a mere one minute and 10 seconds, assisted by the fact that no Annual Report had been prepared to table. Nonetheless, they managed to rack up "the most expensive On On in history" at the Singapore Island Country Club.

Another thing created by the Singapore H3 was the word 'shiggy'. Dick Murphy and Australian Alex Gibb were on trail through a pig farm. According to Murphy, Gibb turned right onto what he thought was a slab of concrete. Alas, it was the dried crust of a pool of pigs' excrement. "Pig shit … *shiggy*!" says Murphy of the term that has come to mean many inclement things to Hashers over the years. "Shiggy" first appeared in a December 1967 newsletter, with frequent references to "shiggy pit" soon thereafter.

Fred Whitaker left for Australia just before this incident. If he'd left like Harry Howell to Sydney the following year, he would have been able to fly on the local airline's brand new toy – the Boeing 707 – and enjoy the stewardesses shapely new *sarong kebaya* uniform. In June 1969, Gastrell left Singapore. But there were still 120 Hashers registered in Singapore. A monster had been created.

A couple of years later, Geoff Whitehead left Singapore for a posting in Bahrain. Despite being avowedly open to allcomers, the Singapore kennel was largely a British bastion, but certainly all-expatriate, until 1971 when former Singaporean Army Major Ratnam Narayansamy joined. At the time it wasn't considered acceptable to mix with the local fillies socially, let alone marry one, as British medico Dr Clyde Lane did. He was reportedly shot in the leg going to visit his wife-to-be in her *kampong* one day. "I mean you'd go down the bars and shag around in the bars but you'd never be seen socially with them," remembers Whitaker. "Some of the single blokes might have had a bit on the side I suppose. But there was still this remnant of the Raj."

In 1972, Singapore Airlines (SIA) was born. And Hashers laughed when the Straits Times interviewed Lim Kim San, then Minister for Environment, who talked of the government imposing a $1 duty on the import of durian fruits. This was because of the skins that were strewn everywhere and reportedly cost the government $14,000 a month in cleaning fees. A Singapore without durian? Unthinkable!

From April to June 1973, the Hash had to choose their r*n sites carefully … a black panther was on the loose and the army had orders to shoot anything that moved. It was eventually caught not far from where Cumming used to live at Bukit Timah. Late in August 1973 the glitzy five-star Mandarin Hotel opened on Orchard Road. Many thought it would never survive: too ostentatious for Singapore they said.

In October 1974, the first record of a female 'guest' was noted on r*n # 669. Des Holloway had invited her and was "merely being polite". The following week, two Hashers – Clyde Lane and Derek Roy – appeared for the r*n dressed as Bugis Street transvestites, in a mock protest.

But while feelings ran high in Singapore, the *circular* achieved new lows with the following dogmatic description of r*n # 677: "Cars come. People in r*nning kit. JM shout, On-on. People r*n. Check. People shout, check. People shout, On-on. People r*n. SCB SC. People shout, check. People shout, On-on. People arrive cars. People drink suds. Talk. Tell lies. Cars leave. People go home, people go On-on. Great." [Asterisked by my dead hand –ed.]

Hashman Jim Raper left Singapore and returned to Surrey in England. A couple of years later saw the hare Gillard react badly to criticism of his r*n, and abuse not only his fellow Hashers [Naturally! –ed.] but also the Fraser & Nieve lackeys in charge of the suds. The next week was a dry r*n as the F&N beer wagon failed to show. This was a contributing factor to the creation of The Order of the Amin Scrotum, a black-balling system for hares. Half a Scrotum was one black ball which disqualified a hare from laying trail for a year. The dreaded Full Scrotum was two black balls and a life disqualification. But the Hash kept growing – despite ineptitude by management who closed membership and raised fees – to about its peak of 210 members in 1978. In 1980, Singapore H3 celebrated its 1,000th r*n.

Despite the original misgivings of its founders, Singapore was obviously fertile ground for Hashing, with r*ns available with different chapters every night of the week by 1982. The expats also seemed a lot more mobile and transient. With Singapore being a major petro-chem centre, the oil crisis of the mid-Eighties saw many expat Hashers packing their bags and heading home whence they came. As a result, according to Bill Panton, about five-eighths of all worldwide Hash chapters owe their existence directly to the Singapore Hash. "Singapore has probably been the father of many other Hashes due to the preponderence and turnover of expats in comparison with other Hashes," according to O'Rourke. Hence its nickname as The Father Hash.

Beer is now about S$40 per jug. Changi Airport is rated as one of the world's best. And the country is famous for its 'clean and green' environment. "Surprising or not, given the irreverent nature of the Hash – and especially the Singapore Monday Hash, which only has three rules; no women, no poofters, no dogs – that the one r*n celebrated on an annual basis is the Gispert memorial r*n, held on the Monday closest to the anniversary of his death," says Andrew Kefford. "Hashmen assemble at the wall in Kranji – which lists Gispert as one of the many whose body was never found – then the GM (or a senior Hasher) says a few words on Gispert's life, his death and what he gave the Hash, followed by one minute's silence. The silence is broken by a lone bagpiper playing the Last Post and then it is back to the entrance of Kranji for the normal 18:00 off and the pack will return to the site for the circle and On On."

To this day, Singapore remains a very 'traditional' chapter with a strong sense of Hashtory, but very few bells and whistles. No names, no horns. But they do hand out the Hash Prick award each week, a large wooden phallus worn around the neck of the offender.

The Cradle of Hashdom.
Within six years of Singapore's founding, 14 new kennels spread like a nasty dose of athlete's foot through Malaysia, Singapore and Brunei. Bill Panton has called this 'The Cradle of Hashdom'.

James Brooke, 'The White Rajah', had r*n Brunei almost as a personal fiefdom in the mid 1800s. In the 1920s, oil and gas – in quantities unheard of outside of a Hasher's shorts – were discovered, setting Brunei and its citizens up for life. Brunei gained self-government in 1959 after a lengthy spell of being a British protectorate. By the early Sixties its citizens enjoyed free health benefits and free education, and almost no taxation. In 1962, their first and only elections were held, ending in a disastrous riot with the Gurkhas called in to restore peace. On reflection, The Sultan decided that he'd keep the reigns of the country as a monarchy after all.

On February 18 1963, Brunei H3 came into being. Colin Berwick and Pip Furse, Hashers from Singapore, were the culprits in this instance, with Peter McManus, Derek Morris and Dave Hobby also being instrumental. They drove around in their Austin rust-buckets and pinned up notices in the various service messes, and even handed out leaflets to expats in the private sector. The first pack numbered about 20 hounds, half of whom were services personnel. Beer was obtained from the NAAFI stores. Ice to cool the drinks proved a little harder to find, but eventually – after a little lateral thinking – was sourced from the local mortuary!

A number of r*ns were held, with pack sizes growing each time. British military man Richard McAllister ran on a couple of dozen trails. "Often heavy drinking affairs," are his memories of this period. "Duke of Edinburgh Bridge on the outskirts of Brunei Town was a good place to consume a few Down Downs. As we sat there with the sun sinking fast, the last rays reflected brilliantly off the golden dome of the mosque. It was a while before someone spotted that the empty Tiger cans we had been throwing into the river were floating in a tidy line with the flow down towards the mosque, some half a mile downstream. It was a race I think we lost – the sun went down before we could determine whether our continuous line of cans reached the mosque. But it was a good effort … "

Obviously not good enough because he was soon transferred to Kluang in Malaysia in 1964. Major Roger Forrest was also on trail before being posted to Singapore, thence Oman in the Middle East. But when McManus left Brunei a few months later in October, the Hash fell in a hole. He was absent for a year, returning the following October and reactivating the chapter which has been continuously active since. The Hash only counts one r*n per week for the kennel's total, regardless of whether it might have been a special event weekend with multiple r*ns or whatever.

No Hash sheets exist for Brunei H3 before 1965, although the founder members have sworn by the start date. Then in April 1966, the first mention of the 'Hashit' award was made in their r*n # 79 newsletter – awarded to hares Nick Rose and John Allum 'for the most Hashed-up r*n of the year'. The humble 'Hashit' would go on to achieve foam and fortune, and become a standard booby prize – accompanied by much shame and dishonour – in many chapters worldwide.

"The Hash Commandments which are now being bandied around the world in various modified forms originated in Brunei in the late Sixties," according to Geoff Feast who arrived there in 1967. "They were put together by an almost de-frocked Catholic vicar – who, for anonymity as Hash Words, went under the pen name of Y. R. Clerk – Eric Cooper, myself and a few others," he says. And plenty of anonymity was obviously needed, Feast recalling one unforgettable recce: "I remember coming across an illegal Iban knockshop up a valley behind Brunei Town. The 'ladies' gave the Hash freebies in return for keeping quiet, an offer which of course was eagerly accepted. Needless to say this area became a very popular area for Hash r*ns."

Its popularity grew rapidly. In 1982 the Brunei Hash House Harriers imposed an upper limit of 150 members. A waiting list for those wanting to join was set up. But ex-BH3 JM John Hughes disagreed with the limitation and invited all those on the waiting list – and any other prospective Hashers – to join him in forming a breakaway group. The Bandar Seri Begawan Hash House Harriers thus came into being. The original Brunei kennel is now known as the Old Farts Hash by other newer chapters in the area, due to its membership, described as geriatric by more kindly souls. Many of the Hashers today are airline employees and teachers, with a large contingent of New Zealanders. While they still drink copiously, the singing standards of days gone by have apparently fallen to a new low. Brunei today is home to no less than seven Hashes.

And this is where it gets messy [Not again! –ed.]. Kuching H3, established by Harry Howell also claims to have laid the first r*n in Brunei, their inaugural r*n having been on May 21 1963. Kuching H3 does indeed have a higher r*n total by virtue of counting all and any r*ns towards their r*n number (which although apparently not in the Hash tradition does make sense) and has been r*nning continuously.

Harry Howell sent out a flier in mid-May summoning hounds for Kuching r*n #1. "All this is a result of a surplus of enthusiasm which has overflowed from the Singapore and KL HHH who have been leading thirsty r*nners out on a paper chase one night a week for many years past," it read. "We would like to make it quite clear that we are not catering for would-be Roger Bannisters – far more for the panting Douggie Clarke's of this world who are occasionally heard to mumble 'really must take some exercise' and are prepared to go any lengths for a beer." It indicated a 40-minute trot over varied terrain was in store.

The flier further directed them to the r*n site one mile up Chawan Road (off Sekama Road) where they were to "look for sickly cream coloured Wolseley 1500 No. K7339."

Foolishly, about 11 expatriate hounds were on this first trail laid by Howell and Sammons and paid over their $2 for beer money. British commando Ray Thornton was on that first trail and emerged from the jungle to r*n as often as he could in between battling insurgents. Mike Dudderidge from Singapore was in attendance, as were Messrs. D. Blatchford and S. Macintosh, among others. Because Monday night was a military officers meeting night, Tuesdays were designated as Hash night. To this day, they still r*n on Tuesdays. Now you know why. "I always started my business trips on a Tuesday," says Howell, "so I could r*n Singapore on Monday and then r*n Kuching on Tuesday. Priorities, old chap," he says.

It was here that a bit of fun was had by the committee with the circular, inspired by Ian Cumming's earlier efforts in KL, according to Howell. One Kuching issue was actually printed circular – a round piece of paper! It was at this time that Howell also started the 'Receding Hareline' terminology that is prevalent around the world today. "I used to put in little things like 'Hare, There and Everywhere', and 'From Hare To Eternity' each week," he says. George Ang took his fare share of turns haring.

Having seen off the Indonesian insurgents, Ray Thornton got a posting to far-off Cyprus in the Mediterranean. They thought it might be the last they saw or heard of him for a while. With Thornton out of the way, the papers announced that Sukarno's self-appointed delegates to congress voted to make him President of Indonesia for life.

About this time, a slender young local chap, Stephen Kueh, turned up, ran strongly and decided to come along regularly. Very regularly as it turned out. Kueh became the first ever Hasher to achieve the incredible milestone of 1,000 r*ns with a single club, chalking it up in May 1989. "Great" and "happy" were the two words he used to describe how he felt when a banner of congratulations was strung up in acknowledgement of the occasion, complete with the finest formica tables, plastic chairs, and a cake. A phallic-shaped balloon arrangement was draped around his neck, and a cardboard tiara in the form of the Kuching H3 logo – a raised middle digit – adorned his head as he gulped several Down Downs that evening.

"Nowadays," he says, "the Hash has been 'Malaysianised'. Of course, there is still a group of hardcore old-time Caucasians like Warwick Anderson, Tim Hatch, Jim Cameron and Robert Basiuk on our r*ns." The committee has also changed. Today Kuching Hash has expanded to 13 committee members – larger than the whole original pack! – with a Grand Master as head of the club. "What has not changed," continues Kueh, "is the camaraderie among all the members irrespective of race, religion or social standing. It does not matter whether you are rich or poor, you will get an equal amount of abuse if, for example, you set a lousy r*n."

Being the eager song-master that he is, Howell had a relevant party piece in the form of Girl From Kuching. "I introduced that song to them and they still sing it to this day," he says.

In 1963, Miri H3 was also formed. Miri is the seaport of Sandakan that had been home to a notorious Japanese POW camp in World War 2, and the site of grisly death marches resulting in thousands of Allied deaths. Ian Nash, who had previously Hashed in Kuching, decided to lay some gruelling death marches of his own in this north-eastern part of North Borneo and the kennel was going strong for a few years in this oil town – often called 'the whorehouse of Brunei'– before fading away sometime in 1966.

It was subsequently revived in May 1973 due to massive demand from the working girls whose establishments had gone awfully quiet with its demise, but most probably when Shell upped its investment in the area. With the revolving door of foreign workers, continuity was fortunately supplied by a strong contingent of local r*nners. These days it is a mixed Hash and the average turnout is about 130, comprising a healthy mixture of locals and expatriates.

In 1964, city authorities in New York proudly unveiled plans for what was to be their city's dominant new landmark – the World Trade Centre towers. Ford's sexy new car, the Mustang, is released but the price tag of US$2,368 was a bit steep for Hashers, even if they could import one. Around Asia, the USS Card was sunk by the Viet Cong and General Westmoreland took over as head of the US Forces in Vietnam.

On June 22, Jesselton H3 was kicked off by George Will and Jim Ambler, who worked for Sime Darby in the East Malaysian town then known as Jesselton. Ambler had been the On Sec in Singapore just the year before. Notices were posted in expat haunts of the day, such as the Shamrock Pub and the Jesselton Club, inviting people to join them for "a gentle lollop through glassy glades and verdant valleys". The poster went on to say that "No strain is involved apart from the imposition of placing one leg in front of the other at a pace slightly faster than normal walking". The run fee was $2, including the shandy bucket.

The core of Hashers came from the Jesselton Rugby Club, where Will and Ambler were regulars [There's a surprise! –ed.]. Many from UN projects in the area turned out, as well as a contingent of Kiwis who were carrying out the Labuk Valley surveys at the time. Dave Ives, Tony Hooper, John Hope, a Mr Bullivant and Ken Floyd rounded out the pack of eager virgins. One of those who fronted for that r*n at Likas Beach was Brian Columbus, who recalled: "Together with a dozen or so others, I engaged in an easy trot along to the end of the beach and back again, a couple of quiet drinks and there you have it …"[76]

The second r*n was held at the Kepayan level crossing. Having missed the first r*n because he was 'up country' a young bespectacled fellow – Andrew Bacon – joined for his first r*n. Afterwards, the hounds repaired to the Shamrock Hotel, which just happened to be the local brothel as well [Nice coincidence! –ed.]. "The ladies entertained the Hash men below," says Bacon, "but few of these, I believe, ventured upstairs for further services."

It didn't take long for the Hash to take a hold on Jesselton's entertainment-starved population, with Hash parties apparently becoming the 'in' place for the expat society at the time. Joe Griffiths was among the regular revellers. At the Jesselton Club, bar manager John held sway, dispensing hot rum toddies after a r*n over Signal Hill in pouring monsoon rains.

Jesselton then became Kota Kinabalu, and the Hash changed its name accordingly. In 1971, worthies such as Peter Thomas, David Cox, Tony Evans, the Gillespies, iron man Mike Pike, and a spritely young fellow named Bob Leonard were regularly 'on'. With the Malayanisation came more 'local' participation. One particularly colourful character was Dr Lieu, who was already in his 60s and once a month used to bring a *sam lok* (stewed dog) casserole for the Hash. George David, a prison guard, got into Hashing in earnest. Presumably he found it a great escape [Groan –ed.]. He would go on to rack up the first 1,000 r*ns in this kennel. Tony Lee, KC Wong, and Thien Bak Yin "were all vocal and solid drinking members," says Bacon. More than 100 of the large 750ml bottles were typically demolished by the thirsty pack at each session.

If that wasn't enough, they'd then head off to The Towkay's Missis, a watering hole at Inanam. Here the large-bosomed wife of the owner would give as good as she got from the misbehaving Hashers. One itinerant oil-rig diver was unlucky enough to receive a large serving of chilli sauce inside his shorts for his troubles. The 'Hash Vomitorium' was presented to Hashers for use in emergency.

Bacon, in the KKH3 500th magazine, said: "Now, nearly 10 years after ... little has changed – except the price of drinks. These have been imbued with the spirit of the Hash, that mad something that drives us every Monday afternoon, to despoil ourselves in mud and rain, and then to fill ourselves with beer, bawling out the choruses of obscene songs, much to the delight and amusement of all in the local *kedai*." Mike Lewis and his rendering of Lavatory Sam was "not to be forgotten" according to Bacon. The other Mike, Mike Pike – an outstanding FRB by all accounts – sadly died at that age of 58 "of neglect and kidney failure" following a too-exhaustive Hash recce.

Sibu H3 was started in 1964 as well, with Ambrose Chung defecting from Nash's kennel in Miri and moving to this part of Malaysia. The kennel subsequently disbanded and sank without trace.

At the beginning of 1965, Winston Churchill went to the big beer stop and cigar humidor in the sky. Britain banned cigarette advertising on TV. Sonny Liston should have sold advertising space on the soles of his boots as he went toes up against Muhammad Ali in just 48 seconds. And Aussie Ron Clarke ran 5,000 metres in a record time of 13 minutes 33.6 seconds.

Thus inspired, January 1965 found the northern Malaysian town of Ipoh falling to the loud calls of "On On" and occasionally "Inn Inn" thanks to Mad Dog Denning and also Mark Olver, who had Hashed in KL since 1947. On the first few r*ns, all were *orang putih* (foreigners) with the notable exception of Loke Kai Heng. Once again, they were a chapter that wanted the minimum of organisation, fuss and bother. "There were no circulars, no beer van and certainly no registered society,"[58] said their Hashtorian. "The starting place of the r*n was notified by 'bush telegraph' and the hare was responsible both for bringing and paying for the beer. Soft drinks had not been invented in those days." After only six months of founding Ipoh, Denning was transferred to Penang.

With his departure, Lok Kai Heng became Grand Master, and initiated circulars and other semblances of organisation. Today, among the almost all-local 110-strong pack, Foo Wan Thot, Wan Sai Pan and Grasshopper are the longest-suffering members.

Things moved at their own languid pace on the Malaysian island of Penang in 1965. Even the workplace was very relaxed as a result of the tropical ambience, with a good lunch virtually slept off by expatriates after lunch most days. Denning – along with some Australian and Malaysian worthies – kicked off the Penang H3 chapter on June 1 1965. Robin Rawlings, who had Hashed in Singapore, and Gary MacDonald, were also partly to blame for the founding. There was plenty of social life at the time and sporting facilities associated with social clubs. "Everything orientated around Hash House Harriers even if you were playing other sports like rugby, cricket, whatever," says Chris Eden.

Eden, a British accountant, worked for the same firm as Denning and MacDonald, and was based in Kuala Lumpur. "I used to go regularly, regularly into The Dog," he says, "but I can't ever recall in those early days anybody talking about the Hash House Harriers. Had I heard of it, no doubt I would've joined." He was seconded to Penang in mid-1965. "I was only visiting for about five or six weeks and had half a dozen r*ns and got to know the trade," he says. "I wasn't on the first r*n, but it must have been fairly close to the beginning. One of the r*ns I went on was on Mt Kedah, the Kedah Peak, and that was a very tough r*n … we went pretty well to the top I think and ran back again." [Sorry I missed it –ed.]

There was no circle after the r*n. "In the early days I don't remember even having circles," says Eden. But Down Downs? "Oh, always! There was certainly plenty of accent on *this*," he says pointing to his beer glass.

It was a *batang* chapter – "definitely male only," says Eden, talking of the added licentiousness it afforded. "Why get yourself into trouble, when you could go into bars, coffee shops … they could not only serve you a very good meal but drink as much Anchor or Tiger Beer or whatever it was at the time, and what would happen is the On On site itself would be a relatively short affair, if at all, and then they'd repair to a coffee shop on the perimeter of town where they'd take over the poor old Chinese *towkay* r*nning the coffee shop, and tell him what to do." Eden left Malaysia in January 1966 and relocated to Hobart, Tasmania.

A contingent from the 75th Squadron Royal Australian Air Force was based at Butterworth nearby, and used to r*n regularly. However, at this stage they disappeared up to Ubon Ratchathani in Thailand to get involved in some airbase construction and activities up there. They started a Hash, which dissolved when they left a couple of years later. Who they were and what they did is lost in the foam of time.

1970 saw a young bloke, Allan Chee, front for his first gallop. His local friends thought he'd lost the plot joining in this "crazy whitemen stupidity". Penang H3 were led for a long time by Nick Boudville, who is thought to be the longest-r*nning GM in the world. He became GM in 1972, and – with the exception of 1982 – has been at the helm ever since.

This remains a men-only kennel. In fact they went one step further and considered themselves a "gentlemen's Hash chapter, subscribing to the belief that Hash can be enjoyed at its very best without resorting to crude and rowdy behaviour."

Penang H3 engenders fierce loyalty and many of their r*nners achieve 500 and 1,000 r*n milestones with the kennel [Either that or there's really nothing else to do in Penang –ed.].

October 18 1965 saw another chapter in Sandakan, Borneo formed. It was called – in the grand creative manner of all things Hash – Sandakan H3. This time Jonathan Grey, who had Hashed at neighbouring Miri, was the culprit. Wes Carter joined them in 1969 and enjoyed the romps through the virgin and recently logged jungles. Apart from plenty of mud, he also remembers "some really strange expatriates in that part of the world, plenty of marriage break-ups and relationship intrigues to add flavour and colour." Sandakan today is host to many varied Hashes in the area and enjoys a good following amongst the locals and expats.

Bonkers in Honkers.

The next significant chapter – in terms of global influence – was started in Hong Kong in 1970 by Louis Thacker, who had recently transferred from Malaysia to the then British territory. The British, who had been trading in and through this city since the late 1700s, considered it rightfully theirs. As the major trading partner with China, Britain had used Hong Kong as a harbour for their opium-trading vessels since the 1820s. Empires such as the Jardine-Matheson trading group grew on the ill-gotten proceeds. Expats poured in on the back of this. Hong Kong streets were paved with gold and adventure. In 1842, Hong Kong Island was ceded to the British crown. Their own little Eastern playpen. In 1898, they signed up for an even bigger deal – Kowloon and the New Territories as well. And the city state grew and grew, becoming one of the world's major financial centres, and a shoppers paradise. The Government required to r*n this needed Civil Servants, British of course. Tunnels, bridges, airports, train systems. Shipping and banks. All required imported expertise. But so much for work, what about play?

"On transfer … I sorely missed the Monday evening's Hash," said Thacker.[50A] "There were a few Hashmen around from Malaysia but the general consensus was that Hong Kong was lacking in good Hash country and the population was too sophisticated. OK, so anyone can make a mistake!"

Thanks to his persistence – and several rounds of drinks at The Pub in D'Aguilar Street – a motley pack of around 22 was raring to go one week later from The Peak car park for the first r*n in February 1970. Hared by John Beavon (who had moved up from Sydney), hounds included Des Robinson, Warwick Artis, Dick Gibb and Malcolm Glass, all of whom enjoyed it enough to become long-term stalwarts on the Hong Kong Hashing scene. In 1971, an Englishman with the Chartered Bank, Michael Ogden, joined them for his first r*n. Other visitors that year included Mike Miall and Fred Whitaker who bolstered the numbers whilst about eight hounds of note left the colony for other postings abroad.

A lack of Hashing countryside didn't stop them from improvising … one r*n had them r*nning in their usually smelly and flimsy attire through the foyer of the ultra-ritzy Peninsula Hotel, owners of one of the largest fleets of Rolls-Royces in the world.

In 1972, Ian Young was transferred to Seoul, Korea, by Pfizer Pharmaceuticals and formed the first Hash there. Phil Kirkland spent a number of years in Sydney before going up to Hong Kong for a few years in the Seventies. Whilst no one remembers much about his tour of duty there, he was famously quoted in the Los Angeles Times in January 1978 as saying: "If you have half a mind to go Hashing, that's all you'll need". This gave rise to the term Half Mind, a perfect description for most Hashers, even if it was *overstating* their mental capacity somewhat. "I was the one who said it," said Kirkland, "but I think I heard it from someone else before... I'm not smart enough to make up things like that."

Hong Kong will also be remembered for hosting the inaugural InterHash in 1978. A couple of other worthies, Ian Hendrie and Chris Rowe, soon after formed their own chapter on the Kowloon side of the harbour for convenience – because there were no harbour tunnels or Mass Transit Rail in those days – and access to the more rural New Territories.

Among Hong Kong H3's highly exaggerated claims to fame are the world's first parachute Hash in 1979 and a helicopter Hash, in which the trail was laid by Lord Lexus who escaped to the air as the pack closed in on him. For the parachute Hash, Chastity Belt remembers about six Hashmen jumping out of a plane, and then r*nning to the beer. Roger 'Flacdem' Medcalf coined the term "*mis*management" to describe the Hong Kong committee, a term which was not only accurate, but was also quickly taken up by other kennels as a better word to describe the mess their affairs were in. "Mismanagement" became an integral part of the Hash lexicon.

In the early Eighties, Charles Earle left for Barnes, in England. In July 1997, Hong Kong was handed back to the Chinese, becoming a special administrative region of China. These days, Hong Kong H3 is still a men-only Hash with a traditional KL back-to-basics mentality. Their membership is also 'traditional', getting on in years now and depleting somewhat with more retirements, fewer expatriates and – of those – fewer expatriates prepared to risk losing their highly-paid jobs by sneaking out of the office early for a r*n on Monday. "The Hong Kong Hash does not sing, hold hands, or play silly games," [51] said Colin Stagg, ex-Grandmaster. "No silly names, no singing … just straight down to the business of the evening – r*nning and refreshment," claims their website. Refreshment is in the form of a Carlsberg beer truck that serves it blistering cold on site.

Apart from siring or inspiring about 11 assorted Hash chapters of all descriptions and persuasions in the territory, Hong Kong H3 outcasts and exiles went on to form a significant number of chapters around the world.

Years of living drunkenly.

500,000 years ago, in the Pleistocene Epoch, an early form of man roamed the Indonesian island of Java. A Dutch palaeontologist found these fossilised remains and gave it the fancy and unpronounceable [Especially with a lisp! –ed.] name of *Pithecanthropus Erectus*, or Erect Ape Man to his friends. After further discoveries of a full skull and other bones were found, he was renamed *Homo*

Erectus Erectus, or Java Man to his Hash mates. Java Man was about five foot eight inches tall (1.73m for those metric types) and his brain was about three-quarters the size of modern man's. He had prominent eyebrow ridges, a retreating forehead, and large powerful jaws [Sounds like most Hashers I know! –ed.].

Indonesia had long been a Dutch colony, since the Netherlands East India Company (VOC) had established Batavia as a major trading port since 1602. The world couldn't get enough of its exotic spices. When oil was discovered in 1920, a household name was born – the Royal Dutch Shell Oil Company. Shell was to become a major home of Hashing over the years in many remote parts of Asia and the world, with foreign expertise brought in to develop and r*n it.

In 1965, an attempted coup started the routing of communists throughout the country which saw 'at least 400,000 people' killed in just six months. No wonder they called it The Year of Living Dangerously!

It wasn't until 1971 that Suharto had the country in some semblance of control, and the first elections under the 'New Order' were held. Meanwhile, an escapee from Singapore had landed in the Indonesian capital, Jakarta – Gordon Benton, thought to be very closely related to Java Man but not as good looking or mentally acute. Jakarta H3 was masterminded by he and Jeremy Pigeon, who was on the r*n from the KL Hash.

March 22 1971 saw Pigeon and John Read lay the first r*n for the 14 eager expatriate hounds at Jalan Telesonic off what used to be Jalan Bangka Raya (now Jalan Kemang Raya). They gladly handed over their Rp500 as r*n fee and gulped down the sacred suds. Five dozen large bottles were seen off that evening.

Pigeon and Marshall Douglas led the hounds in resonant song-fests, fuelled by Bir Bintang. Faces like Ron Strachan and Happy Jack Hunter appeared regularly. A quorum of hard-living, fun-loving eccentrics built up in Jakarta, looking to inject charisma into Hashing at every turn.

Jeremy Pigeon "was known as Birdbrain at that time" according to Ron Strachan, and became the first Joint Master of Jakarta Hash with Benton. A charismatic Scot –"despite his frightfully English accent" – Pigeon usually gnawed on a pipe, and worked with a trading company. His trusty Volvo always got him to the r*ns, and back as well (although perhaps not in such a steady fashion).

At r*n # 71 in March 1973, civilisation took a turn for the worse with the introduction of the dreaded Jakarta Hashit – a phallic Irian Jaya mask, reputedly modelled on Birdbrain's tackle. Of much greater size was the equally dreaded, but much revered, Hashit Mug – The Big One. Two litres of pure drinking performance.

Englishman Phil Riddell arrived from Sydney in 1975 for a couple of years: "Jeremy Pigeon was the Grand Master – very much 'the general' of the Hash there. He just went on year after year, I think it was a mistake." Ole Vigerstole also played a heavy hand at that time. "They had quite a few German people and quite a few Scandinavians who are all pretty keen on strong discipline," says Riddell. "And 'This is vat the Hash does' and 'Now ve vill all r*n together' and 'Now ve will all sing together'."

A few Hashing 'traditions' were introduced around this time. The circle reportedly started by necessity in Jakarta, possibly as late as 1977. "It was out of a need for protection," says John Duncan, "to stop the locals nicking the beer." Literally a circling of the wagons as the Boers had done in Africa a century before [No wonder it was called a *laager* –ed.]. Duncan describes his Jakarta Hashing experiences: "There are a million locals around you," he says. "Even if you go for a widdle, there's one hundred people around you before you've got your zipper down." It became known as The Jakarta Circle, with Down Downs dispensed in the middle, and a ringmaster – later known as a Religious Adviser – to fuel the flames or quell the rioting mob, as appropriate.

In 1978 Birdbrain went off and joined the first InterHash in Hong Kong, no doubt spreading some of Jakarta's songs and practices such as nicknames and circles. Sometime later he himself became renamed as *Burong*, Indonesian for bird. "Because of his outstanding contribution to the Hash he was later named the Godfather," says Strachan.

Tragedy truck when Birdbrain suddenly died aged 40-ish. "He put his heart into the Hash and had most r*ns (326) in his day and most hares/co-hares," says Strachan. "When he died I was the then Hashmaster and it was agreed that there would never be another Godfather in Jakarta Hash. A tin trophy in the shape of a pigeon's egg was designed in his memory and this is still awarded to Hashers 'For Outstanding Contributions and Continued Commitment to The World's Greatest Hash'.

Another by-product of the circles and this eclectic mix of stray dogs – which included Dutch embassy type Cor Schouten from 1980 – was the introduction of not just group singalongs but individual creations and performances, too.

"The JH3 is one of the paramount singing Hashes, requiring the hare to sing an original song in the circle after his r*n," says Marty 'Garfield' Hanratty. "Two or three of the more outstanding products find their way into the JH3 songbook each year. Irian Jaya and I Got the Clap Again are some of the more creative ditties in the book."

Indonesia's r*n of good fortune continued through to the 80s, when oil prices started to fall again. People were laid off, and headed home or to other countries and continents where their skills were needed. Pack sizes of 120 or so were common earlier in the decade, but had dwindled to about half that when Ian 'Konkorde' Roberts arrived in 1988. Not to say that the mayhem had died, though. "I even saw a dead cobra coiled into a beer jug as the evil bastard beer pourer moved round the circle topping up glasses," he says. "Absolutely mad fun." Not to be outdone, he invented the Viking Burial for old Hash shoes. "Set them on fire with petrol even if the Hasher did not want to relinquish them. He got 'em off quick once they ignited though, or hot-footed it round the circle. Mad bastards all." Amen. In February 1989, their 1,000th r*n celebration attracted some 600 Hashers for the weekend. To this day, the spirit of Birdbrain lives on in the Jakarta kennel, as Jonesy still drives Birdbrain's old Volvo to the r*ns each week. Benton is also still part of the furniture.

Through the 70s, Indonesia had prospered on the back of price hikes mandated by OPEC for its oil exports. More expats and contractors came in to work the rigs and refineries. More Hashers! The middle class Indonesians also enjoyed a burgeoning, turning into modern consumers with a desire for things beyond mere survival. Recreation was one of them, and the need to blow off steam against a backdrop of authoritarian government that saw strong censorship in the media, and control by the military. The Indonesians took to Hashing like a Short-Cutting Bastard to the beer wagon. Apart from the Jakarta H3, there are now about five other kennels in Jakarta itself. Directly or indirectly Jakarta H3 became one of the largest sowers of wild Hash oats in the world.

Bandung 1 H3 established itself in 1974, disorganised by John Brinsden and about six (including Michael Ogden and Pigeon) who came down from Jakarta to give it a royal send-off. The Bandung Hash grew rapidly, soon averaging 120 r*nners. Bandung 2 H3, set up in 1984, was r*nning with average packs around 650 in the late 80s. Libra H3 in Bandung grew to a registered membership of 1,300 in early 1987, reportedly attracting an incredible 950 Hashers on one of their normal – that is, not special occasion – r*ns. Their solution to this unwieldy logistics situation was to split the kennel into two different r*n days, bringing their average pack sizes down to a more casual and manageable 550 each! Additionally a Horrors kennel also took up some of the excess, with the Bandung Hash Puppies attracting more than 1,000 r*nners on a special r*n in 1988.

Bandung, with well over 2,000 Hashers in the area by 1990, is easily the densest population of Hashers in the world. "In Bandung now, there exist 19 r*nning clubs like the BHHH," says Sweatie Pie, "some of them very big with over 1,000 members." BH3 records show members from almost all continents: Norwegians, Swedes, Danes, Dutch, Germans, French, Swiss, Spanish, Italians, English, Irish, Scottish, Indian, Chinese, Pakistanis, Malay, Singaporeans, Filipinos, Aussies, Kiwis, South Africans, Japanese, Americans, Canadians, and of course Indonesians. The majority by far are local nationals. The Hash has made a successful jump into the local population, ensuring its viability independent of the ups and downs, comings and goings of those crazy *bules* (foreigners).

The Wild Women of Borneo and other Unmentionables.

Any reader paying attention [That narrows it down –ed.] would have noticed a distinct absence of women in the story thus far. Interestingly, they had participated in the earlier pre-war version of the paper-chase harriers, as had dogs. So what about the exclusion of women on the Hash?

Torch Bennett once said: "We may have been old-fashioned or something – but we were strongly opposed to females r*nning. It was agreed to try it once but it never stopped raining that day, so none turned up."[76] What few women were around in Malaya were probably playing tennis or even hockey for the Selangor Club anyway. Despite the Hash officially being for males only in their association 'rules' [Rule #1: there are no rules –ed.], women were possibly not *non grata*. They were simply just 'not interested' according to Horse Thompson, and John Kennedy doesn't really remember a decision on this as such.

But despite Thompson's conciliatory words, women were strictly excluded.

Batangs-only was the rule of the day on the KL Hash. Even now, a new millennium, women must be referred to as 'Unmentionables' otherwise a penalty is paid. But no one told – or dared to tell – the good folks of Tawau in Borneo.

Tawau in the early Sixties was a very 'backward' place. After independence, the British pulled out in March 1965, leaving behind a multinational force in Borneo of some 18,000 men of whom more than half were British and the remainder were Ghurkas, Malays, Australians and New Zealanders.

The town was booming at that time due to the timber industry's upswing. And where there's money, the women were sure to swarm. "The timber tycoons had lots of money to spend thus night clubbing was the in thing and boozing was a daily affair," says local Hasher, John Yap. Some the of the popular night clubs and brothels of the time included the Wah Yew Hotel, Far East Hotel, Sungei Mas, Royal Hotel Night Club, and the Golden Lotus [Sounds like hard wood to me –ed.].

Tawau H3 was formed by Keith Richmond just before Christmas 1965. According to long-term expats in the area, Richmond had possibly done his Hashing in Singapore previously. George Brown – who worked for the Borneo Company and had Hashed previously elsewhere in Borneo – and Robin Stock were regular r*nners almost from the start, but expat turnover was rapid in this part of the world and most of the key players left soon after. Stock remembers it being a very slap-dash affair with no r*n numbers, no news sheet, no official positions, etc: "The basic requirements of r*nning and beer were adequately covered, I am happy to say."[76]

There is some thought that Tawau might be the first ever example of a 'mixed' Hash, allowing both Hashmen and Hashwomen to happily co-exist from day one. "Ever since it was incepted it was 'mixed' as then Tawau had a very small population and there were only a handful of wankers where they do not mind having [women] in the group," says Yap. "What I was made to believe was that they had some mistresses (bar girls) r*nning Hash in those early days. Definitely *not* their wives as they all had their On On in the nightclubs or bar. They were all casual guests as Hash by then did not have any registration of membership. Till today we do not have any registration of membership."

Later even more bars, brothels and hotels sprung up in the small town, including Hotel Plaza, Hotel Khuhara, Uncle Foo Clan and Tanjong Hotel. "There were about 16 nightclubs for a small town," says Yap. As a result, the On Sec hardly had the time nor inclination to write up r*n sheets. "Well I do not think there were any r*n sheet available now as files were not being kept properly and the On Sec jobs has change hands so many times." So unfortunately, possibly the world's first women Hashers – who remain nameless and faceless, perhaps luckily for them – can't take or claim their rightful place in Hashtory.

It was only in September 1971 when Tai Lin Ngong came on the scene that some sort of formality and organisation crept into the picture, keeping hounds like Old Dog Pang and Choong on trail and in beer. Apart from the bucket, the

Tawau Yacht Club also serves up highly acceptable beer to the local Hashers and has become the adopted home of the current pack of 60 to 80 r*nners each week. "Old timers like us still r*n Hash the way it should be [You mean with a bunch of bargirls? –ed.]," says Yap.

In 1966 ominous strides in the development of feminism were taking place ... Billie Jean King – well known penis-avoider – won Wimbledon [Presumably the *ladies* singles title –ed]. But the mini-skirt had become the big fashion trend thanks to British stick-figure, Twiggy. Mary Quant was credited with the idea, saying at the time: "Perhaps she sees our times something like the 1920s when women, free to smoke, drink and curse, did so in flimsy flapper gowns. Today, sure to keep her shape as long as she is on the Pill, woman is again feeling free." [29]

Many curious wives and girlfriends in Brunei wondered why their men came home late each Wednesday night, reeking to high heaven of assorted beer and curry odours, trailing mud through the house. So it was decided to have a 'joint' r*n, whereby these ladies would be invited to see for themselves what Hashing was all about (and to get them off their backs probably). Despite the Hashers' best efforts, the ladies enjoyed themselves immensely and the sisters wanted to do it for themselves. So the Brunei ladies styled themselves as the Brunei Hen House Harriers and set off for their first r*n on November 21 1966.

An invitation was sent out inviting ladies "to participate in a gentle woodland walk" at mile 3/4 Jalan Gadong. Proof that the H3 abbreviation initiated in Singapore had already caught on, they were told to look for the H3 sign on the roadside. The trail was laid by "interested and sympathetic men", with the further inducement of "finders keepers". The dress code of the day was jungle boots, long pants and sleeves, to counteract the infamous razor grass in the area.

Olive Philips Rodgers was the first Hen Mistress and Hilda Mildrich the first Hen Sec. After the 'walk' they adjourned to the home of the Tiepels in Berakas Road for refreshments as there were no suitable On On venues in Brunei at the time. Husbands of these Hens were encouraged to do the babysitting, and the trend of pussy-whipped husbands meekly coming along to the r*ns with their snotty offspring and waiting dutifully and diligently for Mum to finish her r*n continued for many years. Eventually, the women felt it cramped *their* style and the practice faded out.

Sally Oliver joined in 1970 and would be a stalwart over the next decade. Packs averaged about 12 or 15 at this stage, with mainly expat wives involved along with a few local ladies. Regular galloping Hens included Brenda Ray, Selehan Azia, Margaret Perfitt, and Sue Feast. With plenty of jungle and largely unsurfaced roads in the Jalan Gadong area, many good trails were enjoyed – well, except for one hapless virgin who had a snake land on her. She freaked out and lost her spectacles, only to have the Hen behind her trample on them, leaving her to find her way back virtually sightless. She was never seen on trail again.

The Hens laid pink paper to differentiate them from the men's blue trails in the same area. But while there was a synergy and co-operation of sorts between the men and women chapters, there was still an undercurrent of rivalry. In the early 70s, the Brunei H3 were celebrating an anniversary r*n at the Royal Brunei Yacht Club. The Hens were not invited. In something akin to Mad Magazine's Spy vs. Spy segment, the Hens sent a specially baked cake down to the club with their best wishes. However, a few Hashers found out the hard way that the beautifully iced cake was filled with sawdust, mud, grass and some distinctly unidentifiable substances. Long faces and nights on the couch surely followed in some homes in Bandar Seri Bagawan.

Once the nookie tap was turned back on again, a joint r*n was held, laid (as it were) by the guys who were the hosts on this occasion. Blue trail for the guys, pink for the ladies. All was going swimmingly – pun fully intended – for the ladies until their pink trail led to a large log crossing a stream. It was the only way across. So the FRBs [Is this Front R*nning Bitches? –ed.] dashed across the log and one after another slid unceremoniously into the dirty water. The wily and vengeful Hashmen had greased the pole!

'Where boobs and bums bounce best' was the Brunei Hens' strident motto, although some unkindly folks have noted the sagging of these attributes over the years. With Brunei's booming economy, sealed roads and major buildings sprouted in once out-of-the-way areas, and has also given rise to good On On venues such as the favourite World Wide Club and Tropicana where the fun and frivolity and 'women's stuff' go on. They are no less forward than their Hashmen counterparts, with all manner of innuendo and worse adorning their website and publications.

A precedent was set, and certain parts of the Hashing fraternity soon yielded to the new order. In July 1967 – inspired no doubt by The Doors' hit song of the time Come On Baby Light My Fire – the progressive Ipoh H3 recorded their first 'Hash Ladies Night'. Just over a year later the Ipoh Hen House Harriers was started by Loke Kai Heng of Ipoh H3 [Yes, he's a he! –ed.]. They seconded experienced male Hashers to help with their formation, transferring r*n-laying skills and inculcating some of the Hashing culture in the process. Philip Leong and Bill Lawson set the first r*n on 29 August 1968. It also added a security element that was to prove useful in later years when incidents of molesting by strangers occasionally occurred. Wes Carter was a regular male on trail in 1968 and sadly reports he found himself "in my own bed the following mornings". Maggie Lee, Candy Ng and Lena Foo were the movers and hip-shakers of this fortnightly foray. Within weeks they decided to call themselves the Honey House Harriers (sweet things that they were), with the president called the Queen Bee. However, that idea didn't fly and in October '68 the Ipoh ladies coined the term 'Harriets' to describe female Hashers, which others then evolved into 'Harriettes'. Both words found rapid uptake around the Hashing world thereafter.

The Kota Kinabalu Bunnies was started in 1970 by Olga Floyd-Funk, but they experienced one molesting incident deep in the jungles of Sabah. As a result, while membership is still not open to men, specially qualified Buck Rabbits have been appointed as Bunny Guards. Mary Gove went on to rack up 1,000 r*ns with this chapter.

In August of that year 10,000 women took to the streets of New York to celebrate 50 years of the 19th Amendment [That's a lot of Tippex! –ed.]. The 19th was the women's right to vote. The New York Mayor, for his part, signed a bill forbidding sexual discrimination in public places, which meant that women could now go and drink at any bar they wished, ushering in a practice that was to cost gentlemen a small fortune in the years to come as they tried to woo and bed ladies they had just met in bars with exotic cocktails dripping with fruit and fancy umbrellas.

Hashmen prayed that same Christmas that Germaine Greer's controversial new book, The Female Eunuch, wouldn't end up in their wives' Christmas stockings and pollute their Half Minds even further.

In June 1971 it was the turn of The Ladies Of The Hong Kong H3 to piss off the men folk with their deliberate choice of close-enough-to-be-confusing nomenclature. Hilary Prior was the first Grand Mistress. The Kuching Harriettes first went on trail in June 1972, led by Simon Lee. Then Shirley Burgess, Lorraine Browning and Jean Scott led the Penang Harriettes into action in November.

The Singapore Hash House Harriettes was co-founded by British lass Carol Gurney in October1973. Her husband Gerry was a long-time Singapore hound. Interestingly, one of those instrumental was Clyde Lane's much talked-of Chinese bride. "She got annoyed that he went out every Monday night," says Fred Whitaker. "It's interesting that a Chinese girl starts the socially elite English girls to r*n. That was a completely feminist thing to do at the time."

"At first the Harriers were not impressed," said Margaret Beaman.[76] "In fact they were downright shocked at our intrusion into their world, and did their best to dissuade us. Perish the thought of a bunch of women thrashing through our jungles!" However she did acknowledge the useful assistance rendered by the Hashmen in sharing the secrets of good trail laying and even occasionally joining them on initial r*ns to ward off snarling dogs, snakes and the likes. A small award was even given to the most chivalrous male.

Harriettes found their way to the Holy Ground of Hashing, Kuala Lumpur, in 1974, thanks to English Harriette Veronica Tarry and Australian Sue Harris who gave up on the Mother Hash ever allowing women into their ranks. Tarry's husband, Andrew, had been a long-term Hasher in KL.

Down in Jakarta, the Harriettes came into being a completely different way [Typical –ed.]. Hashers were prohibited from even having their female company wait in the car park for them to finish the r*n, such was the strength of their men-only conviction. But one fine day 'late in 1973 or early 1974', one Judy Prosser turned up at the r*n site in her r*nning gear. Panic set in among the Hashers and the committee, who failed to come to a resolution on what to do with this wayward female. She ran. They tried their best to lose her, but she finished. Then she hung around. They decided to ignore her, hoping she'd go away. That didn't work. Sang some of the nastiest misogynistic songs from their repertoire. That didn't work either.

The following week, Judy was back for more. Then she started to bring some of her girlfriends along. Her brazenness flummoxed the Jakarta Hash. They had unwittingly and unwillingly become a – gulp! – *mixed* Hash. Unbelievably this situation went on for several years until the Jakarta 'Pussy Hash' was finally formed by the renegade ladies at the end of 1977, and they went their separate ways.

Although Hashers had always enjoyed the camaraderie and ample replenishing brews, it was the Harriettes who really developed the social side of Hashing, according to John Duncan. "Within not many months," he said, "the subsequent dinner (the On On) had become almost as important as the r*n itself." [60]

With this increased social element came the need to disseminate more information (and gossip!). So suddenly Hash newsletters expanded to accommodate r*n information, On On information, some fun stuff, and social outings (both Hash and non-Hash related). The inclusive nature of the Hash was taking a hold on Hashers and Harriettes alike. Unmentionables, Hens, Harriets, Harriettes, Hussies, Honorary Gentlemen, HGs – call them what you will – were here to stay.

In December 1975, Singapore H3 hosted the first children's r*n, hailed as a new tradition in Hashing. "Catch them young and train them," was their intent. These children's kennels would go on to assume the generic name 'Hash House Horrors' in many countries around the world, with variations such as 'Hash Puppies' in some parts. The oldest existing family Hash – who regularly allowed children and families to r*n with them – is considered to be Okinawa H3 in Japan, founded 1980.

The greatest concentration of Hash kennels is still found in Asia, about 600 chapters at last count. These include colourfully-named chapters such as the Menstroll (Surabaya, Indonesia) who r*n on the 28th day of each month, the Sangatta Menstrual (ladies only, once a month); The Night R*nners of Benghal (Dhaka, Bangladesh); Tai Koo Wankers Afternoon Tea Society (TWATS) in Hong Kong; Kinky Fully Mooned H3, Hiroshima's Totally Bombed Hash House Harrier Hooligans and JOLLY H3 (Japan Only R*ns Reap Year Hash) which r*ns on February 29 each four years (Japan); Penggaram Wankers H3 (Batu Pahat, Malaysia), The Thinking Drinking H3 (Bangkok, Thailand) and the Miri Wild Women (Sabah, Malaysia).

And Asia continues to be very inventive and progressive with Hashing ... Bike Hashing (or Bashing) was started in Rockport, America but rapidly moved to Singapore in September 1989 when James Tay, Evan 'Barf Balls' Jones and Victor Esbensen – "plus a few other r*nning Hashers with worn-out knees and nothing better to do on a Sunday morning than ride their bikes around town" – saddled up. With the demise of the first American chapter, Singapore Bike Hash is now the oldest Bash kennel in existence.

They've even taken to the water in Singapore with a rowing Hash. "I guess to call it a Hash is a bit of a stretch... it is hard to follow the paper on the water," says Hashman and avid dragon-boater, John McGrath. "But we do have checks." As in the Hash, it is not a race but a lot of skulduggery goes on to sabotage other crews, necessitating some harsh rules such as eggs are not to be hard boiled and must be no more than six months old. Also, water cannon that take up an extra seat will be charged as a person and "anything requiring a crane to get it on a boat will be confiscated and reissued".

The Dirt Road Hashing movement found its genesis in the heady resort town of Pattaya, Thailand [Where else? –ed.]. It was founded by Bob Finch and Derek Miller who were refugees from the Pattaya Mixed H3. The Prince of Darkness wanted a men-only club where not the r*n, nor the On On but the On On On became the focus. And this could happen at any point in proceedings. The celebration of their 50th r*n reportedly went for nigh on three days and three nights from the time the r*n started. Its wonderfully evocative and descriptive title comes from the location of the establishment where they found themselves late in the night after their first r*n – at the dead end of a dusty laterite road. R*ns and ensuing hard-core activity are shrouded in a clandestine mystique, start and end points kept a mystery to deter snoopers, short-cutters and others not of the same ilk. They even take severe action against people trading their t-shirts to others that have not genuinely been on a Dirt Road r*n. They want people to earn their stripes. They also involve an 'Inter-Dirt' component at most major InterHashes these days.

With the ageing of some of the first and second-generation Hashers, the Hash House Hazards were then formed in Petaling Jaya, Malaysia. They are seen as a kindler, gentler type of disorganisation whereby senior Hashers are put out to pasture. Hazards now have about six chapters in Malaysia and one in Indonesia with the reportedly exclusive qualifications being "over 40 years of age, waist line over 40 inches, and possess an IQ of less than 40". They jokingly talk of the next phase of evolution – Hash House *Haggards* for those over 60.

But the one thing all these variations have in common is the *raison d'être*, sweating out the old suds and making room for fresh beer. For over the years, the Hash's unofficial motto became 'The Drinking Club With a R*nning Problem'. But where this strategic mission statement originated is uncertain. "My recollection is that it was originated by a Hash that may have been in, say, Japan, Okinawa," says John Duncan. "It may have been as long ago as the late Seventies, but perhaps more likely some time in the Eighties."

Shooting the Breeze.

There was a whole horde of them, wearing top-to-toe outfits in a striking tiger skin pattern. On closer inspection they were from Rumbai H3 in Indonesia, and their slogan read: "A tiger can kill you, but a little pussy never hurt anyone." It looked out of place on this group of Indonesian ladies, many aged about mid-50s and quite squat. Your humble scribe approached one and asked about the slogan. Yes, she knew exactly what it meant, and we shared the joke with her big group. She then introduced me to her husband, Aritono.

Aritono has had 1,300 r*ns – and counting – with Rumbai since 1976. He was introduced to Hashing by colleagues at the Caltex refinery where expats had started that kennel. "Used to be maybe 200 *bules* (foreigners) before," said Aritono, "now maybe only 10." Their pack is about 300 strong these days. He cites Indonesia's political problems as being one of the reasons that the expats' involvement has been scaled back. As for the tiger skin outfits? Seems that there are still tigers in the jungle around Rumbai – the odd refinery worker has been lost, but no Hashers yet.

Bambang from Malang H3 in East Java was introduced to Hashing by his mother-in-law ... and even attended Pan-Asia 2001 with both his parents-in-law while his wife stayed home to nurse their three-month-old baby. He says their Hash in a rather remote part of Indonesia had about 10 *bule* before but now "about one or two ... I don't know where they went."

Loping Scrotum, an expat hasher in Vietnam from Denmark noted the same thing: "In Hanoi there are more locals these days, but about two-thirds are expats," he says. "But the expats turnover quickly – after two or three years they disappear." He mentions the problem they had when it came to celebrating Hanoi's 500th. "We didn't know how to write our history," he says. "Out of 100 people there were only a couple of guys who'd been there nine years, married to local Vietnamese. So we had to dig around to find the 400th newsletter – and the history there had been stolen from the 300th!"

"Our last two GMs have been Japanese," says Gympy from Samurai H3 in Tokyo, "but you need the American connection for things like accessing duty-free beer from the base and access to cheap vans for the bags and the beer."

Inappropriate is a young Harriette from Michigan married to an oil rigger in Malacca, Malaysia. She had never heard of the Hash in the USA but is now keen to find clubs in her area when she goes back. Her Hash in Malacca is apparently 80 percent locals, 20 percent expats. "Some of the locals just drink tea and orange juice," she says, adding that she thinks some may hang around to get a vicarious thrill. As a modern married woman, what's the attraction of the Hash to her? "You can say anything to anyone and not worry about it ... no one gets bent out of shape. Elsewhere I'm different. Here on the Hash I'm the same."

Despite the incessant shenanigans, dispensation for cultural sensitivity and leniency seems to be accorded to local females, especially Asian lasses whose possible cultural taboos about bare bodies or physical limitations of alcoholic intake are factored in. "Yeah, but that's the same with the Hussies in New Zealand," chimed in one passing Hussy. Unseasoned Harriettes are often let off lightly on Down Downs and icing. "I think there are some cultural issues," says Ivory Ghost who spent five years in Thailand, plus stints in Africa and South America. "Some cultures such as Thailand are not big on public joking and embarrassment."

Edna, a local Harriette from Singapore, works in a multinational law firm by day. "I once asked this guy why he was called Foreskin," she says. "'Do you want me to show ya?' the eager Hasher answered. 'No, I can imagine,' she replied. But because he was from the Hash, and he's a Hasher, I don't find it offensive even if he shows me. But if he's just anyone out on the street, that's a different matter."

Tsim Tsa Tsui Suzie – named after the infamous Suzie Wong character – joined the Selangor Hash aged 17. "At first I was not used to the things that go on in the Hash and the circle," the 34-year-old mother says. But now she happily participates and, in a life-comes-full-circle story, even took her teenaged daughter to Pan-Asia Hash.

Jean is a single Chinese female who has been Hashing around five months with Klang H4 in KL. She sees herself as being "on the open-minded side". Ironically she sees swearing in Chinese as being more offensive than in English. "It's too vulgar," she says of the local dialect. But she likes the camaraderie and warns about taking it too seriously or personally. She admits that outside of the Hash she wouldn't do things like pee behind a tree, "just because I wouldn't".

Ferret, now of Gold Coast H3, says: "I was in Singapore and met this lass, Romeo. She told me about Hashing and I said 'What kind of mad bastards would go around in this heat and humidity?' A few weeks later, it looked like they were having way too much fun so I joined them. I've been Hashing for 26 years now." Richard Jones from Penang in Malaysia said: "I've been doing it 30 years … 1,800 r*ns and I'm beginning to like it!"

Dick the Prick has been a Hasher since 1982, starting in Korea, then Thailand and now Malaysia. He hadn't heard of the Hash in his native America before his first r*n in Seoul. "They were a wild bunch of bastards," he recalls. "I just fit. And when I turned up to the PJ Hazards for the second time it felt like I'd been there for years." He is an avid Hasher who structures his business trips around r*n nights in Asia. "It's an elixir," he says of Hashing. "It clears your head for business the next day." He also enjoys the egalitarian nature of the Hash, especially in a country like Malaysia that has four or five major racial groups. He also recalls his r*nning in Songkhla, Thailand (where he was known as Jurassic Fart) fondly: "The Saturday Hash is the big thing there … everyone turns out. Even all the local bargirls are part of the scene. But there is no distinction … a Hasher is a Hasher," he says. "If the UN was r*n like the Hash, what a different world it would be. Hey, Arafat, you're talking shit – on the ice! Hey, Bush, that's a dumb-ass question – Down Down!"

Teacher, an American in Thailand, had Hashed in Phuket and Chiang Mai since 1985 before moving to Koh Samui and becoming a bar owner. "Half the fun of the Hash is driving back with a can of beer between your legs and a bunch of drunk bastards in the back of the van," he says, enjoying the freedoms of the island paradise. "A friend invited me to Hash in L.A. … why would I do *that*?" he asks.

Gympy is a silver-haired military man, nearing 70. He has been in Asia since the Korean War in 1952. "If I was retired," the lively American gent says over a few cans of Carlsberg at breakfast, "I'd be an alcoholic." He started Hashing 17 years ago. "I was doing marathons before that, but Hashing is so much more fun." He still manages a good pace on the r*ns in Japan, and a lot of nonsense in the circles.

Bomba sees the attraction of Hash differently. "On the Hash, what you hold in at home you can let it go," this Chinese gent from Malaysia explains. "All the swear words they let it out." As a result he says he needs to brief any guests he introduces to the Hash. "Hashman can call each other bastard … but try that somewhere else, die already," he says.

Ball Apart from Penang, Malaysia, says: "When you try to get these buggers to join the Hash, they say 'No … no … ' but when they join they are even *worse* than us – so extreme," he says pointing to Bald Eagle, an Indian gent who inexplicably wears a trademark necklace of 20 to 30 colourful baby pacifiers and a plastic penis head on a string around his neck.

Amazing More of Kuching City H3 and ex-GM of Kuching Harriettes, has a possible explanation: "We enjoy ourselves in a different way," she says of Hashers. "We are like three-year-olds." She likes the way that Hashers are helpful, provide a good networking system, and sees Hashing as the best way to get acclimatised to a new country. "I often travel alone," she says, "and there's a brotherhood link there. Hashers are good people." Getting deeper, she says: "Hash helps me to live through life … something to look forward to every Wednesday. Before that I was on Valium. Hash saved my marriage."

Not everyone has the same experience. A Kiwi ex-Hasher and fervent 'born-again' Christian in Singapore said: "[My Singaporean wife] has become absolutely obsessed with Hash to the point that our marriage and children rank last! She has become an absolute groupie and doesn't care when it interferes so much with family life." [And your point is … ? –ed.]

There are also a couple of less than enchanted travelling Hashmen in Asia. Notable party animal Lord Spicy, from Denmark, was in Borneo once: "After the r*n there was no beer, no circle," he says, incredulously. "Everyone just got in their cars and left. If you miss the r*n, you can get a map of the trail from the hares to r*n it on your own at your convenience. That's *really* Hashing!" he says [Sarcasm meter reading:11 –ed.].

Birdman, was a rubber planter in Malaysia, and ran the Hash in Kluang around 1967. He then spent many years with the Singapore Father Hash before retiring to Perth where he is still Hashing actively. "I recently went back to Kluang," he said, "and it's turned into the strangest Hash I know. After the r*n, there's no drinks or circle or anything. Everyone goes to a local restaurant and has a couple of beers there." However he enjoyed the nostalgic r*n immensely, and reported he was given very reverential treatment as one of the original r*nners of that kennel.

And Shit for Brains, a visitor from Portsmouth, noted: "In Singapore it seems that a lot of people were there for the networking and only about 10 per cent hang around all night singing songs."

So Lifa, an American in Japan, puts Hashing into perspective: "If Hashing interferes with your job, get a new job. You bust your butt trying to make a career but your boss already knows you're not going anywhere 'cause you're a Hasher," he says.

"We're like the Freemasons without the snobbery," says Doggy Dave of Angeles, the Philippines. "The qualification is 'breathing' – you've got to draw the line somewhere … you can't let any old riff-raff in!"

Mike Barrett, OBE, who Hashed with the Himalayan Mixed Hash for several years had a philosophy that is hard to fault. "If you put one foot in front of the other, and if you do this often enough while in the company of Hashers, you will soon find that you are r*nning the Hash," he said[76]. But here comes the clincher: "Once you make this discovery, all other aspects of life become trivial, if not meaningless." Amen.

Law and disorder.

The biggest break in the Hash since its inception was a solid four years from late 1941 to '46 during the Japanese Occupation of Malaya. There are no records to show that the Japanese Imperial Army Hashed in this period, so we can assume it was dormant.

But one can't help thinking that with inveterate Hashmen like Cecil Lee holed up inside Changi prison, the temptation to lay a trail through and around the imposing buildings to break the routine boredom of captivity must have been there. "You know, they were good times, even the war and all that," Lee once said[23]. One wonders whether the call of 'On! On!' was ever heard – even just once – behind the walls.

In the Malayan Emergency period, 1948-60, the authorities needed to tighten up on the movement of people and the assembly of potentially dangerous groups. All societies, associations and clubs had to be registered. Even the Hash. On the official form, the objectives of the society had to be duly noted. Objectives? Don Kennedy – *another* accountant and the secretary at the time – officially registered HASH HOUSE HARRIERS and recorded the following noble aims:

A/ to promote physical fitness among members

B/ to get rid of weekend hangovers

C/ to acquire a good thirst and satisfy it in beer

D/ to persuade the older members that they are not as old as they feel

"Membership is open to all male persons who are interested in taking part in a weekly cross-country paper chase."

So the iconoclastic and anti-establishment tone of the Hash was officially documented for posterity. Along with its sexist intentions.

In the Malayan Emergency period, barbed wire was strung around villages. Road blocks were set up. Special permission in the form of a Curfew Permit had to be issued. "After seven o'clock the curfew was in force," says Bill Panton, "and if you were outside there you were liable to be shot." Fortunately, the Hashers were well connected with constables in the police force. A list of r*nners (and their employing companies) had to be submitted for approval each week. This usually cleared them for the specific r*n area – say, south of Chin Loy Quarry between the hours of 18:00 hours and 20:30 hours – to use an example from July 1957.

Despite the challenges of finding suitably safe r*n sites and securing the permits, no r*ns were missed. Often, John Wyatt-Smith, who worked at the Forestry Research Institute at Kepong, could line up r*ns at short notice in the protected and safe areas under their guard. However in September 1951 –

described as "the blackest period of the 12-year war" [121] – there was one very close shave. In the area of Cheras Road, just beyond the Jalan Tun Razak junction (now a major city intersection), which was then rubber and secondary jungle, the hares inadvertently stumbled over a few men asleep and covered in groundsheets. By the time the hares had passed – and presumably woken the men with a shock – the pack, including Andrew Tarry, saw the same men up and about, but kept r*nning and escaped without harm. One of the FRBs ran to the nearby police station at Cheras Road, raising the alarm. The Suffolk Regiment, who guarded this area, were sent out and set up their ambush positions. The next morning three communist terrorist bandits tried to break out of the area where the Hash trail was, and were gunned down. One of them was a senior terrorist with a RM5,000 price on his head – a large sum of money in those days. As many of the Hashers were not government employees, they were entitled to the spoils. Some reports say they spent the proceeds on a good knees-up for all at the Harper Gilfillan bachelors mess [And they do mean *mess*! –ed.]. Other reports indicate the spoils were divided up among those who were involved and eligible only, to the ill-feeling of others.

In his book The Eye of the Dragon, Dennis Bloodworth describes an occasion when the British Army had set up an ambush on a jungle trail to catch communists. As the soldiers sat, machine guns ready, a patter of feet was heard. The guns were cocked and trained on the path as … 15 harriers appeared wearing vests and shorts "as if they were out on London's Hampstead Heath!"

By 1958, the tide was turned and the communists were driven back out to the hills, leaving Kuala Lumpur to be declared a 'white' zone (meaning communist-free). In 1960, the Emergency was officially over. Cecil Lee's recollections were that "the Emergency cramped our style but did not diminish our activities, and we were even called in for information on various byways in Selangor, but our period of usefulness to MI5 was brief, and our information probably otiose." [28]

In the state of Pahang alone, more than 120 planters had been killed. Twenty percent of rubber plantation managers had been murdered. Ironically, this war against the Brits and their allies helped to propagate the Hash further, with many servicemen and civilians being exposed to the Hash before returning to their homes or usual regiment bases.

From 1962 to 1966 followed the period known as *Konfrontasi*, the war instigated by Sukarno in Indonesia to try to amalgamate Indonesia and Malaysia into a singular Moslem nation. Bring on more British and Commonwealth forces to fight the good fight. During this time, many more in military bases in Malaya and Borneo Hashed or at least heard about Hashing.

Once again life was back in full swing in Kuala Lumpur, and gradually peace restored to the rest of Malaysia. But in 1969, racial riots surrounding elections tore the country apart, resulting in more bloody curfews. This time, the Mother Hash was affected, especially in an intense two-month period in May and June when few dared to leave their homes. Several hundred deaths and massive property damage was rained on KL and other parts of Malaysia. Bill Panton remembers the Hash stopping for two months. Many missed r*ns as phone lines were often down and the mail was delayed so r*n information was not received on a timely basis. "The Hash was suspended then," says Panton, "although we did have a small group up in John Duncan's area – called itself the Klang Hash I think it was. I was in the Government in the Prime Minister's office. I had this official flag – I was able to drive around on official duties after the curfew had been imposed on the city streets and I had this 'Official' notice on my windshield so I went and r*n with them in Klang."

And again in October 1987 the regular Monday night r*n was under threat. Media reports and rumours had it that racial tensions had boiled over once again in Kuala Lumpur, causing problems in the streets and enough confusion and panic to confine most people to their homes. Not 13 intrepid Hashmen, though, who headed for the scheduled r*n at Seminyeh, near Kajang. At the r*n site, the diminished pack agreed to stick together on the r*n in case of any troubles, which did not eventuate. In fact, the story was overblown ... no more than a lone gunman had r*n amok in the notorious downtown area of Chow Kit. Die-hard Dennis Khoo said: "It has been a weekly tradition for the last 50 years for Mother Hash to strictly adhere to r*n on Mondays and I was not going to let tradition be broken as long as I was On Sec." [60]

Penang, Malaysia, still apparently require at least one month's notice from the Hash as to where the r*n site will be. The plus side for the Hash is that the Receding Hareline is therefore necessarily filled up long in advance [That's a change! –ed.].

Down in Singapore, the Hash were in good company with ex-KL Hasher Tommy Voice. He was the Chief of Police in Johore in 1962 when Singapore H3 started, and was known to take a squad of police with him – armed with *parangs* (machetes) – in order to carve a fresh r*nning trail through the wilderness.

Come 1964, Singapore was going through the stormy *Konfrontasi* period. Owing to curfews that kept everyone off the streets, two r*ns were cancelled. R*n # 127 was attended only by the committee and the hares, as the delivery of the circulars to Hashers was delayed by the rioting and general disruption. As a result, this duty-bound quorum polished off the entire allotment of Hash beer!

In August 1965, Singapore was officially granted independence and split from Malaysia. The resulting activities and confusion resulted in a total of only nine Hashers (including the hares) making the next day's r*n, held in the rubber plantations of Johore. The nine were still drinking the full Hash quota of brew long after midnight. In a separate incident around that time, a group of Hashers were driving home one Monday night, absolutely plastered. The driver was perhaps in the worst state, hiccupping often and loudly much to the others' merriment. Along River Valley Road they were pulled over at a police road-block. *Shit, we're done for,* they thought. Not a bit of it – the policeman took pity on this poor soul. "Lucky, we have some water in the car," he said, and trotted off to fetch it. Our hiccupping driver took a few swigs, assured the officer he was now much better thank you, and the policeman then held up the traffic and waved them on their merry way [The skidmarks were not just on the road –ed.].

In late 1967, the hares were laying a trail when they heard Bren guns in the distance. They immediately fled the scene, leaving little or no paper for the hapless hounds to follow home. Later in the piece, 1972 to be exact, the problems were of a different nature. The two hares setting a r*n at Seletar Reservoir were arraigned for polluting the area with small pieces of paper and fined S$50.

One memorable r*n-in with the police was courtesy of Jim Smillie who was reportedly making his way home slowly – and not so surely – from a Brewery r*n. So close to the kerb was he, that he didn't notice the police car parked on the side of the road. The shunting of the car seemingly upset the Hasher's stomach and he generously shared his bellyful of lukewarm Tiger beer and curry with the helpful sergeant who was trying to assist him out of the car.

Easter 1987 saw Pan-Asia Hash hosted in Singapore. Many were a little worried about how the Singapore authorities – reputed to be a few giggles short of full canned laughter – would handle the massed hounds. Others were worried that the beer might be too expensive and that other pleasures may have been banned or eradicated completely. But mostly they worried about whether they would have to pick up the paper from the trail afterwards to avoid a fine for littering. Two Hashers from Pattaya spent the weekend handcuffed to their half-gallon beer mugs, which soon had the local Singaporean Hashers in a fluster – handcuffs are not allowed in Singapore, unless you are a police officer. Later the Pattaya group, obviously not in a compromising mood, led the pack in a spontaneous singalong outside the five-star Mandarin Hotel on Orchard Road. Once again it had the locals rushing for the rule book. "You can't do that in Singapore!" said the officious doorman to no effect, as they romped through the Greatest Hits of Hashdom.

Crossing now to Kuching: "When we first started in Kuching we ran all over the Kuching end of the first division of Sarawak," says Brigadier Ray Thornton, now retired in England. "There were certainly bands of armed Indonesians roaming around there before we persuaded them to leave." Hasher Ian Clark was killed on active service in Borneo in March 1966.

Indonesia, particularly Jakarta, has been plagued by several bouts of unrest and anti-government demonstrations over the years. In early 1987 leading up to the elections, all forms of meetings and assemblies (whether political or not) were banned. Hashing was out. Officially, at least. This didn't stop the Jakarta H3 from testing the limits – it was decided to hold a r*n at a local golf course, but to make it look like they were all individual athletes [A bit of a stretch! –ed.] who just happened to be out for a little jog or a stroll and bump into each other at the same place at the same time by sheer good fortune and coincidence. Thus was r*n # 891 completed.

At the 1982 Jakarta InterHash – Jakarta H3 hares, Teun Botterweg, Alistair McArthur and Piet Verbaarschot, set the 'Blue' r*n which was stopped by the police just as it was about to start as they'd failed to apply for the requisite permit. Cunningly (or stupidly!) two hounds managed to get on trail before the police arrived and ran the course as planned. An unfortunate video cameraman, on duty at the end of the trail to record the r*nners coming in On Beer waited, and waited, and waited – this is before mobile phones were invented, of course. Six hours later he heard the stampede approaching. The hounds had eventually been reloaded onto the buses, and had been driven through the scenic countryside before being dropped off a short distance from the beer. Apparently, the speed and desperation of the short sprint from the buses to the beer has not been seen before or since!

The 1997 Asian financial crisis sent a lot of people packing from Indonesia. Many were evacuated to Singapore thence home as angry mobs demanded *Reformasi* (Reformation) and an overthrow of the government. The only effect on the Hashes was reduced attendance numbers with the worst time being on or around the day of the Jakarta riots (May 14 1998). To this day in Bandung the hare needs to fill out a permit form for each r*n. "It's just a permission form for the local person responsible for the site. Not a biggie these days but it's nice to have something signed in case there is a problem," says Mr Bean.

While Indonesia is a secular state, in Brunei, the challenge comes in a different shape. It is essentially a 'dry' Muslim state, with all the taboos on alcohol attendant. Does that mean they don't drink beer after the r*n? "As for the amber nectar," says Chaztitty, "let's just say that we are all supported by a less than white market!"

Hashing in Vietnam is so revered they even had a permanent trail – the Ho Chi Minh Trail – put in place. So you'd think Vietnam would be Hashers' heaven. But far from it. Australian diplomat Mike Fogarty said: "The Vietnamese authorities, through the Foreign Ministry, put pressures on the Western ambassadors to prevent their staff Hashing. Probably just as well as we were a fairly obnoxious and obstreperous lot – even by Hash standards."[76]

Hanoi H3 started in 1981 but closed down in 1983 after several warnings to curtail their activities. The humour on t-shirts – showing Hashers in conical straw hats in air-raid bunkers – was not necessarily a joke shared with the local authorities. Officially they were closed down as a 'traffic hazard', as it was said the r*nners were interfering with the many bicycles that constituted Hanoi's traffic at that time.

Eight years later the chapter was kick-started back to life by Testicles. Bloody Hanoi from Finland Hashed in Vietnam in the late Eighties. "Back then we had the problem of you can't have too many foreigners together," he says. "I don't think there was an exact number. We did a Tour de Hanoi on bikes once and the very next morning is a note on the Australian ambassador's table to say 'You can't do these things'."

As recently as 1997, Hanoi Bill tells of problems with the military. On a Sunday afternoon r*n outside Ho Chi Minh City, the pack were at full gallop when machine-gun fire rang out, "spraying up the dirt all around them". Soldiers appeared from the undergrowth, surrounding the pack and causing untold damage to the Hashers' underwear, before they were eventually waved on by "a guy with a lot of stripes and badges and braiding who was obviously roused from a perfectly good Sunday afternoon piss-up".

In northern Thailand, near the Golden Triangle border areas, bandits, drug lords and various insurgents abound. This has resulted in the loss of at least one Hasher's life – one Khun Aran from Phitsanulok H3. On that fateful day in 1987 he was the hare, and set out to recce the r*n when reportedly a truck pulled up alongside him, unleashed a hail of bullets from an M16, and left him for dead before speeding away. They returned minutes later to empty another clip into him just in case. The incident was however 'personal' and not directly to do with the Hash. Seems he knew a little too much about some clandestine operations in the area. In true Hash humour, a Situations Vacant ad was posted in Harrier International magazine shortly afterwards: "WANTED. Hare to lay paper for PH3. No experience necessary, free board and meals. Flak jacket supplied." HI Magazine, for its part, awarded the luckless hare a posthumous Hashit award for not completing the trail.

Rangoon H3 in Burma (or Yangon, Union of Myanmar depending on your political sway) has been interrupted by internal turmoil several times. In 1988 they had to fold altogether when the authorities banned any assembly of more than five people. Hash included. There was also a curfew put in place between 10pm and 4am, plus petrol rationing. Far from pissing on the Hash's parade, it meant all-night On Ons because once they were at someone's house they couldn't leave until the next morning. About four years later, diplomatic ties were largely normalised and foreigners and embassy staff started coming back into the country, leading to the resurgence of the Hash in 1992.

In September 1999 a special '9999' r*n was going to be held but was officially cancelled by the Ministry of Foreign Affairs following an incident involving one of the hares-to-be. It seems that Bald Eagle Diver had somehow collided with one of his military intelligence 'minders' who he claimed "walked straight into me". It's difficult to understand how they couldn't see each other as Bald Eagle Diver was illuminated by powerful flash guns from other security personnel at the time.

The restrictions of the past are less in evidence these days. "From time to time we are watched by different local 'security' services," says expat Bo Bo. "Our personal files must be thick with photographs of ourselves drinking beer in the Circle and r*nning across paddy fields. Occasionally villagers will clean up the shredded paper because they are so nervous about seeing foreigners and explaining their presence to the local village/ township/ district/ military intelligence. We are occasionally followed – by someone on an old Chinese bicycle – who has a hard time when we venture onto railway lines or across fields. Often they will show you the route to get you out of their village as quickly as possible."

They also have a problem getting visitors and guests to their anniversary r*ns due to 'visa and travel formalities'. For their 21st birthday they ran into some bureaucratic stone-walling: "The boat we were going to hire had to be cancelled at the last second," says Bo Bo, "because military intelligence wanted four days to vet all the names, and the price of a poor battered old river boat suddenly soared to US$900 for a few hours rental!" The birthday bash went ahead, but in a different form.

Another incident involving the authorities had the Hash r*nning accidentally into a military compound from the unsecured paddy fields at rear. The pack re-emerged at the camp's *front* entrance, where a sentry was on duty. "I still remember the look on the armed guard's face," says Bo Bo. "He was... facing out onto the street to prevent people coming in. Only trouble was we were going *out*. The rule book didn't say anything about preventing people from *leaving* the compound so we ran across the road and disappeared in the milieu of a local market completely unhindered."

The worst incident in Myanmar happened to an Australian Federal policeman who was working with the Myanmar government on various issues. While laying a trail he was arrested by an over-zealous local copper and taken to the local jail. "He was released in time for the r*n to take place," says Bo Bo, "at which the local security officials were much in evidence – they were the ones with handcuffs dangling from their *longyis* (sarongs) or the ones with walkie-talkies in their hands." A grovelling apology was later received from the appropriate ministry.

Nearby Laos is very protective of its borders. Apart from government-related business such as diplomats, aid workers and various national projects, other private sector workers and entrepreneurs found entry difficult prior to the early 90s. However, they obviously let their standards slip when they allowed in a group of Bangkok Hashers for a joint r*n with Vientiane in 1989. But the trouble came more from the Thai side of the border, especially when one of the Bangkok Hashers, who looked a lot like Wallbanger, reportedly gave an Immigration Officer a point blank blast of his Hash horn in his ear.

Okinawa has been much in the news of late with problems with growing anti-American sentiment on the island, especially after a number of rape cases related to the military bases there. Sand in My Crack, of Okinawa H3, found out just where the line in the sand was drawn: "At a Hash Camp in May 1994 after enjoying a beer or 12, I treated myself to a nice little nude dip into the East China Sea. Unfortunately, I was wearing my Beer Goggles and did not notice the restaurant behind me, with many families getting a view of a 'moon' that they didn't need to see. The authorities showed up rather quickly and apprehended me. Luckily they allowed me to be handcuffed in the front, concealing the 'evidence'. They took me back to the station and charged me with indecent exposure. I think I could've got off on a 'lack of evidence' plea. In the military, if you do something that involves the authorities, they call your supervisor. So I begged them to call mine … a Hasher! After my supervisor promised them that he would make sure that I get punished when I got back to work, the authorities made me do some community service for my punishment while I was there. So the next day, for eight hours, they had me raking the driftwood off the beach, getting covered in sand. Since I couldn't make it to the

Hash, the Hashers were nice enough to r*n the trail along the beach where I was and drop off a cold can of our tasty Holy Hash Brew!"

China, perhaps surprisingly, represents little oppression to the Hash. Beijing H3 has had a couple of incidents according to Ratchucker: "One year after the Tiananmen 'incident' there was to be an anniversary r*n. Beijing Public Security Bureau got wind of this and – being the paranoid people that they are – their alarm bells went off. We tried to alert all Hashers that the r*n for that day was cancelled (or possibly relocated). Unfortunately they got hold of everyone except one or two people. So at the r*n site there was a large contingent of PSB and the unlucky Hashers. One was Grog and he had a lengthy discussion with PSB. This is where it comes in handy not to speak any Chinese!"

In 1997, Beijing H3 was going to have a 'handover' Hash to celebrate the return of Hong Kong to the Motherland. The Sunday before July 1 1997 was the designated day and 'away from Tiananmen Square' was the location. The hares Twice in One Night and Chaotic Dog set the Hash at Beihai Lake. This was a t-shirt r*n. Evidently one of the employees of the person doing the t-shirts was a good commie and saw the preliminary designs (something along the lines of 'Hand Over Hash'). Since the Chinese government wanted everything to go perfectly with the handover they were leaving nothing to chance. The owner doing the t-shirts got called in to PSB and was interrogated. PSB found out about the r*n site and the hares were asked some questions. "Chaotic Dog came from the Chinese trying to translate Hash House Harriers," says Ratchucker. "So that Sunday there were about 20 Hashers and 15 or so PSB. All of our local Hashers were asked to show their identification cards and asked questions. While the PSB was questioning the locals, Lao Feng, my driver, was off to the side smoking a cigarette with some of the PSB officials – probably telling them the truth: just a bunch of crazy people that go r*nning and no politics are involved. In the end, we quickly started our Hash and that was pretty much it. The t-shirt guy got deported – more the straw that broke the camel's back – our t-shirts got confiscated, and a few days later Hong Kong returned back to the Motherland."

On the Beijing members list, Ratchucker says: "I'm the only one that has the Beijing Hash e-mail list and never give it out … send everything out usually by blind copy, a bit paranoid or anal retentive over the years."

Further south in Shekou, the Saturday Hashes are set either within the Special Economic Zone (SEZ) or outside, the exact location kept a secret from the pack of 40 to 70 hounds. "If we go outside, passports are required," says Perpetual Poofter, "more to get back into the SEZ rather than to get out."

Of Pakistan, The Wolf says: "In '89 after the dictator Zia Al-Haq got killed in a plane accident, then the drug-peddling from Afghanistan started. Drugs and weapons – that was a dangerous combination. We had one rich guy who came to the Hash with two bodyguards having guns. We didn't want to have any of that, the guy from the American Embassy didn't want to have it, nor the guy from the German Consulate. We had to tell him: 'You're welcome to the Hash but please don't come with your bodyguards'. He stayed away."

Around the same time, in Islamabad a hare was arrested after he laid a trail around Navy headquarters. Islamabad – for the geographically challenged – is about 1,000 miles *inland*!

Over in Korea, since the World Trade Centre incident Hashers have been grabbed many times while laying trail by the Korean National Police because they thought the flour used to lay trail was anthrax. This has forced them to experiment with other means to mark trails. On one night while r*nning the 38th Parallel Hash in the dark up by the DMZ (border to North Korea) virgin hares tried to use bird seed and chalk. "The purple chalk we could not see on the asphalt and the bird seed looked just like dirt," said Jollygreenknob, an American in Korea. "We completely lost trail and finally asked some Koreans – none of whom spoke English – which way to a military base so we could at least find a phone and someone who speaks English. We found our way to a base and found instructions written to go to another military base for the Down Down. Finally we got to the next base and they would not let some of the Hashers in because the threat level had increased and they did not want anyone but US military on their base. We bullshitted our way onto the base for the Down Down, only to have to hurry through it so that the military Hashers could get home by the 10pm curfew."

Apart from curfews, headgear is encouraged on trail, and camouflage "is a bonus" as they r*n north of the so-called 'No Smile Line' at Uijongbu – near the North Korean border. "Come up north and see why we make more than the rest of the Army," dares their website. "As far as beers, well, the logistics of r*nning a Hash is complicated by not having a vehicle," says Slippery Beaver. "So, days out from the Hash, I'd go to the shoppette on post and purchase my daily ration of beer (two cases) days in a row, to stock up. We had to use the pack mule approach to get the food and beer to wherever we ended up, and usually a wanker would volunteer to take a cab with all the Hashers' bags to the end as well. As we got on, the gate guards at a few of the tiny installations up there were quite helpful, carrying bags, food and beer to help out. The On On Ons were non-existent. "We had a few Hashers wander off trail and find themselves in a ROK [Korean] army compound which is typically: not good, not amusing to the ROK army, usually accompanied by the sound of machine guns chambering rounds. No real incidents, they were escorted out."

Dogs of Note.

'Tumbling Bill' Panton.

First r*n Kuala Lumpur H3, Malaya 1954
Founder Washington DC H3, USA 1972
Founder Bangkok H3, Thailand 1977

When was your first Hash r*n and what do you remember of it?
TB: It was '54. Two or three people in the Agricultural Department were members of the Hash and they encouraged me to go with them one evening. We ran from the Agricultural Department Headquarters just on the edge of the Lake Gardens and it was fun, but in those days I was doing surveying in rubber estates and jungle and so on, so the idea of going out on a Monday evening after I had been walking around the jungle all day was too much like a busman's holiday. In 1958 I went up the promotion ladder a little bit, traded in the job I had been doing, and had the urge to keep fit by joining the Hash.
Did you play sports at the time or before that?
TB: Yes, I used to play tennis a little bit … and a little bit of badminton. I played rugby in my younger days … but before I came here I dislocated my right shoulder (twice) so I stopped. Then 30 years later when I had another dislocation – same shoulder – I tripped on a r*n in DC on a slippery rock on a stream crossing. Six months later I dislocated it on the Mother Hash, and then again about a year afterwards I dislocated it when I was r*nning with the Royal Selangor Club Hash. And then six months after that I slipped again and broke the humerus in my right arm and that added to the validity of the Tumbling Bill name … and then finally six months after that I tripped again and had a spasm attack and lost my memory. So a very fitting name – but we don't give names away freely in the Hashes here … you have to earn it. I reckon I earned mine.
You travelled around the world with the World Bank. How has Hashing either helped or hindered your career?
TB: It probably didn't help my career, but it helped me to retain my sanity. Actually when I started the Washington DC Hash the people that put out the monthly in-house journal heard about it and did an interview with my photograph and said what a wonderful idea it was for keeping fit. The beer drinking wasn't featured in that. There were a few recruits in the World Bank who joined in but a lot of them drifted away – they were too darn serious.
You are the recipient of an OBE. Is Hashing in keeping with that station?
TB: Many people look askance at that combination but most people who understand Hashing on a world scale – diplomats and all the rest of it – know about the Hash and many of their staff would be doing it. I think they tolerate it. But there are these characters who might frown on it. Those are the sort of people who stand on ceremony, and don't really have a true sense of humour. There are a few of them about, unfortunately.

Longman's definition of Hashing is as an eccentric British expatriate pursuit. Is it still a valid description of Hashing in the world today?

TB: The majority I'd say drift into it when they get past their rugby or cricket playing days. It's something else to do by way of keeping fit and having a bit of bonhomie afterwards and a few drinks. You can keep on doing this for *life*, I'm evidence of that. You can enjoy Hashing into your old age – it does a lot to keep you fit quite frankly, keeps the old chest and bellows working, the heart ticking over regularly. We've had people do tests on various Hashers and bring along these treadmills and things like that and they've always reported 'You guys are remarkably fit for your ages'.

Has the nature of the Hash always been self-deprecatory or irreverent?

TB: Oh yes. I knew some of those early guys – they were still r*nning when I joined in '58 – but they were not as wild as we are now. The coarseness element has increased in many Hashes, and it's rather unfortunate that it has, and it puts a lot of people off, particularly families now we have mixed Hashes. But then there's room for everything in Hash. Every Hash has its own little peculiarity, and what I enjoy with all the travelling around that I've been doing is seeing how one Hash varies from another and making a record of the differences or peculiarities of any particular Hash. There's no two Hashes are exactly the same, and Hashers themselves are changing with time anyway.

Is it true to the intentions of the founders?

TB: They had no idea this was going to happen, I'm pretty certain of that. It was a very inspirational adaptation on the part of those early guys. And it proved permanent. But in those first 30 years it could have disappeared easily had we not persevered for those few years. But now we don't need to worry … it's so well entrenched.

What's the main thing you've got out of all your years of Hashing?

TB: Friendship. And health.

Have you ever logged how many r*ns you've done?

BP: No. I wish I had started with a logbook. It must be well over 3,000 now. Probably an average of three times a week being a member of four different Hashes here in Malaysia and a couple in the US, where I return for a couple of months each year. At that rate I'm probably doing about a hundred and fifty r*ns a year.

Out of all the different countries you've Hashed in what was the most surprising location, where you've felt 'I can't believe I'm Hashing here'?

TB: Well, I've always been somewhat surprised at the way Hashing has developed in the Middle East, with all these arid desert areas. I satisfied my interest in that earlier this year when I stopped over in Abu Dhabi and went down to Muscat and I did three r*ns over there. And at the end I sort of reflected on that experience and my conclusion was you can do Hashing anywhere if you have the right approach in terms of making it work, but I wouldn't say I relished the idea of those Hashes. I admire the persistence of these guys who continue to Hash in what, by Malaysian standards, is pretty uninviting terrain.

How could and should Hashing evolve? We have Bike Hashes and Splash Hashes … is that Hashing for a start, and is that a natural progression?

TB: Some Hash purists say that is not Hashing. I say as long as it's involving expenditure of muscle power … it's an interesting offshoot of Hashing and good luck to them. Certainly Bashing with bicycles is something that I certainly approve of. But we all have our own ideas on this.

How has Hashing changed over the years?

TB: By the time I joined the Hash in '58 it was very much like [Mother Hash r*n] last night in a sense, but it was a much smaller Hash. I mean we were all expatriate and we didn't go for a r*n and noisy parties in Seminyeh like we did last night. Nowadays, these parties can go on forever and we are a wilder bunch. But the spirit is still much the same – the bonhomie, the leg-pulling, the insulting, and the bawdy songs were enjoyed then, not with the same relish as they are now. In terms of the spirit it doesn't change. The guys who do it – and now the gals – are still cut from the same cloth.

You have used the word 'debased' … quite a sharp criticism of what Hashing has become.

TB: I'm sure a lot of people wouldn't agree with me, but I'm a bit old-fashioned of course. We weren't so shockingly rude in public as people tend to be these days. People don't give a damn for other people's sensitivities. And that peeves me greatly. I'm old-fashioned in these things and we overdo it in some cases and that doesn't make us particularly well-loved in certain sectors of society.

In Malaysia we have certain segments of the population who don't tolerate drinking and if you drink in public then you are offending them. And we should be a little more careful than we are. We're lucky – in Malaysia people are more careful that way. Some countries are more tolerant of these improprieties than others.

The biggest chestnut in Hashing circles these days is InterHash and where does InterHash belong. Some say Asia is the spiritual home of Hashing, therefore InterHash should always be in Asia. Others say it's now global, it belongs anywhere in the world.

TB: Absolutely, that's what I say. Well, it just so happens that most of the InterHashes have been in South East Asia/Australasia because that's been the centre of Hashing until fairly recently. North America is now a major centre – a very, very sizeable community. Cyprus was a good opportunity to test the idea and it worked. I was supportive of Goa when the vote took place two years ago, because I liked the idea of going to Goa. But that doesn't mean I'm against going to Cardiff …

Could it be that people equate a place like Thailand, say Pattaya InterHash, as a great Hashing place because anything goes in places like that, the beer's cheap, the bars are open 25 hours a day and there's a lot of tolerance for excess?

TB: I think it is, for many people, yes. Quite obviously you can really let yourself go, whereas you couldn't do the same possibly in Blackpool in Lancashire.

Does Asia make for a better party though?
TB: It probably does, to be perfectly honest. Pattaya was a great place to go for a party, although the r*nning I wouldn't rate very high. Some people don't give a damn about the r*ns of course, particularly a lot of the people that go to the InterHashes. They're just there for a wild party – once every two years let's just get the hell out of our country and loosen our ties. I quite frankly find that these InterHashes can be a little bit boring – there's too many people.

Stephen 'Uncle Kueh' Kueh.
First r*n Kuching H3 1966

How did you get roped into this, and do you remember your first r*n?
UK: As a young man craving for adventure, I had my first r*n at the Batu Kawa quarry. I heard of the Hash from friends and read about it in the local English newspaper. At first I thought the r*n would be tough and long. After trying it, I found that I did not have any problem doing it. It was a good exercise. My total of r*ns as of 12/3/02 is 1,645 for a single club only.

And what was it like to be the first Hashman in the world to pass the 1,000 r*n mark in May 1989?
UK: That Tuesday was the most amazing day of my life.

You've been a Hashman for so long and all you get is a boring handle like Uncle Kueh?
UK: When a person reaches the age of 50 years, he is entitled to be called Uncle in the Kuching Hash.

Tell us the most enjoyable time in your Hashing memory.
UK: The best, most enjoyable, r*n was our 2,000th anniversary r*n at Kampong Sarig in May 2001 with many old timers coming back from Europe, Australia, Indonesia and other parts of the world. The r*n was through the secondary forest streams, rice fields, a few low hills, a village and finally down hill back to the beer wagon. Everyone was back in less than an hour and no one was lost. In Kuching we mainly r*n outside the city in the primary or secondary jungle. Not like KL where the r*ns are set in oil palm and rubber estates. In some countries the r*ns were set on the roads or streets which were boring.

So what's the main thing you got from all these years of Hashing, Uncle?
UK: Good exercise with fresh air in the jungle, which I do not get sick of. Hashing also provides outings to various places, some socialising and – most of all – a good time.

Being Malaysian, do you think InterHash belongs in Asia?
UK: InterHash belongs worldwide. [In addition to his 1,645 Kuching r*ns, he has also attended 12 InterHashes and 16 Nash Hashes –ed.]

Allan 'Chee Bye' Chee.
First r*n Penang, Malaysia 1970
Member KLH3, Seremban H3
Co-founder Petaling Jaya H3 1977
Co-founder Hash House Hazards 1994

So, what's your story, Chee Bye?
CB: I started Hashing nearly 32 years ago with Penang H3, in my mind the original animal Hash. Weekly Hash trash were always keenly looked forward to, as it was always funny and entertaining. Another old fart, Drainoil, was already a member then and was working with the Hong Kong Bank, hence we were privileged to use the Bank bungalow for our Hash gatherings. Then, I was only one of a handful of locals in the Hash. The rest were mostly British and Australian from the Air Forces – hence my friends would ridicule me as trying to follow the crazy "whitemen" stupidity like r*nning in the rain and drinking beer straight after r*nning as local customs always discourage that.
          In 1975 I was transferred to Kuala Lumpur and after a few r*ns with Mother Hash and Seremban Hash, I decided to give up Hashing as Mother Hash was too fast for me and Seremban was too timid (after the departure of Mike Smith). I met The Bear and Herman Toda one afternoon in the back lane of a red light district. They were also two former Hashers from Seremban. We decided then to start our own Hash and so Petaling Jaya Hash House Harriers was born.
All your kennels seem to be batang-only.
CB: Being a men-only chapter we were actively promoting that mixed Hash and women Hashes should not be called Harriers but Harriers/Harriettes or just Harriettes. Just like YMCA for men only and YWCA from women. This got misunderstood and we became known as animals and drunkards with a r*nning problem. Hey, isn't that Hash? No matter, we took that as a compliment and adopted that as our Hash catch phrase and added 'Animales' to our name. That's why we are now the 'Home of the Hash Animales'.
Any signs of slowing down?
CB: Seventeen years later with many old members dropping out of Hashing, Alex The Bear, myself and a few former Animales decided to form a slower Hash, calling ourselves Hash House Hazards. Originally it was meant for members over 40 years of age and the r*ns to be no shorter than 45 minutes for front members and not longer than 75 minutes. We are not gays but we believe in the original concept of Hash and, like Mother Hash, we are only open to men. We even have a Hash Quack as a "balls checker" to determine the sex of our guests and members.
Sounds like you've had a very rewarding time in The Hash.
CB: Thirty-two years later, and having attended all InterHashes since 1978, my reward is a Hash name of Chee Bye which means cunt in Malay.

Andrew 'Haji Babi' Bacon.

First r*n Jesselton H3 1964
Member Lae H3, PNG; Third Herd Riyadh H3, Saudi Arabia

Great name, how did you get it?
HB: A Haji is an Islam who has made the pilgrimage to Mecca, and is an important and respected person. Muslims do not consume pork and so associated with my surname, Bacon, it seemed to be appropriate, *Babi* meaning pig.

Has the Hash changed since 1964?
HB: Originally it was a group of male expats, joining for some exercise, beer and relaxation. Now it is more a social gathering with the inclusion of women, although r*nning is important and seems to be becoming more competitive.

Does InterHash belong in Asia?
HB: It would still keep the original atmosphere of the Hash. I feel that the spirit of the Hash in the Americas, and Europe, is not the same as in the Far East. Australia does seem to have kept more to the original concept, perhaps since it is closer to Asia.

Is Hashing in the South East Asian cradle of uncivilisation still the best?
HB: Hashing in the original venue – Malaysia – is unique with the admixture of rubber plantations, rice *padi*, sago swamps, mountains, jungle, etc. Other venues cannot compare (especially the dry and rocky *wadis* and desert of Saudi). And although I have Hashed in Scotland, Darwin, Cyprus, and Tasmania, while the venue is different, the whole spirit of the occasion is the same, with local interpretations of the rules.

How many r*ns have you been on. Any idea?
HB: Total r*ns with Jesselton/KK Hash was 707 plus 50 odd with associated Hashes in KK. My total r*ns, counting other r*ns elsewhere, is over 1,250.

And what have you got from the past 37 years of this pursuit?
HB: The chance of meeting many people of different types. The taking of some exercise followed by conviviality over numerous bottles of beer. Also, anywhere in the world you can go, find a telephone and get onto a Hash.

Lisbet 'SpermAid' Kvistgaard.

First r*n Jakarta Harriettes 1982
Member Batavia H3 Hoon, Jakarta; Thank God It's Friday H3, Jakarta; Mijas H3, Spain.

How does a nice girl like you get caught up in a shady outfit like this?
SA: I heard about the Hash shortly after arriving in Jakarta, and was brought to my first Hash r*n by a Norwegian girl. I got my Hash name on a Batavia Hoons r*n (men only but "unmentionables" welcome on the last Thursday of the month) in 1988. Being Danish (the Little Mermaid) and among the small group of females daring to join the challenging Batavia men's r*n ...

Is it possible to select one good Hashing time as the best?
SA: Gee, this one is hard … [Thank you –ed.] One early r*n I still remember is InterHash 1982, when we did the r*n in the tea plantations on the second day. I was amazed at the whole scenery, and the small group of us, who got lost and scaled a very steep hill pushing/ holding/ supporting each other in order not to fall back down into the raging river. The human "horse" race with buckets of tomatoes and whatnot thrown at each other was a scream, and so were the *becak* (tricycle) races over uneven ground. When at the end of the day, all of us held hands and sang Auld Lang Syne it felt like you owned the world.

The annual Jungle R*ns in Indonesia are also very special, because you generally are far away from everything and on a sheer survival Hashing for several days. One stands out as particularly special: The Long Jungle R*n in Ujung Kulon, a national park in the westernmost part of Java. The Long R*n took nine days, and was done by only 17 of us. The planning had been extra hard, because we needed so many bits and pieces of logistics to fall into place. Every day we Hashed quite a distance to reach the shelter for the night. We brought with us more than 50 porters, radio equipment, material to build semi-open tents, and all the other necessities to keep wild animals away during the night. The most incredible thing was that we had cold beer, carried by porters in specially built foam containers with ice through the jungle, and the food was catered by cooks from a French restaurant, so we ate *crepe suzette* on the ocean beach deep into the national park.

So you remember that whenever you have a time on the Hash when you think 'fuck it!'
SA: Well there has never been a time, when I have thought fuck it. But there have been times when I have been sheer scared. In Indonesia two of those times, unfortunately were on my own r*ns. The r*n with the river crossing, when we had our own bridge constructed and took it out to every recce, so it wouldn't disappear. The out and in trails had to cross over this bridge, because it was the rainy season and the river was too dangerous to cross through. Eight recce's assured us that the site was safe. Half an hour before the r*n, it started to rain, but we thought this should be safe enough. Not so, because it has rained in the mountains for the whole day, and when the rain broke through the river, it not only took the bridge but it widened the river by many metres. And where were all the Hashers? On the wrong side of the river! We hoped they got the message of just continuing another five kilometres [Is that all? –ed.] downstream to the concrete bridge, where we had cars waiting. After four hours everybody was back safe.

How does the terrain compare between Indonesia and other places you've Hashed?
SA: Indonesia in general is simply the best. Just sheer excitement. Jakarta, my Hash cradle, is still the most exciting and I would rather fall on a muddy hill than on a dry, stony hill. All the small bamboo bridges are always exciting, although sometimes scary, but then you often have a choice of getting wet by crossing into the stream. Mijas, Spain, the hills are steep and slippery. In the wet season it is so green and beautiful.

Why is Hashing so popular in Indonesia?

SA: In Jakarta, Hash was the main entertainment in the early/middle Eighties. In the Nineties numbers started to go down a bit with so many other entertainment offers, but with the downfall of the economy, Hash seems again to be an important part of expatriate life. The average age on the Jakarta Hashes is somewhere around 50, so we lack young people, although some find their way to the Hash. In the early Eighties the Harriettes seemed more wild and there were more party animals than these days. The days when we would go On and On and On to Jaya Pub and dance on the bar are gone. I guess it's because we all are getting older!

Apart from hangovers, what's the main thing you've got from Hashing?

SA: It is the best way of getting to know a new place you either visit or you are going to settle down in. The people on the Hash are very friendly, easygoing, helpful and a great source of information of the place, where you r*n. When I think back at my 18 years of living in Indonesia, two things stand out: Hashing and travelling in the country. When travelling I have also joined various Hashes outside Jakarta on r*ns. So all in all the main thing I have got from Hashing is friendship.

What are your views on InterHash these days?

SA: I have only InterHashed in Asia – it is definitely easier when the weather is nice and warm. InterHash has become very commercial which is a pity, but I guess it's hard to avoid with such large numbers. InterHash in Jakarta in 1982 was very different, because it had the real InterHash atmosphere, which I guess cannot be obtained these days with such large numbers joining. So now I think InterHash can happen anywhere in the world.

Margaret 'Sweaty Pie' Harisanto.
First r*n Bandung H3 1980

Sweaty, tell us how an Indonesian lass like yourself got involved in this madness.

SP: I heard of the Hash as early as 1975 and I knew a Scottish family where the husband had a cast on one of his legs. He explained that it was the result of r*nning the Hash. How awful, it must be treacherous – no way I'm joining the Hash! I thought it was silly to r*n through the country, fields, to chase paper and drink beer, and I still do not like beer. But in the spring of 1980 friends came over and mentioned about the Hash and I did not know what to do with them. So we went and decided to join the Hash and got hooked. I have more than 1,045 r*ns. The best, most enjoyable, r*ns for me would be the Valentine's R*ns when many expat Harriers were still around. The On In was then taken over by the Harriettes. Besides putting up a show with songs and singalong favourites, all were dressed for the event. This was the time to call in the hares who did not behave in the last year: Master or committee member alike were shown up in the circle for who and what they really were. Besides being a professional and/or manager during the day, exposed then is the other side of their life – for really being one of the pack of wolves and bastards they really are on their off hours. Gossip? No! True stories, yup!

You must have had some shocking experiences over the years ...

SP: Being a hare on elevations of 1,400 metres above sea level, in a thunderstorm at a tea plantation and smelling the sulphur of the huge lightning coming down left and right of the trail. Heavy downpours and tropical storms with lightning striking are really very frightening especially if you cannot hide out or find any cover anywhere. Never again!

What makes r*nning in Bandung special?

SP: To the north and the south you have volcanoes and mountain ridges all around. Besides the rice paddies in the valleys, we have coffee, cacao, rubber, tea and quinine plantations on the slopes of these big mountains. In the valleys, you have the rivers, rapids and clear creeks. Hashing here, whether a half hour or two or three hours, always gives a multitude of choices in terms of easy, medium, or very tough trails through the jungle, up and down steep slopes, rain or shine. R*nning these trails of course is at your own risk and we have no sweepers who find you and fetch you out when you do not show up at the On-In after dark. On several occasions Hashers have ended up sleeping in the jungle overnight because they were lost. But eventually we got them all back.

Andrew 'Snow White' Sheppard.

First r*n Desert H3, Dubai 1983
Founder of the JOLLY Hash (Japan Only R*ns Reap Year Hash)
Member Tokyo H3 and all Tokyo area Hashes

How did you first hear of the Hash?

SW: In Dubai, all of the expats go to the Hash. I didn't know what was going on. And then I had to drive home extremely pissed. Fortunately the cops who stopped me didn't know what beer smelled like. In Japan, it took me a while to realise that there was a Hash – in fact I shared an office with the On Sec for six months before I heard about it. Since then I have r*n with almost 40 different Hashes around the world, and have become a member of mismanagement of all five in the Tokyo area.

Has Japan been your most enjoyable time?

SW: I think the most enjoyable r*n was the one Dog Fucker and I set for the Tokyo Hash 1,300th r*n. There was a river crossing by boat, a choice of four different length trails all set 'live' and a trail we cut ourselves through virgin forest. Before that it was the one also set by Dog Fucker and I for the All-Japan InterHash in 1999 which involved a swim across the bay and culminated in Buster Hymen (aka Pinky) doing a striptease that somehow made all of the guys present unable to have sex for several weeks.

Sounds terrible. But I'm sure you've had worse ...

SW: The Singapore Sunday Hash in November 1997. I was with my girlfriend, Wooden Eye. Unfortunately, we cut the start time fairly fine because I did some shopping beforehand. So it was about 5:25pm when our taxi got to the second of two possible turn-offs for the start. By the time we had driven around the three car parks at the other, we had picked up a virgin [Half your luck! –ed.]. I came back from r*nning around the area, and announced that there were definitely none of the Hash signs promised in the flyer, no sign of hares, beer or cars full of Hash bags, but I had found a trail leading into the jungle. The virgin wisely ducked out, but I offered to carry Wooden Eye's bag as well as my own (complete with all my Christmas shopping, etc). We were managing to follow the trail OK. Then we got to an arrow near a reservoir, and a false trail, and couldn't find trail anywhere so decided to follow the reservoir around. Convinced that the r*n was A to B, I thought we were at a different reservoir, and decided to turn left. We had to follow every creek around, and cross every stream. The ground was often muddy, and at one point I slipped in up to my waist – Wooden Eye thought I had drowned. We got really spooked when we heard these wild animal noises coming from the jungle – we didn't know we were near the zoo!

We came to the West Seletar Pumping Station, followed its access road to the Expressway, and at 1:30am we hailed a cab, covered in mud and still carrying the Christmas shopping. We got home, drank lots of water (water everywhere on trail but none we dared drink), hosed down, opened a bottle of Champagne, and celebrated being alive. I had about 40 minutes' sleep before getting ready to leave for Tokyo again. Looking at the map, we must have been only about a kilometre from the start when we got lost, and would have found it easily if we had followed the reservoir the other way.

What's the main thing you've got from Hashing over the years?
SW: DRUNK. LAID. FUN. FIT. In that order.
So is Asia the best place for InterHash to be held?
SW: Rhetorical question. Of course it is worldwide. It's just that Asia is the best place for it. Other options have expensive beer, bad weather, grotty accommodation and ugly girls. To strike a balance, we should put up with the grot slots about one in three, minimum two, maximum four. For the purpose of this discussion, Australia is *not* in Asia. In other words, Asia should be the choice at least every four years and at worst every six years.

Horst 'Hash Kraut' Whippern.
First r*n ("I haven't got a clue") [KLH3 mid-Sixties]
Founded Port Moresby H3 1973
Member Singapore H3

I know you can't remember your first r*n, but how did you first get into Hashing?
HK: It would seem decades of Tiger Beer intake (with the odd Tooheys and VB thrown in to make matters worse) have affected my brain, or what little there was to begin with. I joined KL Hash around the mid-Sixties and made my presence felt until I left Malaysia in April 1970.

Tell us about the high jinks in KL when you started.

HK: Crazy behaviour … well, in KL no food was served after the r*ns so we had to find our own. Often a bunch of dirty, scruffy, half-pissed and absolutely stupid looking *Orang Puteh* (white men) would descend upon a curry restaurant called Hameedia, located conveniently close to the bars of Batu Road. Here we would be charged outrageous prices for a curry meal, which most of the time seemed to taste quite good. Such dinner outings were usually interspersed and ended with special 'thank yous' to the very tolerant owner by throwing sundry chicken bones into the overhead fans. Thereafter it was off to those mentioned places across the road for a couple of hundred beers, not always to the pleasure of wives or girlfriends who were waiting somewhere.

There seem to be some gaps in your timeline … more 'beer gaps'?

HK: With transfer to Sydney in 1977, my Hash 'career' went into hibernation mode. Upon relocating to Singapore in 1979, I made some effort to join the exalted chapter of Singapore H3 but found them at first sight to be a bunch of stuck-up arseholes, quite cliquey. So, I dropped the idea and concentrated on my business career (honestly!). Only repeated insistence over the years from John O'Rourke – SH3's grand old and wise (?) man – and ex-KL Hasher Des Holloway, convinced me to give it another try in 1989. For almost 10 years I thoroughly enjoyed it, even if the flesh was getting weaker and bones were creaking more loudly. I even let myself be roped in to become Joint Master (a Kraut of all people!). After all it turned out that SH3 was a bunch of nice and sometimes crazy chaps. After transfer to KL in 1998, I tried to r*n with SH3 on my regular visits to Singapore but eventually had to go into Hash retirement with quite a bit of regret.

And what about the 'wurst' of times that you don't miss at all?

HK: On most r*ns I felt 'fuck it!' climbing up a steep hill, sliding arse over tit down a hill, wading knee-deep through mud and slime. One occasion sticks in my mind … when 42 of us got lost around the Klang reservoir, north of KL city, because the hares (fellow Krauts all!) had not recce'd the r*n properly and ran out of paper. As there was no way of finding our way out we decided to camp in the jungle until first light. Incidentally, the hares were politely told never to come r*nning with KL Hash again.

Do you think the Hash has changed over the years?

HK: In some places it has departed from the old 'jogging along' for the fun of it to an element of competitiveness being introduced. This is sad – all we wanted was to sweat out the weekend grog.

John O'Rourke. [96]

First r*n Singapore H3 1963

How has the Hash changed over the years?

JO'R: All in all, the Hash appears to have retained its original form, flavour and style and such changes as have occurred have been largely cosmetic and due to evolution. The original 5:45pm start has become 6pm to compensate for a time zone adjustment in Singapore and Malaysia 20 years ago. However a Singapore Monday seems unchanging with the circular arriving late, a hurried dash in the late afternoon, a slightly different venue, similar bodies and faces, discovery of the checks remaining a closely guarded secret among the front r*nners, and the beer r*nning out far too early every week.

Tell us about the infamous Tuesday lunches.

JO'R: Tuesday lunch virtually disappeared with the Urban Redevelopment Authority resuming the property of such famous restaurants as The Eyes and Piles, Gomez Fish-head, The Rendezvous and Jan's Café. The circulars which emerged from those lunches, influenced as they were by the amber fluid, have now changed into bland if sometimes humorous reviews of the previous week's r*n, occasionally garnished with pornographic cartoons lifted from circulars sent here by foreign Hashes or the internet.

Any particularly good moments in your Hashing years?

JO'R: Ian Hill – Hash and Australian Army Doctor – decided to try the pace of his new (duty free) BMW along Admiralty Road West post Hash one evening. Regrettably a granite bridge bit him as he went past at around 11pm. The Army Hospital located about a mile further on heard the commotion and sent out an ambulance. While the ambulance driver and attendants looked for the corpse, Ian collected the bits and pieces including the hub-caps and placed them carefully in the back of the ambulance, where he was discovered by a nurse who said 'Why, Dr Hill, how did you get here so quickly?'

Another car incident was Gunga Dick who attended an On On at Bill Bailey's Bar (Joe Coco's Rattan Palace) – alas no more – and was suitably distressed when ignored since he had not been introduced. Determined to show his mettle he sped off down the Nichol Highway and demonstrated more than adequately that the road divider was made of sterner stuff than the sum of his TR4's sump, gear box and differential. A kindly soul who drove him home on the back of a scooter decided that Dick's wallet was adequate fare for the journey. However, the Hash compensated for this, providing a chauffered Rolls-Royce for Dick the next Monday.

Any downsides over the years?

JO'R: The termination by Causeway traffic jams of Johore r*ns, which usually surfaced once every six weeks. Also, Mr Ho's on-site r*n catering has displaced the On Ons at disreputable coffee shops or the dubious pleasure of eating *chappatis* wrapped in an old copy of The Straits Times and dipped in curry gravy from a condensed milk tin with a rattan handle, while sitting on the kerb in Bukit Panjang at midnight. This was available together with two large Anchor Beers for S$4.

Wichanee 'Imelda' Charutas.
First r*n Singapore Harriettes 1984
Co-founder Thinking Drinking H3, Bangkok
Member Bangkok Harriettes

Imelda, what were you thinking all those years ago?
I: Where do I begin to tell the story how I fell in love with Hashing and how a chance first impromptu r*n totally changed it all? In April 1984 when I happened to be visiting a very close friend in Singapore, it so happened that my good friend had been Hashing with Seletar Hash for quite some time and that particular weekend the Seletar men were celebrating the baby step of their 200th r*n anniversary. I tagged along with him to the r*n thinking it's going to be some boys' afternoon out and I should be able to convince him to leave after a decent interval of showing your face around. Little did I know, the r*n was open to all, and Singapore Harriettes were there in full force. With some pushing and prompting from the ladies in charge, I had borrowed all – r*nning shorts, shirt and shoes from wives or girlfriends of Seletar Hashmen and joined my first Hash r*n. I used to be a varsity r*nner but the idea of Hashing was quite strange especially with verbal harassment from elderly Hashmen blasting away left, right and centre at every check. I thoroughly got hooked on the idea and decided to check up the local Hash scene in Bangkok once I got back. I joined Bangkok Harriettes, and a week or so later the mixed Monday Hash – the first female member for this primarily men-only Hash.

Did you ever feel out of place?
I: During that time and for several years, very few Thai ladies took to the idea of Hashing. It's definitely not on for self-respecting, prim and proper girls to be seen in public wearing skimpy r*nning outfits and, heaven forbid, be seen in the company of *farangs* (foreigners) who look as if they just came from the Mariner's Club in the Port of Bangkok area. It didn't help that we always ran in the Bangkrachao green belt opposite the port, and many times the Thai girls in the group were met with insults and lewd remarks from the locals thinking that all of us must be street walkers or, in the port area, the rope climbers.

Any cultural problems with work, friends, and so on?
I: Worst greetings ever – 'Ah, Wichanee, I can't recognise you with your clothes on!' This is often heard when I chance upon a Hash friend at social functions in Bangkok, especially when I am with my boss or my elders. Most of my friends gave me a few months of perseverance and predicted that the novelty would wear off and I would meekly go back to the fold seeing how foolish I have been.

You're not Filipino – why the name Imelda?
I: Contrary to popular belief, I don't own as much footwear as my namesake. This Hash name was bestowed on me by Blobbs at InterHash '90 in Manila following a comment from one Hamersley Hasher who saw me at the circle. As the then Grand Mistress of Bangkok Harriettes, I was invited to r*n the circle – and if you can cow the Hamersley mob, you must be something to reckon with!

You're a big fan of InterHash – when was your first one and which was the best?

I: InterHash '86 in Pattaya exposed me to the international Hashing fraternity, and friends made then remain fast and close friends until today. However, my records go as follows: Best InterHash management – still is Rotorua with Hobart as a close second. Best InterHash r*ns – Bali (the organisation sucks, though). Best InterHash crowd – Pattaya (we organised it!). For me, InterHash can be held anywhere in the world if there is sufficient support from the local chapters and travelling there is not too troublesome or costly. For a lot of Hashers, InterHash is the perfect excuse for them to plan a tour which might not be possible without the event. Why do we kick up a fuss about the location when we should look at how the event could be well organised to serve the Hash world in general?

If you had to choose just one best r*n?

I: Best Hash r*n ever – Gibraltar tunnel r*n at EuroHash '93. The trail was under the Rock itself – very few visitors to Gibraltar know that there is an extensive network of trail of 35 miles. The hare must have been high up in British military command to allow us access. I was not prepared and didn't have [a torch] so I had to r*n blindly at the heel of the Hasher ahead of me. At certain times you ran in the dark with your own hard breathing your only company and the hopeless 'Are You?' echoing in the far distance. It's pretty scary! We must have r*n total about six to seven miles – when we entered the tunnel the sky was bright and blue, the sea was calm and enticing. When we emerged onto the dusky mellow of Gibraltar township, we were totally disoriented. I remember stumbling through the deserted streets asking directions from the prim and proper British officers' wives on their way to the Officers Club for the evening drinks. Our sudden burst on the scene must have shocked quite a few people there!

John 'BOF' Lane.

First r*n Kowloon H3, Hong Kong 1980
Member Wanchai H3, Hong Kong; China H3, Taiwan; Taichung H3, Taiwan

At 65, aren't you old enough to know better? Why Hashing?

BOF: Why not. I am foremost a long-distance r*nner having taken up the escapism of the sport when my wife died in 1979. I remember my first Hash guesting with the Kowloon Hash. The On On was at the old Sha Tin Inn on Tai Po Road and I remember climbing up the steel stanchion and crossing over the roof truss, above the whirling fans and down the other side. I did not like r*nning at night so did not join in regular Hashing until 1993 when the Wanchai Hash started r*nning on Sunday afternoons at 4pm. This was ideal for me as I could race in the morning and Hash in the afternoon. R*nner's heaven!

Tell us your best Hashing moments …

BOF: My most enjoyable Hashing experiences have been with the down island Hashes in Taiwan with the China Hash, and the Free China Hash trips to Japan and Guilin. They have all been great weekends with excellent r*ns, rumbustious [No idea either –ed.] circles and mind-bending On Ons. Two Hash-related incidents which are particularly memorable: One was after a Dragon Boat day in Stanley, Hong Kong, when making my way back to my car parked in Repulse Bay after a Hash r*n, dragon boating and much beer. It was dusk and as I ran along the path I came to a stretch covered by trees like a tunnel. The next thing I was sailing through the air, and pitched down the steep cliff, to finish up in among the heap of rubbish at its foot. I managed to scramble back up and get to the end of the path and get a taxi back to my car. After a very painful night I took the ferry to Lantau where I was going walking. I missed the ferry and the group, arrived at Mui Wo late, and decided to take the coastal path to the next bay, Pui O. I puffed and panted up every hill wondering why I was so short of breath. I gave up at Pui O and went home. Another painful night and then my daughter said 'For God's sake, Dad, go to the hospital'. I did and, after an X-ray, was admitted with a collapsed lung.

The other incident illustrates the fact that you cannot always trust a Hash to look after their visitors. I'd just arrived in Chun Mai, booked into a small hotel, and went to find the Hash. After a great r*n through the usual bamboo, rice paddy, streams and jungle, we went back to town. I vaguely remember having a shower with some ladies in a shower show and then – blank. I have one failing when over-drinking: I sleep walk. I awoke next morning on a street corner in Chun Mai in silk pyjamas, with no passport, no money and I could not even remember the name of the hotel. Just as panic set in, a young lady with long hair came into view and asked what in heaven's name I was doing. 'Come back to bed,' she said. I obliged and recovered all my belongings if not my composure.

Yes, Hashing is dangerous for the health but I would not have missed a moment of it.

Ed 'Hazukashii' Howell.

First r*n Okinawa H3, Japan 1984
Founder Aloha H3, Virginia Beach Full Moon H3, Seoul Southside H3, Appalachian H3, Yokota H3
Member Honolulu H4, Hawaii Full Moon H3, San Diego H3, North County H3, Tidewater H3, Ft. Eustis H3, Over the Hump H3, Mount Vernon H3, White House H3, Yongsan Kimchee H3, Seoul H3, Osan Bulgogi H3, Korea Mystery H3, Seoul Full Moon H3, Samurai H3

Where does the Japanese Hash name come from?
H: *Hazukashii* is my original Hash name from the Okinawa H3 and which 17 Hash kennels have either renamed me or just decided not to change. It means shy or bashful, but the Hash is good at eliminating that character trait.

My team of researchers tell me you've done about 1,200 r*ns (including about 250 hares). Must've been some crazy times, but which was the best?

H: I have had so many wonderful times, it is hard to pick just one. I really enjoyed Hashing in China and the Philippines, as well as Tasmania and Kuala Lumpur.

Any life-threatening cock-ups?

H: Ya know, I have said 'fuck it' on many occasions, but only concerning the one trail I was on. I never recall the desire to give up Hashing. Probably the most extreme moment was on the Ball Buster trail at InterHash in KL (1998). We had been on trail an hour or so when an ambulance siren could be heard in the distance, then getting closer and closer. We found out at the end that someone had fallen and broken a collar-bone or leg or something. Too bad. That trail also captured a half dozen Hashers in the jungle overnight. I fortunately made it shortly after dark, but we still had to do a hand-in-hand chain of about 20 Hashers to work our way through a very dark and sloppy stream crossing. I wear that survival shirt with pride.

How do you compare the various places you've Hashed in?

H: The absolute best trails I have ever r*n were in Korea. Plenty of hills, obstacles, and shiggy. The jungles of KL were also very entertaining. Hashing in Africa was very flat, but there was damn little else to do.

What's the main thing you've got from Hashing over the years?

H: The opportunity to see the world. The Hash has been my vehicle to go to so many wonderful locations around the globe, and see stuff a tourist would never see. To show my appreciation for all the Hash has given to me, I gladly host http://gotothehash.net and maintain the Korea, USA, South America, Central America, and Caribbean region Hash contact lists on the web [He got that free plug in nicely –ed.].

Does InterHash belong in Asia or worldwide?

H: I think InterHash belongs in Asia, the rest of the world has their opportunities for [Nash Hashes] … If it were to be in Western Hemisphere, I fear many of the Asian Hashers would not be able to attend, and that would lose the atmosphere that makes InterHash so wonderful.

Nisha 'Two Lips' Khan.

First r*n Penang H3 1978

How did you get into Hashing and what have you got from it?

TL: I was introduced to Hash by none other than my better half – a Hasher himself. Hash has had a tremendous impact on my lifestyle. Any institution which can get you into the jungle and off the back of your families and the world in general for a couple of hours each week is beneficial to a whole heap of humanity. I joined Hash to get rid of the flabby tummy that would not go down after Aida was born. Among the fond memories and enjoyable r*ns and good times were the outstation trips. Like Songkhla in 1984, where it was our night – no care about the cooking, ironing or the children. Those were really the wild fun-loving times we had. The main thing I've learned from Hashing over the years is the big T – TOLERANCE.

Tell us about your Hash name.

TL: In 1991 the Penang Harriets were organising our club's 1,000th r*n celebration. For the souvenir magazine, I was interviewed and one of the questions was 'How would I like to expire?' My answer was 'With a smile on both my lips'.

And then in 1997 you had your own milestone r*n.

TL: In August 1997, I reached my 1,000th r*n which made me the Harriette with the highest number of r*ns in Malaysia and very likely in the world as well. I suppose this sanctified position is reserved for the totally demented. I organised a mixed r*n, a bus ride from Tanjung Bunga to Teluk Bahang, then a long, long r*n back to the beer wagon with t-shirts, food and beer thrown in as added bonuses. Working up a sweat made it worthwhile – better than multiple orgasms. You can get euphoric during a good r*n – it is almost like sex.

So you take the r*nning part pretty seriously?

TL: I am a serious and competitive r*nner, not against the field because that would be unfriendly, but against the clock and therefore against myself.

And what are some of your most memorable Hashing moments?

TL: I have enjoyed as well as cursed some of the most fantastic and gruelling survival commando r*ns, acted as 'Jane of the Jungle', developed Hash rash from poisonous plants, suffered bee stings, fractured my ankle a couple of times, and almost drowned while crossing a big river in Northern Sumatra. But all of these have not deterred me from Hashing because of the love I have for the jungle, and also of the good company and friendship I have in Hash.

John 'Cap'n Squall' Stall.

First r*n Pattaya H3, Thailand 1984
Co-founder Ko Samui H3 1997
Member Bangkok H3

How did you first hear of the Hash and what were your impressions?

CS: Pattaya H3 chartered my 70-foot sailing junk for a r*n on Ko Lan. We sailed back leaving Desert Island Derek lost on the island, which convinced me these guys are weird, just like me. Desert Island Derek was taken in by an island family – who just happened to have two charming daughters – and was fed and put up in the house for the night and returned to the mainland Pattaya the next day. Sadly Derek is deceased, having crashed his car just after laying a Hash R*n on the outskirts of Bangkok.

What was your best r*n ever?

CS: My best r*n no doubt was the outstation at Mae Hon Son up on the Burmese border. As co-hare I laid a tough two-hour r*n and, just as the pack were approaching the finish, I was lying in wait in a dark jungle valley. Each one shit themselves as I leapt out in this bear suit, shaking the foliage. That bear suit cost me Baht 8,000 but the video my co-hare Don Petrie filmed was worth every penny.

Are Hashers changing with the years?

CS: Well, over the years obviously we do find our Hash (as anywhere) getting older. But here on Samui we have a 72-year-old, Derek, who has actually got his young Harriette pregnant !

Alex 'The Bear' Thomas.

First r*n Penang H3, Malaysia 1970
Founder PJ Animals, Malaysia; Seletar H3, Singapore
Member Seremban H3, KL H3

Bear, you're a finely-tuned athlete. Aren't your talents wasted here on the Hash?

TB: You won't believe it, but I was a sprinter in my younger days, school days. I used to clock about 11.2 for the 100 metres.

Yeah, me too. Minutes, that is! So how'd you get started?

TB: I was actually laying a track for my company's annual cross country r*n and to help me lay the route was a Hashman, and he talked about this Hash and got me interested in it. And I never looked back after that. I was not very fit then, but the beer kept my spirits up. We used to drink a great volume of beer, never cared much for food.

Have Hashmen changed over the years?

TB: It was more boisterous, I feel, then. We were banned from several pubs and eateries. We didn't feel we were doing anything wrong but the administrators said that our custom wasn't welcome. In the old days when I started Hashing, one of the things that I looked forward to, we used to gather round the bonfire, we used to sing ... you didn't have to be a good singer but everyone sort of participated ... and that kept us going well into the night. We didn't care much for food then, you know a sandwich or a curry puff. But today, many of the Hashes sit down after a r*n to an eight-course dinner! In the old days, the dining chambers had a dress code, but today the Hash is always out in the country and we don't have a proper dress code. Those who want to shower – it's up to them – and we'd carry on to the wee hours of the morning, whichever place we are. But slowly things are changing, with drink and drive laws being enforced, people get back home a bit earlier.

How many r*ns have those old legs of yours actually done?

TB: I'm 57 now. I've lost track – little bit more than 1,500 r*ns.

So what was the idea behind the Hazards?

TB: In '91 I felt that age was catching up on me a little bit, and a lot of Hashmen were leaving the Animals because they couldn't keep on the hard r*ns so we formed the Hazards. And it was actually meant for the older members ... we limit the r*ns. The maximum time for a first r*nner back is an hour 15 minutes. So you can still get a good r*n, but you know an old fart like me can walk the course in two hours.

Have you Hashed much outside of Asia?

TB: I've Hashed in about 15 countries around the world. Apart from Malaysia, which has excellent r*nning, one of the more interesting r*ns was the UK Nash Hash in Surrey, a r*n set by RoboCop, a fine Hashman and an actual cop. He set a very historical r*n and I think it was on Guy Fawkes Day they re-enacted the attempt to blow up parliament. The worst r*n? We had a r*n with the Animals in the late Seventies where the r*n was over in less than 10 minutes because the hares ran out of paper. We couldn't understand the r*n … we thought it was a check and we got back and the hares said 'That was it'. So we gave them the usual ice treatment.

Don't you ever get tired of the antics?

TB: We all get a little bit childish now and then – it's just a bit of fun. Each r*n is a new experience. A good Hashman is a person who enjoys the r*n, be he a good r*nner or not, and who generally takes part in all these Hash activities. Many clubs try to stick to the ways of the founding fathers, that spirit. For one thing, Hash is not regulated.

What do you still look forward to in the Hash?

TB: The camaraderie. Recently we had the case of a Hashman who couldn't afford to pay his hospital bill, so we all got together and chipped in money and paid his bill. We do that to help a Hashman who's a mate. In over 30 years I've made friends all over the world, and it's nice to meet them now and again when they come to such events like EuroHash or InterHash – renew old friendships, make new friends.

Does InterHashing belong in Asia?

TB: The fact that Hash was 'invented' in Asia, I think doesn't have much bearing nowadays. Hashing has become global. I feel InterHash should move wherever it should go, not to confine the major events to Asia. I feel Asia and Australia had a good share of InterHashes and it should move on. I hope it'll get to Europe and the US.

If you hadn't taken up Hashing, how would your life have been different?

TB: I would've ended up a drunk, you know. When I first started work I found the pleasure of beer, and I used to drink a lot of beer, but I do a bit of exercise now. There has been a wrong perception of the Hash all the while – you know first of all they think all Hashmen are drunkards. When I tell them that 30 per cent of all Hashers in my Hash don't drink at all, they don't believe it [Nor do I! –ed.]. I think there is a lot of negative perception. But Hashers are involved in a lot of charity work, we raise money for some needy paupers.

Paddy 'NasiTurd' O'Kane.

First r*n Madrid H3 1989
Founder Timika H3, Irian Jaya; Milne Bay H3 and Alotau Full Moon H3, PNG
Member Batavia H3, Indonesia; Port Moresby H3, PNG; Taichung H3, Taiwan

You started in Europe then moved to Asia. How do you compare the Hashing terrain between the two places?
NT: I've got poor eyesight so never really noticed. Beer varies from country to country.
How did a boozehound like you slip through the Hash's security net?
NT: From an overweight drinking friend who claimed it kept him fit. Loved it from first, but always did like beer to the excess.
And you've been on trail ever since?
NT: 158 r*ns [in Madrid], current worldwide r*n total 540 approximately. I founded Timika H3, and flew back twice to complete 100 r*ns.
I presume you got your Hash handle in Indonesia?
NT: My birth name is Paddy, fell into a padi field on r*n in Indonesia. *Nasi* being Bahasa word for rice and if you've not fallen in a *padi* field you would not know that they are basically shit.
Was that your worst Hashing moment or have you had worse?
NT: When some sadistic bastard set a 17 kilometre r*n on a bike, being cold, in the dark, a long way from beer, is definitely time to find a different sport.

Dishonourable mentions also go to the following Hashers who have either paid us good money for a cameo appearance or are found to be genuinely of interest by their Hash buddies for reasons which are not too clear …

Louis The Lip, GM of Phuket H3, was given a party on his 65th birthday at Faulty Towers by Hash bar owner, Sybil. Wanda went to the local hospital, and borrowed a wheelchair in which Louis spent his entire birthday. The wheelchair was even brought to the Hash and Louis did the circle in it – a first for a GM? For his birthday on the ninth anniversary r*n, the Tinman Hash had him on stage with five naked ladies who in turn shaved all the hairs from Louis' you know what, and in return Louis shaved the ladies' hairs from you know where. Louis The Lip, who started Hashing in Cambridge, today is 68 years old and still a front-r*nner with 23 years and over 1,000 r*ns behind him and still more to come. Dubai, the founder member of Phuket and Tinman H3, gave Louis The Lip a rocking chair and – in pouring rain – held a circle in it.

Caramba r*ns with Pattaya H3 when he's not diving the North Sea. He was responsible for opening the hatch on the doomed Russian submarine, Kursk.

Chikara from Okinawa H3 once ran in the gruelling Torrii Triathlon. She completed the 41 kilometre course in the morning, garnering the silver medal for her efforts, then later that same day ran with the Okinawa H3 on their annual Halloween r*n – complete with a bunny costume and her medallion dangling proudly round her neck.

Gabriel, of the Hyderabad H3 in India, had already 'r*n' more than 100 Hashes by his third birthday.

Name dropping.

Some have them, some don't. Some earned them the hard way, others just got stuck with them. Either way, a Hash handle may give some good clues about a Hasher's job, behaviour or proclivities. But mainly it sums up the disdain and contempt with which the Hasher is held by his/her peers. Here's a selection of handles from Asia that stood out because they were funny or outrageous on their own, or had a brilliant story behind them – or we included simply because someone bought us a beer:

5 Year Old Shit, Angeles City H3: "In Angeles you have to earn your name and this guy had done nothing. He went off to Subic H3 one day as a guest, and they couldn't believe he'd been Hashing five years without a name, so they instantly christened him."

Acorn, Wanchai H3: "From little things great things grow, apparently!"

Adolph Shitler, Wanchai H3: "He tried to take over the r*nning of the Hash."

Another Fucking Boring Butcher From Perth, Songkhla H3: "We also had a couple of people, called **Another Fucking Boring Butcher from Perth, I & II**. They never returned."

BB, Indonesia: "Surname is Beeby. But when Soeharto was overthrown and replaced by Habibi, the handle changed to **Ha BB**."

Blue Knob Bob, Kerteh H3: "Loves sitting on ice."

Bog Brush, Wanchai H3: "This guy had a very expensive hair-do."

Boomerang, Songkhla H3: "An Aussie – we can't get rid of the bastard, he keeps coming back."

Brain Health, Thailand: Real name – Brian Heath.

Bullet Rash, Phuket H3. "My original name was **Gravel Rash**, then flying from Mozambique to Swaziland a fellow hijacked the plane with a sawn-off AK47. Eventually, the South African security forces stormed on board … guns blazing. I was hit in the arm by a ricochet. I was in the hospital for a couple of days."

Catch of the Day, Wanchai H3: "A delightful Japanese lass."

Creeping Jesus, Balikpapan H3: "I had just arrived in Indonesia, a hippyish-looking guy with a beard down to my navel. I was due to start work at a mechanics workshop. As I arrived on the first day, an Indonesian colleague looked up and said: 'My God. It's Jesus'."

Dances With Dogs, Wanchai, H3: "I was bitten by a bull terrier on a r*n around the time that Dances With Wolves was a hit. I was 'dancing' with this damn dog hanging on my arm."

Digit, Hyderabad H3: "En route for a joint r*n with Bangalore H3, he fell off the train and got his digit stomped on by a passing elephant. After arriving by hired car, he had a surgeon snip off a crushed bone of his digit, loaded up on painkillers, attended the r*n and got renamed Digit."

Dr Sex, Timika H3: This Indonesian Harriette is actually a doctor, who worked in a STD clinic in a tough mining town in Irian Jaya [Not unattractive either –ed.].

EIEIO, Sangatta H3: His surname is MacDonald.

Festering Streaker, Pattaya H3: "Used to be called **Streaker** (apparently he ran naked once somewhere) and then asked for a name change and got the Festering bit added on."

Fitzratana and **Fitzjohn**, Blang Lancang H3: The real name of this couple are John and Ratana Fitzmaurice.

Flatulent Ferret, Wanchai H3: "Has many close lady friends and few inhibitions."

Foreskin, Koh Samui H3: "This guy r*ns some shops which deal in lotions, massage creams and oils … basically everything that is for the skin."

Frank-ly I'm Getting Too Old For Hashing, ex-Bangladesh: Real name – Frank Neal.

Fuck Off, Thailand: "I use the phrase a bit, I suppose. But I got renamed because we went to this pub in the English countryside and ordered a meal, lamb dinner. When he asked for my name I said 'Fuck Off'. 'Scuse me, Sir? That's my name I explained. We came to an agreement that when they came outside to the beer garden at the back with the gentle country clientele they would simply call out '**Lamb Dinner**' instead."

Fukawe, Singapore: "As in 'Where the … ?'"

Getz Off Early, 38th Parallel H3: "Worked three-hour days while on Customs inspection duty in Korea."

Gin + Vomit, Wanchai H3: "The lady ruined a taxi journey home."

Hard On, ex-Pattaya H3. His wife was named **Hard In**.

Harley, Hiroshima H3: "Given Japanese name is Honda."

Hash Kraut, ex-KL, Port Moresby, Singapore: "The reason's obvious – if you keep r*nning in jack boots and Lederhosen …"

Herr Fokker, Wanchai H3: "Just German."

Induces Menstruation, Angeles City H3: "This guy's old and senile and every time he tries to pull a girl out of one of the bars she says 'No, it's that time of the month'."

Itchy Scratchy, Okinawa H3: "I wore my favourite t-shirt from Fisherman's Wharf in San Francisco which says 'I've Got Crabs'. I didn't know it has two meanings. Now my favourite t-shirt is just hanging in the cupboard," says this Japanese Harriette.

Jollygreenknob, Seoul H3: "By wearing green latex shorts. The Hashers wanted to call me **Jollygreengiant** but my tool was not big enough."

Jumping On Men, Taiwan: "She came face to face with a boa constrictor and jumped screaming right into the arms of a fellow virgin Hasher."

Kamikaze, Okinawa H3: Works for the Japanese airforce.

Ketchup, Phuket H3, Thailand. "Had the reputation of going with some of the most ugly bar girls in Patong beer bars … Ketchup goes with anything!"

King Klong, Phuket H3: "He reversed his truck into a *klong* (canal)."

Kinky Traveller, Kobe Harriettes: "An area in Japan that takes in the prefectures around Kobe, Osaka and Kyoto plus a bit used to be called the Kinki region – but when the connotation in English was discovered they changed it to Kansai. She was a domestic travel agent."

K.K.N., Medan H3: "Korrupsion, Kommision, Nepotism – and four other versions, some unprintable."

Knackerwurst, Songkhla H3: "Due to him being German. His wife is **Crackwurst** and their daughter is, quite naturally, **Bratwurst**."

Where the Fuck's Me Keys, Songkhla H3: "I got this due to having lost the keys of my car on an outstation r*n and was stranded until I could have duplicates made."

Konkrete Kock, ex-Medan now Jakarta H3: "My predecessor was a civil engineer, and as they were doing a lot of roads in Indonesia at the time, he became **Tar Balls**. I unfortunately replaced him."

KY Jelly, Kerteh H3: "Married to **Dry R*n**."

Leaky Dick, Jakarta H3: "He was the first of the Welshmen in our Hash, so playing on the leek and he [allegedly] complained of the odd dose. Then his brother joined, so we called him **Dicky Leek**. Another became **Leaky Bum** due to Bali Belly, a common complaint in Indonesia."

Lick Dearly, ex-Seoul, Songkhla, PJ Hazards: Real name Dick Leary.

Liquor Knickers, Kerteh H3: "Works in lingerie department and loves red wine."

Lok Sup Gow, New Territories, HK: Surname is Gow. "Cantonese for 69."

Maid Marion, Bangkok H3: "I used to wear a camel hat with a feather, like Robin Hood's. My GM thought that would be too obvious so he said 'No, you're Maid Marion'."

Mail Order Bride, Tokyo H3: "Moved to Japan to marry a Hasher."

Moose Mounter, Wanchai H3: "He has a large girlfriend."

Nasty Cyst, Songkhla H3: "A (slight) distortion of 'narcissist'. The Hasher in question was fond of blowing his own trumpet."

Nekophiliac, Samurai H3: "Favourite animal is a cat, *neko* in Japanese."

No No Nookie, Soroako H3: "Self explanatory," laughs her husband.

One Floor Up, Kerteh H3: "After one hell of a Hash blast, returned to hotel room without key. Waited for wife to return and fell asleep in the hallway. Was found next morning – one floor up!"

Oral Dysentery, Wanchai H3: "She never stops talking."

Orang Tahilembuh, Kerteh H3: "Bullshit Man – well known for setting r*ns in water buffalo fields."

Pack Pleaser, Wanchai H3: "Has dated rather more than one Hasher."

Pencil Prick, Taiwan: His surname is Woodcock. Previously also named **Timber Tool**.

Already Loaded, Okinawa H3: "One time I forgot that I already had one tampon in and tried to put in another one."

Permanent Press, Taiwan: "A scruffy British gent, has been known to wear the same clothes over and over."

Perpetual Poofter, Shekou H3: "*Poofting* is the offence of placing ones hands on one's hips, in one's pockets, or otherwise fondling body parts during the Down Down. On the day of my christening, I was caught poofting about six or seven times in a row."

Petrified Prick, Kerteh H3: "An old fart, married to **Fossil Lips**."

Pigeon Leg, Kampar Jaya H3: "I'm a tall bloke (6ft. 2in) and have reedy thin legs, like a pigeon."

Pondscum, Hiroshima: "Marine combat instructor of water survival."

Porkfinger, Bali H3: "Real first name Dermot sounds like Kermit, association with Miss Piggy, etc."

Porky, Phuket H3, Thailand: "Had a bar in Patong named Porky's so he often came to the r*n with many of the bar girls who worked for him. The girls were named **Piglet 1,2,3,4** and so on. When his nephew showed up they named him **Pigsty**."

Not Fucking Boring, Songkhla H3. "There were two girls together on the ice for naming. One of them was the girlfriend of a Dutch Hasher called **Boring**. The GM refused to accept the suggestion **Fucking Boring** for her name. But by acclamation the other girl was named *Not* Fucking Boring."

Prime Her, Kerteh H3: "He was involved in painting. His wife was then named **Top Coat**, and his daughters **Stripper** and **Thinner**."

Prosperous Chicken, Malaysia: "Chicken has connotations of young girls on the Malaysian peninsula, but this has nothing to do with that. Prosperous in Chinese is a euphemism for fat and *ayam* is Malay for chicken, pronounced 'I am'. Therefore 'I am fat'."

Pubic Relations, Wanchai H3: "A PR consultant."

Quagmire Quack, ex-Cambodia, Okinawa: "Was almost hit by a truck when crossing a bridge, jumped off a bridge and was named **Swamp Thing**. Opted for name change at OH3."

Red Dickhead, Balikpapan H3: Real name Richard Redhead.

Robbercop, ex-Port Moresby now Angeles City H3: "I was a bank manager in PNG, and had one day off in 12 years of working there – and the bank got robbed that very day. My predecessors were **Deposit** and **Withdrawal**."

Sand In My Crack, Okinawa H3, Japan: "I went for a nude dip once and got arrested by the authorities ... then standing by our cars during Down Downs I did a flip onto the back of my car, breaking the windshield. So they changed it to **Glass In My Crack**."

Screw Ewe, Petaling H3: "Named just after marriage. Husband is **Mother Sheep**."

Shagwell, Vietnam: His surname is Shadwell. His girlfriend is **Well Shagged**.

Sheila Feela, Wanchai H3: "His girlfriend was Sheila – he gave us a problem when he changed girlfriends!"

Shut the Fuck Up, Pattaya H3: "A Thai lady with an abrasive and screeching voice. In the circle they always say 'Shut the fuck up, Shut the Fuck Up!'"

Sir Airhead, Pattaya H3: "Used to be known as **Airhead** (named I think because he talks a lot). He obtained the Sir title after he accomplished his 500th r*n with the Pattaya Hash, likewise **Sir Chicken Fucker** and **Sir Fossil**."

Spread Easy, Wanchai H3: "The lady's name is Flora, a brand of margarine."

Tai Lok, Kampar Jaya H3: "His real name is Tailok Singh. *Tai Lok* in Chinese means big dick!"

Target, ex-Sri Lanka now USA: "It was 1985 when the civil war curfew was introduced in Sri Lanka. Foolishly I was driving after dark and took a wrong turn into a roadblock. I got shot."

The Meat, Ujung Pandang H3: His first name is **Beat**.

To Lose La Trek, Songkhla H3: "Got disorientated after leaving the track and blundered further on through dense bush until, scratched and bleeding, he emerged at a roadside just as darkness was falling. Hailing a passing car wasn't a great problem – but asking the Thai driver where he wanted to go was – he had no idea where the r*n site was. He had no choice but to let the driver take him into town, jumping out at a part he recognised, and walked the rest of the way home!"

Too Boring, Angeles H3: "He wanted to be renamed so we said 'OK, from now on you're **Too Fucking Boring**'."

Torville and Dean, Songkhla H3: "We had a couple of brothers who hadn't made much of an impression and didn't produce any good name suggestions. Someone said 'They've been on the ice so long, we should call them Torville and Dean'."

Vaseline Thighs, Taiwan: "I had a lot of trouble with the tops of my thighs rubbing together and getting sore when r*nning. I decided that the best thing was to coat them in Vaseline. It worked a treat, so at the next r*n I innocently asked 'Anyone for Vaseline?' and held up my jar. Obviously you can picture the response from a bunch of rough hairy-arsed Hashers!"

Wombat, Batavia H3: "From the behaviour of the wombat which as you will all know 'eats roots, shoots and leaves'."

Y Not Undress, Duri H3: Her real name was Ursula Larsen, not Ursula Andress.

And here's a bunch of good names which probably have a good story behind them but no bastard bothered to tell us about. Some make you scratch your head – others, your nuts:

Anal Farmer, Atilla the Hen, Bonking Donkey, Clean Shaven Raven, Cuckoodoodle, Diddler on the Roof, Dilate My Bunghole, Ding Dong Daddy, Dirty Rotten Fucking Muff Diver, Dog Spunk Gozler, Duke of M'Boliako, Ewe Naked Beaver, Fearless Fuckin' Fungus Faced Fred, Glad-He-8-Her, Hannibal Rectum, Horny Gorilla, Just Impale Me, Knacker Lacquer, Let Us Pray, Liberace, Lukewarm Fucking Beer, Malaria Muff, Mistah Lovah Lovah, My Name is Nobody, Operation Lost Cause, Pavarotti, Pig's Asshole, Rupee Wallah, Septic Wank, Sir Bog Diver, Sir Lance-the-lot, Squirrel Nut, Stalin, Super Chicken Shit, Ted the Turdburgla, The Enamel Tamil, Toothless Tiger, Underexposed Goomba, Unsinkable Summertime, Wawa Chiwawa, Witless Wanker, and Woody Wouldn't Pecker.

Hashit happens!

And now a bunch of Hash yarns, idiosyncracies [idiotsyncracies? –ed.], trivia and, well, downright lies from Asia, retold with suitable embellishment, padding and, well, more lies, to make them far more funny and interesting than the worthies and wankers who told them in the first place:

In February 1969, Mother Hash – still notorious for losing people – had a prime example of how *not* to lay a trail. The 49-strong pack set out and, as it was getting darker, still seemed to be heading *out*. But they were on paper, so not to worry, right? Wrong! Five, including Tumbling Bill, who spent his working life researching these forests, voted to backtrack. "I sensed we were still heading out to the hills, which seemed wrong," said Tumbling Bill. The rest soon caught up with the hare and *he* was lost, but still throwing down paper. Darkness rolled in, and they settled down for a restless night as mosquito-fodder (fortunately elephants and tigers in the area did not show up). This got too much for two of the hounds – Gilbertson and Dominey – and their dog. They set off, found an old bamboo raft on a reservoir, and paddled off to the dam where they found a night-watchman on duty. From there they telephoned for a lift home. The rest of the pack – all 42 of them – waited until daybreak before voting (except for one dissenter) to backtrack, eventually finding the fateful 'oops, should've gone left here' turn and the FRBs came in – on paper! – at 7:35am. Others arrived around 9:10am, and the lone dissenter, Bealing, 'from a totally different direction' around midday. To top it off, no beer truck was waiting for them. New boot, Roy Booth, was in deep shiggy when he got home – he'd missed his first wedding anniversary dinner!

We had a r*n in Koh Samui and this guy, Phil, saw us in our r*nning gear getting ready to go. He asked what we were doing. We told him going on a Hash r*n.
"That sounds good," he said, and invited himself, thinking we walked into the bush and smoked drugs. At the circle, we noticed Phil was not with us.
"Anyone seen Phil?" No.
So we backtracked, calling out "PHIL! PHIL!" into the wilderness. No answer. After several locations and no response we decided 'fuck him, let's have the circle,' then went home. The next morning a few of the guys were sitting around at a café in town when Phil turned up. Turns out he had spent the night under a rock in the jungle, and in the morning hitched a ride out on a coconut truck doing its rounds. Our Bangkok guests insisted he did his Down Down right there at breakfast – and that was the last we saw of Phil.

Some Aussie Hashers were visiting Sungei Petani, Malaysia, prior to Pan-Asia 2001. The Aussies were coming over by bus from Penang, a mere 40 kilometres away, to join us for lunch. Dash would pick them up from the bus station. At 1:45 they called to say they had arrived and were at the railway station. Dash's office is in the centre of the town with the railway station behind and the clock tower in front, both 50 metres away. He asked the Aussies whether they could see the clock tower. They said, no, they could only see the Heritage Hotel. Dash looked puzzled. There is no such hotel in SP. He asked the caller to hand over the phone to any local person, which he did. The Malay said that our friends were at the *Kuala Lumpur* railway station – 404 kilometres to the south!

Prince Charles visited Kathmandu in Nepal in 1980, from which two things resulted for the Himalaya H4. Founding member John Wyatt-Smith – who goes back to KL 1940 – was awarded the walking stick used by the Prince on his trek to replace one he'd lost earlier. And the kennel got a new Hashit in the form of the toilet seat used by Prince Charles on his visit. A royal flush!

Seoul H3 used to start the r*n with a Down Down for the first hound in on the previous week's Hash. Then that person was adorned with wings to wear throughout the r*n. Hashers being Hashers, the wings were naturally adorned with all manner of items, representing the full gamut of nationalities and proclivity.

At Sunset of The Empire Hash in Sek Kong, Hong Kong, Armpit fell asleep at the urinal, with people having to step over him to have a piss. Those who didn't know him were horrified – to us, well he does this all the time. We decided to take his watch. He woke up and discovered his watch missing. "Fucking Hong Kong ... bunch of bloody thieves!" he ranted and raved. About a month later, back home in the Philippines, we gave the watch back to him. "Oh, by the way, we found this in Hong Kong." Response not printable.

Balikpapan H3, Indonesia, r*n the first Hash each year. Based on East Kalimantan, they set off at 0000GMT every January 1.

Okinawa H3 occasionally have a r*n on the local US base. The first Hasher and Harriette home win a US Army General's cap to wear, which earns them the right to boss the military personnel around, get them to fetch beer, etc. This is especially popular with the young Japanese Harriettes! For your 69th r*n (and any r*n ending in ... 69), you get a commemorative headband, and get to choose a partner from the circle to go down on the huge purpose-made ice blocks with, in the 69 position. If it's your 269th r*n, you can choose *two* partners, 369th r*n *three* partners and so on.

Angeles City's Hashit award is called the Pillsbury Award, and is awarded to any Hasher found asleep in a bar during the week. This happens more than they care to admit!

A completely dry Hash does exist … the Colla Hash in Bali. Apparently the Hashers are too economically challenged to purchase alcohol for their r*ns, so two soft drinks only are served. Another Bali chapter, the Bolla Hash have a two-beer maximum, once again for economic reasons. It is left to the largely expatriate Bali 1 Hash to make up for them by consuming their own body weight in beer.

The mother of all Phantom Hashes must have been the Haad Yai H3, in southern Thailand. For many years, Malaysian Hashers would head over the border for 'joint r*ns' with the non-existent Haad Yai H3. R*n numbers would be invented and special commemorative t-shirts duly printed up. This put any suspicious spouses to rest. Why would they be suspicious? Only because Haad Yai is notorious (even by Thailand's standards) for its massage parlours, brothels, nightclubs … and little else. However, once Songkhla H3 came on stream in 1981, such joint r*ns have become more legitimate [Well, a little –ed.].

The Rumbai H3 in Sumatra, Indonesia holds a Trans-Equatorial r*n on the r*n day closest to the spring equinox, with the r*n ending up right on the Equator at noon.

Okinawa H3, Japan have a bonehead award. Quite a sight to see Hashers with a big plastic bone in their mouth sitting on the ice.

 In Jakarta for InterHash, we had armed and uniformed soldiers to 'take care of us'. We managed to persuade one of them to swap bits of his army uniform and equipment for our much-coveted Hash gear. He had finally parted with *everything* except his gun, then hopped off the bus never to be seen again. In Jakarta (or was it Jogja?) we gave the Muslim bus driver three beers. He was off his tree, singing, clapping his hands – all of which we realised as we were screaming down a mountain road. A soldier from the back went up front, put a gun to his head, then took away his beer. His driving was a little more focused after that.

 In Malaysia the Port Moresby Hash held a 'Virtual R*n': We met in the pub and got pissed basically. But a cardboard box, fashioned into something akin to virtual reality goggles, was passed around (with nothing at all on/in it) and placed over people's heads to take them on this fantastic virtual voyage of escapism in order to legitimise the r*n.

R*nning with Phuket H3 once, a Hashman arrived at the On In "half covered in vile shiggy" and was immediately given a room key and a whore who was in charge of showering him and returning him to pristine condition in every sense of the word.

At the Manila InterHash, the Pattaya Dirt Road Hash thought they'd be smart and commandeer their own bus. This they did, from the many buses waiting outside, filled it with booze, ice and a few female 'support staff'. Their bus set off with much revelry … then after a couple of hours someone asked where they were going. Destination unknown. *No one* knew where they were going. "Check with the driver, he'll know." The driver knew nothing – he was under instructions to follow the convoy they were *supposed* to be in. They eventually turned back, getting back to the hotel starting point about six hours later and missing the r*ns and circle completely.

On a r*n in Miri, Sarawak, somebody tripped over a beehive causing a swarm. The Hash pack scattered in every direction in thick jungle. The Army was sent in to find everyone, which took up to two whole days to fish them out because of the density of the terrain.

Jakarta H3 once held a Hitler's Birthday r*n, which the hares thought would be appropriate as the r*n fell on that date. Firstly the hares – dressed in full SS Regalia – shepherded us onto a train with flat bogey carts full of cowshit, etc, and we were taken out into the countryside. After the r*n, we were then herded into this fenced-off area for the circle, where a bunch of smoky fireworks were let off. The theme backfired, though – it hit the press in the UK, even Holland. "I was called by the defence attaché at the embassy in Jakarta to explain this strange occultish occurrence," says The Penguin. Many didn't keep the shorts or the t-shirt, and it is still considered taboo to even discuss it by many.

Konkorde remembers the great St. Patrick's Day debacle in Jakarta when a mystery team hijacked the trail and laid a false trail miles across country to another location where they had also sent the sponsor's beer truck. "Two circles at both locations and fighting almost breaking out as to the culprits," he says. "Local alternative Hash Batavia H3 were falsely blamed and spent hours on ice. The real culprits escaped violent retribution until the next AGM when they were granted immunity from prosecution. Only then did I own up – and I was the Hashmaster! They almost strung me up."

A Chinese Hasher named Sergeant T became separated from the pack and spent the night up a big tree in a National Park in Sarawak. He could hear the searchers calling his name, and see their torches, but didn't answer apparently because he thought they were 'jungle spirits' out to get him. The police wouldn't help search, and weren't happy either when they asked for our National Park entry permit. "Entry permit???" we innocently enquired. Sergeant T walked out the next day, and was promptly renamed Major Fuck-Up.

At a Hash r*n in Pattaya, the guys finished the r*n all muddy and dirty as usual, and were directed by the hares to SabaiLand, the famous massage place. The 'professional' clean-up was paid for already by the Hash as part of entry fees for the r*n. But there was a catch – the guys had to put on numbers and go inside the fishbowl to be chosen by the girls. You've got no idea how embarrassing it was to be the last one chosen!

Monday night, Jakarta – driving home from the usual après-Hash debauchery at one of the city's seedier night spots I clipped a fully loaded *becak* (motorised tricycle) going round the Hotel Indonesia roundabout. Being an honourable Hashman (and ignorant expat) I stopped to see if I had caused any permanent damage. In the rear vision mirror I spotted the *becak* lying on its side on the road with the passengers sprawled likewise and a person – whom I assumed was the driver – racing towards me brandishing a large spanner. Again, being an honourable Hashman I decided that discretion was the better part of valour and took off with haste and headed for my scratcher in Bintaro (which I should have done 10-12 Bintangs before). Next morning my driver (where was he the night before?) greeted me in the garage with a huge question mark on his face and pointed at the back of my car. Oh shit, I thought, I must have really pranged my car last night – but no – he was pointing at the bumper bar where the *becak* tyre was still lodged. No wonder the *becak* driver was so angry!

There is a bar in Pattaya called the Caligula that became the first (or last) stop for most of the hardcore Hashmen after the sponsor's product was turned off at the main InterHash venue. One of our team was fascinated by the act in which a beautiful young damsel spat ping pong balls out of her 'you know what'. So intrigued was our friend – a well known perv – that he decided to take a closer look at the anatomy of a Thai girl's nether parts. The girl, with amazing foresight, had added a raw egg to her arsenal of missiles which was duly spat out with great velocity straight into his bearded mug. Talk about getting egg on your face!

 38th Parallel H3 in Korea has a unique promotion scheme: All virgins are considered Recruits. After five r*ns you achieve a promotion to Lance Corporal, then every five r*ns you move up a rank till you reach General after 50 r*ns. Much-coveted dog tags are made up for the Hasher's new rank.

 We were travelling to InterHash Malaysia in '98 and ended up in Bangkok International Airport … five hour flight delay … we drank … we got drunk … we got bored … we decided to have the first Bangkok

Airport Hash. "It wasn't going too badly," says Haggissimo, "until I got a cardboard cut-out of a Sri Lankan Air Hostess and gave it to Scar With 2 T's – who was travelling along the travelator at the time – who was in turn being chased by an irate woman from the Sri Lankan Airways office."

Angeles City H3 once staged a notorious 'Hash To Nowhere', which was the ultimate mystery r*n. They had to pay up front and had to be at Manila airport with "nothing but our Hashing gear on". No other money, credit cards or means of subsistence were allowed. We knew it would be a domestic flight as we weren't allowed to bring passports or any ID either. Just a boarding pass. Trepidation gave way to absolute delight when we found out that when they said *everything* was included for the next two days and nights, boy, did they mean everything – drinks and temporary companions included!

In 1966, a r*n on the Singapore Hash nearly ended in disaster when the Irish hare mislaid the paper – either r*nning out of it or not putting enough down – which led the pack down into a quarry, just as blasting was about to commence. Fortunately, their presence was detected just in time and a wholesale slaughter avoided.

For r*n # 300 in Singapore the hares decided to lay a trail on nearby island, Pulau Ubin. The r*n was straightforward enough, but halfway through, the 'grandfather of all storms' broke out. When they got to the finish, there were no boats to ferry them back to the On On at the Flying Club. There was nothing to do but swim for it – a considerable distance in the rough channel. All but one took the plunge … he spent the night with some local boy scouts under a tree.

Ipoh H3 in 1968 held a r*n right next to the local police Cantonment. After the r*n they discovered that *all* cars had been broken into!

Brunei Hetero H3 started in 1985 with a short r*n to introduce many of the virgins to the concept of Hashing. The second r*n was supposed to be a little longer, but ended up being a monster when the FRBs picked up on a paper trail laid previously by the other Brunei chapter, and off they went into the sunset, leading the 20 or 30 new Hashers horribly astray! [It'll do them good –ed.]

In 1986, which was the Year of the Pig in the Asian calendar, Jakarta H3 decided to ship a huge mechanical *papier mache* pig to the InterHash at Pattaya [Hey it was the Eighties, give them a break –ed.]. Unfortunately, the Thai customs authorities in Bangkok didn't share the same sense of humour and refused to release it without the relevant duty being paid on it. Whether it still languishes unclaimed at Bangkok Port is not known. Unfazed, and continuing the 'it seemed a good idea at the time' theme, Jakarta H3 also built a huge *papier mache* electronic penguin which was transported from Jakarta overland to Bali for the InterHash in 1988. Unfortunately, it didn't make quite the explosive entrance on stage they had hoped … it just sparked and sizzled and smoked in the wings off stage.

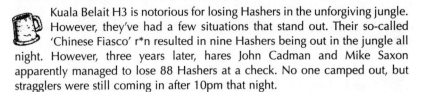

Several years back, Pope John Paul 11 visited Seoul. As it happened it was r*n night, so we had our very own Pope – Pope Blue XX111– fully robed up and dispensing wafers at the wine check that evening.

Kuala Belait H3 is notorious for losing Hashers in the unforgiving jungle. However, they've had a few situations that stand out. Their so-called 'Chinese Fiasco' r*n resulted in nine Hashers being out in the jungle all night. However, three years later, hares John Cadman and Mike Saxon apparently managed to lose 88 Hashers at a check. No one camped out, but stragglers were still coming in after 10pm that night.

Penang H3, Malaysia, which r*ns in hilly terrain, managed to lose seven of its pack once, with howling winds and monsoonal rains pelting down. 14 hours later, the next morning, they made their way down from the hill.

In Limbang, a God-forsaken logging town in Borneo/Sarawak, we used to have an annual Hardcore Hash r*n. The first one 'home' would win a lady in one of the local establishments. However the prizewinner changed his mind after standing in a queue with five dirty loggers ahead of him to receive the services. Thereafter, this prize became the Hashit!

In KL, Jungle Tom had forgotten his r*nning shoes so by the time he got to the r*n site, the Hash was well down the trail. It was an hour later before he bumped into another soul who was heading for the beer wagon. Instead of giving up and heading back for the beer, he charged his way through the undergrowth trying to catch up. Then he slipped, tumbled about 10 or 15 feet, clambered back up, fell another 10 feet, resulting in major bruises and a seriously cut leg and shredded hand. By now it was pitch black, but he found a pool of water to bathe his cuts and bruises, then lay down on the steep incline with ants feasting on his open wounds, and the sounds of nearby wild boars fighting. At daybreak, he went off in search of paper again, through thorns and six-foot ferns. At 11am he reached a clearing, exhausted and dehydrated. Waiting for the midday sun to pass, he then bumped into some lorry drivers – who thought he was some sort of apparition – and reluctantly gave him a drink of water. Through the swamp he arrived at the edge of a golf course, where he got a lift on a motorbike to a main road. It was 3:45pm by the time he could make a phone call, just in time to head off the search about to be mounted by police and rangers.

Bangkok H3 once held a 'Total Eclipse of the Sun' r*n. We had to travel about 200 kilometres to the r*n site and the roads were full as usual. But as the eclipse drew nearer, everyone started pulling over to the sides to view it. Those who couldn't find a space just parked where they were on the road, creating gridlock and bringing traffic to a complete standstill. Eclipse over, we had missed the r*n. We turned up to the site to find the hares still waiting, beer supplies massively depleted.

A one-time GM of the Bangkok Hash had learnt all the Hash songs on his harmonica, much to the consternation of the group, so they all decided one night – behind his back – to sing non-Hash songs, ancient Celtic folk tunes, anything at all, just to shut him up. Come song time, he got really frustrated waiting – and waiting and waiting! – for his cue to come in on something familiar.

In the early Seventies, Low Profile was Hashing in KL and reports that they had to put 100 Hash newsletters in the mail each week. One week, nobody turned up to the r*n – no one had received their newsletters. After a bit of detective work, he discovered that the guy in the local Post Office was steaming off the stamps and reselling them. So they started driving around to more remote post boxes and dropping off around 25 in each one so at least *some* people would get their newsletters each week. It worked.

Doing the Pattaya Dirt Road once, we did a long r*n and at the halfway mark we had a beer stop. We were told to take off our shoes and have a beer. Afterwards, we put them back on again, and this one guy says 'Shit, I'm missing a shoe.' He was the lucky winner – and this fully naked tart was brought out as his prize from the back of the truck. Second half of the r*n optional for him. On In!

Keongsuk in Korea used to have an annual Red Dress R*n. One of the regular hounds, an American Hasher by the name of Mr President had his own dress code: a cum-stained blue dress.

In Singapore in the mid-Sixties, the Hares had put a rope across Thomson Reservoir. They watched as we all clung to it and made our way above and partially in the water. They got us all out in the middle – then cut the rope. Of course half the Hash couldn't swim and it was absolute pandemonium rounding everybody up to the safety of dry land!

At the second Pan-Asia Hash in 1989, the organising committee had assumed that the attendees would be mainly Asian. Thus a conservative figure of six beers per person per night was factored into the budget. "Those days the Asians were not so degenerated yet so we drank less," said Chee Bye[78]. Imagine the bean-counting horror when it turned out that half of the attendees were Australians who threatened to drink the Hash broke with consumption of probably double that. Before breakfast! Fortunately, the committee was saved by a last-minute contingent of 75 light or non-drinkers from Bandung who paid full whack on the day.

Bangkok H3 often used Koh Samui as an outstation venue. "We would travel by train from Bangkok on Thursday night – booking a whole carriage – and I would arrange Eskies of iced beer and dozens of the wife's home made pies," says Cap'n Squall. "By 10pm all the train staff knew where the fun guys were. Vivid memories of David Simister with two female conductors on his lap and the befuddled police guard at our 06:00 arrival in Surat Thani trying to find his hat – the Enamel Tamil had nicked it! We would have a r*n on the Friday and Saturday and a lot of the Phuket Hash, led by Sir Wanda, would always join us and then fly back on the Sunday."

BOF is an over 65 year-old man of amazing stamina, who's always r*nning the Hash, and has completed more than 100 marathons. He also took part in the 'Trailwalker' race which is a charity event where teams of four complete a horizontal distance the equivalent of two-and-a-half marathons and a vertical rise and fall equivalent to Everest, all in under 24 hours. He completed the race one year, winning the veteran's class and – after a few hours sleep on the Saturday night – he went to Macau to r*n the marathon, returning back to Hong Kong on Sunday afternoon. After sinking more than a few beers in The Wanch, he announced that he was going down the road to the Neptune disco. Still in his r*nning gear, and wearing his backpack, he launched himself into a jitterbug on the dance-floor – and promptly twisted his knee. This led to a knee operation which put him out of r*nning for the next six weeks.

The whole of the Kota Kinabalu Hash – all 40 or 50 of them – got lost on trail one night at Madzang on the Sensuron road, where hill ridges rise steeply from the road up to about 1,000 feet. The trail led up to the top of the ridge on the left, but as darkness fell they lost it in the *belukar* and scrub. After much head and ball scratching, the pack came across a makeshift rice-farmer's shack. Following some debate, he agreed to show the forlorn pack the way back to the cars. "So by the flickering light of a hurricane lamp the whole Hash followed in single file down the precipitous route back to the road, arriving at 9:30pm," says Haji Babi. "The poor farmer was delighted, not only to receive free beer, but since everyone contributed one or two Ringgit, he made a fortune collecting in this brief space of time more than he could earn in a month."

Doggy Dave was r*nning on Mt Arayat around Angeles, The Philippines, when he fell off a cliff, or "bungy-jumped without a bungy cord" as one of his sympathetic Hash mates put it. The result was a broken leg in several places, a mangled arm and massive blood loss. Fortunately there were three others with him, including Saput and Bob Smith. One volunteered to stay with him and the other two went for help. One returned with warm clothes and material to staunch the bleeding. The other called Manila to arrange a helicopter to airlift him out, however he was told the airlift would be P33,000. A call to the Philippine Air Force at nearby Clarke Airbase found a chopper crew eager to help out – at no cost (a miracle anywhere, but especially The Philippines). After 20 hours on the mountain Doggy was airlifted to hospital where he spent several months recuperating. A plaque and photo in Mr T's bar in Angeles now commemorates the occasion.

Singapore in the early days had a r*n that resulted in one of the Hashmen, Sandy by name, being lost in the woods. After failing to find him, the hare thought the decent thing to do would be at least call his wife and let her know the unfortunate situation. After some investigation, he found Sandy's wife in the phone book and called her to break the bad news – only to find out that Sandy's wife was in fact his ex-wife! She asked if he could be left out in the jungle longer, please.

The highest Hashes in Asia have been staged in the Himalayas by the Singapore chapter – a country which boasts as its highest peak Bukit Timah, standing at a princely 200 metres. Organised by Neville Watson, the annual series originated in 1974, averaging packs of about a dozen. In 1977, they Hashed South Chola Pass (between Gokyo and Khumbu Valleys in the vicinity of Everest) at an altitude of 18,060 feet. Grand Master was John O'Rourke. A trail was laid with red paper, and even had one check. Special shorts for the r*n were given out on the summit, and they enjoyed a down-down of Tiger Beer … well, one can between them. Over the subsequent years, their efforts were a climb not a r*n, and hence not Hashing per se. A live hare r*n was laid by Magic Hughes in 1987 from Machapuchare Base Camp to Annapurna Base camp. The 1,400 feet elevation rise took them up to 13,550 feet.

"We were r*nning down the Peak in Hong Kong," says Mountain Rescue. "It was dark but we each had a torch. Uncharacteristically, I was near the front. 'What did you say?' I called to the guy in front. Then I realised what he had said but it was too late to avoid the enormous snake. I survived. So did the snake. On reaching the bottom it was curious looking back up the hill to see the distant line of torches making a large detour around the patch where the snake was last seen."

One notable feature of South East Asia's weather is typhoons and Hong Kong receives its far share. Not that this dampens the spirit of the Hash. When the city battens down its hatches and the typhoon 'Signal Eight' is hoisted, the HK Typhoon H3 spring into action. At Signal No.8, gale or storm force winds of 63-117 km/h are expected and gusts may exceed 180 km/h. In

July 2001, Typhoon Utor lashed its way through the Philippines, Hong Kong and Taiwan, leaving nearly 100 dead and more than 300,000 displaced by its gusts of up to 171 kilometres an hour and torrential rain. Nice day for a r*n. Amazingly r*ns are set at short notice. If the signal goes up before 8am then the r*n starts at noon. If the signal is up before noon, then the r*n starts at 4pm. This is do-able because offices close down and *normal* people head for home. 'We r*n for fun when others r*n for cover' is pretty much their catch-cry, with packs of about 20 usually braving the elements. Interestingly, the pack is often split pretty evenly between Hashers and Harriettes.

With the Agana Hash travelling group of 24 hardcore Hashers already quite festive after large amounts of lager, it was only a matter of time before we got into trouble at KL InterHash '98. We decided that we would 'elephant walk' on stage in front of the assembled crowd. Not having a skit signed up presented the problem of access, but we got some other Hashers together and a total of about 30 people made our way to the back of the stage where the transvestite dance group was standing. A man came down and immediately confronted us. We informed him we were next on stage and he informed us we were not as we were not on the list. Minutes went by as he double-checked, and then one of our band came up with, "We asked the emcee from the vomitorium and he said it was okay!" The man went to check and we stripped butt naked, handed our clothes to the transvestites, and 'elephant walked' our naked asses right onto the stage behind him to a flurry of flashbulbs. The transvestites were ecstatic. Security guy not impressed.

One 'rule' the Singapore Harriettes have in place, for men and visitors alike, is that no male may lead the pack in front of the Singapore Harriettes, and Harriettes must be left to find the checks. "But they're quick so there is no problem staying behind them," discovered Bold Fokker from Holland who guested with them. Those found guilty – or even just accused – of leading at some time during the r*n are required to wear lipstick to the On On On dinner.

The Hash decides it's going to do a r*n across Java, a four-day weekend at Java Head where it's only two miles across. "We start off and we hit this tropical storm," says Garfield. "We're in a 65-foot boat, so the waves are coming over almost past the wheelhouse. So everyone takes seasickness pills and it just knocks you out and we all go to sleep." Eventually, they disembarked at the r*n site. "So we r*n across and we r*n back, and we have a little BBQ on the beach. There's a park there and it's an island which sits right in the bay, and the ranger station's over on the island. This mate of mine Fraser Woods, says 'Let's go over'. We're both drunk as skunks – so we went out to this boat, had a bottle of whiskey and we go across. We meet these guys who have this huge boat and they're out there shark fishing, and we have a few beers with them. Then Fraser comes up with a great idea: 'The lighthouse … there's a disco on at the lighthouse!' So off we go and as you get further and further into the Indian Ocean the waves are getting taller and taller, so we cut in and go by this boat – it's sitting there and we didn't think anything of it till we ran into the set net that they had out. So here we are … we got a boat with an engine that's all gummed up with the net, and no one has a knife. We come up with a great idea – we'll just take the petrol cap off and pour some gas on it. It took us a while to find a match, then we lit it. Fuckin' flames all over the place! And I've got all these three guys sitting on my head up the front of the boat. We didn't quite get it off, so we pour a bit more on, and finally get it off.

John Morley says, 'Gee, I've never driven one of these things,' so he starts driving it and starts swerving all over the place, thing flips right over … we're upside down floating out to the Indian Ocean. So there goes the whiskey, there goes the glasses, there goes every bloody thing. And we decide to sit on top of it, and paddle it back to the boat, which is about four miles away. The crew helped pull us in, and take the engine off and put it on the deck, and we go to sleep.

We get up the next morning, and the crew is surly as hell and we can't figure it out. So we go to the back of the boat where there's a big canvas awning covering the deck, and sit down to have breakfast, and there's this big hole in the canvas. What happened is this guy got up at six o'clock in the morning and decided to clean the saltwater off the engine, so fills it up with gasoline, smoking a cigarette, and the engine and the barrel – and almost him – go up through the fuckin' awning. The captain was not impressed with our antics. They let us use the boat but we just had to paddle it around."

"Perhaps the shortest Hash in history was in Brunei," says Mountain Rescue, "from the top of Maura Beach to the water line, generously 25 yards. And the hares were splendidly pissed, shortly followed by the hounds." It was Half Pint's farewell r*n, and he couldn't even complete the trail, managing about 10 yards before collapsing in a giggling heap on the sand.

The Samurai Hash hosted several Hash weekends at Tama Lodge, a recreational facility in the mountains to the west of Tokyo open to US military and US diplomats. The Hash got banned after one unfortunate weekend many years ago when some of the Lodge's furniture succumbed to the weight of dancers, and there was also some structural damage to a number of their buildings caused by collision with a ground maintenance tractor that had been commandeered by a bunch of drunken Marine Hashers.

Attempts to re-establish relations were unsuccessful until persistence from Fu-King Lawyer and new fiscal policies required Tama Lodge to let us back.

The Samurai weekend successfully held its r*n in the mountains around Tama Lodge, partied in the camp site and closed for the night with most Hashers retiring to their tents and a few to their rooms in the luxury Lodge hotel. Some Hashers went to the Lodge disco where a fight started, which resulted in Camel Droppings retiring with facial injuries and Gympy being thrown out. Gympy then staggered out into the neighbourhood looking for bars.

Smarter Than Shit, a Hasher not known for distancing himself from vast quantities of cheap alcohol, meanwhile decided not to sleep in a tent and found that the warmest spot was the barbecue fire. He laid several layers of opened-out cardboard boxes over the barbecue grill and went to sleep. During the night, the weather changed, the wind strengthened and the rain came down. Gympy came back through the rain shortly before dawn, and crashed out in the only place he could find open – the reception area of the Lodge hotel!

The night clerk found this semi-naked pensioner asleep in a pool of water on his hotel's best sofa and tried to rouse him, only to be brushed aside. In a panic he called the hotel manager. Smarter Than Shit was awakened by the wind blowing rain and hot ashes from the barbecue all over him, and went in search of comfort. The hotel manager, none too pleased at being woken before dawn, arrived to find no trace of Gympy, except for the rain-sodden sofa. The manager was abusing the night clerk for allowing this destruction, when the door was flung open to reveal the "wild-haired foul-smelling zombie paranoid alcoholic ex-Marine form" [Average Hashman –ed.] of Smarter Than Shit dripping ash and rainwater all over the luxury carpet.

Needless to say, Tama Lodge did not invite us back.

One of Angeles City's Hashers, Wingnut, died in an untimely air crash in The Philippines. So a memorial r*n was held for him. In laying the trail, we came across a goat's skull. It was duly nailed to a tree with the message: "Wingnut is on back".

In Angeles City, Philippines, Garfield guested on a r*n, turning up to the appointed bar. He takes up the story: "After my beer I asked when the r*n was. 'Oh, when we're done,' came the casual reply. We then upped and moved on … to another bar. Next thing I know, I wake up in my hotel room. I look in the mirror and I'm a bloody mess – my face looks squashed flat on one side, and I've got all these third degree gravel rashes down my arms and body. What the … ? Down at the Hash Pub I ask a few of the morning-after stragglers what happened.

'You were on the A to Z r*n,' they explained. '26 beers in 26 bars … you made it to O then you tried to hail a jeepney … you had a good hold on it, but your legs weren't quite on it so it dragged you about 40-feet down the road …' To their credit, the valiant Hashers were apparently calling 'Let go! Let go!' but I don't remember any of this. 'Then at pub P,' they continued the sorry saga, 'you were walking out, pushed the door that said Pull, hit it head on and passed out on the floor'."

More on our website: at *www.hash-onon.com* you'll find unedited transcripts of the discussions with John Kennedy, David Scourse and Bill Panton, plus extra never-published-before Hashtorical photographs from some of the earliest Hash kennels in Asia that we couldn't find space for in the book.

What'd You Call Me?

The story behind Hash Handles.

Most Half Minds assume that Hash handles are another 'tradition' handed down from the Mother Hash. After all, didn't they have 'Horse' Thompson, 'Torch' Bennett and 'G' Gispert in their ranks in 1938?

However, these were nicknames which they either already had, and carried forward into the Hash, or acquired during their tenure with the Hash but rather as all-purpose nicknames, not specifically Hash-related.

"I believe that the name given to Horse Thompson was a nickname which had followed him from school," says Ralph Wadsworth, KL On Sec in 1963. Horse had a long, rather equine, face. Torch was so named because of his shock of red hair that glowed like a bright flame on top of his head in his younger days.

Cecil Lee, John Kennedy and virtually all others had no name bestowed other than their own. However, there is one famous case of a Mother Hash naming – Arthur 'Belukar' Broome. *Belukar* means "secondary jungle" in Malay. "As far as I know this was indeed the first Hash name," says KL Hashtorian John Duncan (having himself r*n since the late Fifties and remained un-named). "He ran from some time in the Fifties to 1965. He was also a big supporter of jungle walks, in his Hashing uniform, and somewhere that and his Hashing must have earned him the nick-name; it was anyway not one he could have brought with him."

David Scourse sheds some light on this: "Belukar Broome's name arose from the Hash jungle bashing group which usually met on a Sunday. Arthur invariably would follow a compass bearing into dense jungle. Other members would attempt to find an easier route. I think that I can claim direct responsibility for having given him that name… it was not an official Hash name originally, but did become one when names started to be generally used."

Richard McAllister was in Brunei in 1963-64. In one of their earliest news-letters is a reference to a 'Drunken Duncan'. "He was my opposite number in Gurkha Engineers and he had that name before he started Hashing," clarifies McAllister.

Slightly later, Singapore H3 starts dabbling with names and attributives. In their r*n sheet on April 5 1965, Doug Smith's name was substituted on the 'Hairy Jugglers' (hares list) as 'Duck Squiffe'. He was also known variously as 'Dog Sniff', etc over the years. In June 1967, r*n sheet # 274 had reference to 'The Lone Poker' a, er, member who "was surprised at the Tokyo Nights massage centre and nightclub."

"In Singapore we sometimes assigned an attributive, such as Rambutan Smith or Wide Lane," says Ian Cumming of the period up to 1966. Fred Whitaker also confirms that Hash names didn't exist. "We used to have a few odd nicknames but more as a joke. They weren't Hash Names. Cry Drain, Dr Drain was Clyde Lane. Paddy Bye was Baddy Pie. Cockney things. You'd see it in the circular, somebody would make it up ... but you'd never carry it on."

In 1969, John Kingham wrote an elaborate revision of the epic poem about Gunga Din, and thereby anointed Richard Murphy with the handle, Gunga Dick. "In Singapore we didn't use code names initially. I guess John Kingham's parody was one of the first."

By December 1974 the 'Hares to You' list read as: "Ivan Bumbles, Phallic Jalan, Des Hollowhead, and Bonnie Sidelane."

While Hash names did seemingly make an appearance in the late Sixties to the mid-Seventies according to the Great Kahuna, there is only one Hasher in Singapore H3 known to have a name now. Young Andrew, so named as he was the youngest Hasher to be a walker at the back of the pack. Others, like John O'Rourke, have been Hashing in Singapore since 1963 and do not have Hash names.

In Ipoh H3 as early as 1965, names such as Blue Horse and Mad Dog sprung up. Across in Brunei H3 in the period somewhere between 1967 and 1969, the pseudonym 'Y. R. Clerk' was used by an almost-defrocked vicar for anonymity in Hash Words newsletters, according to Geoff 'Father' Feast. "Late 1972 Brunei had Cleanliving Boy, Yank and Jerrard," says Amnesia, now with Bicester H3. "It appears from my collection of Words that nicknames were always around, probably simple nicknames acquired over time. They increased over 1973 and 1974, but by '75 and '76 the real name was a rarity."

It is widely felt that Hash Handles were firstly put into wide and ubiquitous practice in Jakarta to protect the guilty. Geoff 'Father' Feast Hashed in Jakarta between '72 and '76: "A few had Hash names but they tended to be the ultra-extrovert types that made an arse of themselves every time they opened their mouths." Garfield believes Hash names probably started in Jakarta Men's around 1972 when the Hash scribe wrote up each r*n "including the On On and subsequent adjournments to Blok M," he says, referring to the notorious bar and nightlife district of Jakarta. "Needing anonymity, names were assigned which of course the Hashers never divulged to their wives!"

"My records go back to 1973 when most Hashers were named," says Penguin who first got tagged Striker in 1974. "On one of my early r*ns with Jakarta Hash I was named Striker as few could correctly pronounce my surname. But after setting a 'Scottish' r*n, I was renamed Whisky Galore. All r*nners were given names often on the first r*n. Ask The Horn, Sonny 'Runny' Harsono, 'Booze' Erwin, etc." Even Fred Whitaker, who guested with them in April 1973 for one r*n got tagged 'Hot and Cold' in the newsletter as he was involved in selling insulation. Michael Ogden, who ran extensively in Indonesia at that time, agrees: "In the early days we all had names in Jakarta. I was Oggie." But Cambridge's Tampon, who used to r*n with Medan H3, says: "Jakarta names tended to be given by one person, and perhaps spread over the group. It was not an organised naming ceremony." Jakarta's 1972/73 year book shows all of the 50-strong pack to have a Hash handle, with names like Antarctic Owl, 12 o'clock High, The Lone Wolf, and Cauliflower in the mix.

Then the pace of the naming practice seems to pick up considerably. Amnesia, now with Bicester H3 says: "Monkey Glands was part of Serembam H3. It appears to be early 1970s and all the mismanagement had handles (Noodle, Arse Hole, Catweezle). Kowloon in late 1973 (Colonial Boy, Kitbag Kiwi), Panguna H3 had Quack and Zorro in 1973."

Outside of the cradle of Hashdom, Canberra H3 might lay claim to the first real Hash name: In December 1969, Max Stark, a bottle-shop owner, became known as Ruff Red after an On On barbecue in which plenty of vinegar masquerading as wine was consumed. In a curious twist in the tail, the RA's dog was called Spot, so he became Spot around 1972. Having two beings on the Hash with the same name was not acceptable, so the poor pooch, the dog formerly known as Spot, was renamed Fido for his troubles. By '76, the entire pack had Hash names, including JM Jellymeat Whiskas, RA Spot the God, and On Sec Fido Maclean, all curiously named after, or with reference to, their pets.

In Germany, the first kennel there also flirted with names in the period that McAllister was there from September 1971-73. "Hash names were not common and only a few of us picked up names. Mine was 'Wheeze' presumably because of the noises produced under stress and strain of the uphill. Names just stuck if someone came up with a suggestion that clicked; there was no conscious effort to give everyone a name."

But one place that did make a conscious effort was Brisbane H3, where the whole pack had Hash names documented as early as February 1972. "Guilty," says then-president Chris 'Leadballs' Featherstone of who assigned the monikers to Mac the Yak, Rastus, So Solli Mollo, etc. "We used to get Hash Trash from other organisations (sic), particularly Malaysia, and I thought there's a few guys we could hang something on. Generally, they acquired a nickname immediately." Some of the earlier ones he's fond of include Little Arse Play, Bare Bum and Yasser Crackafat (a Lebanese guy). "Either you learned to fight or you had a good sense of humour," he says referring to one of his more tasteful creations, Festering Homo. "Pretty ordinary compared to the names in Sydney," he says.

Indeed there was a strong relationship between the two kennels as Alan Jackman had founded Brisbane, then moved down to Sydney at the end of 1971. John Kingham – who'd named Gunga Dick in Singapore – moved to Sydney in May 1971.

While there may have been some individuals – such as Creeping Jesus and God's Father – named earlier, Sydney's founders Miall and Riddell remember it being a little later that names were ascribed to all its hounds by Ken Scott/Scutt and Rick Thomas, calling this creative duo "a very important ingredient in the success of the Sydney Hash." But French Connection points the finger at JMs Barrie Warden and Brock Bowen. "Definitely 1972," he says, "because I was on committee … we brought in the newsletter and assigned names to all."

Some of those names were the Lachrymose Bellow and Bellicose Bellow (brothers), and Pedantic Circumlocution. "The reasons why the names took off was because how clever they were," says God's Father. "None of those names are coarse or vulgar. If you knew the people they were spot on." In keeping with this tone, when Pink Elephant moved down from Brisbane, he was promptly renamed Puce Pachyderm!

And so the Hash world had yet another 'retro-tradition' which divided Hash kennels in their practice. Whether they adopted these new-fangled things, and how they implemented them, became things to conjure with.

In Asia, Hong Kong came up with its own solution ... simply reverse Hashers' names and see what happened. So Medcalf became Flacdem. That seemed to work. Leonard became Dranoel. Well, let's call him Drainoil. But that practice fell by the wayside over the years. "We certainly do not have boring nicknames for ourselves, we have a hard enough time remembering our own names let alone some childish euphemism," says Colin Stagg, ex-GM of HKH3. "Hash names were a rarity a decade ago, but are now expected, even *demanded*," says Snow White of Tokyo.

Around Oceania, some clubs go to more trouble than others in naming. Mt Isa H3 for instance. "We actually used to compile a little poem/song when naming," says Darwin. "These usually contained unadvertised dirt relating to the Hasher to be named." God's Father would probably be less than impressed with how names have evolved in the region. In Saipan, where there's a strong American influence, the subtly named Sex, of Agana H3, says: "Our names are notably harsher than on other Hashes. Our Hash roster reads like a bathroom wall in a really seedy brothel." Similarly, Fiji seems to have gone the anatomical route. "We have a number of interesting names here in Suva," says Wontok. "A lot are based on the Fijian language and parts of the body."

Many of the names of Hashers in PNG are derived from Pidgin expressions, common in the vernacular. Papua New Guinea itself was named so by the Spanish explorers who thought that they looked like those from Guinea in Africa, and Papua was the Malay word for 'frizzy hair'. So the whole country actually copped a Hash handle!

In Europe and Scandinavia, handles are firmly engrained, and invariably humorous and based on personal events or behaviour. Shag A Wannabe, an Australian Harriette in Tallinn, Estonia is a little innocent in the ways of the Hash world: "All our names have something to do with sex ... are *all* clubs like that?" No, but then not all kennels are run by the likes of their American GM, G String! The Brussels Manneke H3 website features a random name generator, which takes the hard-work and personalisation out of naming a Hasher. And, sadly, the creativity. If you have to know, your humble scribe became 'Eats Strategic Whore', 'Frictionless Guzzler Duck' and 'Unleashed out-of-the-box Wanker'. If these names seem more 'American' in their nature, there is a DC wanker credited for this name generator.

The application of Hash names in the UK follows distinctly different paths. "Our two most loyal Cambridge Hashers, Ron and Ruby Ketteridge, who have r*n over 600 r*ns each, have still to be given Hash handles and therefore remain Ron and Ruby," says Jetstream. "Our Hash names tend to be fairly safe, as we are rapidly becoming a family Hash," says Jumper from Jersey. "Bicester first gave handles only when they were deserved," says Amnesia. "The earliest few were Cashe (renamed Amnesia much later), Milly Molly Mandy, Prof, Juicy Lucy, all named mid-to-late 1970s, but it was the early 1980s before they became general," he says.

Africa and the Middle East seemed to have followed similar timing in adoption of names, with Benghazi H3's second incarnation. "It appears that names did not become regularly used until [1985] and even then they were not universal," says Beetlenut.

The Famous Explorer in r*n #62 newsletter of Morgantown H3, West Virginia said: "We should note that we give each other these nicknames to protect ourselves and our professional reputations when we participate in the sometimes off-the-wall rituals of Hashing." But perhaps the handles assigned in American Hashing are more indicting and offensive than anything the Hasher's themselves get up to. Mention has been made of American handles often being the most anatomically explicit and vulgar. Perhaps if Horse Thompson Hashed in the States he would've been known as Whores Thompson.

Hazukashii rushes to distance himself from this brand of naming. "The Hash in the USA has really gone nasty ... meaning that the names are all just vile. Every name has to have Fuck, Asshole, Cunt, or Dick in it . . . that is not Hash-like if you ask me."

"I was named by Pensacola," says Human Resources, "and the Hashes are basically military so the names are more subtle. Then I meet all these other Hashers called things like Fuck Me Now who think my name's really sick because they don't get it." [She's got big tits, guys. Geddit now? –ed.]

"I prefer it if there's a story or a reason or something behind the name," says New York Harriette, Pearl Necklace. "But often they pick a name and wait for the person who fits it. Other times when there are one-offs or visitors they stick these names on them like Green Eggs and Crotch Cheese or Jizz Mopper," she says, saying that people are sometimes alienated by this. "One lady didn't come back after they called her Short Cunt." God's Father agrees: "The Yankee things are over the top completely. There's no humour in them, there's no relevance to the person." "I was going Hashing in New Orleans once," says Speed Bump, a Harriette from Scotland, "and I was terrified because they had all these really pornographic names – I didn't know what to expect. But they were very funny and friendly," she says of the experience.

Fort Eustis has a link to a 'Wu Name' generator on their website. Type in your nerd name and it gives you your 'Wu' name. The author was immediately transformed into 'Ultra Chronic Monstah'. Perhaps unsurprisingly, Rumson has one of the most unusual practices. "We name ourselves," says Mr Jackson, who's obviously pushed the boat way out, his surname being Jackson [Elephant Dick just went down in my estimation –ed.]. "We think of ourselves as fundamentalists."

Burnt Sox of Mt Vernon H3 wrote a brilliant piece on the glory and honour of Hash handles. "It allows the Hasher to flaunt law, ordinance and customs of society in relative anonymity. It also makes rejection much easier," he surmises. He breaks Hash names down into something of a science with different sub-types: Gifted, Headliner, Hale-Bopp, Speaking in Tongues, Got a Life, Plastic Surgery, Come at Will, Name Yo' Mama Gave Ya, Happily Ever After, Fruit of Our Labor, Dirty Ethnic Slur and Barbra Streisand. "It is the rare Hash name that falls into only one category," he concedes.

Gifted names, he says, arise from a Hash event involving said Hasher, and the name itself is funny or even witty. Example Oar-a-Face who – on her first Hash – was hit in the face with an oar. It has a double entendre obviously with 'orifice'.

Headliner names report a Hash incident, but without the attendant originality or cleverness. Here he quotes his own handle, Burnt Sox, which derived when he burnt his Hash socks trying to dry them in an oven. He also cites Slick Slit "who during a Hash party demonstrated that she really did shave".

Hale-Bopp names arise from a one-time Hash event, never to be repeated. He cites as an example Dahmer, named on the day his Hash retired its bulky, coffin-sized beer cooler.

Speaking in Tongues refers to an unfortunate utterance made by the Hasher in question. Example, Wide Open, so named because as he was justifying his existence at his naming, ended with "If you have any ideas for a Hash name, I'm wide open".

Got a Life names arise from a non-Hash-related hobby or pastime. He cites Pitstop, an auto-racing fan who also has a tiny bladder, and Patio Furniture who is Irish and stays out all night.

Plastic Surgery names refer to a distinguishing and disfigured (or disfiguring) physical characteristic. The example he gives is Owwwww, a Hasher with a stud through his penis, and Heart On who has a tattoo of a heart on her groin.

Come at Will names are those with the word 'come' – or some variation of it – in them, examples of which can be found in abundance.

The Name Yo' Mama Gave Ya is based on the Hasher's nerd name. Witness the Harriette whose mother's surname was Sheets. Naturally she became Stained Sheetz.

Happily Ever After names usually tie two or more people together, be it through matrimony or bloodline. The inherent risk is the ending of a romantic association or a marriage bust-up. He cites the daughter of Blank Check who was named on her 18th birthday – Legal Tender!

Fruit of Our Labor (FOOL) names are related to the Hasher's real-life day job. Hence Pocket Scientist, a researcher for a space development agency.

Dirty Ethnic Slurs, he cautions, should be used sparingly and only with evil purpose as "in my experience no one has returned to the Hash after receiving the Dirty Ethnic Slur". Witness the Hasher of Pakistani descent who copped 7-11. Or the Harriette of Ecuadorian descent who got Spic 'n' Span.

In the absence of all else, he suggests the Barbra Streisand option. "If the Hash fails to determine a name, it should stop trying, drink more beer, and go home. If the effort persists, however, Barbra Streisand is the universally abhorred fall-back name."

For all this effort, insight, cleverness, and resource for Hashers to draw on, it's heart-warming to see that the most common Hash names seem to involve animal excreta – Cowshit, Dogshit and Pigshit would find no problem finding 'twins' on other Hashes. Ditto Sheep Shagger, Deep Throat, and Rambo. And, of course, every kennel has its resident Fossil or Old Fart.

The only real drawback with Hash names is that one gets to meet and know people only by their Hash name, which means when it comes time to contact them in the *real* world – say at their office – people often find themselves requesting of the obliging corporate receptionist on the other end of the line whether, er, Shit for Brains or Scum Sucking Fecal Philiac is there and may I talk to him please? Many a phone call has been terminated at that point. Or, better still, it results in the esteemed Chairman of the Board's Hash name being known to all and sundry in the office. Who said names could never hurt you?

Frozen Ass-ets.

The Hashtory of Ice and Icing.

First there was the Ice Age, but no one remembers too much about that. So we merrily skip to America, early in the 19th century. A Boston merchant, Frederic Tudor, started harvesting ice from the frozen lakes of Massachusetts, New England. He found that people could use it for storing and preserving foodstuffs. They couldn't get enough of it. So he scaled his operation up. And being a big thinker, thought of selling ice to the Eskimos. But first in 1806, he loaded a ship in Boston Harbour with ice, insulated it in hay, and it sailed for Martinique in the Caribbean. Bloody madman, everyone thought. It arrived in one piece, and he was rolling in the dough.

Next, for an even bigger plan – let's ship ice to India. Fuckin' madman was the upgraded consensus. And so in 1833, a ship was loaded with 100 tons of frozen ice blocks, cocooned in hay and sawdust. The ship set sail on its 16,000 mile voyage, crossing the equator twice in the process [Pissed navigator? –ed.]. Four months later, the vessel docked in Calcutta, the hold was opened and – voila! – the ice was still intact, frozen solid. Overnight, iced drinks and chilled beer became part of the Raj. Gin and tonics for everyone! Life would never be the same again. Hurrah!

Tudor benefited from this trade to India, China and other parts of Asia for nigh on half a century until refrigeration technology kicked in, and ice could be manufactured locally, in any kind of climate. The first ice produced mechanically was made in tins which held up to 300 pounds of water, producing ice blocks just a little too large to fit in the average high-ball glass.

And so to Malaya, pre-World War 2. The Hash's vital fuel supply was collected by the hares from Fraser and Neave's warehouse and taken to the run-site, where the beer and ginger beer would be laid in the tin tub of crushed ice. However, the pukka gentle-folk of Mother Hash never saw the opportunity for using ice in any other manner than keeping their drinks cool. "Definitely not here," says Tumbling Bill of whether the practice of icing was introduced by the Mother Hash or elsewhere in Malaysia. "Perhaps Australia." So the trail goes cold for the time being.

Across in Brunei, though, things were starting to get warmer. "'Icing' existed in Brunei during the Sixties," says long-term inmate, Geoff 'Father' Feast. "In Brunei it involved the tipping of the contents of the ice-box over the recipient of the Hashit during his Down Down. The practice eventually had a stop put on it after we nearly killed a young clerk from the British High Commission who we discovered afterwards had a heart problem." But still no mention of bare arses and blocks of ice.

Father subsequently moved down to Jakarta. Here, big blocks of ice were laden in their beer truck in order to keep the kegs cool. "I ran regularly with Jakarta Hash 1972, '73, '74 and spasmodically during '75 and '76," he says. "I don't remember 'icing' at this stage. I think it came later."

Indeed, no evidence of icing exists before the infamous 'Scottish' r*n at which Ron Strachan was named 'Whisky Galore' for his sins against Hashdom in 1978. "I had the experience of sitting on a block after a Scottish r*n where we, the hares, left empty whisky bottles at each check and then proceeded in the circle to spike everyone's beer with whisky, which seemed good fun at the time." To them, perhaps. Their sense of humour was not shared by the pack, and Penguin and his co-hare John 'Cod Liver Oil' Dodds were awarded Jakarta H3's Hashit of the Year for their abysmal effort on run # 364. Their reward? Blocks of ice were ceremoniously requisitioned from the beer truck, and their Gaelic cracks were duly exposed and cryogenically treated. Photographic evidence of this episode exists in the Jakarta H3 1977/78 Yearbook.

"I was given the pleasure of a cool seat in a hot country," he says of the icing event now. "This was a reasonably regular event but by luck not always my pleasure." While this is the first *documented* incidence of a new 'tradition' which has polarised kennels ever since, The Penguin suspects "it was used in Jakarta prior to 1974."

With Whorator as one of Jakarta's ringleaders in '79/'80, it seemed that icing caught on like, er, wildfire. And the ways of using it were seemingly unlimited. At first, it seems that the blocks were placed on top of upended beer crates, requiring less of an Asian squat to inflict the desired effect. "I think we can lay claim also to the ice sandwich – sitting between two blocks of ice," says the ironically-named Penguin. "These ice blocks were BIG!"

But the icing on the cake was Jakarta InterHash 1982. "It was certainly in fashion by the time of the Jakarta InterHash in 1982," says Father, whose first experience of ice-sitting was at that event. And more than 1,000 others at that event would have been mesmerised by the sheer inanity of this dastardly act which required only two items readily available at any Hash – namely an arse and some ice.

News of this practice was beamed around the world, from Hawaii to Helsinki. And never being ones to leave well enough alone, Hashers had to search for new lows. Regal ice-thrones soon made appearances the world over.

"It was something we brought in from Jakarta," says The Bear of the PJ Animals, confirming its origins. They went one step further with the stainless steel ice chair, which added iced water into the tray, meaning the Hashmen's goolies were immersed fully in icy water.

Back in Jakarta, the de-evolution continued in the late Eighties. Ian 'Konkorde' Roberts arrived in 1988. "The ice was in blocks roughly one foot square. Perfect fit for the nether regions," he says. "Bare-arsed was the traditional way, then some got squeamish and thought it unhealthy to plant ones balls and buttocks where some other diseased parts had been minutes earlier." So from there, there have been ice beds for Hashers to lie on, ice sandwiches ("where the incumbent was pressed between layers of ice"), and a communal ice trench ("where a number of miscreants had to lie in at the same time and be buried under crushed ice") was pressed into action. Few who witnessed it will forget the punishment meted out to the Hasher – later to be called Iceman. A new boot, he didn't respond the RA's repeated requests for silence in the circle, so a full-size scale model of a double bed was constructed from ice blocks, down to the detail of pillows, but alas no mint left by room-service. Prone, he then had to Down Down Jakarta's infamous and revered mug, fondly known as The Big One.

"With an average temperature of 30 degrees Celsius, it was pleasant to be cool for a minute or two," says Konkorde. "However, then the iced-water drenching was invented. You sat on the ice and smiled for the camera un-beknown that a large bucket of freezing water was on its way from behind. Jeez, you thought your heart would stop!" Shades of retro-fitting the Brunei practice.

Rolly from Battlestar H3 on HMAS Stalwart once reported their record for sitting on ice – 42 minutes! However, this was easily eclipsed by Whorator, who got a dose of his own medicine in Pattaya one year. Having introduced the practice to the Pattaya Hash, he was on a Dirt Road r*n. His precious Dirt Road Hash shirt had been frozen into the ice, and the only way he could retrieve it was to melt the sucker out. Which he proceeded to do … over a period of roughly a dozen small bottles of beer. (Three *hours*, 18 minutes and 17 seconds by other accounts.) He did not leave the ice during this time, not even to release some of the voluminous amount of piss streaming through his bladder. This was duly recycled directly into the empties.

Butt Pirates H3 in Tijuana, Mexico, went one further. They freeze a real decapitated pig's head into their ice blocks, strategically positioned such that as the ice progressively melts, the pig's snout begins to protrude through the ice.

All a million miles away from simply sweating out the stale piss from the weekend in the tropics. But, if ever you're in danger of being 'iced', just mention The Penguin's name. He'll make sure you get a good seat.

Chunder Down Under.

Hashing in Australia, New Zealand, The South Pacific and The Antarctica.

The Devil's Playground.

Tasmania – or Van Diemen's Land as it was known after the Dutch explorer who managed to miss the *entire* continental mainland of Australia but bumped into this little bit – started out as a prison colony. It was the second Australian colony after New South Wales, and Hobart Town the second major centre after Sydney. Many reminders from the colonial period still exist in the form of bridges, wharves, homes and cottages, ruined prisons, the Port Arthur penal site. And that chap John Kennedy. He moved here from the UK in the early Fifties.

Much of the original charm of the state has remained unchanged since the 1800s and one-fifth of the island is classified as a World Heritage wilderness area [Treehugger's paradise! –ed.]. But the timber and fishing potential of the island state was soon exploited. Hobart began to grow around the Battery Point area of the harbour – where workers' dwellings sprang up – and Salamanca Place, where sandstone warehouses were built.

Fast forward to 1967. Aboriginals in Australia got full Australian citizenship and were eligible to vote for the first time. But full-blooded Aboriginals had gone the way of the Tasmanian tiger in this state. The only difference is that these days there is still the odd sighting of a Tassie tiger, usually on bottles of Cascade Beer.

Enormous bushfires devastated Tasmania that year, with many buildings – and 70 lives – destroyed. Hobart was "a shanty town perhaps" in those days, remembers newly arrived British immigrant, Chris Eden, whom we last heard of in the depths of the late-night coffee shops of Penang, Malaysia. He was in for a bit of culture shock in Hobart, with the infamous Six o'clock Swill having just been renounced. (All pubs closed at 6pm creating a nation hell-bent on getting absolutely pissed before the pub closed then going home to have dinner with their families.) There were precious few restaurants and hotels, either, and women couldn't legally enter a public bar unless accompanied by a male until a few years later. "It was just becoming … human," Eden chooses his words. "It took the Hash of course to fully realise it!"

Hobart H3 formed on October 2 1967, probably the 20th club in the world. Fred Whitaker and Chris Eden met again in Hobart where they had moved after their South East Asia postings in Singapore and Penang, respectively. They had last seen each other swimming through tin mine pools on a Singapore H3 r*n!

Whitaker picks up the story: "When I went down there and I saw Hobart and had to work there, I said I couldn't exist in a place without a Hash – you couldn't exist in Hobart without the Hash!" he says. "It wouldn't be possible in my opinion. Not for a person like me."

"Hash got on the road in October '67," remembers Eden, "although we had been planning it a good six months before that. [Fred] rang me and said 'I'm thinking of setting up a Hash club and I said 'Oh, yes, in fact I have that sort of idea in mind as well'. I was relatively new here and didn't know an awful lot of people but I had joined the Harlequins Rugby Club and it was through them that Fred and I got our initial members. Fred and I together wrote a sort of plea which we passed around to all the potential members at the various meetings we had beforehand. In those days, the Bank of New South Wales [now Westpac] used to have a single men's quarters up in Hobart and occasionally we used to go up there and meet with a few of them, because a lot of rugby players were also bankers," he says.

They were obviously a gullible lot, as a pack of "about 18" were the first to call 'On On' in Australia, their raucous yells echoing off Mt Wellington which towers above the suburb of Ridgeway.

"We chose that spot halfway up Mt Wellington because the On On site we felt was very suitable," explains Eden. "It was right beside a reservoir, a lake, and it was sufficiently distant enough from town – but close enough at the same time – to be able to catch the atmosphere we wanted. We didn't want to be r*nning through built-up areas, and we wanted to give the impression that this was an activity for outside urban areas, where we could make as much noise and do as many stupid things that we wanted to without upsetting the general public."

R*n fees at this point were $1 per annum, plus $1 per r*n "and that bought you as much food and grog as you wanted," says Eden, since renamed The Lord. He and Whitaker loaded the grog and food into the back of Eden's VW Beetle and drove it to the r*n site themselves.

"In those days it consisted really of saveloys boiled in a Hash boiler and 750ml bottles of beer – and ginger beer as well – and we'd mix them together in a bucket," says Eden. The industrious Whitaker recalls: "We used to serve frankfurts because I thought people were not going to stand around in the cold drinking cold beer without having something to eat – so I built up this burner with a 16-pint aluminium pot and methylated spirit stove underneath it made out of an oil can.

"When we'd finished the frankfurts and rolls we put the water aside, Barrel Farrell came along, took his bloody wet shoes off and stood in the hot water." Whitaker also meanwhile busied himself with the r*n sheets as he had at the Eyes and Piles in Singapore. "I was convinced that the circular was very important and so I said to Chris 'I'll make the first one just a copy but I'll have to get somebody to do some drawings'." That somebody turned out to be pharmacist Tony South, who'd never drawn a thing in his life before but rose to Whitaker's challenge. "I said 'Can't you remember Barrel Farrell standing in the hot water?' Anyway, it came out. Magic. He never knew he could draw. From then on he illustrated every week … he was a natural cartoonist."

At the beginning they only ran in the summer months that coincided with Daylight Saving, which Tasmania introduced to Australia. The Antarctica is the next stop south from Tassie, and coincidentally 1967 was one of its coldest years on record with 105 days of snowfall recorded in the Cradle Mountain area – more than double its usual load.

"It didn't snow on the first r*n but certainly sometime during the first half dozen r*ns which were all round this Mount Wellington area, one of them we were definitely r*nning in snow," says Eden, ensconced in a cosy Hobart pub.

The Lord has often said that he and God's Father – as Whitaker subsequently became named – thought that Hobart H3 would be lucky to reach 100 r*ns before folding through apathy and indifference. "But it caught on in a big way – we had the right sort of people generating the right sort of spirit," says The Lord.

"When Alan Rider came and ran with us and left Australian Rules behind they would have liked to have drummed us out of the country," says Whitaker, "because he was the rising star of Australian Rules. The snowy-haired boy. Suddenly one day, Alan Rider turns up and says 'I don't like playing Australian Rules, I'd rather r*n with the Hash' … oh, Jesus." Perhaps tired of the provincial mind-set of the locals, God's Father hightailed it back up to Sydney in 1969.

Pack numbers grew over the years despite the formalities – prospective new r*nners had to be nominated for membership. So cumbersome was this process, a waiting list soon arose. "At that time we felt we really had enough to be comfortable in the summer months as far as transporting food and grog to outlying areas," says The Lord of this austere move. "It was a question really of restricting the membership to a *manageable* number of people so we could transport the pies."

Meanwhile, the Vietnam War raged on. A few of the original Hobart H3 members were conscripted, served over there, and returned to the fold because the beer and pies were better than in South East Asia and the natives friendlier. "And I think they came back with a much better feeling of what Hash was about," says Eden, "because they had been living in South East Asia, seeing what the conditions were, the lie of the land, rubber plantations, palm oil, and so on."

Around '73 or '74, the Hobart Hash yielded to the demand for year-round r*nning, firstly monthly then finally weekly.

"In those days it was all about having a r*n in the scrub, then getting into the piss," says Trembles, a Hobart veteran who started Hashing in 1968. Back then he was an innocent 18-year-old public servant who'd grown up in Hobart. Ten years later, he attended the first InterHash in Hong Kong, but not before writing to the disorganisers to ask if it was necessary to take formal attire with him! "When I arrived in Hong Kong and saw what animals true Hashers really are I discovered the meaning of life," he said[123]. The Lord credits him with bringing the novel idea of a circle back from that InterHash.

And so the Hobart H3 (now known as H4) settled into a nice sweaty rhythm. Until 1982, when that firebrand Easy Rider instigated the formation of the Hobart Hash House Harriers and Harriettes, H5. Whilst normally the formation of another club – and the expansion to include Harriettes – is a positive one, there was something slightly sinister in the fact that the new kennel had also chosen Monday nights as r*n night. Head-on with his home kennel. The H5 inaugural r*n was on April 12 1982, with Mad Dog Bowerman, Plod Duffy and Sarge Sargison defecting to co-found the new kennel.

"It was done on a Monday night out of spite and as a response to the lovable, but non-progressive, rump that was controlling H4 with its men-only attitude," explains Easy. "Quite a few of the influentials in H4 wanted to make it an exclusive men-only club with, wait for it, a fucking waiting list for membership recruitment and vetting to see if they were of suitable social standing to join the club. Many of us subverted this non-Hashing exclusivity by bringing along those who would have had to wait 17 years to get in this weird fringe cult activity. We even fronted with some wildly behaved attractive women which split their previously strong anti-women alliance. Some of the reactionaries claimed their exclusive club would be ruined as a result of not being able to cater for the great unwashed masses who would join if the floodgates were opened. We agreed it would be ruined and it was, thankfully."

On a less vengeful note, Easy also points out that their Hash provided an alternative r*n venue, often closer to the city, with a later time of 6:30 instead of 6pm, thereby enabling more people to get to it. As for Monday night? "Any other night was just not Hash and in many cases people were already occupied with other pursuits." Over the years, different interest groups appeared within the original Hash. A big contingent of Australian Rules referees moved in. And 'yachties', Hobart being a base for many keen sailors.

Boomer was there on the first-ever Aussie r*n. "Hash becomes a way of life," he said[123]. "Keeping fit, trips overseas, friendship and meeting various people, and the fun on On Ons after the r*n." On a recent r*n in Hobart, Boomer tells the story of how he felt a strong stabbing pain across his chest during a r*n, and thought nothing of it. A few weeks later it happened again, so he thought he should check it out. "It turns out all my main arteries were clogged, I had stomach ulcers and acute asthma," he says, laughing, as he walked across a golf course outside Hobart. With about 1,100 r*ns on the board at time of press, he no longer r*ns but also doesn't shortcut, believing that the extra distance does him good and "all you do when you get back is drink beer and eat steak".

Indeed the loyalty and longevity of the Hashers in Hobart is nothing short of amazing. All can tell you to the nearest r*n exactly how many they've done. Thousand-r*n members are more the norm than the exception. Many have been r*nning 20 or 30 years with this same club. "Maybe 'cause we're too poor to move to the mainland," jokes Kiwi.

Mucus Boy, the son of veteran Music Man, is 'the new boy'. Having started at the age of 16, he already has nearly 300 r*ns to his credit and he hasn't finished university yet. Tarzan is also demonstrably proud of his record for consecutive r*ns – over 400 without missing one since 1995, and still counting.

Big Legs kicked off his Hashing in the very late Sixties. "In those days, Hash r*ns were just an excuse for a piss-up, but with the advent of breathalysers, drinking habits become more sober. At the same time, it's become more sophisticated. Gone are the days of saveloys and bread. Now we enjoy a full-scale barbecue and drink from a mobile bar." Indeed, their trailer has beer taps dispensing a choice of three different beers. And plenty of ginger beer is still served up on the side.

In 2000, the 14 Hash clubs now r*nning regularly in Tasmania, jointly hosted the InterHash with great aplomb [That means the beer never ran out –ed.] while alternately terrorising and fraternising with the local populace. In the silent vacuum that followed, the show still goes on. While H4 are very 'traditional' in many senses they have adopted Hash names and used to have a Hashit – although the old toilet seat fell by the wayside some years ago. But no singing – "I could never get singing started in Tassie because I'm not a singer," says God's Father – and no icing – "It's too bloody cold here as it is."

Certainly there's no waiting list any more. That died off about 10 years ago, when they got their own trailer. The r*n fees are now $15 per r*n. "That'll give you an idea of how the costs of living have changed," says Eden.

Although Hobart's H4 is acknowledged as the oldest club in Australia, there are a few clubs with more r*ns because of its original seasonality.

Harbouring Fugitives.
Valentine's Day 1966 – also the day decimal currency was introduced to Australia – was when Phil Riddell, an English Hashman on the r*n from Kuala Lumpur, arrived in Sydney. Michael Miall, also a Pommie on the r*n from Singapore Hash arrived "about the same time".

Australia was in a state of shock following the disappearance and suspected drowning of Prime Minister Harold Holt. Reports of a dingo with an aqualung in the vicinity at the time have not been substantiated.

"It certainly was a great city," says Riddell of Sydney then. "A lot of changes were taking place … a lot of money was coming in to the country." At that stage there were no street-side cafes, and restaurants were just beginning to burgeon. Miall remembers everyone playing the stock exchange. "You'd go down to Sydney for a day and you'd watch things move and you'd buy and sell," he says. "It was a big sharemarket … the immigration was still very high and all the people from Europe and Asia were just starting to bring all their interests into the country."

Something clearly not in the interests of the country, or their adopted city, was the formation of a Hash kennel.

"I had met Mike on two or three occasions," says Riddell. "I rang Mike and said 'I'm in Australia, staying with Bill Davis'. He said, come up for lunch, about 11 o'clock, bring Bill. So I thought, that's very nice, we'll start drinking at 11. Not a bit of it … he had us working for two and a half hours on his fence, which became the rule with Mialls because whenever you went to lunch, there was always two or three hours of fairly hard labour before you were fed. We fell for it every time. One time he said come and play tennis so we had the mandatory two to three hours of work before we played tennis and then we were having a few drinks afterwards.

And that's when Bridget [Miall's then wife] said: 'Well at least you'll be home on a Monday night' and that was it …"

"That started it, there and then," confirms Miall. So Sydney H3 came into being. Miall believed it was "early September 1967, a Monday," which places it before Hobart's formation by a few weeks.

Whitaker graciously concedes that Sydney might have been the first out here: "There were a couple of r*ns here in Sydney but they were never given a number and they were never set down on paper." The Sydney H3 website today clearly places them as the second kennel 'a week behind Hobart'. "If they say they were first, well they can be first," says Miall.

The pack they recruited for r*n #1 was basically a few of their friends. "It gave them the opportunity of not having to be henpecked on a Monday night," says Miall. The first r*n was held in the north shore suburb of Gordon, at the golf course at the end of St John's Avenue. "We just ran across the Gordon golf course and the Killara golf course," says Miall. "The first r*n was only about five from memory." Stuart Ross, Robin and Jim Waite constituted the first 'pack'. Riddell turned up in his Mazda 929, the latest Japanese motoring technology to be imported, with "bottles of whatever beer the pub supplied" and ginger beer in the back. Plus 'the bucket' and "enamel mugs which after six months became a total health hazard," he laughs.

"We just continued on from Singapore and Malaya," says Miall. "Had a bucket, then went to the pub." At the Green Gate Hotel, Killara, it was decided this was a good way to spend a Monday night, so the second r*n was eagerly slated for the following week. With Miles in the building industry – he had been a marketing manager for BRC Weldmesh in Asia – a lot of the subsequent recruits were young and physical. Many were also rugby players. The founders were strongly in favour of perpetuating the men-only practice.

While no subs were payable, a r*n fee of "three bucks or five bucks" was tossed in. "And if you went to the pub, everyone put five bucks on the bar and when it was drunk out you were on your own," says Miall.

Pack sizes grew rapidly, the notion of r*nning though the bush and swimming over the Lane Cover River appealing to many. Soon there were 20 heading down to the pub after each r*n. The whole credo was 'there must be no organisation'. Down at the pub, there were no announcements, no circles, no goings-on. Just a group of guys having a drink, er, in their r*nning shorts.

"All we wanted was to have a r*n, have some drink afterward, have a bloody good evening, drive home on four headlights, and then back to someone's place and play snooker till about three o'clock in the morning," says Riddell. This they did often, and with such delicate finesse that one night a huge plate glass window was shattered during an overly physical game of pool.

While they didn't want to create figureheads and icons, they decided they should hold an AGM, elect a president and get some office bearers in place. "The president was purely the spirit of the Hash and did absolutely nothing," says Riddell. "Absolutely totally honorific." They decided on Bill Davis, Riddell's school friend who had billeted him when he first came to Sydney. "So the position of president was established and Bill kicked it off at the first dinner we had. He sings Welsh songs and stood up and sang a couple of Welsh songs and said 'I'd better give a speech'. He stood up before the assembled Hashmen and said: 'My name is Bill Davis. You wouldn't know me, and I certainly don't know you, but I am your president!'"

Riddell was voted in as On Sec for his troubles. "I was pretty slack. Occasionally the circular wouldn't happen," he admits. "People would have to ring up and check where the r*n was."

As if to test the new committee, the pack grew even more with names like Mike Farrer and John Beavon in the motley mix. Despite the Asian and English roots of the kennel, the majority of the hounds were Australian. Miall remembers on quiet Monday nights at The Green Gate, someone would shuffle up to the bar counter and casually say "Could we have 40 schooners [large glasses of beer] please!" Then when they grew a bit more, they used to give the pub a bit of notice and ask them to do some sausages. "In fact it got to the stage where you had to limit it," says Miall. "We always said you can't just let everyone in otherwise you get too many people and it loses its club-like atmosphere. If people want to say it's an exclusive ... club almost ... fine. But I don't think it was different from KL or Singapore."

"I don't remember Singapore or KL being open slather to anyone," says Riddell. "If you wanted a r*n, you came along, were invited, I mean not just anyone could just walk in. But if you were a reasonable sort of bloke you were in, no problem." And little Singapore-style traditions like H3 neckties were introduced. Anyone who did three or more hares got one.

"It was a very tight little group," remembers Riddell. "We had a lot of extramural activities like golf days – we all had young families – so we actually decided to earn a few points with the women with golf days and barbecues."

In 1968, that well-known rabble-rouser from Singapore, Harry 'God Knows' Howell, made Sydney his home. In 1969 Fred 'God's Father' Whitaker appeared, somewhat relieved to be out of Hobart and back to Sydney where he grew up. And another of the Singapore Hash Eyes and Piles characters, John Gastrell, added a touch of mayhem to the kennel.

By now r*ns had moved away from Miall's place and The Green Gate, and would cover the gamut of Sydney, even – hold your breath Sydney H3 purists! – on the *south* side of the harbour bridge, and Centennial Park in the winter. But the north still had the pick of the bushland r*ns in summer.

One of the most memorable to this day was at the Sphinx memorial at the entrance to Kuringai Park going down to Bobbin Head. Brian Joseph was possibly the hare who wears the blame. "We all got hopelessly lost," remembers Riddell, "and John Beavon as we were stumbling around in the dark was saying [adopts cockney voice]: 'Whatever you do, don't feed the animals ...'. We knew where the cars were but we couldn't get back because it was a very, very steep gorge and it was pitch black." So the Half Minds set off up to Duffy's Forest where one of the pack – an English stockbroker – lived. "He said, 'We can ring up from here and order a couple of taxis' because it was about 15 miles back the other way. We went to his house. There was this lovely smell of food. He said 'Oh, I've got my in-laws here, would you like a little bit of food?' He was cooking up a lovely seafood cocktail entrée – mussels, it had everything in it. Oh, thank you very much. Then a couple more people arrived. 'Would you like a bit of food?' and the word got around – 'Where's the nosh?!?'," he laughs. "We cleaned him out like a pack of gannets – all the food went and his parents-in-law out from England said [adopts posh English tone]: 'What's going on here then?'," he hoots. "About 30 guys poured in and just cleaned him out. The whole dinner went in about 10 minutes. And then we got taxis back. That was hilarious."

Beavon was so pissed off he soon after headed up to cause mischief and lay the first trail in Hong Kong. Meanwhile the hares in Sydney were trying to cock things up even further by introducing bus r*ns, with a difference.

"You wouldn't know it was a straight r*n," says Miall of the sneaky approach. "And then you'd organise a bus at the other end and bring them back. Very often about 80 per cent of the people that started ended up *that* end at the bucket, the other 20 per cent ended up back here without any grog or anything because they'd cheat and come back. You didn't tell anyone, you just did it."

In 1969, Sydney H3 had their first Hash relay in what was to become a proud annual tradition. It went from Sydney to Bathurst – or in r*nning terms from 11pm Friday night to 4pm on Saturday afternoon. "Legends were born then, *real* legends," says David 'Moishe' Donnelly, explaining that 100 kilometre legs with 20 Hashers per team used to be the norm. "The captains used to drink a schooner of beer and eat a pie … whoever won got to choose their team members."

Hashmen Rod Dominish and Pete Donnelly were the keen r*nners behind this – one of them was in the Botany Harriers that organised the official relay from City Hall to Bathurst. "We said, 'Christ we should be in that'," says Riddell, who'd obviously had a few too many. "But what we'd better do is start two hours earlier, and a crowd of us went up and ran early in the morning and we stayed at the Hydro and we had one hell of a piss-up and we were due to be r*nning at six in the morning. They went on an actual real route and we'd say if we cut round the back it'll take off two miles or five miles, and we appeared – the Hash team – about five miles ahead of these professional r*nners. They got very, very shitty!"

In the early Seventies, regular packs of up to 80 were not uncommon. And the social events kept on, including an annual Hash Ball and cricket and football games. "You started off with the Marrieds versus the Singles making up the two teams," says Miall, "and then it was Marrieds with Children or something, then it became Marrieds against Divorcees, then it was Divorcees and Married the Second time, and so it went on. Great fun."

As the Seventies marched on Miall observed that "the second wave" of Hashers went way beyond that level of socialisation until the Hash became "a way of life". While Unmentionables weren't allowed on the r*ns, all the womenfolk were getting to know each other through the regular events.

In December 1972, the Commonwealth ordered equal pay for women.

Orienteering in Australia started in Sydney almost as an offshoot of the Hash. Peter Donnelly, Ken Scott and Ken Warby were the disoriented worthies. Scott – or Scutt, as he was also known as for no-doubt dodgy reasons known to himself and, well, most others – made a name for himself as Hash Scribe.

"His Hash newsletters were unbelievably filthy works of art," says Moishe. "Ken was a masterstroke with the pen." His way with words extended to Hash handles and he anointed everyone with astutely observed Hash names. Miall – named The Little General for his enviable powers of delegation – describes another worthy, Rick 'Creeping Jesus' Thomas, as "a very important ingredient in the success of the Sydney Hash" due to his amusing creativity and brilliant newsletters.

Around that time, Riddell – or Ruptured Duck as he was now known due to his signature song – went up to Jakarta for a two-year stint. In 1977 when he returned, he noticed a lot of changes in the Hashing world.

"Before I went a total new wave of people came through, Hash names were there, then InterHash was starting, Harriettes were there, and Mike and I believed the Hash was actually going off in the wrong direction," he says. "Remember at Silver's place at William Street in the Cross, pies were being thrown ... Christ we used to have a lot of fun r*nning and singing and all this sort of thing. When it came to throwing pies around and stupid things, that was a sort of new wave." Riddell quit Hashing in the late Seventies.

"It became stupid and boisterous," agrees Miall. "And this new wave adopted ... that was their entire social existence. They seemed to have no other friends, they revolved around the Hash, and went to lunches all the time. There's nothing wrong with that, it shows there was a second wave, different wave."

Around this time, the next Sydney kennel formed, south of the Harbour. It was probably they who coined the term 'The Posh Hash' in reference to the more genteel North Shore types of the Sydney H3. "Sydney's had elements of cliqueyness which has been against it over the years," says Whitaker. "There have been some terrific Hashmen here over the years who left it because they felt they weren't, not exactly appreciated, but either jealousy or something like that. I always felt there was an undercurrent."

The formation of this other club, plus the restrictive drink-driving regulations to come in the early Eighties concreted the Posh Hash as a north-side entity. But this didn't stop their sense of adventure and making the most of the terrain and their members' connections. One of their illustrious members was a Commodore in the Royal Australian Navy. He was once in on the hare's plans to r*n the pack down to Balmoral Beach (a northern side harbour beach) and have Navy landing craft on hand to ferry the pack across to Rose Bay (an eastern side beach). "It was like D-Day," say Hashmen who remember it.

In 1984, Sydney H3 – under that baton-wielder from Jakarta, Ole Vigerstole – hosted InterHash with great success. Fred Whitaker headed south to a farm in

Southern New South Wales in the mid-Eighties. Miall quit Hashing around 1986, and subsequently moved north of Sydney.

Virginus Illegitimus avoided joining the Hash – despite Fred Whitaker's exhortations – in Singapore in the mid-Sixties. But back in Sydney he finally relented and has been r*nning since 1968, and even founded Brisbane H3 in 1971 before returning. "When we started out, we always used to go to the pub after the r*n," he said. "Then we used to stop and grab a burger on the way to the pub, then about six years ago it graduated to this," he says, surveying the scene of a bunch of Sydney Hashers eagerly tucking into one of Pilko's famous [That doesn't mean edible –ed.] curry and rice dinners, with salad and bread pudding for afters. Bottles of shiraz adorn each table, lit by gas lamps. The tone is very civilised. The Hash trailer comes fully equipped with a BBQ stove in place, extractor fan, plus tables and benches to seat the whole pack of 60 or more.

With many having racked up 25 years or more of Hashing, they are definitely ageing. Since the beginning of the Nineties, a distinct walkers' trail was also laid. About 25 per cent of the pack now take advantage of that, but not Harry Howell (68 at his last birthday) with about 2,000-odd trails behind him. "When you talk to the walkers it's always 'Me knees, me back, me legs … and they're all the ex-rugby players," he says, counting himself lucky that rowing was his sport of choice. "The Centenary Hash will be in 2038 and I'll be 104 then," says the spritely Howell who still finishes at a fast trot. "How's that for an ambition?"

"I joined at the age of 25," says Moishe, "and that was the average age then. My age is still the average age now because it keeps on creeping up year by year. We'll just keep going till there are none of us left." On one recent r*n, two elderly Hashers walked with the aid of walking sticks. "It's only a matter of time before we see our first wheelchair," he jokes.

Peter Flanagan, ex-pilot and one of the men Cumming pin-pointed as being responsible for creating the anti-establishment persona of the Hash, died in 1999. He was buried wearing his Hash tie.

They do have an orthopaedic surgeon in their ranks who doubtless gets a lot of patients from the wearying bones of these Hashmen. Still, this is not to detract from a bunch of very active cyclists, swimmers and serious athletes in their midst – some of whom think nothing of a 150km Sunday cycle.

They admit they've given some thought as to how to bring young blood in to the group but remain rather selective in their membership criteria. Some joke that until you've been there 10 years you're still considered a virgin and won't be spoken to by the tribal elders. This has created a perception of The Posh Hash as one of the world's most aloof kennels, whereby new potential members are not accepted, let alone named, for at least six months, even a year or more in some cases.

Even man's best friend [No, not the blow-up doll –ed.] was banned at one stage because of their proliferation and people tripping over them, but one dog is now allowed on the r*n. "In fact, *he's* the member, not me!" laughs Pee Dub. The hardworking hound has completed about 60 r*ns over the past two years.

Tradition is alive and well in the form of the bucket with ginger beer shandy and the germ-ridden communal enamel mugs. A Hash horn leads the lost and forlorn. There is no circle – the president simply stands up and addresses the assembled seated diners, and a few (no more than two or three) Down Downs are dished out up the front. Plenty of abuse flies around, and the evening finishes with a few pitiful jokes badly retold. But no singing. "Australians are not great singers," explains the retired Hashman, Ruptured Duck. Howell's mobile phone boasts the distinctive ring tone of The Ruptured Duck, keeping the memory of the founder alive.

Interestingly, Hash names are ubiquitous. But definitely no ice. And no Harriettes. Even joint r*ns with other clubs are a contentious and divisive issue among the grizzled pack, with many boycotting joint r*ns. "A bit inbred" is how Howell once described the group in passing, hardly surprising as almost a dozen of the earliest members are still on trail, weakly if not weekly.

Sydney is now a 'grand-slam' city with at least eight kennels covering the gamut of men-only, mixed, Harriette and Horrors clubs on trail.

Capital Punishment.
Following Federation and the provision in the 1901 constitution for selection of a site for a new national capital, Canberra was designed by Walter Burley-Griffin and situated halfway between the two formerly rivalling capitals, Sydney and Melbourne. That explains why this government city, is literally in the middle of nowhere. Like Las Vegas but without the lights. Or anything for that matter.

On December 1 1969 the newspapers carried an ugly story of the now-infamous My Lai village massacre in Vietnam. Australia was singing along to The Beatles' Come Together and Peter, Paul and Mary's Leaving On a Jet plane rode high on the charts that year. A hippy-fest called Woodstock with peace, love and nudity seemed to sum up the times, with a new face called Hendrix showing that his guitar lessons had paid off quite nicely. The young and the free found their voice in the movie Easy Rider. Sporting-wise, Australia was riding high with Rod Laver having lifted the US Open tennis trophy for the second time.

The third Hash in Australia was established in the capital, which then boasted a population of just 65,000. Karl Henne – an Aussie who had Hashed in KL while being a diplomat on the sideline – was the culprit this time, sending out a detailed two-page typed flyer exhorting people with no direction in their lives to join the Canberra H3 for their first trail on the first day of December 1969. In the section, 'notes for beginners', he advised Half Minds to wear "shorts c/w as many holes as possible" then went on to say: "IMPORTANT: Bring dressing gown or overcoat to stand around in after the r*n."

Winter-wear notwithstanding, he was intent on making it a KL-style kennel, down to the 4"x 4" cut paper squares, the bucket – a large red garbage bin – and a dozen pint mugs, and even "Hash Fags" [Cigarettes not poofters, presumably –ed.]. Otherwise, he wanted complete informality and "a complete shambles" for the only meeting, the AGM. He was not going to stand for office. As a 'PS': "Age is no barrier – about six members in KL are in their fifties *and* flabby. DOGS ARE NOT TO BE BROUGHT ALONG."

And so it was that a bunch of dull-witted pissheads, some of them old and flabby, drove their rust-buckets *du jour* – including a motley VW panel van, EK Holden and Ford Fairlane – out towards Scrivener Dam, looking for Henne's blue-and-white 1961 model Holden.

They set off through pine forests, pine forests, and more pine forests, then up a hill for a spectacular view over the town. And back to the piss and ginger beer, while comparing dressing gowns.

The idea was a hit, r*n # 2 scheduled for the following Monday around Lake Burley-Griffin. The hounds were told to bring their own throat gargle while they sorted out the best way to acquire this, or charge club fees or whatever.

The third r*n was officially announced as the "Inaugural r*n", with founding members including Bob Brookes, Chris Harrison, Graham Bowtell, Geoff Hore, and Max 'Ruff Red' Stark, among 20 others from the embassy circuit, defence forces, government departments and the like. Tony Vincent, an old boot from Singapore, was duly shuffled kicking and screaming into office as JM with Henne. Chris Harrison was voted in as On Sec. An arbitrary maximum 100 members was aimed for, reaching nearly 40 immediately, requiring about 10 32oz. bottles of ginger beer to be procured each week. The pack became all too familiar with the ominously-named Black Mountain, which looms over the city.

A joint r*n with Sydney H3 was touted, each kennel to r*n from their respective cities and meet in the middle. Henne was also keen on fostering brotherhood with other Hash kennels (limited as they were) around Australia and Asia. At one point he even approached KL to ask what the protocol for pewter mugs for departing Hashers was. Hash anecdotes from Singapore and other chapters were included in their circular, which was becoming a major production, each week. A deal was struck up with the Childbirth Education Association – "We owned a duplicator, they could type," says Bob Brookes.

Then in March 1970, the sacrosanct Monday night r*ns were traded in for Sunday mornings "due to failing light conditions and a certain morbid preoccupation with study and football." Barbecues, with the assorted wives/ girlfriends/ mistresses/ dominatrixes typically followed.

Chris Harrison's comments in circular r*n 15 dated 15th March 1970 caused a giggle: "What is all this Sunday r*nning about? Nine out of 10 masochists recommend it, and, what is more, there is a hardcore element that actually gets on. If you've got half a mind to try it, that's all you need." A full eight years before Kirkland – who was Hashing up the road in Sydney before moving to Hong Kong – ripped it off with such global aplomb!

Circular for r*n 19 contained solely a satirical ad for joining the Hash, based on the army ones of the day. "BE IT EVER SO BRIEF, IT'S A MAN'S LIFE IN THE HASH." The text went on to say: "Are you a social failure? A college drop-out? Unemployed? Bitter and resentful?" and carried on before signing off with the same Half Mind slogan. An ABC documentary – a half hour of prime time blood, guts and violence that is the Hash – was aired in 1970 across the nation, ruining most of the pack's chance to ever r*n for public office. A bit of publicity saw their ranks swell again, and on one r*n in July, one Charles George Herridge (who supposedly was on trail in KL in 1938) even turned up as a not-so-new boot. Nan Anderson, an academic from Australian National University, was the first Honorary Gentleman to r*n with the kennel, sometime "early in 1970". So what happened to Henne's chauvinistic directive? "Henne had decreed in our initial operating rules that there were to be no women and no dogs," says Brookes. "We decided to extend that directive to say that there would be no rules either. So women and dogs have always been welcome."

To the best of Brookes' memory, Henne – "a wildly enthusiastic romantic visionary with a laugh like Woody Woodpecker" – moved to Perth in '73 or '74. Then he was posted to Iran. He occasionally returned to Canberra for a r*n.

It was sometime in the mid to late Seventies. The r*n started at about 9:30am on a Sunday in the Uriarra pine forest west of Canberra. The r*n went on and on with no sign of returning. After two hours the pack went past another well-known CH3 On On venue known as Blue Ridge camp. "We knew then that we were a long way from the start," says Greasy. "Soon after the trail continued until we saw the words 'L-O-S-T' spelt out in toilet paper (which was used to lay trails back then) by the hare, Dunapou. The pack then drifted back – a long way – to the On On. I think that it was about 3pm when I got back," he says. Last one home 15.5 hours after the start. "Dunapou is still around Canberra but has not r*n with the Hash for a long time – although his departure from the Hash had nothing to do with that incident."

Canberra's first 'official' t-shirt was for their 'Centenary r*n' in 1977 – '100 Years of Hashing –1969 to 1977'. "We'd have to slap our foreheads whenever anyone pointed out that it was only *eight* years," says Brookes. "The theory was that we might as well celebrate our centenary in 1977 because not too many of our founding members would be able to make it in 2069."

Somewhere along the line, dogs – and plenty of them – found there way on trail. Some owners were even named after their dogs, like Spot Stenhouse in the late Seventies. A unique ritual called 'dog bearing' came into play. "When we had Petals, a 45kg black German shepherd, r*nning with us new r*nners had to pick up the dog – preferably wet – and r*n to and return from a nominated point," says Brookes. "The dog would then be congratulated."

These days, Brookes is the only straggler from r*n #1 still 'on'. The main difference he notices is that there are now more suburban r*ns, given Canberra's population explosion to 315,000 now. There is not as much bushland within reach. "How the Hash is r*n has hardly changed. We don't have circles, singing or in fact any rituals," he says.

Canberra is home to many a colourful chapter, such as Capital Hash and Belconnen H3, both of which – to much original antagonism – also r*n on Monday nights in summer. Plus the ACT Full Moon. Canberra Hashers tend to travel widely – possibly because Canberra itself lacks any redeeming features – and unfortunately crop up all over the world.

Go West, Young Man.

Meanwhile, about 4,000 kilometres west, another isolated town, Perth – dubbed the City of Lights by orbiting astronaut John Glenn – was about to get rudely awoken. "I'd heard there were a couple of people r*nning over in Perth," says God's Father of the very late Sixties. "Somebody had gone to Perth and they had a couple of r*ns in the sand hills. But there were never any circulars or anything like that …"

There is a reference in Singapore H3's 1,000th r*n magazine in1980 talking about the spread of Hashdom: "… and Perth was the first outside Singapore/Malaysia in 1967."

Officially, Perth H3 was kicked off on February 16 1970 – a month after the first direct flight by 747 from New York to London made the headlines – by Mike Farrer. He had previously Hashed in Sydney and took his Hashing skills west when he was transferred by his employers, G.J.Coles. Others in the pack had Hashed in Singapore and/or Malaysia. Membership kicked off modestly with average pack sizes around 10 to 15, including the likes of Sandy Couper, Russell Hume, Ken Peters, Roger Halse, Peter Edwards, Wes Carter and Ian Edmeades.

R*n #1 was around Kings Park, the riverside park area downtown. Subs were $15 a quarter. New potential Half Minds were allowed a free r*n to get the feel of it, and membership grew steadily over the ensuing years, rising to 20 the following year, 30 the year after, and about 40-45 in 1973.

The chapter essentially followed the example set by KL, owing to a lack of imagination on the part of the founders. The big difference, though, was that they were not chasing paper through plantations, but chalk arrows through city streets in the cold winds of winter. The hares were responsible for setting the trail as well as provisions, which were to include "beer, ginger beer, ice and a packet of cigarettes," according to founding father, Peter Edwards.[80] "The cigarettes lasted until health freak Jim Illot replaced them with packets of chips."

The Hashmen would then return home to a nice cooked meal. However, over time, the tolerance of the wives seemed to wear down. One illustrious Hasher's wife reportedly slid his tantalising plate of t-bone, potatoes and vegetables [What, no lobster thermidor? –ed.] into the dishwashing water when her Hashing husband arrived home rather late after Hashing. Monday nights hastily evolved into an 'eat out' night for most Hashers after the r*n.

The Floreat Pub was quickly adopted as the Hash HQ, probably because they rained free jugs of beer on the Half Minds on a regular basis. Then, with a skinful, it was on to someone's home with ample supplies of takeaway beer and sausages. The barbecue would be fired up around 11pm, followed by impromptu games of golf through the unfortunate's house – handkerchiefs designating the greens.

Their first spring r*n was an unmitigated disaster. Set by Peter Pittendrigh and Son of Geoff, the pack came in after five hours resulting in "the very near decimation of the H3 in Perth," according to Ken Peters[80]. However, what didn't kill them only made them stronger. Perth Hashers are invariably intrepid Hash travellers, starting with a pilgrimage to KL's 1,600th r*n. Their original plastic bucket has now grown into a complete trailer equipped with ice-box and full BBQ facilities so they can eat on-site wherever they are and not rely on their wives for nutrition and humiliation.

Whether it was something in the drinking water – or perhaps some passive inhaling of the wafting dope smoke in the air at the time – legend has it that Hunter H3 (in the Hunter Valley of NSW surprisingly) was formed in 1970 by a few of the Air Force personnel from the RAAF Base at Williamtown. Based on the RAAF's exposure to South East Asia, especially West Malaysia, it seems reasonable. The club reportedly ran only sporadically and fought hard to survive in those early days. However, the first *documented* r*n was r*n # 11 on 7 May 1973 at Medowie. This r*n was set by Norm Lawless and Bob Wilkinson. Counting back, as the real story is lost in time, the club has decided that February 1973 was the official date of its inaugural r*n.

Returning airmen also made their mark up in the Northern Territories of Australia. It was "an obvious place to supposedly quarantine those poor inflicted Aussie soliders and airmen," according to Sir Well Pist, GM of Darwin H3[8A]. Many returning servicemen from Butterworth Base in Malaysia influenced the Hashing movement there. Tony Hooper, who ran with Jesselton in its early days, was a leading light in Darwin. Canberra H3's newsletter in May 1970 alludes to a suspected Darwin chapter. By the late Seventies Hashing was evident in Darwin, Katherine, Groote Eyland, Tennant Creek and even Alice Springs.

Darwin H3 is proud of missing only one Monday night r*n since 1973, and then only because the entire city was blown to kingdom come [Read: ceased to exist! –ed.] after Cyclone Tracy ravaged it on Christmas Day in 1974. Physio, of Darwin H3, takes up the story: "Cyclone Tracy struck and devastated the town, completely wiping out all but a few buildings. The next day was a Monday, and a couple of Hashers actually turned up to the r*n site for a r*n. They surveyed the scene – fallen palm trees, sheets of corrugated iron that were once roofs, etc, and said, 'Ah fuck, perhaps not!' and went home," he says.

The Navy, not to be outdone, has also been a virulent force in Australian Hashing with plenty of floating Hash kennels in the Australian Navy. Currently more than 20 floating kennels are apparently 'on' but these come and go as ships are commissioned and decommissioned. According to Wally Kanga, longstanding ringleader of the Fleet Hash, "When they decommissioned the HMAS Yarra, the whole thing [the Fleet Hash] fell apart. But we still get together once a year before the City to Surf in Sydney. Started with about 60 but we get about 200 now," he said, walking along an Aussie Nash Hash trail in Darwin. The Hashers on ships are unlikely to stay on one ship for more than two years, which is a great way of getting rid of a shitty committee [Tautology? –ed]. Some ships advertise themselves as r*nning each week – but the day, city and even country is subject to variation at short notice.

Along the way, Australia with its miniscule population of just 20 million – give or take a few boat people – spread out across this large continent, became home to the second-largest number of Hash kennels in the world. Victoria and Queensland both got 'on' in 1971, the latter state now boasting more than 40 kennels. South Australia brought up the rear, with Adelaide coming on stream as late as 1977.

Ewe Zealand.

1970 – the year that the World Trade Centre towers in New York, still under construction, officially became the world's tallest structures – saw a real spread of Hashing to all parts of the Antipodes.

In New Zealand the first place to fall was its biggest city – then only a small harbourside town – Auckland. Auckland H3 started on August 24 1970 – a month or two before Jimi Hendrix and Janis Joplin fell victim to drugs – and Roy 'Fiveskin' Skinner and Bill 'Great White Chief' Holden are those to blame [For starting the Hash, not for the pop stars' deaths –ed].

In a development that Kiwis are bound to deplore and vigorously deny, Hashing in NZ traces its origins back to Australia. Great White Chief had worked in Sydney before [Unlike most Kiwis who are just on the dole in Australia –ed.] and Hashed with Sydney H3. On his return to Auckland, he sensed something was missing and set about getting Auckland on trail. An invitation went out among friends and work colleagues: "HHH is an international organisation catering for all classes – electricians and astronauts most welcome," it read[8]. "Our couturier notes that correct dress is essential. The costume to be adopted is: Basics – sandshoes and flamboyant scarves. Optional extras – shorts, football jerseys, trench coats, beads and or neckties."

The subscription fee for the first six months was a 'phenomenally low' $2 (a good price considering lamb was $1.50 per hour at that time!). And so it was that Steve Parkinson, Jim Hannah, and Denis McNamara rounded up the first pack at the Exchange Tavern in Parnell, and ran the course set by trail master Clive Magson. Much beer was consumed and it was agreed to meet again the following Monday at the waterfront. Monday night was Hashing night from now on in Auckland. Well, not really. Come that winter, most Hashers dropped out due to rugby commitments or just plain wimpishness, and the Hash packed it in. But when summer reared it's shiny head again, the Hash was revived and has not skipped a beat since.

In 1974, they entered a Hash team in the Round the Bays Fun R*n. This became annual, and they got more and more serious about it, trying to beat their own previous times as well as allcomers. It became an annual institution. Over the years, their disgusting competitive streak has been fortunately mellowed by creaking bones and it was a victory for all Hashdom when the Hash started towing a mini-tanker round the course to keep Hashers in the amber fluid to which they had become accustomed.

A couple of years later, in February 1976, it was decided to lay a trail on Rangitoto, a volcanic island in the middle of Auckland Harbour. That too was deemed an instant failure and became an annual thing. By the mid-Nineties Auckland boasted eight Hash kennels.

Wellington H3 kicked off in 1976 through a bunch of ex-KL Hashmen, including Bret Bestic, John Mills, David Innes and Tremaine. Rotorua was started by ex-Kota Kinabalu stalwart, Tony Evans in 1978. That year five more kennels were formed in New Zealand, including the Auckland Hussies and Wellington Ladies. These were started by bored and disenchanted Hash widows who couldn't get a start in their husbands' misogynistic kennels. Nowadays, both kennels are mixed.

The Kiwis also had plenty of exposure to Hashing in South East Asia as it maintained small forces in military bases in several countries – like Sembawang in Singapore – for many years. At its height as a seafaring nation, it fielded three floating Hashes. Nowadays they've all been called home, and at last report New Zealand had actually sold its Cessna and rubber dinghy so no longer has an Air Force or a Navy!

Masta R*n Amuck.

Meanwhile up north plenty of Antipodeans were finding gainful employment in the booming mining industry of Papua New Guinea. At this time, the dawn of the Seventies, more than 55,000 non-indigenous workers were in PNG.

Appropriately a Black Friday, February 13 1970 saw Panguna H3 on Bouganville Island in Papua New Guinea on trail – interestingly enough [To boring bastards who should get out more often –ed.] 10 days before the British expat bastion of Hong Kong started Hashing. This was entirely the fault of Joe Griffiths who had previously Hashed in Kota Kinabalu. "The atmosphere of a construction camp, large numbers of randy males confined to a small area with little else to do outside working hours but drink, gamble and abuse themselves, provided the perfect culture in which the insidious germ of Hash could flourish," said Michael Bell.[76]

Over several beers they discussed the fate of Apollo 13, which had lost the cosmic flour trail but luckily managed to find the beer back on planet Earth. Panguna changed over the years as the nature of the copper mining community changed around them. Single males in construction were replaced by more married gents to oversee the production phase of the mine, "and institutions like the Hash hymnal have fallen into disuse". Round-the-clock construction noise was replaced by round-the-clock production noises.

Panguna was responsible for the siring of the nearby Arawa H3 in August 1971 – with Don Faulkener and Ted Fulton haring the first r*n – and the Arawa Harriettes (initiated by ex-Singapore Harriette Judy Barge) with whom they occasionally had joint r*ns. They also instigated the Loloho chapter which crashed and burned.

It was at this time that Australia had had enough of being cannon fodder for the USA and announced its troops would pull out of Vietnam. Jim Morrison, a month earlier, had also announced he would be pulling out of this mortal coil.

Port Moresby Hashing started on January 7 1974 with Horst Whippern and Peter Mendl wondering over a few beers how they could overcome the "somewhat dreary scene" of the capital city. Both had previously Hashed in KL.

The expat scene centred on Boroko [Berocca? –ed.] Returned Servicemen's League club where the talk of the time was of those mysterious 'accidental' gaps in Richard Nixon's Watergate tapes. No wonder Nixon had such a long nose.

"In spite of the obvious lack of facilities like curry shops for drunk and hungry harriers, dimly lit *kedais* where a thirsty Hashman can buy beers at outrageous prices at 3am, massage parlours and … girls if you're still capable, HHH seemed like a bloody good idea for this town with tremendous Hashing terrain around it," said Horst Whippern.[82]

Club boards around the town, especially at the notorious 'Sportsman's Corner', helped to spread the gospel, and 16 gullible fools fronted for the first r*n. However, the mix of a gallop and grog "in quantities that would leave a disgusted expression on many Hash faces these days" proved an attractive combination and an extra 14 victims fronted for the second r*n from the Australian Government Offices. Within six months, packs of up to 50 regulars appeared and by r*n # 34 Whippern reports "a big ugly mass of drunks" numbering 150 – many sporting the favoured large sideburns and what-was-I-thinking facial fungus fashionable in the day – singing loudly into the night.

Paul McDonnell, an expat Aussie working in Moresby around that time said that "eight to 10" kegs of beer were routinely demolished by the thirsty pack each r*n night. "I drove home too many times when I don't even remember driving," he recalls, feeling that "something had to give sooner or later." He gave up the Hash six months later.

In September 1975, Papua New Guinea achieved full independence, usually a signal for the economic basket-weavers to move in and get busy on making a tailor-made case. Sure enough, the number of foreigners dwindled and by 1980 only 33,000 – of whom half were Australian – were left.

Over time, Hashing in New Guinea became known for its two-day relay marathons as well as its 24-hour round-the-town relay. Some of the more notable efforts were the gruelling 450km from Goroka to Lae, the 300km from Madan to Lae and the 250km Wau to Lae marathon [A walk in the park –ed.]. Their charity *Helpim Pikanniny* benefits directly from the proceeds.

The Ela Beach RSL burnt down in about 1986 and the Boroko RSL was thoroughly fumigated and sold off in 1995. These days, the main watering holes in Moresby are the Yacht Club, Aviat and Squash Club, all expat-r*n facilities. "As for mellowing," says Aussie Fig Jam, "we used to do three 33-litre kegs a night now we only do two 50-litres a night! With an average of 25 in the circle, when you look at the slow drinkers and those who piss off early, it makes for a hard Tuesday."

With its high turnover of hardcore Hashmen, Papua New Guinea has become one of the most prolific spawning grounds of new Hash chapters elsewhere in the world.

Trouble in Paradise.
Back in 1973, the first Skylab station was being launched, and the Watergate investigators were turning up the heat on Tricky Dicky Nixon. The Solomon

Islands were a sleepy British Protectorate basking in the South Pacific sun. Their doze was rudely interrupted that July, when a small pack of incredibly pale people, led by Brian Leach and Derek Taysum came tearing by, yelling 'On! On!' and completely spoiling the languid atmosphere of the islands. July 11 1973 was that fateful day, thanks to Leach who had escaped from Perth H3. Honiara, the capital, was the first home of the Hash in the South Pacific. Since then, HPM Emery – an accountant who has clearly spent too much time in the sun, just like the Hash founders – has been a long-term player in this kennel, which has continued through the ongoing civil war which now wracks the Solomons.

The newly-independent tropical paradise Fiji came on-stream "sometime in 1974," presumably later in the year as Joe Shaw – who was irresponsible for this whole rabble – had apparently Hashed in Port Moresby, PNG, before moving to Suva, Fiji. (Port Moresby was only kicked off in January of that year.) Joe rallied around and found supporters in the squash fraternity that saw Hashing as a sport that would take less toll on their knees, but obviously didn't factor in the attendant liver damage. So Suva H3 was up and r*nning, closely followed by Lautoka H3 in 1975. It took just three years from Suva's founding for a Harriettes chapter to start r*nning on the island.

Incredibly, Hashing reached the Antarctica, too. Just 20 years after Singapore got on trail, Antarctic H3 came into being at the Davis Antarctic Base. Eskimo Nell, who'd previously r*n in Port Moresby reported their first trail on October 18 1982. Temperatures outside (without factoring in wind-chill) were – 26 degrees Celsius, with winds often gusting to 60 knots. Paper for the trail was blown to kingdom come, so it was decided to use flour. That was invisible on the snow and ice. So they ingeniously decided to tag seals which stand out a bit more – a great idea until they moved! Twenty kilograms of protective clothing were piled onto each Hasher and as a blizzard threatened to close in, blizzard lines were attached, dashing any thoughts of someone short-cutting on the pack! Still, the cold beer went down excellently thereafter. And a Hash golf day was even held around the same time.

Later, Bob 'Danglin' Anglin was posted there in the mid-to-late Eighties. Having previously Hashed in LA, he reported that more than twenty Hash trails had been r*n over the two seasons he was there.

Nowadays, Michael 'Bee Fuck' Stachow is the snow-trail king in McMurdo Sound. He recently attempted to Hash on every continent of the world in the three-month break he had between his two postings down there.

More Arse Than Class.

On the November 13 1978 a very important historical event took place. No, it wasn't the death of 909 Americans in the Jonestown, Guyana, People's Temple cult suicide – in which a potent Hash brew of Kool Aid and Cyanide was concocted. It was the founding in Perth of the Hamersley H3 – undoubtedly one of the most colourful and notorious chapters in Australia – by Ron Duffield. This could be one of the reasons why the cult took such an extreme course. Or it could be explained by the release that year, ironically, of the Bee Gee's song, *Staying Alive.*

Hamersley H3 always prided themselves on being a young, macho and debauched Hash, and they love to sing. "You can't sing 'em down because they'll always have another song, and another one," says Super, Mac the Mouth's wife. "They sing well," she says, " but if you're not strong enough you won't hack it."

And its songs gained fame throughout the Hashing world. From diminutive beginnings at Jakarta InterHash in 1982 where Gunny performed Hamersley's first Hash act and got dumped in the shiggy pit for his troubles, Hamersley have set the low water mark for others to follow. Mac the Mouth points out the Black and White Menstrual Show in Bali, and Hashman act in Manila. "Bar owners invited us to perform in their bars," he enthuses. "It was like the pied piper down the street with little kids following, and jumping over cars in the traffic."

'Envied, emulated, but never equalled' trumpets their website. It is true that Hamersley is the one Hash that Aussies – indeed the world – have a love/hate relationship with. Mere mention of their name never fails to evoke a spontaneous rousing chorus of 'Hamersley take it up the arse ... doo-dah, doo-dah' from others.

And their notoriety is not helped by some of their antics. "In Launceston, we got around in stretch limos everywhere," chuckles Mac of their decidedly non-Hash behaviour. At that same Aussie Nash Hash, Mac the Mouth and others from Hamersley were enjoying the BBQ when they had the idea of taking the pig's heads from the spit roast and stuffing them into the beds of two fellow Hashers. Their laughter was short-lived and revenge was swift. "I had a pig's head in my dunny, one in the fridge, pig's offal in my suitcase," says Mac. "And everything was shoved up against the wall, as if the room was vacant."

They hold an annual Diggers r*n, Palace r*n and the Fish & Chip r*n. The other Hamersley ritual is to always have a lunch on Friday the 13th, regardless of when this falls or where they might be. But it is the Casino r*n is perhaps the most indicative of their ability to cause mayhem. This r*n was held a month after the opening of the flashy new Burswood Casino in Perth. The trail led right up to the door, so the pack naturally assumed it would be a check-back. But ... the door opened! Next thing there was a pack of about 30 or more sweaty Hashers yelling 'On! On!' and bolting past the white-suited and plume-helmeted doorman and through the ritzy casino. There were only about six security guys on duty, radioing each other furiously while desperately trying to chase and catch these errant Hashers.

One guard eventually caught a Hasher, collared him and said: "What the fuck are you guys doing?!?" After a while, the security guy did a double-take and asked his catch, "Don't I know you?" "Yes ...," replied the harangued Hasher, "I'm your bank manager!"

Security at the casino was stepped up thereafter, amid of flurry of media reports on this incident. Fate of bank manager's customer unknown.

"The most fun I had in my life was with Hamersley Hash," says Vodkasplite from Norway, who has also Hashed extensively in Thailand. "How those old farts can party like that I don't know," he says.

Apart from bastards like Hamersley, Australia has also given birth to other quirky – or at least quirkily named – kennels: HOSH (Hash Oldies Still Hashing) in Perth and the Over 50 H3, Geelong Old Farts H3 and Geelong Old Tarts H3 all in Victoria. Hole Shaven Full Moon H3 is based in the Shoalhaven area of NSW, the Wanker H3 is a mixed kennel [go figure –ed.], and one Hash kennel that can truly call itself a kennel – the Dog H3, which is open to Hashers with dogs and donates its r*n fees to Guide Dogs for the Blind. They were raising one puppy called On On [Let's hope the Hash don't r*n past while it's on duty –ed.].   •

New Zealand has not been left behind in the quirky stakes either, with kennels sporting names such as FART H3 (which is actually a *family* Hash!), Not The Rotorua Hash House Harriers Hash House Harriers (NTRHHHHHH) and Not The Navy HHH HHH (N2H6).

One of the craziest kennels must be Ditch H3 – whereby Hashers r*n on the Wellington to Picton ferry crossing, any two restless Hashers forming a quorum. Ditch H3 was instigated by Handle and/or Gee String, who couldn't hack the three-hour trip across the Cook Strait without a sniff of flour or a call of 'On! On!'

The first r*n was June 4 1990, when three r*ns were held in the space of those three hours by Hashers returning from Marlborough's 500th. "Just another excuse for a beer and something to break up the monotony of the ferry ride," explains Gee String. Averagely four to 10 beers per Hasher are consumed on this trail.

And it hasn't been plain sailing along the way – there was a near tragedy once when a steward was found rubbing out the hare's chalk marks because of "the mess".

R*n #60, held post-InterHash had a record 113 Half Minds on trail, having secured the Captain's permission. In January 1997 they chalked up their 100th r*n, and now have nearly 200 on the board due to a walkers trail in the form of a 75-minute fast Lynx ferry.

But Tekapo H3 takes the cake for ongoing madness, claims Jrgee. "The AGMs were the world's quickest, consistently in the sub-20 second range," he says. Feature events at On Ons include the Rabbit Gutting Contests, "a scene of blood and guts to say the least, accompanied by early exits of the squeamish." There is also the Sacrificing the Virgins ritual that is traditionally held at the local Dog Statue. "Unsuspecting tourists are hijacked by the pack from tourist buses, given a shot of medicinal liquid and then given a full body massage by our Hussies or Hounds. First, however, there would be a reading or two from the book of limericks to establish a reverential aura to the sordid event," reports Jrgee.

In the innovation stakes, Phantom and his wife Plunder from Auckland have started what they believe to be a world first – a Splash Hash using kayaks. They field a pack of around 21 kayaks each Sunday, and explore the estuaries and inlets of Auckland Harbour. "It's more like follow the leader," explains Plunder, "as you can't lay a trail." Each paddle lasts about two to three hours, and – like traditional Hashing – serves up its fare share of misadventure. "One lady was washed onto the rocks, bashed around and knocked semi-unconscious," recalls Phantom. "We end up in drains, culverts, streams," she says, "and people come out of their homes and say 'We've never seen kayaks up here before!' We even came up in one place with golf balls flying over us."

Around the South Pacific, one of the more colourful chapters is Agana H3 on the island of Saipan in Guam who bill themselves as the toughest and wildest Hash around. "We are a 'tyrancy' not a democracy," says Sex. "We do not elect anything, our tyrant is in charge until such time as he abdicates to a tyrant of his choosing … no grandmasters, no elections, no B.S.! We have converted Hashes around the world to this thinking. Divine right of the tyrant …" There is a high rate of transitory Hashers … military, expat managers, and teachers, mainly. This accounts for this small island being the father of many other kennels worldwide.

As for some of their peculiarities and proclivities, Sex explains: "We celebrate United Nations Day each year with beer from around the world … let's just say it is not a good night to be in mismanagement as the rabble gets a little unruly and they are drinking from glass bottles instead of the usual cans." Jacksonian Fire Jumping is also popular – involving men and women stripping naked and r*nning and jumping over the fire. "Nothing worse than jumping over a Christmas tree that has just been thrown on," says Sex. "However, if you haven't singed your pubic hair while Hashing, you are doing something wrong!"

Another Guam claim to shame is that the Elephant Walk was started on Guam. "Everyone is once again naked with one hand back through their legs and the other holding on to the hand in front of them. We have done this unannounced at InterHash in Kuala Lumpur and Tasmania with many other Hashers joining in," he says proudly.

On the Agana Hash, all the trails are live with hares getting a few minutes' head-start. "If you are caught while setting the trail, the hounds tackle you and take your shorts which are then burnt in the fire." The fire is lit by a designated fire master, but everyone helps extinguish it at the end of the night. "We piss out our fire when we are done with religion, no water used," says Sex. "We have had women create funnels for this purpose with the most notable being Hot Tuna who could piss with the best of them. Fognozzle is also quite adept at killing a flaming pallet." One of their other chapters, the Berserk Hash, "is insane" says Sex of their long weekend episodes. "A normal r*n finishes some four to six hours later (the longest one thus far is 24-hours straight). Swimming across shipping channels, r*nning on five-foot wide ridges with 600-foot drop-offs on either side, and traversing the island from one ocean to the next is common."

Sex takes pleasure in one particular memory: "Cooter's Cousin, who r*ns weekly on the Agana Hash, once remarked that if he was ever seen at the box for a Berserk r*n again, we were to punch him in the face and tie him to the nearest tree so he wouldn't do more harm to himself."

Drinking Beer and Tellin' Lies.

Walrus, an Australian guru currently resident in India, says: "If we could make Hash the only 'religion' in the world, then all the existing problems of the world would disappear overnight."

Certainly there are a lot of faithful and reverential hounds in Australia, home to the second largest number of Hash kennels in the world. Partly attributable is the fact that 22 per cent of the Australian population reportedly take part in recreational jogging[105]. And if you thought that most Australians were convicts on the r*n, you're quite close – about one percent of the population is thought to be involved in marathon r*nning. But the connection with putting one foot in front of the other goes much deeper than that in this part of the world.

"A lot of people don't realise that the word 'jogging' was coined by a New Zealand r*nner," says Fred Whitaker. That person was Arthur Lidyard, who introduced the term along with the convention of proper warm-ups. "See, we didn't used to go for a 'jog', we just went for a r*n. There was no convention of jogging," Whitaker says of the days when the world was a much simpler place.

But the other factor is sheer distance between places – hundreds if not thousands of kilometres often separate one group of Half Minds from another, so Hash clubs spring up locally out of necessity.

As a result, places like Paraburdoo in the great Aussie Outback of Western Australia, got on the Hashing map. Well, that plus "there was not much to choose from," according to Mother Brown who Hashed there in 1976. Their only other recreational opportunity was pool parties [And you chose the Hash? –ed.]. Amazingly 12 of their 40 hounds attended the first InterHash in Hong Kong.

And right at the top end of Australia, the Hash reached the mining town of Gove. Pamela McDonnell – a New Guinean whose husband used to Hash in PNG before they moved to this remote Northern Territory town – says: "I've seen them r*nning and I always think 'Why are those silly people doing that?'" [Fair question –ed.] For the record, her husband no longer Hashes.

The answer, of course, is that the Hash legitimises what is already a national sport – drinking beer. What hope do they have culturally when (now ex-Prime Minister) Bob Hawke set the world record for beer drinking … knocking back two and a half pints in just 11 seconds whilst a Rhodes Scholar at Oxford University! And a 1998 survey by the Australian Bureau of Statistics found that nearly three quarters of all Australian women drank at 'dangerous levels' [Well, they should get down off the bar counter then –ed.].

But, more importantly, it is the Antipodean culture which predisposes them to being good potential Hashers. The famed egalitarianism. The tall poppy syndrome, in which any prick who gets too big for his r*nning shoes is cut down to size.

"Going out and doing stupid things on a Monday night keeps you sane the rest of the week," says Kiwi from Hobart, to which Sheepshead tells him: "You don't have to go out!" But Kiwi raises an interesting point: "Hashers look younger than they are, because we know how to laugh and relax." Moishe in Sydney agrees: "If you look at a photo of your parents at the same age, they definitely look a lot older."

Mac the Mouth surveys the crowd at Aussie Nash Hash 2001 and points out that the crowd is getting older. "The young guys aren't joining the ranks," he says. "It might be too expensive for the younger guys to spend $30 to $40 bucks on piss on a Monday night." But any InterHash or Nash Hash event will invariably attract a crowd with more time and money on their hands, and more wrinkles round their eyes.

Down in Hobart, The Lord points out: "The average age for H4 is probably 45 or something like that. There are a few younger people, in their 30s and early 40s still coming in. But I think the answer to that is that in Tasmania we have a very huge unemployment rate, so the majority of young people that leave school or graduate from university will generally go interstate or overseas for their first years of employment. And they'll travel – and if they get to hear about Hash overseas, some will come back and join us, but we're not getting too many young people in. That's a worry in a way, a bit of a pity ... it certainly won't die on us."

Lofty, from Perth, agrees that Australian Hashers are aging. An ex-diver, he started Hashing in 1975 and – although he's Hashed "everywhere except South America and Antarctica" – is a bit critical of those who live for the Hash. "Look at the Hamersley guys," he says. "Their whole social life, golf, etc is to do with the Hash and the guys from the Hash. They're even talking about building a Hash retirement village because the single ones will have no one to take care of them," he says. While he now attends some events under duress, "Before, it'd have to be the world ending for me to miss a Hash event," he says.

Sirloin, ex-Grandmaster of New Zealand, notes age creeping up in his local chapter, too: "Dunedin H3 started with a hiss and a roar as we were all much younger then and able to party until three or four on a Tuesday morning. But these days ... most have pissed off home by 10:30pm, back to the old folks home with their Zimmer frames."

Shortplanks from Rotorua agrees: "The dominant feature these days is the amount of grey hair. Why don't young people Hash?" he asks. "It's not the same now, with young people not bothering to play team sport or any other sport for that matter. Will we fade away as the RSL [Returned Servicemen's League] must or will there be another generation of young folk who see the light and stop giving a fuck about anything for a few hours on a Monday night?"

Old Wares, ex-Perth stalwart, only has one regret of his Hashing career: "I was born 20 years too early," he laments, having noticed how many Hash clubs are now up on the web. "I could easily have spent that part of my life now Hashing for a living."

Still, the attractions are there for many, in various forms and guises. "You can create an alter-ego on the Hash," says Hash haberdasher to the gentry, Treadmill. "Like a safety zone."

"All Hashes are different but I am yet to feel unwelcome at a Hash anywhere in this world," says Sex from Guam. "The only form of introduction needed is 'Hi, I'm a Hasher'. I know of few other ways to meet people very similar to myself. There are groups where this is possible around the world ... rugby, Harley-Davidson riders, etc, but none like the Hash."

Pilko from Sydney H3 recalls coming into the office one Tuesday morning. All the blokes were gathered round talking about what was on telly the night before. "What did you watch?" they asked him. "Nothing," he said. "Why, what were you doing?" they asked, a bit bemused. He tried to gather his thoughts about the previous night's r*n and On On On. "Well, I was on a ferry and there was this bird lying naked on the table blowing smoke rings ..."

For Mike Miall, one of the attractions is networking to condense a new society down to manageable proportions. "If you r*n in, say, Vanuatu, anything you want to know or any person, you'll find them. If they're *not* r*nning, they'll also know," he says.

But Phantom from Auckland – who has Hashed a lot in the Middle East – cautions against using the Hash as a business networking tool. "In business if you say you r*n Hash, people that have heard a little bit about it think it's negative," he says. "You have to be really careful who you tell about Hash."

God Knows, intrepid Hashman since the late 1950s, marvels at the Wellington Hash style. "They really know how to turn it on there," says the Sydneysider. "I went for a r*n and there's a keg at the start. You r*n another 200 yards and there's the keg again. Then another 200 and there it is again ... you can hardly even get up a sweat and then you're at the end of the r*n, and into the beer again. Great On Ons."

Copteaser, who Hashed extensively in the UK before moving back to his native New Zealand, loves his Hashing in the Tauranga area. "But, still it is not quite as good as the UK Hash was. The underground made it all so very easy, and allowed for a bit of camaraderie to and from the venue," he reckons. "Also, the country pub r*ns in winter were something special."

A real live Pom, Shit for Brains from Portsmouth, "found Hashing in Australia [Sydney and Adelaide] more formal than in the UK, whereas here [UK] it's more relaxing." Travelling with his wife, he says: "Also, it's more sexist with all the men-only clubs ... old-fashioned like Malaysia in the old days or something."

Floater, a Harriette from Devon in the UK, noticed the same thing. "Hashing in Australia's very different. For a start they r*n from someone's house instead of a pub," she says, based on her experience in Western Australia. "Then there's all these men-only chapters. So it was difficult to get a r*n on the few nights that we were in certain places. But they were great ... very friendly."

New Zealand, by contrast, has only two men-only kennels. "There's a lot of women in New Zealand," says Sirloin, sardonically. "If you just want to play with men, there's plenty of rugby clubs."

But unlike rugby clubs, at the Hash you won't find the same level of testosterone and attendant fisticuffs which often occurs when you combine beer and brawn.

"In 26 years of Hashing I've only seen one fight," says Lofty, "and I instigated it!" It turns out they were organising a country weekend r*n in South Perth and the argument was over how to spit-roast the sheep for the On On BBQ. The discussion reached an impasse. " I hit him and he ended up falling about eight feet into this truck which was full of wet sheep shit. Everyone pissed themselves laughing and so did my 'victim'," says Lofty. "We laughed about it then, and we laugh about it now."

Even Darwin, long considered a redneck frontier town, has cleaned up its act. "Tough town, tough Hash," is how Rhonda sees Darwin H3. "There's animal Hash and there's family Hash – and we're definitely not family Hash. We only stopped guys smashing each other up a few years ago. Before that, if anyone fucked up on the ice or whatever, we'd just drop him."

Perhaps for this reason, Crystal Balls from Mackay looks forward to his annual r*n or so in Asia. "They still have respect for the circle and such, and the traditions of the Hash," he says. "We would grovel at the RA's feet if told to when I first ran. Sadly, most circles (I said *most*, not all) are a rabble in Aussie and other parts. It's a shame because circles can be so entertaining and fun if Hashers would shut up and listen."

Ruptured Duck, partially reformed Englishman says: "Australians are not great singers ... they don't have the tradition the Brits have where singing is just part of the evening, and a lot of us have been up in the East where singing used to go on in bars and so forth."

Shhh!!! No one tell Hamersley they're behaving like a bunch of Pommy bastards.

The Boys In Blue.

Hobart reported no problems with police, officialdom or red tape from the start. "We try not impose ourself on other parts of society and I think that's right," says The Lord. We've had a few complaints about noise and r*nning though property without permission and that sort of thing and we try awfully hard to impress upon hares that they must seek, where necessary, permission to go through an area or to have an On On at a particular site if it involves people outside Hash ... it's very important to do that. Individual members getting into their cars after a few shandies and being booked – that sort of thing has gone on but that's their thing. We've had co-operation from police pretty well right the way through and I guess that's helped via some of members who are police officers."

In Tasmania at the time of the InterHash and the 1,700-Hasher Red Dress r*n, it was illegal for a male to dress in female clothing between sunset and sunrise, according to an archaic law drafted to stop thugs dressing up as women and luring unsuspecting sailors into the dark alleys of the waterfront to rob them. The penalty was a fine of up to $500 or imprisonment for up to six months. This included regular cross-dressers as well as fancy-dress partygoers.

Special dispensation was acquired for the InterHash, and now the law – probably as a direct result – has reportedly been overhauled permanently.

When Sydney came on stream in the late Sixties there were no reported problems with authorities either, although they attracted some sideways glances. "*We* had in fact banned pubs," says Miall of the early Seventies. "We'd done it the other way round. It was that one in Homebush that for some weird reason we were doing a joint r*n with the Harriettes and we'd drink in the public bar – we'd never go to the more expensive one – and they said 'Sorry, women aren't allowed in this public bar'. We said 'Sorry, we're just r*nning and they're r*nning with us'. With that the entire Hash walked out of the pub and we didn't drink their beer which is very stupid of them. I know we had been banned from the Green Gate in Killara, and I know we banned the Homebush pub."

Their next official hurdle was the introduction of random breath testing (RBT) in late 1982. "In spite of the government's attempt to spoil our On Ons we have survived," wrote Wraparound in their 1983 Year Book. "I can remember last December you bastards drinking LA Shandies and lemon squashes and by 8:30pm only a handful of Hashers remaining. We have all come to live with it now, and, if you are not in a car pool then it's back-streets all the way home."

Elsewhere in Australia, there is very little opposition from the authorities. In fact, the Melbourne H3 hares once famously arranged for the trail to go right through a local police station – in the front door and out the back! – passing inmates in holding cells along the way, who were a little bewildered to have their silent contemplations broken by the raucous calls of "OOOOOON! ON!"

In Kalgoorlie, police and the local magistrate are avid Hashers. The local Mayor even founded the Hash. "There are no unnatural sex acts, er … on the r*n," says Leonardo. The Murray Bridge H3 in South Australia probably wished they were so well connected – their first ever r*n (circa 1979) was raided by the local police. Broken Hill H3 got a worldwide ban on behalf of all H3 kennels in the neighbouring town of Silverton. Previously a silver mining centre, it is now a ghost town most often used for commercials and movies such as Priscilla Queen of the Desert, Mad Max, etc.

But perhaps the biggest obstacle in Australia are the stringent drink-drive laws. Lots of returning expat Hashers, chiefly from Asia, are not interested in continuing Hashing in Australia where they'd have to drive 45 minutes across town to the r*n, have a couple of light beers and then head home after an On On or On On On that didn't match the levels of iniquity, inebriatedness or decadence that it might have in Asia.

"We drink about one-third as much as we used to," laments Kiwi around the campfire at a recent Hobart r*n, referring to the drink-drive laws.

Perth H3[80] reported that "due to the introduction of random breath testing we now only occasionally head for a pub after the bucket r*ns dry – probably a good thing." This is in marked contrast to the early Seventies when one of their Hashers, Shorty, left the pub early one Monday night claiming he was getting too pissed. Half an hour later he was back at the pub drinking again. "I can't find my way home!" was his excuse.

New Zealand similarly falls foul of the law only when it comes to drink-driving. In Auckland, they had just completed their AGM when the newly elected Brewmaster hopped into his car and was promptly pulled over by the police and booked for drunk-in-charge and had his licence suspended for six months. "It was a real problem for us as he was in charge of driving the beer to the site each week," said not-so-sympathetic Hash colleague, Phantom.

For the Rotorua InterHash, a heavy police presence was arranged, expecting the usual trouble and flare-ups which go with a big 'sporting' event. Well, the police soon realised this was a slightly different crowd as a) there were no fights and b) they were hysterical because behind every bush they found copulating couples. One lot [Hashers, not police! –ed.] were even going at it on the croquet lawn, watched by hundreds of Hashers and giggling policemen. Soon the police were in the spirit of it, using their cars to taxi Hashers back to their hotels, and one police car was even seen driving with its boot open, "blaring atrocious country and western music".

In Auckland, they had a mangrove r*n around the harbour in winter. The tide comes in fast there, and the trail became lost under the water. Two guys, Demon Dave and Bananas were in a dilemma – they couldn't swim, and couldn't go forward or backward from their waterlogged position on the side of the harbour. Darkness soon fell. A police car was cruising the area, and saw a bunch of guys – who were backsweeping – with torches. They told the police that they had two men missing in action. With that, the police radioed for help and a couple of inflatables were called in to comb the mangrove swamp area. Demon Dave and Bananas were found, clinging to the top branch of a tree (the only branch not covered by the rising tide) with freezing water already up to their knees. As the boat arrived to pluck them to safety, so their branch snapped. The police had to fish them out of the water. The police then took them back to the On On, and joined them for a beer. The event made national news in the paper and on the radio.

The problems escalate for Hashers as one moves further up the Pacific. Following independence in 1975, PNG slid into an abyss of violence, with rebels and *raskals* spoiling everyone's fun. That year Arawa H3 decided to hold a joint r*n with Honiara H3 in the British Solomon Islands Protectorate. The resulting social functions were held in royal splendour at the Governor's official residence, with a rowdy BBQ piss-up round the pool. Not that the Governor minded – he was a keen Hashman himself.

Papua New Guinea Hashers are no strangers to danger. In Lae, "Hashing was much restricted by the activities of the 'rascals' which meant that most of the r*ns were on the roads and in the town area," says Haji Babi of the early-Nineties. "At one r*n, of the 15 participants, 10 had been attacked or harassed by rascals in recent times. I was kidnapped/hijacked and left trussed up in the jungle, and we were attacked six times in the house. The ladies r*ns always had to be accompanied by men."

"We have suffered threats of prosecution for littering, destroying gardens, disturbing the peace and even drinking in a public place, yet the HHH continues to thrive," Port Moresby H3 reported in 1977[82]. The Port Moresby kennel likes to stir things up a bit – like the time they laid a r*n alongside Government House, with short-cutters galloping past startled sentries and heading right into the guard dog-infested grounds [Smart. –ed]. Back at the circle, in came four police demanding answers. Free beer seemed to satisfy their investigations.

"Over the years the police have come to like Hash in Moresby," says Fig Jam, "as the sight of overweight, short-of-breath sweaty old expatriate males r*nning up hills in the heat of the day, yelling 'On On' every Monday was a great source of amusement to them."

Nuku'Alofa H3 in Tonga had the ultimate blessing by the authorities ... the King of Tonga joined them for a Hash r*n. His presence had the side-benefit of making the others Hashers look and feel like finely tuned athletes as the King is, shall we say, royally portly and rode on a bike.

Fiji is rarely out of world news headlines with its Coup of the Week program. The Rambling Rams H3 (off Kiwi Navy ship Southland) was once diverted from Fiji because of a coup by Colonel Ram'buka and ended up in Cairns, Australia, for a r*n instead. But more recently the coup led by George Speight failed to get the better of the Suva Hash. "We did not miss a r*n," reports Wontok, "but were severely restricted by the curfew times and all the roadblocks. So the r*ns for a while were short and relatively quiet. But later on as we got bolder we started to r*n through some of the roadblocks – all the roadblocks were fully armed with machine guns, M16s, etc – so pretty exciting. But it takes a lot to stop a Hasher!"

Dreketi H3 in Fiji faces another mode of extinction ... it has a hard-core membership of 12, but cannot expand this simply because it's a tiny island with a tiny population. Closure of the local pigeon farm reduced its numbers by half! On Nauru, an island in the Pacific, the problems are more physical. "The island is only 11 miles in circumference," says Effigy Snoz, "so we used to have a round-the-island race on the road around it. But being a small place, it was difficult to set a r*n that hadn't been set before. Hash was going strong there in 1978 ... lots of Australians and New Zealanders. Gradually they were replaced by Filipinos and Indians."

"Hash isn't about ... drinking with the idea of not getting drunk," says Wigless, who is a surprising fan of the local police. In Nadi, he says the "police force didn't have a breathalyser." In Suva he says the police "having been supplied with several breathalysers, didn't know how to use them." In Pacific Harbour, where the *apres* often goes until 2am they have a police force "that, having learnt how to use the breathalyser, knows it doesn't have any transport. Having used the equipment and got a reading off the scale, they're sensible enough to realise that locking you up is going to deprive them of their lift home. Fiji – the way the world should be," he says [Where do I sign? –ed].

Vanuatu during 1980 was the scene of a vicious 'coconut rebellion', causing the Santo H3 to halt its r*nning for a while. Arrows fired in anger not only endangered the r*nners but, much worse than that, had everyone thinking they were 'On-Home' already!

It's A Dog's Life.

Fred 'God's Father' Whitaker.
First r*n Singapore H3 1964
Founded Hobart H3 1967
Member Sydney H3

How did you get into Hashing in Singapore, Fred?
GF: We would work Saturdays and we would have half Wednesday afternoon off – go down around 4 o'clock and we'd play golf. And the Japanese were always madly enthusiastic about golf – it was so expensive for them over there that when they came to Australia or Singapore it was so bloody cheap for them to play that they all raced in because it was the status thing to do for Japanese businessmen. And virtually overnight, you had to book and book and book ahead. We just got jack of it … it used to take us three or four bloody hours. I was with an architect playing one day and he said 'I'm giving this away, I can't spend all this bloody time … I'll have to concentrate my exercise into a shorter time, business-wise.' I said 'What are you going to do?' and he said 'I dunno, I'll let you know'. He rang me up one day and said 'Do you want to come for a r*n with me?' and I said 'Come for a r*n with you? *R*n*??? I said what do you do … round the oval or something?' He said, 'No, no, no, it's a cross country r*n.'

That was Singapore H3 r*n # 170. Did you r*n regularly after that?
GF: Yeah, wouldn't miss it. My itinerary for covering South East Asia was based on the Hash … that would be the starting point because I wanted to be somewhere the Hash was r*nning every Monday night, it didn't matter where it was. Penang had only just started and Ipoh was going … and KL reasonably regularly.

Were the r*ns more physical in those days?
GF: Oh yes, some of them were … when you got a bloke like Don Madden setting it, he was a good'un, he was an athlete. But most of us were mainly drinkers.

How did you compare Singapore with KL Mother Hash at that time?
GF: Oh, well, Singapore was pre-eminent because we had such bloody marvellous characters there. I don't know whether you could say it was more British – it could be because there were a lot more servicemen down there [Singapore] which gave it a little bit more of the Fool Britannia instincts. They took the mickey out of the Aussies …

And this was the days before 'the circle'?
GF: There'd be a little bit of humorous statements of a few things by somebody or other, but not an address by the president or anything like that. I don't think I *ever* saw a circle, I was never involved in one.

Does Hashing owe a lot of its culture to rugby?
GF: Yes, I think so – the singing part of it. The thing that made Singapore so bloody marvellous was the tradition of singing at the On Ons … they'd roar all

through the night. There were some good ex-stage singers in the Hash – two or three very good Gilbert and Sullivan singers. They could match it with anybody. And I think that's what captured me, more so than the r*n itself. The people, their attitude, and it was sort of an ego thing – in those days, nobody went r*nning. These days, everybody jogs. But if you said in the Sixties that you went for a 10-mile r*n or something they'd all look at you … it just wasn't done. R*n in the bush??? Christ, that was ridiculous!

Do you think that British-ness has really shaped the nature of the Hash?
GF: Oh, absolutely. To me it goes back to the British background of the thing. Like a Mad Dogs and Englishmen thing. I couldn't imagine the Americans starting this movement anywhere in the world. I couldn't imagine the Germans starting it. I think very much at the core of it is a crazy English light-hearted non-competitive … I think the Australians took to it with absolute delight because it was so ratty we appreciated it. There's a larrikin streak in it that they like.

Do you think the nature of the Hash has changed?
GF: I think so. As a traditional Hash, I don't think there's anyone operating any more. See, it is fundamentally an expatriate thing, you know.

Any particular personal feelings about having started the Hash in Australia?
GF: I thought I did Tasmania a great service. That's something I'm very proud of. Bringing it to Hobart of all places who needed it *desperately* – I think they'll agree, too! Of all places there was a place that needed the Hash … bloody Hobart. Jesus, it was a narrow place in those days … I didn't know I was batting against that when I got the Hash going. Aah, funny days.

Did you have any idea in those days of how the Hash might expand in Australia?
GF: Oh, I was always convinced from the time that I was in Singapore that it would be all over the world. That's why I started to carry the message … I became like a disciple everywhere I went. Because I could see it … to me it was so gloriously unique. Wherever I went I tried to start the Hash … sometimes I was based in places like Tehran, Bahrain, Kuwait, Thailand. I actually used to talk to people and take them out on walks on the weekends and say 'This is what we do.' Some of the ideas fell on fertile ground and years later somebody else picked up the idea.

What about differences between countries you've r*n in?
GF: Well my principle is that I look at a place and think, 'Is this a potential Hash place?' And I always reckoned when I went to Riyadh, and for some reason or another was travelling out near the *wadis*, I looked around and said this would have to be the best bloody Hashing country in the world, because down in these *wadis* you couldn't see where the trail would go. I never thought Melbourne would be very good Hash land because it's so flat, whereas Sydney with its bush … Hobart, magnificent because there's so much variety all around, close in. Other places like Moresby was a natural. Places like that I'd go and assess it and talk to people about forming.

So what or where or when was your best r*n?
GF: Gee, that takes some bloody thinking. The night I met the cows in the

Singapore jungle ... that'd be the one I enjoyed the most. There was the famous second AGM at a roadside stall somewhere with the ice cream man. Right in the middle of it, we're standing around having the AGM and this fellow comes along selling ice-creams. So as the conversation's going on you hear this bell. That was the night they had the meeting up at Nick Bird's flat, it was a sort of mess for one of the companies ... they had this single men's mess, and they sent the *amahs* [maids] out for the night, and they got an army-issue condom and they filled it up in the bath to see how much it would hold. The bloody thing was about as big as the bath by the time they picked it up, carried it out and threw it over the balcony just as the two *amahs* were coming back again and it went SPLAT! There's a period there which was absolutely bloody magic. I'd say for about two to three years ... This is why I look back on what I call the Golden Years of Hashing in Singapore.

Does the InterHash belong in Asia or elsewhere?

GF: We were talking about this in Hobart. The people who were down there were the two r*nners who organised the Bay to Breakers [USA], major movers and serious r*nners, and we were talking about this. And they were saying whether it would be possible with all their regulations and by-laws and stuff, and prejudices with the coppers, they said it would be very difficult – what was done in Hobart couldn't be done (in the USA). Land of the free??? The McCarthyism going on at the present time ...

I've always had an idea that if they ever did have one over there, have a Hollywood Hash and make it like a dress-up thing with a bit of lightheartedness, not-too-serious Hashing, fun and games. The r*nning would be quite incidental to the thing. I reckon that would go. That's the sort of thing I imagine would appeal. I can't imagine going to London or something like that and having InterHash. I think the venue's got to be right.

So where does the Hash go from here?

GF: I was joking about once and I said, 'Who is going to be the first to put on a gay Hash?' Somebody will, and I don't know if anybody's actually done it yet but I don't see any reason why they couldn't, just for the lark [Er, rule # 6 –ed.]. The Hash has moved along with the times, with feminism and all the rest of it, the politically correct side of it. I wouldn't be surprised if there's a handicapped Hash somewhere. I think it's got to keep changing. In another 20 years time it'll be different again. High fashion stuff. High performance.

Speaking of high performance, when did you stop Hashing?

GF: I continued r*nning (in Sydney) right up till when I moved in the middle Eighties down to the farm in Berridale. I could've r*n in Cooma but that stretch of highway is pretty heavily covered with cops. The breathalyser would've stopped me. I suffer from vertigo and that's fine when the light's good. I was finishing – even in the summer sometimes – in the dark and I had some pretty heavy falls and got lost a couple of times, too.

Apart from bruises, what's the thing you've got from Hashing over the years?

GF: Without any doubt, friendships. Infinite numbers of memories that come crowding back all the time for all sorts of reasons. Conversations with people.

A general quality of life thing. There's a certain amount of irrationality in the thing which is lovely, it's ironic, the whole episode of *why* you do it.

Chris 'The Lord' Eden.
First r*n Penang H3, Malaysia 1965
Founded Hobart H3 1967

Tell us about those first uncertain steps into the Hash world, M'Lord, and who was irresponsible for you joining.
TL: Some people who were in Penang at that time say 'You started in Penang? I don't remember you.' I was only visiting for about five or six weeks and had half a dozen r*ns and got to know the trade. Gary MacDonald was in the same company as I was – and another chap called David Denning ... he was branch manager of our office in Ipoh so when he came up he obviously picked up the likes of Gary MacDonald and others.
Is the feeling of Hash still the same?
TL: I think the r*nning side of it remains the same. I would say it's changed in the sense that it's expanded, it's got much larger, it's worldwide, it's not so parochial as it would have been then ... certainly in those days there was no ambition to take it anywhere else than locally. The idea of InterHashes or even national Hashes, any thing like that, hadn't entered anybody's mind at all, and there were perhaps a few occasions when two adjacent clubs might get together for a r*n but that's as far as it went.
Is Hash truthful to the aims of its founders?
TL: We seem to be moving away a bit from the original. The world has changed considerably since 1938 ... It started in very, very meagre surroundings and where there was very little sophistication at all and absolutely no idea at that time of things like financial sponsorship, magazines, putting in advertisements which would help towards meeting costs. People should be kept in touch with what the original concepts were.
How do you feel having started this whole thing in Australia?
TL: Well, I suppose the ultimate for me was having InterHash here ... it was the star in the crown as it were. I was very proud that we did as well with it as we did.
How many r*ns under your belt?
TL: With H4 I've got 1,170 [as of October 2001]. So that doesn't count Hashes in other parts of Australia or anywhere else ... Europe, Scotland, mostly South East Asia, Middle East, Indonesia, Papua New Guinea. Cyprus InterHash.
Which of those stands out as your most enjoyable r*n?
TL: I suppose as far as *real* Hashing goes, the best ones I've done would have been in South East Asia for sure. I can remember one in Singapore where we ran through the tin mine pools and they used to have a rope going across from one side to the other, and those that couldn't swim would have to hang on to the rope, getting absolutely drenched.
What about your worst experience?
TL: That would undoubtedly be here [Hobart], set by probably inexperienced

hares. We went to the top of Mount Wellington and the r*n went over the side of the mountain, down about three or four kilometres and then straight back again.

That's when you really wish you'd done something better with your life ...
TL: My own feeling is that Hash should not the be-all and end-all of your social life or your life in general. I Hash only once a week and I don't want to do any more than that. There are some that will Hash five or six times a week ... got nothing better to do but Hash because they have no other interests. Hashing for me is just an occasion where you can get away on a Monday night from all the mundane officialdom of life and let one's hair down.

What's the main thing you've got from your Hashing?
TL: A very, very wide variety of tremendous friends, colleagues ... a great bunch of people from all walks of life.

Wes 'Old Wares' Carter.
First r*n Kuala Lumpur 1962
Founded Perth Harriettes 1978
Member Ipoh H3, Sandakan H3, Perth H3

It's been a long and winding road, Old Wares.
OW: I'd been consistently involved for 32 years up to 1994. During that time I've r*n in excess of 1,500 r*ns, worn out countless r*nning shoes and probably strained a few thousand litres of amber ale through my kidneys and out the meat tube. Nowadays it's the occasional home brew and stay close to a toilet.

How did you start with Mother Hash in the first place?
OW: Living in the Kuala Lumpur expatriate community between 1958 and 1970, I kept bumping into drunken Hashers, so I thought 'what a good idea, r*nning and drinking, don't beat 'em, join 'em.' Being an Aussie and venturing into the bastion of a British Hashing enterprise was not easy in those days. Antipodean ancestry caused many Brits to close ranks and make fun of our accents and apparent lack of cultured behaviour.

What were you memorable experiences of the time?
OW: Nothing much to report here, all very predictable – lots of r*nning, getting hot and sweaty, drinking, falling over, getting up again, drinking, eating arse-burner curries at the Hameedia Restaurant, and sometimes finding myself in my own bed on the Tuesday morning. To top that lot off, the *amah* refusing to wash my stained and smelly Hash gear. Best memory was avoiding public office on the committee. Besides, committee work was reserved for the Brits, not some hairy-arsed upstart from one of Her Majesty's colonies.

Anything you wish you'd done differently – apart from ending up in a bed other than your own more often?
OW: My one regret is that I did not join [John Duncan] on his popular weekend excursions into the wilds of Malaysia's jungles, complete with condoms fitted to stop leeches from finding a home in your old fella. True story!

And what of other memorable experiences elsewhere?

OW: The first InterHash in Hong Kong, r*nning around the water viaducts in the hills and catching the double-decker buses which had to stop many times to allow the male occupants to relieve themselves. Sixty plus men disembarking – falling out more like it – from a double-decker bus in downtown Honkers, in full view of the local populace, pissing against the nearest wall is not a pleasant sight … neither were the puddles they left. I of course remained seated in the bus during the whole performance, keeping the remaining women amused by pointing out some of the insignificant features of the tools on display. The r*ns around Kowloon and the Chinese mainland were fantastic. The truck full of curry – yes that's right, a truck full of curry – at Sek Kong airfield was a memorable sight and even better tucker [It's all in the presentation! –ed.].

What sort of comparisons have you noticed on your travels?

OW: Hashing in different parts of Malaysia, Singapore, Thailand, Hong Kong, Indonesia, Bali, Philippines are so different from Australian scenes. Being able to lose a kilo of excess body weight through the simple movement of lifting a mug of beer to my mouth had a rather base appeal to me. The hot tropical weather, steamy jungle, shiggy, smelly animal farms (just loved r*nning through pigsties) ensured a good workout during a Hash r*n. Being young and male, extreme punishment was the order of the day for my body. Don't let me put you young blokes off – keep up the punishment for as long as you can, the medical profession loves ya!

So does any good come out of all this?

OW: Strong friendships can be developed and, if you are not just Hashing as some form of dysfunctional hedonist, then the physical benefits from r*nning do have a health bonus for most of us. Community, outrageous fun, a unique lifestyle and good health were the main attributes for me.

Do you think the Hash or Hashers have changed?

OW: For me, being an initial Hash traditionalist … the changes have been more noticeable during InterHash when thousands of men and women from all over the planet get together to r*n, drink, eat, play, make a noise … each Hash brought with them a competitive streak in the fashion stakes, fancy t-shirts, jackets, r*nning gear, embroidered patches, etc. A veritable Hash fashion show now surpasses the scruffy gear of the past. Disgusting behaviour is still an accepted and expected component of Hash.

Unlike the original concept, set way back in the late 1930s, it now appears to be another social diversion that condones a collective form of behaviour that borders on childhood regression. We Hashers give each other permission to publicly thumb our nose at convention and decorum, and act out behaviour that Mum and Dad would probably disapprove of. This is the glue that binds Hashers worldwide, it could even be the forer*nner to world peace (or should that read world piss?).

My long-term tip is that the apparent slick commercial aspects of Hashing will ensure a continuing and prosperous life for the Hash movement. Long may it reign over us.

Barry 'Ferret' Beamen.

First r*n Singapore Harriettes 1974
Founding member of Gold Coast Full Moon H3
Member Singapore H3, Singapore Lion City H3, Gold Coast Men's H3, Gold Coast Mixed H3, Border Hash

What's your sordid tale, Ferret?
F: In Singapore, my wife Margaret came home one day and said she'd met this couple – name of Peter and Sue Eustace – and they were members of this r*nning club and she was going to join and r*n every Wednesday night. I said she was fucking mad – nobody in their right mind ran in the Singapore heat and humidity. She kept coming home on Wednesday nights half cut and telling all these funny stories. So one day I reckoned there must be something in it as she was having too much fun … without me … so I went to their r*n number 50 from Bukit Timah Hill, just down from the Ford factory where Percival surrendered to the Japs in 1942. I was hooked and have been Hashing ever since where ever I can. I have r*n I suppose 2,000 plus r*ns in my time.

Any highlights in that time?
F: The best r*ns I ever had were with the Pattaya Dirt Roaders. I was invited to be a member of this select group of male athletes by Whorator way back in 1980 or thereabouts. The r*ns are long and the circles go on for hours, complete with ice and the odd excursion to a local 'club' for R& R, as you do of course. Another r*n which always sticks in my mind as a classic was a Red Dress r*n organised by Chip Martz in New Orleans. About 200 showed up and we were gathered outside the baseball stadium on the main drag [Poor choice of words –ed.] near the French Quarter all done up like a bunch of poofs, with about three or four cop cars cruising around wondering what the hell was going on. We ran all over town and eventually ran down this street in the French Quarter. I remember BB was with me and the trail went off the footpath into this darkened bar … and by the time our eyes got used to the light we were hearing these 'oohs' and 'ahhs' and ribald comments from all the boys in the place – the hare had led us into a poofter bar! Any negatives were soon forgotten when one remembers the antics and fun we all had.

Sounds like a shocker. Had worse?
F: There was the time Prince Valiant pushed me onto the stage of the Caligula Club on my birthday. Needless to say I was pissed and a bar girl shot me in both upper legs with a dart blown with great expertise out of her vagina as my dear wife – who was there – so delicately put it, while telling me there would be no sex until I had an AIDS test. Then there was the fun we had at Waukesha in 1991 when the Hyatt Hotel made the biggest mistake of its life – letting the Hash in for Inter-Americas. Greg Norman was seen checking himself out prematurely … the local river was awash with yellow cheesehead hats … and so it goes on and on and on.

And what have you got from your years of Hashing?

F: The friendships. It's like family. I can go anywhere in the world and pull out my directory and I have instant friends and company. Like the time we decided to go to Trinidad and couldn't get hotel accommodation … the Hash fixed it and gave us a great time to boot. Marg and I have entertained people from all over the world, and hope to continue to do so.

Has the Hash got better or worse over time?

F: It's just got better. The only thing is the history needs to be kept safe at a permanent Hash HQ and I think that should be in KL. Perhaps a fund should be set up to finance a permanent HQ with a museum where I can bequeath all my Hash shit when I go off to the big InterHash gathering in the sky or where ever the fuck it is.

Jeff 'Cream Puff' Simkins.

First r*n Kuala Kencanna, Irian Jaya (date unknown)
Founder Princeton West Virginia H3
Co-founder Indonesian Fire and Rescue Hash
Member Timika H3

How did you hear of the Hash and your first impressions of it?

CP: I was working as an expat in the Irian Jaya jungle and my friend Duck told me it had some great beer afterwards and good fellowship and 'nice ass Indonesian ladies, too!' It was at a hospital site under construction and the r*n was set by sexy Madame Lash.

You must really pull the Harriettes with a macho name like Cream Puff … what's the story there?

CP: While another Hasher and I were living in Indonesia for our first time, there was a cake for one of his birthdays. As he went to the loo, I placed the cake on the floor and asked some friend to take a snap shot of my bum over the cake so after the pictures were developed he would think about what he had eaten. However, as the photo was being taken, Lip Dick ran up and scooped up three bloody pounds of icing and cake and stuffed it into my bunghole in one quick swoop – a lot faster than one could imagine. It took two days of showering and digging to get all of that from my crack. Hence Cream Puff.

If that wasn't your most enjoyable Hashing moment, what was?

CP: Hashing on the river behind the fire station in Kula Kencanna I was almost caught copulating with a fellow Harriette by none other than Fast Eddy. I thought we were last, but I think the pervert knew what I had in mind. Had he not made so much noise r*nning in the water behind me it would have no doubt been his best sight of blooming foliage ever.

And your worst Hashing moment?

CP: The local clinic had just removed one of my wisdom teeth two days earlier. Right before the r*n the visiting Doc asked me if I was sore and had any problems. I told him lots of swelling and pain. He told me he had just seen the x-rays and part of my jaw-bone had accidentally been removed by the local dentist. After the small r*n, excess Down Downs and too many antibiotics, I swore I would quit.

No wonder they call you Cream Puff. Anything else?

CP: Kuala Lumpur InterHash 1998. I got dysentery during the opening ceremony then straight to hospital and out just in time to fly home.

How have Hashing and/or Hashers changed over the years?

CP: Those who come understand the crowd and have a great attitude. Those who come don't expect a church r*n now … they know what may or could occur – maybe!!!

What's the main thing you've got from Hashing over the years?

CP: As an expat living in a tough situation, the fellow Hashers can get you through anything, and I mean *anything*. Greatest networking known to man.

Peter 'Sirloin' Tipa.

First r*n Wellington Ladies Hash 1981
Founded Dunedin H3
Founding member Otago H3
Member Emeritus H3
NZ Grandmaster 1999 to 2001 ("now xnzgm – even more important!")

How does one get a meaty handle like Sirloin?

S: I said I didn't care what I was named as long as it had a 'Sir' in front.

How did you hear of the Hash and your first impressions of it?

S: I was dragged along by a Wellington Hussie, and thought it was a bit boring 'cause they never drank enough piss. Soon changed that though.

An old fart like you must have done a lot of r*ns?

S: With Dunedin H3 approximately 800. Other Hashes 200 to 300.

Must have been through some shit as well?

S: Can't – and try not to – remember those, but probably the two times I cracked ribs.

How would you compare Hashing in different places you've Hashed?

S: Raratonga's 1,000th r*n – too hot, too muggy but they did have Speight's Beer. Dunedin's 1,000th r*n – too wet, too cold but they did have Speight's Beer.

So what's the main thing you've got from Hashing?

S: Some of the biggest hangovers, married (second time), plenty of friends who I have no idea what their real names are or what they do normally.

They're Hashers, Sirloin – they don't do anything normally! Does InterHash belong in Asia, or worldwide?

S: In New Zealand.

You're obviously a left-field philosopher and visionary – how could/should the Hash evolve from here?

S: We're getting older so I suppose we'll all die.

Hopefully not until they've all bought this book.

Geoff 'Father' Feast.

First r*n Brunei H3 1967.
Member Jakarta H3, Vanuatu H3
Founding member Surabaya H3, Santo H3, Port Vila Harriettes

How did you get into this Hashing caper?
F: I had arrived buggered from London to take up a new job and was picked up at the airport by my new boss and taken straight to the Hash, r*n # 170. The Brunei HHH at that time was one of only three or four in existence. By 1970 the number had risen to about 17 and we all kept in touch with each other regularly by exchanging Hash Words.

You did about 400 r*ns with your South East Asian kennels. How many since?
F: In 1976 I arrived here in Vanuatu and have clocked up just over 550 r*ns – or walks, which they are mostly nowadays.

They found you out early – in 1977 they wrote you up as 'he only makes it to about half the r*ns that he ends up drinking at.'
F: I have obviously got a long-standing reputation as a SCB, for example, from 1976:

A Hasher whose last name was Feast
And was frighteningly fond of the yeast
Would play his cards right
And arrive late each night
*To drink more and r*n quite the least.*

I never had a Hash name until I moved to Port Vila where I eventually acquired the name Father, often intentionally mis-spelt 'Farter'. It was not because I was the oldest or wisest (although I have been the Religious Adviser for as long as I can remember) but because I arrived in the infancy of the PV Hash and was able to introduce some of the Hash traditions they hadn't heard about – basics like paper trails, checking, Down Downs, live r*ns, the Hashit, the Hash hierarchy, Swing Low, etc. At one stage I also had the name Horse after starring in the local adaptation of The Full Monty.

Glad I missed it. Share some of your best Hashing times with us.
F: While living in Surabaya we spent many long weekends in Bali, being only a few hours drive away, and often en masse. Easter 1975 the place was crawling with Surabaya Hash people (it was a family Hash) so it was decided we should inaugurate the Bali Hash. I nominated myself as the hare and set a r*n along Kuta Beach in amongst nude – or semi-nude – sunbathers then through a *kampong* bathing stream.

Last year we had the first and only Yasur Volcano r*n. A group of us went down to the Island of Tanna for the annual weekend of debauchery of the John Frum (local cargo cult) Tribe. We were still there on the Monday, which is our normal Hash day, so we decided we should do a make-up r*n. One of our local Hash girls, whose parents were hosting us in the village, led us on a trail that took us up to the (very active) crater of Yasur Volcano and back down to the village again. The Down Downs were done with kava – which is a traditional local brew made from the roots of a plant, and looks and tastes like dirty dish water with toothpaste in it – and which sends you literally legless.

Sounds like you like to get further afield, then.

F: R*nning round the streets of big cities following chalk or flour marks on the pavement is not my idea of Hashing. Give me the rubber plantations of Malaysia, the jungle of Borneo, the *padi* fields, shiggy and *kampongs* of Indonesia, the coconut plantations and beaches of Vanuatu any day. That's what I call Hashing.

What have you got from your years of Hashing?

F: Apart from countless hangovers and two divorces??? In my younger days I enjoyed the exercise once a week. Now the r*nning is quite incidental – three times round the beer truck is my usual contribution to the r*n, unless there is an obvious short-cut. From a personal point of view I find the Hash to be of great benefit to the professional side of my life as an architect. Many a time I have literally stumbled on the perfect building site while either r*nning or recce'ing a trail.

Rita 'Souvenir' Mendelson.

First r*n Vindobona H3, Vienna 1986
Co-founder Hobart Hash Harem 1999
Member Hobart Hash House Harriers & Harriettes, Hobart Full Moon H3

How did you allow yourself to be dragged into Hashing?

S: I had Hashing friends in Vienna from around 1984. In the early days the Vienna Hash had a reputation for being quite wild and rowdy, but once I joined I found that it was also a lot of fun and that everyone was very friendly.

Must've been, 'cause you've been r*nning like mad since.

S: I did around 225 r*ns with Vindobona, around 250 with H5, around 50 with Hobart Full Moon and around 150 so far with Hobart Hash Harem. Over the years I have r*n as a visitor with many other clubs around Europe, and have attended Hash events in Europe, the UK, Asia and of course InterHashes.

How do you earn a name like Souvenir?

S: Well, my original Hash name was Mindphuck (thanks to a one-time GM who had LSD visions of a character called Mendelson Mindfuck. But when I moved to Hobart I was renamed Souvenir as my partner had picked me up in Cyprus (at InterHash) and brought me back with him.

What are your most memorable moments in Hashing?

S: The one in Cyprus when I met my partner, Spoof of H5. We were both at the GMs meeting on the Sunday morning and were hanging around having a beer afterwards. Along with a number of other GMs we missed all the buses to the r*ns. So Pink Panter and Clepto decided to set a GMs r*n from the Municipal Gardens (IH venue). It was a pleasant r*n, and somewhere along the trail Spoof and I swapped t-shirts. But what made it memorable was that at the first pub we went to, somehow the four women were persuaded to flash our tits – and were rewarded by a round of beers [Talk about spoiling the market! –ed.]. So at the second pub, we did it again – and got another round of beers (this time from the locals). We may have done it again, I don't remember! The ringleader in all this was Blimey, and for the rest of my time in Cyprus, he kept giving me Down Downs for that day.

I have to say my happiest memories are from the times I went down to Zagreb H3 as they are such a fantastic crowd, their summer weekend events on the Adriatic coast are always absolutely wonderful – great r*ns, lovely people, excellent food and beer.

Any big differences in the Hashing experience between Australia and Europe?

S: In Europe people perhaps tend to be a bit more uninhibited, both in language and behaviour. In Europe, we mostly did the circle in the car park immediately after the r*n and then all went on to a pub or restaurant for a meal or drinks. In Tassie at H5 we do the circle (or 'lip session') *after* eating. In terms of r*nning terrain, the summer bush r*ns here can be good but the winter r*ns are often fairly dreary. What amazes me is how the Hash is so widely known and how many Hashes there are in such a small area (and small population).

Have you noticed any changes in the Hash over the 16 years?

S: What amazes me now is that there is such a wide diversity of age groups, from young students to retirees well over 60, whereas earlier it seemed that most Hashers were in the 30-50 category. But it is still an incredible way to meet people from all walks of life. One change is the enormous use of email and the internet, which enables people to contact each other more easily and find out information, too.

What have you got from the Hash?

S: I met my partner through the Hash and would never have come to Australia otherwise.

Surely you'd expect more than just him to show for it!

S: The main thing I have personally gained from Hashing is the friends I have made all over the world, and the network of contacts that I have kept in touch with. The other thing is the places I have visited and the travel opportunities … for example a Hash sailing holiday in the Caribbean arranged by ex-Vienna Hash friends in Washington DC, an absolutely brilliant experience.

Apart from the obvious, are there any fundamental differences between Hashmen and Harriettes?

S: It is true that some Hashmen can appear to be male chauvinists and extremely sexist [That must be just a Tasmanian thing –ed.]. However, I believe that all Hashers are basically considerate of others and that there is no point getting upset by some silly behaviour. Occasionally Harriettes get carried away by the number of available men and go over the top in promiscuous activity – but they usually learn before too long! The great thing about Hashing is that you can do whatever you want and still be accepted.

How come the Hash is still popular with Harriettes in this age – especially in Australia – of increasing political correctness, feminism, etc.
S: I have helped to found a women-only Hash, which I would never have dreamed of in Europe, but there has been a men-only Hash here for 35 years, so now there is equality. Many women like the Hash Harem as they can perhaps be more uninhibited than they would be in mixed company. However, some of us are extroverted in mixed company, too! The Hash in any form is popular with women as they can get exercise, let their hair down, meet a lot of new people with a similar sense of humour and generally relax among friends. Which goes for everyone really, doesn't it?

Rob 'Likka' McNaught.
First r*n Napier H3 1982
Founded Pania Plodders H3 1984
Founder member Rona Island H3; Belfast H3, Northern Ireland
Member Bay Mooners H3, Kool Kidz H3

What do you remember of your first r*n, Likka?
L: It was r*n #77 with Napier H3 at the Criterion Hotel. I left the pub at 1:40am for a 6am start that day. A third of the pack was still pissing it up! Napier Hash (now defunct) was wild, with frequent parties at people's homes after the On On. A great club with great memories; if I could only remember them!
And how does a mild-mannered postal worker get into that group of pissheads?
L: Like most people I guess I heard of HHH by word of mouth – a workmate at the Napier post office by the name of Doug '69' Wright. Doug had stumbled onto HHH purely by chance. On one occasion in early May 1981, about 80 rowdy joggers ran past the main window. They weren't your normal grimacing, pain-stricken, athletic mutants. They were young, vibrant and happy. They laughed, blew trumpets/bugles and yelled 'On! On!' through the main streets. They ravaged the still city night like a plague of festive locusts … then, like a flash of lightning, they were gone again. He tracked them down at Napier's Central Hotel the following week.
So it doesn't take Einstein to figure out that's where your name came from?
L: After the r*n I volunteered to scull 'The Prick' which was unheard of, beating what was then the club record. It was supposed to be punishment not pleasure! Mine was a composite of my surname (McNaught), the above prowess (liquor), and my occupation (licking stamps). Hence McLiquor, abbreviated from Naughty Mick Licker, and known today as Likka.
And you've been on ever since?
L: I've not missed a r*n since the Eighties! I r*n at least once a week, every week, somewhere in the world. This week will be my 777th r*n with Pania Plodders.
On top of about 500 others you've done elsewhere. What do you feel after all that?
L: Fatigue – worn out body (liver and kidneys) from endless Down Downs!!!

Tell us about your famous three-year sabbatical in the mid-Eighties in which you Hashed with 155 clubs around the world. Er, Why???

L: The privilege of being the first self-funded, semi-professional Hasher! And proving such a quest was not impossible! When I'd left NZ it had been a whimsical, 'devil may care' challenge that someone had to do. Why not me? Prove that Hashing truly is an international brotherhood. Best of all do it solo, by the seat of your pants, with a back pack and sod all else. Just passport, your own money and Harrier International's World Directory.

And what was the connection with Tim 'Magic' Hughes?

L: Magic and I had spoken about compiling what was the first international HHH directory. He had the finance to get it off the ground whereas I did not. I updated the directory as I went. He later became synonymous with producing it.

No doubt you had a bunch of good times, met some great Harriettes who took pity on you. I don't wanna know about that – tell me about the shitfights instead.

L: Spending three days and two nights just out of Three Ways in the Northern Territory trying to hitch a lift to Mt Isa, in time for their 500th r*n. I made it, but only just! On night two I came within two metres of being r*n over, while sleeping, by 100 tonnes of road train! The driver had nodded off at the wheel. The previous night I'd been eaten alive by ants, while every day I fried in 46 degrees Celsius with no shelter. I'd arrived in Darwin a week before from Bali with $9.20c to my name. All this with 40 kilograms plus of back pack … for the sake of Hashing the world. Then perils after a Berlin HHH r*n from the Glockenturm. After a few beers, I was deserted by the locals. With no idea which way town was, I slept on a park bench while snow fell around me. Soon after I was woken by an army guy shining a torch in my eyes while two bloody great Alsatians barked their heads off – drooling at the prospect of an early breakfast! I couldn't find my passport which pissed him off: 'Achtung!! Schnell!!' he screamed, ramming a submachine gun into my chest. It was only his realisation that I was too pissed to care that saved me. The heartbreaker … Kuta Beach in Bali. A skinny dip at 2am, with a Hussie who shall remain anonymous [OK we won't ask her name, but can we see some pix? –ed.]. The beach was deserted. Less than five minutes after entering the water we were out again. No clothes … but that was nothing. My wallet containing credit cards and money, my passport packed full of stamps from my travels, and the diary I'd kept about the dozens of HHH clubs I'd r*n with in the last 2 1/2 years had also vanished. The latter two were of no value to anyone else and was likely thrown away or burnt. It was priceless to me, though, as it was to have been basis of a book about my travels entitled: 'THE HASHER'S GUIDE TO THE GALAXY'. I spent all the next day searching but never found a thing.

Arseholes! Cheer us up with some of the pluses you got from the Hash.

L: Friendship – gaining a sense of belonging to a unique fraternity. Amazing people! Travel – seeing the world in relative safety. HHH history – meeting personally many of our founding fathers (Horse Thompson, Cecil Lee, etc) and downing a pint or seven at the Spotted Dog … and another 300-plus pubs!

Where's the Hash at now?

L: Hash is still Hash and there's nothing like it! Attracting the next generation of Hashers to pass the 'torch' to is easier said than done. We have no choice though. We either do or die. Given that we've survived 64 years thus far, that would be a tragedy!!!

So what's the way forward, oh wise one?

L: Promoting HHH publicly, in a positive light such as charity fun r*ns, family outings etc on a regular ongoing basis, is probably our best bet. It needs to be co-ordinated both nationally and internationally though to have any real chance of success. HHH needs to be 'street wise' aligning itself with strong brand names, strong company names, and sports, music or television/movie celebrities.

That's a tall order!

L: Granted – but we need an identity! People, particularly young people, look to such ones as role models. Whatever they do or are associated with is 'cool' and they want to be part of that 'scene'. If HHH can hitch onto their coat tails and share in even one per cent of one per cent of their 'magnetism' we'll attract those very young people who are our future. It works for big business and major sports teams, so why shouldn't it work for us?

Just by way of a little warm-down, what are your thoughts on InterHash?

L: From the moment Hong Kong hosted InterHash '78, HHH was truly and irrevocably international. InterHash is the world – the idea that Hash belongs in Asia is at best archaic! Certainly, Kuala Lumpur, (and by extension Asia) is recognised as being 'mother' to the Hashing world – and that is a unique privilege. It doesn't mean however that they are the be-all and end-all. What chance of Mother celebrating with an international '69' in 2007?

Jon 'Wigless' Orton.

First r*n Durban H3 1971
Founder Pacific Harbour Hash 1999
Co-founder Nadi H3, 1989
Member North Durban H3, London H3, Surrey H3, Sunshine Coast H3, Lautoka H3, Suva H3

Your dad, The Gent from Durban H3, has a lot to answer for I believe.

W: My old man was younger than I am now (Christ – time flies) and was late for one of the r*ns. We spotted the pack on the side of a hill and he probably thought that leaving a nine-year-old in the car on the side of the road wasn't the brightest thing to do, so got me to hop out and join a bunch of old bastards (all of whom were younger than I am now) shuffling around the countryside in their hush puppies. I was bitten by the bug then. The bug mind you, came in the form of the herpes that I claim to have caught while collecting the dregs from everyone's discarded stubbies into one bottle and quaffing it.

That must've been a few r*ns ago now ...

W: Total number is conservatively in the region of 1,200 as I ran with two clubs a week for quite a few years.

And some shocking times had, no doubt?
W: Beer blurs the memory of many. Make that many, many r*ns. You're asking me to resurrect brain cells that died and went to hell on the nights concerned. I vaguely remember a night with the Bangkok Hash which finished up in Soi Cowboy, a sort of downmarket Patpong Road, and a night with the Malacca Hash during which 10 Chinamen challenged me to Down Downs one after the other. It was so bad that afterwards, I was apparently stripped, showered and put to bed by a young Thai girl but can't remember a thing [Wanna see some photos? –ed.].

Talk us through the worst Hashing moments then.
W: Ten years old, high bush – all bush seems high when you're that age – and so far out in the sticks that civilisation was a warm memory. Got left behind by the pack. My manful 'Are you on?' degenerated into a squeaky 'Help!' long before darkness fell. Finally a machete-wielding African cut his way through the bush and led me back to the cars. As I wasn't old enough to be competition for the beer at the wagon I was a bit put out by the pack's lack of concern although, in between chugs of beer, the old man did take the time to ask where I'd been for the past three hours.

How have Hashing – and Hashers – changed over the years?
W: Hashers who started r*nning 31 years ago are now 31 years older. So their r*nning's slower and their hair's disappeared without trace. The capacity for boozing has increased though, so it's all about equal. On a less personal note, Hash seems to be attracting far too many of the wrong sort of women. Those that want to get fit, or look for a marriageable Hasher [Oxymoron? –ed.], shouldn't be allowed or should confine themselves to Harriette groups only.

Speaking of hair disappearing, how does a handsome young bloke like you get a handle like Wigless?
W: Having a natural reverse mohican haircut and being sighted r*nning next to a Fijian bloke (picture all that big bushy hair) whose Hash name was Wig – well, it all sorta fell into place after that.

What's the main thing you've got from Hashing over the years?
W: Chlamydia, and beds in places strange enough that the next morning I was glad I'd been drunk the night before.

Do you think the South Pacific should have a shot at hosting InterHash?
W: Hash is all about meeting different people in interesting places and catching unpronounceable diseases from them. Asia definitely doesn't have it all.

Finally, how could/should the Hash evolve from here?
W: By taking over governments worldwide and rescinding drink-driving laws on Monday nights.

Colin 'Obs' O'Brien.

First r*n Pania Plodders H3 1984
Founded Royal NZ Navy H3 (now Not The Navy HHH HHH)
Member Auckland H3; Seletar H3, Singapore

You could've been an admiral if you didn't mix with the wrong crowd, Obs.

Obs: I was on HMNZS Waikato. The Baron dragged me along, with a quick follow-up from Flinty who rapidly fed me the Auckland Prick three times in a row. Being a drunken sailor that was required to do some exercise, Hash was made for me. I spent from 1985 to 1995 travelling the world Hashing at each port and r*nning with Auckland when home. After they sank Waikato I went onto Wellington (GumBoot H3) then the Canterbury (Can Hash). When I was sent ashore forever I established the New Zealand Navy H3. I now r*n with Auckland H3 and I am at 670 r*ns. Total number of r*ns unknown.

You've covered some ground. Or water. How do you compare the various places you've Hashed in?

Obs: I have only ever known welcome acceptance throughout the world. New Zealand Hashing is different from most in that at least one beer stop is normal on every r*n or it is Hash Shit.

Where does InterHash belong?

Obs: A very emphatic, 'worldwide'. Not all have been as lucky as I to have spent 15 years being transported from Hash site to Hash site. InterHash is a way for a country to display itself. I still travel to Hash events around the world, just not as much.

The Hash world is relieved, no doubt. What sticks in your mind?

Obs: Penang 1,100th r*n. 25/5/85. (No I am not so sick as to be able to remember the date – I have the r*n book.) The HMNZS Waikato called into Penang unexpectedly. After a few phone calls I had a small pack of 14 from the ship organised for an exceptionally drunken weekend of Hashing. A memorable part was on the Sunday morning, three of the expats turning up onboard at 8am to take us to the rugby game which we – the ship's Hash group – had challenged the world on the previous night. Needless to say we were less than enthusiastic about rugby that morning so we plied the Penang expats with mega beer in the hope that they would forget. About four hours later we were told of one of the expat's wives being in the ship's sick bay – she had got bored waiting in the car and had stood by the ship's bow then got r*n over by it. Not too badly hurt, but our medic had her sitting in our sick bay looking at this massive poster of the results of venereal diseases. We still played rugby, and won I think.

One of my earlier horns seemed to upset the staff at Palms Wine Bar at Holland Village, Singapore. The cook in the wine bar asked to look at it then promptly chopped it into many pieces after I blew it once too often.

And when were you Little Boy Blue?

Obs: Ipoh Mens after last KL InterHash. The bastards had me in the jungle until 10pm – two leeches on me, cuts, exhaustion and totally fucked. Luckily the On

On On was good and they sang well. Gave them my Hash horn and I hope some prick is still struggling through the jungle with it.

What's the main thing you've got from Hashing over the years?

Obs: Recurring tropical rashes, damaged back, poor circulation in feet, drunk-in-charge of a car conviction, five severe reprimands from my commanding officers, 30 severe reprimands from my wife, $500 worth of beer fines from mess mates on the ships after bringing Hashmen back, no rum stocks after bringing Hashmen back, five draws full of t- shirts, 100 patches, 10 bumbags.

Sounds like we never learn. Has anything changed over the years?

Obs: Drink-driving and age. I have been driven back to the ship drunk by many drunk people. The Black Widow has been through the gates to the Naval Base at Singapore at speeds that must have terrified the guards. I am not innocent and have been captured by the NZ cops during a Hash weekend. It is just not accepted now and I guess with age we are a little wiser. I have seen the consumption drop considerably over the years except for away weekends.

If we're not drinking as much, what hope do we have?

Obs: Hash needs new young blood. Nor-West Hash in NZ advertised in the paper and got very good results.

Alan 'Easy Rider' Rider.
First r*n Hobart H3 1967
Founded Hobart Hash House Harriers and Harriettes 1982

You were a competitive Aussie Rules footballer. What happened?

ER: I was introduced by my uncle, Super Fart Dart (41 at the time and subsequently deceased at 70 years of age, having Hashed up to within a few months of his death from cancer). Being a youthful 19 at the time I found it essentially an athletic challenge and as H4 was comprised of a core of Harlequins Rugby Union players … it usually ended up being very friendly and competitive. We would collectively be described in contemporary parlance as FRBs. In those unenlightened, politically incorrect days we consumed copious quantities of full-strength beer and if we killed ourselves, or others, driving home it was just part of the daily hazards of life at the time.

Being a youngster then, you probably remember your first r*n clearly.

ER: It was in the Lenah Valley amid blackened landscape, legacy of February 1967 Tasmanian bushfires. Black and white ABC TV footage exists of this r*n and I remember it being shot at the time.

You look like you've racked up a few r*ns since then, Easy.

ER: Total r*ns 700 with H4 and 200 with H5. I've Hashed with all dozen or so clubs in Tasmania. Don't regard myself as the property of, or owning, any.

And where does the handle come from?

ER: Originally known as Red Rag Rider as my still-held socialist views were often vented in those heady radical/revolutionary days of the late Sixties and early Seventies. Changed to Easy Rider with the advent of the movie of the same name.

When and where was the most fun ever had?

ER: There was a r*n in Tijuana, Mexico, as part of Inter-Americas Hash 1995, that had a certain edge to it. We went from San Diego south of the border into Tijuana territory on the light rail train system and did all the usual Hash things with tequilas and margaritas. We decided to return by three or four limos that someone had kindly put on to take us back to further exotic locations. There were about eight to 10 per limo so the champagne had to be rationed – women first and when they didn't want any more we would pick up the dregs. Our calculated gallantry worked a treat as we had been going only a few minutes and all inhibitions loosened … the open-top sunroof was pushed back by bare-breasted Hash babes skulling from the long necks of fizzing champagne bottles. When we arrived at our next exotic location the proprietor rightly judged that we were all too pissed to be of any value to him so he refused entry, chucked us out the door and we went down the street to the beachfront where we continued attempts at 'dacking' [shorts-ing] each other.

And what about the biggest Hashing disaster you encountered?

ER: Rolling a mini-bus containing half the InterHash 2000 committee and consequent serious injuries to all the occupants. Thankfully all have survived and continued Hashing.

Apart from bandages and neck-braces, what changes have you noticed?

ER: It has evolved from athleticism to socialising. It mirrors the ageing process, with renewal occurring at the same time in new clubs and younger participants.

And what have you got to show for 35 years of madness?

ER: Countless hangovers and hairs of the dog. Dozens of lifelong friendships.

Any thoughts on InterHash venues?

ER: Hash belongs worldwide. That's where it was exported – I didn't notice any return to sender sticker.

And how does the Hash evolve from here?

ER: Let it be. Let it evolve. Don't prescribe. Let the market decide. If it disintegrates, becomes too big and impersonal, then too bad. Something is bound to rise out of the Hashes (sic).

DA 'Dagy' Guest.

First r*n Cairns H3 1978 ("Cripes Harry Howell started 20 years before me!")
Founder member Garden City H3
Member Christchurch H3, Slash Hash

You were in the Royal Navy, were you not? How'd you start Hashing in Australia?

D: I first heard about Hash from the Master at Arms on the frigate, HMS Zulu. The Sydney mob had contacted the ship to say that they had a r*n on. Unfortunately, we sailed that day but the Joss Man, as we called him, had taken details of the Cairns club. We arrived in Cairns and went for a r*n in our Union Jack shorts and t's. The temperature as we went over the quarter-deck was 44 degrees C. About a mile into the r*n and someone shouted 'On On' from a car – we did not know at the time what the hell he meant … Damn confusing for a first timer as no one really explained what was going on, but various members helped out during the r*n while trying to scare us Pommy Bastards with stories of snake attacks. A couple of drinks at the end and everyone buggered off, leaving us sailors with a few locals who took us down to a restaurant for an On On On.

So a good impression first up?

D: Really enjoyed it so ran with the Manila Hash and Penang in the following weeks. Personally I thought I was in Utopia. As a good naval man I loved my grog, but I was also a very keen r*nner, orienteerer, etc. So when I found I could combine the two as well as having an outlet for my, erm … extrovert side. Well … "Heaven, I'm in Heaven."

How many r*ns under your belt now?

D: No idea. But I've done 870-odd with Garden City and 350-odd with Christchurch, plus all the others along the way.

And what was your best Hashing moment out of that lot?

D: Sooooo many to chose from. Things like having a naked jelly wrestle at Christchurch Hash's 1,000th r*n. Self, first in naked, but with my guitar and singing. Jelly in guitar, and ended up using it as a cricket bat to spray jelly all over the leering masses. Doing drinking races with 'Dagy's Harem'– self and three Hussies. Always had on the bra, g-strings, suspenders, etc for the mob to look at … and then doing one race with body paint instead of underwear – and guess who did the body painting? Ever tried painting pussy lips with your finger? [This week, or ever? –ed.] Actually, painting Vaseline Elly's tits was the funniest. Painted them but she started to get aroused so I had to keep doing more of her nipples as they grew.

Bringing a crowd home from a Marlborough weekend and Deep Throat (again) was really drunk and fell over, putting her hand on a hot BBQ top. Huge blister over her entire hand, but she couldn't feel a thing. We didn't want to stop at a hospital and waste a few hours so we stopped in at the first [provision store] we passed and bought a bag of frozen peas. She was stretched out in the back of my van – snoring – so we put the bag of peas on her crotch and placed her burnt hand on it. A mile down the road we picked up a couple of hitchhikers. Their faces were a sight when they saw her in the back hanging on to her pussy. A couple of hours later we pulled in to Kaikoura for some fish and chips. By this time we had taken the bag of peas away as they had somehow burst. DT's crotch was soaking and she thought she had pissed herself, so started over the road to find the toilet. Unfortunately she was still drunk and sat down on a picnic bench outside the chippie where we were trying to buy food. Sitting there she shuffled her jeans down enough and pissed through the slats of the bench seat. Mayhem going on around her, with families leaving, the rest of us laughing ourselves silly, and the chip shop owner trying to find out what was happening. By the time she got outside DT had finished and all the chip shop lady could see was a steaming pool under the seat.

My mum would love to meet her. Surprised there's been no bloodshed with you around. Or has there been?

D: Worst Hashing moment was after a full day of fun. Back home to have a barbie with about 40-odd Hashers. We decided in our pissed states to have a go at gymnastics. A few forward rolls and whatnot went well. Then The Baron decided to fly and wrapped a rug around him like Superman and jumped into my hedge. Loud screams, and he came back out with a small branch skewered through his ear. Pulled that out. Then onto the cartwheels … I presume it was because I was so relaxed, but I dislocated my elbow and stood up with the tips of my fingers at waist level and the top of my forearm about at biceps level. Just about made the whole pack spew before they rushed me off to the hospital. I still only have two-thirds movement in that arm.

Another time just after I was made New Zealand Grand Master I went up to Rotorua to r*n with them and see my non-Hashing brother. In those days we used to play a game with the *steel* beer cans called Dent the Can – sit around and bash the can against your head. Do it around the circle, and when you did not put a dent in it you drank. Well, as I got up to speak (standing on a beer crate) the call went out to Dent the Can. Problem … Rotorua drink out of bottles so I said I would dent the beer crate. Easy enough – smash the top rail with your forehead. However, in my drunk state I forgot that the crate I was standing on was upside down. The resultant clash of head against crate bottom resulted in a chunk of my nose being sliced off. Bled like a stuck pig, much to the amusement of Rotorua Hash. The follow-up was that I got a lift back to my brother's who lived in a company village – a cul de sac of identical houses. I staggered down to what I thought was my brother's lounge to find a group having a dinner party. I was in full Hash regalia with pannikin, horn, badges all over, and blood all over everything. I stood there stupefied in dead silence until the man at the head of the table put his knife and fork down, wiped his mouth with his napkin and said: 'You're Rob Guest's brother aren't you? He lives *next* door.'

How come your brother got the good name in the family?

D: DAG are actually my initials and I have been called Dagy for years. I suppose r*nning in NZ I did not need to be named other than that. It is now my business name and there are only a handful of people who call me by my real name.

You've Hashed for half of your 50 years – how has Hashing changed?

D: The lack of r*nning has become an epidemic in the South Island and I see it personally as the downfall of the clubs here. New members have been joining with no thought of r*nning at all – in the end you have a group that walks around the block and perhaps into the nearest pub and then goes back to the On On. Not Hashing in my view. There are always going to be some that cannot r*n and, fair enough, as long as they try a bit and do some of the trail. We older Hashers have done the nine yards before succumbing to the short-cut or walking option. We have had members who walked every r*n but with vigour and with a good Hash attitude and spirit. Nothing wrong with that. But I hope the Hash survives in its present form for many years to come.

Does the Hash need to evolve or is it in good shape?
D: Is the modern evolving world with its political correctness, litigation and safety and health concerns just not the place for a club as irreverent as the Hash? What I need is a good Hash week or so to discuss these things.
What have you got from half a lifetime of Hashing?
D: Friends and laughter wrinkles. Many Hashers I have met are among the finest people I have come across, and the lines on my face are not from pain, but from the happiness they have given me. I thank you all.

Bill 'Crystal Balls' Johnson.
First r*n Mackay H3 1981
Founder Mackay Full Moon H3, Airlie Beach H3
Co-founder Ogmore Animals H3, Lost Patrol H3, Yaamba H3

How'd you get a start in this salubrious club?
CB: I met a bloke named Don 'Puss Puss' Power who had r*n with the Hash in Papua New Guinea and for 18 months we talked of the r*nning, drinking, partying. I thought 'this is for me' (like the Vikings say, 'r*nning, drinking, wanking … that is why we're here'). We talked for hours, over many a carton, about how we were going to start up a Hash club in Mackay. Then in the paper one day an ad appeared, warning people that a Hash club was starting, so we were in like flynn, yaa-bloody-hoo.
And you're still at it 20 odd years later …
CB: The number of r*ns with [Mackay] would be about 700, but have had over 200-plus r*ns with the Mackay Full Moon. The number of away r*ns would be like guessing how many beers, or pisses, I have had. My passion for the Hash is almost fanatical – I attended my first InterHash in Sydney in 1984 and have been to every one since. I have attended all Aussie Nash Hash piss-ups, been to several Pan-Asias, Pan-Indos, and r*n with the Pattaya Dirt Roaders when able.
Is Crystal Balls anything to do with the Dirt Road?
CB: No. Because I own a jewellery store, and I told a joke in the circle about the Gypsy with the crystal ball … you could see him cumming!
I imagine Mackay locks their doors on Hash nights.
CB: We have had some wild r*ns – been banned from several pubs (one pub *three* times) for dancing on the tables and chucking brown-eyes and singing bawdy songs. We had an unwritten commandment that you don't go home until the Hash day is gone (after midnight, for the confused). On our Gispert Memorial r*n in February we had a suitable 2am finish … here's to G and to Tim 'Magic' Hughes, a mate to many.
Have you come close to having your own memorial several times?
CB: The worst, near-death Hash r*n – apart from the time I was bitten by a black snake – was at the Port Vila r*n in Vanuatu. I was on the back of a truck getting a visitors' Down Down with about 20 others, when some goose drove the truck forward, spilling us all off the back. I was on the bottom of the pile. I had my

rib cage ripped off my lung and broken ribs and could barely breathe. It looked like permanent residency in a dark damp hole was likely ... but to the disappointment of the pricks planning the wake, I survived. The thought of all that beer yet to be drunk and r*ns to be r*n kept me going.

Some scary r*ns that come to mind are the time we found fresh tiger prints on a r*n in the Thailand jungle – shit was trumps. The fairly close machine gun fire on a r*n in The Philippines just after the attempted *coup d'etat* in 1990 – the pace was picked up for a while. A r*n through the mountains of Cyprus where we had to negotiate an 18-inch wide track for about 40 feet with a 1,000-foot drop on one side and a vertical rock wall on the other – with the track sloped toward the drop off!

Sounds like Asia is where you've had the most fun. Is that the natural InterHash venue?

CB: I think that InterHash belongs to the Hashing world and so should spread around the world. For those who want to r*n in Asia, there are plenty of r*ns in Asia to go to. I, along with a growing tide of Hashers, believe that some large r*ns (such as InterHash) are getting too big and too expensive. I prefer r*ns that have smaller numbers so you get to see and meet most of them.

Stare into your crystal ball and tell me what you see.

CB: My philosophy on the Hash is simple; you go for a r*n to sweat out the stale beer, you then fill up on new beer, while singing, joking and generally having a good time, then, eventually, you go home. When asked the reason for the Hash the reply from Horse Thompson and Cecil Lee was, 'If your club has bitching, whingeing, and that sort of crap, your club is off the tracks.' [Didn't see that quote in the research notes but we'll accept it –ed.]

Bear.
Border H3, Queensland

I've seen some real dogs on trail in my time, but this one takes the cake.

Treadmill: The illustrious Hash Hound is our very own Bear – a medium size ball of white fluff, affectionately nicknamed Hairy Bum (especially by his mistress Ice Box, our perpetual GM). He is a German Spitz, and a real character. He has the most r*ns of anyone in the club – he even r*ns when his owners are away locally and overseas. I make sure he doesn't miss out on his weekly 'fix' of Hashing. R*ns to date number greater than 200 – the club has only had about 250 r*ns, so that gives you an idea of what a dedicated Hasher he is!

Having contacts on the committee, does he get special treatment?

Treadmill: He hares his own r*n once a year for his birthday. What a treat! His other owner, Hot Dick, interprets the hare's instructions before the start of the r*n, eg, 'Bear says, look for flour trail at doggy height, and he hopes you appreciate the effort it takes to r*n, and spit the flour at the right height, just for your convenience!' We then follow trails that go under bushes (doggy height), etc. The only trouble is, he knows the trail so well he tries to lead the pack!

Nosh is usually a great affair with a luxurious three-course meal to make any Hash Hound drool ... starters: Goodo's dry dog food in rings (actually Fruit Loops dipped in chocolate and rolled in icing sugar), served in twin doggy bowls, along with the obligatory water. Main: Chum (Shepherd's pie) served out of Chum dog food tins. Dessert: Doggy choccy drops. It's hilarious to watch newcomers/visitors stare in disbelief as we plough into the food with glee. 'Oh, great – Goodos and Chum again!'

Let's get to the point of Hashing – what about Down Downs?

Treadmill: He also knows how to do a proper Down Down and even has his own vessel, a collapsible bowl. He waits patiently until we sing him a song, then he's off, no stopping him – and no spillage, either. He usually joins in the song if he can. To top it off, he has his own Hash backpack, Hash coat and various other essentials, which he is personally responsible for, of course.

IceBox: He has his A$1 r*n fee paid for him so that way he can also have food and qualify for his 100th jacket.

Treadmill: Same as any other bone-a-fide [Groan! –ed.] member.

Another dishonourable mention for Hash Dicklickers goes to Boof from Darwin Rural Hash. A Staffordshire Terrier, he's a stocky fella with balls that nearly reach the ground. He has r*n more than 230 r*ns as at April 2001, and counting. He was officially registered on the Hash after his 100th, and wears his '100th jacket' with pride.

Can You Handle It?

Following is a list of Hash Handles from Oceania that passed the 'canine testes' test. Some have been explained by the owner of the name. Others have been told by those who bestowed them. Others have simply just been ratted on by fellow kennel-mates. None are based on truth.

7 Up, Auckland H3: "He was a naval officer who stored up his allocated entitlement of tots of rum. He asked this bird out on a date in the Officers Mess, and offered her a tot of rum – with the warning that rum is strong stuff – and Coke. They drink it. Then another rum and Coke, with the same warning from him. Then another, with increased warnings about how navy guys can handle it, but you young ladies have to be careful. After seven tots, our naval hero passes out. Unbeknownst to him, the barman had been serving his girlfriend only Coke – with a sly wink – since drink number two!"

Anema, Mt Isa H3: "This guy gave everybody the shits and was an animal to boot."

Anti Hash, Milne Bay: "Because she hates Hash but is forced to come by her father."

Aarfabithore, Marlborough H3: "That's what you get for standing on street corners waiting for a lift to Hash with shaven legs (cyclist – my excuse and I'm sticking to it!). Plus the fact that I'm too damn ugly to be a two-bit whore! Not only that, the Hussies get upset with my figure in a red dress (jealousy is an ugly, ugly thing)."

Arson, Townsville H3: "Fireman – accused of lighting them."

Azaria, Agnes Water H3: "This guy is European/Australian so based on 'Ding' being slang for European, through Dingo, through to Azaria (Chamberlain, the baby notoriously taken by a dingo). Then he met a Kiwi lass so became **Dances With Sheep** when they got serious. Three years later they divorced so he became **Bo Peep** and now finally **S.O.L.**, which stands for **Silence of the Lambs!**"

Azmud, Wellington Horrors: Her first name's Claire.

B4, Bushrangers H3: His surname is Mutton. Beef or …

Ballpoint, Central Coast H3: His surname is Parker. His wife is **Refill**.

Bananas, Auckland H3: Something to do with a stripper and a banana, allegedly.

Bandit, Australia: An amputee with only one arm.

Biggus Dickus, Kalgoorlie-Boulder H3: A huge guy with a lisp, named after the character in the Monty Python movie, Life of Brian.

Blowjob, Townsville H3: "Nice girl who used to own a balloon business."

Blue Vein, WA: "He had a rather, er, cheesy experience with a girl before …" says his wife, not overly thrilled at being **Mrs. Vein**.

Bogs, Sale H3: "Had a history of bogging vehicles."

Boltcutter, Australia: "I had a dog that was the ultimate SCB … any chain link fence he was through and away. They called him Boltcutter so I became **Boltcutter's Dad**. The dog's since passed away so now I'm just Boltcutter."

Bottom Blower, Milne Bay: "He constantly talks shit and farts all the time."

Brain Damage, ex-Katherine, now Darwin H3: "There's never a dull moment around him when he has a drink. But he's actually a savvy businessman."

Breaker, Canberra H3: "Had r*n for about 10 years without a Hash name, till he fell off his horse and broke a leg about the time the movie Breaker Morant was doing the rounds."

Bulamakau, Suva H3, Fiji: "Like a cow that's always out rooting."

Bumnut, Sale H3: "Sells farm eggs, is bald."

Bus Driver, Suva H3, Fiji: "Currently his name is **Bus Conductor** which was mellowed from **Bus Fucker** because – after one of our monumental Christmas or family day r*ns at Pacific Harbour where some of the real pissheads got on a bus – this lad decided that the mare beside him was so good looking he decided to throw his leg over on the way home."

Bushlawyer, Rotorua H3: "A lawyer in real life. Bushlawyer was an early colloquialism … Over here we also have a vine in the native bush that is almost invisible but is covered in hooks and spines. It's a shit of a thing – it's called bushlawyer."

Calici, Sydney H3: "We already had a guy called **Bunny Trapper** and then he turned up with the name of **Bunny**. We couldn't have two in the Hash, so we had to get rid of one so we named him after the virus they use to eradicate wild rabbits."

Changi, Sydney H3: "I lived in Singapore, obviously, was real skinny and then got out."

Chocolate Chips, Agana H3, Saipan. "She isn't called Chocolate Chips for nothing … those are fantastic breasts!"

Clueless, Pacific Harbour H3: "Had r*n four to five times and participated in the apres and when finally given a Down Down for a misdemeanour asked 'What is a Down Down?'"

Colonel Sanders, Sydney H3: "I made the mistake once of owning a KFC outlet."

Compost, Wynyard H3: His surname is Heap.

Copteaser, Mt. Maunganui H3: "When I was leaving London I had a farewell party and The Hash was invited. Around 1am there was a knock at the door, a young policewoman was standing there with a stern look on her face. She wanted us to close things down immediately after complaints by the neighbours. Then, in full verbal stride, she started unbuttoning her blouse … and kept going … I had been totally sucked in by a pre-arranged strip-o-gram!"

Corporal Punishment, Canberra: Was an officer in the forces. His wife became **The Rotan**, and his son, **Private Parts**.

Cracka, Sale H3: "Starts work at the crack of dawn."

Cripple, NZ Fleet Hash: "His dick is more like a crippled third leg than a dick."

Crutchless, Australia: "She broke her leg at an On On and used crutches for some months. And then she became crutchless."

Cum On Don, Dunedin H3: "Always calling him on."

Cunstill, Wellington H3: "At the circle everyone would say, is that cunt still here?!?"

Cunt Foo, Adelaide Harriettes: A gent (doctor no less!) of Chinese extraction. "We were in a Chinese restaurant one night having an On On when a food fight broke out. There was stuff flying everywhere. I decided to up the ante and use my chopsticks as a lethal weapon …"

Dame Durex, Dunedin H3: "Used to be **Durex** but married **Sirloin**, had a honeymoon at Slash Hash and became a Dame."

Darwin, Mt Isa H3: "My wife is responsible for this, her name being **Cyclone**. Apparently the old girl told everybody that I was a lazy fuck and she was always on top. So I was named Darwin because everybody knows that Cyclone (Tracey) fucked Darwin."

Dead Ringer, Australia: Carves tombstones and is also a horse-breaker (a ringer in local parlance). Dead ringer is also means 'looks exactly like someone else' in Aussie slang.

Diddly Squat, Wellington H3: "A short thickset guy so we called him **Squat**. Then one r*n, a stripper took his shorts off and nothing happened so he became Diddly Squat."

Dogs Breath, Dunedin H3: "Something to do with stealing food from a dog's mouth."

Door Knob, Agana H3: "Because everybody got a turn with this Harriette …"

Dork, Mt Isa H3: "Photographed at a party with a 12" donger covered with cream poking out of his pants. Only a 'dork' Hasher would do this."

Dosdown, Sale H3: "Is a computer nerd and also falls asleep in chairs, etc. **Blowdown** – her real name is Gail – is married to him."

Double Adaptor, Nowra H3: A late booking for an InterHash event meant he had to share a hotel room with a husband and wife from his kennel. Was reportedly found in the morning sandwiched between them.

Dr Jekyll, Sydney H3: He's an orthopaedic surgeon.

Dumaz, Townsville H3: "Nice lady, but …"

Ellie May, Dunedin H3: "Wanted to be called **Jethro**, from the Beverley Hillbillies."

Fairy Bread, Lithgow H3: "Was due to our past GM serving bread with 'hundreds and thousands' [coloured icing sugar] at one of his r*ns at Wagga Wagga."

Fastballs, Melbourne H3: Surname is Slocock.

Ferret, ex-Singapore, Gold Coast H3: "I was a pretty fit bastard in those days and was forever disappearing down jungle paths whenever we came upon a check … and they reckoned I was like a bloody ferret. Sorry it had nothing to do with long slinky animals disappearing up dark orifices."

Filled Roll, Dunedin H3: "Often pregnant."

First Hill, ex-Gold Coast H3: Morry Tanner was a legend from the Gold Coast H3. Being over 50, he reckoned he was too old to go over hills, so whenever the first hill was reached on a r*n, that was it – Morry's cue to return to the beer truck. But such was his love of Hashing (or beer) that when he passed away, he requested his ashes to be scattered on his favourite Gold Coast r*n site. His anniversary is still celebrated with a r*n over 'his' hill.

Flaps, Australia: Actually there were two ladies called Flaps in the one club, so one ended up being called **Left** and the other **Right**.

Flatbitz, Port Nicholson H3: "We had a r*n in the hills of Wellington. I had to walk up one track, but when I reached the top I started r*nning again. A couple of guys I ran past shouted some friendly abuse to which I replied, 'I only like r*nning on the flat bits'."

Floor Banger, Townsville H3: "Big dick – can do helicopters with it."

Fokker, Kalgoorlie-Boulder H3: "I work doing luggage handling at the airport." His wife is **Cockpit**.

Fresh Fanny, ex-Karratha now Townsville H3: "R*nning through spinifex is very hard so I was sweating and panting quite a bit after. I was wearing those Puma nylon shorts which tend to hang away from your body. This guy had positioned himself on the ground beneath me to get a look and someone asked him how the view was and asked whether 'it' was fresh."

Fuck Knows, Sunshine Coast H3: "We couldn't think what to call him, so we called him this, which he hated. We never saw him again!"

Furburger, Binyup Snails H3: "I cheated and finished a marathon r*n early. As no one else was around, I stripped down to my knickers and went for a dip in the ocean. Then the pack arrived – I had no option but to emerge from the surf with fur hanging everywhere. I don't shave my armpits, bikini line or legs – think of how much I've saved on razors over the years!"

Fussy Not Desperate, Sydney Harriettes: "When I joined I told them I was looking for a man but I was fussy not desperate. After several years I asked for a rename and they made it **Desperate Not Fussy**."

Fuxache, Pania Plodders, NZ: "The first thing this gentleman was heard to say when he was introduced to some of the Hashers was, 'I need a beer for fuck's sake'. We didn't argue with that."

Galloping Tarantula, Sydney H3: "This guy was tall and lanky and ran in a very un-co-ordinated manner."

General Teeth, New Zealand: "Was a dentist in the services. He was a Colonel when he retired – the General was just a Hash promotion because he was a top guy, one of our New Zealand Grand Masters."

Genuflection, ex-Sydney H3: Real name Kurt Zingg (as in courtsey-ing.)

Get Stuffed, Dunedin H3: "An upholsterer."

Ghastly NasalBum, Wellington H3: His real name is Ashley Nausbaum.

Ghost Who Walks, Brisbane H3: "He was held up in somewhere like Nigeria and shot about eight times, and they med-evacced him back to Brisbane to fix him up …"

Great Uncle Bulgaria, Christchurch H3: "Was Hashing in Wellington, with his moustache and headband. A mother and child were walking along the street, and the child called out 'Great Uncle Bulgaria'."

Grewsome, Brisbane H3: "Named in honour of his fellow countryman who, when approached by a fair young lass asking what was worn under the kilt, suggested that she put her hand up and find out. 'That's gruesome,' she exclaimed. 'Put your hand up again,' he said, 'it's just grew some more'."

Gypsy Rose Lee, ex-Wellington Ladies, Sun City H3: "I was fairly mobile and by the time I had done three r*ns with my original home Hash – Wellington Ladies – had done seven away r*ns. That and the fact that I was introduced to Hash by Kerry **'Sweeper'** Lee."

Headjob, Darwin H3: "She's about four feet tall, ie, 'the right height'. Her 65-year-old mother is **Blowjob**, her aunt is **Handjob**, and her father is … **Doc**. No, he's not a medic, just a Dithering Old Cunt that stands next to the beer truck. Headjob has been known to try and pass herself off to members of other Hashes as **Hedgehog!**"

Headjob, Medang H3: "She was my hairdresser and she asked me what her Hash name was going to be. I said, 'Don't tell anyone but it's **Scissors**.' So on her naming r*n where we present a carved wooden plaque, it said Headjob. She actually liked it, but her husband who was with the tax department, and had no sense of humour, hated it."

Hemroid (sic), Townsville H3: "True pain in the arse."

Hold This, NZ: "A navy radio operator who's always looking to help out other people, and always says, 'Hold this', be it a pen, a clipboard or a tool while he pokes around to find the problem."

Imelda Marcos, Townsville H3: "She owned a shoe shop a few years ago."

Innerspring, Suva H3: "As a new r*nner full of energy and bouncing around the place, they tried to get me as a replacement for Hash Mattress but it did not work so I got called Innerspring instead."

Jeeves, Australia: "I drove everyone for a fishing trip, to and from Hash, etc."

Jock in a Box, Auckland Hussies: "I went to a Xmas Hash r*n as a huge parcel, wrapped up in a box and wearing a very pretty bow on top of my head. Being Scottish ..."

Kabawaqa, Suva H3, Fiji: *Kabawaqa* is slang for a girl who swims out to boats in the harbour for sex.

Kava Queen, Auckland Hussies: "While holidaying in Fiji I was the last one up every night drinking kava with the locals when everyone else had gone to bed. It got to the point where they were even wondering when I would go to bed. They couldn't believe that a five foot, 44 kilogram, 42-year-old woman could hack it with the big boys!"

Krabs, Mt Isa H3: "We thought that the tide must have been out with this guy. Was always scratching his balls."

Left Nipple, Pacific Harbour H3: "Based on his name of Geoff Nichol – his wife who also r*ns is **Right Nipple**."

Leftright, Adelaide Harriettes. His surname is Wright, and his partner's called **Centa**.

Leonardo, Kalgoorlie-Boulder H3: "Did my naming r*n On On at **Moana** and **Lisa's** place ..."

Long Time Cumming, Dunedin H3: "His first and second r*ns were about 15 years apart."

Lost Pussy, NZ: "My wife loves cats and we went as guests on a r*n in New Orleans. Halfway through the r*n we hear a cat meowing in the bush so my wife dashes in to find it, and rescues this little kitten and takes it back to the circle."

Lovechild, Hobart H3: "My surname's Leitch but H4 already had a Gilbert Leitch – **Trembles**. The circle said, 'He must be a relation of Trembles. He's Trembles' lovechild!'"

Manumanu, Suva H3: "Means 'animal'– just like one."

Menstrual, Belconnen H3: "The RA reckoned I only showed up once every four weeks."

Miles O'Toole, Brisbane H3: "Is said to be fairly well endowed."

Miss a Bit, Milne Bay: "She always shortcuts."

Mongrel Shoelabels, Sale H3: "Spoonerism of real name Lou Chables."

Moose, Darwin Harriettes: "She turned up at one of our Xmas do's dressed up as a reindeer, but looked more like a moose."

Mother Brown, ex-Paraburdoo H3: Dislocated his knee, tearing his ligaments, at a drunken Hash pool party.

Mucus Boy, Hobart H3: "He's **Music Man's** son so first we called him **Music Boy**, then he disappeared off with a Harriette once ..."

Mudguard, Port Moresby H3: "All shiny on top, all shit underneath."

Muff Diver: "I was visiting Phuket and it was late in the night in the hotel pool and, er, it tastes different underwater."

Muttley, Sale H3: "Speaks like the cartoon character."

Need Her, Brisbane Half Way H3: "I am a massage therapist, so as in 'kneed' but as I was single then, everybody 'needed her' too."

No Balls, Milne Bay: "His wife is the boss of him. She's **Dominatrix**."

One Hung Low, Lithgow H3: "Because one breast is heaps bigger than the other ..."

Oral Job, Dunedin H3: "A dental lecturer."

Organ, Kuranda H3: His surname's Hammond.

Piglet Porker, Karratha H3: "He rooted a copper's daughter ..."

Porky The Human Dynamo, Christchurch H3: "Carries a bit a weight, always short cutting, but always r*ns to the piss stops."

Prik Dokta, Boroko H3: "Because of my profession – an acupuncturist."

Pussy Loa, Suva H3: "Fijian for 'black pussy'."

Pussy, Darwin H3: His son is **Kitty Litter**, and daughter **Kitten**.

Pythagorarse, Townsville H3: "A learned gentleman ..." [What's he doing on the Hash? –ed.]

Rats Ears, Darwin Harriettes: "Is Chinese and serves up a great Hash grub and one of the ingredients she uses is a brown crunchy substance (looks like seaweed) that she called Rats Ears."

Red Light District, Christchurch H3: "She was wearing a red dress one night, with a torch light underneath it."

Retread, Milne Bay: "His father r*ns a tyre repair shop. His sister is **Blow Out**."

Rhonda, Darwin H3: "My first r*n, the trail was set through 12-foot high green snake grass and marked with green – yes, green – tape. Every cunt was lost and they turned to me, a virgin Hasher, and said, 'Help, help me, Rhonda'. Not quite the masculine image you want as a public prosecutor!'

Roachfucker, Suva H3: "R*ns a termite eradication program."

Roadr*nner, Suva H3: "Never *r*ns* a Hash but does the full trail and walks the whole way, finishing before some of the r*nning Hashers."

Rodney Rude, Thames H3: "I went with a couple of friends to see the comedian Rodney Rude and they thought that I was as rude and disgusting as him so when I joined Hash some years later ..."

Roobarb, Noosa H3: "My middle name is Ruby, which I always hated so this is what I got called. **Hotplate** and **Ms Informed** came to pick me up one day and Hotplate's daughter had misheard the 'Aunty Rube' bit and misconstrued it, saying 'Where's Roobarb?'"

Saucy, Tom Price H3: Harriette married to **Meatballs**.

Scottfuckalltodowithyou, Dunedin H3: "Scott is his real name. It just goes down so well when visiting Hashers say 'What's your name?'"

Screwtom Squasher, Karratha H3: "Pronounced as 'scrotum squasher'. I was 18 and still had braces on my teeth – which made me look mean – and did karate. I tripped and accidentally fell on a Hasher who was drunk and asleep on the floor, cracking eight of his ribs."

Scud, Suva H3: "A real womaniser but – like the scud missile – blows apart before hitting the ground, or his woman r*ns off home before he gets the job done."

Sheepshead, Hobart H3: "It was the big curly hair 20 years ago."

Shithead, Capital H3: "Suited him sometimes, but he wanted to be renamed so they called him **Fucking Shithead**. He didn't learn his lesson and asked to be renamed again, so we called him **Stupid Fucking Shithead**. Then he shut up."

Shitlid, Australia: "This useless old bastard was staying with some Hashing friends and stumbled home late one night to find himself locked out. He hunkered down for the night out the back, but towards morning felt the imminent and inexorable need for a dump – so he put the lid of the garbage bin on the ground, did his business, then emptied the contents into his friend's bin."

Shock Absorber, Christchurch H3: "Crossing an electric fence which gave her a shock."

Shortplanks, Rotorua H3: "It's from the expression 'thick as two shortplanks'– I don't know why they called me that!"

Sir Welpist, Darwin H3: His surname is Walquist. His son is **Halfpist**.

Slightly Gaga, Auckland Hussies: "GaGa was the name this Hussie's grandson called her – hence the Slightly was because she wasn't quite old enough???"

Soft & Absorbent, Dunedin H3: "A Hussie who works for a toilet paper manufacturer."

Spastic Plastic, Sydney Harriettes: "Er, I like wearing raincoats … bright pink ones."

Spawn of Satan, Guam: "My husband was a complete ass-fucking-hole … We were both cops so I had a .45 and he had a .32 and we got into this huge-ass fight. I was 19, I was stupid. That's just like one of the Spawn of Satan things …"

Spelchek, Sydney H3: "My name is pronounced M-I-L-E-S but spelt MIELES."

Steelballs, Rotorua H3: "He had the most unusual bandy way of r*nning. After his first training r*n with us our skipper introduced himself with the words, 'I don't know who you are, but you r*n like yer got steel balls'. Turns out his name was Greg Steele. His wife was **Mrs Steelballs**."

Stick It In Jim, Auckland H3: "Originally started out as **Gentleman Jim** but after nine kids in eight years he was renamed accordingly."

Superwoman, Suva H3: "For busting down the office door to get the tickets to the Rugby Sevens that had been locked inside. Broke her hand in the process."

Tnuc, Newcastle H3. "We couldn't think of a cunt of a name for her …"

Toadwhacker, Labasa H3: "He was also a really crap golfer so he would just walk around with us and limit his activities to helping those little toads, which are about twice the size of a squash ball, on their way with a 4-iron. About 150 metres on their way, to be precise – it was a total mystery to me, how he could hit a toad so far and a golf ball not at all."

Tripod, Suva H3: "A reasonably well-built lady whose nipples as well as her box always stuck out – the perfect triangle. Her partner then got called Plumbob because the plumbob always hangs down and in between the tripod!"

Trollop, Suva H3: "Rhymes with his real name and is a real slag bag."

Tukka Phukka, Townsville H3: "Made pies and cakes for a living."

Tunnel Blower, Kalgoorlie-Boulder H3: "Worked in an underground mine here. His occupation was to blow up oversize rocks that fell from the roof of the mine and blocked the tunnels."

Twolips the Dutch Bitch, Rotorua H3: "Self explanatory."

Tyrant F Kramden Sir, Saipan H3: "When they started the Saipan Hash, they had rented a bus and this crazy guy was out of control, driving on the wrong side of the road, etc. So they named him Kramden (from The Honeymooners) and made him the Tyrant. He then declared himself tyrant for life of the Saipan H3 and he has been tyrant ever since."

Tyre Fruck, Townsville H3: "Surname is Archer ... and Robin Hood's right hand man was Friar Tuck so a variation was devised."

Up Front, Milne Bay: "Because she is very forward and she also has huge breasts."

Vaginamite, Suva H3: "Worked in the brewery where the main component is yeast and is also the basis for Vegemite."

Valua, Suva H3: "Means 'pubic hair'– and there is plenty of it."

Vespa, Sale H3: "An adult woman who got her learner motor bike licence and was teased that her bike was like an old Vespa scooter."

Virginus Illegitimus, Sydney H3: "Setting a summer r*n in winter would do it!"

Volva, Rockhampton H3: "My civvie name is Sorrensen, which is Scandinavian, so they reckon I'm a little Scandinavian cunt!"

Wilefing, Mt Isa H3: "Named after he partied pretty heavily on his birthday. Heard the song 'Wildthing, I think I love you ...' but his speech was so slurred that all he could manage to say was 'Wilefing'."

XYZ, Australia: "My surname is Szijarto, and they didn't know how to spell it!"

Yardstick, Sale H3: "Was named after a murder mystery night when she was the undertaker and wanted to measure all sorts of parts while with the corpses."

Yes Dear, Border H3: "Was always making the excuse that his lovely other (non-Hash) half was the reason he couldn't stay after 9pm at night after a Hash r*n."

And here's a list of people with intriguing Hash handles who didn't respond to us, or nobody could remember anyway. So stuff them.

Australia: *Arfuq, Barbie's Chatterbox, Best & Less, Captain and Anchovy, Cop a Whopper, Dearhunter, Dog Muncher, Drip Tray, Duckweano, Far Canal, Fillamacrackin, Frogshit, It's Not Snot, Jonesy the Baptist, Jus Fugly, Kuntri, Late for Breakfast, Laxette, Mazda Bator, Meat to Please You, Miss Baddy 2 Shoes, Mongrel Shoe, Monk Crisp, Pissed and Broke, Plat-a-Puss, Pulpy Kidney, Rice Squad, Root-a-Boot, Rubbersheets, Silver Freckle, Slaphead Cunt, Spermwhale, To the Dump, Twevor Twacker, Vinegar Strokes, Waste of Time, Weak As Piss, Wee Willy Winky.*

New Zealand: *Black & Decker, Blastyffe, Colonel Chicken Shit, Donkey Walloper, Frigid Digit, Golden Showers, Hashputin, Howwouldyoulikea-vibrator, Hydrowanger, IQ20, Mullet Guts, PG Tits, Prickhairyarse, Rangoon Flyer, Somemothers, Trayninweelz, Watafuckinwally.*

Rest of Oceania: *Barney Rubble, Bia Botil, Burma Shave, Busi Busi Bada, Captain Pugwash, Chocolate Mousse and Cream, Krinkle Kut, Madamoiselle Latrine, Mrs Dead Stump, Namabawan and Nambatu, Shoes Arriving, Taqitaqica (Crybaby), Who's That Cunt?*

Anecdotes from around Oceania.

We had a r*n around the Burswood Casino (not *through* it, this time) and discovered its 'darker' side … the trail leading to five or six hitherto unknown – to me at least [Yeah, right –ed.] – brothels. The trail led straight up to these smoked glass doors, which opened to reveal a pristine white-carpeted establishment. "Whatever …," we said, "ON!ON!" The duty officer went ballistic and called for Mama, who of course was in the know. Brave lady. "Go through please." R*nning down the corridors, we were opening doors on complete strangers in the middle of the act, and yelling, "ON!ON!" Between the six whorehouses, I've never known a pack to be more spread out … we even lost the back-sweeper!

At InterHash '84 held in Sydney, Horse Thompson, one of the original founders of Hash, ran the whole trail of the long r*n … he was nearly 78 at the time. On another trail, at scenic Middle Harbour in Sydney, a hot and sweaty Hasher from Malaysia decided a dip was in order, so took off his t-shirt – which he hung on a sign – and dived in. Much yelling and screaming for him to get out of the water quickly ensued. When he retrieved his hanging shirt, he read the sign underneath it: 'No Swimming – SHARKS!' Another r*n had a trail going past on of Sydney's infamous nudist beaches … naturally most of the respectful r*nners stripped down to conform with the required un-dress code for that part of the trail.

Bentabeak from Ipswich, Queensland, is famous for wearing a WW1 great coat and helmet, and playing harmonica. In his act, he starts with a huge harmonica, then progresses down to smaller and smaller ones until he is left with a tiny little one. He then bends over and puts it up his arse and 'plays'. (Unknown to the audience, he has another tiny one in his mouth.) The crowd invariably go wild, at which he says, 'Encore!' and pretends to take the harmonica from his arse and puts it to his lips for another rousing rendition!

In 1975, Noel Peters was haring a r*n for the Goroka H3 in PNG. The trail took the pack around the local airstrip, outlined by plastic cones. However, as he had a pocketful of chalk he didn't want to waste, he scrawled ON ON along the centreline of the r*nway. Next thing, the pack all headed onto the r*nway, earning the irate abuse of the airport officials who tried to shepherd them back toward the grass outside the cones.

We had a huge flood in Katherine, NT, and I saw a few uniformed guys heading into town. Being with the Air Force, I assumed there had been an emergency mobilisation of sorts. So I went home, then walked into town along the railway line to help out a big exercise in the carpark of Woolworths. The waters were rising fast and we were doing our best to stop the flood destroying whole town. Next thing, whoops of 'ON!ON!' are heard and this pack comes leaping over the sandbags and through the waist-deep water. Three of us Air Force guys were actually Hashers so we joined them and r*n for a few hundred metres before returning to sandbagging. At the end of the day, I went to go home along the train line … which wasn't there anymore. I was stuck in town for four days with just the clothes I had on my back.

In Kalgoorlie, they often have a brothel r*n, seeing as how they have actually been sponsored by Stella's Red House for several years. This particular time, there was a 'drink' stop at one of the brothels, and the Mama (who is a trans-sexual and political counsellor) came out with whips, nipple clamps, vibrators, you name it. All 70 of us ended up inside, with the girls propositioning us and so on. We ended up staying for an hour and the r*n fell to pieces!

One night at the Central Coast H3 no one felt like r*nning, so we just went to the pub. Some prick went down to the post office to mail a letter so that counted for the 'r*n'.

For Aussie Nash Hash 2001, we were given an official welcome at Parliament House in Darwin. It was all rather civil to start with. But the waitresses with their silver service trays never stood a chance with the feeding frenzy of drinks taken off their trays. Then gradually Hashers up on the balcony started getting their boobs and bums out. The *coup de disgrace* though must have been the guy who was doing video, who ended up in the fountain doing the 'Roo-ta-ta-taa' and was hauled out by security.

In Hobart for InterHash 2000, we were given the big ceremonial welcome at Government House. Big mistake! For a start, they left the Official Guest Book out for us to sign, so there were all these names like Cuntagious, Fellatio, etc. Then under Comments, we dished up things like 'No Piss'. Pretty much everyone dittoed this, although one elaborated our displeasure a little further with the comment based on the pre-amble: 'The Launceston Mayor gave us piss!' We wonder if they have changed the old guest book or just glued those pages together for future visiting dignitaries?

At Darwin Nash Hash, on Friday night, there was this elderly Hasher who had some interest from a Harriette for their own personal On On On. So he paid a visit to the Gents to load up on the requisite protection. He put his coins in the condom vending machine, but came up 20 cents short. Bugger! He turned his pockets inside out, checked every possible hiding place for a coin, but nothing. He then went back to ask the barman for 20 cents change for the machine and the barman handed it over to the old guy with a knowing wink.

Back in the Gents, he put his last prized coin in, and … nothing. Just then another Hasher came in and offered help. Then another Hasher. Then another. With each successive Hasher, the level of interest, attention and aggression, rose. Soon there were five guys helping out. "Coloured, ribbed or spiral, old fella?" they joked.

"Are the spiral ones threaded left or right?" he asked.

Then another Hasher joined the fray. Next thing, the condom machine was ripped from the wall and violently shaken, turned upside down and smashed. That did the trick – out popped a packet of condoms and they sent the old guy on his merry way.

As of Sunday night at the end of the Nash Hash, no one had spotted the old bugger since. Maybe those spiral condoms were threaded the opposite way.

We had our annual Canberra H3 Christmas r*n on, and the Pale Whale – yes, the name says it all – was nominated to be the fairy on top of the Christmas tree. So he did himself up in the full fairy outfit – wings, glitter, a toilet brush wand, and pink stuff sprinkled all over himself. On the way *to* (fortunately) the r*n, he was pulled over by the police for a random breathalyser test. All the cars ahead of him were tested, passed and waved on, the car immediately in front of him was tested, passed and waved on. Then the copper came to the Pale Whale's car and put his head in the window. With a slight step back at seeing this apparition in pink, the policeman said, "Go now, because if I took you down to the station either you'd never survive, or they'd never believe me. Fuck off!"

We have a r*n just north of Christchurch each year, where the countryside is full of rabbits. And, each year, there is a rabbit-skinning contest, the only allowable utensils being a standard dinner knife. So all these couples (it's done this way) lined up with their rabbits. One guy stripped down to his undies so he wouldn't get his clothes dirty. The starter's gun went off, and he was just watching how the professional competition that he was up against, did it. Seeing how good and fast they were, he said, "Ah, fuck it!" and proceeded to rip off this rabbit's head with his bare hands, and tore its skin off.

He won, but was covered in rabbits' guts and stunk the room out. Much dry retching all round – he certainly put us off the chilli pig barbecue which was to follow.

Organising a pre-amble for Rotorua, our budget was under a bit of pressure. "If we use a removal truck instead of a bus," said Hash Cash, "we can save 70 cents (NZ) per person." We said that was a preposterous alternative … there were no windows, it would be completely dark inside, etc. Completely unsafe and inhumane. Out of the question. Come the big day, what a hoot to watch a pack of 50 Hashers being loaded into the back of a removal van!

On the way from Auckland to Rotorua, 750 Hashers piled onto a train, which then dropped us off at a station en route. From there we went on an easy r*n and ended up at a pub. After we were happily ensconced in the pub, we began wondering how the hell we would get back to the train from there. Next thing, we heard a clanking and a screeching ... the considerate organisers had planned for the train to meet us right outside the pub, with a ton of beers onboard!

Five-Eighths H3 in Victoria, Australia is restricted to those less than 5'8" tall. A mixed Hash, it gives the shorter guys a better chance with the ladies.

On a r*n in Mount Manganui, NZ, we got to the top of the hill, where there was a VW Beetle with four, and only four, cases of beer. "What a rip-off," we moaned, reaching for the last beers. With that, a chant of "MORE BEER, MORE BEER ..." arose.

The GM was looking a little nervous, as if he'd badly under-catered for the thirsty throng.

"MORE BEER, MORE BEER ..." we chanted. With that, he picked up his cellphone in front of the angry pack, dialled a number and said: "We're on Mount Manganui, and it's an emergency – we need more beer, quick!" Barely five seconds later the whop-whop-whop of a huge Wessex helicopter was heard overhead, which then winched down several crates of sacred beer – emblazoned with 'On On' in big red letters – to the delight and applause of the pack.

James Naingulan had been invited to Australia to visit some ex-Timika Hashers. He boarded the late night flight out of Timika and turned up in Sydney at noon, after an all-night drinking binge, and feeling like a rag. "I decided I wanted to take a little shower, opened up my suitcase and ... no clothes, toiletries, underwear nor any familiar article that I could recognise. Turned out Cream Puff had taken *everything* out of my suit case and replaced it with:

1 empty cardboard box
1 bag of Hash paper
2 condoms
Dirty old socks
40 paper plates
Dirty bath towels
A set of ugly sheets.

"Recently, Cream Puff decided that he would take his daughters to Australia for the week and show them how to travel Down Under. A quick bag-switch with his favourite red one saw him enter Australia with:

1 toy gun
2 used condoms
Superman cape

Naked GI Joe doll
Hash paper … of course
A pair of Hooters pyjamas
Bunny, the legacy of the Barksdale family
Toilet paper
Old socks
Goofy hat
A mask."

In Auckland, we boarded a ferry at Westhaven for a r*n, not knowing the destination. Heading off into the harbour, we were soon joined by a chopper overhead with a large net full of beer hanging tantalisingly below it. "Follow the beer," said the GM on the ferry's PA system. We followed it all the way to Rangitoto Island, an extinct volcano, where the helicopter dropped the beer right at the top for us to r*n up to.

R*nning on Christmas Island, we got lost in the rainforest, and night fell. All you can do in that situation is sit down as there is zero visibility. But we had the added problem of the famous red crabs which number in the hundreds of millions and migrate in a big tidal wave at this time of year. So we had to fend those things off as well, which had besieged our circle by now. Fortunately park rangers came searching for us and we were led out around midnight.

In the Fleet Hash, getting to r*n sites is difficult because you don't know the place, and the locals go by car but we have to catch a taxi. This is difficult in places like Seoul, Korea, where all you have is the hare's instructions of how to get there according to odometer readings and you have to explain it to the driver. So in PNG, Sea Dog decided we could – and should – walk to the r*n site. "Well, over what felt like 14 hills and 30 kilometres later, we eventually get to the top of Air Niu Guinea Hill," says Puff, now of Auckland H3, "and the Hash had already left. We ended up going for three hours and we didn't even get to the r*n!"

We were on a Navy exercise in Sembawang, Singapore, with the English, the Kiwis and the Aussies. After a Navy Hash, the usual games ensued, resulting in a biggest dick contest. Each Navy had to put their 'best foot forward' and a clothes peg was used to mark the length on the table. Cripple – a rather shy and reserved Kiwi by all accounts – put his on the table and damn near went over the other side! Since then, we've had him in photo studios doing a 'dick face' (where you put sunglasses and a cigarette on it), and in Bali the word spread and the local girls in the bar insisted on seeing 'it'. They'd then call their friends, and by the end of the evening half the town had come by to see this bloody thing.

We were going on a r*n in Boulder, a mining town in WA, which required a six-hour train trip from Perth and we were absolutely smashed by the time we got there … only to find that the r*n was a pub r*n, which I needed like a hole in the head. The On On was good fun, with topless barmaids, and went on and on and on as more Hashers came off shift and were looking for more. We eventually bailed out at 2am. We awoke the next morning at 8am, and the pub was *still* open and the same people were there from the night before, kicking on. We were saved by the 'help yourself' BBQ which r*ns around the clock to feed hungry miners (and sick Hashers!).

We had gone for a r*n in the Whaitakere Range, surrounding Auckland. First we got on a truck and then loaded onto a train for the rest of the journey there. On the way back, as we were getting back into the truck, we noticed that Piles' bag was there but he wasn't. Drunkin Dunkin was sure he had seen him at the circle, and – in an advanced stage of inebriation – set off with his flashlight to find Piles. Park rangers eventually found Drunkin Dunkin on one of the trails, the batteries in his flashlight long since having given up, around 3am. He wasn't very sure what he was doing there in the first place. At first light, six of us returned to help the search, and along came Piles in someone's car. He had fallen asleep in the forest, and sensibly covered himself in ferns till daylight, before walking out and hitching a ride.

Arkles and Phantom – who was doing some contract work for the New Zealand Air Force – had set a r*n near Ardmore Airport. The piss stop was held beside an old DC3, and they invited curious Hashers on board for a look-see, saying, "Welcome on board," and issuing mock boarding passes. "Strap yourselves in," they said. The pack thought 'yeah, we'll go along with your silly joke' and then once everybody was aboard and seated, the plane suddenly started up, taxied and took off – much to the surprise and delight of the Hashers. ON! UP! After a 20-25 minute scenic flight they landed at Whenuapia Airbase, among some RNZAF fighter planes. They then flew back to the original site and continued the r*n.

This Hasher was a judge, and turned up for work in court to hear a case one Tuesday morning. The defendant was brought in to answer a minor case. The judge called for an adjournment and stepped down from the case citing a conflict of interest – the defendant was a fellow Hasher and they'd been on the piss at a r*n only the night before.

We caught a ferry from Melbourne to Tasmania for the InterHash 2000, and had a couple of beers, as you do. This particular Hash group must have been a little on the thirsty side, because talking to one of the ferry staff at the end of the trip she told me usually they sell $3,000 worth of beer on this trip. That day they did (hic) a staggering $39,000!

In Darwin, this guy was iced in the circle. "As he was about to sit down, I whacked some chilli sauce all over the ice," says Rhonda. "He sat down without realising it, getting chilli sauce all over his nether regions and hit the friggin' roof. He was last seen at a fire hydrant, bent over with his cheeks parted." His Hash handle *was* Atlas, but has now been changed to Assless! They also have this guy who always rides his bike to the Hash. He got pissed once and a car ran into him – the bike was a bit damaged and the Hasher broke his collar-bone. After a few months he was right to go again, turned up to the Hash, got pissed, and stacked into something on the way home and broke the same collar-bone again. His wife now drives him.

In the early Eighties, Fred, a new member of Hobart's H5, was lost, which we discovered after several beers. Sgt Plod, the hare, and some others formed two search parties to backtrack and find him. We were concerned as the r*n had taken us through a river bed with slippery rocks and steep sides. An hour's search was fruitless, and our worst fears set in [What, the beer would be warm? –ed]. We planned to call the police or rescue squad as he was obviously in grave danger. Just then, a car pulled up and Fred hopped out, sipping his beer, casual as you like. Turns out that as he was climbing out of the river, he came across a snake, panicked and ran in any direction as fast as he could, losing the trail. Finally, he located a farmhouse, where the sympathetic owners took pity on him, invited him to come in, have a beer and watch TV and rest a bit. So there he was happy as Larry while we were anxiously searching the bush for him. He was henceforth named Fred the Arsehole.

I had set a good r*n, but the booze ran out early, about 9:30pm. So we all decided to make a dash for the nearest pub. Being in the Tasmanian countryside, the roads were gravel and one of the Hashers lost control of his car on a corner, skidded and ended up on his roof facing the wrong way. Another Hasher came round the corner, saw these lights, freaked out and swerved to miss them, and also ended up upside down next to the first car. "We would've stopped to offer assistance but it was too close to closing time at the pub!" one of his Hash mates reportedly said.

Ohakea H3 in New Zealand once had a r*n, laid by No Reason near a military airbase. We knew we were in for an interesting time when the hare's briefing consisted of the simple instructions: 'The electric fences are live and don't upset the bull!' Sure enough, it wasn't long before we encountered the first of several electric fences, which we had to scale, bringing us to cow paddocks – and face to face with the previously advertised bull. Fortunately he was on the other side of the fence from us. Then we came to a check alongside the airfield's taxiway, but didn't think it could possibly go across one of the country's prime military r*nways. Come to think of it, it was amazing we had got this close without being challenged by security. Chalk on the edge of the r*nway read: 'Stop – look both ways'. So we followed the trail down the r*nway when suddenly a patrol car came zooming towards us, lights flashing. Shit! Not to worry … we see the hare's smiling face, and he's brought beer with him. So we had a beer stop right in the middle of the r*nways, before heading off home.

In July 1985 the Gateway Bridge in Brisbane was due to be officially opened. It was 20 storeys high, and at that point had no sides or lights, with a yet-to-be-finished gap in the middle spanning one to two metres. This didn't stop the Half Way H3 pack of 60 from scaling the fence and r*nning across the bridge. In a later newspaper report in The Telegraph, a spokesperson for the bridge company claimed that the r*n was totally illegal as the bridge was still under construction. "I doubt there are such stupid people about," he said, completely underestimating the Half Way Half Minds! The opening of the Estuary Bridge in Mandurah was similarly upstaged a couple of years later. The navy band had just finished the 1812 Overture and the State Premier was going to do the stuffy official speech-and-ribbon-cutting thing. As he started his speech, the calls of 'On! On!' were heard, bugles and whistles sounded, and the pack headed off across the bridge. The somewhat bemused Premier had to wait for the noisy hounds to move off completely before he could resume his speech.

In Bulsbrook, WA, they once had a special r*n which attracted 200 assorted menfolk. "Part of the advertised attraction was 'women'," says Lofty. "We turned up and there were no women, so we started chanting our disapproval with 'Where are the women we were promised? Where are the women we were promised?' Just then, whop-whop-whop a chopper comes flying in, lands and disgorges six ladies. Oh shit, they think when they see us. 'Oh fuck,' they say when the chopper leaves them. Needless to say we all behaved like true gentlemen – except for one guy who we had to tie up in the corner and took a beer to him once in a while."

In Arawa, PNG, this one prospective Hasher kept on promising he was going to join us for a r*n. But come r*n day, there was always some lame excuse. So we thought fuck it – if he doesn't come to us, we'll go to him. Imagine his surprise and embarrassment when the hares laid the trail to finish right on his front door step! The thirsty and sweaty pack of 30 hounds polished off eight cartons of beer under his house, all the while calling out "IF YOU WON'T COME TO THE HASH, THE HASH WILL COME TO YOU!" I think he got our point.

In the early days of Port Moresby Hash, its first GM – it wasn't old enough to hold an AGM yet – was held. The speed-drinking contest reportedly claimed a victim in ex-Canberra Hasher, Haynes. Having spewed as much as he'd drunk, he allegedly decided enough was enough, and it was time to drive home [After all, he couldn't possibly *walk* in his condition!

–ed.]. Off he sped, only to be disappointed by the boom-gate still being down and firmly in place, making a mess of his car.

Unfazed, he asked the guard where the showers were and cleaned himself up. Subsequent AGMs had to be held at other venues, chosen specifically for their raised boom-gates.

Communication is everything. Port Moresby Hash hold Mondays as sacred. It's always been on a Monday. Well, with one exception: Tangles was the hare and he decided to change the r*n venue at the last minute. Instead of informing the On Sec – a not unreasonable thing to do – he thought he'd r*n an ad in the local daily rag instead. The ad came out with the change of venue, plus an accidental change of date – Tuesday. While most of the pack spotted the inadvertent cock-up, some hounds actually fronted for the r*n on non-sacred Tuesday instead.

To celebrate Hobart H3's 500th, a special event on a Derwent River ferry was held, and a sexy stripper brought in for the occasion from Melbourne. One of the Hashers was in charge of the Hash cheque-book to meet expenses on the night, which were many and various as the evening grew into an alcoholic blur. The next morning at work, the appointed cheque-book guardian received a call – a cheque for thousands of dollars had reportedly been cashed at the Wrest Point casino. He checked, and sure enough, the cheque-book was missing. It could have only been the nasty low-down stripper, who seemed so pleasant when he had dropped her off at the airport that morning. Bitch!

The lawyers should be called immediately, and so should the Commonwealth Police because by now the stripper was on her flight home to Melbourne. The plane had to be stopped. Several calls were made and the grapevine was r*nning hot. He was only a minute away from calling the Commonwealth Police and turning it into an embarrassing interstate incident, when a follow-up call explained everything – a set-up by fellow Hashers! Turns out that two fellow Hashmen had found the cheque-book on the ferry, accidentally dropped by our hapless Hash Cash, and decided to have some fun at his expense.

One of the elders of Hobart's H5 is Tony 'The General' Haig. "It's a rather prosaic nickname but as he's aged he's grown into the part," says Honkers. Another of their number is David 'Doctor Tooth' Crisp – a dentist and, until recently, an Army Reservist. One of the perks of this role was access to the Officers Mess and the tax-free bar. And so it came to pass that Dr Tooth invited a small number of Hashers to join him at the Officers Mess one Saturday afternoon. As the group assembled and set to drinking the bar dry, it was clear the 'locals' weren't altogether happy to be sharing their space with us. The door opened and Tony Haig stepped in. "General, good to see you," boomed Dr Tooth. To a man, the locals snapped to attention and saluted. "The change in attitude was palpable and I don't believe we bought another drink that day!" says Honkers.

Over in Terrey Hills on a Sydney POSH r*n, the pack came out through the bush and – although the track didn't actually lead over the fence some of them went over it anyway – into what was like an old car yard. "Suddenly this fellow with a rifle yells out, and no one took anyone notice of him," says God's Father. "Typical Hashers muttering 'Silly bastard'. So he fired a shot over our heads and all the blokes took off. When we got back someone went off and told the local johns this bloody fellow had fired a shot at us. Anyway, they went out and it was a yard full of stolen vehicles. The coppers were very pleased about it."

In Guam back in 1982 Agana H3 decided to meet Saipan H3 on Tinian Island (from where the planes took off to drop 'the' atomic bomb in WW2.) Most of the r*nways are now consumed by jungle, but two were maintained. Our main r*n was through the strangely 'paved' jungle, but crossed one of the active r*nways. Marines from Okinawa were doing an exercise on the huge r*nways, and pretended they didn't notice us, even when the two hares were fleeing the pack and a C-130 was dropping pallets on parachutes above them.

The circle of about 60 took place on a nearby beach with a fire and ceremonies that lasted for hours. The pickups hauled the 'first loaders' back to the village about 12 miles away. The hard core (about 18 of them) drank more and more, with progressive strip Down Downs, and when the trucks returned we were all standing around the fire nude. Both drivers jumped out of the trucks, doffing their shorts and shirts as they ran toward the fire.

After another case or so, we loaded up the trucks, clothes in hand, plotting to drive through the Marine camp on the way back to the main road. We turned onto a taxiway toward the area where the atomic bomb was loaded aboard the Enola Gay. The tents were dark as we rolled by. Just as we got in the midst of the camp, we switched on the headlights and began making the noise that Arab women make with their tongue (we dubbed it the 'Libyan noise'). Marines started r*nning out of the tents as the trucks sped by. We then made a U-turn and drove through again, but this time they were ready for us – headlights switched on to light our bright butts. We had to grab naked bodies almost toppling out of the truck as the trucks veered and swerved. One of the Hashers, a Continental pilot, noted the blue lights illuminated alongside the road and shouted, "We're on the fucking active r*nway!"

Just then a C-130's landing lights clicked on. The landing plane was headed toward us and drivers were frantically doing 360-degree circles looking for the gap in the jungle where the old road connected. We were convulsing with laughter. Halfway back to the village, we stopped and got dressed, pledging to keep this 'our little secret'. Of course, as soon as we met up with the rest of the Hashers in the various bars and restaurants of San Jose, Tinian (Pop. 800), nobody could stop talking and laughing. We called it the Libyan Raid.

Armidale H3 call themselves the Quiet Hash. They once partied for 26 hours farewelling a departing JM. Must've been glad to see the back of him.

 Belconnen H3, Canberra have an annual 'Tour de Pisse' which involves a bike ride from pub to pub, then have some grub, then get rid of the bikes and then r*n/walk from pub to pub. The third leg is the crawl home. "There's a pack of about 70 and on average it takes 12 hours," says Cabbage Patch. "The t-shirt has a checklist of all the pubs which are then ticked off as you go. It's pretty spectacular … people turn up on penny-farthings, three-seater tandems, you name it."

 R*n with Burnie H3 and you must wear a hat.

 Casuarina H3 produced a t-shirt for their 1,369th r*n with the slogan, 'Licky for some, unlicky for others!'

 Cooma H3 introduced snow Hashing to Australia, with an annual snow Hash each August. They also have a raw-egg-with-beer Down Down.

 At the Darwin Horrors the Down Down – even for parents – is cordial!

 Devonport H3, Tasmania has Christmas topless waitresses, and a double-handed two-litre Down Down mug called the Holy Grail. They all have to wear odd socks for each r*n. Their weekly Hashit award is the Hub, a wheel hubcap that is engraved and worn on the back during the r*n by the 'winner' the following week.

 At Erina, a quiet town on the central coast north of Sydney, the local chapter is called the Wanker H3 [At last, some honesty on the Hash! –ed.]. Incidentally, it's mixed.

 Gladstone H3 in Queensland insist that all their Hashers' names end in '…Dick'.

 Gove H3 use stolen toilet paper to lay trails. They had a huge pig called Headjob who was their mascot – a gift from nearby Groote Eyland H3. On the light plane flight home, it decided to have a dump – 7,000 feet up and half an hour from home. Pilot not impressed.

Grouse Gulf H3 from Weipa, Queensland invited the then-PM of Australia, Bob Hawke, to their 200th r*n celebration. Hawke was in the Guinness Book of Records for downing a yard of ale, although he subsequently became a tee-totaller. Surprisingly he didn't show up on the big occasion. Their award pins for 50th, 100th and 150th r*ns are called the Gispert, Horse and Torch respectively, after the founders. These are hung together like war medals.

Gympie, like many old gold mining towns, has a surplus of pubs. Fourteen in this case. An annual midwinter pub r*n is held, which takes in all 14 pubs.

Ipswich, Queensland, have an Ironman R*n having a beer in each of 19 pubs, plus a stubby (large size beer) stop. If that's not enough, the clock is ticking and this must be completed in less than an hour! Thereafter, they usually retire for a drink and rubdown at a local bar and brothel. This is not a family Hash.

The Kalgoorlie Hashit is a goat's bell. It is conferred by the previous winner. At the AGM they have a pig's head on ice as an award. Their t-shirt usually features the actual 'menu' from their key sponsor, Stella's Red House, and their services and hourly rates.

Melbourne H3 have r*n a Sydney to Melbourne (650 miles) non-stop relay and an 800-miler for Nash Hash '89.

Munno Para H3, South Australia, hold two annual nude r*ns. In 1983, they also staged what is believed to be the first [Perhaps the only? –ed.] brown-eye pyramid on top of the Aboriginal sacred site of Uluru Ayers Rock).

Nowra H3 in NSW drink their Down Downs from an ex-morgue bucket. God only knows what's been in there before. The winner each week must r*n the next r*n wearing a greatcoat and carrying a house-brick, not easy when you have to wade through swamps and creeks.

Ohakea H3 have an annual Scentril Syphari r*n each year. One year it was attended by a pack of 150, not including two dogs and – only in New Zealand – a lamb!

Palau H3 in the South Pacific have two special titles: that of Tide Master and Fire Master. Occasionally they have r*ns on outer islands, and overnighters too, so this person needs to advise on tidal movements to avoid catastrophe. A part of their ritual is also making almighty bonfires, so a resident pyro comes in handy to keep things under control.

Port Vila H3 in Vanuatu was celebrating their 50th r*n at the Rossi Hotel, the oldest pub in Port Vila. As usual the celebration got out of hand, resulting in the publican giving them mops and a bucket to clean up their mess on the terrace bar. A squashed beer can proved to be the perfect puck, and they were in business – a game of ice hockey! Now, every 50th r*n in Port Vila is celebrated with a bone-crunching game of floor mop ice hockey.

 Sunshine Coast H3 in Queensland used to advertise its r*ns in the local rag in the Personal Column classifieds under 'Beautiful Young Asian Lady …' No doubt this helped its, er, membership grow.

 The Sydney South Harbour H3 'Larrikin Hash' was formed by a splinter group from the Sydney H3 'Posh Hash'. The rivalry continues whenever possible, annual Hash relays being a good example. In 1984, the Larrikin Hash chartered a helicopter to make sure they got in ahead of the Posh Hash!

Wagga Wagga H3 call themselves the Gaberdine Hash because about three-quarters of all r*nners wear gaberdine overcoats!

Lik Lik and his Pommie sidekick Tulips set a reasonable r*n though the back streets and settlements around Hohola, PNG. After the second halt check the pack ran down a small hill into a settlement, all calling, "On! On!". The villagers grabbed their children and ran for lives and – before we exited the settlement – it had been cleared … all the local inhabitants had disappeared and a deathly silence had descended. Hashers thought it was a bit strange, as normally the children r*n out to greet us for high-fives and sometimes lollies.

On the other side of the settlement the trail just stopped – no more paper, nothing.

Later upon interrogating the laughing hares it was discovered that while setting the r*n on the Sunday afternoon they were held up by knife-wielding locals and had their watches, and r*nners, stolen. The thieves then stole the haversack which was filled with the shredded paper for the trail, hence the trail had finished and it was On On home.

No wonder the villagers had vacated the settlement, in terror – with 40-odd expatriate males r*nning into their settlement screaming at the top of their voices, they obviously thought it was payback and we had come to rape, burn and pillage to exact our revenge for the atrocities carried out on the previous day.

 For about 15 years Auckland H3 have held an annual Sex r*n, whereby they get strippers from notorious Karangahape Road to entertain them on/after the r*n. "I haven't been to a bad one yet," beams Hugo.

An old joke in Australia goes, "Where's Yeppoon?" The answer: "With your knife and fork!" [Groan! –ed.] A new H3 has just been formed in Yeppoon, Queensland called ... wait for it ... the Cutlery Hash.

Wewak H3 once Hashed up Mt Wilhelm, PNG's tallest mountain at 15,000 feet.

The Port Moresby Extreme Hash did a scuba diving Hash to Tufi Dive Resort, reportedly one of the best dive spots in the world. "We did a r*n, followed by a dive in the middle, followed by a r*n again," said an excited Deep Throat.

Hurricane from Lake Macquarie H3, NSW, was a real Hasher in the crazy, madcap, live-life-to-the-full sense of the word. After a r*n in 1983 he was allegedly 'pissed as' in the lake, and drowned. The Hash has been renamed 'The Hurricane Hash' in his honour. What is eerie is the club logo, designed well before this incident, depicted a drunken Hasher in the lake.

On a Sydney H3 r*n, everything proceeded as normal [? –ed.] one Monday night. After the bucket, the On On was about to get under way, when suddenly Terry Morro stood up and made the announcement – he's getting married. Now. With that he produced a bride, a celebrant and all the accoutrement, and the service proceeded, with us – all male Hashers – as witnesses. Nobody knew anything about it beforehand. "It was the only way I could get him to marry me," were the reported words of the blushing bride.

At an On On after a Sydney H3 relay from Liverpool to Ranelagh House, about 100 Hashers, wives and children were enjoying a rowdy time. Jeff Pearl was banging away on the piano, and everyone was in fine voice. By that time quite a lot of glasses had been broken over the floor, round the piano, singing away when suddenly – from the right – appeared Philthy Wilson. "He'd get so excited with a few drinks so he'd have to do something quite spectacular physically," laughs Phil Riddell. "And he came *roaring* through and did this enormous swallow dive in front of everyone on the cut glass. I couldn't believe it – that was one of the most amazing sights I've ever seen."

When Darwin Don from Sydney [Makes sense –ed.] had his 60th birthday, the hares laid on a special r*n for him around Forest Hills, where they made sure the trail went through as many retirement homes as they could find, not to mention cemeteries bristling with old gravestones. "The bastard's still going strong," lamented a fellow Hashman recently, almost 20 years later.

Sydney H3 lost a fond member, Toothprick, who was a bit of a greenie environmentalist. He had stipulated he wanted his coffin to be plain unpainted plywood. The Hash went along with this request, but adorned it with about 100 old Hash t-shirts, dirty r*nning shoes, etc to give him a send-off to Heaven H3 in style.

During NZ InterHash, Pongo laid a r*n from Lake Tikitapu to Okareka. Pete the Pom and Steakman were on piss-stop duty. On day one, the super-fit FRBs pulled up, hoovered up most of the water and what they couldn't drink there and then, they took with them. Of course, the struggling hung-over pack behind them had no options apart from beer to drink – and they were only halfway through the r*n, with no short cuts to be had. On day two, the same r*n was laid. Did Pete and Steakman plan to serve more water? "The shit they did," says Shortplanks. "They poured out the water from several bottles and refilled them with hole-in-the-wall vodka. It tickled their tiny brains no end to see a heap of super-fit Hashers pull into the drink stop on Sunday and guzzle half a bottle before they knew what they were drinking. The sight of a dozen or so poor bastards doubled over puking made their demented weekend."

At Rotorua '94 an Aussie Hasher was aboard the train from Auckland to Rotorua when he slumped into unconsciousness. His mates realised this wasn't the usual 'too much beer' slump and he was rushed from the train to hospital where he lay in a coma for a couple of days. Coming round, he not only found he had missed the whole InterHash, but also his drinking days were over – they had diagnosed diabetes. It gets worse … he had reportedly just bought a pub before going to InterHash!

On the train to Rotorua, the train ran dry of booze about halfway at Waharoa. On spotting the Waharoa Tavern, some Hashman pulled the emergency chord – the train ground to a shuddering halt, and the bemused drivers poked their heads out of their windows to see five hundred Hashers hightailing to the tavern to restock. The carriages were a bit of a mess after this episode so the management extracted a promise from the committee that next day's train would be 'non-drinking'. True to the committee's word it – unbelievably – was. Until the train broke down at Putaruru – a town with *two* pubs. The Hashers drank themselves stupid, depleting the two pubs' stocks, emptied the off-license, and arrived every bit as shit-faced as the previous day's arrivals.

"That was the pissiest train trip I've ever been on," says Ferret. "As we sat awaiting departure from Auckland, some reckless sole decided to breakout his duty free supplies. By the time the train left, over an hour late, the party was raging … cocktails of all sizes and colours were being mixed. At some drunken stage down the line I decided I fancied this Harriette, Breeding Stock from Houston, and we decided to get 'married'. Argus from Brisbane was the celebrant, dressed up in his monk robes (the ones with nothing in the rear where his arse is) and the one-and-only only Sewerage was my best man. When the train stopped [See story above –ed.] my bride and I staggered up to the engine compartment and had our 'marriage' certified in writing on a beer coaster by the Engineer.

"It was at this point that Sewerage thought it would be a good idea to set a r*n while the train was stationary. Trouble was in his drunken state he decided to start the r*n from the top of the train and, having managed to scale the ladder at the back of the last carriage, promptly fell off the thing. He must have landed on his rather portly beer belly as he survived the rather long drop – he did however pass away that very year having succumbed to an aneurism of the brain.

"I'm reliably informed I divorced Breeding Stock before we got to Rotorooter … just as well as Romeo probably would have booted her out of our motel room if I had been brazen enough to bring her home!"

Perth's 200th was an inventive r*n involving a train ride, a bus ride, and not one but *two* swims across the mighty Swan River. A virgin r*nner – "we don't even know who he was or where he is today," said Ken Peters – decided to cross the Guildford Railway Bridge instead of swimming the river. Half way across, he met a Perth-bound train and leapt into the river to save his bacon, avoiding a near fatality.

For the 2000 Sydney Olympics, a contractor was needed to make the flame cauldron, and supply props, men and machinery for the opening and closing ceremonies which were to be beamed live to a global audience. Sensibly, the committee chose a Hasher from the Sydney H3. Under a cloak of secrecy he asked people at the next r*n if they could help out, it would require a few practices, etc. "What a con job," says Four X. "It turned out to be three times a week for about three months." They improvised these rickety old combined harvesters into shape for use in the arena. Not wanting to let the opportunity slip, the Hashers stuck these huge letters saying 'ON ON' on the back of the lead vehicle just before it went on to the world stage before billions of viewers.

At InterHash in Tassie there was a 'clothing optional' r*n. "Problem was that the Malaysians came along but were definitely not prepared to take their kit off," says Haggissimo. "They were prepared to practically stick their cameras into each and every orifice of the female Hashers however." So how can we get them back? It was a dry day and the Hash had been r*nning over some cow-fields and there were quite a few dry cow patties lying around. "So off I went with a sack and collected 20-odd of the damn things. During the circle we started placing them in a line and at the end all the naked Hashers lined up for a photo opportunity and just as the Malaysians were lining up their shots we ran at the dry cow patties and kicked shit all over them … there was cow shit flying everywhere. It's on the Tassie 2000 video but it's not very clear what's happening … now you know."

Then there was the poor American Harriette who came to Hamersley and persuaded the RA that she'd do *anything* to r*n with the famous Hamersley men. I don't think getting her pussy shaved in the circle was quite what she had in mind.

Then there was the time that a Hamersley man showed up with a brand new mountain bike. He was persuaded to attempt an Evil Knievil-type jump across the winter bonfire but he slipped on the ramp and his bike ended up in the fire. Not to be outdone by this, Young Dags decided that he'd body surf up the ramp – a table with two legs turned down – clear the fire and roll out the other side. What he'd never contemplated was the chance that the table legs might collapse (which they did) and he'd end up flying through the embers on his belly (which he did) or that he'd end up lying face down in a pool of red hot embers (which he did) or that some of the embers might end up inside his shorts (which they did) and those same embers might blister his favourite body part (which they did). Anyway we had to get him to hospital but his request for ice to cool the throbbing was met with the response, 'Fuck off – we need that to keep the beer cold. But since yer a mate and there's no Sheilas here tonight you can have this wine cooler.' He ended up in hospital for a month and needed to have some skin grafts … all because some stupid bastard brought his new mountain bike to the Hash.

All Moresby Hashers love a r*n in the bush so a r*n at Sabusa Sawmill in the Heron Ranges – about 21 kilometres out of town – attracted about 40 r*nners in 18 cars. The pack stayed together over the well-marked trail, back through a gate in the fence at the road and On Home down a short road through a gate into the sawmill property. Eventually Outlaw called on the pack to form a circle and the festivities got under way in earnest. But because of the distance from Port Moresby, none of those in attendance wanted to have too late a night, so it was agreed with Hash Booze that only one 50-litre keg would be consumed – the rest would be saved until next week.

Just before the keg was emptied, Snatch 'n Grab decided to head off back to Moresby. His boss was out of town, and Snatch was driving his boss's new Pajero 4x4 and didn't want to risk a *bia*-induced prang on the way home. After Snatch departed, the pack was sorting itself into small groups for the return trip in convoys to Moresby.

Suddenly a vehicle came charging back into the pack and stopped in a cloud of dust! Snatch 'n Grab jumped out and exclaimed that he had been attacked by a group of *raskals* (local name for thugs, thieves, rapists, murderers, etc) positioned at the gate into the sawmill property. Fortunately for Snatch, his boss's new Pajero was only slightly damaged … his decision not to drive through the *raskals* in his boss's car probably saved any real damage to the vehicle. He said we would be sitting ducks for the *raskals* if anybody attempted to leave the property.

Mobile phones were not used in PNG at the time, but Snatch 'n Grab had his boss's radiophone and Shotaway also had one. The radio phones were used to talk to wives in Moresby to alert police to our plight. It was estimated help would be about an hour away ... so Hash Booze unloaded the cooling equipment and set up the next keg.

The pack stayed in a loose group guarding the keg as only true brave Hashers would. In less than an hour flashing blue lights appeared – help had arrived in the form of two police vehicles from Boroko police station. In the back of each utility were policemen armed with M16 rifles. The pack wanted to know how they came through the two gates without harassment. "The *raskals* have now disappeared," said the police.

With the second keg of *bia* finally finished, the empty kegs and cooling system were again loaded onto Hash Booze's utility and one large convoy was formed for the trip to Moresby. In the lead was a police vehicle, with flashing blue lights and an armed policeman in the back; then followed 18 Hashers' cars some with police in the back and the second police vehicle brought up the rear – all with loaded and cocked M16s, fingers on the triggers. Thankfully no Hasher lent out the window and yelled out 'bang'.

"What a sight as the convoy snaked its way to Moresby through the night," says Fig Jam. "It makes one wonder where else in the world would 40 drunken Hashmen in 18 vehicles be escorted over 20km by armed police for the Hashers' protection?"

More on our website: To read the full unedited transcripts of our discussions with Tassie Hash founders Fred 'God's Father' Whitaker and Chris 'The Lord' Eden, plus Sydney founders Phil 'Ruptured Duck' Riddell and Mike 'The Little General' Miall, go to our website at *www.hash-onon.com.*

Fabricating Evidence.

Keeping abreast of Hash couture.

"There was no such thing as a t-shirt with a message on it," says Fred Whitaker of his formative days of Hashing in the mid-Sixties. "And I reckon, if you really trace it back out, where was the first t-shirt with a message on it? By Christ, I reckon it would be pretty close to being a Hash one. But if you think about it, what other group of people would bother to put a message on a singlet, you know what I mean?"

There's a reason t-shirts have become the Hashers universally adopted uniform. Once again it's got to do with beer. In the early Sixties, Budweiser Beer started selling t-shirts in America as a novelty, emblazoned with its name. Soon, t-shirts caught on among the Californian youth, and at beaches in Florida. Youngsters wore their proclivities not on their sleeves but across their chests. Plain t-shirts as worn by Brando and James Dean just weren't cool anymore.

According to Des Pearson, former screen-printing magnate from Sydney, t-shirts just used to be plain and single coloured. Then, people felt a need to be more creative and expressive, and the first t-shirts were more one-off designs (in mainly block lettering) of the iron-on variety which could be done at suburban shops while you waited.

Thinking it was a beer-wagon and not a band-wagon, the Hobart Hash was soon in on the act. In their inaugural year, 1967, Alan 'Easy Rider' Rider, had signed up and soon started sporting his own distinctive Hash fashion. "I don't remember any others in the pack doing it. Most of the pack were rugby union players, so what would you expect? It took an Aussie Rules player to start a visible written history," he says of hist first crude Hash shirt designs. Why? "My sense of history and enjoyment derived from discussions arising out of the record of what actually happened at those Hash r*ns as opposed to the bullshit usually spread by The Lord to enhance his standing in the mythology of Tasmanian Hashing."

"You will see that I started hand-printing my personal record along the waistline of the garment. I slowly realised this would end up a total mess, and I really wasn't sure how long the writing would last, so I stopped."

The Lord says: "T-shirts in those days were the old, fairly thick material, and over the years we developed badges and designs to go on those t-shirts. Before they even used to have badges and overprint shirts, we used to paint things on or sew things on. We originally had a black felt circle backing on which were sewn yellow plastic figures viz: 50, 100, etc indicating the number of r*ns reached by individuals. Alas, they fell apart very easily in washing machines, and I am not aware that there are any of these left now in a recognisable condition."

"I remember having a 50 r*n patch with plastic numbers sewn on. It would have been 1970 as I moved interstate in October that year," says Easy Rider. "The Lord used to run in shorts with hand-emblazoned 'ON ON' painted on the cheeks. They have probably disintegrated (as you would) being located around a Hasher's arse."

So they progressed from hand-written marker pen, to sewing plastic numbers and letters on felt cloth, and then to screen-printing, but they have no recollection of when Hobart's first screen-printing effort might have come into play.

Ipoh H3, Malaysia, lay claim to the world's first Hash t-shirt screen-printed for the whole pack. Yellow with simple black lettering and a hare and hound illustration, the shirt was issued in "early 1967" according to Boney. No one remembers what the occasion was, and there was no documentation of its issuance. One still exists in the collection of Foo Wan Thot.

R*n #15 Canberra H3 newsletter (15 March 1970) talks of founder Karle Henne missing a r*n. "Wonder if it had anything to do with the ASIO [Australia's CIA] investigation as to how a singlet with HHH on the back was found up a flagpole of the Russian embassy." Upon probing, it turns out this was just fanciful talk, although founding member Bob Brookes does remember some hounds doing their own home-made designs, a la Hobart.

Then the big revolution came with newly available and affordable silk-screening technology. 'Backyard operators' sprung up and went into business, able to offer good-quality shirts for A$10 in the early Seventies.

On August 21 1971, Fred Whitaker visited Singapore H3 on the occasion of their 500th r*n. A trip down memory lane for him. And it's still one he remembers because [Dadaaaaa! –ed.] the first issue of t-shirts on the Hash was *recorded*. White, it had an illustration of a Johnson's outboard boat motor on the front and red lettering on the back. It was sponsored by Johnson's because John Beavons (who had previously r*n in Sydney and Hong Kong) was the Johnson representative in Asia, according to Whitaker. The r*n sheet also credits "by arrangement with Tony Wicks."

To put this into context, it was nine years before Ken Done – the celebrated Australian designer who's sold billions of garish t-shirts to the Japanese – first ran off half a dozen shirts for the media to promote his first art exhibition.

Singapore Hashers had to wait almost another two years till r*n #600 to get their second t-shirt, a red singlet this time. A far cry from these days where t-shirts are dished out at almost every r*n, free of charge, thanks to sponsors within the ranks.

Mid-1971 also saw the production of the first Perth Hash H3 t-shirts, owing to the newly available screen-printing technology. They were white with a simple blue graphic of a dog holding an HHH logo with a little 'WA' (for Western Australia) in the corner. "Hash t-shirts were produced mid-1971 with the help of Jim Illott's wife," wrote Wes Carter.[80] While this *may* have pipped Singapore to the post, the date of its first airing is unascertainable. "I have been trying to get an exact date for you without success," says Cans of Perth H3. "The original guy (whose wife designed the t-shirt) is dead. I have been unable to contact her. Any of the other bastards who have been running as long as we have probably have similar memories to myself – useless!" This design was reprised to celebrate the kennel's 25th anniversary.

The next documented t-shirt came from Sydney H3. Their 250th r*n on July 10 1972. 'Where beer is a spirit' it read on the front, with a quite elaborate stylised beer tankard design in red on a yellow background. They believed it was the world's first, and claimed as much when they reprised it 25 years later. What is interesting is that Whitaker ran with Sydney for many years after his Singapore days: He says he tried to set the record straight by pointing out the existence of the previous Singapore one.

Jakarta H3 printed a simple HHH design for their 111th r*n on 29 April 1973. "Thanks to Mr Glasso for the nice new shirts," said that week's newsletter. "What was so special about the r*n!!!? Why not celebrate r*n 111 …" Sponsorship was arranged by Reimer 'Reindeer' Kohlsaat.

Malaysia's first t-shirt was in fact produced by Mother Hash for their 1,500th r*n on June 23 1973, to celebrate a gathering of the clans. "On that occasion we distributed what we have always believed to be the first Hash t-shirt, a very simple thing of some towelling material with very basic lettering, but which we always thought to be a Hash milestone," says John Duncan. "A number are still in existence, and Tumbling Bill has one in his collection."

By now the world in general was catching on to the t-shirt craze. By 1975, "anyone wearing a t-shirt this summer that does not advertise a product or make a political statement might very well feel naked" said one media report at the time[29]. Running shoes, beer, sex, airlines, and sports goods manufacturers gave it a whirl. One of the biggest selling designs that year? The Fonz from the Happy Days TV show.

"Things went through the roof and merchandising came into its own," says Pearson. In the late Seventies, rock band shirts were in, Harley-Davidson prints, and smutty prints. "Then in the mid-Eighties licences kicked in and people were taken to court. Before that, you'd market anything that came along."

These days, the Hash t-shirt empire must be worth millions of dollars. Trading of prized event r*n shirts happens at a voracious pace. People want souvenirs of kennels and cities in which they've r*n or guested. Most importantly, a Hash t-shirt can give you an alibi for where you were on a certain date. Some hardcore Hash addicts have entire wardrobes and closets overflowing with Hash t-shirts. One Harriette reported, with a roll of her eyes, that they had given over an entire room in their house for her husband's Hash shirt collection.

As Dare Jennings, founder of the Mambo surfwear empire, once said: he had set out to prove that "almost any idiot could make a few dollars by sticking a picture on the back of a t-shirt and selling it."

That may be so. But it takes a Half Mind to wear one.

More on our website: For a selection of all these early t-shirt designs, go to *www.hash-onon.com*. Don't worry about the smell – we've had them fumigated!

Asia

"A tiger can kill you, but a little pussy never hurt anyone"

— Rumbai H3

"Non-Hashers just don't understand."
—Jakarta H3.

"Give us your tired, weak and weary and we will completely destroy them."
— Medan H3.

"You're only young once, but you can stay immature forever."
— Songkhla H3.

"Cogito, ergo imbibo."
— Thinking Drinking H3.

Australia and Oceania

"If normal people scare you join the Hash House Harriers"

— Hobart H4

"100 Years of Hashing – 1969 to 1977"
— Canberra H3.

"No licking my ear, no touching my boobs, no sucking my nipples, no grabbing my butt, no biting my arse – and YES, a root is out of the question!"

"Semper in excretum est."
— Brisbane H3.

Europe and Scandinavia

"When God created Hashmen she must have been joking"

— Oslo H3

"I used to jog but the ice kept falling out of my glass."
— Full Moon Zombies, Norway.

"Helping ugly people have sex since 1999."
— Flensburg H3, Germany.

"What you can't remember you never did."
— Norway

"Farting, Blowing, Hashing! On!On!"
— Hanover H3.

"We never r*n ... out of beer."
— Brussels Manneke Piss H3.

The United Kingdom

"Per Mud
Ad Pub"

— Harrowgate H3

"Wot do you mean Where's Effing Donnington?"
— Donnington H3.

"Normal for Norfolk"
— Norfolk H3.

"Hashus Elginatum non marbilensii'"
— Elgin H3.

"Cursor Semper in Orbe Diminuente Currat"
— Stannary H3, Devon.

"Short R*ns – Long Piss Ups"
— London ex-Athens chapter.

Africa and the Middle East

"Hashing is Life.
The rest is just
details"

— Durban H3

"The Hash that does it in little spurts"
— Accra H3.

"The only Hash where the pussy eats you!"
— Harare H3, Zimbabwe.

**"The Comrades is for people too scared to r*n with
the Durban Hash House Harriers."**
— Durban H3, South Africa.

"No Muff Too Tuff"
— Muff Busters H3, UAE.

The Americas

"If you've got half a prostrate, that's all you'll need"

— Rumson H3

"I'm not as think as you drunk I am."
— Washington DC.

"1,000 r*ns, countless beers, no f&*@$ broads."
— DC's 1,000th

"The meek shall inherit the earth... after we're through with it."
— Waukesha H3.

"Don't shoot – I'm only Hashing!"

"Life's too short to drink cheap beer"
— Pinelake H3

Eurotrash and the Scandihooligans.

Hashing in Europe and Scandinavia.

A Right Royal Pith Up.

OK, seated comfortably in a nice chair? Ready for a bombshell? The first European kennel – and arguably the *second* in the world – was the Royal Bordighera H3 in Italy, started by British military officer, Captain Gus Mackie.

That very month, April 1947, the man responsible for selling 29 million cars before the war died. Henry Ford – whose conveyor belt system Stalin said was the foundation of the Allied win – kicked the galvanised tin Hash bucket. Without his mass production methods, millions of cars – which needed rubber tyres which needed rubber trees which needed rubber planters – would not have been sold and the Hash arguably would not have come into being.

The Mackies were English but had lived in colonial Kenya, and were schooled in South Africa, then sent on to Cambridge to sandpaper the rough edges down. Brother Rupert – a keen sportsman about five years older than Gus – had been stationed in Kuala Lumpur in the Thirties working with one of the big rubber trading firms (possibly Dunlop), and passed his interest in the Hash on to young Gus. Gus had distinguished himself at Cambridge in cricket and rugby and was serving in a Gurkha regiment in Pahang and Trengganu. During leave, he'd go up to KL to visit Rupert and join the intrepid Hashers on r*ns in the jungle that then surrounded the city.

During the war, young Gus – who had become interested in politics and apparently could rattle off about nine or ten languages fluently – became a Captain dealing in 'intelligence' and was stationed in Anzio, Italy, although he travelled far and wide through the European theatre. According to some reports he was captured then imprisoned in Italy, meeting on the inside the grandson of Emmanuel Vittorio 111, one Giovanni Paradiso, an officer in the *Bersaglieri*.

After the war Mackie decided to stay on in Italy, near Ventimiglia, and considered Bordhigera very much his home. And why not – he had inherited a beautiful old villa in the hills from an aunt of his who was part of the Raj in pre-World War 1 India where her husband was stationed with the army.

"Gus said that inheriting the villa from the aunt he had never met was the best stroke of luck in his life, and he was a man who was naturally lucky," said his long-time friend, Lieut-Col (retd.) Anthony Reid Page.[88]

Post-war Italy was in a state of flux. On the back of a succession of huge military wins against formidable foes such as Abyssinia and Albania [They were obviously going in alphabetical order which came as a relief to Zambia and Zimbabwe! –ed.] a peace treaty was signed with the Allies in 1947, and a new constitution put in place that would see Italy become a republic the following year. Back in England post-war austerity measures were in place. With the left-wing government in power, Mackie was no longer flavour of the month, and didn't see eye-to-eye with their dealings. There has been talk of him 'having to leave' England at that point. In any case, the sunny climes and great food of the Italian Riviera beckoned.

Not so lucky was his brother Rupert, who was captured in Singapore and spent the rest of the War relying on the notoriously iffy Japanese butler service. He came to the temperate climes of the Mediterranean to recuperate with his brother. There must have been sibling chat about the fun times of the pre-war Hash, and Gus decided to round up some of the many British expatriates then resident around San Remo for an inaugural trot on April 4 1947. A lot of these were ex-services men, and possibly included the likes of Ken Latimer and Eric Batchelor. "I don't know whether Rupert would have been strong enough to do any r*nning," says Reid Page. "I suppose he was strong enough to organise the drinks, though."

Because the Italians have not exactly threatened the Germans in the gold-medal beer-brewing stakes, the colonial stock-in-trade gins and whiskies were wheeled out instead. Some of the local wines were found to be quite suitable, too. The club was social rather than athletic from the outset, and they were chuffed to have Giovanni Paradiso – a member of the Italian royal family no less! – join them. It was then decided that the club should henceforth be called the *Royal* Bordighera Hash House Harriers. Sadly, Rupert never fully recovered from his wartime injuries and privations, and died around the age of 40.

However, life was just getting interesting for Mackie, meeting and marrying a local lass of not unsubstantial beauty, Anna Maria, many years his junior [Nothing wrong with that –ed.]. At 'home' in the UK, Winston Churchill had just been returned to office as well, meaning Gus was politically on-side again, recalled for some more of his famous keyhole work. He travelled extensively to the Far East and Central Europe, disappearing for lengthy spells. Reid Page says: "He certainly knew a bit about the Burgess and MacLean affair and he did know Philby and Cairncross." These were some of the biggest national security scandals to rock Britain in the Fifties and Sixties.

As a result, the Hash back home was being neglected. "Gus was much younger than a lot of the British expats so the others must have tired quicker than he did," says Reid Page. As members died or moved on, there was scarcely anyone left who knew how to *follow* a trail let alone lay one. "Afterwards it just became a drinking club and it was still going when I retired here in 1966. The chaps invited me to join their group which they still called the Royal Bordighera Hash House Harriers but in my time we never did anything more athletic beyond a stroll along the seafront. So the name was just a joke for going out for a drink. We used to meet in a certain bar on Thursdays, just the men." [Sounds just like the average Hash so far –ed.]

Gus Mackie himself died in July 1971 – two days after the jazz trumpet virtuoso who was raised in a bordello, Louis Armstrong, blew his last – leaving a bequest for his estate to send 50,000 lira each year to buy a good old boozy lunch for his mates. A few good knees-ups were had but as inflation bit into that powerhouse currency, the Italian lira, it gradually got to the point where all it could buy was a round of drinks. Then, it was not worth even sending because the inter-bank remittance charges were higher than the amount remitted.

Anna Maria sold the inherited villa around 1980 and moved to be closer to her family in Genoa. And so the sun set on an illustrious chapter.

From a genealogy aspect, Tumbling Bill's Hash family tree shows Royal Bordighera as a forlorn lone chapter that stopped where it started, with no further bloodline as there was no continuity in personnel from the old chapter to the new. However, where it gets messy is that Royal Bordighera boldly claims to be the second oldest Hash kennel in the world, as do the Singapore 'Father' Hash. This is an emotional and divisive issue [Among those who care –ed.]. They were indeed set up before Singapore, but the other side claim that Singapore has been *continuously* r*nning since its inception.

Ian Cumming, the founder of Singapore: "The story of the 'second' Hash is totally in keeping with the spirit and the myth of the Hash – my only wish is that I had had the wit and imagination to have invented it myself!" Robin 'Tone Deaf' Duff, current GM of the disputed kennel and proud Scot, says: "Sounds like sour milk. Did you know a Scotsman found America 100 years before Columbus set sail? And *he* might not have been the first. He wasn't approved by the English monarchy so it wasn't on record. One could draw parallels here. Anyway I've seen Gus's ghost and so would everyone else if the video battery had not r*n out."

Enough said. But these days *most* Hashers – apart from those in Italy and Singapore – are happy to grant them each equal second place.

Royal Bordighera H3 lay dormant until 1984 when the Bordighera Arena for Science, Technology, Arts, Research and Development was set up. Expatriate social life was typically much less organised on the Italian Riviera side of the border, compared with the French and one had to make one's own fun. So, in the fabled Year of Big Brother – as the tyranny of terrorist groups such as the Red Brigade waned – the chapter was revived by Guiseppe Casagrande, a friend of Anna Maria's. Straight away they had about 40 starters, and over the years Sergio Casagrande, Peter Johnson and Claudio Biancardi could regularly be found at the beer wagon on r*n night. One of their number, Fabulous by name, claimed to have family in the Liguria area related to Anna Maria Mackie's family. That was good enough for them to claim direct lineage and bloodline descendants from the original chapter.

Meanwhile in 1990, Milan – a city not too distant – was basking in beautiful spring weather. The peace of Lago d'Orta was however shattered by a group of loudmouths speaking in strange tongues from the furthest corners of the planet. Closer inspection revealed these to be Zimbabwean accountant Rob 'Dirty Words' Walker and Australian Mark 'Posh Marvi' Stigwood. They had been GM and Vice Master of Mombasa H3 in Kenya previously. But now Dirty Words (or Bwana as he became known) and Posh Marvi were heading in separate directions – Alfa Romeo-driving Bwana had a job in Milan with Coopers and Lybrand, and Posh Marvi was off to Tanzania. Fuelling the discussion was John Murphy (who worked for The Informer newspaper) and an American friend of his,

Dana Quinn. The lads were enjoying a warts-and-all reminisce of the great days of Hashing past, which was too much for the politically correct Quinn. Accusations of male chauvinist farm animals that go 'Oink' in the night were levelled at the Hashers. They retorted with the only credible intellectual defence – "No women or dogs on the Hash. Full stop." Starting such a disgusting and degrading activity in her adopted city? Over her dead body, said Quinn.

She had a point. And Bwana had his doubts. After all, Milan is known as the capital of style and sophistication, two words somewhat under-utilised then, now – in fact *ever*! – in the same breath as Hashers. "Northern Italians are very serious about sport, and looking good, wearing the right (most expensive) gear, being seen in the poshest clubs, etc is as important as the sport itself," says Bwana. The place was full of Yuppie poseurs and *fashionisti*, who would sooner be seen wearing last week's trend than be sweating and r*nning through mud. However, Murphy pledged he was on board and would put the whole weight of his media empire behind the cause. Posh Marvi said it was just the beer talking, and bet a case of beer [A serious stake in anyone's language! –ed.] that he would have a Hash up and r*nning in Arusha, Tanzania, before these wankers got off the ground.

On that same trip, Bwana and Posh Marvi joined the annual Bibione fun r*n staged by the *Podisti di Robbiano*, a r*nning club in Brianza. Our two intrepid Hash hounds stood out like the proverbial canine's nethers, what with Posh in his Aussie bush hat with dangling corks, and Bwana in his usual scruffy Hash gear. However, they got the Italians' attention, and soon the idea of the Milan H3 was mooted to the *Podisti* crowd. "We got a lot of interest from the Italians," says Bwana, "but we didn't tell them about the beer or they wouldn't have come. Absolutely no one combines drinking with sport in Milan."

One couple, Bruno and Marg Pinel, were so enthusiastic they offered to co-hare the first r*n. The fact that neither had ever seen a Hash r*n in action before was not deemed important – like any naïve, gullible and innocent virgin volunteers, their services were immediately snapped up.

And so it was that on June 23 1990, Bwana and Bruno Pinel laid a long trail of flour through the muddy woods around Lago Annone. Then they waited for the inaugural pack to show up. And waited. The Soccer World Cup was being hosted in Italy at the time, representing some stiff competition by way of an alternative to the Hash, it must be said. Surely John Murphy of The Informer would turn up. After all, he had sponsored the t-shirts. But no. Even *he* didn't show up that day.

However he had r*n an ad in his rag as promised, and that 'over my dead body' woman, Dana Quinn, came along dragging a contingent of colleagues from the US Consulate. Some of them, including Roy Waygood, had Hashed in the Middle East before. Some hardcore Hashers – including Randy Mayfield – even made the trip down from Bonn, Germany, to be part of the foundation r*n. In all a pack of 37. Half local *Podisti*, half expats. The Bonn crowd took over the circle and gave the whole pack a Down Down on the basis that they were Milan virgins or visitors. Fair cop.

Soccer fans might like to know that West Germany hoisted the silverware that year, beating Argentina 1-0 in the World Cup final.

But with the encouraging turnout, it seemed that Hashing could take root in Italy after all. "A lot of expats joined the Hash to get away from the formal Italian style," says Bwana, who mentions the early-morning starts and dress-codes typical of other r*nning clubs in Italy as contributing factors. So monthly r*ns were instigated. Each Saturday in summer, Sundays in winter. August was cancelled due to lack of interest.

Bwana and Bruno laid six out of the first 10 trails, often ending up at the Banker's Bar in Piazza Fontana. John Murphy had still not attended a r*n, but kept r*nning his ads which brought out a strange type of tyre-kicker. People who saw the ad, liked the sound of it (or had nothing else happening in their lives) and came along for a r*n. Naturally they got a virgin Down Down, but then disappeared for good. The incidence of this was too high for Bwana, so it was decided not to waste precious Hash beer on one-time-only voyeuristic virgins. "You have to cum twice to lose your virginity," said Bwana [Hash logic! –ed.]. Furthermore, to encourage loyalty it was decided that 15 r*ns – remember this is monthly – earned you a tankard with your name engraved.

Despite this wealth of enticements, newspaperman Murphy didn't show up until r*n # 100. Conversely, and ironically, Dana Quinn became an avid Harriette and now goes by the name of Sex But No Grappa.

A committee was voted in and Bruno became Hash Italian and was named Broken Knee for his troubles. The Australian Consul, Alan MacDonald, was named Vice Master and took to the task like a Ferrari to a Formula One title. His first divine inspiration was to provide two cases of tantalisingly chilled Foster's Beer at a beer stop half way through the r*n. This was first trialled on a trail through the famed historic Castello in the middle of Milan, and held up under severe scientific scrutiny to be a bloody good idea. It immediately became a tradition in the kennel. As did singing. A Welsh RA and a huge contingent from the major rugby playing nations ensured that, and the suitably-scruffy Samson's Eritrean Bar became a favourite demolition site. Kudos, the bar owner, was made an honorary Hasher. "We could sing and dance in the restaurant all night, and Tone Deaf and I saw the dawn in at Samson's quite a few times," says Bwana. "Eventually, Kudos let us take over the back wall of the restaurant, which is now decorated with footprints, Hash photos, t-shirts, even a photo of the first Hash House in KL!"

Feeling that the Hash was becoming too soft, Bwana instigated Monday evening r*ns, alternating with the standard Saturdays, which took the pack through 'Rat City', the seedy back streets of Milan.

The kennel became a home to all manner of stray puppies, including Canadian Dave Bowden who treated the Hash to all 60 – yes, you read that right – all 60 verses of Eskimo Nell when he could.

In April 1991, changing seats quicker than a Hasher on ice, Italy welcomed its 50th post-War government. Then in September 1991 came the turn for Fabulous to host an away r*n at a family property [How many cousins and houses does this guy have? –ed.] at Liguria. Hashers came from far and wide – well, Rome and the French Riviera – and it was during this r*n that mention was made of the Royal Bordighera H3. What? Another Hash in Italy? That's preposterous. At this stage, Bwana made a pilgrimage to South East Asia and met with Tim 'Magic' Hughes. Magic confirmed the existence of the Bordighera kennel and suggested that something be done to save it from extinction. After all, it was a key historic piece in the Hash puzzle.

Meanwhile, the whole country was headed south with a moral crisis evolving. No less than 2,500 politicians, government officials and businessmen were behind bars.

In 1992 – after more than 500 r*ns – the only straight, honourable and dependable committee in the country, the Milan H3, met up with the Royal Bordighera folks and it was decided to merge, the new entity to be called the Royal Milan and Bordighera Hash House Harriers. As with any good partnership it was decided that all the spoils should go to one party – Milan – and Bordighera would get a token singular annual r*n on home soil at Liguria to maintain their proud tradition.

Death Roll, the loud-signing Welsh RA, at this point came across an old pith helmet reputed to be from Gus Mackie's war days. It was battered and bruised, but a worthy symbol of their proud past. It was decided that each r*nner surpassing 75 r*ns with the new kennel would receive one of these helmets. Bwana, with his African connections, could ensure a good supply.

Their website is adorned with the pith helmet logo and a scroll reading 'In Gus We Trust'. Interestingly, 'Mackie' appears in various forms – including 'McKay' and 'McKey'– throughout the website.

A memorial r*n is held for Gus Mackie each July 8. His widow was named Honorary GM and Hash Mistress, and attended special occasions till she was past 70, reportedly drinking her Down Downs like a seasoned Hasher.

Tone Deaf says: "Ghost On the Coast started about 11 years ago. That place is along the Italian Ligurian Riviera coast from Bordighera and is reputed to be near where Gus and Anna Marie had their holiday home. We found a ruined house which fits the bill and it resembles a Scottish castle, near Manie, so must have been theirs."

Bordighera itself has been ruled out as a Hashing venue. "RBH3 must have r*n in the town or in the country further away," says Tone Deaf. "Either that or the foliage must have been more accommodating back then. I co-hared a live r*n in the 'hills of thorn' behind said town and – having had the arse ripped out of the flour bag – the trail went dry and the pack got lost and ripped to shreds by thorn bushes before getting to the On In in the dark." All this was witnessed by a complete village from the other side of the valley, while seated at their dinner tables during a festival. "We eventually regrouped and held our circle while they looked on in disbelief," he says.

More recent On On venues, apart from Samson's, tend to be Irish pubs such as Crazy Patrick's and McDuff's, where a few drinks are typically had before the r*n. "The Hash now has quite a few Italians, but they are rebels enjoying the break from mainstream Italian culture," says Bwana. "Hashing is never likely to attract the majority of expats in Milan, and RMBH3 will stay a relatively small Hash because many expats have become totally absorbed in the local culture, including the 'image consciousness' of Italians. They become more Italian than the Italians themselves and are often openly critical if they find us doing our circle in some quaint village square, or singing hymns in a local trattoria after the r*n. Italians find these parts of Hashing hilarious – once they discover we are not dangerous football hooligans, they usually join in the singing and post-Hash party. Good food, wine and lots of singing – this is the flavour of Milan Hashing."

No Man is an Island.

On January 30 1967 at Cape Kennedy, the Apollo space mission started off on the wrong foot, the last reported words of the astronauts being, "Get us out of here," as Apollo 1 burnt on the launch-pad.

Across the oceans in Cyprus, a more successful launch was taking place, although arguably with more hot air. The second European chapter, and possibly only the fourth outside of Malaysia, was to be Dhekelia H3. So Cyprus – which had been inhabited for 7,000 years since the Bronze Age – was about to take a step backwards in evolution, and became host to Europe's longest continuous-r*nning Hash.

Going back to World War 2, Cyprus was under British protection. However it was granted independence in 1960 after a brief guerilla war, a power-sharing arrangement between the island's 130,000 Turks and 590,000 Greeks being the cornerstone. Some people are just not supposed to share a bed together and, within four years, the UN had sent a bunch of peacekeepers in to referee the ensuing shitfight. The Brits had wisely retained sovereignty over their two military bases – at Dhekelia and Akrotiri – all the while.

That eager young military commando, Ray Thornton, got his marching orders from London to Dhekelia in 1967. He had Hashed in Singapore and Kuching before. Just a couple of weeks later, with a little more time on his hands, Thornton sorted out the lie of the land – there were no pubs around and the garrison was miles from everywhere. A bleak outlook.

As a junior officer, he went prudently cap in hand to outline his plans for a Hash kennel to his senior officer who was Deputy Commander, British Forces in Cyprus. In other words, a big shot. "We had a great commander in that place, one Brigadier Gris Davies-Scourfield who had to approve the formation of such a thing," recalls Thornton. "But his response was to agree straight away and appoint himself a founder JM, and a very good JM he was too." Phew! That didn't go too badly, then. Davies-Scourfield had not Hashed elsewhere previously. "Who had, in those days?" asks Thornton.

"We took our beer from one of the Dhekelia messes and borrowed a three-tonner to get us all out and back," says Thornton of his Monday forays. Garo Choporian, Armenian t-shirt maker to the gentry, joined virtually at inception, while others performed musical chairs around him. One of the first to rotate was the boots-and-all JM, Davies-Scourfield, who was posted within six months of his first Hash to another garrison on the other side of the island, at Episkopi.

At the same time, the peaceniks were gathering momentum. The Beatles ruled the airwaves with All You Need Is Love. The Stones competed sonically with Ruby Tuesday. Supersonically, the world 'ooh-ed and ahh-ed' as the Concorde airliner – the FRB of passenger aircraft – was unveiled for the first time.

By 1968 the arranged marriage of the Cypriots was on the rocks, and the Turks set up an 'autonomous administration' in the north of the island. It's been a ding-dong battle ever since, ensuring a steady supply of military Hash recruits.

In 1975 the island was divided into two states, the Republic of Cyprus and the Turkish Republic of Northern Cyprus. Despite the reduced deployment of British Forces on the island, the club remained staunchly a 'military-style' Hash. It therefore had trouble attracting hounds from the local expat population, mainly retirees looking for something a little more free and easy.

An ex-officer and long-term resident of Cyprus arrived around this time, going on record only on condition of anonymity [Don't worry, we'll *all* still be anonymous after this book comes out! –ed.]: "Shortly afterwards, I was encouraged to join the DH3. As a former officer, I thought this was most appropriate. The Hash was billed as a 'male bachelor officer-only r*n', a garrison Hash within the British Sovereign Base area, in keeping with the true traditions of the Hash."

He found that of the 10-15 r*nners, only two were actually serving officers. One of those retired within a couple of weeks, and the other transferred a year or so later, leaving a majority of civilian school teachers – who locally are accorded officer status – in the pack. "As a majority, they regulate the Hash around the frequent school holidays, when they zoom off the island in pursuit of other interests," says our man on the ground.

"The smallest Hashes I recall – always at holiday time – comprised Garo Chaporean, a British pilot and myself. Garo would attend to the BBQ, one of us would lay the trail, and the other would find it! [Hey, I could be an FRB there! –ed.] At times, the three of us would declare a Hash away-day, r*nning with the Larnaca H3 instead, but getting a signed certificate from their Hash Master stating the DH3 hadn't defaulted – we were 'on' that week!"

He proposed the insular kennel – which was "so bloody pretentious"– should open itself to all comers and save itself from extinction. Especially with quite a few other Hashes now on the island to compete with. Reluctantly after much discourse it was agreed to state that Dhekelia H3 were a 'gentleman's Hash', to try to attract more un-entitled outsiders. "Whether they were a 'gentleman' was to be defined by any potential new members having to be introduced by an existing member, for them to be vetted and approved by the others." The decision was also made to change Hash night from the sacred Monday to midweek Wednesday, and their next ploy was to try an "open Hash special" – to allow Unmentionables to r*n. "I believe that on the first r*n there was one female; on the second special, two or three came along with the kids."

"As you may gather, I feel pretty emotive about all this," says our mole. "The DH3 is the oldest continuous-r*nning Hash in Europe. They couldn't wish for a better lineage," he says of founding members, Thornton and Davies-Scourfield.

"Dear old Garo still toddles along when he remembers!" he says of the kennel's long-suffering stalwart, a figurehead of continuity in an otherwise rapidly rotating membership over the years.

The Old Man Down the Road.

Episkopi H3 – the third-ever European chapter, and about the 20th worldwide – was kicked off on November 13, 1967 by Davies-Scourfield, who had just transferred to this other garrison on Cyprus after his brief stint at Dhekelia. He was to become Brigadier Gris Davies-Scourfield, CBE [You'd have to be a British military officer with a name like that –ed.].

A month later, the first heart transplant was performed by Dr Christiaan Barnard in Cape Town, South Africa. This gave Hashers hope as they tackled the rugged countryside in the Limassol-Pissouri vicinity of the garrison, chests heaving to breaking point under sweaty t-shirts. With their military origins, and a will to be true to the grand Hashing tradition, they are a men-only kennel, and have not missed a Tuesday since inception.

On record-keeping, Tom McSherry says: "In the early days they did not seem to deem this a very important activity and some of those records are quite sketchy." However they do have some living history in the form of Jack Blocki, an impressionable young man who drifted into this rabble early on. Carbon dating puts it around 1977. "I never believed it could be done in more than 40 degrees," Blocki says. "Nearly died, if it wasn't for the beer!" However, the chilly winters were another story, and he was nominated Hash Ash, keeper of the fires lit in the local *bondu* (bush) which harboured the notorious thorns – known to Hashers as 'JC' – slashing legs and arms with each passing. "Not that we are religious, but each dash through them causes shouts of 'Jesus Christ!'"

Gordon Casson, Peter Robinson and Barney Bruce were also early internees and long-term inmates of this kennel. Despite the likes of them setting low standards and failing to achieve them, the 'officers and gentlemen-only' code was still in place. Honorary Gentlemen were only allowed as guests if they were regular r*nners with another Hash.

In the late Eighties, at the ripe old age of 75, Blocki notched up his 1,000th trot with the kennel, the local museum expressing interest in him for their ancient history section. In 1987 there was a particularly memorable r*n, when both hares went missing in action on the trail. The *bondu* had swallowed them up. A search party was duly launched, and after a late-night search effort, one of the hares was found in the bedroom of the wife of his mate. A particularly good effort considering Episkopi r*n on Tuesdays at 3:30pm in summer, and half an hour earlier in winter – indicating that most of the Hashers are either retired or unemployable [I imagine the latter –ed.]. In fact, Episkopi hounds are mainly part of the expat British community that lives locally, averaging 40 to 50 per r*n, and the Keo flows freely.

Unlike their insular friends down the road at Dhekelia, EH3 is much more open – relatively speaking – with family away-days in spring and summer, the odd street party, and away-weekend celebrations. But some still see Epi Hash as exclusive and a bit "us and them".

Because of these extra events and r*ns, EH3 now have numerically more Hashes under their considerably expanding belt than Dhekelia. Their 2,000th celebration is scheduled for Easter 2004.

In the last few years they've even started producing a magazine year book. Perhaps this is so that old farts such as Jack Blocki, Richard Stenton, Brian Liddell, and Pat Craft will somehow be able to account for their misspent lives. "Wouldn't miss it for a fortune," is how Blocki sees his Hashing days r*nning with Nicosia, Dhekelia and Episkopi kennels. "But sadly it has become more of a race than the noble art of bringing everyone to the beer within a few minutes."

Many of the hounds remain retired on Cyprus. Others return to the Old Dart, where they have an Episkopi Exiles Hash which meets once a year in the south of England for a family Hashing weekend.

Harriettes will be pleased to know they can get a regular r*n with the third kennel to be set up on the island at the Agios Nicolaos British base. The Polygon H3 (named for the shape of its home base) was founded in the early Eighties by two Hashmen disillusioned by not being able to take their wives or girlfriends [Or both? –ed.] on a r*n.

This island of just 3,572 square miles is also home to the Larnaca, Amathus, and Nicosia kennels which all started in the late Eighties.

So that bloke Thornton has a lot to answer for.

Meanwhile, Back On the Mainland.

In September 1971, American President Pinocchio Nixon realised this whole automotive caper started by Henry Ford had got out of hand, and signed a bill to cut auto fumes by 90 per cent in the next seven years.

Over in the land of Volkswagens – a car designed on the bug-eyed facial features of Marty Feldman – Lübbecke H3 in Germany was the first modern diagnosed case of Hash outbreak on the mainland of Europe. Lübbecke is in the federal state of North Rhine-Westfalia and was home to a British garrison until the late Eighties.

"On arrival at HQ 2 Division in Lübbecke I founded the Lübbecke Hash," says that intrepid military gypsy, Richard McAllister, who had earned his Hash wings floating beer cans down the river in old Brunei Town.

"The Headquarters Mess was above the small town of Lübbecke, a typical north German town with a very limited British military population – just the Headquarters and Signals squadron and transport support. The Mess was a splendid building which Hitler had used as quarters for his Hitler Youth training staff. It was set on the hillside of the Teutebergerwald, a long range of hills including the strategic Minden Gap. The main ridge was heavily wooded and a great favourite for German walkers." For Lübbecke r*n #1, a stockpile of

Lowenbrau and Becks beer was brought in as reward for the new boots, who eagerly piled into it after their first taste of Hashing.

"They thought we were mad, of course," remembers McAllister of the local townsfolk's reactions. "By and large there was so much ideal Hashing territory around the mess that most r*ns started and finished there. Occasionally we would go further afield in which case a car would be loaded with the necessaries." McAllister's brand new Rover 2000 TC proved to be more of a chick-magnet than his old Ford Popular. As it happened, his wife-to-be was teaching at a British school just a few miles from Lübbecke. Hash Pash's, evening events which included partners, were a big part of the social life.

Further south in Munich that year 6,750,000 pints of beer – along with two million sausages – were variously poured and stuffed down throats at Oktoberfest [Sounds like a mixed Hash On On On –ed.]. Along with the purpose-built *Bier Leichen Zelt* – literally 'beer body tent' – it is clear that Germans were born to Hash. And as if the beer were not enough, Lübbecke is also famous for its schnapps, such as Doornkaat and Steinhager.

But this was not a happy time for Germany, economically rising phoenix-like from its smouldering Gothic architectural ashes. The notorious Baader-Meinhof Group, the Red Army Faction and the German Socialists Students Union all managed to provide enough smokescreen so the Hash could r*n undisturbed. Chancellor Willy Brandt sought reconciliation with Eastern Europe, signing a treaty with Russia.

A little later, there was some redeployment from the East, and a number of boots who'd previously been exposed to the garrulous Singapore Hash found their way to Lübbecke. As usual, the Hash thrived on mayhem and adversary, and the hares proved up to the task of some tricky Teutonic times. "The Lübbecke hounds paused around the gate leading to the GOC's house," recalls McAllister of one particularly memorable r*n. "They could see the trail went in through the front door but didn't believe it so they went next door to the mess, while the hares and GOC enjoyed their beer. Only the non-appearance of the hares and beer encouraged them to knock on the General's door!

"I was in Lübbecke for two years before going to Northern Ireland where Hashing was certainly not on the menu," says McAllister. While Lübbecke flourished on trail for a few years, they subsequently sank without trace partly due to the decision to scale back deployment of troops east of the Suez by 1972. "I have no records as they were left with my successors," McAllister rues after his 1973 departure.

It Helps To Be a Little Cuckoo.

Over the border from Germany lies Switzerland, best known for multi-bladed pocket knives, cuckoo clocks, triangular chocolates and cheese fondues. And dodgy bank accounts [As if any Hasher has two beans to rub together –ed.].

While the notoriously neutral Swiss decided against joining the United Nations, they were happy to have a number of UN bodies set up in Geneva. In 1971, the World Economic Forum moved into Davos. That same year, government elections were held at which it was decided that Unmentionables could vote – and even get elected! – at a Federal level. Nasty right-wing factions emerged which touted a curb on foreign workers and aliens in Switzerland, rightly fearing the undesirable likes of Likk'mm moving in.

One former KL Hashman, Werner Krebs, managed to slip through the net and moved to Switzerland in 1972. Showing massive creative flair, it was decided to call this kennel – wait for it – Swiss H3. It was based in the Lucerne area.

At the same time, Switzerland developed another tourist attraction called the Bare Mountain Walker [That's a BMW I haven't heard of before –ed.]. Hikers, tourists and day-trippers in the Alpine trails near the village of Kerns would often be surprised by this naked apparition, clad only in straw hat and tennis shoes. As suddenly as he had startled them, he would disappear into the rocks and hills. Funnily, he and Werner Krebs were never spotted in the same room together.

Switzerland being the birthplace of the fun-loving bohemian Calvinist movement, it was natural that Hashing, once introduced, would spread like a nasty rash from a Reeperbahn whore. But no. Swiss H3 fizzled after five years. In true Swiss style, all records were meticulously shredded to protect the identity of those involved. Well, almost all documents. One Joseph Felber – who was probably On Sex – of Buochs in Switzerland was listed as the Swiss H3 contact in one of the world's first Hash magazines.

A follow-on group emerged in the early Eighties, comprising about six Hashers (mostly exiled from Penang, or Malaysia at least) and scattered throughout Switzerland. The group folded as they got older and the drinking interfered with the distances they had to travel between them. One of these players was The Incredible Hulk. Subsequently, Lucerne was then 'on' again, and Hashed for four years without anyone even knowing about them (well, apart from local villagers a little perplexed by the accented calls of 'ON ON, On On, on on, n, n,' echoing through their valleys).

Behind the Iron Curtain.
Going back to 1941, Adolf's mob and those unstoppable war heroes, Italy, got together and sliced up Yugoslavia, ruining a perfectly good afternoon. The slice – which looks more like a rather messy hatchet job – they called the Independent State of Croatia. Five years later it became a republic within federated Yugoslavia. But this wasn't enough and they still wanted more autonomy, creating internal conflicts.

Zagreb H3 – in what is now called Croatia – was the next kennel on trail, amazingly behind the formidable ideological Iron Curtain. A New Year's Eve party in 1974 was where Peter Armstrong and Paul Redmond met and, in the process of getting to know each other, found out that not only had they both lived in KL before, but both had r*n with the Hash there. It was immediately decided to get Croatia on trail.

Having shaken off their New Year's Eve hangovers, and dying to do it all over again, Armstrong and Redmond got this small chapter going on January 2

1975. Their first r*n was from the top of a road called Pantovcak. A large percentage of its pack were local booze-hounds who were on trail from the start. Nikola 'Sir John Shooter' Strelar joined on the third r*n.

Speaking of legless, the country's leader Tito shuffled off to the big brewery in the sky in 1980. Now the gloves were off, and the Serbian leaders were trying to stare down the Croatians who wanted no part of this. Ten years later the commies were defeated and Croatia moved to secede from the federal republic. Then the ethnic Serbs within Croatia threatened to secede from an independent Croatia. A punch or two was thrown, some nasty names called no doubt. Then the federal government ordered Yugoslav troops to disarm paramilitary groups in early 1991, and stoic Croatia gave them the big greasy middle finger once again.

Croatia declared independence on June 25. Over 10,000 people had given up their mortal parking spaces. Those nice chaps with the blue berets were called in at the start of 1992 to referee again and two years later a ceasefire agreement was reached. After the fighting was finally over in 1995, the UN retained the capital Zagreb as its regional headquarters. Always good news for recruiting Hashers. Zagreb H3 organised the 1995 EuroHash.

Veteran Dutch Hasher, Blimey – having been kicked out of several cities from A to Y – ended up in the last possible alphabetical refuge, Zagreb. As perhaps no clearer indication of how far *perestroika* has come, their RA, Bummer McAgram, livens things up by dressing from head to toe in a fluorescent hot pink outfit for any big event or special occasion [I know the name of a good shrink –ed.].

A regular pack of about 20 is still 'on' these days, enjoying a regular Hash program plus social away Hashes – such as cruising the stunning Dalmatian coast and Hashing many of its 600 small offshore islands. One of their traditions is that each January 2 there is a r*n from the original starting point at Pantovcak, to honour that first trail of their founders, whose subsequent fate is unknown. Sir John Shooter still goes through the motions as the kennel's longest-serving Half Mind.

Land of the Midnight Fun.
Meanwhile, a bit to the north and to the left, the first of the Scandinavian chapters to form was in the capital of Finland [Cue Monty Python song –ed.], Helsinki.

Finland – or *Suomen* as the locals call it – also has a history as chequered as the Croatian flag. Interestingly, the area where modern Finland stands was settled about 10,000 years ago by tribes from Asia [That would explain the, er, blonde hair and blue eyes –ed.]. Then in 1323 the treaty of Pahkinasaari made them a part of Sweden for 500 years which they were no doubt absolutely thrilled by. When it came to the Great Northern War, which ended in 1721, the Swedes showed their gratitude, respect and friendship by ceding Finnish Karelia to Peter the Great [Modest Hash Handle! –ed.] of Russia. During the Napoleonic wars, Russia – having seen the beautiful Finnish womenfolk – said 'We'll have more of that' and annexed the rest of Finland. It was only after the

Russian Revolution in 1917 that Finland got independence and became a republic, nestled side-by-side with the big Russian bear.

The year was 1977 and Juhani 'Screw My Bike' Vanska – who had started Hashing when he was with the Finnish Embassy in Washington, DC – suffered severe salmon withdrawal symptoms and moved back to Finland. He, Ulf 'Dirty Old Man' Burmeister, and Osmo Jalovaara – who between them had Hashed in Singapore and Washington DC – kicked off Helsinki H3.

At that time Screw My Bike was still doing his national service, so Dirty Old Man – a respectable figure in the financial world – had to arrange his evening pass so he could leave camp to attend the Hash r*ns.

For his part, Dirty Old Man reflects: "Our biggest obstacle was overcoming the competitiveness of the Finnish people." He had started Hashing when the DC kennel had only about 100 r*ns on the board. "I modelled everything on DC. It was a gentlemen's club then … no Down Downs, and very close to having black tie dinners sometimes. But we had our AGMs and they lasted forever," he says, his weather-beaten face crinkling round the eyes.

As with most Hash chapters, there were a few expats at the beginning – but Helsinki managed to rope in no less than the Norwegian and Canadian Ambassadors. "The Norwegian was a very shy guy and didn't fit in," he remembers. "Then we had the cold winters in the early Eighties which were down to the –30s." While this didn't dampen the spirit of the Hash, Screw My Bike moved off to America again in 1981 just to be on the safe side.

Around this time, a happy accident led to a new tradition. "For Helsinki's 500th r*n," says Dirty Old Man, "I had two secretaries working overtime to mail out to *every* club and Hasher around the world to join us. And only *one* foreigner came – French Kiss, a French Canadian lady. It was the first special occasion we allowed females. The spouses were still there in the sauna when we finished, so we said to French Kiss, 'You've got 15 minutes'. Then one of the guy's wives said 'If you don't go in now she'll never come out'. So we all piled in – the first *mixed* sauna!"

Over the years, nothing much has changed with this 'traditional' chapter. Helsinki H3 celebrated their 25th anniversary in 2002. Still men only. Still r*nning hard 10 kilometre trails, with Screw My Bike back in the fold again. "Now, we have very few expats," observes Dirty Old Man. "Of the active members, zero." And they don't come more active than him: "I've been GM since the beginning but they refuse to change me. I have tried but they just give me a Down Down," he says.

Another bunch of lively Scandinavian wankers is Helsinki H5. This kennel rose from the ashes of the old *mixed* Helsinki Hash House Harriers. "When I kick-started this mixed Hash I changed the name into H5 as it wasn't 'Hash logic' to have two kennels with the same name in one city," says Dutch ringleader, Blimey.

Started from his house in 1992, Helsinki H5 now claim to be the only Hash in the world with a mixed sauna after *every* r*n. Finding saunas large enough for the pack, which averages up to 40, can be a bit of a challenge and this dictates the sites for their more leisurely five or six kilometre trails.

They only once had to throw out a Hashman who seemed to think it was open season in the sauna. But several Hashmen have been known to cross their legs and clasp their hands in front, surrounded as they are by glistening Scandinavian female forms.

Needless to say, they get a lot of visitors. But their biggest drawcard is their Hole in the Ice escapade, staged each February since Blimey introduced it in 1993.

Revolta, from England, talks us through it. "It was between minus nine and minus 14 degrees Celsius outside at night," he remembers. "After the r*n, you go into a sauna then out into this hole which is about two metres round. The water is about minus five! I got in up to about here," he motions at shoulder height, "before everything was saying 'It's time to get out now'. Then it's back into the sauna and repeat procedure. Plus, there's no hats and gloves in the circle. Next time I'll bring my *apres* ski boots because all the heat escapes through your feet in the circle."

"Picture 85 Hashers," says Obscene Sex Craver from Milan, "r*nning totally starkers from the sauna into the ice. Every European Hasher should do it at least once," he enthuses.

But not everyone's a fan. "Noooooo way, I'd never do that!" says Wimpy Limpy, a thin-skinned Finn living in Frankfurt. One Hasher reportedly made himself very unpopular by attempting video close-ups of Hashers' pathetically shrunken and shrivelled members as they emerged from the ice one year [They weren't any more impressive after they'd thawed out, fellas! –ed.].

And the nudity doesn't stop there. On Helsinki Full Moon Hash – featuring a lot of the same, er, faces – there is no *r*nning* unless you're naked. They've had a couple of r*ns where the whole pack (usually about 10) was in the altogether. "In the Finnish summer it's not too hard to persuade people 'OK let's enjoy'," according to Dancing Queen.

But one place you wouldn't want to get naked in is Turku, which – being near the Arctic Circle in uppermost Finland – is the world's most northerly kennel.

It took a long time for Hashing to spread throughout the rest of Scandinavia. The first Swedish kennel kicked off in 1986, and the Danes and Norwegians were late to the party, starting only in 1989. However, it wasn't long before differences were set aside and the first Inter-Scandi Hash followed just a couple years later in Oslo, Norway, in 1991. The Europeans were also a little slow on the uptake, with Paris hosting the first EuroHash a year later in 1992.

Even Iceland was on for a while, thanks to Bill 'Wild Bill' Higgins, with the Fire and Ice Hash which ran from one of the US military bases there. But it melted into an amorphous puddle after Wild Bill left as they hadn't got a strong core of locals involved.

That's the Spirit.

Europe and Scandinavia have their fair share [perhaps more! –ed] of colourful characters and mad dogs. But as a kennel, the windswept town of Aarhus in Denmark, would make a great case study for a psychiatric convention. "Aarhus … in the middle of the street" are a real personality Hash, like Rumson and Hamersley in terms of visibility and, well, just getting the party swinging.

Denmark started as they planned to continue – the Danes had been seafaring warriors since the fifth Century. By the early 11th Century, the whole of Scandinavia and England were united under Cnut The Great [Great he might have been, but he couldn't spell for shit! –ed.]. Nothing much has changed, although these days they fly instead of row longships. And Danes sink two billion bottles of beer a year, making them sixth in the world order of beer drinkers.

Aarhus is roughly half way up Denmark and in the middle somewhere, overlooking some body of water. It's windier than Lord Spicy after a hot Indian curry and they have summers which soar to 17 degrees Celsius to look forward to all winter. No wonder they drink so much and have to Hash for their sanity.

They give Hashers the prefix of Sir when they reach 75 r*ns and Lord when they reach 100. For Harriettes, it's Dame and Lady, respectively. Their previous Hashit was the Brick of the Week, which was a big foam square painted to look like a brick wall and worn on the head. But their ultimate Hashit for really screwing up big time is to get the pack to form two lines, each with a beer-filled sock, then the offending Hasher has to crawl down through the lines as they whack him/her with their soggy socks.

One of the biggest coups they ever pulled off was to bid for the hosting of the *German* Nash Hash 2000. The eagle-eyed will immediately spot what's wrong with the picture. Lord Soaked Arse takes up the story: "This fact has baffled a few people who have a geographical knowledge above the level of an American high school student. Since the mid-Nineties the *Danish* Aarhus Hashers had regularly bid for the German Nash Hash. This was first written off as joke and not taken seriously. But the Danes seemed determined and they escalated the campaigns and popularity year after year. This resulted in the scandalous voting at the 1999 German Nash Hash. Some mediocre German Hash had put up a bid and got about 30 votes. When the votes for the Danes were to be counted, almost all hands were up – and if it hadn't been for the courageous ballot counter who simply stopped counting at 29, the German Nash Hash 2000 would have been in Denmark. Some say he just got thirsty of all the counting and went for a beer."

To prevent this happening again, a couple of patriotic and nationalistic Aarhus Hashers sat down and formed the Flensburg H3 to r*n for the next German Nash Hash. And they proved their point: at the 2000 German Nash Hash the Aarhus Hashers didn't even attend, and the Flensburg HHH took the German Nash Hash 2001 home with them. "The mismanagement was appointed and after a thorough search for a suitable site they settled upon Ry in Denmark," says Soaked Arse, cheekily. "What more cruel revenge could have been invented for the Danish Hashers? Not only did the Danes lose the

GNH2001 to Flensburg HHH … Flensburg HHH rubbed the defeat in the face of the Danes by saying 'Lets do it in their own backyard!'"

Eagle-eyed Hashers would note a lot of facial similarities between the Aarhus hounds and the Flensburg hounds. However, Aarhus deny this implicitly, pointing to the separate entity of Flensburg: Every Hasher in FH3 has a German-sounding Hash handle, for instance. But linguistic deduction pointed to the fact that Charlie Brown became Carlheinz Flottenheimer, The Last Boyscout became Pfadfinder, BoneUs became Sparpreis , Viking Puker became Kotzer, Soaked Arse became Nasser Popo, and so on ... An elaborate ruse, but, as anyone would tell you, real German Hashers have English Hash names. Just ask The Wolf. Or Pink Panter.

The German tax on beer and wine is lower than Danish taxes. For that reason many Danes often go to Germany – preferably to Flensburg – to buy Danish beer cheaply and re-import it to Denmark. The most popular strong beer in Denmark is the (Blue) Ceres Royal Export. Ninety per cent of the production is exported, only to be imported again by thirsty Danes, mainly Hashers. "Due to this traffic the Flensburg H3 actually has done quite a few r*ns," says Lord Spicy, referring to the practice of any member visiting Flensburg grog-shops having to do a 'trail' around the carpark. "Unfortunately no one has been able to keep a number on them, so the actual number of r*ns is not known. There is a very relaxed attitude to the administrative tasks in FHHH," he says, probably unnecessarily.

Aarhus these days is also home to the berserk warriors known as the Full Moon Howling H3. Who look remarkably similar to the Flensburg Hashers. Who look remarkably similar to the Aarhus H3 Hashers. Still, Aarhus were the first kennel to hijack another country's Nash Hash.

With all that time spent boozing rocket fuel in the pub, no wonder colourful kennel names abound throughout Europe and Scandinavia. These include: West Zealand H3, Denmark, who call themselves the Lav-Fart Vikings (which actually means 'Slow Journey' in local parlance, although their logo does depict a beer drinking viking on the 'throne'); Athens Honeys and Twin Cheeks Moonshine H3 in Athens, Greece; Riga Beerslayers H3, Latvia; Warsaw Not So Serious H3, Poland; the Honourable Hot and Horny in Hungary HHH and Harriettes (H8) now unfortunately extinct, Monteith Mini-Me H3 in Belgrade (UN Peace-keepers); FILTH (Fully Illuminated Luna®tics The Hague) Full Moon H3; Zagreb Strollers, Croatia; Gonad H3 (Going Nowhere Always Drunk) and ASSHOle H3 (Alicanta Sometimes Sober Hash Ole), Brussels; Nicosia Horrible H3, Cyprus; ASS (Amsterdam Sometimes Sober) H3; Bloovane H3, Adana Big Lick H3 and the Ankara Bastards Evening H3 in Turkey; Drunken Ramblers in Foreign Territory Every R*n (DRIFTER) H3 based in Germany (who only do away r*ns); and Copenhagen H3 who win the accuracy award with their nickname, The Viking Wankers.

Talking a Common Language.

Virgil, the great European philosopher who espoused the theory of Arcadia as Utopia, once said: "Why not go forward singing all the way. It makes the going easier." While there is no documented evidence to show he started an Arcadia H3, he certainly could've been a Hasher. But if it wasn't Virgil, perhaps someone else sowed the seeds of Hashing anonymously and mysteriously before.

"I was in a place called Fichtenau in Germany," says TNT from India, "200 miles north of Frankfurt. They have a r*n there – it's not a Hash, the r*n is 20 kilometres and the walk is 10 kilometres, and they come back and sit together and drink a lot of beer until late in the afternoon then they split. They have a mayor in charge of about 14 villages, then once a year all the villages get together like a Nash Hash. They are not aware of the Hash – they've not even *heard* of the Hash, but they do something very similar. Excepting the circle, everything is there including the marked trail." Must be a stray harriers offshoot.

A great story which is testament to the clandestine spread of the Hash involves Three Holes, who used to r*n many, many years ago in Kuala Lumpur. He was passionate about his Hashing, and meticulous about filing his Hash newsletters and memorabilia. He then returned to his home country in Scandinavia and got married, at which point he filed all his Hash stuff away as ancient history, a closed chapter of his life. Nearly 30 years later, he was in his boss's office and saw a Hash newsletter – he had no idea the Hash existed outside of Malaysia, nor that his boss was a keen Hasher. He's now back into it.

English Hashman Revolta – who has Hashed in 19 or 20 countries, "all but two in Europe" – also has a tale to tell about the value of working for a Hashman: "I was once working in Prague and doing nine to 10 hour days, six days a week. I needed a blowout," he says, "my brain was just shit." [Apparently inoperable –ed.] "So I told my boss I was going to Budapest Hash anyway and was not working the next weekend for *any* amount of money. We had a big argument – one of the reasons I'm called Revolta – and in the end he drove me down there, about five hours. He was a Hasher!"

"Hashing is a must," says Dirty Old Man, an ex-World Bank executive, adding some lofty perspective on the matter. "Business is just, er, … business," he says.

Likk'mm, generic Swiss Hasher, would surely agree. Although American, he has lived in Switzerland for a couple of decades, and managed 130 r*ns in the year 2000, including about 20 Hashes in 21 days based around the Tasmania InterHash. A prodigious traveller, many of his r*ns are 'away' r*ns in Europe and further afield.

Particularly with the new passport-free European Community, more venues are within easier striking distance.

An American Harriette now living in Germany, Two Holes, finds the accessibility particularly appealing. Speaking at UK Nash Hash in Winchester, England, she said: "One reason I've had more opportunities to travel is because I'm in Europe. When you're in the States, Canada, Australia, Russia, China you're so far away from so many places and the vacation time is more restricted, the expenses are higher. So now I'm somewhere where you can get cheap mass transit, centrally located, more vacation … that makes it easier for me to travel. I can see the world Hashing and I don't have to go on some kind of a boring tour with people that have nothing in common with me, that are a different age or whatever. I can go anywhere and there'll be a group of totally varied individuals from all over, and I want to go places that I would've never dreamed of going. One of the Hashes near Machu Pichu – I'd like to go do that. Maybe Asia. Coming from the Mid-West near the Canadian border, this is all so extreme. Most of my friends can't imagine even visiting me in Germany …"

Ironically, there are a lot of American Hashers in Europe, primarily involved through the military bases dotted all over the continent. This makes many of the kennels hard r*nning, hard living and certainly hard drinking. But the Europeans, and Scandinavians in particular, take it up that one crucial notch with the addition of spirits on top of the sacred Hash nectar, just for good measure.

High-octane aviation fuels such as aquavit, Jaegermeister, and schnapps are prevalent in Hashing circles here, and are thought to go particularly well with corn flakes at breakfast. A good example of this predominance of spirits is the practice of a travelling Hash started by Tone Deaf and his missus, Sofa. "We decided to call it AWOL H3... Absolut, Water Of Life. Sofa is Swedish hence the Absolut. I'm Scottish, we live in Italy, and whisky and grappa are called the same thing – *acqua vite* (water of life)," he says. "The Down Downs are Absolut vodka, whisky, grappa or plain water … one chooses what to drink, how much and the circle goes on until all four bottles are finished."

On Hashing culture, Easy Rider from Frankfurt says: "People assume that Germans are very conservative and when I go away to events such as UK Nash Hash I find out it's not always true – it's often the opposite."

"Germans think that the Englishmen are conservative," agrees veteran German Hasher, The Wolf, "and once you are here [UK] you see a lot of crazy Englishmen and probably the Germans are more conservative. Here the value of the Hash and the situation is quite a different one than in Germany. Germany just ignore the minorities, here it's part of society. Like Australia and New Zealand, it's part of daily life."

However, cultural differences are possibly no more extreme than two separated by a narrow strip of water called the English Channel. France is one of the bits on the map with relatively few H3 pins stuck in it.

There are four active Hashes in the Paris area, and only four or five throughout the rest of the country. Paris H3 had just over 500 r*ns on the board at press time, indicating a mere decade's worth of trail-sniffing in *la maquis* (the scrubby underbrush). But it hasn't taken off with the locals in France, like elsewhere – the hounds in France are notably nearly all expatriates.

Chris Destrieux was born in France (and subsequently resident in South Africa, New Zealand, Tahiti, Singapore and Australia) and, although not a Hasher, as an ex-journalist and travel marketer, is able to articulate his thoughts on French culture and the non-burgeoning of Hash in France clearly [Unlike most Frenchmen, and certainly unlike most Hashers –ed.].

So, is it just because the French don't like the British? "The French don't reject British stuff at the higher level," he says. "In fact amongst the bourgeoisie it has some cachet. There are a lot of British things the French have adopted such as tea, whiskey, pets and golf. But, as expats, they would tend to stick to themselves mainly because of the language factor," he surmises. "Also, French expats are not the most sports-minded people, so they wouldn't go out in the midday sun. Also they are traditionally not into clubs, and don't have that level of social cohesion the English have, with clubs and societies. They're very individualistic … it's an enigma … unlike the Germans who are more into the Anglo-Saxon things, and doing group things together. Food and wine are inextricably intertwined – the concept of 'going out on the piss' is not French."

Brian Gray, a once-avid Hasher now retired to France, says: "The Hash is Anglo-Saxon culture and humour. It is not intellectual – the French, because of their education, tend to intellectualise everything, even rugby. They have lots of alternatives, eg, cycling and tennis and basketball. At weekends they do lots of family things. They like to be dignified in their sports dress [Hey, I iron my t-shirt every leap year –ed.]. Hash culture is related to rugby culture and one would expect a Hash potential in South West France and … there is a Hash in Pau."

Indeed the Schlumberger company, headquartered in Versailles, has been indirectly responsible for propagating the Hash, with several kennels r*nning from its facilities in remote parts of the world. Interestingly, the French have also made a big contribution to Hashing in Africa, where large numbers of them still live and work in the ex-colonies. But, either they never return to France, or – when they do – they don't bring the desire to Hash with them.

The Wolf agrees that in France and Italy there are only a few Hashing spots, "but now East Europe is coming up," he notes. "Now it is open for us to travel there without a visa. Halloween at Dracula Castle was quite something, and then a weekend in Romania is so cheap. Going out to a disco in Frankfurt is more than spending a weekend in Transylvania."

Before a kennel was established in Bratislava, Slovakia, Vienna used to set r*ns there. Bratislava H3 was only officially set up post-communism, and membership has risen rapidly since, a pattern seen in many former communist bloc countries.

"As we grow older I have declared that we are the last resort of real sportsmen," says Dirty Old Man. But while Europe doesn't have the problem of ageing packs like most, because it is relatively new to Hashing, it does face problems of finding enough of the right people. Man in Black from Helsinki talks of recruiting virgins and the problems of keeping new recruits: "Only about one in 20 virgins stay – it takes a certain mind," he says [Don't you mean Half Mind? –ed.]. Likk'mm adds: "In Switzerland we have trouble getting people on the Hash because there is so much to do … movies, hiking, travelling to other parts of Europe. Plus, of course, the family thing." In his adopted home-town of Bern, their pack size is often in single digits.

Ironically, the notion of competing attractions also raises its head in several Eastern European countries, including Poland. "When I first started r*nning here in 1993 we regularly used to get 30 or 40 people," says Overdrive. "Now we get 12 to 15... although we did manage about 100 for our 1,000th r*n last September. I guess there are just too many other things going on in Warsaw these days, and yet the city is not large enough to have a big group of 'natural' Hashers." Gigolo, another Warsaw Hasher, says the place is "wild" since the political changes came in. Made up largely by expats, the pack is decreasing, "because there are so many other things to do in Warsaw now."

Hot Dog, an English lass working in Prague, points out that in many Eastern European countries, and in her own Hash in Prague, Hash membership is actually declining as there become more and more other things to do as these places develop. She also cites longer working hours as an intrusion.

Smurf from Brussels counters this. "The Hash does very well to keep it innovative and creative," she finds. As a result their pack sizes have grown from about 20 to about 35 in the past few years. She has recently been sidelined by bad knees but that hasn't stopped her. "I offered to lay three or four r*ns a year on my bike," says the Hash enthusiast and Belgian beer lover, even though she lives 25 kilometres out of Brussels itself.

But sometimes it's just a matter of size [As we Hashmen are told so often –ed.]. Tallinn, the capital of Estonia, attracts an average pack of about 15 Hashers. "Tallinn's a small town," explains American GM, G String. "We don't care if we get one or two people, just as long as we r*n."

And a lot of these new, emerging, and volatile marketplaces bring with them another problem of rapid turnover. "We have quite a high turnover rate with some Hashers only lasting a matter of months in Bucharest," says Big Mac. "Only two or three BH3 members have been with us from the re-start in 1999."

"The turnover is very high because of the international community," says Smurf. "So if you stay away six months there's nearly a complete change of faces," she notices. "They say 'Welcome, are you new?'"

Man in Black started Hashing about four-and-a-half years ago. "I went to a party at the British Embassy," explains the Finn, illustrating perfectly the lack of skill required, "and gave my card to the wrong guy so I got on the Hash list. Anyway, my boss was a Hasher so I thought 'Give it a go' … that's six countries and about 30 Hash clubs later." He likes Hash for its "lack of politeness. It's like what you do to your mates all the time," he says.

"Either you love the Hash or you r*n for your life," is how Estonian Harriette Infrequent Comer, puts it. She works for the European Commission and has been Hashing for a couple of years. "I turned up for a r*n, then not for the next two months, then ran, then not for two weeks. But I just introduced three friends last week and they loved it."

Icehole is a Harriette from Germany, now living in Helsinki. "Hash is a good way to meet lots of people quickly," she says. She was introduced by Greta Garbo, a friend of a friend. "She said 'It's sort of r*nning but not serious'. It was fun, really nice people and nothing too bad." She's now been Hashing for two-and-a-half years.

Doggy Style is a Scot living in Amsterdam, where he started Hashing. "It was a beautiful sunny day and I said to this guy from work, 'I wish I had something to do today' and he said 'I've got just the thing'. That was over nine years ago now."

Rug Burns, an English lass with the embassy is now based in Tallinn, Estonia. Previously she had Hashed in Turkmenistan, and has also lived in Kazakhstan, and other 'Stans' where there was no Hash. "I always saw it as an overseas/ expat thing," she says, in the courtyard of medieval old Tallinn. "I wouldn't have thought of Hashing back in England." Although the Hash in Tallinn is largely expatriate (Americans and Australians) she enjoys it as a way of meeting locals who become friends. "The Hash in Turkmenistan, and here in Estonia for that matter, was great in that it opened up a group of 'friends' and a social life immediately I arrived, which is terribly useful, especially when you are working alone and don't know anyone in the country," she says.

More importantly, of the value of Hashing in Turkmenistan, Rug Burns says: "It was also a great relief after the oppression of the week. Turkmenistan, being r*n by the megalomaniac dictator Turkmenbashi, was a very difficult place to work, very frustrating and oppressive. The Hash was a great escape from that. At least we didn't usually see the 20-foot pictures of Turkmenbashi peering down at us from every building when we were on the Hash."

Hashes tend to be mixed in Europe and Scandinavia. In fact, there are virtually no men-only chapters on the continent. Vodka Splite, noted party animal from Oslo, Norway, notes: "Hashing is exactly the same all round the world. But 'men only' is only good in Asia," he says, having spent a bit of time in Thailand. Part of the attraction to Man in Black is the mixed environment, and the mixed saunas afterwards. "Why would you want to r*n men only?" he asks rhetorically.

Disrespect For Authority.

"By the time I started Dhekelia H3, EOKA [pro-Greek terrorist organisation] had really given up," says Dhekelia H3 founder Ray Thornton. "However there was still a radical pro-Greek element abroad … I was required to clear each r*n area each week with the civil Chief of Police in Famagusta. When I once wanted to r*n in a rather difficult area, the head copper suggested we park our truck in the police compound at nine mile point. We did. It was a chilly night and the police sergeant in charge invited us in. 'The place is empty, he said, make yourselves at home, use the cells.' We did. An hour and far too much beer later our Brig JM came up to me: 'This guy has only got to lock the front door, ring up his boss and report 30 drunken British officers, say that he's captured the lot, and his future is assured. I think it was time I was off!'"

As this book went to print, talks were being held to end 27 years of division between Greek and Turkish Cypriots, so hopefully resolution is near. However, both sides were probably united briefly when InterHash came to Cyprus in 1996 – a common enemy they could agree on: "At the Cyprus InterHash, something like 240,000 tins of beer were drunk in six days," says Pissoles. That averages about 80 cans per person. He says the police turned up in force, expecting trouble a la Hell's Angels or football louts. "After two days they didn't bother turning up anymore," he says. "And we (the Hash) jealously guard that reputation."

On the European mainland, The Wolf from Germany has his say about the

Hash dealing with officialdom: "In Germany, we've had a little bit of problem with the media, mainly to do with the consumption of alcohol," he says. This seems a little hypocritical in the home country of Oktoberfest. "We are not doing any harm to anybody, no violence ... OK, we might drink more beer than the average but... we are used to drinking mainly beer because we want to have fun, have a good time, but we don't drink because we want to get drunk ..."

In Munich, "Police often come to investigate noise complaints," said one local Hasher. "But they end up taking off their hats and joining us for a couple of Down Downs." This seems to be a fairly common reaction in other German cities, too.

In Finland, where the first Scandinavian chapter kicked off, the Turku H3 hares were once suspected of laying dog poison – and were written up in the local press as such – when in fact they were just scattering their flour trail.

However, things weren't so simple when Zagreb H3 parted the Iron Curtain and had a good snoop around. On-going civil war in Croatia, and repeated breakdowns of ceasefires in the early Nineties, had made some Hashing territory – such as their favourite island, Hvar – out of bounds altogether.

One of their famous r*n-ins with the law actually happened in Poland sometime in the Eighties when the Iron Curtain still existed. "About nine Hashers went to Warsaw to join one of the special Warsaw weekends," says Blimey. "Two flew, and the others rented a minibus. Because of a fuel shortage in most of the communist countries they had to drive through, they decided to take a few hundred litres of diesel with them in jerry cans. These were put on top of their sleeping bags and other stuff, not aware of the fact that a number of the jerry cans were leaking all over their gear. The person who signed the contract for renting the car insisted on driving all the way to and from Warsaw.

He was so pissed when it came time to drive back to Zagreb on Sunday afternoon that he couldn't find his way out of Warsaw, so asked a traffic policeman for directions. Shortly after, the police stopped the minibus and the driver was arrested."

While awaiting the driver's fate, they had a couple of drinks in the Hotel Forum and, it so happens, met a high-ranking police officer who was a keen r*nner. They explained to him that they were r*nners as well and that the way from Zagreb to participate in a r*nning event in Warsaw, mentioning the plight of their arrested fellow 'athlete'. "After some hours this officer had arranged the release of the driver without a fine or other punishment. So the next morning after the driver was sobered up, they left Warsaw for Zagreb, where they arrived with a delay of only about 24 hours," says Blimey.

Nowadays: "There have been police checking, before anthrax and now," says Sharkfin, "but nothing bad ever happened, and we always make fun of it. Dogs are a greater danger when we r*n in remote areas."

The recent spate of anthrax scares has also set off alarm bells in other countries. Bergen H3 in Norway now has an official licence from the city police department to strew flour through the streets of their town.

Elsewhere in Scandinavia, the r*n-ins with authorities have been of a different nature. Copenhagen's 1,000th r*n coincided with the official state visit of US President, Bill Clinton. So, naturally, a big banner was hung up in the street saying, 'Even Bill Clinton's coming back for the Copenhagen 1,000th!'. On the r*n itself, his effigy was proudly displayed and carried along in the pack. The organisers reportedly received a fax from the White House politely asking 'What the fuck is going on?' or statesmen-like words to that effect.

But the one common battle in Scandinavia is against their notoriously stringent drink-driving laws [Why bother making Volvos so safe if you can't drive pissed? –ed]. In Denmark, Loping Scrotum – who lives in rural North Zealand but commutes to Copenhagen for his r*ns – says: "There is not much beer because nine out of 10 people drive to the r*ns and there are strict drink driving laws ... 0.03 you go on probation and 0.05 you lose your licence. So for a guy like me even one beer I have to think about not driving for the next one or two hours," says the wiry Dane who spent time in Vietnam. "Sometimes maybe five people will share like one can for the Down Down."

On the subject of legless, mines are a scourge through parts of Europe and Eastern Europe that have gone through conflicts and battles in the past few decades. Sarajevo (now the capital of Bosnia) is no stranger to danger. The assassination of Archduke Francis Ferdinand here in 1914 led to World War 1. Showing no guts at all, Sarajevo H3 went defunct during the latest war, and restarted again in 1997, thinking the coast was clear and it was safe to come out of their bunkers. "Almost all the r*ns were in the city," says G String, a US State Department official. "'Cause outside of that you don't know where the mines are – about two million mines were left around Sarajevo."

Mines also affected Belgrade H3 in Yugoslavia. They disbanded in 1991 because of the increasing incidence of hares being harassed and often beaten up, "and inadvertently straying on to minefields," adds Likk'mm for good measure. Also in Yugoslavia, two hapless Hashers were arrested for carrying some 'technical equipment' in their car, which was mistaken for espionage gear. Hashers around the world were alerted to their plight and emailed the authorities to rally for their cause several years ago. Sensibly, they now have a Belgrade Exiles H3 that meets in different European locations every two years.

For all that, though, Wormcrusher – an American in Yugoslavia who came close to stepping on a mine found on the slippery path outside their compound – talks about Europe overall being nice and relaxed when it comes to the big issue of Hashing and authority: big groups drinking in public. "In the US when you see the cops you have to hide the beer," she says.

The Iron Curtain coming down has freed up a lot of activity and made things easier for Hashers. In Bucharest H3, Romania, membership was limited to expats only for security reasons as On Ons were invariably held in embassy grounds, and most Hashers were on diplomatic service. "I recall hearing tales of the Securitate (evil state security force) attempting to follow Hashers on trails around the city in pre-revolutionary Romania," says Big Mac.

In the new Slovakia, the Hash is also on the rise: "I guess you could say that without the fall of communism there wouldn't have been anybody to establish the Hash in Bratislava, so attendance rose infinitely," says Jim Gladstone. "The only problems with authorities that we have had are with the *babickas* [old housewife types] who yell at us for wasting flour."

But nowhere was the Hash more acutely aware of the perceived oppression to its freedom than in the Commie grand-daddy of them all – Russia. In September 1984 Hashing in Moscow was well supported by many of the embassy staff and private sector business. This took pack sizes up to about 80, terrorising the streets of Moscow on a weekly basis. Especially as their r*ns were at peak hour, with heavy traffic, the Soviet Ministry of Foreign Affairs conveniently saw it as an accident waiting to happen. The Ministry then 'suggested' (as only the Russians could) that the r*ns should be held only in the beautiful and spacious Gorky Park area.

This was taken out of context by the foreign media, and next thing the Moscow Hash was all over the TV, radio and press as having being corralled and curtailed by the Russian authorities. In London, many sympathetic UK Hashers – who were fed the misquoted stories – rallied outside the Russian embassy against the seemingly oppressive regime. In New York, Rumson H3 lent their voice with placards and chants outside the Russian embassy.

Soon after – whether directly related or not – came the edict from above that there was to be *no* drinking in *any* public place *anywhere* in the USSR. The Hashers were then forced to retreat to the sanctity of the embassies for their On Ons and ritual excesses.

The Moscow Hash were actually great supporters of the KGB … they thought it stood for 'Keep Getting Boozed'! Dirty Old Man, who Hashed in Moscow during Soviet times, says the oppression of the Hash is no longer. "That was the old days," he says.

Sensibly, some Half Minds in Prague decided this was a good time to start Hashing in Czechoslovakia. To be fair, much deliberation was done by founder Fantum and his wife – who had just come from six years of Hashing in Indonesia – before deciding to go ahead and lay a trail. Halfway through setting the first r*n, sure enough, the dreaded local police turned up for a question and answer session. They let him carry on, although they kept a beady eye on the group for months. Their Czech RA was almost arrested once doing his circle in the middle of Town Square. Gatherings of that nature were outlawed in those communist times, with several question and answer sessions reported.

"There have been so many incidents," says Bouncing Czech. "Like at the time of the anthrax scare, [some virgin hares] set the r*n on the Sunday and on the Monday in the newspapers appeared an item that in Prague 6, firemen and police had been called out to examine a pile of white powder but later discovered it was flour. On the Wednesday, Czech TV announced that someone in Prague 6 was still putting down white powder. But of course we knew it was put down on Sunday. The Hash was never caught, and we did not own up, of course! Since the Iron Curtain came down the effect on Hashing has been that people can r*n anywhere. Today there is no need to look over one's shoulders."

But they still have the odd r*n-in with the law: The pack had gone via bus to the r*n site in Budapest, and the bus had parked under a bridge on the freeway while waiting for them. Soon enough, a police car pulled up and two strutting officers got out. "You can't park here ... move on," they commanded the driver. The bus driver tried to explain he was waiting for the group, but the cops grew more threatening and officious. With that, one of the Hash group stepped forward, pulled out her Austrian diplomatic passport and thrust it in the face of the two officers.

"Do you know who I am?" the feisty Harriette barked.

"Er, yes," the officers quivered.

"Well, this bus is under instruction to wait here until we are finished and ready to go ... if you want to make trouble ..." With that the police just nodded and retreated back to their car with their tails between their legs. It turns out our heroine was a humble *secretary* at the embassy!

Iceman, the founder of Warsaw H3 in Poland, found that in getting the Hash off the ground there, the problem was not the law initially. "The year prior to me getting it up and r*nning a bloke called Andy Smith from the Brit Embassy tried to get one going but, on the day of the r*n, only he and two other blokes turned up, plus a mongrel dog. They still went for a jog, the dog tagged along and the poor pooch dropped dead of a heart attack half way round. Totally discouraged and depressed they gave up after that," he says. Around 1983, Iceman gave it a go. "The following year we started off with a pretty small bunch but we stuck to our guns. It was not unusual to have between 40-50 r*nners and sometimes more. We had an absolute ball and there was no trouble from the authorities until they got wind that their comrades-in-arms had banned similar gatherings in Moscow. So, we turned up one Saturday morning and there – looking rather threatening – were two burly coppers. The poor buggers tried to follow us around but became totally confused and returned to their vehicle to await our return. When the throng had gathered we offered them a beer (Foster's) and they were over the moon. By the time we left they had their jackets off and were doing Down Downs with the best of us. After that, it was always the same two blokes who turned up to report on our subversive activities – they eventually confessed that they never told their mates at the station about the free beer, food, etc. In those days a square meal washed down by several icy cold Foster's was beyond the wildest dreams of your average Pole. They were certainly fun days."

But perhaps the ultimate authority for many is God. And his representative on earth, the Pope. So, of course, to create the maximum potential for disaster Rome H3 – being good Catholics – r*n on a Sunday. In early 1987, they took the pack through a packed St. Peter's Square in The Vatican City where the Pope was saying mass, and subsequently invited the Pope and his cardinals to join them for a Hash. Surprisingly, they never turned up [Must have been piss-poor directions on the r*n sheet –ed.].

So instead they took the Hash to the Pope, repeatedly – one of the most memorable r*n-ins being at the first Italian Nash Hash in September '92 . "On our Hangover/Halloween r*n," says Efes, "the pack arrived in Vatican Square and – to our horror – found 100,000 pilgrims celebrating the beatification of four Spanish saints with His Holiness. Now imagine the scene … this is a fancy dress Hash so Hash flashers, nuns, transvestites and various animals are following flour through St Peter's as the service is taking place. Chaos ensues. The security service begins to round us up as disturbers of the peace. Luckily Crocodildo Dundee, dressed as an angel, produces his diplomat's immunity card and waves it at the police with the words: 'I am appealing to a higher authority (even than the Pope)'. With this we were ushered out of the Square to our On On," he recalls, still with great mirth and incredulity.

Great Danes and Dobermans, Dalmatians and Alsatians.

Wolfgang 'The Wolf' Gust.
First r*n Seoul H3, Korea 1972
Member Karachi H3, Pakistan; Oslo H3, Norway; Frankfurt H3, Germany

Seems like you've been Hashing for a hundred years, Wolf. Actually when and how did you start?
TW: I had moved to Korea and had a German shepherd puppy, training him on the weekend and ran into a bunch of expats, and I knew some of the faces. Monday in the office I called them up and said 'What was that all about?'. So next Saturday I joined them, and didn't stop r*nning since then in 1972. I was allowed to r*n with my shepherd.

Is that how you got the name?
TW: They started looking for a name, Wolfman, and Wolfman didn't mean anything to me – a famous American disc-jockey, Wolfman Jack. They thought my English is too poor and they just settle for The Wolf.

Then you moved to Seoul. How was that?
TW: I was GM in Korea – it was difficult because it was 99 per cent Americans and I think they wanted an American being their GM, then I moved back to Germany. There was no Hash at that time in Frankfurt. So I Hashed only when I travelled.

What about your time in Pakistan?
TW: It had a British influence – besides a lot of British guys, a lot of the Pakistanis have their British education, so I was again one of the outsiders. I had to improve my English. The best social life I had from all my foreign assignments was Pakistan … social life was excellent.

When was the first InterHash you attended?
TW: I attended the first InterHash in '78 and didn't stop visiting the InterHash since then, so I am one out of five who attended all InterHash events, the five Survivors.

Of all the InterHashes, which had the best memories? Or Mammaries?
TW: I remember about '78 more. One specific thing was in the very famous old Chinese Merchant Seamen Club, where they used to have the American

soldiers from Vietnam on the R&R mission and for years they didn't come anymore. Then the Hash came. And I talked to one of the Captains in the restaurant and he said 'Sir, it's the first time we had for many years smashing tables and chairs, beer flowing, body-surfing on the floor...' I met Chee Bye from PJ. The other thing is we went to the Chinese border, the Gurkha camp, and then '97 for the Handover of the Empire to the Chinese we visited that camp again and the memories came up.

With great guys like Chee Bye on board, I guess you don't see the Hash as just an eccentric expatriate pursuit anymore?

TW: No, possibly not. In Malaysia and Indonesia, every little village has a Hash. I just ran in Port Dickson, for instance, where it's 99 per cent locals. In Asia I try to stay with the locals. Of course, working for Lufthansa, I can meet my colleagues at the Goethe Institute or the German Consulate, but I mix with the locals.

So how many Hashes have you done now?

TW: I am reaching the 30 year mark, so I think I pass easily the 1,000 mark.

How many different countries have you Hashed in?

TW: More than 50. With a Korean wife, my second home is Korea. If I'm 50 per cent Korean there's not much time for Pakistan and for Norway. But I have good friends in Norway and I have been there two weeks ago and I will be going there soon again.

What have you got from these years of Hashing?

TW: In Korea I met my present wife, not exactly on a Hash but through a Hasher. The Dragon Lady was given her name on a train ride to Phuket.

Best time? (On the Hash I mean, not with your wife.)

TW: What comes to mind is the Inter-Scandick. I was the founder of Inter-Scandick in '91 in Oslo and we moved over to Tallinn in the early Nineties and hired a train which took us to Narva on the Russian border. Then when I finally reached the station of Narva, I relieved myself on the station building. I thought nobody saw it but the police were there and grabbed my passport. I was only rescued by the Dutch embassy [Blimey's best work –ed.]. Then we went to a sauna and my right heel disappeared into a sink which was covered so I had a very bloody injury. The wife of Dr Anderson, an American military doctor, saw it and called 'Jim, Jim, The Wolf is bleeding, The Wolf is bleeding,' and Jim came over and made his diagnosis. He looked me in the eye and said 'Wolf ... amputation or vodka?' 'Vodka!' 'OK, give The Wolf some Vodka.' Later I had a few more vodkas and we looked for a taxi and tried to explain where our hotel was – and actually we were just standing at the back side of our hotel! He only drove us to the main entrance. That was Narva. It was a KGB Sanitorium ... it didn't have guests for four years, we were the first.

How has Hashing changed over the years?

TW: Communication is much easier now. Even up to the early Nineties we had to make photocopies and send out faxes and mail information, or leave them. In Seoul we'd leave it at Chosun Hotel or US Kim Tailor Shop near to the US Army Base, where they were laughing 'Ha, ha, ha, the white man's Trash'. Now 99 per cent of Frankfurt we are on email.

Is Asia the spiritual home of Hashing?

TW: For me, Hashing belongs to Asia. I lived for so many years in Asia. My wife is Asian. I have been to so many countries off the beaten track – for me Hash is Asia. But look around in England, for instance, how many groups are existing. For years I always voted for Asia. For 2004 might be the first time that I vote for Cardiff.

Why is the Hash thriving in the face of increased political correctness and societal regulation? [Gosh, tough question for a Hasher –ed.]

TW: It's not a closed group. Hash is open to everybody. If somebody doesn't feel at home with a group then he stays away by himself. Very seldom a Hash has to kick out somebody … it never happens. Hash is not doing any harm to anybody, Hashers are happy with themselves. If there's newcomers they're welcomed by old farts. If I do something foolish, I know some friends there would protect me or tell me 'Wolf, you went beyond what you should have done'. Hashers do not create the problem – they might argue with the taxi driver about the fare, but that's the maximum. There's no physical violence on the Hash.

At EuroHash 2001 I went to the caretaker who did that for 25 years. He said 'At any carnival party or sports club, things are damaged … showers, toilets, lockers, vomiting – nothing at all, the cleaners had an easy job'. The only thing was spillage of beer and they had to wipe the floor. But we didn't do any damage.

So you're looking forward to another 30 years of Hashing, Wolf?

TW: In '95 I experienced a little problem with the ticker … maybe I should reduce the alcohol intake.

Paula 'Greta Garbo' Kankaanpaa.
First r*n Helsinki H5 1994

When, where and how did you first hear of the Hash?

GG: In 1993 in Malaysia. At that time I only heard that there's some guys r*nning in the rubber plantations outside of Kuala Lumpur. Stupid me, I didn't bother to find out more about it at that time … but one year later in Helsinki a friend of mine wanted to take me along.

How did you get a name like Greta Garbo?

GG: It was my second or third r*n and, for some reason, I got pulled front and centre many times. I wished not to get too blasted so I mumbled 'Leave me alone'. The RA of that time was a film freak and he recalled those lines being one of Greta Garbo's most famous ones …

Now that you're Grand Mattress you're probably getting even more blasted in the circle! How has Helsinki H5 changed?

GG: Our annual events have been growing towards more international direction, more participants, more fun. Internet has been playing part in this development. Hashers, I don't see that they have changed in spirit over these years that I've been involved. The same, keen [Talking about Hashers? –ed.]

Malaysia

The Selangor Club Chambers, aka The Hash House, where it all started over lunch in 1938. Thought to be the only remaining photograph of the original Chambers since records were trashed in World War 2. The building was demolished in 1974.

'G' Gispert, felt by many to be the real founder of the Hash House Harriers. He was killed in Singapore while serving with the Argylls. Remembered by Cecil Lee (bottom left) as having "a great sense of fun and humour but underneath noble instincts". Torch Bennett, the great organiser (bottom right).

Photo reprinted from On! On! Jubilee magazine

Photo reprinted from Singapore H3 1,000th magazine

▲ A Hash group after completing the first Malay Mail Big Walk, 1960. John Wyatt-Smith centre right.

Photo reprinted from On! On! Jubilee magazine

▼ Horse Thompson (centre) with some of the KL H3 Mother Hash committee, celebrating 50 years of Hashing in 1988.

Photo: New Straits Times, as reprinted in KLH3 3,000th magazine

NEWSFRONT

NST 28/4/88

Mother Hash turns 50!

By PAUL SINGH

KUALA LUMPUR: The oldest Hash Chapter in the world, the Kuala Lumpur Hash House Harriers or simply Mother Hash, is 50 years old.

Founded in 1938 by C.H. Lee, E.J. Galvin, H.M. Doig and A.S. Gispert at the Selangor Club padang, the "mother" has since given birth to 460 Chapters not only in Malaysia but all over the world.

Come June, Mother Hash will open its arms to all members of the 460 Chapters as it wants to relive its past and let them share the magic and experience of running with the original Hash Chapter.

There will be a grand celebration to commemorate its 50th anniversary.

Among the highlights will be a road relay around Peninsular Malaysia, involving some 1,000 runners, both local and from overseas, two celebration runs (to give the visitors a feel of how it is to run with the original Hash) and a host of other social activities.

The Hash House Harriers (HHH) is basically a social group, who meet once a week in the countryside to run for an hour or so following a paper trail that had earlier been laid by another member.

'Horse' Thompson (centre) with four committee members of Mother Hash

Singapore

John Gastrell (left), veteran of many good sessions at 'The Eyes and Piles' and Singapore H3 founder, Ian Cumming, after a trail through a Singapore kampong, mid-Sixties. *Photo reprinted from Singapore 1,000th magazine*

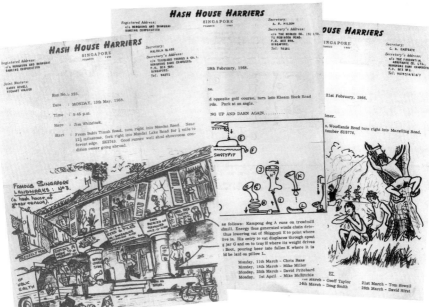

Singapore newsletters 1966-68. The word 'shiggy' first made its appearance in December '67. *Newsletters courtesy of Fred Whitaker*

Australia

Sydney H3 – invariably off the rails, but on track here in 1969. Barry Warden (FRB) Phil Costa (second) Jim Juniper (fifth)
Photo: courtesy Mike Miall & The Daily Mirror

◀

They caught the annual relay bug. Seen here at start of a Sydney-Bathurst r*n, 1969.
Photo: courtesy of Mike Miall & The Daily Mirror

▶

The world's first Hash shirt, belonging to Alan 'Easy Rider' Rider of Hobart H4. Note personal r*n record along bottom edge. "I realised this would end up a total mess, so I stopped."
Photo: courtesy of Alan Rider

▼

Europe / Scandinavia

The first Hash chapter on the European mainland, at a British garrison in Lubbecke, Germany. Founder Richard McAllister back row, right. ▶ *Photo: courtesy Richard McAllister*

◀ They don't call it the Manneke Piss statue for nothing! The Hash in Brussels had the honorary Hashboy pissing real beer. *Photo: courtesy of Higgins*

Fire and ice at Helsinki H5's annual Hole In the Ice extravaganza, where many a Hashman (like Schniedelwutz from Frankfurt) has been cut down to size by the freezing water. They thaw out with a mixed sauna. *Photo: courtesy of Schniedelwutz* ▼

United Kingdom

The pack from Longmoor H3 r*n #1, the first-ever Hash on English soil.
Prolific kennel-founder Richard McAllister is back row, left. Note doomed whitewash sprayer at right. "Utter failure, but useful in the garden."

Photo: courtesy of Richard McAllister

Mad Hasher's tea party at Westcombe Park H3, 1972. They are still not sure why they thought the dress code was 'fancy dress' and to this day they wear silly hats each outing. Still Hashing are Alan Gaunt (far left), John Ward-Turner (sombrero) and Mike Payne (lying on ground). *Photo: courtesy of John Ward-Turner*

Africa / Middle East

An early Durban H3 pack, featuring – gulp! – women and children. Hash Brat Wigless, the kid on the left, started Hashing because his dad, The Gent, couldn't leave him alone in the car park. *Photo reprinted from Durban 1,000th magazine* ▶

Here's mud in your eye! English Hasher Cock Sure receives a 'welcome back to Riyadh' in 1984. "That shit took some getting off!" *Photo: courtesy of Harry Shaw* ◀

Muscat H3's Bandar Jissa trail through the wadis was hot and dry but soon turned cold and wet when a navy landing craft plucked them off the shoreline. *Photo: Muscat H3 500th magazine* ▼

USA

The pack from r*n #1 in the United States, November 1971. Virgin founder Major Francis Arnold is centre left with hands in pockets.
Photo: courtesy of Francis Arnold
◀

One of the earliest American Hash trails through Fort Eustis, 1972.
Photo: courtesy of Francis Arnold ▶

The Rumson Hash display Hash solidarity at a protest in New York following the infamous Gorky Park Moscow H3 incident in 1984. A protest was also held in London. Communism and the Cold War ended shortly thereafter. *Photo: courtesy of Gil Jackson*

approach on r*nning, enjoying outdoors and most of all enjoying socialising... well, and maybe drinking beer … and everything else that comes with it: enjoying life!

You're having loads of fun, that's the main thing.

GG: One of the most enjoyable r*ns … as a result of the one particular r*n my washing machine got clogged from all the swamp filth and mud. Well, it was a r*n in Helsinki – 'organised' by three French Hashers to honour the French National Day in 1995. The whole world knows the organising skills of French, *excuse moi, j'aime tout mes amis Francaise, mais …*

I love it when you talk dirty, Greta. Do go on …

GG: The r*n was due to start at 4pm and the crowds were on the starting spot around that time. We were waiting a good while, but the hares were non-existent. Someone even took his car around to look for them without a result. It took more than one hour when the hares returned from laying the trail. So, finally the trail started – on and on and on we went … we toured over the hills, deeper to the forest and even more deeper to the forest, so deep that we didn't hear no traffic, no nothing. At that point the trail crossed through a muddy swamp – couldn't go under it, couldn't go round it, had to go through it! And, gosh, we had to crawl in the knee-high muddy water for about a kilometre before we finally got to dry land. Rest of the trail was boring, r*nning next to a motorway.

You've spent time in Malaysia. Does InterHash belong in Asia or worldwide?

GG: Worldwide. But all the anniversaries, ie, 70th year of Hashing in 2008 should take place in Malaysia.

Cor 'Blimey' Schouten.

First r*n Jakarta H3 1982
Founding GM Brussels Manneke Piss H3
Co-founder Abuja H3, Nigeria
Member Islamabad H3, Pakistan; Helsinki H3 and Helsinki H4, Finland; Lagos H3 and Lagos Thursday H3, Nigeria; The Hague H3 and Amsterdam H3, Holland; Zagreb H3, Croatia

I feel tired and thirsty just looking at that list, Blimey. How many r*ns?

B: I started Hashing 20 years ago … about 1,000 r*ns worldwide.

Talk us through some of the highlights with some of those chapters, starting with Islamabad.

B: We organised a Hash weekend in Hunza, Northern Pakistan, where we stayed in the Royal guest-quarters of the Mirh of Hunza (ie, the Aga Khan). Although Pakistan is a 'dry' country, our host – the Deputy Mirh – was very pleased with the champagne we brought him.

Then you spent some time in Finland, where you were very involved.

B: There used to be a mixed Hash – called the Helsinki H3 as well – which was not that active any more. Restarted the mixed Hash as Helsinki Hash House Harriers and Harriettes (H5) in December 1992 from my place, with the introduction of a *mixed* sauna after the circle activities. The H5 mixed sauna became world famous – at least in Helsinki. I was also founder of the annual Hole in the Ice' r*n in March 1993, and H5 celebrated the 10th Hole in the Ice r*n in 2002.

And around the same time, you instigated the first r*n in Estonia, correct?

B: I organised the first ever Baltic Hash r*n in Tallinn, Estonia, in March 1993. Then we organised a Gispert Memorial weekend in Narva, Estonia, in February 1996.

Tell us of your fun times in Africa.

B: Flying from Lagos to Abuja for the inaugural r*n, we had Down Downs at an altitude of 33,000 feet. A Hash record?

Yeah, give or take a few thousand feet. And you're planning something a bit more down to earth at the moment ...

B: Co-organising with Zagreb H3 at the moment the – as far as I know – first ever 100 per cent Hash cruise, in the Dalmatian Sea. The trip will take eight days (including 10 r*ns) and will bring the 90 participants to seven islands. Hashing only, and no sight-seeing tours planned. Three boats, all with their own draught beer equipment, are chartered for this trip.

Great Hash name – where did you get it?

B: Having lived in mainly former English colonies, it cannot be that difficult for you to guess. My Christian name is Cornelis which, at least in the Netherlands, means you're called Cor. When I introduced myself in Islamabad as Cor Schouten to one of the Brits he answered 'Cor what??? Ah ... forget about it ... Cor Blimey!' So it's been Blimey since.

Irena 'Bouncing Czech' Brichta.

First r*n Budapest H3 1991
Member Prague H3

Great Hash name, how'd you get it?

BC: Although I was born and brought up in the UK, when the Budapest H3 heard my parents were Czech ...

How did you hear of the Hash and what were your first impressions of it?

BC: I heard about it when I first went to live and work in Budapest in 1991 and was persuaded to go along. My first impression was I loved it; great people, great r*n, great atmosphere.

So you've done about 250 Hashes so far?

BC: With both Hash chapters – probably in total with away Hashes about 280.

Can you pick a 'best time' out of all of those?

BC: Very difficult to say – each r*n is unique and has its special points. Our annual Prague Hash weekend Saturday r*n is always great. Warsaw 1,000th r*n was great – flat! Waterloo r*n at 1997 EuroHash was great – hot and long! [How can that be 'great'? –ed.] Cambridge Grunty Fen 2001 was very, very flat – great! Finale Ligure Saturday r*n, 16 kilometres in October 2001 was stupendous! And the joint Sydney Hash r*n December 2000 was a winner! The beer is great everywhere, including Brussels. I love the Manneke Piss pissing beer – that is really special in his special Hash costume.

What's the main thing you've got from Hashing over the years?

BC: Some really great friends – it's great to visit different parts of the world and share great r*ns. And share the atmosphere together over a jar or two or three. Hashing is really about being amongst friends although, of course, you get out of it what you put into it. And it takes all sorts!

Do you think the Hash needs to evolve in some way?

BC: Carry on as it is. After all, there are no rules! It's a social club for meeting people (and they are always interesting). After all, where else would you get such a collection of weirdos who are out to enjoy themselves, ie, good clean fun, well, most of the time! Plus, isn't it incredible how many Hash romances and Hash marriages there are?

James 'Likk'mm' Waddell.

First r*n Zürich H3 1991
Founder Generic Swiss New Year's Day H3
Member Bern H3, Lucerne H3, Zürich H3, Switzerland, BerZuBa Triangle H3, Geneva Leap Year Day H3
Inaugural participant Swiss-Franc(e) H3, Leman-Geneva H3, Basel H3

What were you thinking, Likk'mm. Was it a moment of personal weakness?

L: I had met this babe at a friend's party and she invited me to come along. Visualising an opportunity not to be missed, I seized it with only slight trepidation, as I have always been a generally non-athletic type, keeping the tone up only with a weekly set of sloppy tennis. As life would have it, she showed up with her boyfriend. Scratch that one. Somehow I got the impression that I was supposed to wear jeans as, if I didn't, the trail would rip my legs to pieces. (Needless to say, I was slightly intoxicated at that party.) So I proceeded to show up in jeans that weren't that loose, and ran the ball-buster that the hare-iette had set. Then for the next week I could hardly walk – the last time I had done any duration r*nning had been 20 years prior, under duress, in high school.

Are all the Swiss Hashes much of a muchness?

L: I am nominally a member of most of the Swiss clubs, making regular visits monthly. I call Bern H3 my home Hash, but am just about as closely involved in the Lucerne H3. The Hashes do vary in style within Switzerland and I feel the LH3 suits my mood most closely at this time.

How did the Generic Swiss New Year's Day H3 come about?

L: At one point it turned out that I had set five consecutive New Year's Day r*ns in various locations in Switzerland. As this event had turned out to be unusually popular (where were those hangovers?), and I was having regular conflicts trying to do it under the umbrella of another group, I got my wild hare to form a new group, meeting once a year. And now we're already up to r*n #2002!

So when did you become this prodigious, omnipresent Hashman?

L: I hung out with this [Zurich] group for a year before someone organised an away trip to Paris for EuroHash. It was a bit overwhelming, but ever since I took this step I haven't looked back. When I travel, I travel Hashing.

And you took just over a decade to reach 1,000 r*ns – you must be about the quickest in the world. [That's what his girlfriend tells me! –ed.]

L: I reached my 1,000th personal r*n in February 2002 at InterGulf.

From those that you can actually remember, which was the best time?

L: Undoubtedly the best r*ns are the ones you get laid at. But besides that, the best weekend I've done so far has been Inter-Africa '99 at Victoria Falls. Everything fit – the accommodation, the food, the beer, the entertainment, the crowd, the weather, the r*ns, the atmosphere, the organisation.

Speaking of laid, tell us about your handle?

L: I only give personal demonstrations of the technique which got me this moniker, preferably with females in a darkened room.

Apart from not getting laid, what constitutes a bad r*n for you?

L: Generally, I cannot take the humidity so Hashing under those conditions takes the lead here. One particular memory is of a Zürich Hash in relatively cool weather, where we were kilometres deep in the woods. The heavens opened up and it began to pour. We were all drenched to the bone – all the stuff I was packing was, too. And we had to continue on like this for 30 minutes or so. At the end it was fun – you couldn't get any wetter – but it was cold.

The worst event for me overall was the Berlin H3 # 666. They made a valiant effort, but it was a camping weekend (30-person tent with no cots,) rained the whole time at a moderate temperature and featured 'Invasion of the Annoying Ants' in the tent. I'm not a camping type of person.

What's the biggest contrast of terrain you've found yourself in?

L: I've Hashed in waste-deep snow (Helsinki) and then at 35 degrees (Qatar) the next day.

And how would you compare the Hashers in the various places you go?

L: I seem to find the most compatible Hashers in Europe and Africa. I find the expat interaction most stimulating. Hashing in the US and Oz is nice, but somehow just doesn't do the same things for me. I have had little experience in Asia, but that bit has seemed a bit stilted other than with people I already knew.

What's the main thing you've got from Hashing over the years?

L: Social openings [My favourite, too –ed.]. I like to travel (comfortably) and through my Hashing now know people all over the world who I can contact and buy a drink for, and they'll let their hair down with me. I've also gotten my job, flat and main hobbies through the Hash.

You haven't Hashed too much in Asia – any thoughts on where InterHash 'belongs'?

L: Who cares? 'InterHash' is the name of an event. The only thing that makes it big is the name and its built-in PR. If the Belize Nash Hash would be looked upon by the Hashing world in the same light, we'd be asking the question about it. I choose my trips mainly by destination (secondly by estimation of quality of event based on my criteria), not by the name of the event.

Happy with the way the Hash is – or any room for de-evolution?

L: It should stay free-format and unorganised. It would be very useful if a couple of central facilities would be available for all to use to simplify putting on events – a cheap haberdasher and a clearing house for payments. The information sources are already all out there on the net.

Pierre-Marc 'Higgins' Lefebvre.

First r*n Brussels Manneke Piss H3 1991
Co-founder Alicante Sometimes Sober Hash Ole
Member Bonn H3, Germany; Copenhagen H3, Denmark; GONAD H3, Brussels

You get around. I see you and your rubber chicken *everywhere* ...

H: I now have approximately 800 r*ns under my belt ... 350 as visitor of 141 chapters across 36 countries, the northern-most being Helsinki H4 (Finland) and the southern-most Hobart H3 (Australia). 1995 must have been my 'Get a life' year with 51 r*ns abroad, 23 of which were over the August/September period. The latter included a 10-day Hashing trip in Scandinavia immediately followed by two weekends in neighbouring countries as a warm-up for another 10-day Hashing trip around Inter-America in Orlando. The subsequent two weekends in Belgium and Luxembourg completed the destruction job nicely. It took me five weeks to completely recover.

How did you hear of the Hash and your first impressions of it?

H: You probably mean 'de ash'. Having 'tested' me over a few after-hours drinks and office parties, Semi-Column asked me nonchalantly what I was doing the next Sunday. He then proposed me to join him for a bit of r*nning. I immediately replied: 'You're no r*nner, you're a party animal!' I guess this was the right answer since Semi-Column smiled and arranged a meeting point. In those days the hardcore of Manneke Piss used to drink until 2am after each Hash. Probably the most (un)memorable of these after-Hash drinks was my first visit to an Irish pub. That evening/morning ended up puking in the pub before being thrown out and puking again in my car while driving home. (Drinking and driving was stupidly part of the Belgian party routine in those days and was not high on the police priority.)

And 'ow does a French-speaking Monsieur get a name like 'iggins, Master of Disaster?

H: When I joined Manneke Piss H3, this little Belgian was sporting a small moustache and a receding hairline. I was pointed out as a younger replica of the former British army sergeant major converted into a butler for the rich and famous in the American TV series Magnum P.I. Much later Try A Fuck unofficially added the title of Master of Disaster for my repeated drinking performances.

So when did Higgins first thrust himself on the unsuspecting world?

H: Copenhagen # 666 was my first Hash weekend abroad – my first meeting with a few high profiles in central Europe at that time. By then I had realised that Hashing was not only local but global. However, in those pre-internet days, getting to know about HHHappenings outside your own territory was usually a mouth-to-ear job.

Luckily, someone in Brussels gave me a copy of Magic's newsletter where I read about EuroHash II to take place in Madrid, May 1993. It was really fun and a great opportunity to expand my address book of European Hashers. I even had the 'privilege' to share a room with Rong Jon from San Francisco (King of the Gypsiesssss, man!). So many drunk people and still no trouble – a new concept!

From there, I heard about the World InterHash in New Zealand. With Neptunus and Hot Lips I made it to my first Hash trip outside Europe and had a mouthful of international Hashing flavours, including stopovers in Los Angeles ('What you mean, no drinking in public?') and Fiji ('Sorry Sir, this is a member-only club … ah, you're visiting Hashers! No problem, do come in.')

Have you ever been told what your most enjoyable time was?

H: The ice throne at Copenhagen # 666; the mock bullfight involving a crate of beer at EuroHash '93; Iguana-Lu-Lu bundle of r*ns in Oahu, featuring the impressive volcanic rock trail, short-cut by train and synchronised butt-chugs involving six 'couples'; rubber chickens flying formation during French Nash Hash 2000 in Champagne – Squadron leaders Urine and Higgins going where nobody had drunk before with the help of three anatomically correct rubber chickens …

I won't ask – carry on …

H: Anal Condom's trail through the *Dentelles de Montmirail* including two wine tastings and a Belgian chocolate stop in the middle of nowhere in Provence. But two extraordinary memories – for their uniqueness – will ever remain my 'timeless classics': Mt Maunganui H3 World InterHash Monday r*n, New Zealand [See Oceania chapter –ed.] and the Eeerie H3 shiggy r*n, pre-InterAm 1999 [See Americas chapter –ed.].

And what does it take to wipe the smile off your face?

H: BMP H3 icing for 20 minutes in winter, under falling snow, while nursing a serious hangover on tequila; Stockholm H3 warm beer during InterScandi '95, one of the hottest summers of last century in Sweden; Munich H3 1997 Oktoberfest 'rented chicken' incident (or, why magic cookies and steins of beer don't mix well. I should have known better – they couldn't be regular cookies if Chainsaw was offering them.); Oslo 600th self-termination on beer, rum and aquavit poured over an empty stomach. The start of a new sensible life (for a Hasher, that is) after alcohol poisoning.

Any other strange or exotic experiences?

H: Nothing beats Rabat, Morocco, in 1994. While on a two-week business trip in Casablanca, I had decided to join the Rabat H3 for its usual Saturday outing. At Rabat's train station, I was picked up as planned by an American translator. As we reached the venue, a posh villa in the expat neighbourhood of Rabat, I realised I had no local money on me – searching my bag, all I had was 20 Deutsche Marks and a couple of Magic's Hash directories. Fortunately, there was a high demand for Magic's publication – often heard but never seen in Morocco at that stage – plus half the Rabat Hash then consisted of German nationals. Cost of living in Morocco being low, I was now in possession of enough Dinar to pay the fee, attend the party and take the train back to Casablanca.

You've Hashed over frozen seas, volcanic lava, even ketchup. Any words of wisdom on Hashing terrain?

H: Hashing definitely brings you to places you'll never go on your own (or with a r*nning club). Either because you don't know there is a hidden path leading to a green patch in that big city or simply because it would look insane to r*n in a swamp or a sewer. The new trails I discover in my own city by venturing in unchecked places always amaze me (and the pack as well, since they can't shortcut).

Does InterHash belong in Asia or worldwide?

H: WWWorldwide! Personally, I believe this discussion is a little bit outdated now that each (sub)continent has it's biannual gathering. Isn't Pan-Asia the answer?

How could/should Hash evolve from here?

H: More beer!

Caitlin 'MaBouche' Clarke.

First r*n Paris H3 1998
Member Paris Full Moon H3, Sans Clue H3

My schoolboy, er, French suggests something oral about your name.

M: Something to do with eating a giant Toblerone. MaBouche was changed from MaBush when George W came to power.

How did you get yourself into this mess, and how did you find it once you were trapped?

M: Through a colleague. It was everything I wanted from a club, and I should have thought of it myself. Done over 100 r*ns with Sans Clue Hash, plus several with Paris, Paris Full Moon and away Hashes.

What makes for a good Hashing time in your view?

M: We generally have a good time, especially when it's not too cold. Best [event] ever was Luxembourg 500th in 1999. Perhaps this answer will be different after Sans Clue 450th.

And what pisses you off?

M: Extremely long r*ns, none quite so bad as EuroHash 2001's Saturday r*n [A 16km death march –ed.].

So you're probably not a big fan of Frankfurt as a result, but how would you compare other places you've Hashed in?

M: Home is where the heart is. In UK and South Africa, I miss the mix of nationalities. Benelux Hashes are lovely. But they use some bizarre markings. I have no preference for street or country r*ns … as long as there's a beer stop. Hashes without one aren't the same!

What's the main thing you've got from Hashing so far?

M: Drunk. Is that a trick question? No, I am also going out with my RA for nearly three years.

Does InterHash belong in Asia or worldwide?
M: Worldwide. It's Europe's turn.
And how do you think the Hash should evolve from here?
M: Organically, with no thought input.
Rest assured, that shouldn't be a problem!

Juhani 'Screw My Bike' Vanska.
First r*n Washington, DC H3 1975
Co-founder Helsinki H3 1977
Member New York H3

When did you first get involved in this nonsense?
SMB: I have been Hashing since 1975, so my total number of r*ns must be
somewhere around 1,000 (26 years, maybe 40 r*ns per year).
Who's fault was it for introducing you?
SMB: Ulf Burmeister, who was at that time working at World Bank in
Washington and had been Hashing there already a year or so, introduced me
to HHH. It was love at first sight [Er, with Ulf or the Hash? –ed]. I wanted to do
something but hated to r*n alone. Beer drinking was already my sport so to
become a 'beer drinker with a r*nning problem' was a no-brainer.
What do you find so attractive about your bike?
SMB: In summer time we often bike to the r*n. Drinking and driving (a car) is
a no-no here. So once we were served cold Heineken by our hare (a Dutchman
called Blimey). It was so good I had troubles biking home. So I was
complaining that there must have been something wrong with his Heineken as
I could not bike properly, and he said 'Screw your bike!'
How do you compare Hashing in different parts of the world?
SMB: It is pretty much the same all over the world. Hashers are tuned to the
same channel no matter where they Hash. Of course, snow (and sauna) are our
specialty. As we are males only – like the original Hash – some family Hashes
seem strange to us.
Do you think the Hash itself has changed over the years?
SMB: I am not sure whether Hashers have changed. I have been Hashing with
esteemed Hashers like Ian Cumming and Bill Panton and they have given me
great perspective to Hashing as they started already in the Sixties [1860s! –ed.].
And what did you get from the last quarter century of Hashing?
SMB: Great time with good buddies. Plus great cholesterol values. So I believe
in moderate physical exercise and drinking.
Do you think InterHash should always be held in Asia?
SMB: No it does not belong to Asia. Actually it should be more often in white
mans' places (not too hot).
And, finally, is there something that would improve the Hash?
SMB: More Hashes. It is a great break to a business trip when you can go
Hashing in a strange city. So there should be a Hash in every city where
business people go.

Peter 'No Mercy Master' Venton.

First r*n Vienna H3 1989
Co-founder Vienna Full Moon H3
Member Milan H3

I've always liked your Hash name. How did that come about?
NMM: Two gorgeous-looking Scandinavian girls turned up at the Vienna Hash. I was renowned for making the Down Down rule – 'in you or on you' – stick. So the girls were new, got their virgin awards, and failed to drink the beer. I would stand behind people in the circle with two cans in my hand. If they failed to complete the Down Down I would squeeze the cans out onto them. At the time with these particular girls it was minus 10 or something, ie, butt-freezing cold, and one of them started to cry. At which point I poured even more beer onto her. Needless to say, the two of them never came back. So I got named No Mercy, and as I was Grand Master the Master bit was added to the end.

Who roped you in for your first r*n, and where was it?
NMM: A colleague at work. In the Vienna woods somewhere – loved it.

And how many misadventurous outings are you up to now?
NMM: My r*n total in Vienna was some 250 (I think). I know I had about 30 with Milan, plus all the InterHash stuff, it must be up to 350 in total. Became Grand Master of Vienna until I left for the US, about two years later.

What was the best time ever had on the Hash?
NMM: This is a difficult one. I would say the most spectacular r*n was being r*n up a ravine in Petra, Jordan, and arriving at the end of Petra where the Indiana Jones movie was filmed. I immediately recognised the temple carved in the rock face upon getting to the end of the ravine where it opened into the valley.

Your worst Hashing moment or r*n?
NMM: Madrid in '99 or '98? Some Spanish asshole slapped my girlfriend, Cheeky. It was difficult not to beat the crap out of him. But I believe that the Hash is a very good example of non-violent entertainment, so I had to grit my teeth. Under normal circumstances I would have gone berserk.

Compare Hashing terrain conditions and the overall vibe in different places you've Hashed.
NMM: They definitely vary. The Milan Hash was always really good – I think it has a lot to do with the GM and associated main organisers. To be honest the Americans are better organisers than the Brits hence Hashes r*n by US citizens tend to be better. Although Milan was very good – but the 'leader' was actually a white Zimbabwean.

How has Hashing changed in the few years you've been involved?
NMM: It's becoming more personalised and reaching a larger audience. I feel this often weakens the Hash. It was, after all, a thing for expats – it was meant to be tough fun – merciless!

Apart from instilling fear in others, what have you got from the Hash?
NMM: Fantastic trips to foreign countries with instant companionship. It is

undoubtedly one of the best ways to see the world. If I won a lottery tomorrow I would buy a laptop, book up InterHashes in the coming months and travel. One other thing … I got married on the Hash! We did an 'away' from Vienna just over the border in Bratislava, Slovakia. We did the r*n through the town for about an hour. Then came upon a check with a large 'W' (ie, Wedding) – all piled into the registry office, complete with Hash attire. My wife and I got dressed in suit and gown and we got married. Then carried on with the r*n and did the circle.

What is it about Hashers in Europe getting married on the Hash? Shakespeare and More Knickers from Madrid H3 not only got married on a Hash, but also had a baby without missing a *single* r*n!

The Name of the Game.

A bunch of wacko names from around European and Scandinavian chapters which illustrate how dangerous too little sun and too much alcohol can be:

3 And Out, Etra H3: "Went to her gyno for a pap and her doc said that she was too small to be sleeping with her Hasher boyfriend. Doc recommended only three times per week."

Absolutely Pathetic, Riviera H3: "I was just **Pathetic** before, then collapsed 15km into a 20km race and spent three days in hospital. **Absolutely** was then added to my name."

Axe Murderer, Tallinn H3: "My lawyer said not to comment. But I think it's got something to do with my tennis backhand."

Bald Fokker, The Hague H3: "I worked for Fokker airplanes in The Netherlands."

Bam Bam Thank You M'am, Bern H3: "Wore Pebbles underwear to a r*n."

Bare Pussy, Warsaw H3: "Her real name was Kitty Koala, or at least that's how it sounded. So..."

Big Balls, Helsinki H5: Once carried two huge convict-style balls and chain on an Australia Day r*n.

Blow My Bagpipe, Heidelberg H3: "I was wearing a kilt when we met and she kissed my ball sac on a dare."

Bum Boy, ex-Cambodia, The Hague H3: "I used to be **Biggus Dickus** and that was good with the women. Now I'm called Bum Boy I get nothing!"

CUNT, Slovakia H3: "A fellow from the USA by the name of Todd was attending an InterHash and needed a name. One fellow from Geneva asked why Currently Un-Named Todd needed a name???"

Cellular Brogues, RMB H3: "Adrian was getting a Down Down since he forgot his trainers and ran in his brogue shoes. He was still in the circle when his wife phoned to say she was in the car and just a few seconds away and waiting to park."

Chainsaw Massacre, Zurich H3: "Try sleeping in the same room with him – you'll find out."

Chilly Willy, St. Petersburg H3: "This GM was found in minus 20 degrees Celsius with just his shorts on, hugging the radiator."

Crocadildo Dundee, Rome H3: "A British exile to the Antipodes and while in Rome insisted on wearing a Paul Hogan hat for every Hash. Given his general leering nature ..."

Crossword, Lisbon H3: Her husband is **Clueless**, the daughter is **One Across**, and the son is **Two Down**.

Cunt Dracula, Turkey: "This guy was the Managing Director of Tampax in Turkey."

Dakota, Oslo H3. "He used to fly for SAS in old Dakotas ... and also he can still get it up at 80!"

Dancing Queen, Helsinki, H5: "He and his partner once won second prize in a dance contest."

Dick Stand, Heidelberg H3: "He was 'gifted' ... but he wanted a rename and because he was such a whiner we now call him **Maxi Pad**."

Doggy Style, Amsterdam H3. "Perambulating [I think it's legal –ed.] through Vondel Park and I had a head-on collision with a golden labrador, and went weeeeeee and fell with style."

Double Dick, Oslo H3: "He fathered twins."

Drunk and Desperate, Helsinki H5: "I met my husband at a sleazy bar, so they said I must have been drunk ... then looking at him, they said 'And Desperate!'"

Effin Thong, Riviera H3: "It was first **Financial Times** (because of my initials) then became **Effin Tart** (because I ate a lot of apple tart) then became **Effin Twinset** (because I wore matching top and bottom jogging suit) then became **Effin Tranny** (because I played a female part in a play) then became **Effin Thong** (because I stripped down to my underwear at a Rocky Horror party and converted the underwear into a thong)."

Eiffel, Cyprus: "Amazonian lady ... very tall."

Elephant Clitoris, ex-Moscow, Helsinki H5: "When she moved to Helsinki she claimed she didn't have a name – then we had some Russian visitors who said 'Nice to see you again, Elephant Clitoris!' She had tried to hide it – she had been eating this big hot dog sausage on a r*n."

Eric The Viking, ex-Copenhagen, ex-Surrey, now London: Was originally **Eric the Half B** due to male pattern baldness, and Surrey renamed him **Eric The Retard**.

Fissed As A Prat, Rome H3: "Spent the entire Italian Nash Hash on Sardegna under the influence of alcohol." [Standard operating procedure? –ed.]

Flying Chicken, Oslo H3: "At Berlin 666th On On On there was a food fight with chicken flying everywhere. I'm also a keen bike rider and my friend thought that's exactly what I looked like riding."

Forest Dump, Geneva H3: "He used to be called **Daddy Long Legs**, then came back from a r*n one day without his t-shirt. His explanation was that he'd had an 'emergency' and had to leave his t-shirt behind."

Forest Gimp, Geneva H3: "As he jumped into the circle one day, his knee gave way and he writhed around on the ground. He was in a full leg plaster for a while after that."

Frequent Comer and **Comes Infrequently**, Tallinn H3: Two Harriettes whose attendance is regular and erratic, respectively.

Frostbite Foreskin: An American in icy Finland.

Fucking Incest, Helsinki H5: "She once shared a room with her brother at a Hole in the Ice event."

Full Body Condom, Helsinki H5: "Something to do with my sleeping bag."

Gagarin, Oslo H3: "They said I am always in a different orbit!"

Gonorrhea With the Wind, Heidelberg H3: "His wife was not happy, and he demanded to be renamed, so we called him **Penisillan**."

Gorky Foreskinski, Heidelberg H3: "He was a Russian Military Intelligence guy."

Guerilla Groupie, Helsinki H5: "Something to do with a terrorist in Sudan wearing a t-shirt from the same Hash as I used to r*n with, and some guy in Estonia wearing the same shirt."

Haggissimo, ex-Assen H3 Netherlands: "Being a Scotsman there were several Hashers named Haggis or some derivative thereof. Since I had a top with a Latin inscription that ended in '-imo' that was appended."

Horny Goat Weed, Drifter H3: "Horny Goat Weed is a natural aphrodisiac, so I go around handing that out. Before that I was **VirginsSuckMe** because I went to bed with a virgin Hasher and ended up with a neck full of love bites in the morning."

Hot Lips, Madrid H3: "She was always wearing spandex trousers that were too tight."

Icehole, Helsinki H4: "My naming was at the Hole in the Ice r*n."

Immaculate Cheesehead, Bern H3: "Name is Mary, comes from Wisconsin."

Jesus, Helsinki H5: "He once short cut across a very shallow stream and it looked like he was walking on water. He's also Hash Cash hence our slogan 'In Jesus We Trust – Others Pay Cash!'" He also looks amazingly Jesus-like with his long hair and curved beak.

Justin, Madrid H3: "His surname is Case and he was renamed about 15 times … **Brief, Suit,** etc."

Keen Incurable Nymphomaniac Dipsomania: "My name was **Kind** (pronounced 'kint') and they decided I needed something longer." [Don't we all, fellas? –ed.]

Knitwit, The Hague H3: "Wore an 'Absolut Idiot' vest during circle."

Lonely Brain Cell, Bern H3: "Just talk to her … ha ha."

Loping Scrotum, Copenhagen H3: "Have you seen him r*n?"

Lubrication, Tallinn H3: "She was in charge of marketing for all Shell Lubricant products in Estonia."

Man in Black, Helsinki H5: "I wore all black on my first r*n, at the time of the movie Men In Black. Whenever a t-shirt is made for a r*n now, a black version is made specially for me."

Mr Doldrum, Torrana H3: "This guy was completely unnoticeable on the Hash; never did anything."

Mrs Unlucky, Zurich H3: "Married to **Festering Fish Face**."

Muff Diver, Germany: Works as a diver on oil rigs.

Obscene Sex Craver, RMB H3: "Well, um, you know …"

Paint Job, Milan H3: "Removes his clothes at the slightest provocation – the very first time I ever met him, he was naked in a bar in Sweden – now known as **Paint Stripper**."

Pierced Brosnan, Bitburg H3: "He's full of body piercings – here, there and everywhere."

Pippi Wrongstockings, Rome H3: "Everytime I came to the Hash I was wearing some weird pair of tights (including under my toga for the Ides of March r*n) – orange or bright pink or something. Since I am tall and have reddish hair and am kind of crazy …"

Pope-alactic, Zurich H3: "Once was a Swiss Guard at the Vatican."

Pork Chop (Harriette), Bitburg H3: "Because a pork chop is a bit of white meat that is flat on both sides."

Precious Pouch, Helsinki H5: "Started to get a hard-on in the mixed sauna and ran out, covering his bits."

Professor Panic, Aarhus H3: "I had been to a work conference and got these free caps and t-shirts with 'PANIC' on them, which I brought to the Hash."

Pussy Foot, Grand Duchy H3: "Came back from Thailand with an infected foot – stood on a sea urchin."

Really Stupid, Heidelberg H3: "He'd emailed before his naming r*n, really paranoid, saying he was worried about his naming and that they could call him anything, unless it's really stupid."

Scrotineer, Riviera H3: "She once famously said 'I can tell the boys apart by their balls …' referring to two identical-looking male dogs on a r*n."

Self Rising, Bern H3: "Professional chef."

Shag-a-Wannabe, Tallinn H3: "She's an Aussie, and 'wannabe' was close to the Australian animal wallaby. And who wouldn't want to shag somebody important like her?"

Sharkfin, Zagreb H3: "One weekend Hash on the Adriatic coast I was the hare. Last part of the r*n was getting out of the forest to a pier where you had to jump in, and swim for 100 metres to a small peninsula to make the last part of the r*n. I was r*nning with a surf-flipper but in the water it looked like real shark fin, so people started screaming and r*nning like hell …"

Shit Britches, Heidelberg H3: "His son is **Son Of a Britch**."

Shitluck Holmes, Budapest H3: "He chose the wrong way on all nine checkpoints on one Hash – bad luck/no investigative skills – voila."

Sideways, XABEA X3, Spain: His surname is Crabb.

Sister Bianca the Fuckin' Nun, Heidelberg H3: "We had a Halloween r*n in Heidelberg where she wore a full nun's get up, plus garter belt, etc."

Snow Angel, Helsinki H5: "I usually r*n naked from the sauna into the water or snow, creating a bit of a scene."

Sperm Bank, Oslo H3: "He's a banker and just bought a yacht. That makes him a seaman (semen), right?"

Standing Ovation, Stockholm H3: "The clap. I used to keep it a secret but that's over 10 years ago now. The worst official secret in the Hash."

Strawberry Foreskin, ex-Milan H3, Athens H3: "They got me drunk one night and I suddenly took to the idea of getting a tattoo. Booze bravado helped me decide to have a neat snake's head on the foreskin. But the tattooist wasn't keen and persuaded me to have a honey bee instead. The deciding factor was the special ink he had which tasted of honey, he said. So I went ahead. Unfortunately he must have got the inks mixed up and used a strawberry flavoured one instead. Sounds a bit far fetched? Well, send me a nice young lady and she can have the opportunity to check this out personally …" [Happy to work on commission basis –ed.]

Tiny Tank, Rome H3: "His inability to hold even the smallest Down Down in his bladder for anything more than five minutes without sloping off behind the nearest tree."

Tone Deaf, RMB H3: You should hear this guy sing. There again, maybe just take my word for it.

Two Bit Shit, ex-Turkey, now Drifter H3: "He was wearing a dress and the police threw him in jail. Behind bars he was like 'Do you want to see my pussy? It'll cost you a quarter' which, in American parlance, is 'two bits'."

Vicar Licker, Bucharest H3: "Vicar Licker is a bubbly, buxom lass who embarrassed the Vicar from the local Anglican church by going down on her knees in the pub and trying to gobble him, in full view of his weekend congregation. He still blushes at the mention of her name …"

Viking Puker, Aarhus H3: "Vikings go half way round the world raping and pillaging and puking. I do the same."

White Fang, RMB H3: "After a Hash sex offence with a dog!"

WYBHALAIH, ex-Jakarta, RMB H3: "Short for **'When You've Been Hashing As Long As I Have …'"**

And, once again, a bunch of slack-arses who we couldn't contact to get their story [And/or no-one rushed to their defence –ed]. But we like these names anyway as they sound like they might have a good story behind them:

37½ Inches, Bananaman, Baron Avalanche, Beergasm, Big Chill Mamma, Bring Me the Hotel Manager, Caligula, Cellular Sex, Chief Dances With Foreskin, Dame Swinging Tits, Dim Sum, Does It for Money, Dr Feelgood and Dr Feltgood, Dr Feels Good, Dying Cockroach, Ee-Jack-Yer-Late, El Ultimo Paso, Even Dumber Blonde, Florida Cocktail, Fucking Lost Cause, Fucking Paddington, Gentleman Bugger, Grunt Grunt, Hashputin, His Bollocks (from Afghanistan), Hobbledehoy, Homo Amo Beerus, Hurdy Gurdy, Juan Hoonose, Jura-sick Pork, Karma Queen, Keep Up With the Jones, King of the 'Roid, Kinky Boots, Kus Boku, L'il Nuts, Lady Go Diver, Lamb Buggerer, Laughing Gas, Let's Go Party Ken, Look At Those, Lumpy and Lumpy Jumper, Madame Ovary, Major Monkey, Marie Tamponette, Mary Pop It, Miss Mozambique, Missed Phantasy, Mount 'n Groan, Octopussy Arms, Orangutan, Pheelthy Frog, Pillsbury Doughboy, Randeedextrose, Roger the Cabin Boy, Rolls Rice, Rumple Foreskin, Scrottweiler, Semen On the Pew, Sgt Pecker, Shitting Bull, Sister Punk, Slippery Seaman, SlowFuckYa (from Slovakia), Smooth Bastard, Spunk on the Beach, Tampon Bloody Tampon, Tar Baby, The Gorgeous Three Holes, The Lame Bugger, The Uncouple (real name Tony Randall), Things Go Better With Jim, Too Fuckin' Short, Towering Infernal, Trash Can Man, Trucking Desperate, Wanchai Stud, Working the Bar, Zizi Jambon.

Anecdotes from Europe and Scandinavia.

Bwana gave Paint Stripper and Tone Deaf 300 RMB H3 shirts to sell at EuroHash Brussels in 1997. However they sold only one, and that for just 40 Belgian Francs (a cup of tea cost 45BF at that time!) "But it was a great profit however since a Danish dentist in Milan had spent 1,800,000 Lire sponsorship on them and put his tiny logo on a sleeve for the privilege," says Tone Deaf, Scottish to the last.

They got pissed instead. "Paint Stripper then carried me and the t-shirts back to our hotel. Somehow the next night we lost the lot." Some reports have them gate-crashing a wedding and featuring in all the wedding photos holding up RMB H3 shirts. The bride wanted one of the shirts, so they gave her one [A shirt that is –ed.] in exchange for a kiss. Then *all* the girls wanted a shirt, so they lined up for their shirts and kisses. They gave away just about every last shirt they had.

"Paint Stripper returned to Milan and I went on to Edinburgh and surrounds where I got multiple Down Downs – standing on my head – from the RA whose Harriettes all seemed to be wearing the lost shirts," remembers Tone Deaf.

Bwana confronted Paint Stripper in Milan, demanding the great profits from their sojourn, to be told that there wasn't any because of one (or all) of the following excuses:

1. They were stolen by Brussels / Mexican / Moroccan Bandits
2. They had to give them away at EuroHash because they were designed by a famous Italian who, following his murder in the States only the week before, was discovered to be gay … and, well, Rule 7 applies … no poofters on the Hash.
3. "Er, em, I don't know nuthin', Bwana."

Bwana was upset, but apparently stopped going on about it when a Milan Moroccan walked off with 25 shirts he put down on the pavement during the circle outside Samson's, their Hash house.

"I'm still making 'Versace reject EuroHash freebie No. xxx of 300' patches for all those girls who turn up wearing those RMB H3 shirts," says Tone Deaf.

A weekend trip to Sicily, a r*n on the 3,000m Mt Etna. "All the hares and 45 hounds were US Navy, with the exception of three of us visiting hounds," says Obscene Sex Craver. "We're on the summit. This volcano is smoking. It's two degrees Celsius. It's pissing with rain."They gave the hares a 15-minute start before taking off across the lava field, devoid of any reference points except for the toilet paper trail. It wasn't long before they were all lost. Suffering from thin oxygen and three-metre visibility. No maps, no compass. Gashes on legs bleeding from the glass-like lavascape.

"Eventually we found the hares – from the best navy the free world knows – huddled in the foetal position," says OSC. They had been lost for three hours.

"A few of us kept walking down till we found a road, and hitchhiked for an hour before a car picked us up. We finally got back to our cars and came back to fetch the others."

At the Madrid 1,000th the place was going off. About 350 people partying, including a large contingent from Sarajevo – mainly mine-defusers looking to let their hair down and get among the womenfolk. A few Spanish women were sticking olives in their navels and dancing seductively on a table-top. No Mercy Master, from Milan, said: "I can do better than that!" and reportedly proceeded to jump on the table, drop his trousers and whip out his tackle. He then tucked an olive up his foreskin. His female partner then removed it orally, according to onlooking Hashers, much to the delight of the crowd. The Spanish hosts didn't see it the same way – and No Mercy Master and partner will reportedly no longer be Hashing in Spain. *Ever*!

What about the Hasher from Lisbon, Portugal, who they reckon wears a XXXXL sized t-shirt … and even then it's a tight fit.

A game the Norwegians often play at the On On is a team relay where you drink a Down Down, then put your bottle on the ground with your finger in it, and r*n around it 10 times. Usually there are teams of four, but one guy decided to play on his own as he couldn't find three team-mates. He collapsed on the spot after the fourth consecutive skol and spin!

A Hasher from Aarhus H3, Denmark, started off the r*n and, seconds later, it was all over for him – he ran smack bang into a set of traffic lights and was whisked off to hospital for seven stitches to his head and face. That's nearly two stitches for every metre he ran!

The Athens H3 in Greece managed a rare feet: Two years in a row they held their AGM in a favourite local tavern. Two years in a row they managed to break the *same* front window of the bar. Although much beer had been consumed, both were put down to 'accidental' causes. Will tavern management have them back a third time?

In Germany, On Ons are often held at the hare's house. Two visiting Hashers got there first one night and the main door was closed, so the two of them went to another door on the side, which was open. As no one else was around, they helped themselves to the fridge. Still no one turned up so they had a few more beers. Then a husband and wife turned up – she, screaming in terror. Turned out the Hashers were in the wrong house! After some explanation they calmed her down and actually had a couple of drinks together – turns out the husband and one of the Hashers did work for the same company.

In Helsinki, Man in Black was going to fellow Hasher Dicklomat's apartment. "I turned up to this quite fancy building – which houses many expatriates, embassy officials and the like – and realised I didn't know the apartment number or the guy's proper name," he says. "I had no option but to push each intercom button in turn, politely enquiring: 'Are you Dicklomat?'" Lucky he wasn't looking for his other kennel mates such as Magic Poofter, Sly Sausage Sucker or Drunk and Desperate!

In Germany, Heidelberg H3 did a great version of Singing in the Rain once. The hares had arranged for the local fire brigade to turn up and spray the two or three hundred Hashers with water. This led to some serious complete strips, especially from the Swedish contingent [Please send photos! –ed.].

The RA of Helsinki Full Moon is called Jesus. So naturally on their Easter r*n they crucified him – made a big cross and tied him to it – and he conducted the circle from there. After 15 minutes he said, "My arms are getting tired, please let me down," so – after considerable debate – they did.

In Tallinn, they'd done the circle and were enjoying a good On On in the Bermuda bar/restaurant when suddenly someone came in around 10pm and announced that a car had been broken into and all the Hashers' bags (about five of them) and *everything* had been taken. The police were soon there, statements taken. As some were overseas visitors, there was the matter of lost passports, etc. Those affected were all cordially invited down to the police station in town, where the session continued. Fortunately, there was a Finnish Hasher who kept disappearing and reappearing with booze, booze and more booze. "So we had a great piss-up in the police station till about 6am when the paperwork was finally done and we were dismissed," says Goldilocks.

In 1984 the Manneke Piss H3 of Brussels dressed that city's famous 'Peeing Boy' statue in Hashing gear and used the fountain as a piss stop. Literally. Unknown to many of the disbelieving visitors, it had been specially geared up for a festival beforehand, so Hashers' jaws dropped when they saw a keg loaded into the plumbing system and a fountain of beer for them to drink from. Hashing Heaven!

In Brussels, they had just named Hedgehog at the r*n, complete with the flour and beer and everything to baptise her. "I said she could use my shower to change before she flew out," says Revolta, "then she noticed that her flight was due to leave in just over half an hour ... so it was a mercy dash to the airport, where she checked in – still covered in flour and beer ... and God knows what."

On the Gulf of Norway, they were r*nning at the narrowest part once, where cruise ships pass by very slowly and very near by. "A pack of 70 of us lined up, waving and smiling at the tourists on board, dispensing much salutation and goodwill," says The Vicar. The tourists waved back happily, pleased with the overt friendliness and hospitality of the locals. "Then, at the pre-arranged sound of the air horn, it was down-trow for a mass mooning. All 70 of us at close quarters!"

Helsinki H5 were returning from a weekend r*n in Estonia, taking a 6pm ferry back on a Sunday night. The trip normally takes about four-and-a-half hours. Under normal circumstances the ferries are strong enough to break through the ice, however, that evening The Baltic Sea was frozen solid. The ferry left on time, and they got stuck into the piss. "After a couple of drinks, we noticed that the ice was moving as fast as the ferry was," says Blimey. A closer look at the situation revealed that the ferry was actually *stuck* in the ice – and not moving one inch.

At 7pm 'happy hour' started and an hour later 'happy hour' was officially over. "However we convinced the purser of the ferry to continue 'Happy Hour' as long as the ferry wasn't moving," says Blimey, to the cheers of the Hashers and other passengers. At around midnight they were 'saved' by another bigger and stronger ferry. The remaining part of the trip back to Helsinki took them until 7am the next morning – Monday, a working day. "We had a great weekend," says Blimey. "The only problem was all of us on the ferry were shit-faced and had to be in our various offices by 9 o'clock."

Grandslammer from Cleveland H4 flew to Frankfurt for EuroHash 2001, and spent the afternoon getting over his jetlag the best way he knew – by getting drunk. Then he decided to get ready for the Red Dress r*n and turned up at Alte Opera – in the middle of the high-powered financial belt of Frankfurt – in his fetching floral sun dress and straw hat, offset by his lush beard, and sat down at an outside café table. He got many raised eyebrows, and became fluent in saying 'Don't ask!' in German as he sat and waited on his own. And waited. And waited. Until he realised something was seriously amiss. Yes, folks, he was a whole day early for the Red Dress r*n!

On a flight from London to Larnaca, Cyprus, for InterHash there were about 50 or 60 Hashers on the plane – 35,000 feet above the Mediterranean. After about half an hour Pissoles noticed the guy next to him, sitting in an aisle seat, started tearing up a napkin, and was putting all these little pieces into a bag. Pissoles asked him what he was doing.

"We're going to have a Hash," the Arizonan Hasher says. "What's your name?"

"Pissoles," said Pissoles, proving he at least remembered his name.

"Right, you're the hare."

With that the American stood up in front of the 150 unsuspecting passengers: "Ladies and gentlemen. This here is Pissoles and he's gonna be the hare." So he handed this bag of paper to Pissoles, who jumped up, ran down the aisle and laid a trail.

"We're in economy class, so I r*n into business class laying the trail, and all these Hashers are r*nning after me," Pissoles says. "We get into first class, go round the corner and all these Hashers are still there, we go round back into business, back in to economy – some bastard, an ordinary passenger not a Hasher, had put these papers into like a cross check.

"Ah, On BACK!!!"

"The plane's wavering around as we go again through business, first class round the other side all the way back to economy. Finally an air hostess comes up to me and says in this stern tone: 'Have you nearly finished?' I should've said 'No, we're about to have the circle!' but we really thought we were going to get arrested."

Merdeka Reunion H3, The Netherlands, is a kennel of ex-Jakarta Hashers. They r*n once a year on the r*n day closest to Indonesia's Independence (*Merdeka*) Day and reminisce. As Indonesia is a former Dutch colony they often get up to 100 in the pack.

Bitburg's 69th in Germany was going to be a good weekend, with the American Air Force, lots of party animals, and lots of nudity because it's an American Hash. Gonna Come was Hashing on the Friday night and he decided to swap his t-shirt for a Harriette's sports bra at a clothing check. And he wore this sports bra for the whole weekend until the Sunday – when they had another clothing check, so he swapped his sports bra for some other bras. On Sunday night they all got back to their crash space, and he took the bra off and had tan lines! He was going to have to go back to Britain the next morning and explain to his girlfriend – who was laid up with a sprained knee and couldn't Hash – why he had tan lines in the form of a bra. Outcome unknown.

R*nning through a beautiful city park on a Red Dress r*n in Frankfurt, they were on trail and looking for flour. Lovers and after-workers were strolling everywhere, and one young guy in jeans and blue shirt had passed out on a park bench, sleeping face down. The hares had given him a generous dollop of flour on his backside, so he was awakened by masses of r*nners – in all manner of red attire – screaming 'On! On!' as they passed over him. The confused look on his face was apparently priceless.

In Cyprus for InterHash, a large South African Hasher was heading down to the Hash pub to meet his mates. He got one of those sleazy taxi drivers who offered him a much better time with some young ladies at this place he knew. No, resisted the Hasher, he was going to meet his mates. The taxi driver persisted with his offers of gorgeous young European girls. Showing the willpower for which Hashmen are renowned, he eventually succumbed and went along for the ride – ending up in this 'establishment' where he was introduced to the very comely Natasha, a young Russian lass. He had a beer, Natasha had a 'champagne' (funny, no bubbles). Another drink for the lady? Why not. And another? Why not. After three drinks, he asked for the bill. Time to go see his mates.

The bill duly arrived – for 800 Pounds! A big argument ensued.

"800 Pounds for three fucking drinks – that's ridiculous," he stormed. "I want to see the manager."

"You'll have to see … Mr Big," the waiter said in a hallowed tone.

"Bring him on!" the angry South African challenged.

He was ushered out the back to an office. The door was opened and there sat this stereotypical Mr Big with his sunglasses on, flanked by two beefy henchmen.

"Get rid of the gorillas, I'm only talking to you," said the cocky Hashman. The two sidekicks left the room. What ensued next is not exactly clear. However, our intrepid Hashman had his bill reduced a mere 200 Pounds for three champagnes, and was allowed to leave. Trap for young players. Lesson learnt.

Ephesus in Turkey have a toga r*n in June each year through ancient Roman ruins. "All these tourists see about 100 guys r*nning around in togas," says G String, "and they're like 'Hang on, what's going on here?' It's really good."

In Verberg, Sweden Hashers often have a sauna after the r*n, then dip into the sea. The slight catch here is that they do it in *winter*, when the water is near freezing point!

Almansil Area H3 in Algarve, Portugal, have an annual Easter bonnet r*n.

Bucharest H3, Romania, often finish the r*n with a game of broomball on a nearby iced lake.

In 1989 the Guadiaro H3 from Spain held their inaugural Incontinent Hash. This involves Hashing in Morocco, Gibraltar and Spain – three different countries and two different continents – on the same day.

Friday 13th H3 often do a pub crawl r*n with a murder site reconstruction done at each stop, sometimes laid by a Hasher who is an ex-Scotland Yard guy. They have also been known to do ketchup r*ns. After their first ketchup r*n in Cyprus, the hotel guy said 'You can't come in here like that – wash yourselves off in the pool …' By the time he said 'Only joking!' the whole pack was in the pool, which had turned blood red. On another r*n from Pattaya to an island by boat, they used 60kg of ketchup on 40 guys according to Vodka Splite. "I actually thought it was a '*catch up*' r*n, until I saw the state of the pack getting back in," says Haggisimo.

Riviera H3, France, take their On Ons seriously with gourmet/cordon bleu catering, and usually kegs of local red wine instead of beer. In Spain, the Burro/Mija H3 on the ritzy Costa Del Sol is a swank affair with champagne and caviar an essential part of the On On.

Rome H3 traditionally don't count their r*ns, and tend to r*n at the time of the day when others are enjoying their siestas … so there's less traffic pollution and – more importantly – less chance of being r*n over in the maelstrom that is Rome's traffic. In true Hashing form, an award is given each week for the best short cut.

The setting was the Oslo Ski Hash 1999 at a snowy mountain location [A good place to ski –ed.] north of Oslo. They'd finished a 1.5-hour trail on cross country skis through tracks, forests and over frozen lakes and were now back outside the cabins for the circle. "I had plenty of material for the Down Downs," says The Vicar. "A multitude of sinners adorned my list and plenty of cold beers to dispense. One of our regular Harriettes, Coffee Tea or Me, had recently given birth and as a result was sporting a magnificent pair of lactating tits. The circle was going well, I had their attention, people were laughing and the atmosphere was buzzing … I felt in control. That was soon to change. On being called up for her second Down Down, Coffee Tea or Me decided enough was enough. Completely without warning, she unzipped her ski suit, pulled out her right tit and – using both hands – directed a perfectly aimed stream of mother's milk right into my unsuspecting face. I don't know if it was the stories of spitting cobras from my Africa days or what, but the surprise made me lose balance and I heard the hysterical laughter as I keeled over, crumpled on the floor. I was completely gob-smacked. Several tissues and some reassuring counselling from the mismanagement and I was able to regain my speech and even persuaded to resume the circle again. Well, after a few beers."

The Slovensky Raj weekend in eastern Slovakia in June 2001 was unforgettable for all the wrong reasons. The directions were a bit hard to follow, so Hashers were arriving at all hours of the evening on the first night – including one guy in a Mini with *three* passengers all the way from Vienna! The next day, the group separated into walking and r*nning groups. Neither the walking nor r*nning hares had ever pre-checked the area so were at the mercy of a local guide. And what a surprise they had – the walkers, who had the option to spend most of the day in the pub and were expecting a nice wankers trail, were led through precarious cliff-side goat tracks, lacking safety barriers, and with only metal crampons to step on. Having completed this ordeal, the hapless group finished two hours *behind* the r*nners, who marvelled at their wonderful challenging experience tackling the rock face of the river gorge. Needless to say, the r*nners and walkers did not see eye to eye that weekend!

Bucharest H3 had a trip down to Mamaia when a car full of Harriettes, driven by Bob, reportedly experienced a blowout and rolled off the road. Everyone escaped with little more than cuts and grazes, although the car was a write-off. The car in question, a Romanian four-wheel drive, inspired their very own Hash tune after the name of the car – Aro (pronounced 'arrow'). "Every year at Mamaia we have a rendition of 'Roll out the Aro', much to the amusement of the survivors of the crash who are, of course, psychologically scarred by the accident and won't ever get in a car with Bob again," says Big Mac.

Pub crawl r*ns are usually a bit of a trot and a giggle. But the live hares of Ram H3 in Germany had something a little more in mind for the 20 or so wankers on this trail. Sure it sounded like the average pub r*n, with 12 pubs to be covered, but here's the catch: Each pub was at least a mile apart, some possibly two miles apart. A litre of beer had to be consumed at each stop. Do the math – that's a major marathon in every sense of the word. No fatalities reported. Hounds not happy.

"It all began just before the Rome 200th in May 1992 when we decided to do our first Pope t-shirt," says Efes, ex-GM of Rome. "Tiny Tank penned the famous Pope design with the Pope raising a glass and under the caption 'Blessed are the Rome Hash for they are On...' We needed his Holiness's blessing for this so we duly arrived in Vatican Square for his Sunday morning session and held up our boxes containing 250 t-shirts. He blessed the t-shirts, along with the other few thousand pilgrims. Thus we advertised 'T-SHIRTS BLESSED BY THE POPE' for the 200th r*n … at a significant premium of course."

In Milan, the circle was in full flight when the Hasher soon-to-be-known as Cellular Brogues was summoned into the middle for his naming. Just then his wife called to say she was about to arrive and pick him up. When a car drew up seconds later, the occupant got out and the RA embraced this blonde (but rather butch-looking) wife with the pageboy hairstyle whom he had never met before, and made a big fuss over her. No one else had met her either, so it wasn't until another woman – the Hasher's wife – appeared a minute later from the car parked alongside that the case of mistaken identity was discovered. The RA had been passionately kissing and hugging and welcoming an unknown 'guy' [Did 'he' sign up for the Hash yet? –ed.].

In March 1991 the Brussels Manneke Piss organised its first special event (50th r*n). The Sunday Hangover r*n (with over 100 Hashers) was an 'A to B' r*n, taking them from the host venue to the centre of Brussels.

After the r*n it was back to point 'A' by tube train for the circle. They sang some songs and, at the third last station, Blimey started singing The Cow Kicked Nelly. Clepto stood on one of the benches with his video camera taping the action. "The singing became louder and louder and at the second-last station the driver got out of his cabin and threatened us that he would kick us out of the tube if we wouldn't stop our singing," says Blimey.

As soon as the tube started moving, the singing continued louder and louder. At the next station the driver stopped his train abruptly, ran out of his cabin again and shouted at the hounds: "Out, all of you or I'll call the police!" As meek as lambs over 100 Hashers stepped on the platform and walked to the exit of the station. "The driver – who probably thought that he was well in control over 100 plus idiots – wasn't aware of the fact that we were at our final destination," says Blimey.

In February 1996, a Gispert memorial weekend was disorganised in Narva, near the Russian border, in Estonia. Thirty-six Hashers, including notorious Half Minds like The Wolf, Pink Panter, Blimey, Periodical, Vodka Splite and the Three Oslo Nurses joined this event. On a freezing Friday afternoon, they left Tallinn by train for Narva, a four-hour ride. As seats couldn't be reserved, they shared seats with members of the local community [Cue groans from the public and demands for refunds –ed.]. The beer sponsor for this event provided a mobile bar which, of course, was promptly pressed into action on the old Russian-built train. With the swaying and rattling, there was more froth than beer but, hell, they had beer and life was good. Until the grouchy conductress turned up – she was pissed off about the bar, saying it was occupying the space of at least one passenger.

"I offered her to pay for *two* passengers instead of one (total amount about 20 Euro cents)," says Blimey. With a smile she accepted this offer.

The train had one toilet only and, because of the mentioned rhythm, it was hard for most Hashmen to piss in the pot. The nearer they got to Narva the more kidney-filtered beer was flooding the toilet floor. In the sub-freezing temperatures, the liquid became more and more of a slush. Then The Wolf wanted to go for a leak. When he saw the state of the toilet floor, he said, "I'm not going to pizz in zere!" and walked back to his seat, nursing a bursting bladder instead.

Upon arrival in Narva, it was pitch dark, snow knee-deep, and the temperature close to minus 30 Centigrade. The Wolf jumped from the train, ran straight to the wall of the station building and started pissing the piss of his life. His relief was short-lived as two pairs of hands gripped him by his shoulders – two Estonian policemen, who said something to him in Russian and took him to the police station.

While the other Hashers went to the waiting bus, Blimey and the Estonian representative of their beer sponsor [Just the sort of character witnesses you want! –ed.] went to the police station. The Wolf had been arrested for pissing in public, against a public building. He had to see a judge the next day and had to spend the night in the police station, they said. His passport was confiscated.

The Estonian beer man and Blimey took one of the officers aside and apologised. They offered to pay a fine and advised them to release The Wolf. A fine – the equivalent of one Euro – was paid, a receipt issued and The Wolf was released. (So pleased was he, he didn't notice that Blimey had retrieved his confiscated passport, too.)

As soon as he got on the bus, he remembered his passport. "I told him that the police would consider returning the passport the next Monday," says Blimey. The whole group was in on this joke, except the poor old Wolf. As he had to fly back to Oslo on Sunday he wasn't too pleased with this idea and was quite grumpy the rest of the evening and on Saturday morning. Not wanting to see his grumpy – and possibly dangerous side – they decided the joke was up and returned his passport after breakfast. Wolf happy.

German Nash Hash was again held overseas, this time in Prague, Czech Republic. It was the first-ever Red Dress r*n through Prague, and a beer stop had been organised. So 60 Hashers in all manner of sleazy red attire invade the bar, where there's also a 21st birthday party going on. The Hash thinks the food that's laid out is a big spread for their benefit … WRONG! Bouncing Czech had to quickly restore diplomatic relations with the management, the party and practically everybody else in there. "There's two fat bastards at the bar that look as if they play as linebackers for the 49ers," says Haggissimo, "and they're not happy that their quiet convivial after-work pint has been disrupted by a bunch of noisy smelly bastards. Unfortunately, and accidentally, I brushed my sweaty arm against his as I passed, and the bigger one starts letting off steam. I notice that he's wearing a red top and by way of an apology I say to him 'I'm sorry I thought you were one of us'."

Haggissimo got a full pint of beer straight in the face. "Since I had a red dress on at the time …"

"I have to say one of the best Hash weekends I've been on was the wedding of No Mercy Master and his bride Cheeky in Bratislavia, Slovakia," says GBH. "I was charged with ensuring NMM was drunk before we left the first pub. After a couple of 'games' I played with NMM, he was not only drunk, but dressed only in my old rugby jock strap and a dickie bowtie, with the words 'CHEEKY' written on his bum. The streets of Vienna, where the stag took place, closed their eyes. The final circle saw the newly weds in the centre. Each of the 65 guest Hashers shook the champagne bottle from their goody bag, and all together popped the corks. For one magical second or two the spray of champagne met in a complete dome over the bride and groom."

Chromedome was at the Paris 500th r*n, which was a beautifully organised affair, and stopped at every major tourist sight in the centre of Paris. The pack was just enjoying a beer check inside the entrance to the Louvre when an American tourist turned round, saw them, said, "Holy shit, honey, it's the Hash – here, hold my coat, will ya," and waltzed off in his Brooks Brother shirt, slack and loafers to r*n with the pack all the rest of the afternoon and well into the evening. What a Hasher!

As the Half Minds were waiting for the last of Hash buses back to the hotels after a Red Dress r*n at Brussels EuroHash, Show 'Em from Munich reportedly poured her beer over the windscreen of a limo – with four mafia types inside – that bumped into her. She and her boyfriend got thumped for their efforts, he being chased and jumped upon by one with a gun. They were on the ground, gun to Hasher's head.

"That man's got a gun – call the police, call the police!" a nameless Hasher said, bravely r*nning for a taxi. The taxi driver sat impassively: "I haven't heard a shot yet," he said.

One of the other thugs pulled a huge sword out of its sheath and started waving it in front of the Hashers. Cries of terror from assembled Harriettes. Taking stock of the situation, and with the three other occupants occupied with the rest of the crowd, Tone Deaf – pissed and dressed for all the world like a brolly-wielding Super Gran in his bright red Royal Stuart tartan kilt – went into action and managed to get the guy with the gun on the ground. He stood on his chest like a conquering knight until the police arrived. Turned out the gun was a toy. He was questioned by police and thrown onto the last Hash bus home.

"I met an Aussie Hasher later in that year who told me I was lucky I wasn't knifed by one of the other *mafioso* coming at me with a sword stick," says Tone Deaf. "This Aussie told me he was too late to book for EuroHash to get the plastic EuroHash '97 mug so he received a real glass one instead [Sounds like Hash logic –ed.] and the handle was all he had left holding after taking out the passing hood."

Tone Deaf was renamed Tone Deaf the Brave Fart for his heroic deeds that day. But, tragically, his first pair of prescription glasses – bought at great expense just two weeks before that EuroHash – had been found "a scratched and mangled mess".

"When I got them from Dollis and Aitchison the opticians (Burt Reynolds does the advert) their guarantee said 'You break them, we fix them'," recalls Tone Deaf. Back in Edinburgh, three weeks after purchasing them, "D&A gave me a new pair and didn't even have the courtesy to ask how I managed it!"

More on our website: at *www.hash-onon.com* you'll find more never-published-before Hashtorical photographs from Lubbecke H3, naked Hole in the Ice action, and a whole bunch of other Hashit.

Beer: A Potted Pisstory.

Stone tablets from Babylonia (ancient Assyria) describe in detail the brewing process for what we now know as beer, the amber nectar, the golden throat oil, the sacred suds, the holy water. Hammurabi, the Grand Master of Babylonia at the time, realised the importance of this feel-good fluid for the progress and development of society, so came up with a bunch of edicts concerning the brewing of beer and had these laws cast in stone. Literally. These were inscribed on a column at Susa, a ruined city in Iran. No wonder the area is known as the cradle of civilisation.

So civilised were they, in fact, that any beer vendor who overcharged customers for beer was drowned. Anyone found to have watered down their beer was caged in their own vats. And heaven help any high priestesses found loitering with intent in a public drinking establishment – they were burnt at the stake.

Beer is also mentioned in some of the earliest records from places as diverse as Egypt and China. The Egyptians were kind enough (or pissed enough) to let on the state secrets of brewing beer to the Greeks and Romans, and suddenly those two were the biggest empires and strongest forces to be reckoned with. Mere coincidence? Surely not.

In Northern Europe, beverages made from cereal go back to the pre-Christian era. The excavation of a peat bog in Denmark uncovered a girl clutching a jug of beer, which has been scientifically dated as coming from 1370 BC. We then have to fast forward to around the 12th century, to when brewing of ale became a popular pursuit in England. Firstly it was trial-and-error homebrew, which some got the knack of, and decided to share it with the world in establishments called taverns [Old English for 'temple of worship' –ed.]. 'Getting pissed down the pub' was born! A nation of Andy Capps was launched.

However it was several centuries later again that America got civilised. The first brewing in USA got going in the 1630s. Not surprisingly, as they were so new to it, the beer tasted like the stale dregs from a race-horse urine swab. They stayed away in droves. Well, until the 1840s and America was flooded with Germans (unlike the 1940s when Germany was flooded by Americans). The Germans had been at this beer caper for quite a while, and knew how to brew a decent lager. It caught on, and the Americans now had a good excuse for their loud-mouthed behaviour. Their pursuit of perfection was cut short, tragically, when the 1920 Prohibition was brought in. The Prohibition meant that people actually drank industrial quantities of more dangerous rocket fuels behind closed doors rather than sipping a few cold ones in public. Another triumphant moment for bureaucracy. So for the next 13 years, the staple was a very low-alcohol product called *near beer*.

However, across the Pacific, in 1931 in Malaya it was the Chinese year of the tiger. Malayan Breweries started as a joint venture between Fraser and Neave Limited (F&N) and Heineken NV of Holland. The original brewery was opened in 1932 and Tiger Beer was launched shortly after. This was god's own nectar which made otherwise-sensible residents of the colony want to r*n around in the jungles and rejoice with shouts of 'On! On!'

And so the world entered a new era of uncivilisation.

Today, Iran is a fundamentalist Islamic state, where consumption of the sacred nectar will earn you the ultimate Down Down – the death penalty.

Unfortunately the American breweries never fully recovered from the restrictions of Prohibition, and today the best they produce is still only *near beer*. Its consumption is still governed by archaic laws drafted in Abyssinia, and enforced to the letter by over-zealous park rangers and police.

The rest of the civilised world is happy to consume mass-produced frosted horse piss and declare it good. Twenty-four beers in a case, twenty-four hours in a day. Mere coincidence? Surely not.

Fool Britannia.

Hashing in the United Kingdom.

Young Farts in the Old Dart.
It was the British – albeit sun-drenched colonial ones – who discovered Hashing. But who are the Brits and why did they inflict this strange behaviour on the world? The best explanation comes from looking at their ancestors, ice-age humans who crossed the land bridge from Europe to England when the weather was nice. In turn these were the Lower Paleolithic hunters [close relatives of Phil Davies from West Sussex H3 –ed.], Neanderthals [The immediate family of Twonk], then finally *homo sapiens* [See rule #6 – no poofters].

They buggered about with the copper age, the invention of the wheel, and so on. By now they were standing on their hind legs, and cricket – a sport even weirder than Hashing – was invented by this lot. Football – or soccer, to some – was actually invented by the Chinese ('*cuju*' during the Han Dynasty), but it was a crap game anyway so a cheeky student, William Webb Ellis, picked up the ball and ran with it in 1823 and invented an altogether better game – rugby. Then a couple of world wars, rule the waves, that sort of thing.

Next we know, in 1966 Prime Minister Harold Wilson declares a state of emergency to quell a dock strike, and President De Gaulle says *non* to allowing Britain into the EEC in 1967. A couple of years later, rioting by Catholics and Protestants in Ulster sees British troops sent into Ireland. In a few short years, this would include Hashman Richard 'Mountain Rescue' McAllister, but first the Army sent him from Kluang, Malaysia, back to the home country, England.

His posting in winter 1968 was to Liphook in beautiful Hampshire. The Longmoor area surrounding his new camp was flat, with a mixture of open and closed countryside. Bitten by the highly contagious Hash bug in Brunei and Kluang, it wasn't long before his fevered mind began fomenting plans for a Longmoor Hash kennel. Undeclared to quarantine and customs authorities, he was bringing a strain of eccentric tropical madness back to the motherland for the first time.

"Getting it going was not difficult," recalls Mountain Rescue. "I was a member of the instructional staff at the Operations and Movements Wing of the School of Transport. We had a captive source of potential in the form of some 22 newly commissioned officers directly out of Sandhurst. As it was completely new to all of them, and also to most of the staff, I used one period of instruction to give a thorough briefing on how to Hash."

And so it came to pass that the first Hash on British soil was in the wooded area around the Mess of the Longmoor camp sometime "around September 1968". His service records bear this timing out. "This was a great area with lots of good Hash countryside," says Mountain Rescue. "The trail medium did cause a bit of a problem – we could not use paper because that was against the new litter laws. I tried whitewash dispensed from a garden spray but the mix could not be made strong enough to show up on the ground and still pass through the tubing. Utter failure, but the sprayer was useful in the garden."

Close to 20 virgins, of varying degrees of eagerness, fronted for that first UK trail. To aid his cause Tony 'Fruit 'n' Nut' Case was his co-conspirator, plus there were a couple of others who had run in Kluang and Singapore before. In fact, the kennel's style was very much based on the Kluang Hash's style – meaning at the end of the r*n they just got stuck straight into the beers, Courage Light Ale in a light blue can in this case.

They dug into their pockets for the two-shilling weekly sub (which covered the Hash piss). Then it was off to the Officers Mess for jokes, stories and unrestrained singalongs. "The reluctance of some was quickly replaced by dedication to the cause," says Mountain Rescue. "Most of them came back for more after the first meet and many have gone on to Hash around the world."

Each week, he drove his second-hand Ford Popular to the local supplier where he purchased the beer in bulk. When that ran out they'd go on missions to an Officers Mess in the area for emergency reinforcements. "It was a one-man band and I did all the convening and Hash notes, and accounting for Hash Cash." He also had to sit down and devise a better way to mark trails. "So I went to the carpenter's shop and got some sawdust which did the trick and that is what we used for years, dispensed from two old haversacks."

Soon they were exploring countryside further afield from the mess area. A couple of miles up the road from Longmoor was the Mechanical Transport Wing of the school at Borden and some of their staff used to join the Longmoor H3's trails. This helped supplement pack numbers, which could be down to about half a dozen when there were no students to second.

June 1970 saw Edward Heath triumph over the Labour party and get a costly docker's strike as a welcome present. "The Labour government had just put us on to a military salary rather than the old system of pay and allowances. As a bachelor I was suddenly financially far better off," he says. He traded in his trusty [Rusty, more like it –ed.] Ford for a gleaming new Rover. In early autumn 1971, Mountain Rescue was shipped off to Germany for a stint.

Later on, the hardcore Half Minds from Borden started their own pack and eventually subsumed the Longmoor Hash when the camp was closed down. The kennel later became known as the Borden H3 and all of Mountain Rescue's early documents were handed over to them. That Hash kennel didn't last long either, and Longmoor's meticulously recorded Hashtory vanished without trace.

Call In the Marines.

Decimal currency was introduced to England in February 1971, with inflation and unemployment rising immediately – not that it affected the largely unemployable Hashers anyway.

The previous month, Ray Thornton was posted to Plymouth, Devon, to form a new regiment within the Royal Marines. It was to be called the Commando

Logistic Regiment, which he was to command. Astute readers will recognise the colonel's name. He had previously Hashed in Singapore, Kuching, and founded Dhekelia H3, Cyprus.

Within a few short months, he was up to his old tricks again, forming the Commando Forces H3. "As far as I knew there was no other Hash in the UK at that time," he says, feeling – along with many others – that they might have been the first kennel in Britain. The exact start date of Commando Forces H3 – and all documents – have been lost in the beer-foam of time. "I did not return to Commando Forces until January 1971. I can assure you the first r*n was in the spring of that year from a pub on Dartmoor," now-Brig Thornton said recently. Thornton travelled to and from r*ns in his old minibus – "to move the family and our wolfhound dog" – and the pack used their own cars or military vehicles to get to r*ns which were always from pubs in the Plymouth and Dartmoor areas.

1971 saw the first of what was to be a sadly familiar headline – a British soldier was killed as a new wing of the IRA waged a campaign of terror against British troops. By September, 100 victims had been claimed. IRA members were locked up and their marches banned. This didn't stop them from setting off a bomb in the London Post Office Tower. In November, two Irish lasses in Belfast were tarred and feathered for dating British soldiers.

While not directly involved, the Hashing Commandos had other battles to contend with. "That Hash was based on the Commando Logistic Regiment that, even in those early days, was continually totally or in part deployed in UK, to Cyprus and to north Norway," explains Thornton. "The trouble was that we spent much of our time deployed, not so much as a unit, but in a number of detachments. We ran when we could. As the regiment grew and assumed a full role the workload became heavy."

England was thrown into darkness in early 1972 due to a miners' strike which led to blackouts. A black day soon followed when the British Army parachute headquarters in Aldershot was bombed by the IRA, killing seven.

Thornton himself was transferred to another garrison in the Bicester area in April 1974 – leading to the folding of the CFH3 – and went on to greener Hashing pastures. "Considering its role then and now it is little wonder that it folded," says Thornton. This is typical of many military kennels around the world, which tend to peter out as postings decimate the membership.

A Piece of Old Hat.
It was the week before Christmas, 1971. With the bad weather rolling in, and turkeys bracing themselves for the seasonal stuffing, most people were content to stand around the fireplace with a snifter of brandy and feel the warmth seep into their bones. But not Mike Read. Oh no. Evidently still reeling from too much jungle juice in East Africa, he thought that Westcombe Park in Kent needed a Hash to liven things up. It's believed that he'd done his Hashing in Lagos, Nigeria, previously but this doesn't tally with African Hashtory as we know it.

So he sat down and penned a note inviting some fellow members of the Westcombe Park Rugby Club to a Hash r*n. John Ward-Turner was one of the unlucky ones to receive the invitation, changing his life irreparably. "It was thought for some long-forgotten reason that we should arrive in fancy dress," he says. Perhaps Read had had a few too many at the club when he sent these out.

In any case, 10 liver-support systems masquerading as potential Hashers turned up on December 19 at the appointed spot. Most wore some form of silly hat. One Half Mind apparently got it wrong completely, turning up in a fine pair of pin-striped trousers, which saw him completely out of contention through the shiggy, but a clear winner in the *concours d'elegance* stakes. Hash Master Read pissed everyone off royally as he overtook the pack in his car, beer bottle in hand, and sped off to the end. He was awarded Westcombe Park's first Hashit for this unworthy exploit. However, he was partially forgiven when he dished up some vaguely potable home brew at the bucket afterwards. Capitalising on this recaptured high ground, he dished out fines to Messrs. Brett, Hadaway and one PC Pat, for breaches of Hash etiquette on trail. He also slipped in the small matter of starting fees for Hashers each r*n. In the case of profits, these would go toward the cost of procuring some floodlights so the pack could see just how gruesomely ugly their Hash pals were.

Whether it was the weather or not, is not known, but it was decided to hold r*ns monthly instead of weekly. Although Tasmania had set a precedent for seasonal operation, no Hash had previously r*n just once a month, a practice which they continue to this day. So, although Westcombe Park H3 is regarded as the longest-r*nning H3 kennel in the UK, it has logged significantly fewer r*ns than other clubs.

From that original acorn of miscommunication, a huge oak of fashion victims has sprouted. "Today we still r*n wearing a hat, and a different hat must be worn each month," says Ward-Turner. "The local Oxfam shop does very well out of us." Some of the original hounds from the first outing still front up groggily each Sunday morning at 9:55am for a heart-starting brandy.

The walking wounded (they are mainly ex-rugby players after all) then have a bit of a walk or trot until they meet the hares at some ill-defined halfway mark, where medicinal shots are once again dispensed. Then it's a slightly meandering trek to the end, where the smiling hares greet them with what's left of the brandy to polish off. "There are a lot of old farts in it these days," says Pete the Pilot, a Kent resident who also r*ns with London H3. "A two-hour gentlemanly stroll through the countryside I regard it as nowadays."

"We then retire to the hare's house where we bathe, we then have a meeting when people are fined for bad behaviour, and the next month's hares are selected," says Ward-Turner. By this time, they're getting stuck into a keg of beer. "We then sing a song which has been written by the Hash Musique which tells of escapades and activities that occurred on the previous r*n." This replaced the slavish r*n reports which Read used to write each month.

Numerous beers are consumed from the keg that travels with them until they adjourn to the hare's local pub somewhere in Kent, Surrey or Sussex.

"I suspect our Hash is r*n on similar lines to all the others" says Ward-Turner, Hash Master these days, showing a flimsy grasp of reality [Apart from shots of brandy and sombreros once a month on a Sunday morning, yes, possibly –ed.]. However, he does concede that they have a few peculiar practices. "We carry a Hash Card with us at all times – this must have your name and photograph on it. You can be challenged at any time or place by a fellow Hasher to produce your card. Failure to do so requires you to buy the challenger a drink. Should the challenged have his card upon him then the challenger must buy the drink." The Hash Card Challenge has been used to devastating effect as far away as the Greek Islands, when two holidaying groups accidentally bumped into each other.

They also have a claim to foam. Prince Charles has an estate, Chevening, near Sevenoaks. The Westcombe Wankers wrote to Jug Ears asking permission to r*n on his property during the Queen's Silver Jubilee. They also suggested he join them for a trot [He could borrow one of his mum's hats –ed.]. "He declined the offer to r*n but did give us permission to r*n on his land," says Ward-Turner. "The halfway sip was served in the middle of a field on a table decorated with bunting on which were three silver bowls, each with a red, white or blue drink in them." The dress code for the day was similarly patriotic. "We have managed to remain strictly men only, seeing this as our stand against the intrusion of females into a man's world," says Ward-Turner. To this traditional misogynistic end, their committee even has a Hash Porn installed.

Picester at Bicester.

In March 1974, Britain went to the polls again, with the bitter coal miners' strike the big election issue. Harold Wilson won by the proverbial bee's dick.

Bicester H3 in Oxfordshire was founded the following month by the irrepressible then-Lieut-Col Ray Thornton, who moved with his family and dog and minibus up to Oxfordshire. "The army sent me to Bicester to help make a computer work," explains Thornton. "It was the only thing that kept me sane after chasing binary bits from morn till night." Bicester H3 was based at an army garrison but it was decided to also throw the membership open to civilians to augment the pack and ensure some sort of continuity. Thirty Hash virgins were conned into joining.

Appropriately, the first outing was on April Fools Day. "When it started Bicester was 95 per cent military," says Thornton, who laid the first trail with his garrison commander, Brig Paddy Minogue. Getting permission to cross land all around that area proved difficult so they decided to base the first r*n around the Officers mess, and lay a figure eight trail.

"Paddy and I laid the top half and then crouched down behind a roadside hedge to wait for the pack to r*n through before laying the bottom loop. Just as the front r*nners approached, a quiet voice behind us said 'Would you gentlemen mind telling us what you are doing?' Two police officers had driven by and didn't like the look of us. 'Certainly', said Paddy, and his voice would have convinced a sinner of the second coming. 'If you crouch down here with us, you'll see your boss r*n by in a moment.' We got a suspicious look, but slowly they sank onto their haunches. 'Bloody hell, it's Alf' said one as the Chief of Police – a personal pal of Paddy's – led the pack and disappeared into the trees.

'Come and join us next week' we called to the policemen's retreating backs," says Thornton. Then it was back to the pub to get stuck into some Hook Norton ale, "a brain-rotting brew with a gentle aperient effect."

With many army officers in the pack, the r*ns had to start at 5pm so that they could get a r*n in, have a few pints at the pub, and still be back at the barracks mess in time for the gruel that masqueraded as dinner. It was agreed to do this crazy r*nning and drinking thing weekly. But on the second outing, there was no sign of Alf the Chief of Police, Paddy the garrison commander or the two chastened bobbies. No one remembers exactly why Alf and Paddy gave Hashing away.

Around that time a bomb blast in Birmingham – the worst yet – killed 17, and a new Prevention of Terrorism Act was introduced.

Soon Bicester H3 was r*nning from all and every pub within a 20-mile radius of their camp, with the addition of Honorary Gentlemen in the pack at r*n # 44 in 1975. Sue Roycroft (daughter of Brig Roycroft) was the first. "Girls came into Bicester due to the 'Why the hell can't I come too?' logic," says Thornton, who was happy to go along with it.

One Monday night thereafter, the pack was straggling down a slope and plodding across a major road, to the fury of one driver who pulled up and vented his spleen on a somewhat overweight Hasher, Sambo. He screamed back "LISTEN! Don't you support your Olympic team in training?" With that the motorist offered his profuse apologies and best wishes, and Sambo motioned the tail-enders to cross.

In 1994 for Bicester's 1,000th pack regular Half-a-Fuck penned a ditty which seems to sum up this lot:

The legendary Hashers of Bicester
Could not give a stuff for the vista
Of countryside seen
Through a sweaty red sheen
They'd rather get picester and picester

"I was one of those few civilians who were invited to join Bicester H3 back in 1974," says Gordon 'Prof' Williams, "but it took me until 1977 to get round to doing so – I now regret missing out on being a founder member," he says of the second-oldest existing – and oldest *weekly* r*nning – Hash in England today, with some of its original hounds still on trail.

These days, the kennel is much changed. With a largely civilian profile, summer r*ns set off on Mondays at 7pm, then in winter, Sunday mornings at the highly civilised hour of 11am find them at the starting pub. In winter they only r*n fortnightly because of the unbearable creaking of the joints in faithful old hounds such as Dick Dick, Knobhead, Wha'd He Say, and Monkey Glands.

Bicester is now also home to a Full Moon chapter, the Bicester Unofficial Moonshine (BUMS) H3, and a bike kennel.

Thornton, meanwhile, had been sent off to Donnington in 1976, where he couldn't help himself again, and got that kennel up and r*nning.

A Sorry Sight.

In January 1975, one Jim Raper – a financial type who had just returned from loading his bags of gold in Singapore – placed a classified ad in the Personal column of The Times announcing the 'Surrey Hash in formation ...'. The newspaper turned down the ad, suspecting it be some sort of undesirable drug-related subversion. Fortunately, he persuaded them to r*n it.

The following month, an unmentionable with a pointy nose, rodent-like teeth and bouffant hairdo took over the Tory leadership from Heath. Her name was Maggie, or Margaret to her friends [Her husband Denis just calls her 'Yes Dear' –ed.].

In April, Surrey H3 came into being with a complement of four. A further inquiry from a female nurse had been dismissed because they were intent on it being a male preserve. Raper himself had r*n in Singapore, but the others – Ron Walters, Don Weir, and Kerry Bagshaw – though interested participants, had never been on trail before. This was also before the big jogging craze had begun to sweep the world so a lot of explaining was required [Duh! Put your left foot forward, then your right foot ... –ed.]. Neighbouring Westcombe Park H3 was invited to join the inaugural r*n and supplement the numbers. They rallied to the cause with half a dozen of their hat-wearing members responding.

And so the pack assembled at the Old Rectory in Little Bookham for the first r*n. More than a little competitiveness was evident but "they duly allowed themselves to be instructed in the mysteries of the Hash," said Raper[103]. Other visitors from the Far East also helped to inculcate the Hash philosophy the beer at the end is more important than who gets there first. Following KL's tradition it was a shandy bucket waiting for them at the end (albeit lemonade was substituted for ginger beer). R*n subs of 50p each week were applied, according to Bumble.

However, contrary to KL tradition, they chose Sundays as r*n day to circumvent the Monday evening traffic. Shortly thereafter, they also chose to admit Harriettes to the chapter, as it was on Sundays that they were stealing the men away from their families. It is not known whether the originally dismissed nurse ever joined their ranks.

The following year, 1976, London was on with its first kennel – London H3.

A couple of years later, on a r*n near Epsom, the Surrey Half Minds were tearing through the countryside, filling the air with lusty cries of 'On! On!' when an elderly bespectacled gent stopped them and inquired whether they were the Hash House Harriers. Indeed they were. And who was he? "I am C.M. Lee, one of the founders," the gent told the gob-smacked pack. They hastily accompanied him to the nearest pub for drinks and extensive questioning. This is the area Lee had retired to in 1961 after his post-war career took him from Kuala Lumpur, to Sandakan, thence to North Borneo.

One of their military members, Lt-Col Willie Couper was posted around 1980 up north to Edinburgh. In 1981 Surrey hosted the first UK Nash Hash. With close ties to Asia, Surrey's members were also the first to attend an international InterHash.

In April 1982, Britain proved it still ruled the waves and the Commando regiment (formed by Ray Thornton) sent the Argentineans packing from the Falkland Islands [Argentina, in a post-mortem, ordered a flotilla of glass-bottomed boats to improve tactical co-ordination between its navy and air force! –ed.]. This turned out to be a cunning front for extending the Hash to this furthest remaining bastion of the old empire, with Bunter taking the opportunity to lay trails in the Falklands in the reconstruction phase. But while Britons excitedly wave the Union Jack again, the miners went on another strike – this time for a year.

An example of how well kept a secret the Hash can be happened in 1983 when Charles Earle (ex-Hong Kong H3) got his tennis-playing mates together to form Barnes H3. The first r*n was to be at the Green Man pub, Putney Heath, South West London. Someone leaked this news to the local press, the story being that the first Hash in the UK was to be started. This information filtered through to the well-established Surrey Hash who turned up in force to show these 'upstarts' how it really should be done, and how it was in fact being done already in the UK. Hence the friendly rivalry between Surrey (Sorry) Hash and the Barnes (Yuppie) Tennis Club Hash. Many of each membership now r*n on both.

Today, Surrey H3 is the oldest year-round *weekly* Hash in the UK, and hence have more r*ns on the board than Bicester with their wimpy winter schedule [Isn't that all year round in England? –ed.]. Long-term bingers and whingers include Gerry Gurney (who, like Raper, was also from Singapore H3), Richard Piercy, and John Buss.

Scotland the Depraved.

Hashing came late to Scotland, but what they lacked in punctuality they've more than compensated for in single-malted mayhem and madness. It seems that, according to some dipstick research undertaken by Olymprick and Sheena Gillespie, the Aberdeen Haggis H3 – founded in November 1978 by a KL escapee – might be the earliest example of McHashing. However, it crashed and burned after just four outings and never registered on any 'official' radar.

More officially, it was February 8 1981 a rather chilly Sunday morning in Edinburgh when Lt-Col Willie Couper decided that a little exercise was in order, along the lines of the KL tradition. He had just moved up from Surrey H3. So he parked his car outside Holyrood House, and he and a pack of two other military types, suspected of being Ken McGukin and Allan Thomson, tore around the Arthur's Seat landmark. They sweated a little, they had a couple of beers, and felt all was right with the world. They voted for doing this each week, but felt that the group should be expanded to make a little more noise and a little more fun.

So a classified ad was taken out in the local paper. Success! Seven turned up on trail the following week, including Thomson's partner Susan, and Susan Vye. It was a rather tame group by all accounts, the kennel persona shaped and dominated by the rather Presbyterian and old-school military Couper, who was GM. Gradually, the pack swelled, with The Brewer and some irrepressible characters such as Mad George Wilkes joining the ranks. What Wilkes saw at Jakarta InterHash the following year opened his eyes to a whole bunch of nefarious Hashing practices that only encouraged him more, much to the chagrin of the conservative and rather pukka founders.

Edinburgh's 100th was a tame affair, well short of the expectations of the visitors. With the onset of the Falklands War, Couper was transferred out. Wilkes became GM and pushed the Hash to a level of behaviour which was not only unseen in Scotland, but animalistic even by seasoned Asian Hash standards, when they attended UK Nash Hash 1983. Cambridge H3 said: "Members of the Edinburgh H3 should be separated from the normal human beings at away thrashes."[76] They had arrived! The mould for true Scottish Hashers had been cast in mud. And lots of it. The Scots lined up like so many lemmings for a chance to Hash. Soon, Edinburgh decided to cap their membership off.

And so it was that on Wednesday 11 April 1984, an off-shoot group called The New Town Hash set off from the home of one of their members and ended up well oiled in Kay's Bar in The New Town [New, meaning only 230-odd years old –ed.]. This new mid-week format proved popular, so Bad News and Nut Case – decreed the founders in the absence of anyone else wanting to take the blame – decided to declare the TNT Hash open for business officially on July 4 1984, making a mess of the Preservation Hall Tavern.

Soon 70 to 80 Half Minds were wrecking the Wednesday evening quietness. Costume and theme r*ns added colour and quirkiness to the kennel, which celebrated its 100th r*n with an On On at Edinburgh Castle, no less. Over the years, The Argyle and The Golden Rule reaped the benefit of the TNT Hasher's intemperance.

Meanwhile, the original Edinburgh H3 kennel kept steaming on, making a name for itself with special events like the Commonwealth Games Hash in 1986, and the 1989 UK Nash Hash. Mr Nuisance, Radar, Railroad, Ayatollah, Cock of the North, 70 Shillings and 80 Shillings making a regular, well, nuisance of themselves at their long-standing Hash House, The Brewers. But Charlie 'The Brewer' Tuck's liver has taken more direct hits than anyone else, racking up 1,000 r*ns on the same day that the kennel celebrated its 1,111th! These days, while the mixed EH3 still keeps to its Sunday morning 11am heart-start, Edinburgh Hashers can find a trail or an event or a pub-crawl just about every night of the week, with a lively cross-pollination [In every sense of the word –ed.] between all chapters.

Aberdeen Anguish.

With Aberdeen being one of the world's major oil centres, it was inevitable that 'oiltrash' coming in from the Middle East and Asia had been infected with the

Hash bug, and would be looking for treatment before withdrawal set in. The BP refinery was home to Egypt H3 exile Mark 'Tortoise' Thompson and nearly a dozen other slippery customers, and – over several cans of McEwans with Phil 'Tonto' Townsend – the plan was hatched to have their first r*n in Kirkhill Forest on January 23 1983. From there it got out of control, with Wild Local setting the pace for this mixed chapter, which begat a hundred shiggy-loving characters, all far more unattractive than Lifeboats [So we won't mention the ugly bastards like Olymprick and Ronnie Robb –ed.]. The pack, which averages around 40 hounds, couldn't make it round the trail without their obligatory beer check strategically placed about two-thirds the way round. Offenders receive the Down Down finale and have to don the much-feared never-washed Hashit t-shirt.

McIlroy Was Here.

'Oiltrash' was also responsible for Glasgow getting on trail. Roger 'Big Mac' McIlroy blew in from The Hague to enjoy the spoils [Or is that spills? –ed.] with BritOil which had just set up shop in Glasgow. They began making plans for their first r*n, pinning notices up around the Britoil premises. Additionally they started a scurrilous whisper campaign, building up hopes of "free beer, free Hash and even the much sought-after free love" for attendees.

Simpson and Big Mac laid the first trail in Pollok Park on August 26 1985, and took a case of beer along for good measure. The hockey ladies turned up, as did Graham Dean, Wol Chaffe, John Nieto and Christine Flint. Whether any free love eventuated is not clearly documented, but it was decided that this should be a regular thing. After the fourth 'dry r*n', they felt the Glasgow H3 was ready to take on the world and declare themselves open for business. Yes, only in Scotland is r*n #5 considered r*n #1, and Founder Member t-shirts were duly r*n up, Hash sheets produced, and Down Downs duly dispensed. This brought more names into the fold, such as Maw and Paw Broon, plus Carolyn Grant. Glasgow was up and r*nning. Then, in true 'oiltrash' style, it was time for Big Mac to move on. The local sheep were much relieved at the prospect of a break, and the Hash Hashed on.

There are now approximately 15 hard-drinking, shiggy-seeking Hash kennels in Scotland. Lt-Col Couper would be wriggling in his slippers, wondering just where he went wrong.

But perhaps no kennel is more indicative of the spread of Hashdom than the Falkland Islands, Britain's own little piece of the Atlantic Ocean. The Falklands started on trail in 1985 with the building of a new airport following the Falklands War. Bunter, who had figured in Cambridge and Bali previously, was the driver in this case. A couple of years later – with the completion of that project – the chapter folded. However in late 1989 Red Leader and The Tin Man, who had been part of Bunter's previous hound pack, got it going again briefly before it folded. With the land now all privately owned, or permanently fenced-off because of landmines, it became un-Hashable.

As the self-acclaimed eccentric capital of the world, Britain is not lacking in colourful chapters, full of weird and wonderful idiosyncrasies, and world-class Hashers. But we'll mention these chapters instead:

The Sub-60 H3 is based in Weymouth. Its r*ns have to be completed by the hounds in under the hour. Penalties are given to the *hare* for setting too long a r*n, ie, over an hour. "If there is a drink stop – and there frequently is – r*ns do go on longer," says one regular. "But the time for on-the-r*n drinking is subtracted … sort of."

The Hemispheral Umbral Shadow H3 (*HUSHHHH*) is a Solar Eclipse Hash, founded by Spoons. "The idea was hatched by myself during Truro H3 eclipse week after drinking too much of Skinners – Who Put The Lights Out? – specially brewed for the eclipse," he says. "We've had two Hashes so far," he says. Bottles of said brew were taken to Zambia for r*n #2 for special Down Downs to host Hash, Lusaka H3. Spoons says the advantage of the Solar Eclipse Hash is they are the only Hash that knows *years* in advance where and when their r*ns will be (although things are still organised last-minute in the great Hash tradition). Their receding hareline currently reads as follows:

#3 December 4 2002 Mozambique/South Africa
#4 November 23 2003 Mirnyy, Antarctica
#5 April 8 2005 San Carlos, Panama
#6 March 29 2006 Kayseri, Turkey
#7 August 1 2008 Xian, China
#8 July 22 2009 Jabalpur, India
#9 July 11 2010 Easter Island
#10 November 13 2012 Cairns, Australia
#11 November 3 2013 Pakwach, Uganda
#12 March 20 2015 Torshavn, Faeroe Islands
#13 March 9 2016 Sampit, Borneo
#14 August 21 2017 Scottsbluff, Nebraska, USA

"R*n #4 is posing quite a challenge," he says, " but one or two Hashers are making inquiries about getting to Antarctica."

The Drop Zone H3 in Scarborough r*n the day after one of their lot – presumably a Harriette – 'drops' a baby. "When the news is out," says the aptly named Pampers, "I immediately hit the printers and job the t-shirts and we r*n the next day. We also name the baby (something innocuous) and print it a tiny version of the t-shirt."

The Brits love their acronyms and exploit them for all they're worth when naming their kennels. Witness: Cambridge Randomly Active Bash (CRABS), First UK Anti-Lunar Light (FUKALL), South Monmouth and East Gwent (SMEG), South of Devon Anti-Lunar Light (SODALL), South Oxfordshire and District Official (SODOFF), Currently Unnamed North Thames (CUNT), Westerham and North Kent (WANK), Bicester Unofficial Moon Shine (BUMS), Fosse Annual R*n by Torchlight (FART), Portsea Island Seriously Social (PISS), Scottish Hashers in Temporary Exile (SHITE), First UK Organised Formation Flying

Squad (FUKOFF) … and *Second* as well (SUKOFF), South of River Thames Extremely Drunk (SORTED) aka Staggers North of River Thames Extremely Drunk (SNORTED), and Forth and Clyde around Falkirk (FACAF). Other kennel names include Hooray Henley (r*n a few times a year including the Henley Regatta), Far Canal from Wales, Haunch of Venison Mountain Rescue (named after their pub), Slut & Pimp, Jersey Crapaud, and Black Nose Taxi H3.

At last count there were 206 chapters (including eight bike Hash chapters) in the UK. "An increase of 10 per cent over last year," says the Prof in his foreword to the UK Hash House Harriers Directory 2001. "So overall Hashing is continuing to grow at a very healthy rate."

Singing in the Rain …

While life in the colonial tropics bred its share of eccentrics this was often blamed on them being out in the sun a bit too long. But on home soil, the British are equally inclined. So much so that an annual contest – Best British Eccentric – is held annually. Toe wrestlers with inflated yellow gloves like a chicken's comb on their head compete with men who dress to look like baked beans who in turn look normal compared to the gent who cycles his Edwardian tricycle-turned-catamaran down the River Thames. Bernard Le Vay, who describes himself as an expert on eccentricity, said: "We should all be extremely proud of Britain's eccentric heritage. Throughout history, our spirit of eccentricity has produced great thinkers, writers, inventors, explorers and scientists – and, of course, our famous sense of humour." Surely, Hashers were inadvertently overlooked in that list but he could be talking about the Hash when he goes on to say: "We could all learn a thing or two from their alternative approach to life and help make every day just a little less ordinary."[(105)]

Surprisingly – given that most of the Hash's expatriate founders were British and the long heritage of Hares and Hounds – England got into Hashing very late. "I would think it may have been due to the very existence of these H&H clubs which inhibited the H3 development," says Hashtorian Prof, of Bicester H3. "Whereas the social life in the colonies was very laid back and often centred on the Hash, those returning to the UK – being from many different companies – were dispersed widely and the only existing clubs individuals had access to were these highly competitive Hare & Hounds r*nning clubs and not the socialising clubs they would have preferred. It was only when the army units returned from the Malayan war (sic) that there were large groups of people who could establish viable H3 clubs based on their barracks. Even then it was only those which threw their membership open to civilians which have since survived."

But isn't it paradoxical that something so lax and ill defined as the Hash should find so many fervent fans in something so ironed and polished as the British Army?

"I don't think it paradoxical that the military have been responsible for much of the propagation," says the English Hasher who has probably done more to expose the civilised world to Hashing than any other, Mountain Rescue. "The military can recognise ill-discipline and practice it as well as the next man if they put their minds to it. The fact that we do travel a lot naturally leads to a general spread." The other prominent military figure, Ray 'The Brig' Thornton, sees no paradox in the military being involved in such a disorganised shambles as The Hash: "Not at all! Those Hashes I have known that were primarily military in origin accepted the spirit of the Hash wonderfully," he says. "I have never experienced a rank problem but, in my experience, the British Army was always able to work this miracle in sport."

Half Pint, a retired Lieut-Colonel in the Winchester area, says: "A lot of military Hashes were officers only, and men officers only at that," as they usually went back to the Officers Mess for their On On beers, and fraternising with lower ranks was not the done thing. "It was also a good way for them to behave really stupidly away from their men." Like himself – who had postings in Germany, Brunei and Bahrain – there are a lot of returned military in the area looking for a Hash. "You can Hash every night of the week here," he says, happily adding: "I used to be a serious r*nner, but I'm better now!"

Candy Floss, pony-tailed globe-trotter of Yorkshire H3 says: "I spend a third of my salary on the Hash. I've done 300 r*ns with my home Hash, and probably almost as many on away r*ns." Lately he's been seen all over the world draped in a Welsh flag, giving the Cardiff bid a boost. Fat Bastard, who has Hashed in Saudi as well as his native UK, also takes his Hashing seriously. Dressed in an outrageously coloured t-shirt [More like a bad acid trip –ed.] at UK Nash Hash he said: "At registration they asked me for my name. I said 'Fat Bastard'. They said 'No, your *human* name'. I said 'I don't have one because I don't exist outside of the Hash'."

Speaking of the outside world, Paella, a statuesque blonde Harriette said: "People must wonder what I get up to … I'm always covered in scratches on my legs and my back!" And despite the national dress of Scotland being very skirt-like, the Red Dress r*n still raises eyebrows there. "People can't believe what they're seeing," says Oxford. "The problem is there's so many events. If I was single I would be at Hash weekends *every* weekend. If you were a single guy you wouldn't have to worry about your social calendar … Hashing supplies it all."

But there is wide variance in the sociability of UK Hashes. Weybridge H3 holds no circle. After the r*n they just disband and adjourn to a local restaurant. "What's the point of that?" echoed a number of English Hashers at UK Nash Hash 2001. "*That's* not Hashing!" However, Vicar from Guernsey defends their similar format: "We're only nine by five miles and we see the same 20 or so people each week, so we don't bother with Down Downs and circles – it's just a waste of drinking beer. Besides we're not there for just two beers – we're out for the whole night," he says of the notoriously hospitable chapter, who always turn on a good party at major events. "Plus, we're all on bicycles home these days." [Perhaps wheelbarrows would be better –ed.]

"We have about 16 chapters in Devon," says Redlight, a Welsh Harriette, "but they're all totally different. TITS doesn't have circles and Down Downs … just a beer and that's it," she says, pointing out that many of its members are commandos who are more interested in keeping fit. So what's it like being a single Harriette surrounded by so much testosterone on the Hash? "Verbal is OK, touching is not," is her philosophy on acceptable Hash behaviour. "Just because I'm a Hasher there's no need to touch me. But you give as good as you get. To me I have a rule ... never shag a Hasher. That lasted five years."

To Pure Genius, a Harriette from Guernsey, the Hash means "I can go out every week, I don't have to worry about putting my make-up on, I just put my t-shirt on, r*nning shorts and I go out, meet some great friends, have a good laugh and be myself." She got introduced to the Hash by her sister who was r*nning in Phuket, Thailand, at the time. When her sister came back to the UK for a while, they looked up the Hash book and went along. "What a load of nutters," was her first impression, after overcoming her initial fear: "Everyone gets a bit scared when you say 'a r*nning club'. But it's nothing like that – I've never even r*n for a bloody bus!"

Of Hashers, "A jollier bunch of people you couldn't hope to meet," wrote Will L.B. Bogarde[1]. "These are just the folk that you wanted to bump into, particularly if you're new in town ... whatever you wanted to know – the best pickup joints, the cost of a bonk, or the address of a reliable VD clinic – someone on the Hash is bound to know." He should know – he called Bicester H3 home, with his other home Hash being Manila, Philippines.

But Wigless from Fiji came up against some good old English frostiness when he ran with London. "Visitors made themselves welcome by talking to each other," he said of the "crappy vibe". However elsewhere, notably Surrey, he found a much warmer reception. "I even had women wanting to drive me home – that's never happened anywhere else."

When Old Wares did a Hash tour of the UK he also had mixed feelings on the way they operated. "Most had no experience of overseas Hashing, so it was a little on the formal side," says the Asia and Australia veteran. Formal or not, intrepid travel writer Bill Bryson – an American who lived in the UK for 20 years – brings up a point about the Brits: "If there is one golden quality that characterises the Brits," he says, "it is an innate sense of good manners and you defy it at your own peril."[75] This partially explains the noble instincts of Hashdom.

"Apart from Eric the Retard there's nobody really violent on the Hash," says Revolta. "It's always good natured and good fun."

"Two punch-ups in 20 years is not bad," says the accused, who has averaged four r*ns a week since 1980 [My calculator doesn't go that high –ed.]. "Life is good on the Hash," says the one-time NASA consultant enjoying a mid-morning beer in the Bengal Tiger pub restaurant in Helsinki. "It makes you wonder why you didn't join earlier."

"We *look* like lager louts, especially when there's a big group of us," says Low Profile – a Brit who's lived in Malaysia and Nigeria – on trail in the Forest of Bere. "But no one gets a bop on the nose. Hashers are good people from all kinds of jobs. After the Hash get together there's not a trail of blood – maybe just a pile of peas and carrots!"

To Sir Cluggs, an MBE recipient with the British High Commission in Africa, the attraction is the egalitarianism of the Hash: "Put on your shorts and a t-shirt and we're all the same," he says. However, *under* those shorts and t-shirts is where things get more interesting. Hence the phenomena of Hash romances and, often, Hash weddings. At UK Nash Hash 2001, a Hash wedding was held, uniting Pork Torpedo and Horny. The ceremony was celebrated by several hundred Hashers dressed in the nominated theme of The Rocky Horror Show. Fishnet stockings and suspenders were the order of the day – and that was just the guys. Ghouls and transvestites aplenty filled the room.

"As I'm a social worker I need my Mondays," said Horny – the blushing bride who wore a red PVC outfit that could hardly contain all her womanly curves – who's been Hashing seven years. "It's a stress-buster." Pork [Or Mr. Torpedo to his bank manager –ed.] first heard of Hashing on a stopover in Morocco.

Their proud families were in attendance to witness the wedding. Any resistance from them? "Not at all," Pork Torpedo says. "I got a little bit wary as they've got no real idea about Hashing," said Horny immediately after the ceremony. "But they're all smiling and they liked it."

Why was it important to them to get married at a Hash? "It was something Horny's done for quite a while, and she got me into it," says Pork Torpedo. "I'm a submariner in the navy so my basic instinct is to be stupid, be a child, and just be ridiculous, and it just fits in," he says. "It's just so good to get into a different circle of friends with the same mentality, I don't have to be anyone I'm not, I don't have to change myself to be anyone different." For the record, the bridal waltz was a mass rendition of the Time Warp ('Let's …do … the time … warp … agaaaaaaaain') and they spent their first night as a married couple doing a naked midnight Hash and sharing a tent with their best man!

After the lively celebration Lesley ("Just Lesley") the vicar shared her thoughts on this Hash wedding. "I'd much rather have honesty than hypocrisy and people making vows and promises they don't intend," she said. Her thoughts on the Hashing crowd? "I've never met quite such a friendly crowd," she said, admitting she'd never heard of the Hash before. "I asked for their respect and they gave me their respect and that really chuffed me."

Within the United Kingdom, Hashing is noticeably less successful in Ireland than in other parts. Surprising, as it is a country of renowned boozers and peat bogs, ie, perfect Hashing conditions.

Over a pint or seven of Guinness in Mulligan's Bar, Dublin, Polly – who has lived and Hashed in the USA, Asia, Middle East and Australia – explained the factors inhibiting Irish Hashing. "Firstly, we are very active socially and we are a very family-oriented society." As if to underline the pull of family life in Ireland, he now considers himself "half a Hasher" since he got married. Polly is convinced it has nothing to do with 'Irish versus British' attitudes. Those who do Hash in Ireland are also ageing, and it usually befalls the same old faces to keep things moving in the Emerald Isle. "I wish there were a bunch of single 20-year-old-guys who could take over, organise away weekends, and so on," he laments.

Stick the Tongue In is an Australian based in Dublin, and she has enjoyed many great Hashing moments in Ireland. "We had 80 of us on the Millennium Bridge doing Father Abrahams for our 600th r*n," she says. "We even got the harmonic wave going." Another fan of Hashing in Ireland is Fag, from Washington DC, who spent three years there. "I miss Ireland so much – the mud, the shiggy … and no poison ivy," he says holding two thumbs up.

But the shiggy doesn't come any better or thicker than in Scotland. The expression 'happy as a pig in shit' could be applied to Scottish Hashers. But at least the pigs have an excuse – they actually cover themselves in mud in order to lower their body temperature. Scottish Hashers use beer and whisky to try and achieve the same aim, giving them a reputation for being rather rowdy and boisterous. Oxford, of Edinburgh H3, jumps in to defend his countrymen: "We have an occasional fling, and at the big events we do generally have fun," he said through an interpreter. "Some of it can be outrageous but I wouldn't go as far as saying our Hashing as such is over the top. Scots enjoy themselves and that's what Hashing's all about. It's just an ongoing event."

The Hashing schedule in their area is busy. It was six nights a week, but that was found to be not enough. "We've started one new Hash just to fill in a date we never had on a Thursday evening." And the packs are nicely balanced between Hashmen and Harriettes. "Everyone's a Hasher, male or female … we all want to enjoy each other's company is the prevailing attitude," the Hasher of five years says of the mixed kennels. But the faces tend to be the same ones. "I don't think we're bringing enough young people through into Hashing, and that's a concern," he says. Another concern is that the Office of National Statistics[111] reported that "Scotland shows up badly for heart disease … and alcohol-related death partly because the Scots are prone to binge-drinking more than those south of the border."

In fact, beer consumption in Britain has hit a 30-year low [Pathetic! –ed]. But it's not that the Brits are moving away from booze … just moving onto a tipple of wine and fortified alcohol instead [No poofters on the Hash! –ed.]. Still they must be drinking enough to come up with hare-brained schemes like the English kennel who are talking about hosting UK Nash Hash in Belize … a British Protectorate in central America!

And Pampers (Gary to his Mum) from Scarborough Full Moon H3, shows no signs of slowing down: "My mum once said 'I'm really glad Gary's started Hashing – it's given him something else to do apart from drinking. In fact, she doesn't know that it's given me a passport to drink in every country around the world!"

R*nning the Gauntlet.

Since Ray Thornton's first r*n-in with the police while crouching behind a hedge-row in Bicester, the bobbies have been conspicuously absent as far as the Hash is concerned. Like any civilised country, drink-drive laws are in place in England, but don't seem to be the bugbear they are elsewhere for two reasons: for those Hashes in the countryside, nipping home undetected down back lanes seems to be a satisfactory option. Or else the village itself is so small, one can ride home by bicycle or even stagger the short distance. In the larger English cities, the public transport system is the central nervous system which functions well, covers a broad spread of areas, and it's an agreeable option for most to climb on board with a skin-full after a Hash. That way, inner-city parking nightmares are also avoided.

Irate landowners are possibly the most regular brush with the law the Hash experiences. The law in the English countryside states that the public has rights to 'peaceful passage' through many parts of the land. Obviously the Hash does not quite qualify under this definition.

Surrey H3 once laid a r*n south of Shere. The map showed a footpath, but this had long since fallen into disuse, leaving the pack to fight its way through a fully grown wheatfield. Emerging relieved out the other side, the Hashers' joy was short-lived as they came face to face with a farmer, aided and abetted by a shotgun and Alsatian.

Shagger from Surrey H3: "Our On Sec at the time received a letter from the National Trust claiming that we'd r*n on NT land on December 18 1988, despite their repeated requests that we shouldn't including, they say, having written on 18/7/85, ie, 2½ years earlier. The matter was referred to their management committee and we got a letter in February 1989 saying we were banned. We did r*n there again in 1998, sending out scouting parties for wardens ahead!"

Commercial Whale from North Hants tells of a r*n through a field of cows one evening. "We thought no more about it until we received a lawyer's letter saying that our antics and noise had startled and killed a prize bull and the Hash was to blame." The Hash wrote back saying a dangerous animal such as a bull should not be kept on a public passage of land. So there. "They wrote back demanding our membership list and threatened to sue us for their loss. We replied saying we have no membership list per se, but we could possibly give you names but no addresses. Also, we don't know for sure who attended the r*n on that night. Another point – they claimed it was morning but we only r*n at night, so there was another yawning gap in their case. We just stonewalled them at every juncture until it went away."

The Friday 13th Hash organise 'Murder r*ns' [Most r*ns are murder for me –ed.] in which famous crimes in London such as the Jack the Ripper series are re-enacted. On a recent r*n the hare, Robocop, was surrounded by a large pack while describing a particularly grisly crime which took place near Scotland Yard. Seeing a large gathering on the CCTV monitor, two officers were dispatched to check it out. A panda car screeched to a halt and a stern looking WPC leapt out, obviously deciding no one should be enjoying themselves and enough was enough (the other officer was less concerned and immediately joined in with some Hashers at the back). She marched up to Robocop, who was all covered in shiggy and stage blood, and demanded: "Who's in charge here?". This elicited a gale of laughter, and she responded by telling the pack they were causing an obstruction and a breach of the peace. She pulled out her notebook, pointed at Robocop's chest and demanded to know his name. Robocop replied by pointing out that her understanding of the law was flawed, she was breaching police regulations by not having any identifying insignia, and there were over a hundred independent witnesses who would verify that the main points to prove for obstruction or a breach of the peace were absent in this case, and that he would appreciate it if she would let them get on with some real crime investigation!

She begun to suspect that he had some knowledge of what he was talking about and she asked him if he was "in the job". He then had a quiet word in her ear and she beat a hasty retreat, apologising profusely. Robocop is in fact a *very* senior police officer in his other life. Her shocked face was a picture, better than all the grisly make-up worn by the other Hashers.

In Scotland, the law is less pervasive. "Very little" is how Oxford from Edinburgh rates intervention by authorities of any type. "We're very conscious of the farmland in areas we use," he says, "we respect their land, we ask them first. They've always been very good to us."

"There are no laws of trespass in Scotland which might make it easier when the SCBs club cross land one had previously agreed to keep away from," says Thornton who Hashed there recently. As for drink-drive rules, different parts of Scotland work on a different system of detection and enforcement. "To be honest, I couldn't tell you the [blood/alcohol] level," says Oxford, whose home Hash, Cairneyhill, works on a car-pooling system.

"Ten to 20 flour-spattered and sweaty Hashers crying 'On On' is unlikely to set the men from the PSNI quaking in their boots," says Sex Reject of Belfast H3 in Northern Ireland of the police and authorities there. "As it's not a political assembly of any kind, we are not constricted from laying trail and Hashing anywhere that's open to the public. We've never tried Hashing through or near any kind of military or security force installation, so that's never been an issue." They do, however, have some restrictions on drinking alcohol in public places "but they're nowhere near as bad as say the US."

And we can't forget England's little piece of windswept paradise in the Atlantic, The Falklands, where the Hash found support at the highest possible level. "The Governor (Sir Rex Hunt) was an ex-Hasher from Kuching," says Bunter. "He was thrilled to find a Hash was formed there but did not r*n. It was the only game in town and the pack swelled to over 100 while I was there. The Army put a coach at our disposal on Monday nights so we could visit more remote parts of East Falkland."

Post-September 11, Clepto called for a self-imposed global ban on the use of white flour in the wake of the anthrax scare in Britain, USA, Australia and a few other countries as a gesture of social responsibility.

Lager Than Life Characters.

Richard 'Mountain Rescue' McAllister.
First r*n Brunei H3 1964
Founded Kluang H3, Malaysia 1967; Longmoor H3 England,1968; Lübbecke
H3, Germany 1971; Dharan H3, East Nepal 1983; Buller and Aldershot District
H3, UK 1985
Member Ft Eustis H3, USA, Kathmandu H3, Deepcut H3, UK

How'd you hear of Hashing way back then?
MR: I first heard of Hashing in Singapore before we were deployed to Brunei in
1962, but I had better things to do at the time, didn't have a car to get to the starts
and was not particularly interested anyway. Ignorant youth. Little did I know …
You were known as Wheeze at one point, but your handle has changed.
MR: At the end of the first Hash in Deepcut we came across a 'McAllister's
Recovery' vehicle and because I had recently been involved with the British
Joint Services Everest Expedition …
What are the Hash moments indelibly printed in your mind?
MR: I think Lübbecke produced one of the best and it was followed by a Hash
Pash to which our partners were invited. Now that was a party! Some of the
meets in Malaya were great and were invariably very beery affairs. We had joint
military and civilian masters and many of the civilians were planters so we had
plenty of real estate and good drinking bases. Drinking and driving was not a
problem then. Kathmandu had some memorable scenic r*ns.
And what about the not-so-good times on trail?
MR: Probably when laying a trail with a rather weighty planter in his estate and
we came to a raging stream after a downpour. There was a bamboo 'bridge'
crossing the torrent which he was about to cross. But he was far too heavy so
skinny me volunteered to try first. Halfway across the bamboo cracked, leaving
me hanging from a convenient vine in the middle of the stream. My predicament
made my co-hare giggle which was very infectious and did nothing to help my
plight. I managed to swing on over to the far side and safety. He walked 50 yards
downstream and crossed over the vehicular bridge just round the corner. His
come-uppance came a little later when he hopped over a narrow stream only to
find that the far 'bank' was floating grass. Up to his armpits in shiggy, in a real
panic. We later used the same stream to excellent effect on the pack!
How has Hashing changed over the years?
MR: The main differences in Hashing have been caused by laws protecting the
environment from litter and the roads from drunken drivers. A couple of pints
and that's it. 'Duty of Care' also means that the hares tend to accompany the
hounds to make sure they don't get lost or into trouble. Sex discrimination
allows women to join in now – pity someone didn't think of that sooner!
How does it feel to have introduced Hashing to the motherland?
MR: I'm not sure I have any great feelings about having introduced Hashing

into UK (and Europe – I think Lübbecke was the first). It was certainly far from my mind when starting up and I had no idea then that I was perhaps going to get my place in history. I suppose I'm quite chuffed! The sad thing is that the meticulous records I used to keep have probably been discarded as our bases have closed down. I was not aware of being anything of a pioneer at the time. I was more aware of the US connection when I first introduced myself as a 'proxy father' of their Hash.

How would life be different if you hadn't signed on for the Hash?

MR: I may have got married sooner! I would also have grown up fatter and with fewer friends. In fact my now wife was a teacher at Bünde (just a few miles from Lübbecke) British Army school. She wouldn't, and still doesn't, Hash!

Ray 'The Brig' Thornton.
First r*n Singapore 1962
Founder Dhekelia H3, Cyprus 1967; UK Commando Forces H3 1969; Bicester H3 1974, Donnington H3 1976; Looe & Liskeard H3 1981
Member Kuching H3

How did you first hear of the Hash in Singapore?

TB: A chum sandbagged me. In 1962 I was posted to the staff of HQ 3 Commando Brigade, then stationed in Sembawang in Singapore. I'd been there for three days when a chum, Mike Dudderidge, took me to join the Singapore Hash. I don't think I ever fully recovered. The mismanagement comprised only an On Sec and two JMs. GMs were unknown, nicknames were not used and Down Downs unheard of. If we objected to somebody we simply chucked him in the nearest deep water.

And how did you find yourself in the wilderness of Sarawak?

TB: In 1963 we were on exercise in up-country Aden when that somewhat minor unpleasantness started in Indonesia. We were flown back smartly and airlifted into Kuching and spread around Sarawak. With a number of others I helped form the Kuching Hash and ran with them until my first commando tour was up. It was about this time that I really thought that I was cured – I was then on the staff of the Adjutant-General in London and that had my full attention. Then came a dreadful remission. I was promoted and sent to Cyprus, Germany and other sybaritic hell-holes. It's said that, in the army, the best and worse move frequently. I claim to have been in neither group.

Any regrets from your time spent Hashing?

TB: When I reached the age of 65 I made a great mistake. I gave up r*nning. Never do it. L2H3 of course went from strength to strength as I watched it with an ever more drooping eye. Then I read a piece I had written some years ago boasting that I would still be r*nning when I was 70. Since this was due to hit me in seven months time I realised that I had better sharpen up. Getting fit again is a young man's sport. It took Jules (my wife) and me three months to get to the stage where we could at least make a token showing in the SCB branch of the Hash. I've read that a heavy drinker, taking his first drink after a long abstinence, is welcomed back into the heart of the disease as if he had never been away. So it is with Hashing. It's nice to be back.

What were the best times on trail?

TB: Sarawak, with dissidents in the jungle. Cyprus with EOKA on the loose.

And what's the main thing you got from Hashing?

TB: In no other sport (?) will you find so different and entertaining a membership.

David 'Short Cut' Scourse.

First r*n KL H3 1957

Member KL Harriettes, Petaling Jaya H3, Tamar Valley H3, Stannary H3

You joined Hash at a low ebb in its life?

SC: In 1957 only one Hash club existed, Mother Hash KL. It had about 20 active members, though numbers could become 10. Hash nearly perished. Late '58/ early '59 we had a recruitment drive and numbers improved to around 25 and Hash survived, but only just.

Are there any positives to the numbers being smaller?

SC: Numbers being around 20 meant you knew everyone very well and a good Hash spirit existed. Later clubs became very large (100 or more). The best Hash club is still around 30 Hashers with all members forming a close-knit club. Numbers in many clubs are very large and inevitably 'cliques' of members have formed and members contest positions in the club organisation structure. Early KL AGMs used to be completed in the shortest time possible – the record was under a minute on the basis that valuable drinking time should not be used up for the AGM.

Tell us about Cecil Lee, with whom you ran briefly, who was a director of your company's group.

SC: Cecil was a great example of Hashing … treated all Hashers with a genuine greeting. He was very pleased to see how the basic concept of Hash had become such a major worldwide club. HHH is one of Malaysia's most successful exports but never really recognised as such.

You have an interesting story about The Hash House photo.

SC: The Royal Selangor Club did not have any pictures of the original Hash House. The Jap occupation plus a major fire in 1970 had destroyed all records. We checked with the Malay Mail – again no luck, records lost during Jap times. I was on leave in the UK in 1980 and r*nning with Tamar Valley who, to my surprise, had a picture of 'Hash House' displayed at each r*n. It came out Torch Bennett had retired to Belstone, a village about 20 miles from my house in the UK and he had provided the picture. I took a copy back to KL and the enlarged version is in the Hash Bar, and has appeared in many Hash publications since.

You've done around 2,500 runs. Any real shockers?

SC: This was r*n # 1272 [When the whole KL pack was out in jungle overnight, February 1969 –ed.]. The diesel engine heard during the night was assumed to be a marine launch searching for drowned Harriers. 'Hope they are alright,' I said, 'as I would not like George Gilbertson in my water supply!' Roy Booth's night out for his first wedding anniversary was to be attended by Jane (my wife) and I, so I got it in the neck for having taken Roy along to the Hash.

How has Hash changed over the years?

SC: KL prided itself for many years in having a very relaxed approach. The only count on members r*nning was the cars parked, and when the beer on site had r*n out you looked at the cars that were left to ensure all r*nners had returned, and a search party – if required – was organised. This did result in John Duncan being left out overnight as he had arrived late at the r*n and parked some distance away from the main site!

Any other changes?

SC: It was taboo to discuss business on the Hash. Drinking, sport, sex, limited politics. No commercialisation in any form was considered. Our founding members must be turning in their graves at books/directories being produced, especially for profit.

What's the main thing you've got from your 100 years of Hashing?

SC: In '58 we had a High Court judge, director of forestry, senior police officer, with Hashers of all levels, including me, a very young and junior new arrival. The Hash did not care what level you were provided you could r*n a mile or so and drink a few beers over a yarn after the r*n. Nobody used rank – you were an equal in the Hash, which resulted in many lasting friendships, now worldwide, being formed. In later years, when Malaysians of all races became Hash members, this was very good in breaking down racial barriers, and most of my close Malaysian friends originated from the Hash.

And did your children inherit the same passion for Malaysia and the Hash?

SC: My son Robert is resident in KL, and a keen member of the PJ Saturday Hash. He is in fact engaged to a Malaysian girl he met on the Hash (not like '57, no ladies allowed).

Ron 'The Penguin' Strachan.

First r*n Jakarta H3 1974
Co-founder Jakarta Harriettes 1977; Indo-Nostalgia H3 1993
Member Muscat H3, Aberdeen H3

How did you get yourself into this mess?

TP: I first heard of the HHH when working in Bahrain in 1972 but, from what I understood, this was an activity which was not for me. Even when I moved to Jakarta and heard of this group again I avoided making contact as I wasn't much of a r*nner and the antics were – well – just too childish for me! It was an Australian Embassy girl who eventually persuaded me to come along one night to a special r*n, the Jakarta 200th, and that night I became addicted and have never looked back.

And you were on the first r*n in Oman of all places.

TP: I was in the fortunate position in 1975/76 to be working in the interior of Oman when I heard the rumour of a Hash starting up near the coast by some army personnel ex-Singapore based near Muscat. I found my way by Land-Rover over the untarred track the 80 kilometres or so to join their first r*n.

How did you get the name The Penguin?

TP: I took to the habit of always wearing a sarong after the r*n. I have to admit that being short in stature wearing a sarong with two short feet projecting beneath and a peaked cap, I did resemble a penguin.

Tell us about Jakarta's heyday.

TP: Around 1980/82 Jakarta Hash was recognised as being probably the largest in the world with a regular 200 Hashers r*nning each week. I was Hashmaster at this time and, believe me, finding adequate car parking space and controlling a circle of 200 thirsty, noisy r*nners was not always easy. We had a wait-list to join and many tried bribery to no avail [Bribery in Indonesia? I'm shocked! –ed.]. With such large numbers it was only a matter of time before an alternative men's Hash would start, which did happen in 1986. I left Indonesia in 1992 having r*n more than 750 r*ns with Jakarta H3 alone and with a total of more than 1,000 r*ns in Indonesia. My world total is now around 1,750.

And you're one of the 'InterHash survivors'?

TP: I have attended all InterHashes from 1978 to the present, except for Phuket, which I had to cancel at the last minute to arrange my mother's funeral. In such circumstances I have been accepted as one of the 'Survivors' together with Drainoil, Wolf, Philthy, Whorator and Cheebye, who calls me the sixth of the five survivors.

How did the Indo-Nostalgia Hash get started in the UK?

TP: When I left Jakarta in 1992 I became a regular with Aberdeen Hash but my thoughts always returned to my 20 years in the East, and I would find any excuse to return to Jakarta to Hash there. It was good old Tampon who came to the rescue in 1993. He had Hashed in Medan and Merapi in Yogyakarta, one of the most male chauvinistic, vile Hashes in the world at the time. Checks on the r*n would be placed in the middle of the most filthy whorehouses that could be found. A fine Hash! Tampon was also bored to tears on his return to UK, and he contacted me to ask if we could not set up a Hash in the UK which would conform to Indonesian standards, where the circle after must be longer than the r*n, and anyone who had Hashed in Indonesia would be welcome to join.

Jane 'Thunderthighs' Akroyd.

First r*n London H3 1978
Member London H3, West London H3, FUK Full Moon
Co-founder Royal London Harriettes 1989

Tell us about your first Hash outing?

TT: September '78 at Jack Straws pub in Hampstead. Four to five miles – I was last, and shattered! I was a member of IVC [Inter Varsity Club]. Hashing was a sub-club. In the end the only thing I did with IVC was Hashing so I left and just Hashed. I started Hashing to lose weight, but over the years the opposite has happened.

How many r*ns ago was that?
TT: I plan to celebrate my 1,000th with London H3 in May '03. Probably done 1,500 or 1,600 worldwide to date.
And your best time out of that lot?
TT: 1988 in Bali, the night Hooray Henry won the world Down Down. Fantastic! Dancing in that wonderful venue to Fartin' Martin and the Booze Brothers, then in *bemos* back to the hotel – all jumped into the pool naked and drank champagne out of Henry's two-litre silver cup. Best Hashing has been in Malaysia, ie, hardest and longest. But you can't beat the English countryside.
Any worst moments you wish to forget?
TT: Seeing photos of my huge 'love handles' while putting on a celebration t-shirt (back to the crowd) at my 900th r*n celebration last year.
How is the Hash changing or evolving?
TT: Hashing now has as many female Hashers as men. The concept of girlie bars, etc is slowly dying, thank goodness, although I'm sure the dirt is still thriving. The Hash has already evolved – Magic's directory has shown us that. In the Eighties it was the bible, but the web has taken its place. I think Goa will take us back to basics and the meaning of Hashing.
What've you got from your years of Hashing?
TT: A bloody long Christmas card list!

Nick 'Half-a-Fuck' Storr.
First r*n Bandung Men's Hash 1980
Co-founder Labasa H3, Fiji 1982
Member Manila H3, Bicester H3

Your Hash name is intriguing. Share the gory details.
H-A-F: Initially based on a physiological abnormality … a dick of incredible length, but with a width varying between that of an HB pencil and a fibre optic strand, depending on its state of excitement. Completely independently of this, Numb Nuts asked me what my Hash name was. 'Don't have one,' was the intelligent reply, 'but me real name's Nick.' 'Well, you're Half a Fuck, then …' *Nick-Nick* means 'fuck' in Arabic.
What about your most enjoyable time on the Hash?
H-A-F: When my trusty mate, the indefatigable Chromedome, and I were told that the two hares intended to set the Manila Men's 1,000th r*n at Colonel Arsenio's Sleazy Hotsprings and Notional Eating Establishment 70 kilometres south of Manila, and that the 150-strong [? –ed.] pack would be looking for some 'bumpy company', we knew just what to do. So it was Hi! Ho! for P. Burgos Street to place the task of choosing some jolly bonk-machines in the capable and ever-grasping hands of the *mamasans* of three bars.

The transport turned out to be an off-duty yellow school bus, so Chromedome and I duly collected our baggage, which consisted of 61 assorted bar-girls from various bars, at three in the afternoon and trooped off to board the bus. We had already carefully provisioned the bus with 10 cases of San

Miguel Beer, 12 assorted bottles of Tanduay Rum or Ginebra (a local spirit that also has several industrial uses and is outlawed under the Geneva Convention for use against enemy troops), 70,000 pesos and 432 condoms.

Buying the condoms had been an unusual experience. I was at that time a staff member of the rather po-faced Asian Development Bank, which is based in Manila, and the bank had a commissary conveniently located in the basement. I was the first customer in, at 9am sharp on the Friday, grabbed three packs of 144 condoms each, and headed for the check-out desk.

Chromedome and I shepherded our loving crew down to the On On, and we threw our lissom and willing companions into the boiling bouillon just at the right moment at the end of the Circle – talk about a feeding frenzy! David Attenborough, eat your heart out! However, the normally not-over-reflective Chromedome put it very nicely a day or two later. "You know where we went wrong, Half-a? (We have long been on first name terms.) There we had been, driving happily down the optimistically named South Super Highway, with 10 cases of beers, a dozen bottles of hooch, 70,000 pesos, 432 condoms and 61 highly trained and desirable women. What we *should* have done is to have shot the driver, flung his mate out by the roadside and just kept on going. Bugger the Hash, whose woeful lack of nookie would have been their problem, not ours. We could have stopped off near Lipa City and founded a dynasty somewhere up in the hills with those kind of assets." Men have done far more with far less of a start!

What about your worst Hashing moment?
H-A-F: Like the booze I've drunk, the company I've kept or the women I've known, I really can't remember a bad one!

How has Hashing changed over the years?
H-A-F: Not much; older Hashers stop Hashing or die (generally, but not always, the former first), but there's always some new and carefree ones coming along. There was a period a few years back when the droning of the Hash-bore, ie, those sad gits whose social life revolves entirely around Hashing, rose to intolerable levels. Can you imagine Gispert and the other founders talking about nothing else but Hashing all week long? No fucking way! The Hash was invented as an amiable way of passing some time and nothing more, and that's what the institution is still best at.

How would you compare the Hashes in different places you've visited?
H-A-F: There have been obvious physical differences on the Hashing territory available to the 40-odd different Hashes that I've attended, but very little difference in the ethos. In some places, local conditions such as rabid Muslims or anti-drink driving laws make it harder to drink and enjoy yourself, but everybody still always seems to get suitably plumptious [Sounds fun to me, whatever it is –ed.] and rat-arsed no matter where the Hashes have been.

What's the main thing that you've got from Hashing?
H-A-F: A guaranteed laugh and the sure and comforting knowledge that wherever I am in the world someone just as tacky as me is only a phone call away!

Is it safe to assume you're a big fan of InterHash in Asia, or elsewhere?
H-A-F: Anywhere in the world, of course! Just think of the stunning rumpy-pumpy to be found in South America! Borrow the money and go there and check it out, instead of wasting time asking a lot of damn-fool questions.
[Footnote: Half-a-Fuck sadly died in June 2002, soon after completion of this interview.]

Richard 'Gunga Dick' Murphy.
First r*n Jesselton H3 1965
Founded Princeton University Class of 1951 H3
Member Singapore H3, Kathmandu H3, Surrey H3, Weybridge H3, Guildford H3, Barnes H3, Brunei H3

You are possibly the first American Hasher. How did you get into the Hash?
GD: Some bloke saw me r*nning in Jesselton and asked me if I liked keeping fit. 'What the hell do you think I'm doing?' was my polite rejoinder. At my first Hash r*n, which was a nine-miler, I asked myself how the hell did these guys lose their empire?
You've done 1,605 r*ns so far. Any of those stick in your Half Mind?
GD: In June 1991, aged 61, I laid four consecutive live r*ns in four days for four different Hashes in four different venues (Surrey, Guildford, Weybridge, Barnes). I am not aware of this being done by anybody else, of whatever age.
You have another claim to shame which is something to do with attending two Hashes the furthest apart within a 24-hour period. What's that all about? And why?
GD: My long-distance Hashing event was to r*n two Hashes within 24 clock hours with the longest airline distance in between. I did this twice from both Dhaka (via Dubai) and Bangkok [5,912 miles –ed.] linking with Surrey back in 1987 and 1988, respectively. Time zones have been converted so that we are talking about 24 actual hours. Why? Why, indeed?
What about low moments in Hashing?
GD: 1997 Nash Hash in Devon when East Grinstead H3 and the Aberdeen H3 turned the r*n into a mud-bash. I wrote this up. Characteristically, both Hashes adopted my tirade as a banner. I turned up at the East Grinstead 500th, where Aberdeen were guests of honour, to find that my comments were displayed on both club's t-shirts. We are now good friends, which shows the positive power of Hashing.
How has Hashing changed over the years?
GD: Mixed instead of all male (Good). Collapse in the standard of circular writing (Bad). There is a danger of Hashing being a one-generation event.
And what have you got from this rabble?
GD: Companionship. A Hasher in a foreign country who loses his wallet and passport can always get a bed, a meal, and a cash advance. Hash is a religion, a way of life.

Terence 'Bunter' Kavanagh.
First r*n Cambridge H3 1978
Founder Falkland Islands H3 1985
Co-founder Cantabrigensis H3 1992
Founder member Indonesians In Exile H3 1994
Member Bali H3

You're a grand old man of 65 now and r*nning a pub. Beats r*nning to the beer, eh?

B: I very rarely Hash nowadays – save for big events. When I did, I always considered myself something of a Hash fraud as I detested the r*nning bit and was a Short Cutting Bastard from my first r*n. I will admit the beer tastes better after a canter, whether it is the superior British bitter or the 'frosted horse-piss' that masquerades as beer obtainable in foreign climes.

Whose fault was it for getting you out on trail?

B: In October 1966, I had a drink in the Royal Selangor Club in KL. It was a Monday night to boot and I never met any Hashers. Had I done, my Hashing CV may have started earlier! My old friend Howard Taylor who had recently returned from Bangkok decided to start one in Cambridge. Prior to Hashing I imagined that it always pissed down on Sunday mornings and I used to hit a local pub at 1pm. Surprisingly enough it seldom rained between the hours of 11am and midday when the Hash ran so it was a bonus visiting pubs within a 20 mile radius of Cambridge on a Sunday.

Where was the most Hashing fun had?

B: Probably on Bali. Prior to my first r*n, Bali GM Victor Mason addressed the pack as follows: 'RIGHT! Shut your variegated brown and yellow holes as the GM is speaking'. I couldn't believe it, but the locals and Chinese loved him dearly. A beautiful r*n and an On On outside a temple with the scene lit by a tilly lamp is hard to beat. Bali ran between 4pm and 5pm, the same time as the Balinese girls bathed in the rivers. Many a time the pack have leapt in with them to shrieks of laughter and half hearted cries of '*Nakal!*' (naughty). The local farmers thought that 'On On' was some form of greeting like 'hello' and always cried out to us whether on trail or not. Bali never needed gimmicks for enjoying a Hash – there were always temple ceremonies going on and a lop-sided shack selling lethal shots of arak every 200 yards all over the island!

Tell us about the Falklands. I can't believe that was fun ...

B: Memorable is a trail that was laid through a minefield. The Royal Engineers had kindly co-operated and laid two parallel lines of red tape through a cleared section of the field although you could see plenty of the nasty things propped up against fences and sticking out of the ground. My Hash Master's address went as follows: 'Right, you Hashers. You think you have balls? Well, if you don't stick between the red tapes during this r*n you won't have any balls left at the end of it!' All good fun. We found loads of spent ammo and live ammo during our r*ns, and a couple of crashed helicopters.

What about the extreme conditions over there?

B: At Fitzroy Sound, I was the hare and – with the help of the locals – laid a trail that returned over a 100-yard inlet as the tide was coming in. I had allowed for the pack to show their respects to the Welsh Guards memorial at nearby Bluff Cove and barely managed to get back across the inlet with the pack hard on my heels. They however, did not! I have never seen a tide come in so quick. They had to back track for a mile to cross over the bridge they went out on. They did not like it and I had to eat a penguin egg before my Down Down.

Looking back over your 500 r*ns (plus about 50 hared r*ns), what have you got from this motley crew?

B: Friendship plus a few beers and a few laughs. It has been unlike any other social club I ever belonged to. There is a code among Hashers and long may it remain.

Let's talk about your favourite topic, hosting of InterHash, which you and Warren Dosanjh from Cambridge hold strong views on.

B: If a genuine InterHash is to exist, then there is no valid reason why it could not be held in any part of the world where a healthy Hash exists and is in a position to organise such a huge undertaking successfully. Hashing is now a worldwide fraternity (some in Europe formed before many in Asia) and, in spirit, there is no difference between a Hash in Malaysia and those in Europe, Africa, Central America, New Zealand and … Australia. If the very word itself has any meaning, it means all Hashes, and not a self-selected elitist few who are within a cheap plane ride from where Gispert and Lee originally did their thing.

There have been InterHashes in Cyprus and New Zealand [And Australia twice –ed.] that were successful. The main problem with InterHash is they have got too big. You cannot have amateur organisation with so many involved and this tends to lose the casual concept of Hashing. Don't get me wrong – they are always enjoyable and a chance to meet old friends but I feel they should be more imaginative as against the stereotype stadium, food, stage show of ghastly rock music, and overlong r*ns.

How do you think the Hash will evolve from here?

B: I don't think it will. I notice in Britain there are many break-away groups who are moving back to the original concept – r*ns being an hour and minimum organisation, and less rugby club syndrome. There are also many special Hashes like the Indonesians In Exile Hash and full moon Hashes that are enjoyable mainly because they are small, have minimum organisation and are a lot of fun. Originally Hashing was stag only and from this evolved the 'wildman' Hashes in the Far East where all forms of nefarious activities are indulged in. They are a lot of fun.

Barry 'GBH' Pope.
First r*n Royal Berkshire H3 1988
Founded South Oxfordshire and District Official H3 1996
Member Swansea Jack H3

How did you get in with this lot, then?
GBH: I was in a very posh South Oxfordshire school talking privately to the Welsh headmaster about reducing the waistline and getting fitter. We agreed to meet that evening in the pub to discuss it further. A voice from behind me said 'HASHING!' I turned to see this interfering English bastard in a suit, who told me where the r*n was that Sunday. That was Shep. I turned up and soon discovered I had found the nicest, craziest bunch of people … and I knew on that first day, I had found the answer to what do I do now I cannot play soccer or rugby. Shep is now like a brother to me, and introduced me to more mischievous methods in Hashing than anyone knows.
And how does a big softie like you get called GBH?
GBH: Being an ex-police officer of 30 years I knew a few 'antics'. I went to the New Forest on a Hash weekend where another bloody Englishman tried winding me up by saying 'You're Welsh, aren't you – I fucking hate the Welsh!' Tell me more, I replied. 'You're a copper, too … you've got no chance …' As I did not wind up to this, another guy (later discovered to be the RA) asked those present 'What would you do if you were insulted all night?' Someone replied 'PUT HIM OUT!' I hoisted him onto my shoulders, securing him in the fireman's rescue lift, took him outside, and lowered him gently (?) onto the pavement. For causing the GM 'Grievous Bodily Harm', I was immediately named GBH. How was I to know what a GM was? I had been set up and again that GM is now one of my best friends.
How many r*ns have you notched up now?
GBH: Not sure how many r*ns exactly, but over 1,000 around the world.
Any truly memorable trails r*n or laid?
GBH: Together, Shep and I became famous for our Braille trail. At that time in Berks. H3 there was a blind man, Queenie aka Red Rum, who I believe has r*n over 100 marathons. We thought it a good idea to find out what it is like to r*n blind [As opposed to drunk –ed.]. At the North Hants UK Nash Hash we laid a Braille trail, and blindfolded half the Hash. We explained that halfway the blinds changed over, so those with eyes, had better make the most of it in the first half. I will always remember one Hasher's comment: 'I can't see a thing, but I smell something fucking awful!' Yes, they went through the shiggy chest-deep while their partners were crawling – dry – along the side. Shep and I were thrown in the shit, I can't understand why.

Robert 'Le Voisin' Neighbour.

First r*n South Herts. H3 1985
Member Berkshire H3, London H3, West London H3, Barnes H3, High
Wycombe H3, Marlow H3, South Oxfordshire H3, R2D2 H3, North Hants H3,
Hursley H3, Worthy Winchester H3

What got you into the Hash in the first place?
LV: I was a member of a r*nning club and one of their members turned up with
a New York Hash t-shirt on. He explained that while living in the Big Apple he
had laid a Hash through the Waldorf Hotel, and this grabbed my attention. He
told me that the next Hash was from Tring Station. The next Saturday when the
Hash was due to take place it snowed heavily. I thought no way will there be a
Hash in those conditions, but a voice within me said to go. After a treacherous
journey by car in the snow, there they all were huddled together in the cold.
The trail was laid in lentils and I knew from my first Hash that Hashing was for
me.

Why the fancy French Hash name?
LV: Berkshire Hash organised a charity Hash from Windsor to Reading carrying
a bottle of Beaujolais Nouveau to be raffled off for Guide Dogs for the Blind.
We had a bus supporting us, complete with alcoholic refreshment. We were
required to dress up in French gear. Wally, a Berkshire Hasher, demonstrated
his advanced knowledge of the French language by calling me *Le Voisin* which
is French for my surname and it has followed me around ever since.

**What's the strangest, worst, weirdest moment on the Hash (that we can
print)?**
LV: My worst Hashing moment was attending Hairy Fairy's memorial service
after he so tragically was killed in a climbing accident on Christmas Day. My
most potent memory of a Hash spent in his company was in Chalk Farm,
London. The Hash had been uneventful but in the pub afterwards I chatted up
this lovely lady whom I discovered was the girlfriend of a drug dealer who –
much to my dismay – suddenly appeared in the pub from his chauffeur-driven
Chevrolet with his minders. I extracted myself from this dangerous liaison with
Hairy's help by chatting up the drug dealer, and then beating a hasty retreat. We
then went on a pub-crawl and when we eventually broke up I caught the train
home, went to sleep and woke up in Aylesbury, four stops beyond where I
wanted to get out. The next train back, which was the last that night, was not
for another one-and-a-half hours!

How's Hashing changed from your perspective?
LV: The standard of trail-laying has deteriorated over the years and the Down
Downs seem to have got longer and longer. What is often disappointing are the
Hash trails, which are often too long, are laid as r*ns rather than Hashes. Some
Hashes have never heard of back-checks, bar-checks, arrow-checks, regroups,
short cuts, etc.

Harry 'Cocksure' Shaw.

First r*n Riyadh Megamob H3 1981
Member Cairo H3, Dubai Desert H3, Creek H3, Abu Dhabi Island, Al Ain H3,
WASP H3, Jeddah H3, Amman H3, Muscat H3, Khasab, Sharjah H3

What were you thinking?
CS: I was working as a quantity surveyor in Riyadh, Saudi Arabia. Some of my
colleagues were already members of Riyadh Megamob, and were encouraging
me to come along with them on their weekly r*ns. The clincher was when they
told me about a celebratory event to be held to mark the 100th r*n and the big
do was to be held the night before the actual r*n, so the only obligation to do
the r*n was a moral obligation. What followed that night opened up my eyes
to a world I didn't know existed. Here we were, in a country that boasted 'the
driest Hash in the world', and there was available just about every drink you
could wish for, all of it home-made, with an amazing amount and variety of
food, as well as several 'variety' acts to entertain.

I don't remember much about it except someone blew a horn and everyone
else dashed off into the desert. I managed about 100 yards before collapsing,
but I had gasped the all-important phrase, 'ON! ON!!!'
And you've filtered some piss since then, no doubt.
CS: I seem to have r*n over 1,150 Hashes, in at least 24 different countries and
with at least 44 Hash clubs (plus those who hosted World InterHashes). Due to
my innate wanderlust (or perhaps because no one would employ me for long),
I have had spells all around the Middle East including Saudi Arabia, Egypt,
Jordan, Oman, and the United Arab Emirates. I have also been lucky enough to
have been able to travel to many other places and attend many worldwide
Hashing events. For instance, a round-the-world jaunt in 1988 allowed me to
visit and Hash in KL, Hong Kong, Beijing, Tokyo, Honolulu, San Francisco and
Memphis.
So are you in better or worse shape than when you started Hashing?
CS: R*nning on the Hash seems to have nurtured a long-neglected liking for
exercise, and given me the confidence to participate in such events as 10
London marathons and even two Highland Games (perhaps a dram too many
beforehand, or maybe not enough).
What do you consider your most enjoyable time?
CS: I can't remember my most enjoyable r*n or good time. The only ones I can
remember all ran out of beer (or, as in the case of Saudi Arabia, didn't have any
in the first place). Whatever I thought of the r*n itself, I always remembered that
a fellow-Hasher had spent some of his or her spare time setting it so give credit
at all times, even though you may not have felt like it at the time.
And your worst moment on the Hash?
CS: I had arranged an extra r*n around the hotel so that the next milestone
WASP Hash r*n would be on a certain date. Me and the missus went home for
a little rest which lasted a bit too long and we got back a wee bit late. Some

WASPERS had done the circuit but we rounded up a couple of strangers and set off for two laps of the building, no mean feat in the condition we were in. Duty done, we repaired to the bar only later to discover that the beloved and revered WASP Hash horn had gone missing. No amount of searching and press appeals ever revealed its whereabouts so, whoever may have this unique instrument of great sentimental value, please take good care of it as it cost a Yorkshireman some (I won't say how much) money to replace. That was almost my Hashing swansong in the Middle East.

My spies tell me you were involved in the Highest Hash ever?

CS: This evolved as the Creek H3 was en route to Manila. Here we were, cruising along at 600 mph, 39,000 feet high, having drunk the galley dry and therefore at what might be termed a loose end. 'Come on, lads,' came the cry,' let's have a Hash'. Of course, we couldn't set a trail using normal methods but handy material lay all around us on the floor in the form of discarded and empty beer containers. A trail of sorts was laid along the aisles and up the stairs to the top deck, not too many falsies because of space limitation, and at the sound of the horn (or maybe someone farted) off we all went in a mad scramble in hot pursuit. The r*n didn't last very long, perhaps because of the sound of 'MAYDAY! MAYDAY!' coming from up front where the bloke with the steering wheel was probably having eggs at the thought of a riot on his lovely, new aeroplane.

And, this doesn't surprise me, you were also involved in the, er, lowest Hash.

CS: This was a planned operation organised by the Hashemite H3 where the r*nners drove from Amman down to the Dead Sea and Hashed around the pond for a while before partaking of the waters, as they say. The Dead Sea is about 1,300 feet below sea level and you can't get much lower than that without getting wet. It is quite possible to float on the very salty water while reading a newspaper and this gives rise to some amusing photographs.

Any feelings on where InterHash should or shouldn't be held?

CS: Hashing is a worldwide pursuit and cannot be confined to a particular country or continent. However, it should be acknowledged that there is more freedom to do silly things in the less-developed countries and get away with it than is likely in, say, England.

Whither Hashing?

CS: Just keep on going along. Sixty years and more have passed since the lads Hashed around Selangor, and any changes that have transpired in the meantime have been more beneficial than otherwise. Hashing will always be King.

Graeme 'Olymprick' Thain.

First r*n Berkshire H3 1986
Co-founder Aberdeen Seriously Social H3 1992
Member West London H3, Edinburgh H3, Aberdeen H3,

How did you become Olymprick?
O: On a weekend away on the Isle of Wight I returned to the circle round the campfire having r*n round the campsite with a burning toilet roll held aloft on a branch. On my homecoming r*n, I was re-christened MasterBaker – pink, green and chilli pies were introduced to Hashing.

You seem to do more than your fair share of away weekends.
O: I spent 1988 on the road. From Bangkok to Bali, a couple of months in Sydney, r*nning with most of the Hashes there. The motorcycle trip around Australia got as far as Adelaide before being hijacked back to the central coast for the Aussie Nash Hash. The annual Alice Springs downtown night-dress r*n was a once-in-a-lifetime event for me. Terry's house in Darwin had *five* fridges, two exclusively for food. I paid my rent in VB, the local brew, for 10 weeks. The return to Sydney stopped off at various Queensland and New South Wales Hashes. It was a *great* feeling riding back over the Sydney Harbour Bridge and returning the borrowed tent. Then I spent a month hitching and Hashing around New Zealand.

How many r*ns do you think you've done?
O: Probably in excess of 1,000 worldwide, but never really kept count. A flick through the world Hash directory several years ago came up with 80-ish individual Hash chapters which I'm sure I've r*n/drank with. The figure is probably nearer 100 by now.

You seem to prefer to be a hare than a hound.
O: Haring is probably in the hundreds, but it is the quality not the quantity that matters. Getting Aberdeen into the Denburn (our underground river) three times, ranks highly. The AH3 500th Royal Deeside r*n, set with Michelin Man and Penguin, was a classic, with the inner tubes down the rapids a memorable finale for all involved.

How come you're famous for shiggy?
O: In 2001 at Winchester, I joined forces with East Grinstead to set, possibly, the greatest shiggy r*n ever.

Any unmitigated disasters?
O: In 1996 at Cyprus InterHash, Shit for Brains and I set the Aberdeen 600th. Over 300 r*nners short-cut the beer check and left over 100 beers undrunk.

Dishonourable mentions go to the following Brits for services to Hashing well below and short of the call of duty:

Andrew Markham who spent three years going round the world Hashing and playing soccer. Also Phil Baker and Howie Lock who spent 18 months Hashing round the world.

Lt. Rupert Williamson started a floating Hash when aboard the warship HMS Gloucester. He probably got a bit more support from colleagues on board the Gloucester than he did from his previous vessel, none other than the Royal Yacht Britannia. While he didn't have a floating kennel [What about the Corgis? –ed.] he did reportedly Hash while on port visits with the Royals aboard.

In 1989, Hashers Boon and Bubbles, from West London H3 and London H3 respectively, ran with three separate clubs in one day. The first r*n was with Haslemere H3 at 11am, followed by North Hants H3 at 3pm, and finally London H3 at 5:30pm. To top it off, it was New Year's Day.

Phil 'Londoner Phil' Davies was born in 1911 within sound of Bow Bells, and at 91 years of age, is possibly the oldest regular Hasher in the world today. He still r*ns regularly with Wessex H3 and Dorset Hospitality H3 in England, having completed some 400 r*ns. He has also r*n four marathons since the age of 80 and has a place in the 2002 London Marathon, which would make him a record breaker. Amazingly he only took up r*nning at 75 years of age.

Sticks and Stones May Break My Bones ...

A random assortment of British Hash handles that tickled the fancy of kennel-mates enough for them to spill the beans. Some Hashers were even drunk enough to spill the dirt on themselves!

Annual Fisting, Milton Keynes H3: "I have quite small hands and they named me this but later said 'We've been waiting to call somebody this for ages'. My wife is **Madame Sin** because she's associated with me and she works in the *Vice* Chancellor's office."

ATANS: "Short for **All Tits And No Silicon**. Her tits are GG. Her partner is called **SATAN** or **Creamy Tit Wanker**."

Barmitzvah, Stannary H3: "Circumcision at 27 years old was no joke – the memory of the op still brings tears to my eyes ..."

Big Bollocks, Winchester H3: His wife is Beaver Bollocks.

Billericay Dickie, Bicester H3: She was born and raised in Billericay.

Bloomers, Barnes H3: "Auntie's Bloomers, for cocking up the shipping forecast at the BBC."

Blotting Paper, Mash H3: "Because of his staggering ability to soak up vast quantities of liquid, preferably alcoholic."

Bodily Functions, ex-West Rhine, now UK: "Don't r*n behind him, that's all I'm saying."

Boggers, London: "I used to be **Bog Brush** because of my spiky hair after the r*n."

Boris, Bicester H3: "In real life he's a Russian spy – no, not really, but he used to work at a top-secret rocket research station and he understands Russian."

Bulldozer, ex-Beirut, Moscow, Cairo, West London H3: "During reconstruction after the war in Lebanon I took a shortcut to the drinks stop, and came in sitting in the bucket of this bulldozer with my legs swinging over the front."

Bums and Roses, Stannary H3: "A quiet, unassuming college lecturer but give him a guitar and he turns into Eric Clapton."

Butane, Mash H3: "Because he constantly farts."

Carlos, Gloucestershire Gourmets: "Expert in having his car stolen … as in *car* loss."

Carmen, ex-Auckland, Copenhagen H3: "I appeared on stage in an opera for six weeks, so when they asked where I'd been I copped a lot for being a poofter, etc. It also has a double entendre for Australians as Carmen was the name of a famous Kiwi transvestite who moved to King's Cross."

Chastity Belt, Barnes H3: "For wearing knickers in the bath 'cause I had promised my husband I would not drop my knickers on my first weekend away from him and the kids, having been married for seven years."

Chippendale, Surrey H3: "Played Rocky in Rocky Horror Show at UK Nash Hash fully dressed in posing pouch, cuffs and bow tie. Then got completely wrecked and generally behaved like a tart. Named the following day for 'enjoying myself too much while dressed like an old piece of furniture'."

Cocktail, Bicester H3: Real name Iball.

Codpiece, Learned Lyngby H3: "I'm Faroese. 95 per cent of Faroese export is fish."

Commercial Whale, North Hants H3: A big guy given to r*nning in only white shorts. Once surprised a group of girl guides who thought he was a flasher, then a couple of Japanese girls took his photo. This happened at a time when the Japanese commercial whaling fleet was re-negotiating its terms.

Cornflake, Hardys H3: "Fainted in a cornfield on her first Hash."

Crackin' Pussy, Swansea Jack H3: "Based on the dubious reasons that I'm the owner of a three-legged cat and I was a fan of the program Dawson's Creek (affectionately referred to as Dawson's Crack by friends).

Creamy Bristols, City of Leicester H3: "Her family name being Harvey, and herself being amply provided up top, our minds instantaneously thought of Bristols … Harvey … Bristols, argh Harvey's Bristol Cream … hence Creamy Bristols."

Deadeye Duck, Worthy Winchester H3: "I used to be a shooter and my surname's Huck."

Depth Gauge, Surrey H3: "He is only 5'2" tall, and once disappeared completely underwater on a r*n when the tide had come in. A warning to all those shorter than him to take an alternative route."

Dick Dick, Bicester H3: "His real name is Richard Fallas (ie, Dick Phallus)."

Digby's Dad, Scarborough H3: "This guy's a complete twat – we're not related at all but now I'm forever associated with him."

Dingaling, Bicester H3: "He discovered that ringing a small bell placed on the bar of a remote country pub in the New Forest resulted in a fresh pint being poured for him, so naturally he kept ringing it."

Disappointed, London H3: "Wife of **Wee Cold Member**!"

Dissa Peer, Surrey H3: "Has something to do with his ability to r*n."

Dizzy, Winchester H3: "I had my dark hair dyed blonde at the time, and the other options were **Black Box** and thus **Inflight Data Recorder**. I'm glad they chose **Dizzy!**"

Do You?, Surrey H3: Her surname is Ball.

Doormouse: "Is very quiet and has been known to fall asleep standing up – any time, any place."

Dormobile, Bicester H3: Real name Peter *Van* Kerkhof (Dormobile is a popular van type in the UK).

Edna the Inebriate Woman, Cheltenham H3: "We Hashed from a pub in Gloucestershire one Sunday and when I went up to the bar one of the locals said 'You look just like Patricia Hayes!' He enlightened me by saying that she was 'Edna the Inebriate Woman'. When they christened me, they dressed me up in a sacking skirt, duffle coat tied round the middle with string, headscarf and carried two plastic carrier bags full of empty beer cans!"

FO, Surrey H3: "As well as the obvious she works at the Foreign Office."

Faking It, Guernsey H3: "I went to a sports shop and bought a London Marathon t-shirt, and then I wore it to the Hash. I never ran the marathon, of course."

Fetish, Hardys H3: "Rides an ancient Harley-Davidson motorbike. He turned up late for a Hash once and ran in his full motorcycle leathers. He decided he enjoyed the sweaty feel of leather on his skin …"

Find a Stool, Stannary H3: "Works as a radiologist, particularly on intestine areas."

Fireindahole, Cambridge H3: "A red-haired Harriette who used to r*n with Cambridge. Although it is rumoured that she dyes her hair blonde this does not extend to her pubes which (allegedly!) remain red."

Fishcake, Bicester H3: Real name Salmon.

Flashman, Barnes H3: "Because he's an Essex boy and always wore gold medallions and drove a Lotus 7. However, he got renamed **Dafadil – Does Absolutely Fuck All And Does It Loudly**."

Forget Me Not, Bath H3: "A seldom-seen flower. Just like the r*ns she sets."

Forrest Dump, Jersey H3: "Was in his tent late at night and badly needed to go to the toilet … he only got as far as the nearby trees."

FRB, Guernsey H3: "He's not a Front R*nning Bastard, he's a Fucking Rich Bloke."

Fruit 'n' Nut, Deepcut H3: His surname is Case.

Fu Man Chu, Plymouth H3: "I did a tour of duty of Hong Kong and Singapore with the RAF. My wife's **Enter the Dragon**."

Furbag, Wirral & Chester: "Her real name's Cobbledick – what do you do with that???"

Ginger Plonker, Malvern H3: "Made a bit of a fool of himself one day and says, 'I'm a bit of a Ginger Plonker' as he has ginger hair. It can obviously be interpreted differently."

Goldflinger, ex-Bangkok H3, Cambridge H3: "Got his handle on the Bangkok Hash, I think for throwing money about."

Green Giant, Sheffield H3: "He was a rather tall travelling salesman … his peers thought he resembled the illustration on one of the cans of produce he was selling. He would often turn up to Hash with a boot-load of this canned sweet corn."

Groin Biter, ex-West Rhine H3, now UK: "My boyfriend fell off his bike and got a huge bruise from the handlebars all around his groin. They naturally accused me of all sorts of things!"

Gunpowder Plod, Cambridge H3: "First name is Guy, but he is an ex-Hong Kong policeman, hence Plod."

Gyrabonk, Barnes H3: "She was in a cabaret and had to do various movements which in turn looked like she was gyrating her hips in a very interesting manner."

Hash Poof, Berkshire H3: "Didn't like his name, so on account of doing a swimming shortcut one day we gladly renamed him **Aqua Poof**."

Heather on the Hill, ex-Cape Town now UK: "My partner was Billy Hill so they called him **Hill Billy**. My name's Heather so … but I got renamed in London after that relationship ended – at a Halloween r*n I went as Frankenstein and, as sweat and adhesive don't mix, I lost my bolt [I know the feeling! –ed.]. So my new name is **Screw Loose**."

Hold it for Me, Cambridge H3: "Arrived first at a check and requested the next arrival to hold the check while he ran ahead. Occasionally referred to as **Hold Shit for Me** on account of his two dogs who r*n and shit on the trail. He always carries a plastic bag in which he pops the poop in order to avoid fouling the trail!"

Honey Nuts, Surrey H3: "Stung on the balls by a bee …"

Hughie Blaaaaaaaaargh, Glasgow H3: "On January 2 I bought a guest to the r*n whose name was Ralph. I went missing, and they naturally presumed I was feeling poorly and was off being sick somewhere. So they called him **Ralffffffffffffff**. People often think my real name is Hugh Blair and book hotels and things under that name for me."

Jailbird, Mash H3: "Because I spent a weekend in a Saudi prison cell."

Jumper, ex-Berkshire H3, Jersey H3: "Berkshire Hash initially called me **Jersey**, 'cos that's where I came from, then it was changed to Jumper – 'cause a Jersey is a sort of jumper (sweater)."

Khaw Fucker, ex-Songkhla, now Aberdeen H3: "I went on holiday to Phuket for three weeks and just couldn't get a tan. *Khaw* (pronounced 'cow') is the Thai word for white."

Kipper, Hardys H3: "A retired fish pathologist."

Lagerlout, Hardys H3: "Chairlady of the Campaign for Real Ale."

Leatherback, ex-PJ Animals, East Grinstead H3: "They named me after a slow old turtle."

Liability Joe, Stannary H3: "Joe volunteers for everything, however, rarely comes up with the goods."

Lifeboats, Aberdeen H3. "My real name's Mandy, as in Man De Lifeboats."

Little Johnnie: "When going to a nightclub, it's not so cool to ask for 'one adult'."

Little White Bus, Surrey H3: "My surname is Buss and I used to drive a white Subaru van for years."

Living Bra, Wirral and Chester H3: "Well it's not quantity if that's what you're wondering. Picture the scene … warm autumn day Hashing across the gentle fields of rural Cheshire when 'splat!' I'm hit in the back by a wet smelly cow pat. I removed my t-shirt and continued the trail. A short while later, I was grabbed by a Hasher and held over a muddy wallow. I emerged and, as my bra was full of mud, I leaned forward and released the bottom of it and some bugs and things fell out."

Looberty, London H3: "Did a theme r*n dressed as the Statue of Liberty, with a toilet brush and other adornments."

Lord Raleigh, Surrey H3: "Goes *everywhere* on his bicycle except into the pub. Raleigh received the Lordship after having successfully piloted the pack across Lord Halpern's front lawn."

Low Profile, ex-Malaysia, Surrey H3: It took him 15 years to be named, such was his unobtrusive nature. Eventually got named while visiting in New Zealand.

Massive Chew Sets, Stannary H3: "Because of the teeth – breaking them in for a horse or what?"

Megasaurarse, Edinburgh H3: "A young lady on an Edinburgh Hash had, to put it politely, a generous rear! One particular r*n she suffered an unfortunate slip and bounced down a steep slope, over rocks and all sorts, on the aforementioned rear."

Messiah, Surrey H3: "A look-a-like."

Monkey Glands, Bicester H3: Real name Gibbons.

Monsieur Perfectionist, Mash H3: "Because he spent the entire first Cross-Channel Hash in Belgium whingeing about the trail."

Mother Brown, Surrey H3: "Short for 'Knees up Mother Brown' after kind Aussie Hashers had inadvertently broken his legs."

Mouse Trap, Truro H3: "Her mother hash is Basel, Switzerland – they always had cheese at the beer stop and she dropped a piece once and rubbed it on her shorts to clean it, right next to her privates. The Zurich lot wanted to name her **Cheesy Pussy** but as Basel was a family Hash it got softened."

Mr Minty, Truro H3: "Hashing in Venice we all got goodie bags. In mine was a minty flavoured condom. My missus and I used it and I was overheard to say 'Yeah, Steph said it was really minty!'"

Muff Diver: A diving instructor.

Nil By Mouth, Sannary H3: "A nurse … does post heart attack work."

Nookie, ex-Norfolk, London H3: "Originally it was **Nookie Bare**, being the opposite of 'No Fuck', where I was named. Gradually it shortened to Nookie."

Not Another One, Plympton H3: "There are 12 midwives in this chapter. The first was called **Push Harder**, then **Baby Boomer**, etc. When the 10th midwife joined, they groaned and said 'Argh, not another one!'"

Numb Nuts, Surrey H3: "Let's just say his other half is known as **Cool Box**."

O'Duracell, Hardys H3: "Irish with seemingly everlasting energy."

Organgrinder, Hardys H3: "We went on a pre-marital holiday to Greece – sun, sea, sangria, sex and sand … Our GM decided that the last two on the list would require my (now) wife to become Organgrinder – I still have the scars to prove it!"

P60, Stannary H3: "Was a tax inspector (P60 being the form filled out for tax returns). Now retired, perhaps we should call him P40 (the unemployment form).

Pete the Pilot, London H3: "I used to be in the Marine Pilot Service."

Pirelli, Glasgow H3: Surname is Callender.

Polly, ex-Kuala Belait H3, Dublin H3: "After being thrown off the high dive board at the Ghurkha pool for two times without a name, some bugger called Wedge Lee asked 'What's his name?' 'Hadfield' was the reply. 'Fuck me, I knew a bloke who went to Hatfield Poly' said Wedge, and like shit to a blanket ..."

Pork Scratchings, Truro H3: "She's currently dating **Pig Pen** (a common trait here – it all goes wrong when they split up!)"

Pork Torpedo, Teign Valley H3: "I'm a submariner with the navy."

Puffer, Surrey H3: "After Monika Seles."

Pure Genius, Guernsey H3: "I get Guinness on prescription because I have an iron deficiency. They even deliver it!"

Rambina, Surrey H3: "Her husband is **Rambo**."

Rapunzel, Yorkshire H3: "I have (somewhat balding now) long golden locks."

Redlight, Plympton H3: "At an On On I went to the kitchen and got the chips and eight Hashmen immediately descended on me. One of the guys said I couldn't do better business if I had a red light above me."

Right Hand, ex-Hamburg, Edinburgh H3: "In Hamburg the H7 (Hansestadt Hamburg Hash House Harriers Hummel Hummel) were a small bunch of lazy gits. As the GM, RA, Beer Master, On Sec etc weren't available at all times, I was eager enough to substitute their positions. On top of that I had a demanding job (24/7/365) and the only way to go Hashing was to be hooked up to a mobile. Then about two months later they discovered that my fiancée still lived in Scotland while I was in Hamburg ..."

Ringpull, Surrey H3: "After finding 24 cans of beer on a r*n ..."

Road Enema, Bicester H3: "Poured himself into a culvert under a motorway in order to avoid the long r*n-in over the bridge."

Ryde, London H3: "We had an away weekend in Ryde which I didn't initially plan to attend, so I drove 200 miles down there at the last minute, got the ferry across and had to hitch from there to the r*n site. I only got there five minutes before the first r*n. Lucky it wasn't held at Fishbourne ..."

Scaredy Custard, Glasgow H3: "Very good r*nner who ran off from a bunch of thugs encountered during a Monday night trail, leaving the girls he was with to fend for themselves!"

Scud, Surrey H3: "Apparently someone seemed to think he was always going off course."

Sergio, ex-Thailand, Nigeria, Aberdeen H3: "You need to wear a lot more clothes in this part of the world, and I wore a Sergio Tachinni tracksuit top."

Sex Goddess, Glasgow H3: "Was the director of family planning Scotland."

Sherpa, Bicester H3: Real name Susannah *Van* Schaick (Sherpa is another popular van type in the UK).

Shiddy, ex-Saudi: "I was a midwife in Saudi and *Shiddy* was the Arabic word for 'Push, push!'"

Shirtlifter, Plympton H3: "I'm a sailor ..."

Shit for Brains, Portsmouth H3: "It's just one of those names you get given and it sticks. My wife is **Tits for Brains**."

Short an', Surrey H3: "She's short, and her husband's **Curly**."

Skidmark, Barnes H3: "Used to be known as **That Bastard from East Grinstead**.

This was however too long to fit on the Barnes circular masthead. Saddlesniffer, on noticing my shorts after a mud battle with the North Hants boys, had all the ammo he needed for my new name."

Souffle, London H3: "He rises early then falls in a heap … he has been known to do several circuits of the London City Circle asleep."

Spanish Fly, West London H3: "I hadn't been named yet and was speaking Spanish to another visiting Hasher."

Speed Bump, Scotland: "I crashed into a few speed bumps once. They're trying to change it to **Speed Hump** now."

Squits, ex-Lagos, now Norkfolk H3: "The name is very recent after I poisoned the Lagos Hash."

Stevie Wonder, Glasgow H3: "First name is Steve. Really named as a result of his girlfriend – a top triathlete who kept winning medals and was called **Golden Wonder**."

Swollen Member, ex-Bangkok H3, Cambridge H3: "An ant bit me on the end of my foreskin which swelled up alarmingly to resemble a baby elephant's trunk. I believe the photographic evidence still exists in Bangkok."

Tampon, ex-Medan, now Cambridge H3: "I strongly deny that laying a trail with used tampons and subsequently holding the circle around a 10-foot tampon effigy (later worn by Froggy who caused mayhem when he ran around Blok M during the On On On On) had anything to do with my being called **Tampon** – it was the other way round. I had been named Tampon a couple of years previously in Medan by Dubai due to certain habits which I have kept secret all these years due to the joy of hearing all the wonderful stories made up."

Taxidermist: "I got hit by a taxi. At first the driver was worried that he had killed me, but when he realised I was OK he got nasty because I had completely stuffed his taxi."

Teepee, Teign Valley H3: "Her initials are T.P. So her husband became **Wigwam**. He then introduced a guest and the inventive RA called him **Migman**."

Tequil'over, Surrey H3: "He organised a Tequila drinking contest, and was demonstrating to participants over and over how it should be drunk with style. He then proceeded to show us, all in perfectly good style, how to keel over."

The Boy from Brazil, London H3: "I was born in Brazil and was only about 19 when I started Hashing."

The Invisible Man, Surrey H3: "Aka Lord Tracksuit. Will disappear when elected to any position of authority."

Three Buttery Nipples, Suffuck H3: "Unfortunately nobody was able to confirm whether this was due to her physical attributes or for her performance in downing three cocktails of the same name (Butterscotch liqueur and Baileys)."

Thrush, Berkshire H3: "He's an irritating cunt!"

Toed Bedsores, Cambridge H3: "Kept complaining that his real name, Ted Bradshawe, was always being misspelt so he was renamed to avoid further errors."

Top Gear, Surrey H3: "Drove a quarter of the way round the M25 wondering why her Metro was suddenly not capable of more than 50 mph before realising she was still in third gear."

Transit, Bicester H3: Real name Roger *Van* Schaick (would you believe Transit is yet another popular van type in the UK).

Tub Thumper, Glasgow H3: "Pissed at a party once and kept falling down but getting back up again as in the song 'I get knocked down but I get up again, ain't never gonna keep me down …'"

Velcro, Hardys H3: "She sticks to men."

Vidal Sassoon, Barnes H3: "I had my hair cut and drastically restyled."

Waterbed, Hardy's H3: "Woke up while on a Hash camping weekend and decided to have a pee in the corner of her tent rather than go outside – forgetting that the groundsheet was attached to the tent so that bedding was soaked."

Wellie Wanker, Hardy's H3: "We had a Wellington Boot throwing contest outside a pub in Weymouth. Wellie threw his over his shoulder. It smashed through an upstairs window and landed on the dining table where the landlord and his wife were eating their lunch. We had the window repaired and later gave them a Down Down – drinking from a child's Wellington boot."

Yabbadabbadoo, Truro H3: "Looks like Fred Flintstone."

And, once again, there were a bunch of wankers and diddlers who just plain ignored our requests, or proved utterly elusive in our *exhaustive* searches – which consisted of a single email to someone who may or may not have been in their kennel. Anyway, we're sure these names are far more interesting than the people behind them:

19th Hole, Bad News, Betty Swollocks, Birthing Blanket, Bloodknock, Captain Cook, Community Chest, Condom and Femidom, Cream Soda, Croc Tosser, Daffy Dildo, Daft Wader, Doggie Bag, Duck Walk, Endosperm, Flying Pharmacist, Foot in Crutch, Foxes Glacier Mint, Frau Gouda, Gulab Jamoon, Hard Core Bomber, Herr Flick, Human Sponge, Jammy Tart, Jetslag, Johnny Fart Pants, Kiltlifter, Look If You Like, M'Bongo, McWot, Mecca, Miss Whiplash, Monsieur Merde, Mr Creosote, No Relation To, Oink, Pickled Fart, Please Sir, Pleasure Gnome, Postman Splat, Randy Memsahib, Red Snapper, Sewer Rat, ShaginaJag, Sloppy Seconds, Snakehips, Squirrel Shit, Stand in Shit, Straddle Various, Sweet Black Angel, Taxi Tosser, The Vaseline Queen, Triple Dick, Utterly Butterly, Vicky Vomit, Virgin Expert, Wandering Grizzler, Wedgiewood, Wine Wine Wine, Winja Turtle, YakkyDah, and Yokelbonker.

Anecdotes, trivia and a bunch of stuff
from around the United Kingdom.

Past Master was laying a trail and was accosted by an old lady walking her dogs who assumed he was laying rat poison. Vigorously denying her challenge, and claiming it was only good old harmless flour – which of course it was – the only way to refute it was to eat some himself in front of her. Naturally, his mouth turned into a jar of glue. "That's one of the few times I've been speechless!" he said at the time. The little old lady went on her way.

Hashing in the North Hants countryside one day, we came to a field with a horse in it. The three Harriettes in front of me pulled up, afraid of what the horse might do if they entered its paddock, but couldn't see a way around it. "Step aside, ladies," Commercial Whale said gallantly, "I know how to deal with horses." With that he strode up to the horse and quietly said: "Fuck off, horse!" It promptly galloped off leaving the ladies most impressed.

Dragonarse of Dorset (ex-China, Bahrain and Balikpapan) used to carry his son on his back during Hash r*ns. The poor little fella received his first icing at the grand old age of nine days, yes, *days* and his first words were 'On! On!' He'll go far.

The day that Hashers were upstaged. At UK Nash Hash, the band Bad Manners had been hired as the evening's entertainment. Their larger-than-life frontman – Buster Bloodvessel to his mum – finished his show then proceeded to a seat near the bar and got stuck into the free beer. By around sunrise, he had seen off the last of the Hashers and then started to call out for *anyone* to join him for a drink. A bleary-eyed Hashman was on the way to do his teeth (it was a camping Hash) and thought 'Sod it, I'll join him'. Bloodvessel then proceeded to down between 16 and 18 *bottles* of white wine on his own before evening fell again, leaving his chair only twice to make room for more in his bladder. No one recalled seeing him eat. He was immediately adopted as a Hasher, christened Cat Funt (he must weigh 150kg or more), but unfortunately missed the bus for the ball-breaker so never actually got on trail.

Olymprick once set a r*n while on the ferry from London to Paris. The ferry conveniently had a bar on each level. One sugar cube and you were 'on'!

The Scots love their shiggy and set a Scottish Shiggy 'A to B' Special at UK Nash Hash in Winchester. We got to the beer at the end, and then proceeded to clean ourselves off. The hares then told us the buses were waiting for us just down along the beach. Unfortunately this meant going

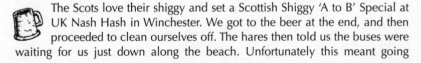

through this estuary at low tide. More fuckin' shiggy, and there was no other way around. "I almost lost my shoes in this thick sticky mud," says Le Voisin. "Then the bus driver starts making noises about not letting us get on his bus." A Catch-22. So the hares tell us that there's a fire station just around the corner, maybe they could help. Obviously they'd been briefed on this, and set upon us with high-pressure hoses, cleaning bits which hadn't been cleaned for years. One of the Harriettes wanted to marry the fire hose! "It was the most unique end to a r*n I've ever had," he said.

 A Winchester area Hash had at one stage a judge, a solicitor and a barrister on a r*n. An old lady was complaining about the noise they were making, so they decided to give her a full impromptu hearing, with the Hash acting as judge and jury of course. One of their legal eagles, Blue Tits, was called forward and asked if she could proffer any legal advice to the complaining lady. "Yeah, fuck off!" was her summary judgement. Case closed.

 The pink skirt wearer is an exalted position of high standing in the City H3, London. It is passed, week to week, from r*nner to r*nner to ensure it is always held by the idiot most apt to represent the Hash to the world at large. It has undergone various manifestations over the years, variously accompanied by hula flowers, diamond tiara and sometimes a wand.

 When Col. Phil Spooner, founding member of the Chichester Hash, died, the church was full to overflowing with Hashers paying their last respects – all resplendent in their Hash shirts at the request of his Hashing widow, Sue.

 Charlie from West London H3 ran until he was nearly 90, still proudly bearing the handle of Hash Letch!

 Plympton H3 has a Hashit which is a wooden pole with check-back and arrow signs on it. It has since been progressively adorned with a couple of pairs of knickers and other paraphernalia from its 'winners'.

 Edinburgh TNT H3 is not happy with just one Hashit. It has three, including the Ding-a-ling (a hat covered with bells), the Sleeper (a used mortuary sheet) and the Wendy Wig (details upon application).

 Arthur 'Belukar' Broome, an old stalwart from KL in the Fifties, was honoured by the Ashburton H3 with a special r*n for his 80th birthday. True to form, the old bugger got lost in the woods and missed his party!

 Yogurt from Cairneyhill H3, Scotland, once completed a r*n on skis.

Likka attended the Commonwealth Hash 1986 in Edinburgh, at which a Hash Olympics – loosely based on the Highland Games – was held with everyone assigned to one of four teams. Hilarious! "Even funnier was waking up at 4:30am with nobody left 'alive' and trying to pour myself a beer at the bar," he says. "At that precise moment a Hashman (who had been sleeping behind the bar) stood up like Dracula out of his coffin and said: 'Can I help you sir?' It was, as Monty Python would say, something completely different!"

GBH had gone on a weekend Hash to the New Forest. While the Hash pack revelled and cavorted in the middle of a small lake on the r*n, he noticed a Harriette – Circuit Breaker, who he didn't know – happily watching all this from the sideline, totally dry and clean. Going up behind her, he caught her unawares, threw her over his shoulder and carried her to the middle of the lake where he let go, depositing her in the muddy water. A frantic scream came from another Harriette: "SHE CAN'T SWIM!" GBH turned to see Circuit Breaker struggling in the water and went to her rescue. They were married on April Fools Day shortly thereafter.

In Cardiff, with the countryside out of commission during the foot and mouth crisis, the hares came up with a novel solution to laying a city trail. They took a list of public phone boxes, and rang each one successively when the Hash arrived. On two occasions the phone was answered by a member of the public, who have since become Hashers!

The Cambridge Hash started in a strange position, in the personal column of the Cambridge Evening News. Wedged between 'Gentleman, forties, wishes to meet lady …' above and 'Widow, aged 60, wishes to meet gentleman …' below was the advertisement 'HASH HOUSE HARRIERS. Isn't it time there was a Hash in Cambridge? Interested r*nners please call Taylor. Comberton 3636.' Howard Taylor previously had been on the Bangkok Hash, and the newspaper thought he was r*nning drugs from Asia. Lewd Silverspoon claims it was the advert *underneath* the Hash one that he was interested in, but he phoned the Hash by mistake …

More on our website: For the full story from Ray Thornton and Richard McAllister on the origins of Hashing in England, plus anything else they could squeeze from their brain-cells, go to *www.hash-onon.com*. Also lots of pictures of assorted insanity through the ages.

Don't Bore Us, Get to the Chorus

How the Hash developed its anthems and butchered some classics.

Like ice, singing is another major trait that polarises Hash kennel types. Simply – some do, some don't. Mostly, you just wish they didn't! It often depends on their founding fathers, their Hash kennel ancestry or sometimes their nationality. But why has what can loosely be termed 'music' become such an integral part of Hash culture?

Ian Cumming, one of the more acknowledged song-meisters in Hashdom, sets the tone: "Hashes sing because rugby clubs sing. Rugby clubs sing because there is a little bit of Hasher in every rugby player – just enough to differentiate him from a soccer player, who leaves it up to the fans to create the mayhem. Whether a Hash is a singing Hash or not depends largely on how it starts out – whether the founders can pick singable keys, know the words and don't mind the resistance of the softer-mouthed of the pack."

Fred Whitaker joined the Singapore H3, drawn in by the musicality of Cumming's mob in the jungles of Singapore. But, ironically, he himself can't hold a note, and therefore the Hobart Hash which he co-founded never became a singing Hash. But he admires the American music tradition and American singing Hashes and bemoans the lack of singing Hashes around these days. "They have a great tradition of university glee clubs. People like Cole Porter, and all those, that's where they came from. Rudi Valle. Particularly the Connecticut Yankee area, the Ivy League universities – the Harvard Glee Club, the Yale Glee Club, and all that. Clever songs, brilliant songs. They're not rugby songs. Rugby songs are purely an English phenomenon," he says. That may be true, but it seems a lot of the repertoire were imported from Stateside.

"The transfer to UK took place in the second half of World War 2 when countless Fleet Air Arm pilots were trained in US bases," says Cumming. "Most Hashes [in the US] sing, largely the songs that repeat obscenities loud and often, but also there is a strong following for ballads that tell a risqué story, permitting them to be sung in semi-public locations. Not only are the songs largely traditional, they have in the past introduced a wealth of songs now part of the UK and Aussie rugby repertoire. Think of Mobile, I Used to Work in Chicago, Way Down in Texas, Way out in West Virginia and Lil Was a Gal. The dirty song cult here is ancient. Even the national anthem was originally a bar room ballad!"

While none of the typical titles which are trotted out with boozy bravado can claim great antiquity, the oldest of all is The Lobster Song, "the quintessential dirty song," according to Cumming. "It has been translated into every known live and dead language on the planet – even Indian tribal dialects in Peru. The oldest written version is on a Sumerian vase, recognised by chance by a Cambridge undergraduate doing time on the dig. He played rugby and was therefore well familiar with the context." For some reason, Cumming observes, rugby players are far better educated in the matter of singing. He should know – he played with the Esher Club, west of London, from 1944, off and on until 1967.

"As a 'colonial' I was permitted to play for a somewhat casual team called the Expendibles. You had to be over 40 or suffering from some permanent physical disability (which included colonialism) and we played in a league of similarly handicapped teams. As early as 1945, when demobbing was beginning, the first-team captain required each team captain to pick up one new rugby song at each away match. We wound up with 11 teams – not less than 100 new songs per year! Swing Low was performed at least once a week at Esher as early as 1944, and therefore most likely was a carry over from earlier times, introduced to us by some other, unknown club. The actions were not as elaborate as the final version, but generally included the masturbation antics. I don't remember it being sung at Mother Hash when I was there (1959-61) but somehow it crept into Singapore before I left in 1966. Its popularity as an exit song most likely developed at some InterHash in Thailand and, because of its total irrelevance to anything (an admirable Hash-like attribute), became the closing hymn for most Hashes worldwide."

One of the unsolved mysteries to Cumming "is why Swing Low and not Just a Song at Twilight, which has the same opportunity for sexual innuendo (see last line of chorus: 'Comes love's sweet song/ Comes love's old sweet song')? It was always sung in conjunction with Swing Low, in a crowded men-only bar, at Esher in 1944."

What of the other Hash staple, Why Was He Born …? "We know it was dyed-in-the-wool rugby before 1967," says Cumming, as it formed the title of a well-known rugby songbook first issued that year. "Did it start with the Hash? It's doubtful, but who knows?" Father Abraham was originally a children's song, used in much the way the Hash often use it – as a warm-up. "It appears in several nursery school handbooks, and is, I am told, a staple in Young Ladies Camps in the US and Canada."

While Cumming admires the consistency of lyrics across countries, across different services over the decades, he notes – perhaps not altogether surprisingly –that "as soon as the Hash gets hold of a song, it starts to change immediately". Usually the moment tone-deaf Hashers open their mouths. Tremendous variances then develop between kennels and between countries.

"Hash songs are the victims of the usual Hash misorganisation," says Cumming. "In 1997 ZiPpy in Colorado took a year's sabbatical to try to straighten this mess out, and refereed a free-for-all with at least 30 major contributors, all of whom were convinced that their version was the word of god. ZiPpy took the trouble to root out the earliest version under dispute and, while to make peace in the end on two occasions he printed two versions, he was able to compile the other 419 songs (excluding special local Down Down chants and 10 pages of limericks) to everyone's reasonable satisfaction. Sadly, ZiPpy relinquished editorship in favour of a life and his monumental work, The Definitive Hash Songbook, now lies collecting dust. This may not be a bad thing, for what other aspect of Hashing is so clearly defined. No rules, no regimentation, no control, says Mamma."

And *that's* music to Hashers' beers, er, ears.

InterHash.

Group therapy with drinks.

In 1966, at the end of the four year *Konfrontasi*, KL was due to celebrate its milestone 1,000th r*n. To augment numbers and make it a r*n to remember, they decided to invite Hashers from Ipoh H3 and neighbouring Singapore. It was the first joint r*n on record, and "the response was splendid" according to Duncan. Twenty-four sozzled souls made their way up on that infamous rail journey from Singapore to Kuala Lumpur. Even so, Hash Crash managed to accommodate all the bodies. Some call this, the weekend of March 11-13 1966, the first InterHash.

Jeremy 'Burong' Pigeon was at that event, and despite finding the r*n up Bukit Besi hard going, obviously enjoyed the brotherhood of the expanded piss up. In Jakarta's 1972/73 year book he wrote: "Something for the Singapore Hash to consider. How about inviting us all along for your 750th (or 1,000th) r*n? A genuine International Hash Extraordinary would be a really great occasion and Singapore the best spot for it, perhaps, unless Hong Kong have other ideas. (Singapore's 750th fell in May 1976.)

Then, in June 1973, to mark KL Mother Hash's 1,500th r*n – and 35 years of Hashing – they invited for the first time not just local and regional clubs, but many international kennels as well. At this time the Hashing world consisted of approximately 35 chapters in 14 countries, largely in Asia. Hashers from Singapore, Brunei, Jakarta, Perth, Hong Kong and even Washington DC turned up, making up 300 attendees. It was the first time that guest r*nners had ever outnumbered their hosts. The seed was sown, which got Hashers thinking about the international brotherhood, and making more out of what was then a relatively small, tight-knit community.

"John O'Rourke and I got talking about this," says Fred Whitaker, who was back in Sydney by this stage. It was something he remembers thinking even further back in the Sixties. "We were chewing the fat one day and I said we ought to have a meeting of all the clubs, in the early Seventies, and we decided to have it on Bali – there wasn't a Bali Hash then, but we thought it would be a nice place to go for all the people up there and all the people down here and meet on common ground. It's a holiday place, we thought it was a great idea. We called it Hash International. And what we were going to do was charter one of the Singapore Airlines aircraft through Peter Flanagan [Singapore airlines pilot and Hasher]. He was going to do a r*n around and pick everybody up and bring them to Bali."

Whitaker produces a file of correspondence and administrative paperwork to prove it's not all piss and wind. O'Rourke in Singapore and Whitaker in Sydney exchanged voluminous letters. "I've got people interested over here, he's got people interested over there. We had a starting date and people ready to put their money down, had it all organised, how much it was all gonna be," he says. "Then, one of those things, I went travelling to the Middle East or something and sort of lost track so it never quite happened. It *nearly* happened. It would've been a good piss-up," says Whitaker.

By 1977 there were 91 chapters in the known Hashing world – every single continent, except for Antarctica, was 'on' with a mushrooming amount of kennels in each. Inspired no doubt by the Kuala Lumpur joint celebration r*ns, the San Miguel Beer-inspired notion of an international Hash meeting came out of Kowloon H3, the idea being to invite everyone one in the known Hashing world to come together for a long weekend of Hashing festivity and excess in Hong Kong during Easter 1978. Wes 'Chairman Pasttit' Parfitt and Barrie Griffin were recognised as the leaders of this endeavour, bringing it to fruition and galvanising the Hashing world.

And so with those two having claimed the kudos, it was left to the rank-and-file Hong Kong Hashers (mostly from Kowloon) to organise and implement the first InterHash in 1978. The first thing they realised was that laying on meals and transport and beer for up to 1,000 Hashers was an expensive business. They sent out a letter, saying that a 'levy' of HK$50 [then US$10] would be applicable for each attendee.

The KL Hash were incensed that HK were actually charging visiting Hashers for beer and wrote to complain. Stuart MacDoull wrote a polite letter back from Hong Kong, in a conciliatory tone, but organised it such that the first letter of each paragraph, when read downwards, read 'FUCK OFF'.

While the fiscal issue still fumed, a good time was had tearing through the territory by day, and laying waste to Wanchai by night. Eight hundred Hashers made pigs of themselves on that 'inaugural' event. Over the years, it's become like Woodstock, with seemingly thousands claiming to have been there. At the end of the weekend, the Hash decided it wanted more of this. Where? When? It was decided every two years was about all that most Hashers would want to see of the others.

KL decided to host the next one in 1980 to show that Mother could do it best. One of the first things they did was send out invitations outlining the 'sponsorship' fee of MR$92 [around US$50] for attendees! Suddenly, the glove was on the other foot. Or the boot was on the other hand, or something.

Undeterred by this cost for four days of Hashing in the Motherland, more than 1,200 Half Minds turned up. Jakarta took its turn in 1982, securing massive sponsorship from Anker Bir which defrayed costs. 1,300 partook of the suds, of whom 20 percent were Harriettes. Then, controversially, it was decided to host it outside Asia for the first time. Sydney was to be the host in 1984, at which stage it was estimated that about 380 Hash kennels were terrorising 76 countries across the globe. Sydney attracted a different mix of hounds, with around half being local round-eyes. Still, more clubs and more countries than ever before were represented. 100,000 cans of beer found their way down 1,650 throats in just four days. And, still under the influence, they decided to hold the first Aussie Nash Hash the year after. It was no surprise that Thailand, with all its exotic charms, would host InterHash sooner or later. It had its chance in 1986, with Pattaya being the preferred venue over Bangkok. Of the 2,100 hounds only five per cent were from the host country. Whitaker and O'Rourke's pipedream came true in '88 when Bali hosted InterHash. Unfortunately, Whitaker could not attend. By this stage, a full 25 per cent of attendees were Harriettes. Another interesting aspect was Bali's fiscal proposal of a sliding scale of registration fees – US$60 now or US$150 on the day. More than 2,400 hounds – a full 25 per cent of whom were Harriettes – soaked up the sun and suds on Bali. In the absence of buses, the world's largest fleet of *bemos* with police side-riders provided the transport to and from r*n sites.

The solid uptrend of attendance figures was dashed only in 1990 when Manila hosted InterHash. Figures range from 1,400 to 1,600 who eventually made it, with many others being put off by yet another coup, random murder of Americans, and a travel advisory for Americans not to go to The Philippines. However, numbers were solidly up for InterHash 1992 in Phuket, with 2,500 intrepid hounds going back to Thailand for a second dose, as it were. After several unsuccessful bids, the Kiwis got the sympathy vote for 1994 and, much to many people's surprise, the largest contingent to date turned up at the gate, baying for beer. At that time, the Hashing world had almost tripled since the Sydney InterHash, reaching 1,100 chapters in 157 countries. Given the distance, and the small home Hashing population, it is nothing short of incredible that 3,650 Half Minds made the trip to Rotorua. Beer was served from 5,000-litre semi-trailer tankers with chiller lines at the main venue. Additionally 130 x 50 litre kegs, and 15 palettes of cans were wheeled in. A total of 37,000 cans of beer were delivered to r*n sites by way of a little refreshment. Jose Cuervo was a major sponsor, shifting six thousand bottles of tequila from their makeshift cantina in three days.

Cyprus was a slight backward step at the turnstiles, but it proved that Hashing had truly come of age internationally, with 3,000 pissheads finding their way to this little island in the Mediterranean in 1996. It was fitting that the Mother Hash should host a turn on its 60th birthday, so it was back to KL in 1998. Perhaps they were seeing double, but no one could quite believe it that 5,500 Hashers would turn up to pay their respects to The Dog and to the Mother of them all. Dick the Prick points out that at the KL InterHash, which ran for 10 days including pre and post events, "there was not one incident with the police".

InterHash 2000 headed back to Australia – Tasmania this time. About 4,400 Hashers terrorised the neighbourhood, the Red Dress r*n alone attracting 1,900 r*nners. And so to Goa in 2002.

One of the biggest chestnuts around the beer wagon is where InterHash belongs. Some are resolutely of the opinion that Asia is the spiritual home of Hashing, and therefore should stay in Asia. Father, currently resident in Vanuatu, says: "I am a firm believer that InterHash belongs in Asia where it all started and where the *apres*-Hash delicacies are most abundant. Who could ever think that Cardiff could offer anything like the 'attractions' of Goa?"

Others believe that Hash is truly an international phenomenon now, with no geographical powerbase. Furthermore, following Tumbling Bill's Hash genealogy chart, the explosion of Hash clubs that are born after InterHashes in a local area can almost be plotted. So InterHash belongs to the world and serves the longer-term interests of propagating the Hash better.

But the more germane question is *why* do people fly halfway, or more, round the world for a weekend of Hashing? Why is InterHash, or indeed a larger conglomeration such as a Nash Hash, so much fun?

According to those sociologist wankers Calhoun, Light (Beer) and Keller, a Hash group would likely fall into the category of being an expressive crowd, similar to a rock festival, revival meeting or Mardi Gras celebration. "The emotionally charged members of an expressive crowd get carried away by their enthusiasm and intense feelings, behaving in ways they would consider unacceptable in other settings. Expressing their feelings becomes their primary aim."[100] And you thought it was just the beer!

Further Le Bon, cited in the same text, says that involvement in a crowd puts individuals "in possession of a collective mind". Well, make that a collective *Half* Mind for Hashers. He says that waves of emotion sweep through crowds in what he calls social contagion. "The thin veneer of civilisation falls away, allowing primitive motivations and antisocial impulses to rise to the surface." Hashers wouldn't have it any other way.

Another bunch of ivory-tower dwellers, Turner and Lewis, go on to say: "The crowd begins to define the situation, to develop a justification for acts that would in other circumstances seem questionable."

The role of Tim 'Magic' Hughes in creating and perpetuating leagues of itinerant Hashers cannot be under-estimated. A Bangkok-based Englishman, Magic got off the corporate fast-lane lifestyle and made it his life's work to document and propagate Hashing around the world. He published a magazine, Harrier International, which reached out to more than 50,000 Hashers at its peak. Importantly, he galvanised the Hashing world and gave it a semblance of structure, painstakingly compiling worldwide directories and contact lists. That this was done largely in the days of the phone and fax without the aid of the internet and email is nothing short of Herculean.

Through Magic's effort, for the first time Hashers were able to find out what their counterparts in other countries were doing, publicise special upcoming events, and link up with Hashers when they found themselves on the other side of the world. The modern Hashing community was largely born through this, and the concept of the travelling Hasher became a phenomenon. Likka from New Zealand is but one prime example. Around the early Nineties, Magic said: "A Hash t-shirt is as good as a passport. It currently allows its wearer to enjoy a r*n and a few beers in 136 countries." [76]

Magic literally lived for the Hash. His Bangkok office – in the premises of Bangkok Hasher Tony Erswell's accounting practice – was filled to the ceiling with files and folders and boxes of Hash newsletters and misinformation. And his apartment was filled with Hash t-shirts by the thousand. In recognition of his efforts, the Pattaya Dirt Road Hash bestowed upon him the Phhh. D honorific.

Unfortunately, his health was not the best and he died of a heart attack soon after leaving an AGPU in Bangkok in 1998. His priceless collection of Hash memorabilia was subsequently gathered up by Colin Snow, Bill Panton, John Duncan and Fu Chee Cheng in Bangkok and transferred (at the latter three's own cost) to the Tim 'Magic' Hughes Memorial Library, which is currently housed in Tumbling Bill's residence in Kuala Lumpur.

Flying Booger recently made this statement to his fellow Hash publishers' circle: "There'll probably never be another Magic. You met the man and you knew you'd met the archetypal international Hasher, the classic expat Hash character. He put out a world directory so excellent that to this day those Hashers who are lucky enough to have one (no matter how old or out of date) carry it everywhere; their favourite, most prized possession. And we're happy to stand in the great man's shadow!"

We'll close this global topic with some Hash logic from Screw My Bike who journeyed from Finland to New Zealand for InterHash '94: "If it was any further away, it would have been closer!" Yes, quite.

The Dark Incontinent and
and the Arabian Nights.

Hashing in Africa and the Middle East.

Hashes to Hashes, dust to dust.

Libya has been around since time immemorial but was mostly under Italian control in recent history. However, their brave soldiers suffered a rare defeat when pushing from Libya to Egypt in World War 2, so they lost the lot. After the war, Libya was lumped together as the United Kingdom of Libya, and at the end of 1951 King Idris was installed as its first hereditary leader. Any questions?

As financial and economic aid was required, the Brits and Yanks were quick to say 'Yes, have our money, on condition [there's always a catch, isn't there? –ed.] that we can maintain military bases on your sacred soil'.

In a further cruel blow for the vanquished Italians and their rapidly diminishing lira, oil was subsequently discovered in Libya in the Sixties. With increased private wealth and burgeoning middle classes, social tensions arose. Young radicals wanted their king, Idris, to pile in on the Israelis in the Six-Day War in 1967. But he didn't. Whether this would have made the war shorter or longer is an interesting point, the answer to which will never be known.

"A number of Brits went over to work in North Africa to r*n bases that had previously been entirely British Army," says Ray Thornton, at that time basking in the Mediterranean sun on nearby Cyprus. And so Libya was the first African nation to be terrorised by the calls of 'On! On!'. The Benghazi H3 came into being in 1968 – just a year after the first modern European and Australian chapters – but also thanks to the British military garrisoned in this Mediterranean city. Ironically, in January of that year, British PM Harold Wilson had announced that Britain would withdraw all its military forces from East of the Suez by 1972. (This essentially meant the Persian Gulf and Singapore.) It was abandoning its role of peacekeeper in the area because the currency had devalued and the balance of payments was wishful thinking at best and an oxymoron at that.

History clouds who was personally irresponsible for Benghazi H3, but Dhekelia H3 was where they had been exposed to the Hash previously.

Mid-year Bobby Kennedy was shot by a Jordanian, Sirhan Sirhan, making way for the election of Richard Nixon. Jim Hines blitzed the field at the Olympics and set a new mark for the 100 metres of 9.8 seconds ... a time matched only – unofficially at least – by front-r*nning Hashmen whose nostrils detected miniscule particles of beer in the air near the On-Home. On the BBC International service in their camp at night, they would have heard the strains of a very hirsute Paul McCartney crooning Hey Jude or Marvin Gaye grooving his way through I Heard it Through the Grapevine.

The following year, in September 1969, with the unrest in the country continuing, a coup was mounted and King Idris was deposed. The gallant young army officer who took control was one Col Muammar al Qadhafi (Gaddafi to most), who formed a Revolutionary Command Council. The first thing he did – with scant regard for the Hash – was to close the Western military bases and send them packing – 'at the request of the regime' – in March 1970. The Libyans refer to it as 'British Evacuation Day'. An Arab nationalist ideology was then installed. The Hash bit the dust.

A few years later Westerners started crawling back into to Libya despite its evolving political stances. These were probably embassy types and others brought in to help on petrochem projects – chiefly the Libyan National Oil Corporation founded in 1970 – which pretty much controlled the country's oil production. After a bit of scratching, it was once again time to get the Benghazi H3 back on stream again. Austin 'Haj' Hurley was one of the earliest Hashmen in the renewed chapter, and Adrian 'Odd Balls' Keane was another early member who hung around Libya for a long, long time. They were not the founders, but lingered around the crime scene long enough to have the smoking gun planted on them.

Packs soon numbered around 30, "mostly athletic types and no hangers on," recalls Haj[15]. The Grand Master pretty much ran things on his own, minus the entourage and committee that he enjoys today. "His main task was to ensure punctuality and who was hosting future Hashes." Interestingly, they ran on Tuesdays, and only every other Tuesday at that.

Haj recalls it being a men-only kennel: "In the Seventies the Hash was very much male chauvinist," he says. "It was not only considered distasteful for women to be seen r*nning about Benghazi, but also frowned upon if they appeared or were known to have contributed towards the bash afterwards."

The hares were armed with "a couple of rolls of bog roll", and also had to supply drinks and food after. Post-r*n formalities were kept to a minimum – no Down Downs and no 'special occasion' r*ns. "The Hash itself was similar to today's, but not quite the booze-up one would expect considering it was men only." [Bunch of amateurs –ed.]

A coup against Qadhafi in 1975 was unsuccessful, and he started taking a hard line against his opponents. Neighbouring countries got twitchy. Foreign workers got twitchy. The pack got down to around six each r*n, with some of those wanting to boost the ranks and On Ons with Honorary Gentlemen. As far as Roger 'Taxi' Duffin can remember BH3 (Mark Two) folded over the issue of females on the Hash, or more particularly the bash afterwards. In 1980, the advancing sands of the desert swallowed up the second Benghazi H3. As a direct result of this shabby treatment of the Hash, Britain and the US severed diplomatic relations with Libya in 1981 and 1984, respectively.

Amazingly, there were some mercenary souls – obviously being paid in large denomination US dollar notes (used and not in running sequence please)

– who stuck to their guns in Libya. So Benghazi H3 started for the *third* time on St. Patrick's Day 1984. Alun Phillips was the culprit, and his partners in crime were Andy 'Golden Balls' Butler, Mike 'Pilchard' Pinard, and Scotsman Fin 'Mombasa Handshake' Niederle.

Haj and Odd Balls were still in Libya, and – having not learned their lesson the first time round – signed on again. The r*n was held at North Lakes Beach, not too far from where Pilchard lived. It was still a men-only affair, the air reportedly being more one of a gentlemen's club. But this time round it was weekly, on a Saturday. Numbers grew rapidly, and after much deliberation and discussion, Harriettes were admitted into the Benghazi H3 for the first time. The pack soon numbered 80 expats from all corners of the globe, even Bulgaria and South America. Dave 'Headband' Lyons made his mark as an RA who had the pack – which included the venerable Slap Head – withering.

The Daewoo Golf Course and the Daewoo Quarry behind the airport were popular r*n sites at that time, as was Shell Beach. Other often-used sites included "the broken dam, the top of the Jebel, the concrete pier and other beauty spots such as the rubbish tip by Hash Crash Corner where Alan 'Moonadagaree' Foulds' car came to a sticky end. The power station road, the outskirts of Kuywayfiah village, the Roman ruins, and Wadi Katarah – seasoned Hashers know them all."[15]

For Benghazi H3 Mark Three's 50th r*n, a special theme was put on – all Hashers had to r*n in their national costume. "Where else in the world would you see a mad scouser, a waiter complete with tea-tray shouting 'tea?,' a Welsh-man wearing a pith helmet and a leek carrying a rugby ball, an army officer, and a lunatic Scotsman with his caber r*nning round the desert?" asked that week's Hash Words[15] write-up. "Would any normal right-thinking person even *dream* of donning collar, tie and suit to r*n for an hour through sand, mud and water?" Needless to say, it was the talk of the chattering classes in Libya for weeks.

Libya was continually accused of terrorist attacks and, after attacks on Rome and Vienna airports in late 1985, the US ordered all Americans out of Libya, and – as they tend to do – sent the air force in. Benghazi itself was bombed in April 1986, killing 30. Qadhafi was temporarily chastened. Growing economic problems [The problem being that they *weren't* growing economically –ed.] meant a further expulsion of foreign workers. But somehow, people like John 'Geisha Girl' Shepherd, The Human Vibrator, Baldilocks, Handlebars and Irena Lenciova managed to keep their jobs and stay on. R*n #150 featured their first 'live hare' experience.

By 1988 economic reforms were put in place and private enterprise was allowed a freer reign. Hash numbers peaked around 70 to 80, but with trouble in the country the pack size fluctuated as expats and contractors got shipped in or out. The pack was very cosmopolitan due to the nature of the expat community, reporting about 12 different nationalities in a pack of around 35 in the early Nineties. Other key players over the years were Dave 'R2D2' Hughes, Graham 'Full Toss' Bowler, Trevor 'The Martian' Moore, Roger 'Taxi' Duffin, Kenny 'Off the Leash' Brown and Bill 'Dolly' Barton.

In April 1992, the UN imposed sanctions on Libya because Qadhafi was singing from a different hymn book. Around this time, Milestone signed up. He remembers an awkward and embarrassing moment for the club: "I remember RA John 'Geisha Girl' Shepherd, and we actually have a r*n site named after him – the John Shepherd Memorial R*n – so named because it was reported a few years ago that he had died. This was later disputed by a returning visitor, who advised the Hash that he was *alive* and still r*nning somewhere out in the big bad world." At least, it's nice to be remembered.

The pack size currently hovers around the 20 to 30 mark. Says Timberdick: "Our numbers have reduced substantially in the eight or so years I've been a member. As a guide, the amber nectar consumption has reduced from a barely adequate 60 litres to around 20 litres, although 30 litres can be consumed if we try hard enough!"

The present Hash membership is drawn from personnel working for contractors, consultants, the local oil company, the Ministry of Public Health and the British School. Nationalities involved are Brits, Irish, Canadians, Australians, Poles, Germans, French, Maltese, Italians, Bulgarians, Ukrainians, Czechs, Slovakians, Filipinos, Swedes … and possibly others. There has been a dramatic reduction in the number of overseas contractors, giving them problems in finding On On venues – which take place (usually) indoors and away from the actual r*n venues. "This is due to the official attitude to amber nectar and the like and there are very few r*ns where we can have a Down Down session at the end of the r*n in public, so we have to adjourn to private premises," says Timberdick. "Formerly these were company messes, nowadays we use private houses. The days of beer fights in the premises of the Great Greek Shit House Owner, etc are sadly gone."

Some memorable episodes are etched in the Half Minds of Benghazi Hashers, none more so than Antipodeans Cockodile Dundee and Slam in Lamb being 'discovered' in the kitchen of Southfork, and Sophia's impromptu strip act – much to the delight of the Hash choir – on being awarded the Hashit.

Possession of alcohol in Libya is illegal, conditions in which resourceful Hashers come into their own. Non-alcoholic near-beer is available in supermarkets, and malt could be purchased as 'baby food' from pharmacies to produce the desired convivial effect. A Hash Amber recipe was posted in the Hash Trash, with 40 or 50 litres required to lubricate the choir's finely tuned vocal chords at that stage. Dire Straights decided that instead of using 8lb of sugar he would use 8kg instead (more than twice as much)! "The result was a delightfully potent brew of about nine to 10 per cent alcohol," says Timberdick. This was duly dished up at Terry Towel's mess about 20km out of town. "We ended up with most of the Hash absolutely legless, propped up against walls. Several had to stay at the venue overnight because they were too pissed to *crawl* to their cars never mind drive them!" Dire Straights, given a serious Down Down for his efforts, was last seen "sitting in the middle of the floor, giggling and laughing with tears r*nning down his face at the jokes he was telling himself!"

In the new millennium most agree that life on the Hash in Libya seems to be more restrained, however the Hash still forms an important focus in expat life. "My, my, how the world has moved on," says Timberdick. "We've even had HGs dishing out the Down Downs, by special invitation of course." They are hoping that with an improved trading situation and the removal of UN sanctions more projects will come on line and there will be an increase in expats and potential Half Minds.

Comrades in arms.

From the top to the very bottom of the continent. South Africa had become a republic in May 1961 and had left the Commonwealth over its criticism of their apartheid policy. "South Africa was spoken of in *sotto voce,*" according to Illucidious[38]. They were on the verge of sanctions which would see them out on a limb politically, and sitting in the grandstand while other sporting nations took their place on the field. Riots – and their automatic accompaniment, the riot police – greeted South Africa's rampant teams wherever they toured in the 'socially aware, man' late Sixties.

Durban, a seaport on the east coast, was next on trail in 1971. In South Africa it was still pre-television days. However, in the UK the BBC had brought down the full force of censorship and banned Sesame Street for two years because of its alleged authoritarian aims. With all that spare time on their hands, South Africans probably read Erich Segal's Love Story that year. 'Watching the radio' was a popular pastime, too, aural wallpaper coming in the form of Jesus Christ, Superstar; Joy to the World by Three Dog Night [I've had one of those! –ed.] and Maggie May by a skinny young Scottish git with sandpaper for tonsils experiencing a bad hair life.

In August, Jamaican Don Quarrie set a blistering new mark of 19.8 seconds for the 200 metres. At home, Durbanites had their own home-grown rite of passage – the Comrades Marathon. This is a gruelling 88-kilometre race from Durban to Pietermaritzburg (and vice-versa on alternate years). And it's not flat. The steep, undulating roadway goes through the Valley of a Thousand Hills… a good hint that this is not for pussies.

Quantity surveyor Peter Dominey had just returned from a stint in KL where he had Hashed. So distant was the Hashing fraternity in those days he was not aware of the previous Libya chapter or even chapters in the UK having started up. "We still believe we were the first Hash in Africa, as Peter had arrived from KL Hash with strict instructions to get one going on the African continent," says Brian 'The Gent' Orton, a work colleague of his.

On a winter Sunday afternoon in September 1971, Dominey rounded up many of his lackey co-workers, and a few hounds who had blown back into South Africa from oilfields abroad such as Baghdad and the UAE. The Gent arrived in his gleaming chariot, a Chrysler Valiant VIP. Women were not included among those first 12 hounds – this was men's business. "The pack was all male and littered with young good-looking athletic types," says The Gent.

Reg Sweet who was the sports editor of the Daily News and Alan Kidson, who was on the Sports Desk, both ran that first trail.

The inaugural venue was an Umhlanga canefield, now lost to the developers of a shopping centre. Umhlanga Rocks, a quiet little beach resort a few minutes north of Durban, was then famous for its towering red-and-white striped lighthouse and little else.

The trail set off into the green canefields. Soon, the r*nners were dripping with sweat in Durban's sticky humidity. At the end, a roaring trade in Castle Lager was done from the boot of Dominey's Alfa, a princely 20 cents changing hands for each 340ml bottle.

After a few r*ns, Stewart Walker – in a tilt towards traditionalism – introduced the shandy in a bucket. Being die-hard South Africans raised on full-strength beer instead of being breast-fed, this was too much. The bucket and the shandy lasted about two r*ns before being unceremoniously ditched.

The word got out about this group having fun in the *bushveld* to the west of the city and the great cane country to the north of the Umgeni River. The Hash headaches, the hell of organising r*ns and getting newsletters out, kicked in. This was still the age before email and fax, before even the photocopier. "The weekly write-ups had to be roneo'd off," said Wigless, son of The Gent[38]. "Ink everywhere – you'd come out at lunch looking like a deranged counterfeiter on speed. On Secs had their work cut out to ensure that their draft was typed and copied, that they'd addressed all 50 of the envelopes by hand, and that the circular was in the mail by Tuesday lunchtime for the Friday morning post." Failure to meet that timing meant that you'd have just the On Sec and the hare at your next r*n.

Regardless, there was one unwanted visitor they just couldn't shake. An Unmentionable, at that. Ann 'Safety' Knott "caused such a nuisance factor that it was decided to humour her," according to Illucidius. However, instead of buggering off after one r*n, as they had tried with Unmentionables in Jakarta, she is still Hashing avidly, nearly 30 years later. Honorary Gentlemen were officially accepted sometime after 1971.

The country, too, was undergoing major changes. Petrol rationing was introduced, and The Gent had to get rid of his gas-guzzling Valiant in 1973. In the mid-Seventies South Africa was to be one of those few countries in the world that went straight to colour TV without the usual black-and-white phase in between.

Dave Bagshaw, a regular winner of the Comrades Marathon in the Seventies, was a Hasher with Durban H3 (although he presumably did his serious training elsewhere!).

Durban H3 at that time also thrived on some macho hare behaviour, usually as payback for previous r*ns. Hare John Tatham laid a trail at Queensbergh Quarry, which r*nners still talk about. Somehow expecting Hashers to be fully equipped mountaineers, he had the On-Home r*n take them up (and hopefully over) a near-vertical quarry face, about 40-metres high. And Gordon Wiseman's r*n through the entire length of a train tunnel in Mt Edgecombe would also take a lot of beating. The tunnel was about one kilometre long, and the interior was in complete darkness. No torches. Then, with the pack all in the tunnel he started yelling: "TRAIN COMING!!! TRAIN COMING!!!"

It was only in the early Eighties that a fully-fledged circle began to take a hold in Durban, introduced by guys such as Tin Ribs who'd Hashed in the Middle East and attended overseas InterHashes. More beers, Down Downs and the Toilet Seat Hashit were introduced. A split between the young and the old formed, with the oldies reportedly grumbling in the corner at the childishness of it all. However, they eventually saw the light and embraced the concept of the circle, so it's now happily a 'six-pack circle' for all concerned. But it was a catalyst for the formation of the North Durban H3, with the ageing bones – and years of rugby injuries – catching up with The Gent and his good pal, Garth Berg who "disliked women and ceremonies and dogs on the Hash and who also disliked record keeping."[38] They decided a more relaxed, strain-free Hash was more in keeping with their advancing seniority. There was no need to call 'On On', you just followed the sound of the creaking knee joints. "Durban HHH began to attract the ladies (which is not surprising since some of us were extremely sexy and macho) and yet us MCPs, well, we just missed the old male camaraderie," says The Gent. So Tuesdays also became Hash day, with over 1,100 r*ns – "invariably geared to the abilities of wrecked rugby players" – on the board now.

Back at Durban H3, the fun and games continued, with novelty r*ns such as the annual Beano being introduced. It's essentially a 15km fun r*n, champagne breakfast and then a pub crawl from Pietermaritzburg down through the valley back to Durban on a bus. Prizes are given to Hashers who finish closest to their nominated time. Usually six or seven pubs are visited, with a compulsory Down Down beer at each, and a compulsory beer on the bus between each pub. "Additionally, every one has a number, and all these numbers are written on the tyre of the bus, so when the bus stops, whoever's number is pointing straight to the ground gets an additional Down Down," says Camel.

They still laugh about the time the busload of boozed up Hashers pulled into the 1,000 Hills Hotel and Bill 'Bollocks' Brackenridge – "who cannot keep his clothes on after a few pints," according to Headbutt – tore his gear off in such haste and wild abandon that his underwear got irretrievably caught up in the ceiling fan!

But it hasn't all been beer and skittles. Two Hashers have died on trails in Durban, both in the excessively hot and humid month of February. Graham 'Blue' Campbell, after having set the r*n and while chaperoning the pack, collapsed in a tunnel under a road, where he died. His daughter, Kylie 'Klippies' Griffin was a young girl then and has remained a Hasher. "My father, set his r*n in the morning and ran it in the afternoon," said Klippies. "He keeled over half way with a heart attack and was dead on the spot. We spread his ashes on a Durban H3 Hash r*n. It was his *second* preferred way to go!"

Another unfortunate loss was Nobby Clark who died while on a r*n near the SPCA. "He was r*nning next to Pom who was telling a joke," says

Headbutt. "Pom says he heard Nobby laugh and then disappear from beside him. When he looked around, Pom found Nobby had collapsed and subsequently died."

In the early Nineties, Torch Bennett – one of the original founders of the KL Hash, for those flirting with Alzheimers – attended Durban's 1,000th r*n. By then he was well over 70 and passed on the chance to r*n.

And their circles evolved to new levels of craziness. Gadget made a name for himself as a ruthless RA in Durban where, wearing his clerics 'dog collar', he has moved from using a little water pistol to a fearsome multi-coloured SupaSoaker to keep the rabble in line. His successor, The Rabid Rabbi, performed his duty in a Jewish yarmulka and a local *sjambok* whip. He tended to go on and on and on in the circle. So they hatched a plan to hijack him one week. Halfway through another monologue, a group wearing balaclavas and 'armed' with guns and axes, burst into the circle and hijacked him, giving him an unpleasant but suitable lesson involving a lot of mud and flour and humiliation while charges against him were read out. However, he apparently hasn't reformed… Stopcock, a plumber, has taken it one step further as RA with pieces of rolled clay that resemble turds, and are rubbed on the arse of the offender. There is also a fully flushing cistern – full of ice-cold water and 'mystery shit' which is flushed over offenders, who lie on their backs on the ground for their punishment. Christening involves another manoeuvre known as 'The S Bend enema'. Suffice to say it's not a pretty sight!

As of the time of writing, The Gent still r*ns regularly. Newsletters have recorded each week's r*n since inception, "and I have all 1,588 of them!" His son, Wigless, and grandson actively Hash in Fiji. Many Durban Hashers still r*n the Comrades Marathon, mostly in serious fashion. Others have chosen to r*n in flip-flops [rubber thong sandals], one in a kilt, one even as Santa Claus. Scrotum, who has r*n 27 Comrades Marathons, is also a regular in this party-loving mixed Hash pack.

Mainly because of South Africa's political and economic isolation there was little contact with Hashers in the outside world. Indeed it wasn't until the Eighties that the proliferation kicked in … there are now five Hash kennels in Durban alone. Cape Town H3 was started by an exile from Durban H3, Big Bang Bob. The Jacaranda H3 in the nation's capital, Pretoria, was started by a Brit who had been 'thrown out' of Russia following the Gorky Park Hashing incident.

Horseplay in Nairobi.
A month after Durban had started on trail in 1971, the talk in sporting clubs around the world was of Rocket Rod Laver becoming the first tennis millionaire. A group of long-haired ne'er-do-wells going by the name of Led Zeppelin went into a recording studio and recorded one of the longest rock songs ever, Stairway to Heaven. This would bring untold pleasure to millions of head-bangers around the world in the years to come, and earned the band enough money to buy out several Third World countries.

On their shopping list might have been Kenya. Kenya was home to the earliest known ancestors of the modern Hashman. Stone Age and Iron Age cultures thrived here. Originally settled by Arabs and then Portuguese traders, news of this place from returning missionaries was too much for the English to ignore. Soon the British East Africa Company was trading large volumes in the area, and the ever-altruistic Brits set up what they called the British East Africa protectorate in 1895. Within 25 years, it was a fully fledged colony with white settlers from England and other African colonies moving in for their share of the spoils. The settlers had brought in indented Indian labourers to help build railways and other infrastructural projects. The locals got a bit pissed off with the settlers living in large stately homes overlooking scenic valleys, and sipping gin and tonics, while the native Kenyans sat around scratching their nuts, with no jobs to go to and no roof over their heads.

Rebellion bubbled like a pot of maize-meal porridge, until one fine day in 1952 the Mau Mau made themselves known. They were the Land and Freedom Army, they said, restoring land to Africans. This seemed to mainly involve killing white settlers and anyone who appeared to side with them. It was, in retrospect, black Africa's first war of liberation. A state of emergency kicked in for the next eight years. In 1963, Kenya became an independent country and Jomo Kenyatta (who was imprisoned for organising the Mau Mau – a charge he always denied) was made President. His rallying cry for nation-building was '*Harambee!*' ('Let's all pull together!') [Brings back a few memories of boarding school days –ed.]. At this time, more than 40,000 whites lived in Kenya. Before long, the usual *smorgasbord du jour* of racial riots, government corruption, and political murders was under way. In neighbouring Uganda, a towering lump of lard – and potential Hash stage-tyrant – called Idi Amin came to power.

English expatriate Nigel Cross recalls the day Hash came to Kenya: "There had been a Hash at Karen on October 9 1971. 'Long but nobody actually lost' is what I wrote in a letter at the time. We would take a few crates of Tusker in the car boots ready for the finish." Fortunately he was a rather prolific correspondent and these letters have enabled the reconstruction of events that have long since been relegated to a very dark corner of his memory bank.

"I am not sure when the first Nairobi Harlequins Hash took place but I wrote in a letter that I am quite certain that the original idea to try a Hash at 'Quins [The Harlequins Rugby Club, Nairobi] came from a new club member who had worked in Brunei," says Cross. This turned out to be Gareth Rendell, a Hashman who was an engineer with Howard Humphrey & Sons working on the new Brunei Airport, who was transferred with the same firm to Kenya.

Several keen rugby players were recruited. All were enthusiastic drinkers, seeing off large bottles of Tusker with deftness and alacrity in the small rugby clubhouse, where – in English club tradition – jacket and ties were often worn, along with the often-dubious facial hair of the time.

Recalling the first Nairobi r*n, Cross says: "It took place off the Ngong Road and must have been a success because it became a regular 'out of season' event attended by wives, girlfriends and children. Later, as joint (non-playing) social member on the committee, I laid several trails with Geoff Partridge (a player), sometimes helped by Bob Miller from the USA." Key hounds, who often lowered the tone of the club with their casual dress code and boisterous behaviour, included Bill Maynard, Douggie Hamilton, Dave Lawless, Lew Huddlestone, Bob Sheppard, and Tony Glover.

One particularly colourful memory involves a horse [Illegal in most states! –ed.]. "My memories of having a couple of horses at a Hash are a bit dim (perhaps it was a morning after a club night before). We can't have actually laid the trail while mounted as the forest was too thick to even r*n in and I remember being on my own, and totally lost, at one stage. But as we waited for the Hash to finish I was on a horse, walking it slowly down the track the cars had used, when some well-meaning person came up and said 'Hi Nige – it should go faster than that!' and promptly slapped the horse on the rump. I managed to stay on and eventually stopped, but not before the insides of my legs were raw and bleeding. I was walking round like John Wayne for a week after. I learnt two things from this – don't get on a horse without knowing how to ride, and don't try to ride wearing shorts."

The Nairobi Hash also enjoyed visitors from far and wide, the Harriettes enjoying enormously the January 1974 visit by a rugby team from HMS Dido [They would've enjoyed HMS *Dildo* a lot more! –ed.], and the February 1974 visit of a team of randy rugger-buggers off HMS Dinae. At this r*n, a sailor stripped off on the side of the Ngong Road to display his full fox-hunting tattoo, which ran up over his shoulder and down his back, with the fox's tail "disappearing to ground in a suitable orifice".

Then the Hash fell into a dark hole of its own. Relations with neighbouring Uganda had deteriorated, and the East African Community (with Uganda and Tanzania) was also on the verge of collapsing. Asian shopkeepers who hadn't taken Kenyan citizenship had their businesses confiscated and were essentially told to go home. "Quite a few of us left Kenya about that time heading for Australia, USA, Botswana, even some back to the UK," says Cross, who himself left in May 1974 and took up a teaching post in Essex, England. Then, suddenly, the Hash chapter went into hibernation.

In 1976, Kenya – which lived or died by its coffee crops – hit the jackpot when South American crops were decimated by frost. Prices for its coffee went up 150 per cent in less than a year. The government went on a spending spree. Kenyatta died in 1978. His Vice-President, Daniel arap Moi, stepped up into the big chair. He saw the need to form close ties with Western allies, especially the United States. In came the expats and foreigners again.

Nairobi H3 restarted on October 2 1978 under the guidance of Arthur Schrock. Bill Drake was also a part of the furniture in this second incarnation, r*nning the most consistently for many years through the turbulent times, corruption and coups that followed. Rape, pillage and plunder were commonplace as Kenya struggled to find its feet. Tourist dollars were deemed to be the big saviour, with the country's abundance of wildlife and safari parks.

However, the murder of the odd accidental tourist in the mid-Eighties made the outside world a little nervous.

Although the Hash was now unbundled from the Harlequins Rugby Club, the format changed little. "We would go to a place, r*n the Hash, and drink a few beers or sodas brought by someone in the boot of a car," says Nuisance. "Then the hare would announce the venue, usually some cheap dump downtown, and all would drive there for more beer and food."

There are now two kennels in Nairobi itself, and a further two elsewhere in Kenya, such as coastal Mombasa. Others spring up and die according to special projects further afield. The Hash now has a noticeably large local following. Kenyans themselves have become renowned for their long-distance athletic prowess, usually leaving other competitors in a cloud of dust in major marathons and the Olympics.

Bah humbug.

At the Munich Olympics in 1972, Mark Spitz – an American with a thick black moustache and a hairy chest to match – had seven gold medals to show for his efforts in the pool. Neil Young ruled the airwaves with a song called, appropriately, Heart of Gold. Showing an equally competitive streak, in December '72, Apollo 17 splashed down to Earth after the longest lunar mission in the series. Astronaut Eugene Cernan was the last man to leave his footprints on the moon.

But we need to backtrack more than 50 years to put all of this in context. Bahrain – peopled by indigenous Persians – had been ruled by a merchant family from Qatar, the al-Khalifas, for a couple of centuries and the novelty was wearing off. Just as the Persians were about to contest it, the Brits – the global referee in those days – stepped in. Bahrain was a vital pearl and fishing centre in the Gulf, so Britain made all sides sign an agreement that they would not fight during fishing season (after all, it might scare the fish away). This seemed to work and Britain withdrew, leaving Bahrain to become independent in August 1971. Bahrain had long been an oil-producing force, which gave Iran the idea it might like to annexe it a couple of times, but otherwise it has led a peaceful existence. This *relative* stability in a region known for its volatility has in turn made Bahrain attractive to offshore banks and businesses to set up shop.

On a hot Saturday, December 2 1972, Bahrain H3 was started by Geoff Whitehead, who worked for the Gulf Technical College and had done his Hashing in Singapore previously. Many thought he was out of his Half Mind… r*nning in the stony, dusty desert in incredible heat. It wasn't exactly tropical Singapore or Malaysia, now, was it? Still, he persevered with the idea, driving his blue Holden estate car along the Zella Road from Awali, and turning left to take him past Sakhir and the Sheik's Palace. A couple of miles further, past the old airstrip he placed his HHH sign, and parked to lay his trail in the Jebal Al Dukan area.

His invitation had advised people to wear "lightweight footwear ie, tennis shoes (with stockings)". No one was perhaps more surprised than he when 16 gullible fools turned up for r*n #1 at 4pm that afternoon. Among them, Andy Bisson and Bruce Rolph, who were to become Hash Words and Hash Cash respectively. Strangely, Whitehead's precedent of haring solus stuck for many years.

That singular moment was the beginning of what Christopher Dickey[40] called "a local obsession". A couple of years later, Saturday r*ns switched to the Monday night slot. By this stage more than 400 members were on the books, with a raucous pack averaging 280. "It was difficult to have a signing-in system and so we do not know how many r*ns we have done," says Mad Cow, who has r*n with this kennel since 1986. With more than 60 percent of the country's workforce being expatriates, Bahrain's capacity for Hashing was immense and it was soon the largest chapter in the world – and remained so until early '87 when Bandung H3 in Indonesia took over that mantle.

Intended as a men-only chapter, Rule 10 of their constitution reads: "Women, children and dogs will not be tolerated". It was to everybody's surprise then that they found themselves with a woman RA in 1989! [Apparently no camels were up for election –ed.] The kennel has had some long-term members, few more venerable than Dave Corless over the years. Now resolutely a mixed kennel, Budget Davis, Margaret Timmings, Mad Cow and Silly Old Moo have been key members, keeping the publican of the Londoner Bar in the Bristol Hotel in retirement funds.

Bahrain is the Gulf base for the US Navy's bristling don't-look-at-me-like-that Fifth Fleet. This means the Hash has also had more than its fair share of short-term members and guests, augmented by hundreds of military personnel in the area, especially round the time of the Gulf War. With nationalisation of the workforce under way, "now we are down to a membership of less than 100 and a pack of about 60," says Mad Cow, who brings his BBQ along each week to keep the party going. Today, Bahrain is home to two Hash chapters, the other being the Bahrain Black H3.

I ran from Iran.

In the mid-Seventies the Middle East was not a happy place. Or rather, some were just downright miserable, meaning that just about everyone who wasn't a Hasher was in some liberation group or another. Terrorism was going through the roof. Hijackers had to take a ticket for the queue to get to the cockpit.

Iran was in a period of unprecedented modernisation – including greater freedom for women, and land reforms – under the progressive Shahansha. The Shah. The King of Kings, whose family dynasty had presided for 2,000 years. Since 1914, Britain had acquired a controlling interest in the Anglo-Persian Oil Company through a lucky carve-up of the country which gave them influence in the south of what was then known as Persia. Persia became known as Iran in the Thirties after its leader, Reza Shah Pahlavi, tried to grovel to the ascendant Germans [Iran actually means 'Aryan', trivia buffs –ed.] Britain and Russia got suspicious of this cosy arrangement and at the earliest available opportunity, 1941, invaded Iran, and Pahlavi abdicated in favour of his son.

The son – the young Shah – embarked upon a nationalisation program. One of the prime assets was the Anglo-Iranian Oil Company, which Iran nationalised in 1954 and agreed to pay compensation to what became known as British Petroleum. A consortium of seven oil companies was created to r*n the existing AIOC operations, hence creating a strong dependence on Western technology and know-how.

The Shah also launched into his program of reforms, with progressive Prime Minister Amir Abbas Hoveida holding the reigns for a decade from 1965. In the background, this Westernisation and secularisation was not well received by the Moslem clerics. And Americans were in Iran in large numbers. Two of them, Guy Woodford and Adrian Hromiak got together with an Aussie, Karl Henne, and discovered they had something in common – they'd all Hashed in Asia before. Woodford worked for the Chartered Bank, and previously ran with Hong Kong H3. Hromiak had Hashed in KL before, and presumably knew Henne who had Hashed in KL before setting off to establish Canberra H3.

1975 was an election year in Iran, and around March, the Hash flag was flying in Tehran. It was time for the cries of 'On! On!' to compete with the election spruikers and calls from the *muezzins* of Tehran.

R*ns were held weekly from the start, and only those in possession of the requisite amount of testosterone and testicles allowed to participate. With a few close calls, the following were soon in and 'on': Alan Holmes, David Williams, Per Odd Kjoeraas, Steve Kitching, Hans Lillebye, S.S.E Green, J. Carney, Kevin Latham and Doug King.

"We have always had a certain amount of (drunken) imagination and bravado (stupidity) about us, during those first few months which determined whether the Hash succeeded or failed in Tehran," wrote Joint Masters Green and Carney[(109)]. "As it turned out, the combination of extrovert, totally idiotic guys that were attracted to Hashing, and the complete dearth of anything which approached the Hash as an excuse for getting a bit of exercise and a lot of booze mid-week catapulted the Hash forward …"

In June, the Suez Canal was opened for the first time in eight years by Egypt after closure for the Arab-Israel War. Even the Elburz Mountains were still OK to r*n in. In September, civil war broke out in Tripoli and Beirut in Lebanon, between Moslems and Christians. The following month, Springsteen released an unofficial Hash anthem, Born to R*n.

Apart from men only r*ns, family picnics were also frequently held, even ambitious away weekends to Ziba Kenaring on the Caspian Sea. This served to butter up the womenfolk nicely, and got the Hashmen off the hook for their weekly r*ns.

As the crazy turbulent year of 1975 was drawing to a close, pro-Palestinian terrrorists broke into OPEC headquarters and took 11 ministers hostage. Even though they asked nicely, they didn't get the aeroplane they asked for and gave themselves up. The following year, Jimmy Carter, the world's most famous peanut farmer – and perhaps the only with teeth all his own – was elected President of the USA. Immediately he was on the phone to Iran and a

$10 billion arms deal was concluded. Almost as immediately, three US civilians in Iran were killed by guerrillas.

Henne was posted to Belgium. Tennis fanatic Hromiak headed back to Washington, DC, around the same time, but later resurfaced in Egypt where he got Cairo H3 going.

Tehran H3 received an invitation to join Penang H3 for their 600th celebration r*n. But it was deemed too far and too expensive. Soon after, Bahrain invited them to their 200th – it was close enough but the silly buggers held it mid-week which was impossible for our industrious lot in Tehran to attend. Additional Hash activities in the form of a Ladies Night and a Hash Christmas trip to Singapore and Thailand gets all the Hash widows on side.

However, they get offside with at least one person described in their Hash Trash as "the poor bastard in the black tracksuit who got lost on his first r*n with us in Tehran Pars". He – *whoever he was* – was not seen on trail again. Unfortunately he hadn't paid his subscription fees. But that's OK because, with 75 paid-up members in the winter quarter, the Hash was almost up to its capacity. Come summer, that number reached 85, averaging 50 mad dogs on trail each week. Rainer Bruchmann was one of the more instrumental Hashmen at this point.

With the outbreak of the Islamic Revolution in 1978 – and the ayatollahs calling for greater modesty and the return of Khomeini – Carter's grinning effigy was burnt along with that of the Shah, thousands of robed clerics and bearded demonstrators chanting and burning the American flag. Shah, meet Ayatollah Khomeini – the Shiite head in exile. The Shah knew he couldn't win and fled the country. The Hash pack shrunk overnight from 80 to about 20 due to enforced evacuation.

Still, for the hardcore Hashmen left behind, it was possible to get a drink at any hour of the day or night in the international hotels of Tehran. Vodka and caviar was served aplenty. "Walking into these temporary sanctuaries was like stepping into a time machine," wrote Claude Salhan[18]. "Elegant Iranian women, clad in the latest Parisian fashions, consumed alcohol and tobacco." Speaking of alcohol and tobacco, journalists and news teams poured in from all over the world. Not a good omen. Eventually in late 1979, the Hash ceased activities altogether. The Tehran Hash never survived the revolution. In 1980, when all the news cameras were in place, the Iran-Iraq war broke out and the cries of 'On! On!' have not been heard in that country since.

Oh, man, what fun!

Just south from Iran, across the narrow Gulf, lies the Sultanate of Oman. Ever since most people could remember, Sultan Said Bin Taymour had been rescuing Oman from the jaws of progress, keeping it nicely in reverse. Paved roads were a rarity. There was only one school. Its one hospital was nearly two decades in the building. Women were barred from education and couldn't go out alone at night. Music, dancing and television were banned. And while you're at it, you'd better take those sunglasses off as well [Doesn't sound like a great venue for InterHash so far –ed.]. However, the Sultan was doing alright, thank you very much. He reportedly kept more than 100 concubines. With all that bonking, who *needs* progress?

The giant wooden gates of the walled capital Muscat were shut at sundown each night. Unless you held a lantern up to your face to identify yourself, you were liable to be shot by the Palace Guards. Qaboos, the Sultan's son, was an Oxford man and knew that there had to be a better way to r*n the place. Fortunately, the Sultan's bonkathon was cut short in July 1970 when Qaboos – with a little bit of help from Britain – staged a palace coup. Soon schools and hospitals were springing up everywhere, political exiles were granted amnesty, and skilled professionals – not to be confused with Hashers – were paid truckloads to bring in their expertise to get highways, communications and other infrastructure projects off the ground. All of this was paid for with petro-bucks – the Straits of Hormuz, whose azure waters wash Oman's eastern coast, are a vital and strategic sea lane. Two-thirds of the free world's oil needs to pass through here.

The British military – which played a significant role in the coup – once again got down to the serious business of setting up a Hash in their garrison. And so it was that the Muscat H3 was started on October 25 1976, with Major (later Col) Roger Forrest being the acknowledged ring-leader. He had previously Hashed in Brunei and Singapore and was now working at the Base Ordnance Depot of the Sultan's Armed Forces.

He cranked out a letter on his typewriter inviting all regiments in the Muscat area to join in. "It does not matter whether you are fat, 50 and never r*n a step in your life!" it read. "Either boots or plimsolls are acceptable" was the dress advice.

Most of the original r*nners were reportedly military officers, with Doug Mann and John Johnson – an ex-Singapore Hasher from the Embassy – and Ron Strachan among those on r*n #1. At 5pm on that Monday evening, they rendezvoused outside the MAM perimeter on the north side, having followed the H3 signs from the old Nizwa Road.

The following week, Forrest reported: "The Oman H3 is now well and truly established" with 12 fully paid-up members. (A nominal cost of three Rials per quarter was charged to cover cost of drinks.) After a few beers had eased the pain of the r*n, it was decided to hold r*ns weekly as opposed to fortnightly, his original plan. Strachan, who had started Hashing in Jakarta a year earlier, hared r*n # 2, which was "a hard fast r*n with an agonising gallop over the jebel," and had Hugh Myers doing the limbo under some barbed wire. Slowly the pack developed a steady core, with about 15 regulars on trail by the time a young turk named Tony 'Chopper' Fellows joined in 1977.

Like many other Sultanates with limited recreational diversions, the Hash caught on like wildfire. At one stage 250 members were registered, with an average of 150 Half Minds having a dash each Saturday in the early Eighties. "Supplying enough cold Tiger for an evening in the desert could be a problem," says Chopper. "It could not have been achieved without the military. We owned five or six freezers and they were kept in a disused hut on one of the bases – free electricity! We also used to BBQ after each r*n."

Over the years, the mixed Muscat chapter included Chris Blettney, Helen Rogerson, Sue Chapman, and the delightfully named Gonzo T. Wattychops. Severe restrictions on tourism and visa requirements meant that visitors were few and far between. But officialdom, in the form of His Majesty Sultan Qaboos, was on side with the Hash. GM Brooke Saunders, with the Ministry of Defence in Muscat, once attended a Royal Garden Party, with VIPs and dignitaries aplenty, military bands, and a sumptuous spread in the grounds of the palace. The formal introductions were made and the event was under way. "It was a scene of grace, dignity and distinction and one I felt honoured to witness," recalls Saunders[67]. "I suddenly felt, rather than saw, an impressive figure approaching from behind. He had the presence and the bearing of a man of influence. He stopped behind my chair and bent forward. 'Stone me,' I thought, 'they've realised it's only little old me!' He bent close to my ear; at least I was going to be asked to leave discreetly. After a long moment of dreadful suspense he spoke: 'On, On,' he murmured." She turned around to see the Sultan in his formal regalia, cutting a distinctly different figure from the r*nning kit he normally wore to Muscat r*ns.

In the mid-Eighties a r*n was laid at Jissah, taking the pack down the *wadi* to the sand and water's edge, where the trail simply petered out. Much confusion, milling about, and ball-scratching [Typical 'checking' behaviour, then –ed.]. Suddenly a thunderous roar of engines was heard, and from over the horizon came two navy landing craft. All aboard! 200 Hashers clambered in and sailed off to the On On, frightening the life out of the locals who thought an invasion was under way.

Many of the members were pilots, aviation engineers and the like. In 1987, the Hash's big 11th anniversary bash was being planned at the Civil Aviation Club. The decoration committee was doing the rather ramshackle place up, including giving it a good coat of paint, when out of the skies dived an F-27 plane. It headed straight for the clubhouse, only banking away sharply at the last minute, and leaving the odd pair of soiled trousers in the Hash working bee group. The man behind the controls was none other than GM, Steve Kruger.

A subsequent GM, Andy Crate, introduced the stocks – a humiliating medieval punishment device – to the Hash circle, making a Down Down something to be feared indeed.

The only time a r*n was never completed by this chapter was in 1994. The hare, Wadi Adei Bob, apparently laid the trail not with white chalk but some sort of living, breathing mass of what looked like "heaving putrefying lumps of pestilence"[66]. The pack followed the trail for as long as it took them all to get screwed up. Soon, the trail was lost – the creepy crawlies having upped and left the spot where they were unceremoniously dumped by the hares. The trail was abandoned.

Oman is still very much 'on' as a vibrant family Hash with about 1,350 r*ns on the board at time of writing. Many r*ns are held from Airport Heights, and even the local sewage farm has been used as a r*n site. The r*n fee these days is one Rial and the Hashit is the Big Red Pencil. Each week the pencil – a large red phallic object – is passed on to an unsuspecting Hasher who becomes the Pencil for that week's r*n. Their job is to write a piece for the Hash Wurdz about the r*n. "Using font size 356 to reduce words is not allowed!" say their Hash Rules.

Escapees now meet once a year in the form of the Muscat Reunion H3 in the UK.

Coup blimey.

Like Bahrain, Qatar found themselves under the influence of a branch of the Bani Utb tribe who moved from Kuwait to Qatar in the middle of the 18th century to broaden their fish and pearl empire. Those nice chaps who brought you the Empire, the British, managed to muscle in again in the 1870s. Within 50 years they had a signature on a document that gave them effective control [Unlike Hash Mismanagement –ed.] of Qatar's foreign relations and security. Another protectorate was born. Again, a lucky stroke for the Brits in that oil was found here in 1949, relieving the Sunni Moslem population of the dreariness so often associated with having no food or money.

In 1971, the State of Qatar gained independence. Within a year, a coup took place, one cousin (Shiekh Khalifa bin Hamad al-Thani) shafting another (Sheikh Ahmad) for rights to use the palace as a crash pad. The nationalisation of Shell Oil and the Qatar Petroleum Company meant loads of dollars for developing the infrastructure, so they were off to a flying start.

"I arrived in Qatar in 1975 and it had no Hash," says Mike Ogden, a banker who had started Hashing in Hong Kong, then Hashed extensively in Indonesia. "Unfortunately the first year in Qatar was very busy down to a local colleague who died and had defrauded the bank by some £2m. After a year, we got going with Hashing."

Qatar offered little in the way of entertainment and recreation for expats then. "The Rugby Club was there and that's how we met up with John Frith, although he was a customer and so was Tony Westcott." The latter was a quantity surveyor. Qatar H3 got underway on June 6 1976, disorganised by these three. A pack of six trail-hungry r*nners were on r*n #1, laid within sight of Doha, then just a fledgling city. "It was June, very hot, and started at 5pm, in the desert just to the south of the C Ring Road on the road to Wakrah. I laid the r*n and provided the beer and took the cash for it," says Ogden, who had piled the supplies into his distinctive yellow Subaru coupe.

"The first six months were sheer murder in trying to get more than 10 people r*nning each week," he remembers. "At least three people who ran on the first r*n were not r*nning by the fourth r*n. John Janes, a colleague, missed the first r*n because he was still trying to balance the accounts from the month-end and ran on subsequent r*ns." Ben Blyleven, whom Ogden had known from the Jakarta Hash, became the first Master. Such was the turnover of expats in Qatar that co-founder John Frith left "possibly 1977" and a year later Ogden left Qatar with 93 r*ns with 'his' kennel under his belt. Tony Westcott Hashed on.

Shelagh 'Gin Bin' McComiskey joined in 1977. "I remember it was a hotly contested issue," says Timberdick of allowing Harriettes on trail in Qatar and to the On On. But the Unmentionables won out, and Muscat H3 (as it was now known) had grown to regular packs of more than 100 in the early Nineties, despite the heat and ankle-breaking terrain. Their 1,000th r*n came up in January1994, with Half Minds like Rambo, Wildman, Vancock, Getahead, JFM, Mansion, Tubular Tits and Tubular Balls, among others, holding the thing together.

Qatar itself is under new mismanagement with the Crown Prince taking over more responsibility from his father. This has resulted in a bigger focus on Qatar as a sport, recreation and tourism centre. The US military deployed aircraft here in 1997 and has been busily constructing military installations ever since, adding to the potential Hash pool. "It is still operating and has spawned the UK-Qatar Reunion H3 which we r*n with annually in the UK," says Ogden. Qatar these days is perhaps best known to the outside world as being where the influential Arabic TV channel Al-Jazeera broadcasts from.

Making a molehill out of a mountain.

This first example of a 'colourful' kennel in this region is living proof that tse-tse fly bites are bad for you, causing fevered imagination and hallucinations in its unfortunate victims. You may remember Bwana and Posh Marve betting a case of beer on whether Milan or Tanzania would get 'on' first. We know the Milan story, now let's meet its Twin Hash, Kilimanjaro H3.

Bwana took a trip to Africa to see Posh Marve at the hotel the latter was r*nning on a remote mountain in Tanzania, and to confidently claim his case of beer. Posh was quite unfazed when told about the Milan Hash, and asked Bwana in turn to come and r*n with his Kilimanjaro Hash. A little taken aback by its existence, Bwana happily agreed. "When do you r*n?" "When can you make it?" was Marve's reply!

When Bwana arrived at the r*n site at the agreed time, there was Posh Marve, alone. Well, he wasn't exactly alone – he was there with his dog, but no other Hashers in sight. "I think one of the Americans is coming, so we'll wait!" he said. Sure enough, a lone Yank tourist arrived, and the r*n began ... a truly spectacular trail round the rim of a volcanic crater. But Bwana smelt a rat. The trail had a curiously used look about it. Upon intensive interrogation, Marve cracked and had to admit that indeed the trail was an old one, set in lime, and that he was currently the *only* permanent member of KH3! "But the *tourists* love it!" he said. "Sometimes I get two or three!"

It was agreed that as KH3 was registered in Harrier International, it was a fair try, and the case of beer booty was duly split. Such is the curious twin of RMBH3, no longer listed as active with Marve now at Arusha H3, Tanzania.

The Kigali fields.

On a lighter note, in 1994, Rwanda experienced genocide, with an estimated half million Rwandans killed in a 'state-orchestrated ethnic bloodbath'[(90)] in the former Belgian protectorate. Andy 'Diable' Plitt had been the Hash Master in Abidjan, the Ivory Coast, in the early to mid-Nineties, and arrived in Kigali in September 1995. "The country was still in intensive care some 14 months after the slaughter," he says. "There was r*nning water and electricity in the capital, but only about six to eight hours per day. Ninety-five percent of vehicles on the road were either RPA (Rwandan Patriotic Army), ICRC (Swiss Red Cross) or international relief NGOs. None of the traffic lights in town worked, and a large percentage of buildings were still showing their scars from bullets and mortar hits."

Real problems still lay ahead. De-mining was just getting under way, and there were daily radio reports of children and farmers being maimed or killed by mines and unexploded ordnance. "Most Rwandans were psychologically numb after the horror. Needless to say, Hashing was not on my mind," says Diable.

Of course, life went on with the American Club and the ICRC hosting parties. Local bars were open and some nightclubs were frequented. "But most Rwandans were very wary of expats – collective resentment for leaving them to the machete." Gradually the general atmosphere improved, and life around town began to gain a semblance of normality.

Herman 'Van Der Belge' Van Brandt, a Belgian who was in Kigali before the war, reported that there was a Hash back then – a very family oriented event on Sunday afternoons. There was also talk that some expat had made an effort to get a Hash going back in late '94, but it was too early and people were too busy trying to survive.

In the spring of 1996 the American Club got an Aussie couple r*nning the American Club, and one of them – the future Madame Lash – goaded Diable into getting the Hash up and r*nning. "I put together some flyers for distribution at the American Club, and the first Post-Genocide Kigali Hash House Harriers r*n was 'on'," says Diable proudly. Some 14 Half Minds showed up for the event on June 1 1996 – all expats including Americans, Belgians, Germans, Brits "and a Half-Brit/Half-Frog". Most were aid workers or on diplomatic assignment. There was also a contingent of investigators from the International Criminal Tribunal for Rwanda, and other UN organisations.

The trail was set by Diable, Van Der Belge, and a US Navy officer who Diable knew from Abidjan, Kommanda It Just Doesn't Matter. Lynn 'Legs' Williams is also credited as founder. The primarily urban 45-minute trail, marked with shredded paper, hugged the main hill of Kiyovu, with a beer stop midway through.

A nominal fee paid in Rwandan Francs [Bongo Bucks –ed.] was collected to cover the hallowed Mutzig Beer. "The post-r*n celebration consisted of placing toilet seats marked KHHH around the necks of notable sinners, and of course singing them the Hash song as they slugged down the Mutzig beer," says Diable. "The American Club gave us a good price on the chop (*nyoma choma*, or grilled meats) and we all hung around, had more beer and got to know each other."

In the fall of 1996, the Hash went through some lean weeks as a massive refugee-return stampede from Zaire saw most Hashers deployed to the western provinces to assist in the emergency. "But even when only two of us showed up for the r*n, we drank Down Downs, sang the song and called it a Hash."

With time they got more brazen, and started doing more Hash r*ns in the bush, but some Hashers were not permitted to attend because of the wimpy security restrictions of their organisations. That was the case when two Swedes and a Russian from UNDP showed up at a Lake Muhazi Hash in 1997 wearing UN flak jackets and helmets. "Of course it was all in good fun, and thankfully, we never had any accidental de-mining incidents," says Diable, "though I used to hold my breath whenever the Hash shreddie strayed from a well-worn path."

When Diable left in late '97, Uranus took over the reins of this 40 to 45-strong motley assortment of lunatics. The American Club is still very instrumental, with Hobbit and Spank playing an active role in recent years. Not quite the gentle walk in the park of your average Hash.

Africa InterHash was conceived in 1995 by Marty 'Garfield' Hanratty, then of the US Embassy in Addis Ababa, and Mike 'Sister Michael' Fotheringham, GM of Addis Ababa, who were bemoaning the state of Hashing in Africa. "The event itself, which was called the East Africa InterHash and included 128 Hashers from four countries, was a resounding success," says Garfield. It kicked off with a "30-second tour" of one of the local breweries whereafter the Hash remained in the hospitality room sampling different brewery products for a further two hours "to show our appreciation to brewery management." Since then, Africa InterHash has been a firm function on the African Hashing calendar, with meetings in Machakos (Kenya), Dar es Salaam, Zimbabwe and Durban. As for Inter-Gulf Hash, this was first staged by the Qatar H3 in November 1979 in Doha.

Funny kennel names are not too common here, but there is the odd one that surfaces and survives: Khamis Mile High H3 (Saudi Arabia), Muff Busters (UAE), Heliopolis Atomic Breakfast H3 (Cairo), Desert Rats (Tripoli), Desert Dust Devils (South Africa), and Hho Hho (Swaziland). And where would we be without an acronym to flavour things up: Swahili Northwest Kenya (SWANK).

The Beat of the Jungle Drums.

It seems to follow that the more boring the place, the fewer competing attractions, the bigger the Hash pack. In which case, some of these Middle Eastern countries must be deathly dull, especially for expats and contractors in some God-forsaken outpost away from a major conurbation.

"As the beer started to work its magic, we lapsed easily into the camaraderie of drinking by a fire, telling jokes and singing bawdy songs. For the expats of the more remote reaches of the Gulf, beyond the domain of golf courses and tennis courts, the Hash had a riveting appeal. The rituals were set as a fraternity party, an Animal House on the r*n, built around a steady flow of beer – over bodies as well as into them – and humour as raw as home-brewed gin: racist, sexist, not-giving-a-fuck-about-the-wogs, for a few hours at least, stewing in sweat and hops there by the campfire." So wrote Christopher Dickey[40] about

Hashing in Oman, but it might have been about any number of Arabian or perhaps African states.

Desert H3 in the United Arab Emirates highlights how much the Hash is their social epicentre. In the late Eighties, in one year alone, the Hashing calendar included two weekends away, a progressive dinner, a treasure hunt, an auction, a quiz night, a casino night, a sponsored walk and charity marathon, a dance night, annual dinner dance, a New Year's Eve party and a hockey match [In, ahem, drag – please see rule #6 –ed.]. And this was *on top* of their weekly r*n schedule.

East Coast H3 in the early Nineties fielded a pack of about 12 hounds, yet they'd have an additional 20 or so people turn up just for the circle, which gives you an idea of its lack of competing attractions. Hashing as a spectator sport – an interesting concept.

In the 'dry' state of Riyadh, each of the three chapters was attracting average packs of about 150 to 175 r*nners on different nights of the week ... healthy numbers at their peak, but closer scrutiny revealed that many of the same faces appeared in all the kennels. Many of these kennels don't even have the added variety or novelty of visitors on trail due to the difficulty of obtaining just a casual 'visitor's visa' for most Middle Eastern destinations.

So it's either go Hashing, or stay home or in the compound and watch the region's top-rating show, 'Who Wants to Win a Million?' In fact, this is the highest-rating show in the entire world, with 80 per cent of the Arab world tuning into the Saudi-owned MBC satellite channel to see its slick host putting contestants – often in full-face *burqha* veils – through their paces. No wonder Hashing is so attractive. And so it is that the Hash has reached everywhere from Burkina Faso to the holy land, Israel. While now dormant, r*ns were held alternately between Jerusalem and Tel Aviv.

"I thoroughly enjoyed my 15 months of Hashing in Morocco," says American, Schwarzkopf, currently serving with the UN in the demilitarised zone between Iraq and Kuwait. "I have also been back on vacation a few times in the past three years since I left." He talks of the enthusiastic participation of Moroccans, concluding: "Perhaps the ultimate highlight of the Hash is the stunning Moroccan women that frequent it. In fact, I met my wife, Petite Nature, there."

Colin Richardson, who ran with Muscat H3 in Oman, summed it up beautifully when asked why we Hash. "Under the uniform of our daily dress is a Hasher trying to burst out," he said[67]. "With the multitude gathered in shorts we can forget the pips and the epaulettes, forget the business suits and ties, forget the Corolla or the Range Rover. It's a form of escapism ... a voyage into the unknown that titillates the desire of trapped urban man to r*n free with the wind in his hair." Or his shorts.

For others, the attractions are more spiritual in nature. "When I left the Harare Hash, at times they would rise to the occasion and start up a sing-song," says Garfield, a veteran of great singing Hashes such as Jakarta H3. "This usually was not in the circle but at the On On after being anointed with substantial amounts of the amber fluid. Unfortunately, this was often accompanied with the remainder of the food being flung around the restaurant and expulsion from the premises – a fitting tribute to a good r*n and On On. The Hash often talk with pride of the numerous places that they have been evicted from."

While this sounds like typical expat behaviour, it is interesting to note the shifting sands from expats to locals in Hash kennels. In the mid-Eighties there were surprisingly more whites living in Africa (with the exception of Mozambique and Angola) than during the colonial era. Many of these, though, are now short-term contract-based expats as opposed to long-termers or even residents.

And where local meets foreigner – especially a Hasher – culture clash is sure to follow. As Mathilde Hassoun, a Lebanese Harriette from Beirut relates: "I had an English boyfriend before and I got the idea that Hash was this very bad thing. I always went to the pub on Friday and they convinced me to join. My sister doesn't like it and when I came home with the Pink Potty [Hashit] one week my parents said 'What kind of people are you socialising with?'" She reports that the make-up of the Beirut kennel is now 60 per cent locals since the end of the war reconstruction projects. Before it was 80 per cent expat and 20 per cent locals.

"Ten years ago we had about 75 per cent expats," says Stoker, GM of Nairobi H3, "and now we're about 90 per cent 'local'… it's working well." He sees this turnaround as the result of burgeoning middle classes in Kenya since independence, as they aspire to a higher quality of life which includes recreation, such as golf, etc. "White people – or 'international employees'," he says, choosing his words carefully, "are called *wazungu* … people that come and go, because in the old days they'd see the district commissioner passing through their villages every few weeks." Even the Nairobi Hash logo has changed to reflect the new reality. What was previously a white man in pith helmet and beer is now a "more Africanised" figure with traditional Masai dress and *shuka* (weapon).

In fact, such is the growth of Hashing in Kenya, the Nairobi pack had grown to about 160 regulars when it was decided to split them into two separate r*ns. Mainly this was for parking convenience, although he does concede "you can park anywhere there's a hole" in Kenya. Every five or six r*ns they have a joint r*n.

Mad Cow in Bahrain also notices that expats today are different: "They just come in for a couple of years to build a building and then they're out again. Unlike me, institutional with the government," says the resident of nearly four decades. Of Bahrain's pack about 10 per cent are locals, he reckons. "They're the boozers, of course, but they don't bring their wives, with the exception of one of them."

Uranus, ex-Kigali in Rwanda and now r*nning in Malawi also highlights the turnover: "The average tour of a KH3 Hasher was one year because most were expats working for PVOs, NGOs, embassies or UN organisations."

Burkina Faso has a similar eclectic mix of Half Minds. In its regular pack of about 40 are diplomats (especially Danes and Americans), French military, business and aid workers, North American 'do-gooders' and an encouraging number of Burkinabe and other African participants. Rarely are there fewer than 10 nationalities. The kennel has always had a majority of expats, about equally divided between French and English speakers. André Adell, a Frenchman who taught at the technical university, was the spirit behind the Hash for many years, which raises the question about the Frogs and Hashing again.

"Ah, the French and Hashing are quite often like oil and water, t'is true," says Diable, who spent much time in their company in Abidjan. "Abidjan was an exceptional place for Hashing in the early and mid-Nineties. The Hash turnout used to be 100-150. The majority of Hashers were Francophones, though the Hash Masters (of which there were four to five) tended to be Anglophone or at least good English-speakers. There was about 40 per cent African participation, so it was a great mix of people. When the Frogs organised a r*n, it was usually a good one – with wine and cheese stops in the middle of the bush, or with a buffet dinner afterwards. I'm told by an English friend who was recently reposted to Abidjan that the Hash there split into two kennels in recent years – more or less along Anglophone/Francophone lines. Pity, really."

Still, the biggest divide in Middle Eastern culture is not so much race as gender. Hasher in Asia and New Guinea since 1964, Haji Babi, says: "Hashing in Saudi is very different. Firstly, there are the restrictions over alcohol so that the usual post-Hash conviviality is missing. Secondly due to the extreme restrictions over females by the authorities, it is used as the only social outlet that many of the girls have. They are less interested in the physical side of r*nning or walking, but more on meeting people and socialising."

Elizabeth Bassett of the Jeddah Hash spoke eloquently of the attraction of Hash, especially for women, in the Middle East: "The Hash is a great escape in a society which provides so few," she said. "No restaurants, concerts, movies, bars, and of course, no drinking. Women must wear very conservative (read hot, bulky, confining) clothes when they are outside their homes, so the mere freedom to wear shorts and t-shirt on our r*ns in the desert was not taken lightly … to be able to r*n every week, away from the prying eyes of our host society, was as close to being carefree as we ever felt."[45]

Tulip Eater might have felt carefree, but mainly he was thirsty: "In those days, there was not a lot to do – Hashing was everything. In Jeddah you *wanted* to get a Down Down in the circle 'cause that's the only way you get a drink," he says. "Otherwise, it's soft drink unless you bring your own home brew."

Cock Sure, who joined the Riyadh Megamob in the early Eighties, not only enjoyed the piss-ups but the added lifestyle dimension that the Hash represented. "The social life was really good with a party most Thursday nights followed by a wander round different compounds on Fridays, a drink here, a bite there, perhaps a dip in a pool. How different life suddenly became … there was another life outside the office!"

And different people come by this in different ways. Friki Da Priki, is a

Nigerian from Lagos. He ran a restaurant that the Hash used to use, and sometimes used to do on-site catering for r*ns. Did the Hash trash his restaurant? "No, they behaved pretty good," he says. "Then I decided to join them three years ago. Now I'm hooked!" Now he's also the GM of the Little Boys Hash on Thursdays, a r*n especially "for managing directors and bigwigs of companies like Shell."

"I'd never heard of Hash until I was introduced by a little man called Two Inches," says Still Waters of Johannesburg, who has been Hashing about two years and hardly missed a r*n. "I was hooked from day one, and now you look forward to meeting other crazy people like yourself." She also highlights an interesting point about the geography of her own city. "I've got to know Jo'burg better because you can go down these little side streets and alleys that you wouldn't dream of going down otherwise." Johannesburg, which encompasses the suburb of Soweto, is notorious for its inner-city crime rate – one of the worst murder rates in the world. "You feel very safe in the Hash environment," she says.

The like-mindedness also snared Gandhi from Cape Town H3, now 10 years down the trail. "Some people turn up for Hash and you know that they just don't or won't fit in, and they're not there the next week," he says. "But those that stay are all the same – there's a common thread."

Huggy Bear from Durban agrees: "It's a bit like the Masons ... a secret society. It doesn't go out to propagate itself, but if you know someone you think to yourself 'they might like Hash', so you invite them. There's nothing secret, but it's about being likeminded." His friend John ("Just call me John") agrees, expanding his philosophy. "We don't care if you're a r*nner or not – 'social' is the middle name. In this world we're trying to fight each other or fuck each other."

Drawing a Line in the Sand, or, R*n Like You Stole Something.

"Sadly, Africa has not known a single day of peace since the independence era began," wrote David Lamb,[110] a journalist who spent many years on this continent.

In April 1986, an American strike on Libya put Benghazi H3 out of action for a couple of weeks. The Hash "went underground" in the war-torn city as fighter planes zoomed overhead and the crump of artillery shells was heard nearby. "Saturday nights were spent frothing at the bit ready for the off, and some even developed 'Hash withdrawal symptoms'– not a nice disease – which only Hashing could cure," said Tina 'The Tigress' Irving.[15] "Only a few braved the aftermath of the war beyond the village of Nwagia. In fact we ran twice there in successive weeks."

The following year, they were still keeping their heads down, their noses clean. "Only a couple of times have we r*n into trouble with the local authorities, which is quite an achievement." UN sanctions were imposed in 1992 and many expats left in light of the unpredictable government and policies of Qadhafi.

"Our present Hash is very cosmopolitan but explicitly excludes Libyans," says Timberdick. "Not because we are racist or specifically anti to the host nation nationals, but because it is considered a serious offence by their authorities to supply them with amber nectar and the secret police are all over the place. They know more or less what goes on and so long as we don't involve locals they ignore us.

"We've been seen off by the army at gunpoint (twice!) for being in the wrong field. There is a military installation at this location and for some reason they claim a perimeter a field width from their actual gate. The field is in middle of prime Hashing country. Taxi, being unaware of any restrictions, laid a false trail into the field and no one said anything. The following day the Hash ran into the field, found it was a 'falsie' and started to r*n back to the previous check. Meanwhile the army, alerted by the shouts of 'On! On!', decided they were being invaded and set out to intercept the r*nners who, of course by this time, had turned around. The squaddies went tearing after them shouting something to the effect of 'Come back or be shot!' Up puffed these two lads, in full combat kit with all sorts of weaponry and grenades hanging on their webbing. Stern and upset, they asked us not to go there again." Unfortunately, being a Hasher, Taxi has a short memory and some months later he again laid a 'falsie' in the very same field. "This time they sent an armoured car, and as the officer explained that it really was his field, the turret turned from side to side covering us all. He also mentioned words like 'military prison' so we've not been back there again! Taxi was awarded 'Hash Shit' again," says Timberdick.

One r*n-in with the police ended a little differently. Irritant had been on a trail 30km out of town, and had taken a pounding from the RA, with several additional Down Downs dispensed to him for 'alternative choiring' with Milestone. After the bash, he had to navigate his way back into town, with police checkpoints on the city boundary on every road in and out of the city. The barriers are a chicane of steel tubular fencing set so that motorists have to slow to a walking pace to negotiate them. Irritant, feeling that warm post-Hash inner glow, failed to negotiate the bend and embedded his VW Golf among the steel-work. In his Geordie dialect, Irritant tried to explain to the officer that the barrier must have somehow moved into his path as he approached it, earning him an invitation to the policeman's office where the matter could be discussed at greater length. Sensibly, Irritant chose this moment to relieve the mounting pressure in his bladder – intending to anoint the crumbled mess of steel which was his car. His aim was a bit off (as it had been all night) and he peed on the policeman's trousers and shoes instead. Irritant then found himself enjoying 'bed and breakfast' at the local police station. The following day his employer was contacted and they were requested to provide him with a single ticket to "Anywhere but Libya" at their soonest possible convenience. "The Hash were most upset … he never took his Down Down for 'desertion'!" says Timberdick.

Down in South Africa, a country often in the news in the 30 years since the Hash flag was planted there, Durban H3 has covered most of the territory in the urban and suburban areas, but stays well clear now of places such as Kwa Mashu and Umhlazi, which are a little too gang-ridden and notorious to contemplate.

Stricter drink-drive laws were brought in in the mid-Seventies, after a sky-rocketing road toll. The Hash contributed a couple of those statistics. Andrew 'Wobbs' Webb had left the Highway Hash one evening after a r*n, popped in to visit a Harriette, then apparently lost control of his car on a bend, and was killed instantly. The unfortunately named Tim 'Killer' Watt had just enjoyed Durban's Christmas Hash r*n when he left on his motorcycle, failed to negotiate a bend (merely 500 metres away from the revelling pack) and hit a tree. He, too, died instantly.

Sensibly, buses are used to move the Durban pack en masse for their annual Beano r*n. Still, it doesn't keep them out of the law's long grasp. One year, pissed as parrots, they reboarded the bus to go the next pub on the crawl. A police car was behind the bus, and someone mooned them. Next thing, the bus was pulled over and the police demanded to know who the offender was. Hashers to the last, no one owned up. However, one of their quick-thinking and helpful number suggested to the police that an ID line-up of bare bottoms should be held in order to positively identify the offender! This suggestion was gratefully declined and they waved the bus off in disgust.

In Kenya, the unsolved murder of Foreign Affairs Minister Dr Robert Ouko in February 1990 proved too much for the local populace, thinking 'Here we go, here we go, here we go...' again. Anti-government riots flared in Nairobi and other provincial centres. The government responded in the fairest and most even-handed manner, banning *all* gatherings and demonstrations. However, the Hash reportedly ran gallantly each day of this episode. Of that period, David Lamb[110] wrote: "In Nairobi a man calling the police station to report that his house is under attack by a band of bandits with machetes is told he will have to drive to the station to pick up some officers." So a few drunken Hashers was unlikely to result in an all-points bulletin.

As a general observation on law and order, visiting American embassy worker, Jollgreenknob, has this to say: "Kenya has no laws so you can pack up the truck with as much beer as you want, drive off road to some Masaii river and camp for free, and be as loud or naked as you want." However, Hash rule #6 [No poofters! –ed.] is alive and well. Homosexuality is punishable by five years in prison and up to 100 lashes.

"The police do turn up and say 'What are you doing?' sometimes," says Mad Cow of their relationship with authorities in Bahrain. "But the fact that there's a lot of white faces and we don't appear to be a threat, the Bahrainians are very, very tolerant." It was only towards the end of 1995, when Bahrain had been experiencing quite a lengthy period of civil unrest, that there was a significant police and army presence on the streets – and in the air. The Hash circles were frequently buzzed by Bahrain Defence Force helicopters eager to check out any unauthorised gatherings.

In Iran, SAVAK – a secret police force created in 1957 – had helped to keep the opposition lid from bubbling over. But by 1978, massive demonstrations, riots and strikes demanding the return of the exiled Ayatollah Khomeini saw martial law declared, and ultimately the death of the Hash there. But it was not before they had caused some strife. In the late Seventies, the notorious Shah of Iran had a private game reserve where he could view all his favourite animals at his leisure, away from the heat of international politics. Being near Tehran, this was considered by one hare as fair game for Hashing territory. So the course was duly laid through the reserve and the stampeding pack reached the Shah's reserve, yelling 'On! On!' and startling the guards. Animals scattered in every direction and guards yelled at the pack. They yelled back. Well, until the guards' guns were levelled at them. The hunters became the hunted and the pack scattered in every direction, looking for the nearest hole in the fence to escape through. Fortunately no one was lost, injured or killed.

Soon after, the revolution was in full swing. First was a call to ban all alcohol in the country, a blow to the Hashers who enjoyed their American and European beers. They were forced to drink the local alcohol-free variant. However, when the evacuation of all expatriates came in early 1979, a die-hard core of Hashers remained. According to the Daily Telegraph "They salvaged 60 cases of beer from the brewery before it was burned down and they don't want to leave them behind."[76] It was only when they were given their marching orders by the British Embassy that they reluctantly departed.

However, the story has an even happier ending. Funds were still in the Hash's kitty and, years later out of the blue, all ex-Tehran Hashers received an invitation to form a one-off reunion Hash, and drink all the remaining money which was with Hash Cash in Brussels. Many took up the kind, albeit belated, offer of a free piss-up and r*n in Brussels. To this day, there are 109 offences that carry the death penalty in Iran.

In the Sultanate of Oman, the Hash needed a PO Box for their correspondence. The application form required them to be a registered society and to state the aims of their society and why they needed a mailbox. It didn't take too long to realise that the Hash would not be getting a mailbox in a hurry, so the idea was dropped.

Around 1979, Phantom (now with Auckland H3) recalls a gent from the UK arriving on a Monday night to begin a two-year contract in Muscat. He went for a r*n that very evening with the local Hash chapter and got lost, ending up turning *left* into a local military base instead of *right* where he would have found the Hash in the British Air Force base. He could offer the competent authorities no convincing explanation as to why he was there, who he was or what he was doing. Still in his r*nning gear, they put him on the next British Airways plane out. It was two or three days later before all the pieces of the story came together and his company realised he was not only missing, but had already been deported on suspicions of espionage.

One-time Muscat H3 GM, John 'Jaws' Dorr, ran slightly afoul of Oman's customs officers. He was waddling through customs with ominously bulging luggage, when he was pulled aside. A quick search revealed 1,000 Hash beer-coolers which he'd had made up. Quizzical looks from customs officers. A straight-faced reply from Jaws: "Hey, I'm a Hasher, these things wear out!"

The Sacred Nectar is the biggest sticking point in Islamic countries, but there is a wide variance in applied laws and practical tolerance. There are some genuinely dry chapters in the Middle East which don't have replenishing suds every week but will have a monthly camp-out in the desert where they drink with impunity. Qatar in the Arabian Gulf is a 'dry' country, although expats are allowed a monthly quota which is consumed with gusto on the Hash. Jeddah is a 'dry' Hash being a fundamentalist Islamic state. So Down Downs are a soft drink or non-alcoholic beer.

Groper – who was in Saudi from 1984-89 – remembers the evil 'gunge' that they used to concoct in the absence of alcohol for Down Downs. "It was flour, water and food colouring, and this would be poured over the offender instead," he says, laughing at the recollection of how vile and stubborn this stuff was.

But still, you wouldn't be a Hasher if you didn't r*n the gauntlet for even the vilest lukewarm horse-piss imaginable.

During a r*n with the Road R*nners in Riyadh 1989, Fanny Rat managed to Down Down a few quiet ones in the diplomatic quarter. On the way home to his apartment, he had a blowout and bumped his car. He pulled over and 'a third country national' offered help, which he declined. This guy then called the police and told them his breath smelt funny. While changing the wheel, flashing blue and white lights approached and he was nicked: Handcuffed and shackled. Then it was off to the clinic for a blood test, and into the slammer for a couple of weeks. Saudi Arabia has a total ban on all alcohol. No questions. Full stop.

"I did manage to get through the long hour upon hour with constant visits and gifts of food from my fellow Hashers, and was finally released because one of them worked for the brother of the Governor of Riyadh. One day I had a visit and was told that I would be out the next day. Sure enough, the next day I was out. To him I will ever be indebted. Trouble is [my employer] didn't show any compassion and booted me out of the country," says Fanny Rat.

"There are no locals," says Mr Mohammed, an American in Jubail H3, Saudi, "because what we do is illegal. No booze is allowed or women in anything other than black bean-bags. Gatherings of more than five expats are unsanctioned. And men and women – especially single ones – cannot meet." Still that doesn't stop them from rounding up 120 gallons of beer, and 100 one-litre bottles of home-made wine for the Quad Hash gathering of four Hash chapters. "Plus a live band, generator, huge Bedouin tent in the middle of the desert," he proudly points out. "A few times when squad cars can see something like a bonfire or gathering they'll have a look, see we're Westerners and turn a blind eye to it."

The biggest battle in the Middle East lives on quite fresh in the Half Minds of many Hashers. The Gulf War. Kuwait H3 (Q8H3) ran on August 4 1990, just two days after Iraq launched its attack and annexed Kuwait. One of the co-hares, Alan 'Dubai' Cook, was missing as he was sensibly waiting for instructions and developments at his home [Unacceptable Hash Behaviour! –ed.]. He and two other Hashers, Reg Baker and John 'Condom' Johnson, were later to evade the Iraqi occupying forces and flee the country. Condom takes up the story: "The situation was very simple – we ran out of things to drink and decided that since we never seemed to be in time to buy the Effes Beer the Iraqis were trucking in, it was time to go," says Condom, now ensconced in Indochina. "Since we had two vehicles between us four, we invited a number of others to join us, one of whom was Alan 'Dubai' Cooke, and made up a small convoy of four vehicles and 13 people, three of whom were kids. We left on August 10, quite late in the morning. We had been scheduled to leave the previous day but the Motorola crew (all Brits) had decided to finish the boss's home-brewed wine the previous night and were all suffering serious hangovers! Leaving towards midday, the hottest part of the day, we figured that the Iraqis would all be napping after lunch. In reality, we didn't see any of them, except for a solitary tank. We eventually struck the right desert route towards Saudi the second time round, and then met up with some Kuwaitis who blazed the way. We arrived at a border camel crossing post after about five hours, where we were herded into a 150-car convoy to enter Saudi at a legal border checkpoint. The Saudis gave us entry visas, free petrol, water, food and even car repairs if they were needed. They had refrigerated trailers giving out the stuff to all and sundry. We then drove all night via Jubail to Dharan/Alkhobar, Eastern Province where we separated. The most emotional part was in Jubail where we 'phoned home' and related our escape. The Saudi-British Trade Office in Dharan also interviewed us, and we gave them a hand-drawn map of our route."

In Jubail, Saudi Arabia, the Hash had been a relatively quiet and obscure affair since 1984, but once the Gulf War started they were in the hot seat, as Jubail is the site of one of the world's largest desalination plants and supplies drinking water for the area. Obviously a key target for the enemy, so many military reinforcements were sent to the area. Jubail H3 temporarily renamed itself Desert Strike H3.

In Iraq, Basrah H3 closed down in December 1986 when the artillery activity got a little too intense and most of the expats evacuated. While some expats chose to stay (no doubt earning excellent danger money) most didn't see the point as the local brewery was closed anyway. With the start of the Gulf War, a pack of 50 Hashers with Baghdad H3 were photographed with gas masks doing Down Downs in Iraq. As the tide turned against the aggressor, the Baghdad, Babylon and Assyrian H3 kennels were affected. None are 'on' anymore but there is an ex-Baghdad Reunion chapter in England.

The Hash kennel in Kuwait suspended its activities for several months until Kuwait was liberated again, by which time the retreating Iraqis had set fire to each and every oil well, filling the sky with acrid smoke and fumes, which in turn made breathing difficult for r*nners on those early post-War trails.

Beirut H3, Lebanon, closed down in the mid-Eighties as diplomats and expatriates left this war-torn city in droves. It was dormant for a number of years before people were game to stick their heads out again. Rebuilding brought with it a number of mainly British finely tuned athletes and, quicker than you could say 'more beer', Beirut H3 was back in business.

In Khartoum, Sudan, they've been 'on' since 1980 and only missed a couple of r*ns. The hare was unfortunately arrested laying his r*n while the authorities were trying to retain control in the face of a coup against then-President Ga-afar Nimeri. The r*n was called off. Meningitis outbreaks, locust plagues, and an ongoing civil war peppered with the usual accompanying riots and coups also couldn't deter the Hash until the early Nineties when martial law was imposed and gatherings – such as a group of sweaty r*nners – were banned in the interests of national security. Even then, only a r*n or two was missed. Although Shria law bans the sale of alcohol in Sudan, they're not a dry Hash because they rely on home brew which is eagerly consumed by, but not strictly *sold* to, Hashers.

Ra, of Cairo H3, says they don't experience any problems of freedom of movement in Egypt. "About the only thing one must be careful of is military installations. If you see a barbed wire fence with military personnel and/or vehicles – stay away!" is his simple advice. Still, Egypt has seen its fair share of Hashing misadventures. Ferret recalls a big visiting contingent post-Cyprus InterHash. "About 500 of us went to Egypt on a big ferry we called 'The Love Boat' and partied all night long with Hash r*ns all over the ship. We then landed in Port Said and got on about 16 buses for a wild ride into Cairo, with a police escort of several trucks loaded with troops with nasty looking guns … it seems they were worried we might be a target for the extremist groups [The Hash *is* an extremist group –ed.] which gunned down those people around that time. We arrived at the Pyramids and set out on a big looping trail which took us out into the desert and back via the Sphinx and all the time we had to contend with these wanking bloody camels and their unwashed drivers galloping along beside us yelling, 'You want camel, eh? Why you r*n eh?' The fucking beasts stank. One bright spark from California called Fungus Humungus [sic] decided to forgo the r*n and climbed the largest pyramid. We all thought the cops would arrest him when he got down, because there were signs everywhere telling you not to climb on them. We had a great party in the car park after, and the poor drivers couldn't round up all the drunks to get them back to the ship for the return to Cyprus."

Cock Sure, no stranger to Middle Eastern misadventure, also has a Cairo story: "The Cairo Hash was tracking through a cultivated area, within a javelin's throw of the Sphinx's nose, when this extremely irate woman came at us, wielding a very nasty-looking machete (of the kind we could have done with on the ball-breaker r*n). Needless to say, her actions soon cleared the allotment of trespassers. The Hares received a well-deserved Down Down for putting so many lives at risk."

In Yemen, Walrus and his co-hares came even closer to grief. "We were setting a r*n when three mortars were fired at us over some land dispute," he recalls. The three rounds whistled in perilously close overhead but the r*n went on. "We just had to go round the side of where they were," said Walrus. Another time, a Hashing family (including the wife and a two-year-old child) were taken by the military for questioning. "We didn't realise they were missing until they called," said Walrus.

In Rabat, Morocco, Diable says the local gendarmes sometimes show up "scratching their heads, but generally leave once they are clued in." The most interesting r*n-in with the authorities was when the Hash circle was asked to move deeper into the woods at a site near a highway as the gendarmes were clearing the security area for a convoy carrying Yasser Arafat from the airport to a meeting with the king. "I guess Yasser doesn't have his Hash name as yet," he jokes.

The other universal 'no no' in Islamic states is anything remotely pornographic, a matter quite close to the, er, bone with most Hash publications. Unfortunately, a Hash Trash magazine attracted some undue attention from the authorities in a bizarre manner one year. "Seems that some folks left the event mags in their hotel room after a previous event," says Likk'mm. " It was picked up, photocopied and sold at the local market in Bahrain – of course without 'anonymising'. The parties responsible for the mag were reportedly sought out and requested to leave the country." At Inter-Gulf 2002 they put out the event magazine ("right bawdy it is") on CD. Password protected. Most Middle Eastern Hash websites carry the same precautionary password protection.

In African states, the issues are not so much religious as pure survival in a continent racked with downward-spiralling economies, factional civil wars and warring neighbours. Luanda H3, Angola, reports a "lack of suitable places to r*n thanks to a proliferation of land mines." This is in stark contrast to the early Eighties when it was highly regarded: "There was, in fact, no more striking urban view – and no more pleasing life style – on the entire continent."[(110)]

In Bujumbura, Burundi, the war caused the Hash kennel to go 'underground' for four years from 1994. It subsequently restarted but with the renewed Rwanda/Burundi situation, mines and fighting outside of the city means this lot are currently "confined to barracks."

Kigali H3, in neighbouring Rwanda got restarted a little sooner with its first post-genocide r*ns in 1996. "We did have Hashers who ran in flak jackets and blue (UN) helmets," says Uranus. "When we said 'Stay on trail' no one dared get off because of the fear of land mines or falling into body pits. Setting Hashes was a very tricky affair. We always consulted with the de-mining team before going into a new area."

Nigeria also throws up issues of personal security for Hashers. Blimey, attached to the Dutch Embassy there, says of the capital, Lagos: "Because of security, we often r*n the same areas over and over again on the island. So your trail arrows must have the date written next to them to avoid confusion." This in turn creates headaches for the scribe.

"We always r*n the same streets, so being the scribe for the r*n each week takes some imagination," says Leisure Suit Larry, formerly from Washington, DC. And the problem is not just with 'bad guys'. Several versions of a story exist of the pack r*nning through Bonny Camp army barracks on Victoria Island. Some Hashers were apparently arrested and charged with spying, while others continued the r*n. The Australian High Commission was instrumental in getting them off the hook the next day. Ikeja H3, also in Nigeria, proudly claim they ran every day through the last coup in the early Nineties without any mishaps.

Hashers in Mozambique, an ex-colony plagued by civil disruption for decades and now under socialist/Marxist rule, also refuse to be daunted. "It kept going throughout the Civil War here," says Bwana. "Its motto '*Á Hasha Continua*' comes from Miriam Makeba's famous song of the Mozambique wars '*Á Luta Continua*' ("The Struggle Continues"). It must be the only Hash with a Hasher carrying a machine gun ducking bullets as its logo!" More than 100 Hashers, a very international bunch, front up weekly in Maputo, the capital. Outside Maputo is where the prime Hashing country is, but rebel guerrilla activity still rages on. Government force patrols have often pulled up hares at machine-gun point to demand an explanation for their unlikely presence there. Most times, this is easily explained. Sometimes not. Resulting in the odd hare being taken away to explain himself to a higher-ranked authority before being released to continue laying his trail. Two unfortunate hares were given a thorough interrogation by the local commander, and by the time they were released were too late to finish their trail. R*n cancelled.

While many of these skirmishes barely rate a mention in media outside the local area, Somalia is one country that was scarcely out of the headlines in the early Nineties. "I was there in '92 to '93 during operation Restore Hope," says American Hazukashii. "Life was rather bland, but the commanding general happened to be a former Hasher and – with a little prodding by the Aussies that were in the coalition – he approved a Hash r*n around the embassy compound and over to the university compound. The trail was less than two miles long, but it was a welcome break from the daily grind. We ended up at the Swedish Hospital, and they had a spread of fresh fruit and goodies. That was the best eats I had the whole time I was there."

However, he had a more dangerous experience in February '93, which he dealt with in true Hash style. "I usually finished up my day about 10pm and was wandering back to my tent when a stray sniper round cracked over my head (we had become accustomed to them by this point). As I looked up I noticed it was a full moon. Being the Hash slut that I am, I took a leisurely jog around the compound and called it a Full Moon Hash. I made a little write-up of the event and sent it back to Flying Booger to whom I had passed the On Sec duties for the Aloha H3 before I departed Hawaii, and it was added to the next Hash trash."

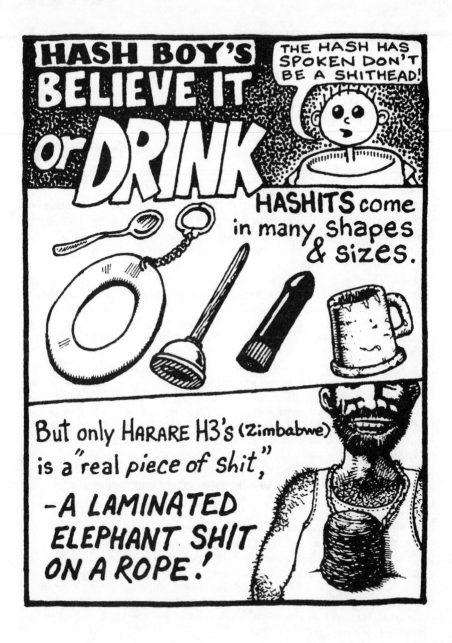

Wild Animals on the Loose.

Michael 'Dog and a Half' Ogden.
First r*n Hong Kong H3 1971
Founder member Bandung H3 1974
Inaugural r*n Surabaya H3 1975
Co-founder Qatar H3 1976
Member Bandung H3, Kuala Belait H3, Mbabane H3, Wessex H3, UK-Qatar H3

Your Hash name is Dog and a Half. Pray tell.
DAAH: In Brunei I got One and a Half Dogs Fucking because I took a dog on the Hash. In 1992 I transferred to Swaziland and started Hashing at Mbabane and my Hash name was changed to Dog and a Half as this was a family Hash!
You've done several hundred r*ns on several different continents. Any times particularly stick in your mind?
DAAH: There were many. First the r*n when I returned to Bandung in 1981 – I went back and told them I had been on their inaugural r*n. Well, they didn't believe me. So, next week I brought the tankard, which then evinced a number of Down Downs for me. Also in Indonesia, the inaugural r*n in Surabaya in March 1975. Forty-three of us flew from Jakarta on a chartered F-27 from Pelita for the day!

In Brunei, we got lost in the jungle on one r*n up at Labi in the jungle. Fortunately we were able to extract ourselves after about two hours, but about 20 of them were still in there after midnight. Two of them did not stagger out until 4am. Those two were a man and … a woman. And that spawned a relationship which led to marriage and we had a Hash wedding!
Sounds like quite a lot of beating around the bush! What about your worst Hashing r*n?
DAAH: I broke my ankle in 1972 in Jakarta on a r*n.
Do you enjoy Hashing in the UK after those other exotic locations?
DAAH: Personally in the UK I do not like Hashing from pubs, which we are forced to do, as that provides a watering hole and a car park. In Asia we met *anywhere* and we hired drinks suppliers to bring the drinks to the site.
What's the main thing you've got from Hashing over the years?
DAAH: Visiting those places that few other people ever get to. It has been for me the most instant social club I have ever known – arrive in a place knowing nobody and, in a few hours, have r*n with people and enjoyed their company. It is the greatest leveller I know. It did not matter what job you did or how important/unimportant you were in a company. On the Hash, you were at ground level with everyone else.

Brian 'The Gent' Orton.
First r*n Durban H3 1971
Founding member Durban North H3

How does a big bloke like you get bullied into joining the Hash?
TG: I happened to work with Peter [Dominey] and got dragged along to that first Durban r*n by the promise of a good party afterwards. We all thought the r*n was a hoot with its 'On Ons' and 'falsies', but it was the beers afterwards that really clinched it for me, I'd say.

Just between you, me and the website, any wild adventures along the way?
TG: Don't expect anything particularly wild 'n' crazy in South Africa. We're a bit inhibited compared with, say, Thailand or Aussie Hashes.

Is that why you got called The Gent?
TG: My Sunday Hash name was given to me when I draped my old dressing gown over a puddle in a cane-field clearing. Must've had one beer too many! The lady Hasher who thus kept her dainty toes dry as she climbed into her car, said 'Oh, what a gent' and the name stuck ever since. I can't say I'm overly fond of it. My Tuesday Hash moniker, Orterknowbetter, also grates a bit.

Tell us about your worst Hashing moment.
TG: Lost after dark in a reed-bed along the muddy edges of the Pani Dam. I never felt so shit-scared, not even when I was lost at sea off the coast of Venezuela back in '62.

How has Hashing changed over the years?
TG: I can really only speak for Durban Hashes and Hashers when considering how things have changed in 30 years since that first On On. We are definitely less macho for instance … one crazy hare took us half a mile through a railway tunnel and, in the pitch dark, yelled 'A train's coming!!!' The ensuing panic as the pack wet themselves failed to deter a single Hasher from pitching the following week.

Apart from soiled trousers, anything else you've got from the Hash?
TG: Hash should be off-road and in parts tough to negotiate. For me, the main thing is the challenge. R*nning *per se* leaves me stone cold. I've learned to love the bush, or *veld* as it's called in South Africa. Setting trails has always been the main thing for me, though. Making them as different as possible, too, and then seeing how the pack handles it, that is what I never tire of even though I'm now 68.

And what does the future hold for Hashdom?
TG: The essence of Hash is its ability to attract people with a sense of fun and who don't take themselves too seriously. Keeping everything as informal and 'laid back' as possible must remain the main aim of any Hash … How Hash evolves is best left to the new Hashers who enjoy this 'escape' from the workaday world with all its stresses and pressures. Long live the Hash, and eternal thanks to the Selangor Club that brought it to the unsuspecting and grateful world!

Alan 'Dubai' Cooke.

First r*n Medan H3 1981
Member Bahamas H3, Creek H3 and Desert H3,Dubai; Tin Man H3 and
Phuket H3, Thailand

How did you get yourself into this mess in Indonesia?
D: From people talking – I thought they were idiots. I tried it once and was
hooked for life.
Of all the places you've Hashed, how come you're named after Dubai?
D: I constantly complain about what a shit place Medan was (true!) and what
a great place Dubai was.
Tell us about your worst moment on a Medan trail then.
D: I decided that the inside knowledge of it being an 'A to A' r*n could be put to
good use by short-cutting across the nearby paddy which should put me on paper
ahead of the pack. To this day, I don't know what went wrong. I ended some 15
miles by road from the r*n site; sun long gone, not a word of the language. Reaching a small village on the main road I stopped. No traffic, all quiet, everything all
closed up. Blast! I spotted a light on in a café (of sorts), a car parked alongside,
great. Imagine, this European man walks out of the jungle, late at night, no money,
no identification, covered in mud and mosquito bites, sweaty and smelling like a
sewer, unable to speak a word of the local language. Unable to explain who he
is, where he has come from, where he wants to go. Voices get louder as the
questions go unanswered, doors and windows open, lights go on. The village
elders, in fact the whole village, are all of a sudden standing around me.

Fearing I might get lynched I thought to make a r*n for the jungle and hide
up over night. Impossible – I'm shattered. And anyway I need a beer. I
remembered that the other building next to the start of the r*n site was a lunatic
asylum. My driver had told me that to indicate someone who is mad the
Indonesians put two crossed fingers to their forehead. So I explained loudly in
slow clear English what I wanted, and put two crossed fingers to my forehead.

The mob went quiet, then started talking away in their own language.
Suddenly four of them rushed me and bundled me into the back of the car –
two smelly villagers each side of me. After a bit I started to recognise roads and
buildings. Then, ahead, the lunatic asylum. The gates opened, and we charged
in. I piled out – ran like I'd never ran before or since. I had to make it through
those gates before they slammed shut. And did, just – but they were right
behind me shouting and yelling, determined to get me back where they
believed I belonged.

Fortunately I was not far from where my car was parked and – with the mob
in hot pursuit – I made it, grabbed my wallet, pulled out money – lots of money
– and threw it into the air. Now if there is one thing that will stop Indonesian
villagers dead in their tracks it's stopping to pick up money. The day was saved.
As I rejoined the Hash, the last beer was drunk, so I had yet longer to wait for
that much needed beer.

How has Hashing/Hashers changed over the years?
D: I have not been paying attention. Evolution is a natural process – let nature take its course.

Alan 'Baldrick 2 Dogs' Holden.
First r*n Jeddah H3 1994
Founder Kuwait Full Moon H3, Bedouin Black Hash
Member Kuwait H3, Sulaimaniya and Third Herd, Riyadh

So, Baldrick, how did you get roped into this?
B2D: In Jeddah I was taken along by a co-worker who suggested it was a good way to pass time in the Magic Kingdom. It was their 666th r*n and there were all these weird guys in devil outfits – I thought 'hey, these are my kind of people!'
So I guess the Hash has been a waste of time for you, like most people. How many r*ns have you done?
B2D: Approximately 500 r*ns – who's counting!
How does a good-looking bloke like you get a Hash handle like that?
B2D: I got the initial name Baldrick in Jeddah due to a passing resemblance to Black Adder's sidekick. I arrived in Kuwait and they already had a Baldrick, so I was on their books as Baldrick #2. Then after a while I was caught shagging around with a couple of 'not the prettiest girls on the block' and became Baldrick 2 Dogs.
Any life-threatening moments in Kuwait?
B2D: Me, Slapper and Floppy Dick held a pub crawl r*n in 'dry' Kuwait including six drink stops – one at each of our houses and three out of the back of our cars in the Kuwaiti streets!
Excellent work. What about shit-fights on the Hash?
B2D: Setting trail with Slapper and Baht Loy. We laid the Saturday Hash trail on Wednesday evening (we had a busy weekend planned). It rained and washed the trail away. We laid it again on Thursday. It rained again. We laid it again on Friday. It rained again. This is a desert remember! We laid it again Saturday an hour before the r*n. It rained again, then stopped five minutes before the start. We ended up live haring after a whole weekend on the pop!
Is it true that once you've Hashed one desert you've Hashed them all? Where else have you experienced?
B2D: The only thing in common between Kuwait and Riyadh is the damned heat! Other than that I've Hashed in jungle in KL and Pattaya, up a waterfall and about 3,000 steps in Hong Kong, through cow-pats and rivers in the UK. But, regardless, I've enjoyed each one for what they offer.
What's the main thing you've got from Hashing over the years?
B2D: Friends! Lots of them – 'Come stay with us when you are in the area' seems to be all the go. That, and the only exercise I do each week.

OK, enough of the easy questions. Does InterHash belong in Asia or worldwide?

B2D: Oh come on! If it belonged in Asia it would never have left. It's the multinational, multicultural aspect that makes Hash what it is today. A Filipino cleaner can be on equal par with a British bank manager or Venezuelan cowboy!

Happy with the way the Hash is or does it need to evolve to survive?

B2D: Evolution suggests change, and change for change's sake is a bad idea – 'If it ain't broke, don't try and fix it!' All it needs is new blood encouraging to promote healthy chapters – unfortunately, the expat side of things seems to be on the decline, especially in the Middle East, and much as we would like to encourage the local community to take part, we know it would fuck up our party!

Fanny Rat.

First r*n Riyadh H3 (Megamob) 1986
Member Jebel H3, Muscat H3

What did you think after your first outing?

FR: What the hell is this all about? – especially as the Down Downs were done with soft drinks. It was not at all what I expected, as I had visions of people racing around the desert. I think it was all the competitive baggage that I envisioned when the term Harriers was mentioned.

How did you come by that tasteful Hash name?

FR: In Riyadh I was christened Mr Smoothie as I was always tapping up the ladies. In Oman it was much the same, but as the Jebel Hashers were more inclined to lower the tone, I was re-christened Fanny Rat. This is not to be confused with the American meaning of fanny! The Muscat Hash were a bunch of wimps, and to me Hashing was more than sitting around drinking tea after the r*n. What a bunch of old women!

What was your favourite time out on trail?

FR: All the r*ns were enjoyable in Riyadh. The countryside is quite stunning in places and the chance to r*n around oases and *wadi* is something that should not be missed. Every so often the Hash would have a camp-out over the weekend where there would be a couple of r*ns and a ding-dong of a session during the evening. As you well know, alcohol is not permitted in the Kingdom of Saudi Arabia, so there were no special drinks for the evening's festivities. Not!!! We all brewed our own beers and fermented wines and some people were craftsmen, producing brews that some of the top breweries would be proud of. One of my compatriots, Ken, worked for the company that supplied the fire safety equipment to the King Fahad Airport in Riyadh. On one occasion Ken and I prepared our evening beers by filling a couple of stainless steel fire extinguishers, priming them with CO_2 and marking the handles with lead seals. These were then transported to the site and, voila, draft beer!

How would you compare Hashing between the Middle East and the UK?

FR: I'd highlight the difference of mindset between Mid-East expat/contractors and 'home' crowd in UK. Hashing in the UK has grown over the past 15 years but it is still frequented mainly by expats. Probably those expats who have done a stint abroad, found the Hash and enjoyed it and wanted to get back into it in the UK. If you counted the number of expats to non-expats, I expect there would be a 95 per cent to five per cent ratio. Each Hash I've visited holds to the traditional methods pretty much alike. In the Middle East people appeared less inhibited and more willing to enjoy themselves. That's not necessarily true in the UK with the 'embarrassment' culture that we have here.

What's the main thing you've got from Hashing over the years?

FR: The friendships that spring up from being a part of the Hash is something that would make you a fortune if it could be bottled. I believe that this stems from everyone being on an equal footing. Company directors to the least skilled technicians [That's me! –ed.] mingle together as like-minded people and don't care about the daily pressures placed upon them.

Shelagh 'Gin Bin' McComiskey.

First r*n Qatar H3 1977
Founder member Delta Hash House Harriers, Egypt 1984
Member Bahrain H3, Edinburgh/TNT H3, Kuwait H3, Hashemite H3, Mainland H3

You've done at least 1,050 r*ns. How did you get started?

GB: First heard of the Hash in Doha, Qatar. Read a Hash sheet, couldn't understand a thing about it, and decided to go along to find out what it was all about. Thought what a bunch of lunatics, this is for me!

What moments of inspired lunacy do you remember?

GB: Cambridge Nash Hash, watching George Wilkes in a dish-dash get arrested on arrival in Edinburgh Waverley train station by the police for flashing after climbing a signal in Newcastle. Hurray for George! We hired a bus to get us down, but in those days they had no toilets. So we got a five-gallon container with a funnel marked 'ladies'. Halfway down the motorway we asked the driver to stop. 'Do you need the toilet?' he asks. 'No, we need to empty this container!'

Another good outing was a Mainland Hash *dhow* trip where we pissed it up all the way there, went ashore, had a barbie, and came back to find our crew had also been at the beer and were as pissed as we were! Very amusing until we found out the engine had broken down. Since the crew were incapable, it was left to an ex-navy Hasher to fire up the engines and get us back.

And what moments do you wish to forget?

GB: InterHash Rotorua. After flying for 22 hours to NZ, having chosen the r*n carefully – mountains, lakes, BBQ – then proceeded to get completely shit-faced trying to outdrink a New Zealander on Margaritas. Spent the rest of the night with my head down the toilet, then watched out the window of the bungalow with a white face while the rest of EH3 went off on my chosen r*n to have a great time.

How has Hashing, or Hashers, changed over the years?

GB: You meet the same crowd with larger beer bellies than the last time you saw them!

Yourself included?

GB: The main thing I have got from Hashing is a great bunch of friends all over the world … and a gin bin from the 20-odd years of Hashing.

So where does Hashing go from here?

GB: I think Hashing should just follow its natural course – more drinking, more r*nning, no poofters.

Michael 'Pissoles' Petzold.

First r*n Blantyre H3, Malawi 1989
Co-founder XABEA X3 (sic), Spain
Member Nelson H3, NZ

How did you hear of the Hash and what were your first impressions?

P: Introduced by Andy 'Sideways' Crabb in Blantyre shortly after BH3 was founded. First impression? 'This lunacy will die a natural death…' I began by making excuses not to r*n but shortly realised that Hashing was what I had secretly lusted after for years.

With nearly 500 r*ns under your belt, what have you got from Hashing?

P: PISSED, and extremely fit.

Tell us about the most fun you've had with this rabble.

P: The first Api-Api H3 post ramble at Kota Kinabalu (after KL '98) takes a lot of beating, for sheer masochistic exhilaration, variety of terrain and scenery: climbing through steamy rain-forest up a 60-degree slope, grappling for tree roots, swinging on lianas, scrambling ever upward through several vegetation strata, finally emerging in the cool heather-covered highlands, then down again via numerous check-backs and false trails (by this time you're on your own – you've seen no other Hasher for 20 minutes), urged on by a distant faint cry of 'On! On!' and encouraged by an occasional tiny scrap of paper. The final orgasmic dive into a glorious rock pool, with crystal-cool water and local mermaids (Harriettes) to welcome you beneath the waterfall. At the circle we were honoured by the presence of the Prime Minister of Sabah, who welcomed us and was duly given a Down Down for pitching up in his official limo, dressed in suit and tie. (I often wonder whether there were repercussions after we sang 'He's a bastard through and through …')

How would you compare Hashing in the different places you've Hashed?

P: It doesn't matter where you r*n as long as the spirit of Hashing is preserved. No two clubs or r*n venues are the same. Everywhere is different. That is part of the charm. That, and the beer. In Africa, it's difficult to convince the

multitude of snotty *piccaninnies* r*nning past you that Hashing is not a race. And it's a job to stop the dogs eating the flour the hare uses to mark the trail.
How has Hashing changed over the years?
P: There seems to be a desire among Hashers for more extreme r*ns and behaviour. But the pendulum swings. For instance, Blantyre went through an ultra-crude phase in the early Nineties – numbers dropped off, probably as a consequence. Their act was cleaned up – visitors have even called it 'tame' recently – but numbers are increasing again and the r*ns are great.
How could or should Hash evolve from here?
P: Hashing is an expat thing and I believe it will remain so. Hashing will continue to develop as a healthy outlet for the stressed, and a normal reaction to political correctness, posers and poofs. How *should* it evolve? Ask me again after Goa.

Robert 'Bwana' Walker.
First r*n Nairobi H3 1983
Founder Milan H3 1990 (merged into Royal Milan & Bordighera H3 1992), Hippo H3 2000
Member Mombasa H3, Durban H3, Maputo H3

How did you hear of the Hash, and what were your first impressions?
B: I heard of it from someone in my office in Nairobi. I thought I had finally found the meaning of life! In 1984 I left Nairobi for Mombasa, where the Hash was in trouble. With the help of the existing members, who were a mix of races and cultures that you can only find on the African coast, the Hash regained popularity and became a great focus for regional Hashing, with a lot of passing navy from the first Gulf war passing by and providing some really wild visitors. This was my first real experience of Hashing.
Where when and why did you get called Bwana?
B: When Milan H3 merged with RMBH3 we thought the event was momentous enough that all Hashers should receive new names. I was dubbed Bwana because I kept talking about Africa and I had a tendency to wear a pith helmet.
You've done nearly 1,000 r*ns – any favourite times?
B: Opening InterHash 1998 on stage with the 'Pope' (our RMBH3 RA). Bibione Hash, where RMBH3 annually takes over an international fun r*n and 100 pith-helmeted Hashers get on stage to sing Swing Low and give a Down Down to the mayor. A Mombasa Hash around the summit of Mount Kenya. The incredible 'Two Millenniums' Hash, where RMBH3 went to a sand dune in the middle of the Kalahari and set a r*n in the desert, which started at 23:30 in 1999 and ended at 00:30 in 2000, after a champagne stop by firelight at the stroke of midnight. Of all these I think my favourite Hash event was the 1999 Africa Hash in Victoria Falls, Zimbabwe. This trip started a tradition of 'Bwana Safaris' in which RMBH3 Hashers join me for Hash Safari in Africa which still continues.

What about your worst Hashing moment or r*n?
B: One cold rainy winter night in Milan I was the hare and by half an hour after the start time there was still no one about. This was fairly usual for Milan, and Fabulous had called me to say he would be late, so I knew that at least there would be one hound. So I left a big check marker, put on my knee-length plastic mac and ran off with the flour. The rain got worse and I was soon covered in dough, and the lightweight plastic mac was stuck to me. After about 40 minutes I started looking for a beer stop. We usually used any small bar that was open, but in the seedy areas there weren't many around. After a long time, I found one, and made huge flour marks on the pavement to indicate a beer stop, and went inside to wait for the hounds.

Now you must picture how I looked. Not a small person, covered in dough, with shorts and t-shirt covered by a small plastic mac, giving the impression of a dirty wet mini-skirt. So I ordered my beer and stood at the counter. But after a while I realised I was the centre of attention, and the awful truth dawned. This was a gay bar! The only 'women' around were transvestite prostitutes, and the whole bar was waiting to hear what exactly I wanted in my wet plastic mini-skirt, and whether I was buying or selling it! I tried some half-hearted explanations – but no one believed me. I said a lot of friends were following – but they just giggled. I sat like this for what seemed like ages. I had marked the beer stop so I couldn't leave, but I had no idea if anyone was following, or even if they'd find the place. The longer I sat, the louder the giggles and mutters got. Finally, to my great relief I heard a Hash horn, and in came Tone Deaf. But now the giggles turned to outright laughter – he had taken to r*nning in a kilt, made by his girlfriend, which was much too short but he insisted on wearing it. Still, the worst was over. Then Fabulous turned up. That was the whole pack – two! – and the whole scene started to seem hilariously funny.

How have Hashing/Hashers changed over the years?
B: Hashers are getting older. As long as they don't grow up mentally that doesn't matter, but one or two established Hashes are getting a little staid.

What's the main thing you've got from Hashing over the years?
B: Fantastic fun, an instant set of friends whenever I move location, a great way to get to know a place and meet people when I travel, a worldwide set of loyal friends, two long term girlfriends and one wife. Not bad!

How could/should Hash evolve from here?
B: We should be mindful to keep young people joining. A determined effort to avoid becoming 'cliquey' is needed among older members. Hashing should be uninhibited fun but Hashers should realise that the object is not just to be as coarse and vulgar as possible. This tends to put off some people and is not the Hash tradition. I think the increasing trend for bigger and bigger InterHashes (including all the continental, sub-continental, Nash Hashes, etc) has gone far enough. The best away Hashes have no more than 200 people, often far less. Huge events are daunting to organise and expensive to get to. They will turn Hashing into a business and a rich man's sport. I wouldn't do away with the

InterHash or the better Nash Hashes, but no more mega-events should clutter the calendar to stop us getting on with real Hashing.

Shaun 'Tinkerbell' Burgess.
First r*n Blantyre H3, Malawi 1991
Member Harare H3, Kalahari H3

You're coming up for 500 r*ns. How was your first time?
TB: It reminded me of my first year at university. My second r*n was the worst, though – I leapt off a bank onto a concrete block … my feet missed, my face didn't. Still, I made it back for drinks after the stitches.

Did you have any good times to make up for that?
TB: Yes. Cape Town during the Inter-Africa '99 prelude. Arriving on the cliffs above Gordon's Bay with the whole of False Bay stretched out beneath us on an absolutely clear day.

So, on balance, what have you got from your Hashing?
TB: A beer gut.

Which goes so well with the name Tinkerbell…
TB: I got named Tinkerbell because I'm petite and beautiful. Nearer the truth is more arcane – I used to r*n with keys in my pocket, the jingling earned me the name. I did however have a second christening as Master of the Universe. This was because I was personally blamed for the collapse of Malawi's currency.

Any similarities or differences on kennels you've been on?
TB: I think every Hash has its own personality. The smaller and more remote the Hash, the more friendly it seems. The InterHashes have become more professional. I'm not too sure that this is a good thing. Mind you, Goa will probably disprove all of this!

As Master of the Universe, any changes you would make?
TB: Maybe we should develop a lobby to repeal the drink-driving laws.

Does InterHash belong in Asia or worldwide?
TB: Worldwide, but every second one at least should be in Asia.

Malcolm 'Mad Cow' Britton.
First r*n Bahrain H3 1986

You've done more than 750 r*ns, nearly all with Bahrain. Don't you ever get tired of it?
MC: Since being a Hasher I have not lived elsewhere and so have not been a member of any other Hashes. I have been in Bahrain for 37 years, man and boy. I hardly miss a week.

How and why'd you get into this?
MC: I first heard of Hashing through my next-door neighbour. My children were in school in the UK and used to go with him to the Hash when they came out on holiday. What did I *think* about Hashing? I thought that it was revolting. What does one think when one's 12-year-old daughter comes home saying

'Guess who was Wanker of the Week, daddy?' The children however seemed to enjoy r*nning around in temperatures of 40-degrees Celsius and 90 per cent humilities (sic), getting covered in shiggy and sweat. I thought that it was bloody stupid.

After about four years my next-door neighbour was to leave Bahrain and, to enable me to take my children the next time that they came out on holiday, I went with him on the Hash to get orientated. I went twice and never looked back. I thought that it was brilliant. My children, now grown up, live in Scotland and r*n with the TNT Hash in Edinburgh. Hashing is the main focus of their social life.

Apart from the involuntary twitches, why are you called Mad Cow?

MC: Apparently I was making a fool of myself and was groping a bit too deeply at a party and was accused of behaving like a mad cow. My wife's name is Silly Old Moo. She has this name because of the number of silly things that she does. For instance, before we met she moved into the flat above me and soon after went out with the taps r*nning in her bathroom. The water eventually flooded into my flat and brought down my bedroom ceiling. We met and got married. One of our friends said to her once 'Do you know Moreen, if you ever got Alzheimer's, we would never notice. Silly Old Moo is approaching 70. There cannot be not too many 70-year-old ladies prancing around the countryside laying flour and shouting 'On On'. She considers that when she dies she should be cremated, the ashes mixed with flour and a Hash trail laid in her favourite area.

What was your most enjoyable time on the Hash?

MC: In 1999 when, after the India Nash Hash in Hyderabad, we did a Hash train trip, called the Great Dravidian Rail Jerk, for about eight days. The idea was that about 40 of us would travel at night and sleep on the train and during the day sightsee and Hash. Well, the daytime sightseeing and Hashing worked, but there was no sleep to be had on the train – too much drinking and shenanigans.

How do other Hashing venues stack up against Bahrain?

MC: We have travelled to all the world InterHashes since Rotorua in 1994 and have been to InterGulf Hashes, Pan-African and India Nash Hashes. We have very limited terrain in Bahrain and I am quite envious of the possibilities available at the places that we visit. However I do not like the idea of Hashing in cold climes. I prefer to have the gather-round alfresco and have a barbecue after. For me Hashing in a warm climate seems to be more natural. However, those people I have Hashed with in Scotland thoroughly enjoy it.

You're in a fairly unique position to judge how Hashing has changed around you, being in one locale.

MC: Hashing has certainly changed quite a bit in Bahrain. Fifteen years ago we had a membership of about 400, with packs of 300 each week. The pleasure of Hashing has not diminished though. Also Bahrain is a small island and, with the development taking place, the area that we have available to lay trails is continually shrinking. The age group is also on the rise. We seem not to be attracting younger people to the Hash, and the type of expatriate coming to Bahrain is changing. With 'Bahrainisation' of jobs here, most expats now come here on short-term contracts and save money and do not want to get involved with the place.

How could or should Hashing evolve?

MC: Hashing should evolve naturally, and any particular group should not impose change.

Reid 'Rambo' Whitlock.

First r*n Colombo H3, Sri Lanka 1983
Co-founder Bamako H3, Charlottesville H3
Member Dar es Salaam H3, Abidjan H3, Dakar H3, Seven Hills H3, Richmond H3, Larrikins H3, Global Trash H3, Mt Vernon H3, Internet H3, Iguana H3, Naked City H4, Founders H3, Hanoi H3, Ikeja H3, Ouagadougou H3

You can't blame yourself, so who's fault is it for getting you 'on'?

R: I was introduced to Hashing by Peter Ridley, a British resident golf pro and buddy I had met through weekly soccer friendlies in Sri Lanka. First impressions: Great terrain. Seemed to be good entertainment for the locals through whose rice paddies we Hashed. Well suited to my temperament.

And there's been a lot of beer through the kidneys since then?

R: I have no real idea how many Hashes I've participated in. In 1998 my home Hash gave me an award called the 'Triple Hundred' which recognised my having hared 100 times, visited 100 different US Hashes and visited 100 different non-US Hashes. This might give some idea of the number of Hashes in which I have participated.

How, why and where did you get your heroic handle?

R: Awarded in Abidjan. I had just finished hare-ing in the animal park outside the city. It was particularly shiggic (sic), close encounters with carnivores, inextricable mud, slippery logs on which to cross slime pits, that sort of thing. The name seemed to fit, in the Half Minds of those present ...

What was the most fun time for you?

R: Iguana H3 r*n in Taos, New Mexico, was good for the combination of the site (all to ourselves with a proprietor who became 'one of us'), the spectacular scenery of the actual Hash, the weekend of virtual total nudity for all participating (including naked *pinata* bashing!), and the sex with the locals. Also Calgary H3. They treat their visitors like royalty – even if their trails are sometimes boring pavement pounders. Pittsburgh Anniversary ball-buster in June 1995. A most-excellent, true epic. The Inyaka Hash Weekend with the Maputo H3 in spring 1996.

Any dud moments?

R: Showing up in Puerto Gallera, Philippines, *one week* too early for their huge anniversary Hash weekend, and having to content myself with the regular trail of the week before the big event (which did have some great mud, by the way ...)

How would you compare Hashing in the different places you've Hashed?

R: There are just too many sights, smells and sounds to give more than the tip of the iceberg! In England, *forcing* people to drink alcohol who are non alcohol-drinkers. Bad form. In the US, some of the best and worst – from post-apocalyptic wasteland (good) to sidewalk shiggy (bad) and from sexuality and nudity-relaxed (good) to 'family' Hashes (bad) – who *invented* that concept anyway? Tricycles, nursery rhyme Down Downs, home by five, yada yada yada … Warsaw: finishing with an outdoor barbecue of Polish sausage, whatever the weather! Cairo: extends the Saturday Hash into Sunday with a Hasher-only booze and lunch cruise on the Nile …

How have Hashing or Hashers changed over the years?

R: The stealing of Hash banners, flags and totems seems to have (happily) died down. People seem to respect the personal property of others more. People seem to respect the property through which they Hash more (though trespassing remains *de rigeur* …). There are more verses to Yogi Bear and Balls to Your Partner.

What's the main thing you've got from Hashing over the years?

R: Permanent scars on my shins.

How could/should Hash evolve from here?

R: I hope the people who pioneer colonies on Mars have some Hashers in their group ready to scout out and lay trail! I would also like to see more 'one-time event' Hashes that permit people to explore some of the ever-dwindling truly dramatic locales still remaining on the planet. People would simply convene on some patch of Brazilian rain forest, for instance, for a weekend, then return home.

While we didn't want to waste too much paper and ink, dishonourable mentions in Africa and the Middle East must be made of the following characters:

Oh Yeah from Rabat H3, Morocco, drives a bright yellow MG proudly sporting his Hash name on the number plate. His long dreadlocks make him look a lot more like a Rasta man than a Moroccan and he has been known to quit the circle to go and pray and shortly return to continue Down Downs.

Tom Holbrook, who had been a Hasher in Laos, started the Nouakchatt kennel in Mauritania. He and his wife, Cathy, ran on the Hash one hour after their official marriage in 1986.

Admiral Hal Bernsen, commander of the American Fleet – deployed in the Gulf around 1987 – was a regular with other naval commanders on the Bahrain Hash, and turned up for their 800th r*n celebration where he copped a nomination as 'Wanker of the Year' for his troubles.

Been Called Worse.

If ever you needed proof that a collective sense of humour was lacking with these maladroit under-achievers, this list of Hash handles proves it conclusively:

68 and a Bit, Q8H3: "Lost the tip of his tongue."

Akin' Dick: His significant other is **Akin' 4 Dick**.

Arse-onist, Durban H3: "She's a pyro-technician, and during the Millennium celebration a warehouse caught light and she got blamed for it."

Ben Hur, Durban H3: "This American couple used to r*n with us with their little kid, about four years old. Because the terrain includes rivers, barbed wire fences, etc, a little chariot was made for him, and he was pulled everywhere, so dad became Ben Hur and mum became **Ben Him**."

Birdbrain, South Africa: A gent that breeds pigeons.

Brokenstick, Zululand H3: Real surname Birkenstock.

Bullet Proof, Durban H3: "While employed as a security guard he shot himself and survived."

Buzzer, Durban H3: "Behaves like a bee round a honey pot."

Byclops, South Africa: "I was r*nning with my sunglasses on, when one of the lenses popped out. People immediately thought **Cyclops** but then thought, 'No he's got four eyes minus one lens, that makes him **Tryclops**. After protracted debate, they compromised."

Camel, Durban H3: "Our family are keen caravan vacationers, towing our caravan around for decades. One time coming back we were late for the r*n, so went straight to the site, caravan and all..." His wife, who attends but doesn't r*n, is **Carguard**.

Cesspit, Riyadh H3: His significant other is **Suckcess**.

Cock of the North, ex-Sri Lanka, Bahrain H3: "I was wearing a Sid The Sexist t-shirt for the r*n with the caption on the front saying 'If the lady wants a baby I'm the Cock o' the North. Being born in northern England it stuck ..."

Cumsfersure, ex-Creek H3: Wife of **Cock Sure**.

Deceased, ex-Brunei, Nairobi H3: "My name is Haywood, which they mixed up with Rita *Hayworth* who had just died. So I became **Rita Deceased** and over time the Rita just dropped off."

Dinosaur Don, ex-Bahrain, Harare H3: "My name is Don, and when in Bahrain we used to do a lot of camp-outs in the desert where the rocks – that formed a backdrop to the site where we set up the disco which I did – were shaped like a dinosaur..."

Diplomatic Bag, Bahrain H3: A Harriette who works at the British Embassy in Bahrain.

Excess Baggage, Q8H3: "Her husband went to the airport for his 'excess baggage' and came back with his wife."

Eyefull, Durban H3: The official photographer for his kennel.

Floppy Dick and **Floppy Flaps**, ex-Qatar: "They had a moment of ecstasy and produced a daughter. Floppy Flaps was still Hashing while pregnant in Kuwait, where the norm was to name a Hasher after 10 r*ns. It was deemed that as the bump was quite pronounced, it must have done 10 r*ns and was duly named **Floppy Foetus**!"

Fuck You Tu-Tu, Creek H3: His surname was Bishop.

Fruit Machine: "I heard this scream from the bathroom. She had been cutting her toenails, foot perched on the edge of the toilet when she slipped and jammed her foot in the S-bend. She stood there, starkers, arms waving around like a windmill – and fractured her wrist on the bathroom shelf. She pitched up for the next couple of Hash r*ns with her arm in a sling, like a one-armed bandit = Fruit Machine. Geddit?"

Helicopter Coming, Bahrain Black H3: "It was my naming r*n and I was in the circle, after dark, deep in the desert. The Hash circles were frequently buzzed by Bahrain Defence Force helicopters eager to check out any unauthorised gatherings. Then came the familiar whir of approaching helicopter blades. 'Helicopter coming!' went up the Pavlovian cry. 'That'll do' said the RA."

Hindenberg, Q8H3: "More hot air than a Zeppelin."

Honey Pot, Durban H3: "Wherever she goes, there's a man."

Hops 'n' Malt, Zululand H3: Real surname De Beer.

Huggy Bear, Durban H3: "I had been at the rugby one day and was totally pissed. When I get pissed I get all emotional and was going round giving everyone nice big hugs." [He didn't mention he's also about 130kg –ed.]

Ice Box, Lusaka H3: "Friday night is panty-free night for Harriettes. One night I was going on the town after the r*n so changed into a mini-skirt. We were then made to sit on the freezing floor of the circle hall, and everything was unfortunately on show…"

Incognito, Benghazi H3: "Driving home after the Hash he arrived at a police check point with the correct papers for the car (not his own) but without *any* form of ID for himself. No licence, no passport, no alien documents, not even his office tag. Fortunately, we managed to get him out of what could have been a naughty situation, like a night in the cells. It didn't even cost the normal packet of cigarettes which was just as well, none of us smokes."

Incuming, Baghdad H3: "Named shortly before the war."

Jabber the Slut, Q8H3: "Used be called **Zit** but we renamed him this after a TV incident in which he was beaten up by the WWF wrestler, Vader. Has a double meaning in Kuwait as Jabber is the name of the Royal Family!"

Kucking Fiwi, Muscat H3: A New Zealander.

Leaking Johnny, Bahrain H3: "A Harriette who blamed a leaking condom for her pregnancy."

Mamma Hen, Nairobi H3: Saw a bunch of young Harriettes heading for certain trouble with too much drink, the threat of impending disrobement, etc. She advised them to drink some water and have a lie down [Spoil sport! –ed.]. Her husband, approximately half her weight and a bit shorter, is **Papa Hen**.

Miss Maggot, ex-Ethiopia, UK: "I went to a dinner party in Malawi and someone served up de-legged cockroaches. A few weeks later I had a really itchy back and blotches so went to the doctor. He said the only thing that causes that is syphilis, but we had to wait three weeks for the test results. When they came back, it turned out to be maggots – and they removed 60 from my back and my bum."

Miss Whiplash, Bahrain H3: "A Harriette who abuses her male committee colleagues at every opportunity."

Moses: "Looks for all the world like the biblical character Moses with his shaped white beard and hooked nose. His partner naturally is **The Red Sea**."

Mudguard, Durban H3: "Shiny on top, full of shit underneath!"

No Bells Prize: "Something about her boss only drinks Bells Whisky and she forgot to order it for his farewell party."

No Relation, Muscat H3: His *real* name is Mick Jagger!

Nurse Prick in the Arse, Bahrain H3: "A Harriette who gets her enjoyment sticking her pricks (needles) in Hashers' arses." Married to **Dragon Arse**: "Smells and flames continually emanate from this Hasher's arse. The offspring of both Nurse Prick in the Arse and Dragon Arse was thought to be too young to be named an arse and so was named **Baby Bum**."

Pink and Shaven, Q8H3: Her other half is **Pink and Furry**.

Pissoles, ex-Blantyre H3: "It had something to do with piss holes in the snow but is also a play on my surname, Petzold."

Pizza Piss, Q8H3: "Tried to get Pizza Hut to deliver to a vague bit of desert … and finally succeeded at the third attempt."

Quality Blowjob, Barbie H3, UAE: "After a liaison following a night out at the Alamo, a local nightspot and a favourite for Harriettes. The victim that night was known to have reported that it was indeed a quality blowjob." [Note to self: visit Barbie H3 –ed.]

Ring Sting, Durban H3: "I cook a mean chilli…"

Samson, Durban H3: "A strong man with long hair. His wife is **Delightful**."

Schindler, Q8H3: "Always walks around work with a list."

Shark Shift, Durban H3: "I work on security part-time at King's Park, the home ground of the Natal Sharks rugby team."

Sir Clugs, ex-Seoul, Milton Keynes, Lagos H3. "I was named **Cunt Lugs** after a very drunken night in Itaewon, Seoul, of which I remember nothing. I suspect they were just winding me up. When I went back to Milton Keynes it was deemed unacceptable, so it became **Clugs**. Then I was called down to Buck Palace by the Queen, so they splashed beer on both my shoulders and said 'Arise, Sir Clugs'."

Snap and **Ditto**, Durban H3: Identical twins.

Something Meaty, Durban H3: "A pizza lover who got her name from a pizza menu."

Swallow My Leader, Jordan: "She was an ex-White House intern stationed with the embassy in Jordan."

The Bearded Clam, Cairo H3: "**Bearded Wonder** was originally given to this Brit and it just sorted of migrated unofficially to the more Hash-like name."

Thumbprint, Durban H3: "His wife was not a Hasher and used to sit in the car until the r*n finished and he was allowed 10 minutes or one beer (whichever came first) before she would ferry him off. So he was very much under the thumb…"

Thunder and **Clap**, ex-Assen, Nigeria: This couple's surname is Newman, as in the musician Thunderclap Newman.

Tubular Balls, Bop H3: His surname is Oldfield, as in Mike Oldfield the musician who created the Tubular Bells album

Ugwagwa, ex-Kigali H3, Rabat H3: "We had just started to get some Rwandan participants at that time, so one of them spoke up and said that '*Ugwagwa*' was the Kinyarwandan word for 'banana beer'.

And, now, a bunch of Hash handles that we really wanted to find out more about, but on balance decided a trip down the pub was preferable:

1986 Desert Super-Masturbating Piledriver, African Bart Fart, Ahpisto, Ass on Line, Bang on Bob, Blow Beans, Blue Ass Fly, Bowel Trowel, Cap'n Birdseye, Captain Sober, Cardinal Sin, Corny Thunt, Dingo Bum Sniffer, Dog Walker, Donkey Dick, Dr Livingstick, Ewe Trollop, Feelya McCrapsky, Flying Flacid Flanger, Gattling Gob, Grape Ape, Gussett Gobbler, Hard Astern, Heavenly Body, Hee Mah, I Beg Your Pardon, Ice Quim Licker, Jolly Green Grunt, Knob Jockey, Luton Airport, Micro-Orgasm, Mind the Wet Patch, Off the Leash, Open 24 Hours, Orrsunkunt, Pox Doctor's Clerk, Putt Putt, Rough Knight, Singing Dwarf, Space Monkey, Supremous Blobus, Turd Hurder, and Watersports.

Anecdotes From Around Africa and the Middle East.

In Yemen, Walrus was on trail and found himself being chased by a couple of "crazy women" – one throwing a rock at the back of his head, and another with an AK-47 with the safety off. The husband was away and apparently the women were in charge of the *qat* farm. "*Qat* is a tree that produces a leaf which gives you a high five times stronger than coffee," says Walrus. "It is banned in every Moslem country except Yemen, so it can't be too good for you."

At the Africa InterHash in Zimbabwe, a killer r*n took the pack for about 7km through hot African bush. Firstly, as they left the hotel they ran into three elephants. A yelling, screaming, abusive pack, with camera flashes blazing, did not deter them and they moved off in their own sweet time. Then through the bush, dodging more elephant shit as they went, until finally they came to the beer at Victoria Falls Boating Club, on the Zambesi. The inviting waters were off limits for a refreshing dip, though, with signs everywhere warning about crocodiles. The ball-buster trail had to be re-routed because there was a wounded Cape Buffalo in the region which could not be found.

Then there was also a sunset booze cruise down the Zambesi River one night. The area is notorious for its large man-eating crocodiles and hippos. In fact someone had been taken by a croc just one month earlier at exactly the same place. Out in the middle of the river – several sacred nectars later – one notorious South African decided it was time for a swim. He dived in and started swimming round the boat. The organisers and crew were hysterical. The pack wasn't sure what to make of it … hero or bloody idiot?

Thus encouraged, he decided to do another lap around the boat, before hauling himself unscathed up and over the boat's pontoons to safety.

In Nigeria, a petrol tanker had rolled over, spilling its flammable load and blocking the road. A car-load of Hashers, driving to a Hash r*n, decided to go slowly around it, while another chose to go down an adjacent exit road. As they were passing, an almighty explosion erupted, resulting in three dead Hashers and a further two who were permanently med-evacced and not likely to be Hashing in Nigeria (or anywhere else) again.

As part of the pre-amble to Africa InterHash in Durban, there was to be a r*n in Port Elizabeth. Two guys were appointed to lay it and, through some miscommunication, didn't. Ordinarily it would be a straightforward crucifixion but … one of the guys owned the brewery and had sponsored 6,000 litres of their favourite beer, which this guy had concocted and brewed himself. "Understand, this man is a God to us!" said one of the locals. A stand-in hare laid the r*n, getting in 10 minutes before the FRBs. The defaulters were given a two-pint Down Down, then they kept the *other* guy (ie, not the brewery God) up for a half-pint Down Down with every other fine in the circle. There were at least 10. By the end of the evening he was completely legless and unable to drive his big beer truck home, so they made him sleep it off in the back of his truck until the next day.

On the Maseru H3 in Lesotho, this Hasher was 73 years old and extremely fit … in fact, still an FRB with the aid of a heart pacemaker. He found that his pacemaker needed a bit of tweaking upward in order to keep pace with his demands. Unfortunately he was killed in a car accident.

On a r*n in Mbabane, Swaziland, the hares laid the trail along a mountain and down into a steep valley. They had studied maps and aerial photographs before laying it, but fucked up royally … they hadn't counted on the terrain being so steep so they had to build in a zig-zag up and down the valley. The FRBs came in about seven hours later. The walkers were shepherded to a shortcut and spirited out of there. Fortunately there was only one injury – a sprained ankle near the end, resulting in one person being carried the last kilometre. The sympathetic hares comment? "Fuck them. If we had to do it, the pack has do it!"

In Sudan – which is now 'dry' – we used to have a Monday night r*n with beer supplied by the British Embassy. It was Tuborg Lager, but very old and in rusty cans, probably past its use-by date. But, hey, it was beer. On Tuesday mornings we'd have to do a ring around the prisons and hospitals to see who didn't make it as a result.

At Richards Bay, South Africa, for an Africa InterHash post ramble, we all stayed at Mvubu (Hippo) Lodge on this tidal estuary. Big signs all over warned about crocodiles and not to swim. The management and GM cautioned everyone this was for real, so take heed. The next morning we indeed saw a couple of specimens swimming quite near the bank, much to everyone's touristy delight. Post-r*n, Garfield was called for a Down Down because all the red ink had r*n from his new Perth 2004 bid shirt during the rainy r*n. In disgust, he threw his much-prized shirt off into the lake where it floated forlornly for a few hours. Many beers later, Slabeye decided he wanted that shirt. Stripping down to his shorts, he got onto the balcony railing and dived in. Tone Deaf heroically stood by with the remaining ice from the circle, ready to ward off any attacking crocodile. Instantly sobered by the cool water Slabeye reached the shirt but realised he couldn't just climb back where he dived from … he needed to go round the side of the club building, through the reeds and out the side of the river bank. You've never seen a big guy – or *any* guy for that matter! – swim so fast.

In Lagos, Scouse Git had been 'on the wagon' for 10 weeks when he had his turn to lay a r*n. "Right, I'm gonna play catch up," he said, "and have a r*n with 10 beer stops in it. I'm the hare – I can do that." All r*nners basically walk-jogged from beer stop to beer stop, getting ticked off at each one. The prize at the end for those who had a fully-checked card was … a beer! "It was the most hellish circle we've had for a while," says Beerhound.

In Nigeria we were all r*nning like mad in a Hash pack when, walking the other way, was this Nigerian bloke – big, black, and strong – and stark-bollock naked [Any pictures for the Harriettes? –ed.]. On seeing us, he covered his *face* with a newspaper he was carrying, leaving all the other bits on display. A different form of modesty.

After a particularly bad Hash they retired to Everything But Big Tits' flat for food, where they were treated to some succulent *haram* meat. After a while the host (an American diplomat of some sort) announced that he had a cool box full of beers. He lifted the lid to expose a tempting choice of Becks or Holsten. Slapper was due to have his medical the next day for a visit visa to Saudi. "Sod it," he said as he started to down a Holsten, "if it shows up, so what, who wants to go to Saudi anyway." It was only pointed out to him later that the beer was actually the alcohol-free version, so all his worry was in vain.

In Alexandria, an English hare was laying a trail once when a mangy dog pounced on him. With rabies being a common affliction, he was subjected to a battery of anti-rabies injections. He soon left for Cairo. Dog seeking treatment and counselling.

On an away weekend in Bahrain [Mmmmm, *real* beer! –ed.] the Q8 Hash took part in the Bahrain Marathon Relay race (a 60km road race in high-40 degree Celsius temperatures). Public drinking is not allowed in Bahrain, but this never stops the intrepid Q8 Half Minds, who have a couple of slabs on the bus to follow the team, along with bottles of Baileys, port and tequila! One particular year – despite their anchor man twisting his ankle after just three feet and Tug falling asleep in the shade of the handover point – they managed to finish in the top half of the field. Naturally, an official complaint was lodged immediately with the organisers – they finished too high and wouldn't accept the judge's decision!

Q8H3 has only two Kuwaitis r*nning with them – one is a policeman (always handy to have around) and the other a local TV personality. The latter was once involved in interviewing WWF wrestler, Vader. During his questioning on live TV, our intrepid Hasher asked 'It's all rigged isn't it?' to which Vader replied 'You think *this* is rigged?' He grabbed our Hashman by the neck and started to throttle him. Eventually the two were separated, and our Hasher then proceeded to sue the wrestler.

At Africa InterHash in Zimbabwe, the r*nners were warned repeatedly by the hares during the trail talk that this was prime elephant country and, if encountered, just stop and move off the path into the bush and let them pass by … do not make noise, do not bother them. "We had a very large contingent, about 50, from a country in Asia widely known for its many Hashes," says Kojak. "The r*nners were off and sure enough about 15 minutes into the r*n a large herd of elephants was coming in the opposite direction. Most r*nners did exactly as briefed, moved off into the bush, behind trees and lay low. Not our 50 Asians. The words 'Take pitture, take pitture' were heard over and over as groups posed in front of the beasts, people in and out to pose or shoot photos, while the elephants, trunks raised and trumpeting, ears flapping, feet stomping were about to have Asian lunch. Somehow our Asian visitors managed to escape any injury and, to this day, think those African elephants are nice friendly beasts and they have the photos to prove it. The hares, however, are still recovering and having nightmares about what they thought was going to be one hell of a disaster."

One of the hounds, Jollygreenknob, ran unsuspectingly right up onto a few elephants. "One of them was within three feet of me," he says. "She flapped her ears and stomped her foot and then did a fake charge. My friend next to me panicked and went right into the bushes to get away from the elephant, which was dumb because the terrain was mined. The elephant finally backed off and all was forgiven."

 Abu Dhabi Island H3 claim to have the biggest knitting circle in the Gulf – *there's* a claim to fame!

 Bamako Area Sahelian H3 in Mali use a compressed-air boating horn for their Hash Horn.

 Cairo H3 in Egypt hold an annual raft race on the River Nile.

 In Kuwait, the Xmas Hash in 1985 featured a huge campfire, seasonal carols at each checkpoint and mulled wine for Down Downs at the end.

 Ikeja in Nigeria has a poof's hat and a handbag which Hashit offenders have to wear on the r*n.

 In Tanzania, Hamna H3's Hashit is an awful statue/monstrosity carved from black ebony. Winners get to carve their names in it before returning it.

 Harare H3 Zimbabwe's, Hashit is literally that … a large piece of elephant shit. "I found it in the jungle around Lake Kariba," says Garfield. "I took the thing home and gave it 15 or 16 layers of varnish to laminate it." It's slightly smaller than a soccer ball and hangs on a rope around the weekly winner's neck.

 Kalahari H3's Hashit is a bright pink shirt.

Niamey H3 in Niger set r*ns with live hares. If they are caught, they have to r*n naked. A big incentive to lay a good trail. They also hold r*ns where hares are decided on the spot by the drawing of straws, and then have to immediately set an impromptu trail.

 Riyadh Third Herd H3 usually wear full Arabic robes and 'dish dash' to InterHash events and are often seen carrying inflatable plastic camels on the r*n as well.

Cairo H3 claim the world's first complete underwater Hash in the Red Sea, in Shark's Bay in Sharm el Sheikh in 1991.

Rabat H3, Morocco, punish 'religious transgressions' by forcing the Hash sinner to wear the sinner's *jelaba* – an incredibly nasty, ugly, unhygienic and uncomfortable accoutrement – during the entire Hash. Sinners are invited to sign and date the *jelaba* after wearing it.

Africa InterHash at Victoria Falls, Zimbabwe, drew 470 Hashers from 18 different countries. This huge logistical effort required beer to be specially trucked in from the brewery in Harare, 800km away. This nearly ended in a mutiny before it had begun on the Friday when thirsty Hashers (and sweating disorganisers) still had seen no sign of the hallowed beer truck. Fortunately it turned up just in time, to cheering Hashers and relieved organisers.

"We went to the Richards Bay, South Africa, #1 Hash that Bwana had arranged," says No Mercy Master. "I already knew about the drink Amarula and immediately went on a shopping trip to the local shops and bought every bottle of Amarula the local shop had – some 20 large 1.5 litre bottles. Bwana said we were mad and would never drink that much." Four days later No Mercy Master had proved him wrong, consuming the last of the highly-potent liqueur, made from berries known to sedate elephants in the wild. With reinforcements, the next three weeks followed the same pattern. Soon, Cheeky (now his wife) was pregnant. "We put this down to the fact we were drunk most of the time, with Amarula being the offending drink," says No Mercy Master. "Several months later we attended the Africa InterHash in Durban and went and did a Richards Bay Hash again. This time my wife was very pregnant and the story got out about how she had got pregnant. So they christened my unborn child with the Hash name of Amarula! He even has a small Hash T-shirt with his name on it!"

Hashers get started all sorts of interesting ways. Driving a bus from Capetown to Port Elizabeth, the lady bus driver was not sure what had hit her when her cargo of Hashers boarded. Nervous glances in her rear-vision mirror and quizzical glances at this motley crew of drinking and singing Hashers and Harriettes only heightened her curiosity until she just had to ask who they were and what the hell they were doing. After a quick explanation, she was into it, boots and all, joining in some of the singing. They even invited her to join in the circles after some of the r*ns on the route, and christened her Sugar Bush. "I can't wait to get back to Cape Town and start Hashing," she said. So who's going to drive next time?

After Cyprus InterHash '96, a group of Hashers from Hardy's H3 in the UK took a side-trip via cruise ship to Egypt. One night on board, they had a bit of fun and games, including an unsuccessful human pyramid. As a grand finale, they stripped off for a nude Hash round the deck of the ship, much to the delight of other passengers and crew. Not.

On trail in Yemen a 65-year-old Harriette just walked off a 20-metre cliff in front of the pack. "Yes, literally walked off the cliff and rolled five times, hitting her head [Luckily, not a important organ for Hashers –ed.] on the way down," says Walrus. "We had a doctor on the r*n and he dived to try and catch her but, alas, missed and managed to break *his* ankle. She landed flat on her back and we all thought the worst [What, that she hadn't paid her subs? –ed.]. But on rushing down to her, she casually sat up – blood gushing from her head – and said, 'Sorry, hope I didn't cause any worries'. She survived to r*n many more Hashes."

In Port Harcourt, Nigeria, Haggissimo decided to stage a Nigerian Nash Hash. The word went out on the old jungle drums. "We were expecting about 40, maybe 50 Hashers to turn up," he says. "Well 50 Hashers did turn up, *plus* about 150 nationals who'd hiked it to Port Harcourt from Lagos, Jos, Abuja and further afield on the promise that there'd be free food, drink and accommodation to be had for the week-end … talk about a fuck-up."

"While posted in Helsinki, I started making Blimey's fruit punch," says the man himself. "It's easy to make – three litres of orange juice, three cans of fruit cocktail and three litres of any kind of alcohol (vodka, gin, rum, etc). Living in Lagos, I decided to make a punch using *fresh* fruit only, for after a Christmas r*n at the Australian High Commission. One thing I had never realised before was the fact that fresh fruit, in combination with alcohol, starts fermenting in your stomach. The next day I received a call from the hare to thank me for helping redecorate the bathroom of his house as pieces of fruit were stuck all over the walls. Apparently not even on the ceiling was exempt from these decorative projectile patterns!

Le Mistral, an ex-GM of Maputo H3 committed suicide recently. "He was an ex-Foreign Legionnaire who had been here throughout the civil war," says Bwana. "He had no known family, was in perfect health mentally and physically, but had reached 60 and decided that it was time to go. He had made meticulous arrangements – disposed of his things to the poor, gave his servant the day off, and sent a note to the French Vice Consul (another Hasher) and the current MH3 GM to come to his house at a certain time, where they found him. In the absence of relatives, the VC had Le Mistral cremated and was left with the ashes.

"As all his friends were Hashers it was decided that a Hash send-off was the only thing to do. After the 850th r*n, a Hare of the Dog r*n was held at a spot Le Mistral had found, a lovely waterfall in the hills. The trail led up to the top of the falls where an "Ash 'old" was called, and a rousing chorus of a Frenchman Went to the Lavatory was sung (with the French Vice Consul singing along, standing to attention). A short, highly-irreverent, poem was read by Chuck Speers commemorating some of Le Mistral's more dubious feats, and the ashes were tipped over the falls along with a can of beer as the final Down Down. Then we did the 21-gun salute. Twenty-one of us stood in line on the edge of the waterfall, and, as the GM called out numbers, each one mooned (or flashed tits, according to sex) in the direction of the disappearing ashes. At the call of '21', the whole row did one final flash, and then we continued with the r*n.

"The circle was pretty normal, but the RA declared Le Mistral the Hashit, and a representative Frenchman was named to drink in his place. No one mentioned the Ash Down Down at all. This was perhaps the strangest thing – it was all done with the greatest respect, and there seemed to be no reason to comment afterwards. Just another day's Hashing in Africa!"

The Steppes in Benghazi is common land used for grazing animals, usually sheep, brought to the city for market. Now and again there are camels about. Amnesia and Timberdick had laid a trail on a Friday morning for their Hash the following day. They had noted a couple of flocks of sheep and – quite far off – a large herd of camels. It is worth noting that when they lay trails they don't use paper, flour or rice, ie, something environmentally acceptable, they use emulsion paint because it is more permanent so they can lay a trail in advance of the actual Hash Day.

"During the pre-r*n briefing we mentioned the camels and said if you see them 'don't r*n at them – walk!'," says Timberdick. The pack was shuffling along together when, on breasting a rise, they found the camels. The camels saw them too. "Most of the Hash slowed to a walk, but not our two 'Calgary cowboys', Wild Bill and Two Bit Mick, who continued at full gallop. The camels began to move away despite the protestations of their minder mounted on a tiny donkey [Hope it was a good-looking donkey –ed.]. Suddenly the camels took off towards Egypt about 600km away with the donkey-rider in pursuit! As the dust cleared we saw the owner of the camels emerge from his Bedouin tent. He shouted suitable abuse at us and then started to fire his rifle, in the air, towards us. We decided to seek the refuge of the cars and beat it quick while he was preoccupied in recovering his 100 stampeding camels."

Benghazi H3 hasn't used that venue since.

The Cairo Annual Rehydration R*n features 10 checks out in the desert, each operated by a different nationality serving their favourite tipple. At sign-in every Hasher is given a plastic mug to take with him.

"Traditionally the first check is always the Scottish (I used five litres of Scotch for it on one occasion)," says Sir Clugs. "The second is the English, usually with G & T or Pimms. It goes downhill fast from there. Aussies, Germans, Dutch, Damn Yankees (Long Island iced tea), Southerners (bourbon), etc. The sixth check is usually a Saudi check (unmanned, with cases of bottled water under the only tree in the *wadi*).

"One year 100 per cent of the Zimbabwe Embassy in Cairo (32 men, one woman and a dog) was to do the ninth check, and airfreighted in some Zim beer specially for the purpose. However, a couple of days before the event, Robert Mugabe decided to come to Cairo for his periodic check of brain tumours at Mansouriyah University Hospital, and the Zimbabweans had to drop out [Did they find his brain? –ed.]. I was relating this to Sister Michael and Bondage Queen from Tel Aviv Hash after picking them up at the airport for the event – they took one look at each other and asked if they could do an Israeli check in their place. (They had brought some Israeli beer and some Tequila.) Great, I said. So after the Damn Yankee check, we shot ahead with my old Range-Rover and stuck it as far as we could up a gully out of sight of Egyptian army observation posts.

"When the first Hashers came over the top and spotted the Israeli flags on the aerials – just 20 miles outside Cairo! – they nearly threw a wobbly. Anyway, they spotted the Macabee beer and came on down to sample it. They were also offered shots of Tequila. 'But that's *Mexican*,' they said, at which we linked up our arms and gave them a quick burst of that traditional Israeli song: 'Have a Tequila, Have a Tequila …'"

More on our website: Not a hell of a lot more, it must be said. But go to *www.hash-onon.com* to see early pictures of the Nairobi H3 in action at the Harlequins club, and some other Hashit.

The Beer Necessities.

Why Hashing and Beer Hurts So Good.

"That was for the energy," says Clementine at a drink stop on a UK Nash Hash 2001 ball-breaker run, discarding an empty bottle of isotonic sports drink. "*This* is for the pain," he says opening a can of bitter. Sensing that he might be onto something here, we went in search of some scientific understanding of the effects of mixing r*nning and drinking. The Karolinska Institute in Stockholm found that laboratory rats show the same behaviour on r*nning wheels – a taste for natural highs, such as those experienced by joggers, encourages a taste for artificial ones, such as alcohol. Using a bunch of alcoholic rats (because their control group of Hashers never turned up) the Swedish scientists found that the rats eagerly racked up 10 kilometres per day on their treadmills, but then hit the bottle of ethanol *twice* as hard as the rats who did not exercise. Just thirsty? No, water was available but the rampaging rodents turned their noses up at it.

So is drinking and r*nning any good for you? Well 200,000 Hashers couldn't be wrong. Could they? Over to our resident sports science guru, Hammer from Honolulu H3:

"Beer and Hashing. Two inseparable partners that lean on each other. Let's have a beer. *Mabuhay! Cheers! Salute! On, On!* Before, during, and/or after? What's yours? At the Hash, beer almost always tastes good, and at times even better than others. In fact, if restricted to one word to describe that beer, universally the Hasher is probably apt to say '*good*'. But, *beneficial*, that's another question – a question that has no simple yes *or* no reply.

As any well-travelled Hasher knows, it starts out as piss and ends up as piss. It's the in-between that we'll consider here. First off, what's in the beer? An average 12 oz beer has about 150 calories (light beer about 100). Most of the calories come from the alcohol, of which an average beer has four to five per cent alcohol, or about ½ oz of pure ethanol. But, unfortunately, very few of those calories can be used for energy. We depend primarily on carbohydrates and fat for that. And as for the nutrient value of beer, sorry again, beer is just about bereft of nutrients. Yet it has been jokingly said by some – who would rather not rely on the findings of chemical analysis – that beer has in it all five of the major food groups: carbohydrates, fat, protein, vitamins, and minerals. But that's just not so. Those calories are just *empty calories*.

It would be quite handy if those calories in alcohol could have been used for energy since the alcohol in beer gets absorbed so quickly. About 20 per cent is rather immediately absorbed in the stomach (especially if the stomach is empty), with the rest rapidly absorbed by the small intestine. Once absorbed from the gut into the blood, the alcohol meets several fates, all of which have as their objective reducing the amount of alcohol that you have in your blood.

This is accomplished chiefly by your liver, which in a 154 lb (70 kg) person, can metabolise about 1/3 of an ounce of alcohol per hour, in a process rather judgmentally called detoxification.

Since there's about half an ounce of alcohol in a beer, drinking more than one beer per hour causes alcohol to accumulate in your blood. And, for every beer that you drink in excess of the *one beer per hour*, your blood alcohol content (BAC) increases by 0.025%. So that, for instance, drinking four beers more than the one-beer-per-hour pace would bring your BAC to 0.10, or make you legally too drunk to drive in most developed societies. With the job of eliminating the alcohol from our blood, the liver does get some assistance from our lungs and sweat glands. We breathe away and sweat off from three per cent (while sitting still) to 10 per cent of the alcohol in us during vigorous r*nning. This is why you may have noticed that the volume of beer that you drink has less of an effect on you when you're in torrid climes – much of the alcohol is eliminated via sweating.

Now, back to the question of whether or not beer, or alcohol in any other form, actually facilitates (or hinders) the physical performance entailed in Hashing. Over the years, certainly, many athletes (and a disproportionate number of Hashers) have suspected that alcohol just may improve physical performance. Perhaps by giving us more energy for the effort. Well, truth of the matter is that alcohol is metabolised so slowly that it's not able to contribute very much to our energy requirement. As it's metabolised some of the alcohol, however, is converted to fat, a rich source of energy, but who among us would look at that as a benefit? All of us have more than enough fat for energy delivery to begin with. The upshot of this is that physiological studies have shown that one to two beers or drinks prior to exercise have no significant effect on exercise, one way or the other. On the other hand, going beyond the one to two beers prior to exercise does have a negative impact, one which gets progressively worse as blood alcohol content rises. High concentrations of alcohol in the blood can impair the pumping action of the heart and also interfere with your muscles getting enough glucose (sugar) to keep contracting.

Alas, the argument for having a beer or two prior to or during the Hash run is not lost entirely because there is no verifiable physiological benefit. The real bonus to having one or two beers is the *psychological* one (especially if you've shown up for the Hash hung-over). And here the dosage is very important. Technically, alcohol is a narcotic, a central nervous system (our brain and spinal cord) depressant. But, paradoxically, in low doses (one to two beers for example) it's a stimulant. We feel stronger and more alert. In these low doses, alcohol also reduces what's called our *perceived exertion*, that is, it makes the effort *seem* easier. So then, why not have a few beers before and/or during the run/walk? [Now we're talking! –ed.]

Now, it's after the outing, and everyone is getting back in varying states of dehydration, so no one's counting the beers! For rehydration, it must be said that beer isn't as good a rehydration choice as non-alcoholic beverages, but it's close enough. And, in sufficient volume, beer does quite an adequate job.

Now, there are a couple of other 'drugs' to be considered. During the long, strenuous Hash r*n, the body has itself been manufacturing two other significant chemicals, namely, adrenaline and endorphin (our body's endogenous morphine). Happily, the beer blends ever-so-nicely to produce the best imaginable post-workout cocktail: alcohol, adrenaline, and endorphin. No worries now! On, On ..."

Dr Larry Fee, M.S., Ph. D., ACSM
Aka Hammer
Honolulu H3, Hawaii.

So, Clementine, you were right all along. And you managed to nail it in just 10 words. Now, some scientific proof from Hammer that Front Running Bastards (FRBs) are wasting their time: "The energy expended on Hashing whether you're the FRB, the last Hasher in at the Hash, or some place in-between, the formula for just how much energy you've spent is the same. For every kilogram that you weigh (1 kg = 2.2 lb) it takes one calorie to run one kilometre. So, if you weigh 70 kg (154 lb) and you ran 10 kilometres, you would have burned 700 calories. And that's true whether you r*n very fast or very slow."

So, Front R*nning Bastards, the only benefit is that you may get to the beer a bit earlier. Although, admittedly, that's a hell of a benefit!

Nude World Order.

Hashing in the Americas.

The Beagle Has Landed.

Amerindian tribes were the first to settle the Americas, after they crossed the Bering Straits from Asia. They went on to establish elaborate cultures such as the Aztecs in South America, and others remained simple nomads roaming the plains. Western civilisation first reached the shores of America with Columbus at the end of the 15th century. However, real refined civilisation as we know it began when rugby was introduced in 1874 to the United States thanks to Harvard and McGill University, Canada, just three years after the formation in England of the Rugby Union. This free-flowing, r*nning, kicking and carrying game caught on big time with Yale, Princeton and Columbia joining in. However it was soon dwarfed by its derivative, American football – gridiron – as the prescient Yanks knew that there were not enough stoppages in a good game of rugby to allow for all the commercial breaks the televised game would eventually require.

"I arrived in the US in 1967," says British expat in Washington, DC, Ralph Wadsworth, "and occasionally thought about starting a Hash." He had Hashed for five years in Kuala Lumpur before and believed American civilisation needed to be taken to its ultimate stage of enlightenment. "However, I travelled globally three to four months a year, and I was committed to playing three racquet sports."[Tut, tut. Priorities! –ed.]. "In addition, based on my observation that Americans love to play competitive sports – and to win – I felt that the Hash would not appeal to them."

The prevailing thought, according to Wadsworth, was that "Americans were too sensible to be attracted to such a crazy pastime!"[(122)] History shows that he would eat those words – plain, without catsup, ketchup, or chilli sauce. And no fries with that.

April of the following year saw Martin Luther King, Jr – a civil rights campaigner – assassinated. In July 1969, the United States – in fulfilment of JFK's ambition to have a man on the moon by the end of the decade – got Apollo 11 and Neil Armstrong to take a giant step for mankind on the lunar surface. Many saw this as just a recce for a future InterHash venue.

"I'm not for women in any job. I don't want any of them around. The reason … is mainly because they are erratic. And emotional." Just another chauvinistic Rumson Hashman mouthing off? Hardly. These are the words of President Richard Nixon in September 1971, as quoted in The Rehnquist Choice by John Dean. The context was the search for a replacement for retiring Supreme Court judges. But he told the Attorney-General that it could perhaps help him swing an extra percentage point or two if he nominated a woman, Mildred Lillie. She never got the job.

The US – in a burst of patriotic fervour with the Vietnam war raging on – also announced that it would deny passports to anyone refusing to take an oath of allegiance to the country. Ambitious peace talks began, with the release of POWs a priority. This led to the most intense battles and bombings from both sides so far. A total of 541,000 US troops would eventually see combat in Vietnam, including 32,000 in Cambodia. Talk was now of an all-volunteer army. It was against this background that Fort Eustis H3 in Virginia became America's very first Hash in rather strange circumstances.

Firstly, Major Francis Arnold was a *British* exchange officer on temporary exchange at the fort. Secondly, he had *never* Hashed in his life before! Not even one trail. "I knew about H3 at Longmoor, but due to a demanding job r*nning and lecturing in the Advanced Transport Course – and no particular interest in r*nning – didn't get involved," he said.

"Major Frank Arnold had heard of the Hash when he was also a member of the directing staff at Longmoor," says Mountain Rescue. "Although he never Hashed with us in England, he came to me to ask what the 'rules' were and went off with copious notes." This differs from Arnold's own account. "I was aware of the basics. I genuinely don't remember being briefed, but I did write to Longmoor to state my intentions," he says.

So, despite many other recreational opportunities for the American soldiers and himself being available, this Operations Officer – who worked at the HQ of a transport group – single-handedly conspired to get the New World on trail. "I saw the introduction of Hashing as an opportunity for something different, new and typically weirdly British," he said. He went to his boss, Col Pat Delavan ("an Anglophile") and got full support. In shades of Thornton at Dhekelia, Delavan even wanted to participate himself.

"I was confident of success, at least for the first few Hashes," says the virgin founder, then a fit 42-year-old. "There were some 'r*nners' who joined up including two very keen and experienced young captains."

The receding hareline for r*n #1 was duly chosen: "One captain, one lieutenant, both balding. They accepted the joke with very good grace." And so it was that the first Hash on American soil took place on November 7 1971. A Tuesday – "Tuesdays suited us all," being the simple explanation. Fourteen masochistic hounds fronted to find out what it was all about. The virgin hares took off through the woods in Fort Eustis's extensive training area, and the pack never caught them that day.

At the end, beer and other drinks were served up, plus some snacks. With a positive reaction, it was decided to make some appointments for each r*n. Hares, obviously, plus a couple of assistants consisting of Purveyor of Hash Thrash ("drink and grub") and Maker of Hash Musick ("deliberate spelling and something to listen to during the thrash"). Like a revolving committee in other words. Arnold took it upon himself to produce the weekly newsletter.

Just before Christmas 1971, GM [That'd be General Motors, not Grand

Master –ed.] recalled 6.7 million Chevvies. Fortunately Arnold was not affected as he drove a Rambler Ambassador in those days.

Live hare r*ns became the norm on their Tuesday r*ns. The penalty for hares, if caught, was to be thrown into the nearest body of water available. With several lakes on post, this was never too far from hand. "Very often this ended up in a marvellous free-for-all with everyone enjoying the 'splash-in'." Arnold also remembers "many very inventive Hashes both on and off post." Their post-r*n thrashes evolved, with the pack getting into the spirit of it. Being Maker of Hash Musick brought out the worst in people, with creative offerings coming in the form of tape decks, bagpipes, accordion playing, trumpets, and saxophones. But the one that everyone remembers was Arnold's boss, the full-bird Colonel who upped the ante with "a go-go dancer from a downtown strip joint!"

A few months later, Arnold was promoted and moved to Post HQ, working for a couple of generals. "This enabled me to extend the Hash base considerably," says Arnold, showing true priority and commitment to the cause. They went beyond just the men on base, too. Families began to get involved, including wives and children. "I well remember the panic of two wives (one of them mine), then our two teenage daughters, as they heard the 'On! On!' baying of the pack chasing them."

The hardcore Half Minds also got involved in other r*nning events, such as a Fort Eustis cross-country race (Arnold taking the trophy in the over-40s division), and entered a team in a local 10-mile event ("which we won hands down") and an off-post marathon.

Up until the end of his two-year posting in 1973, Arnold took part in just about every Hash, taking his fair share of haring turns as well. He watched with satisfaction as the pack of hounds grew, aided and abetted by the variety of quirky entertainment by each week's Maker of Hash Musick. He bid a fond farewell to Fort Eustis and America, eventually becoming a colonel himself. He organised a few Hashes thereafter, "but never regained the special flavour of Fort Eustis. It was a privilege to introduce H3 to the USA and an enormous pleasure to be part of it and knowing it's continued and developed."

By 1975, Saigon had fallen and the last of the American troops had been withdrawn. More than 46,000 Americans had been killed, more than 300,000 wounded.

Mountain Rescue, the proxy mentor of the Fort Eustis kennel, ironically took over from Arnold on rotation about 10 years later. "I joined Fort Eustis for two and half years and notched up over 100 r*ns with them," says Mountain Rescue. 'Hashregs' stipulated a maximum two false trails. "The trouble here was that they were very competitive and live hares used to get two minutes start if they were lucky. It was into the nearest body of water if hares were caught. OK in summer, but in winter…"

There were other land-based incidents, too. "As one of the foreign exchange officers it was decided that it would be more prudent if I was the one to explain why the senior officers' golf was disturbed when the pack, in extended line, crossed over the fairway. Fortunately, the Commanding General was, and still is, an Anglophile and I am a fully paid-up Anglo," recalls Mountain Rescue. "I teamed up with the Australian exchange officer, Peter Burdeu, and we became adept at cheating (most un-American!) and were never caught, quite. We decided once we would screw the pack and settle for a barbecue. Because we were somewhat older than all the Americans they generously gave us a three-minute start. We ran off round the corner, laid a false trail into the car park, and a hidden trail to the front door of the Officers Club. We entered the bar. Within 60 seconds of leaving the pack we had beers in our hands, and our ears to the emergency exit which led to the patio where the pack was still assembling. 'Come on, let's go.' 'No. We said we'd give them three minutes.' 'Well, two is enough!' and they were off. We took our cans with us out through the exit to the nearby barbie area. It took the first one a good 10 minutes to cotton on, and the rest came in later. Some, much later. They all got over it once they had a beer and a bun in them."

This sneaky duo also once laid a trail by bicycle. "The Americans were not impressed when they spotted us on bicycles laying the trail. Well, as 'live' hares we had to keep ahead of them somehow and we hadn't managed to cheat by laying most of the trail earlier in the afternoon."

But for all this fun and frivolity, it was kept to themselves. The Hash world at large knew nothing of this chapter, not even its very existence, until 1988. They operated in splendid isolation, notching up something like 850 r*ns on the board before word got out to the rest of the burgeoning Hashing world.

Long & Hard says: "I started Hashing in Korea in early 1988. I enjoyed it so much that I knew I wanted to find a Hash when I returned to this area so I could continue. I did some research but was unable to track down the Hash. I did have a magazine that showed there was a 'Norfolk HHH' but there was no contact information. There were also no internet resources to use. Finally I heard about the Fort Eustis HHH and that they usually ran near the post and they sometimes hung out at an Italian restaurant in Denbigh (now called Carmella's). I almost made contact one weekend in late 1989. I heard they were doing a r*n in Northern Newport News, and went to the area of the Italian restaurant, but they were doing their 900th r*n on Fort Eustis. I was finally able to meet up with the Hash the following weekend."[(42)]

At that stage, Tuesday evenings in the summer and Saturday afternoons in the winter were the moments of mayhem for this mixed kennel. The pack was composed of more than 90 per cent military (active-duty, retired and spouses).

The make-up of the hounds today is more like 60 per cent military, including members who are military dependents or military retirees. Very few are from the fort itself. "I believe it was Desert Storm in 1991 that changed things drastically," says Preparation H. "When they mobilised, it was left to the airmen from Langley AFB and the sailors from the naval stations, and a few civilians, to keep it going. Attendance dwindled to a small handful in the early Nineties but picked up and is about 25-30 on average." As that military population evolved, members came in who wanted to be able to continue to party on-after the Hash, so in 1999 Fort Eustis changed to a year-round Saturday schedule.

Through all of the ups and down, a weekly trail has never been missed, taking them over 1,625 r*ns as of time of writing. The Fort Eustis area is full of Hashes such as Tidewater H3 and Virginia Beach Full Moon H3, and hard-core Hashers can get a r*n three or four times a week.

Seedy DC.

In March 1972, the US Senate passed the Equal Rights Amendment, meaning that repression of white Caucasian men must stop and they must be given a fair go. One American lass who did give the guys a fair go that year was Linda Lovelace, who starred in Deep Throat – a movie which launched a thousand Hash names.

On May 19 1972 a bomb exploded in the Pentagon. But that wasn't as much of a shock to the residents of DC as what was to follow a week later ... Washington DC H3 – 'the second-oldest regular r*nning Hash in the New World' – got its first sniff of flour on May 27 1972. Tumbling Bill Panton, who had started Hashing in Kuala Lumpur, was to blame for this infestation.

Posted to the World Bank, the British expat depended on his colleagues there to round up numbers for the first trail. "But a lot of them were too serious to take this Hashing mystique too literally and I didn't have all that many contacts among the American public at the time," says Tumbling Bill. Like Wadsworth before him, he harboured nervous feelings of whether Americans were too competitive to be Hashers.

The first DC r*n was remarkably staged only a few weeks after Tumbling Bill had arrived in the States. He was then living in a rented townhouse close to the Linden Hill Hotel in Bethesda, so the r*n started from there ... out of its recreation room, in fact. From there, across the hotel car park, through a hole in the fence behind the Alta Vista Elementary School, then south down the Georgetown Pike, down through the NIH grounds and back up Connecticut Avenue to welcome Pabst Blue Ribbon beers and pies in the basement.

The r*n was kept short and simple for good reason – there were only five in the pack, and of those, only three had r*n Hash before. It was also uncharacteristically hot for that time of year. Tumbling Bill was the hare, but ran with the pack to make sure things went according to plan. Doug Gray and Doug Gold were in the pack. "As it happened, I found most of the checks," jokes Tumbling Bill. "Something I had never done before or since!"

Ralph Wadsworth, one of Tumbling Bill's former KL buddies, was instrumental from the start, going on to become Grand Master. It was a welcome return to Hashing for those who had not Hashed for several years in the interim, but whom Tumbling Bill had persuaded to get out from behind their desks at the World Bank, IMF and various commonwealth embassies and join him. "We did pick up a few kindred souls in the locals (lawyers and ex-military types) because the Vietnam War was more or less coming to an end and lots of veterans were out and about doing various things, and were willing to get involved. Some of these had heard about the Hash, possibly even been members of the Hash in those days in their Vietnamese experiences, so we managed to get locals coming in," Tumbling Bill said.

Mother Hash practices were followed for the DCH3, with the exception that initially r*ns were held fortnightly, but with the building enthusiasm and numbers growing steadily, weekly r*ns were started within a few months of inception. However, it wasn't all beer and skittles. Many potential recruits never showed up a second time. One reportedly fell behind the pack at the first check and was never seen again. But it was Tumbling Bill's enthusiasm and perseverance that won through, until a couple of years later when America led the world into a r*nning and jogging boom. The Hash coasted along on the coat tails of this lifestyle change, with new boots such as Finnish expats Ulf Burmeister and Juhani Vanska showing up on trail.

"Hashing was aided, in terms of footwear, by the jogging craze enthusiasm which started around the very late Sixties, early Seventies. And then the shoemakers came in with all their fancy gear and these trailblazer type shoes are ideal for Hashing, they cushion your feet far better," says Panton.

"Let me put this in context," says Wadsworth. "In the mid-Seventies the r*nning boom hit America, which subsequently had a major impact on DCH3. Guys r*nning 10km, 10-Milers and marathons 'discovered' the Hash and could not believe their good fortune – a relatively easy r*n, a fun group and beer drinking after, for them, modest exercise!"

Washington, DC, being a major political centre, became by default a huge propagator of the Hashing movement, with a lot of politicos, World Bank officers, and armed forces personnel fanning out from here. Tumbling Bill himself moved with the World Bank to Bangkok in 1977 and started the renowned Bangkok H3 chapter. At Panton's insistence, DC remained resolutely a men-only kennel. Within months of his departure, a Harriettes chapter had started, with a number of men defecting across. Some wag nicknamed the mixed Harriettes chapter the AC-DC Hash.

When the world decided to go through its next craze, aerobics, in the Eighties, Washington became a notorious city due to its infamous 'crack wars'. This had nothing to do with the proliferation of moonings and browneyes by Hashers, but more to do with territorial fights by drug lords and their peons in some of the desperately poor neighbourhoods which had sprung up in this increasingly multi-ethnic and cosmopolitan city.

Following this ethnic bent, the Hash held a Hawaiian-themed r*n, with a Polynesian-style après site set up in a wooded clearing. Anne, the fiancée of DC kennel's resident character, Bob Santos, was one of two women who greeted the Hashers after the r*n in a grass skirt. *Just* a grass skirt. She and her compatriot handed out *leis* to the runners as they entered the clearing.

Their 500th r*n celebration in 1982 was described by Hugh 'True Blue' Robinson as one of the two best parties he'd ever attended. Other clubs in the DC area were invited, and Philadelphia H3 and Rumson were well represented. DCH3 had rented a boathouse on the Potomac River for the event. There was plenty of barbecue at the end of the run and about six kegs on the boathouse balcony overlooking the river, with Bob Santos ensuring that any empties were immediately replaced. The DC Hashers had recruited women from the area to ensure there were dance partners for the predominantly male group. "I don't think I ever sat down except to finish another beer," says True Blue.

Rumson H3 were up to their usual tricks, having stolen a box of commemorative mugs, and later appeared *en masse* on a balcony inside the boathouse and mooned the dance hall. At midnight, the band announced that their time was up and got ready to pack up their instruments. As no one was ready to see the party end, a hat was passed and enough was collected to keep them for another hour. "It was sometime during this last hour that I happened to look up from where I had taken one of my infrequent pauses and noticed an extremely fetching young woman (looked somewhat like Audrey Hepburn) in a diaphanous dress being twirled around the dance floor to a Glen Miller style tune. She and her partner were making it look easy – a la Fred Astaire and Ginger Rogers. A second glance revealed that her partner was one of the Rumson crowd and he had neglected to put his knickers back on after the mooning of a half hour ago. Both were totally blasé," says True Blue, a tad incredulous.

At a r*n a few months later, Santos' game fiancée was wheeled into action once again. "She rode one of her horses through a check at a r*n out of Bob's home dressed as Zorro, but again, couldn't seem to find her top," says True Blue. Not to be outdone, Santos once showed up at DC's annual Halloween r*n, dressed (thankfully!) as Zorro on a big black stallion.

Through this all, DC thought they were the oldest kennel in the USA until Fort Eustis's existence came to light in 1988. In the Nineties America moved into its next health craze, yoga, with 15 million Americans including yoga as part of their get-fit or keep-fit regime[119]. Not so good for the health in 1993 were the 67 million handguns owned by private US citizens which resulted in 10,000 murders a year. DC became the murder capital of the USA [Isn't a Down Down enough any more? –ed.].

Today, the face of the DC men's Hash has changed somewhat. Washington DC is a club with a keen sense of history and seniority, with founders such as Bill Panton and Ralph Wadsworth going back to Kuala Lumpur in the 1950s and 1960s. As a result, they created a special membership category called Hashman Emeritus. Those who graduate to these lofty heights pay no subs yet receive all the membership benefits and literature, and can attend any r*n or On On.

The expatriate communities from the World Bank, and other similar organisations, have declined. Because of that, and others simply wanting to get out of the place, Washington, DC, has been one of the most prolific spawning grounds of new Hash chapters. "Now it's pretty well all local guys living in the Washington area," says Panton. One such local is Hops. "As a group, we are old, set in our ways, and do not participate in the annual DC-area Red Dress r*n," says Hops, colouring the kennel a bit grey. He's a keen proponent of the Red Dress movement in DC and enjoys the variety of Hashing on offer in the area. Hugh Robinson, more of a traditionalist, compares DCH3 with Seoul H3 and says: "Both stand out as premier clubs – both all male and with a camaraderie few other organisations offer. In both clubs, many of the members had military experience which provided a sense of history and most held positions of responsibility in their daily lives."

"Now there are about 10 Hashes in the Washington area," says Tumbling Bill, "and that's probably more saturation than there is in the Klang Valley in KL itself and Petaling Jaya."

It now seems that the ill-fated predictions of the viability of the Hash in America were a little off. "I could not have been more wrong!" the venerable Wadsworth says. Tumbling Bill also throws himself gladly onto his sword. "I was completely wrong! There were a lot of them – it's great! And the combination of the opportunity to have a few beers after exerting yourself goes down as well in America, if not better, than anywhere else. It's a true thing that there are more Hashes in America right now than any other country in the world. OK, the size of population helps, but it hasn't caught on in Russia for example."

So how does Panton feel now that it turns out he wasn't the first to introduce Hashing to the New World? "Well, I'm still not convinced that what Fort Eustis have got now is the Fort Eustis that existed in the very beginning, because they haven't produced that evidence that I would like to see. But I take their word for it – if they say they were the first and they are the same continuous group, then OK, I'll accept their word. Of course, as a genealogist I have to be circumspect here."

Getting Their Rocks Off.

In August 1974, Pinocchio Nixon quit the presidency, the first US President to do so. He had undone himself with the Watergate scandal. Only one other President, Andrew Johnson in 1868, had faced impeachment but he survived the process. Gerald Ford took over the big desk. Meanwhile a trial is heard of those American Indian leaders who took part in an armed occupation of the Wounded Knee Indian Reservation, a name most battle-scarred Hashers could readily identify with.

The third Hash in America – and the first Hash west of the Mississippi River – was about to get underway, in Little Rock, Arkansas, with a total of around 40 kennels in the world at that stage. "I was aware of DCH3 having been made aware of its existence during my last week in Korea where I had been r*nning with Seoul H3," says Hugh 'True Blue' Robinson, a Yank from northern New Jersey. "The Hash Trash handed out at my farewell r*n announced that some wanker named Bill Panton had started a club in Washington, DC. This news was probably the incentive I needed to try to start a Hash upon my return."

The 34-year-old arrived with his family in Little Rock to r*n the military personnel office at Little Rock Air Force Base. At that time 40 aircraft and 1,000 of his colleagues were sent to Cambodia.

"I became a regular at the base gym during the lunch hour and continued r*nning, while missing the Hash. I had noticed that a pilot whose locker was next to mine was a strong r*nner and struck up a conversation. I told him I wanted to start a r*nning club and asked if he was aware of a location where r*nners congregated. He told me that a group got together at a local school's track on Friday evenings to informally compete." Robinson went to the track that Friday. "Entering the field, I approached the first r*nner I noticed, introduced myself, and told him I was interested in starting a r*nning club called the Hash House Harriers. Before I could begin to explain the concept he had replied, 'On On' and was laughing wildly." This was Bob Rooke, who had recently arrived from KL where he'd r*n with Mother Hash.

Rooke was a Brit who had attended the University of Colorado. After a stint in India with the Peace Corps he had moved to Malaysia to work as a mining engineer. "Bob and I proceeded to describe the Hash to the other r*nners and convinced enough of them to give it a try. I also managed to get an article on Hashing published in the air force base newspaper which brought out a few more of the curious," says Robinson.

Little Rock H3's first trail kicked off from Robinson's house in North Little Rock on Monday, August 19 1974 at 7pm. A dozen prospects – including one Bill Brass – pitched up, lured by some spurious and grossly exaggerated promises. Robinson and Rooke went about replicating their experiences in Korea and Malaysia, respectively. The trail was pre-laid, "with false trails used to a great extent", and they ran with the pack to bolster the numbers and to preclude any disasters among the virgins. "We did lose one guy who got so lost he called a cab and went home. We were afraid he had drowned or fallen into a hole," says Robinson. However, back at the cooler, Schlitz beer washed away any and all concerns. In what became a time-honoured practice, Down Downs were few (usually just to welcome new boots), and hotdogs and burgers were dished up.

Decisions taken that night were to make this a weekly thing, to be held on Mondays, and to limit the membership to men only – a traditional Hash. The unique Hashing concept garnered some play in the local press.

The first few months saw growing attendance, Rooke and Robinson usually setting, or at least co-haring most trails. Then winter's frosty fingers dictated that Sunday afternoons at 4pm would be a better Hashing time. Pack numbers began to drop. "I suspect competition with televised football and occasionally nasty weather may have prompted many to stay home," says Robinson. "We once ran with a pack of six, *including* the two co-hares. We persevered, however, and with the spring of '75 the numbers began a gradual increase." Several high school and college cross-country r*nners had joined and recruited others of a like mind.

In 1978, a clean-living saxophone-blowing gent called Bill Clinton became Governor of Arkansas. Robinson upped and left around this time, happy that LRH3 had 200 r*ns under its belt, 50 suckers on their mailing list, and 15 to 30 of the usual suspects on trail each week. "The buggers admitted women two weeks after I left," says Robinson.

Some time after, Little Rock enterprisingly began sponsoring an annual 10km r*n with a built-in short cut. "The short cut guaranteed a shorter course but not necessarily a faster finish as it usually included water, briars, or hills. It became a very popular event and helped with recruiting."

One of the problems with becoming a mixed pack is it exposed innocent and naïve Hashmen to hitherto unseen problems. For their 900th r*n a boat was chartered to take the rabid pack on a dinner cruise around a lake near Hot Springs. Reverend Bob succumbed to the excitement and passed out. Some of the Harriettes couldn't resist the temptation to paint his toenails red. The next morning when Reverend Bob discovered what had happened, he drove all over Hot Springs asking for toenail polish remover. It seemed all he could find on the shelf was *fingernail* polish remover. Finally, after a number of stops, a sales clerk explained to him that they were the same thing.

And it was through a Harriette that LRH3 had one of its biggest claims to foam. On August 2 1992, just before his election to the White House in November, Bill Clinton was jogging down Cantrell Rd with two secret service agents. Hillary and Chelsea were following on mountain bikes, en route to a family BBQ at Hillary's parents' house. "The Little Rock Hash emerged from a wooded area – frequented by homosexuals and transvestites, and known to be a 'homeless Haven' – in all their glory to find Mr Clinton on the same r*nning trail," says Yo Adrian. "He joined the r*n for about six blocks, and was accompanied by many secret service vehicles. After speaking to old high school friend, Lunchbox, he assured his secret service agents that the Hash 'posed no real threat' to himself or his family." They reminisced about her auntie's apple pies and how he should call her and get her to make some. The Hash invited him to the 'On On' in the parking lot of the Cajun's Wharf (a local restaurant) on the river. Mr Clinton said he'd love to, rather than go to dinner with his out-laws, but declined due to family commitment. "However, the secret service agents were not above a good time and joined the Hash for the On On after trying to follow the trail in four-wheel-drive vehicles," says Yo Adrian. A t-shirt was made to commemorate the r*n: "Clinton did Hash, but didn't inhale!"

In 1993, Slick Willie Clinton won a resounding victory in the US presidential race. At 45 he was younger than most Hashmen and promised a 'new season of American renewal'. He seemed to confuse election promises with erection promises. At that stage homosexuals [Let's call them poofters! –ed.] were banned from the armed forces, and he moved to rescind the ban, which was an unpopular call in the shower blocks of US bases worldwide. He also scrapped the Star Wars defence program, and – without consulting the Hash – approved the closure of 129 domestic military bases and more than 90 overseas bases.

Not letting any of that dampen their enthusiasm, Little Rock H3 celebrated their 1,000th r*n that July. Hugh Robinson came back for it. "It wasn't the same. Many of the folks from the first four years had departed, and the presence of women had changed the ambience," he laments. "I started in a traditional club and hope to hang up my shoes in a traditional club." Since the 1,000th he's had little contact with LRH3 which he describes as "a curious social club".

A good example of that is the *double* wedding they once had on a r*n. Imagine the whole pack decked out in their finery, including full-length gowns (and that was just the guys). The grooms wore those printed tuxedo t-shirts. The bride and grooms' families also joined the r*n, and the service was performed against the backdrop of a mountain by Ogre, who is (believe it or not) an ordained minister. At the end of the r*n, a full reception was held and much more drink and fun had to make it a really memorable wedding.

Year-round now, Sunday afternoons are their Hash slot, with a US$1 donation weekly. Bob 'Missing Link' Rooke is still in Little Rock, and still shows up on occasion. Bill 'Brass Balls' Brass, another r*n #1 veteran, also still r*ns regularly, and they can't seem to shake that guy with the coloured toenails, Bob 'Reverend Bob' McKinney.

An Englishman in New York.

The next place to go to the dogs was the Big Apple, New York. Banker Charley (Chuck) Woodhouse and his wife Barbara returned from a posting in Singapore. He had Hashed with Singapore H3, she with the Singapore Harriettes. As it happened, the founder of Singapore H3, Ian Cumming, lived not too far away in the Westchester area, so naturally they got in touch

Saturday, January 31 1978 was the big day, with 25 souls – of whom only one *wasn't* a virgin – braving the weather for the dubious pleasure of a r*n and a sip of some cold suds on a freezing day. Dot and Paul Janis, Peter Callaway and Bill Falter were in the rabble, with a few children in amongst the pack, making up numbers on NYH3 r*n #1.

"For convenience this started from the Woodhouse home," says Cumming.[74] "Charley laid the trail the day before, marked with paper strips and paper plates on the ground. It snowed eight to 10 inches in the night and we immediately recognised that there were conditions under which Hashing worked better in the tropics than in our climate. With the cunning of a fox, Charley relaid the trail starting at the end using paper plates pinned on trees. This ruse was most effective for the first 100 yards, but after that marks were superfluous; the pack followed the backwards footprints in an outright race for the beer." Except for one who was "never seen again after the first check – we don't even remember her name."

The first r*ns were held on weekends, either a Saturday or a Sunday, and usually a fortnight or more apart. These were nice cosy family affairs with barbecues and screaming kids, but not the primal gathering to which Cumming had become accustomed in his Singapore days.

In 1980, they resolved to start a Monday night group in addition to the weekend r*n (if any). This new group eventually supplanted the old one. Their 7pm starts meant that for a third of the year, not only would they finish the r*n in darkness, but it would actually *start* in darkness! "We had an unwritten rule that anybody can bring along a flashlight but they must leave the batteries with the hare," says Cumming.

This wasn't without its hazards as obstacles such as clothes-lines, chained entrances and low-level road signs ruined the odd Hasher's evening, not to mention their facial features. Darkness also induced Brice Faller to lay a trail under the third rail on Metro North, crossing four tracks three times. "After the first crossing we abandoned the trail, sought out a cheap pub and waited for him to find *us*," reminisces Cumming.

Back at the beer, Cumming and his mates from the St James choir led the hounds in lusty song. "Here in New York, the founding pack contained eight members of a church choir. They already knew the tunes, they only had to learn the words. They were used to being called upon with full mouthful to sing cohesively and tunefully as often as anyone could think of a song. To our embarrassment we frequently get standing ovations in bars – but not many free beers. The important part is that *everybody* sings. The cacophony of the tone deaf is absorbed into magnificently spread chords so intricate that *any* note will fit in."

Among the early legends was the 'shirt tail' Hash. Bill Falter was the hare on a Saturday r*n. At some point on the On-in trail he ran out of paper markers and proceeded to rip his shirt apart to provide enough to get home. Next he started on his shorts, and only a last-minute shortcut saved his underwear.

"In 1981 I moved to New York," says Finnish Hasher Screw My Bike, "and saw an article in the New York Times on the Hash in New York. It felt like I was home," he says.

"We have a lot of singers, inspired by Ian Cumming," says Pearl Necklace of NYH3. "Many are from a choir and they even talk about the acoustics of a room," she says. But the imprimatur of Cummings is very much felt, not just in New York, but on American and Asian Hashing.

Along the lines of Mother Hash in KL and the Singapore Men's Hash from which Cumming came, New York also shies away from horns, whistles, Hash names, and so on. "Ian always takes it back to the basics, the singing, etc," says Pearl Necklace [Named in Houston, before you say 'I thought they didn't have names'–ed.].

She reports that the NYH3 has had a rough patch lately with people getting married and settling down, a lot of corporate changes and consolidation, plus the jitters of September 11. This has effected pack sizes "so some people have stepped up and set more than their fair share of r*ns," she says. However, some homeless puppies never strayed very far and are still on trail a quarter of a century later: Dot and Paul Janis, Peter Callaway and Bill Falter, who Hashes only occasionally these days. And Cumming himself, of course.

In the New York area, Hashes have been set up in Fairfield, Ridgefield and Hudson Valley, Manhattan, Litchfield Hills, Newark, and Long Island, among others. Keith Kanaga, a veteran from KL, has been instrumental in setting up many of these.

None of the Greater Gotham (New York City) Hashes have any membership or subscriptions and "freely and incestuously" r*n in each other's Hashes on a regular basis. Instead all On Ons are financed by splitting the bill, except in Ridgefield, where everyone brings a covered dish or beer to the r*n.

South of the Border.

But did South America come first? Hashtorians have talked about El Salvador having a lively chapter of British Hashers r*nning from a garrison there in the late Sixties, which subsequently died off. However, Brig Ray Thornton dismisses it: "I cannot imagine what the British Army would be doing in El Salvador in the late Sixties. We did have a small garrison in Belize around that time and perhaps this is the origin of the South America story." Grapes of Wrath, presently with Salvador H3, says: "I arrived in San Salvador in 1998 and revived the SHHH for what we refer to as the fourth instalment. I was able to acquire all the known history of the SHHH and who was involved when. We have no history that I am aware of prior to the mid-Eighties when our present numbering began."

The first place to officially fall in Central America was Costa Rica, a land settled by Mayans and Incans over 10,000 years ago. Christopher Columbus even dropped by on his last trip to the New World. The Spanish were so interested in the potential of this place they named it Costa Rica (the Rich Coast), but soon lost interest when all they found was coffee and bananas. Costa Rica rid itself of Spanish rule in 1821, and has been living relatively peacefully (compared to its turbulent neighbours) ever since.

The 1978 presidential elections saw Rodrigo Carazo Odio win the hot seat. With the Sandanistas' victory in neighbouring Nicaragua in 1979, relations with them got icy, and border skirmishes resulted.

San Jose H3 in Costa Rica started off in February 1979, less than a year after Hashing reached New York. Ian Young and Bill 'Barbie' Barbee were the Half Minds irresponsible. A pack of five hounds made up the numbers on that first trail. A couple of years later, they had the likes of Rick 'Chapa Chatty' Chatham, Peter Groenendyk, and the inveterate ex-African Giles 'Patchwork Quilt' Paget-Wilkes in their cosmopolitan fold. By 1983 the country's brewery stocks were doing well, but the country's economic crisis worsened, and border skirmishes increased. Thanks largely to Patchwork Quilt, they found themselves initiating and hosting the first Inter-Americas Hash in 1983. He was unable to attend InterHash at that stage so thought a Nash Hash in Costa Rica would be the next best thing. It attracted 60 *overseas* Hashers, including Tony Webb from Surrey, England and Paul Ghannoum from West Beirut. A total of about130 Hashers attended. A lot of bullshit must have been sprouted around the beer-taps at that event, because that same year, Hash kennels mushroomed in Venezuela, Mexico, Panama and Ecuador.

Over the years, the mixed San Jose pack has reached membership of around 80, with nearly 20 nationalities represented. Jorge Salazar was rarely not at a Hash, chalking up 235 consecutive r*ns at one stage. His colleagues said of him at the time: "He never gets sick, never takes a vacation, never does anything. Very boring guy."[76] However, they had two colourful old Hashers in their kennel until recently: Sauerkraut had been a radio operator aboard the notorious German pocket battleship, Panzer Schiff Admiral Graf Spee, when she was fatally damaged by British warships in the Battle of the River Plate at Montevideo, Uruguay, in 1939. According to Rogelio Doctor Salvador, former Hash Quack and Costa Rica's present Minister of Health, Sauerkraut still plays tennis occasionally. Creep was a US commercial airline pilot when he retired as a *pensionado* in Costa Rica during the early Eighties. Quite the distance r*nner, at age 65 Creep won the silver medal (20 km) at the World Masters Championships in Puerto Rico. Shortly after his arches collapsed. "Unfortunately these two colourful characters (now in their 80s) retired from Hashing around 1990," says Chapa Chatty. San Jose founder Barbie is still around to this day causing mayhem.

On Again, Off Again.
Lima has been the capital of the Pacific coast nation Peru since the days of the Spanish conquistador Francisco Pizarro in 1535. In pre-Columbian times, it was part of the Inca Empire; the imperial capital of Cuzco was in present-day Peru. Things have been quiet since then. In the 1850s the treasury prevented financial collapse of the country and the economy by trading the foreign debt for a pile of guano. A French firm eagerly accepted. Peru has been plagued by economic problems ever since. This led to a military junta in 1968, led by Gen Juan Velasco Alvarado. He set about nationalising US company assets and sweeping land reforms. Hurrah! But being all out of guano, the economy was now reliant on fishmeal, copper and sugar which wasn't fetching a good price at the market. Boo!

Unconfirmed reports have it that in 1974, Mike 'Yasser' Yetman and John Pilk kicked off Lima, Peru, South America's first Hash kennel. In 1975, Gen Alvardo was given the army boot and replaced by another general, Francisco Morales Bermudez. Austerity measures were brought in to quell growing foreign debt. Somewhere along the line, the chapter fizzled out.

In 1980, President Belaunde Terry returned to power, hoping to get International Monetary Fund support [A great political vision! –ed.]. More instability and strikes followed. The following year, Argentinian Juan Carlos 'Pinchy' Valdivia and his wife 'Daisy Duck' arrived in Lima from their posting in the Philippines. He ran an ad in the paper announcing the formation of the club, and got six Half Minds on trail #1 of Lima H3 (Mark Two) on or about June 9 1981. In this tiny pack was David Hartford, John 'Hashcrash' Gill, and his wife, Elizabeth. The Gills subsequently moved back to Tucson, Arizona, whilst Pinchy and Daisy Duck moved on to La Paz, Bolivia.

Other reports have Yasser and Pilk starting up Lima 2 H3 only in 1993, not two decades earlier. In any case, that incarnation disappeared down the gurgler once again, in unknown circumstances around mid-'95. Yasser has been spotted Hashing everywhere from Ethiopia to Canada. Pilk has been spotted in The Hague and Indonesia.

Enter Tom 'Ivory Ghost' Fallon, who'd Hashed in Bangkok and Abidjan in Africa, previously. "In March 1996, I – along with Marisol Diaz and Victor Tenorio – decided to kick it off again (for the third time in its history). We've been going fine ever since and generally have about 50 participants." On a rare occasion they might attract 100 hounds. Marisol Diaz is with the US Aid office in Lima, as is Stool Sample, who transferred from La Paz, Bolivia, where he coincidentally Hashed with Pinchy. Stool Sample describes Lima H3 as "a relatively tame Hash", despite the copious quantities of Peruvian nectar such as Cusquena, Cristal and Pilsner that disappear down the sinners' throats at a restaurant or On On at the hare's house. Occasionally, they'll be in fine voice in the circle and Father Abraham will raise the rafters until after midnight [Not a bad effort considering they start at 2.30pm –ed.].

A major gas project by Shell and Mobil was closed in the late 1990s, resulting in a mass exodus of expats and contractors. The pack these days is 80 per cent Peruvian, and "more informal and more relaxed with less international participation," according to Stool Sample.

Far Canal.

Panama came on trail sometime after 1980, thanks to a Singapore escapee, Steve Coates. The US has had a significant military influence over Panama since the late 19th century. With the completion of the Panama Canal, even more military might was needed to protect shipping and American business interests. Especially as the country had had four elected governments overthrown, and one president impeached. Then in 1981 Col Omar Torrijos Herrera, who had been named 'the Supreme Leader of the Panamanian Revolution' was killed in a plane crash, claimed to have been engineered by Manuel Noriega. So it is perhaps no surprise that the Canal Zone was a men-only military style Hash. They managed to r*n intermittently over the following years, and it was only in August 1983, when the Panama City Hash was started by Bob Macintosh, Patchwork Quilt and others, that a critical mass developed [And very critical they were, too! –ed.]. The following year, the two kennels came together to form the mixed Panama City H3 and shared their stocks of Panama Beer.

But Chile was *possibly* already on flour by this stage. The capital, Santiago, was founded by Pedro de Valdivia in 1541 a few years after the Spanish conquest of the country. However, the Army of the Andes, led by the nationalistically confused Bernardo O'Higgins, reconquered it in the early 1800s. Since then it's been pretty much civil war, coups and dodgy dictatorships. In 1973 a military junta, headed by Augusto Pinochet, was installed. He immediately banned Marxist political parties, and all other parties in 1977, curtailing civil and human rights in the process. Against this rosy backdrop in 1978, Don and Peggy McGillivrey apparently kicked off a family Hash, according to one source. However, other sources have three possible start dates (with March 31 1986 being the most likely) that Ian Lewis, his wife Marina, and Liam O'Brien from the American Embassy got Santiago on trail, perhaps for its second time. This might have more credence given that Chile was rebounding from its foreign debt crisis of the early Eighties. Pack sizes grew to a respectable 40 for their Monday evening summer r*ns and Sunday morning winter r*ns.

They were on consistently till the early 90s, then either switched to a fortnightly schedule or were interrupted by the civil situation, as it took several years to rack up their next 100 r*ns. Today, they are still on, with Fintan Bohan and Akos Zahoran being the key protagonists.

In short, Central and South American Hashtory is as mixed-up as a bowl of refried beans, and shows the long-term ill effects of consuming too much Tequila.

Northern Exposure.
To understand Canada and its country-folk, it helps to know that its first European settlers were Vikings [Possibly relatives of Moose from Norway? –ed.] who gatecrashed Newfoundland in the 11th century. Then during the American Revolution, tens of thousands of those loyal to 'The Empire' came up from America after losing their property there, and brought their anti-American sentiment with them. Then they had the Quiet Revolution in the 1960s, which was to do with intervening in an increasingly antsy Quebec, which – in true French fashion – wanted to r*n its own show. This led to kidnapping of British diplomats, the murder of a cabinet minister, as well as a terrorist bombing campaign.

In 1982, Queen Elizabeth signed the Constitution Act in Ottawa. The doors were now open for Hashing in Canada, the world's second-largest country.

Almost a year later to the day, Calgary H3 was founded by Mike 'Oombala' Carr. Oombala earned his Hash wings in Jakarta, Indonesia, and soon set about corrupting Calgary with other Half Minded bean-counters, mainly from Clarkson Gordon (now Ernst & Young). Their first r*n was on May 30 1983, starting from the Portuguese Society of Calgary, in south-east Calgary. Fifteen stray hounds – including Stuart 'On In' Crichton – went searching for the elusive flour strewn by Oombala and Mike Manderson.

Prime Minister Trudeau was voted out of office in 1984 and replaced by Mulroney, who was much more our kind of guy. A series of sex and financial scandals soon followed.

Despite its Jakarta roots, Calgary did not develop the habit of a circle after a r*n. Instead, the Hash gathers at a pub (or other suitable On In venue) and Down Downs are administered there. Ice is used only occasionally. The Hashit is a toilet plunger. After Down Downing a beer from it, the Hashers must carry the Hashit on every r*n until it is given to the next recipient. The worthy Hasher must embellish it suitably before handing it on.

But they did inherit some musicality from their Jakarta parent, albeit a strange mutation. "We're a singing Hash, we love karaoke bars," says King Shit. "Calgary does not have a Red Dress r*n, however we do have an annual Karaoke and Krossdressing r*n." They also have an annual Beer and Chilli Fart-a-rama, and celebrate everything else going from 'Rubbie Buns' Day to Grey Cup football, to themes such as gap-teeth hare r*ns.

One gets the feeling that these finely tuned athletes are really selling themselves short. Their shortest-ever Hash was laid by Dreary and Lakey: "We didn't quite make a full lap around the building that held the bar," says King Shit. "Yes, there was a check on trail, and I ran the falsie!"

Stuart 'On-In' Crichton is the only relic who was on the first CH3 r*n. Mike Carr now lives in Houston, Texas. Mike Manderson lives in Aberdeen,

Scotland. So badly affected were they by this madness, that neither of them Hash any longer.

Hashing outbreaks have now been detected by Health Authorities in at east 20 Canadian cities, despite some of the severest weather conditions on this planet.

"A lot of Hashes in the States, especially Texas, started in the early Eighties when Singapore went into recession," points out Hedges, himself a Hasher since '77 in Korea, the Philippines and Singapore before moving back to Dallas. Singapore was a major petroleum rig and refining centre. In mid-'87, in a period of just a few weeks, something in the order of 16 new kennels were added to the Hashing world.

Although a late starter, the USA now is the country that is home to the largest number of Hash kennels. Combined with Canada, North America is now home to about 550 kennels of errant hounds and sick puppies [If they'd just stand still for a minute, we could count them –ed.].

The Hash even reached Bermuda in 1986 in a way that testifies to how Hashers have infiltrated and white-anted all societies by now. Hooray Henry yearned to Hash again so ran a little classified ad in the local rag. Imagine his surprise when that little outing flushed ex-Hashers from Malaysia, the Middle East, the South Pacific, and even Scotland, out of the woodwork in Bermuda. The Hash has even reached Trinidad – the furthest geographic point away from its KL origins.

Kennel names that raise a chuckle on this continent include Blood, Sweat and Beers, Get a Life, On the Rag (women's kennel that only r*ns on the 28th of each month!), Pelvic Congestion, PMS, Puget Sound No Balls (women-only kennel), Rude Puss, Arizona Larrikins Mr Happy Pick Up Hash, Toontown (Saskatoon, Saskatchewan), Upper Bum Fuck, Rocket Shitty, Frozen Chosen (Anchorage, Alaska), Chapter 13 (runs 13th of each month), Gypsies in the Palace, Hot Dry Hump, Humpin', Vandenberg Village People Pickup Hash, Winers (Napa Valley), Damn It's Monday, Delawhere?, Corned Beef, Foo Foo Harriettes, Slow Old Bastards, Blooming Fools (Bloomington, Indiana), Lost in the Bush, Mad Anthony's Irregulars, Three Mile Island Nuclear Meltdown, Happy Heretics, Caribbean Liming Imbibing Touring (CLIT), South Bay Poofters, and the Prison Bitch H3 ("I work in a federal prison, and many of them are fellow co-workers, not inmates!" says Wet & Dry.)

A Howling Success.
Hashing in the USA has often been described as one big party, a frat ball in r*nning shorts. And much of the hard-core party aspect can be traced to the Full Moon Hashing movement, who truly put the 'r*n' in 'drunk'.

In one of those inspired moments, as simple as the invention of the paperclip, Mr Spock and Van Go claim to have come up with the idea of r*nning a Hash during the full moon. Voila – Full Moon Hashing. Dr Spock tells us how it came about way back in 1986: "Van Go and I were r*nning mostly San Diego H3 at the time. We ran Friday night and alternate Saturdays/Sundays.

It was family oriented with kids always there. Then we went to InterHash in Pattaya, Thailand, and were exposed to Hash singing and rowdiness, etc. It was great. Then we came home to the kids…"

Dr Spock moved temporarily from California to Washington DC and ran with adult-only kennels there, when Van Go called and asked him if he was interested in starting a group "to Hash more like in Asia". Does the Pope shit in the woods??? Do the Kennedy's have the funeral home on speed-dial???

"Of course!!!" said Dr Spock. What did he have in mind? Van Go had heard of a group that ran on special occasions only and thought to have it around the Full Moon, end in a bar and sing. So when Dr Spock came home on vacation their first outing was staged on October 19 1986 – attracting 56 Half Minds, mainly from SDH3 and La Jolla H3, starting out at the county administration building on the San Diego waterfront. "We had a downtown r*n ending in the Princess of Wales pub. Good beer, English food and singing. We were in a back room having drunk way too much and I was leading songs from atop a table. Even the employees liked it. I had on a '69' shirt from Little Rock H3. Never sang like that again, disappointingly."

And so they commandeered the Full Moon dates regularly. "We had it on the full moon for quite a while until San Diego got so many Hashes that one got their feelings hurt when we got too many of their usual attendees. So we moved to the nearest little-other-Hashed night. Saturday and Sunday were always fine because others Hashed in the morning, and two in one day was just right. Even three on special occasions," says the Hashing lunar-tic. The kennel became Full Moon H3 (FMH3).

R*ns were always 'A to B' to create uncertainty, taking in the city streets and alleys, and along the railroad track for a bit of dirt. And they had a strong viewpoint on the holy water. "We had been drinking cheap beer up to the Full Moon start. At FMH3 we encouraged finishing at places with better beer, and *usually* did. But some were recalcitrant and didn't get to hare without pre-approval." Dr Spock was the self-appointed Down Down Master and GM. And later he teamed up with Deep Throat to heap a never-ending torrent of abuse on the congregation. Visitors came and checked out the concept of running during a full moon, and liked it. The gospel spread. So now the kennel is known as the Original Full Moon H3.

Dr Spock puts its success down to several factors: Firstly, the hares had minimal responsibilities. "SDH3 r*ns were getting to 100 – too much for many to do food, beer, etc. There was also the novelty of their logos and shirt designs: All the first ones were black using glow-in-the-dark ink, "best seen upon arrival home in the head while peeing before turning on the lights". These they sold cheaply, always just up to the next dollar above cost. "At first we were collecting money for the Down Downs and to get our effort for America's InterHash seed money. When that was over we gave away stuff – shirts, hats, random free r*n, free beer. The unexpected. Never known until we showed up with something and the treasury was large enough."

Anniversary r*ns are always hared by the founders and usually start from the original County Authority building with a check at the Santa Fe Station, the rail depot, "with a million ways out and always a great check". After about five years, they noticed a new phenomenon appearing in their ranks: An exclusive Full Moon Hasher. "He was named PMS – Hashed only every 28 days."

So how does it now feel to be irresponsible for a worldwide empire of howling dogs? "There are FMH3s everywhere now. Even more than Red Dress r*ns," says Dr Spock. "It is fun. The founder of the First UK Full Moon Hash came over in the early Nineties. Brought me an English pint glass and gave me a Guinness Down Down with an egg. I finally made it to theirs, and bought a dozen eggs since you couldn't buy just one. Forgot them in the hotel, remembered on the train. Found a store walking to the start. Bought six more. Short-cut and got lost on the r*n. Went back to the start and drank while *they* held Down Downs out in the woods. Ma fello 'Mericans, did get my just due."

Apart from the Full Moon movement, the USA has also brought many other Half Minded notions to the Hashing world. Colorado has a rollerblade Hash, the Colorado Roller-Blade Asphalt Shiggy H3 – otherwise known as CRASH! Bike Hashing was also started in the US with Cape Anne Mountain Bike H3, in Massachusetts in 1988. Although it didn't last, the seed was planted from there, with more than 100 Bashes worldwide. Then, of course, most 'colourful' of them all, the syndrome which goes under the banner of Red Dress r*ns, of which more in the next chapter.

As far as character Hashes go, the States looms large with legends. But none larger (in their own minds) than Rumson H3, New Jersey. Kicked off in 1978 by ex-KL Hasher Keith Kanaga and Gil 'Mr Jackson' Jackson, it's one of very few men-only kennels in America. With the attitude and eye for trouble of a horny pit-bull spotting a perfectly-coiffed and perfumed poodle on the other side of the road.

"They are the most original, inventive, and fun-loving Hashers I've ever associated with," says Kanaga. "It's been a real thrill watching them evolve from a group of somewhat athletic middle-aged men into an elite corps of confirmed barflies who can't r*n more than 50 yards without stopping for a beer." Or perhaps something a little more potent – Rumson must be the only kennel that has regular *joint* r*ns on its own!

"The tag 'The Hells Angels of Hashing' came in after a Philly joint r*n and we trashed the place," explains Mr Jackson. "We have the reputation as Animal House – we started with middle-aged alcoholics, divorcees with drug problems and we did some shit. We used to go on bus trips but could never use the same bus company twice!"

One such occasion was their 50th in 1979. They chartered a bus to Bear Mountain State Park in northern New Jersey. "All of us exited the bus totally naked to the surprise of the many picnickers." Crazy Eddie, a United pilot, dived out an open window, not realizing it was on the second floor and was slightly injured. Another of their number stood on a chair holding a pitcher of beer, told some jokes, then threw the beer into a very large fan. "All were soaked. The bar owner, hearing the bedlam, tried to get into our room but we had bolted the door.

On the trip home someone ripped the toilet seat off the bus toilet and hung it over Kanaga's neck and proclaimed him 'asshole of the year'."

'SEXISM IN THE RUMSON HASH' was the headline in the Redbank Register, written by a female sports reporter who turned up but they refused to let her r*n because she wasn't a Hasher. "It was the best fuckin' thing that happened to us – great publicity," laughs Mr Jackson. "We allow visiting *bimbos* to r*n with us. We don't use the term Harriette. One said 'I'm not a bimbo!' and I said 'Well, you are to me!'

Rumson's pack sizes are pretty small, round about 10 or 15. "Obviously having no women cuts the pack size in half," concedes Elephant Dick, but they relish their notoriety and would rather hang onto it than compromise for survival. Their 500th r*n was a three-day, three-night piss-up with a solitary one hour r*n at the halfway mark of the long weekend!

Never short of an opinion, the Rumson Hash protested outside the Russian Consulate in New York after the '84 Gorky Park Hashing incident. Nearby was the Russian Tea Room café, and Elephant Dick paraded outside with a sign bedecked with beads which read, 'FREE RUSSIAN JEWELRY!'

They play up to their tag, with a skull and cross-bones logo, and black Hashing gear. Their average age is now about 55 "but show no signs of slowing". "We're all beginning to look alike!" jokes Chemical Mike, referring to the increasing greyness of hair and onset of Alzheimer's.

Ironically, given their advancing age and decrepit states, they've only lost one of their number on trail. "He was only 32, he was one of our youngest members and looked to be in great shape," says Jackson. "We were r*nning, he stopped, sat down, fell over and that was it. The irony is that our oldest guy is 80 and he's at the Hash every week."

And death nearly visited six of the Rumson pack in 1994, including Jackson and Crazy Eddie, the pilot. "He rented a plane to take us to a Pittsburgh Hash weekend. The engine gave out and he made an emergency landing. We just made it."

Then there was the animated blow-job by Nancy on Ronald Reagan in the rear window of Bobby Reid's car. And the time Lunar Don found a dead rat on the street at Inter-Americas '85 in Atlanta. It became the Rumson mascot for the weekend. At one point, the rat was tossed off the motel balcony into the central pool where families were among the frolickers. "We scheduled a rat race in the pool with competing Hash teams using the rat as a relay baton, but it never happened – we hid the rat at the beginning of the Sunday r*n because some of the more squeamish types wanted to get rid of it. Rumour has it that one of the many dogs at the r*n found it and did what dogs do to dead rats."

Another time, after a Hogtown Hash in 2000, six Rumsonites were leaving Toronto. "Elephant Dick set the drug sniffing dog into a frenzy," says Jackson. "They hustled him into a private room and the rest of us headed to the bar, expecting not to see him on our plane. As he tells it they told him to give him whatever he was carrying and if they found anything else he was in big trouble. He gave up his small stash of grass and they proceeded to go through his three carry-ons. You'd have to see what Elephant Dick brings to Hashes to believe it. They pulled out a blow-up sheep, handcuffs, dildos, bras with only one cup, a porcelain bulldog where he had extracted his stash from the asshole, and dozens of other bizarre items. No, he is not a sex addict, but these are his props from his world-famous skits. The final item was a cigarette lighter that they tried to light and a plastic dick popped up. The customs agent who tried it was a woman – until then they had been stony faced, but this cracked them up and they let him go and he made the flight."

Elephant Dick was involved in another airport drama leaving Amsterdam after a Hash event the following year. "He put his boots in the overhead locker and fell asleep," says Jackson. "The stewardess was closing the bin, noticed them and asked who they belonged to. He was five rows away and unconscious, so no one claimed them. They evacuated the plane and woke him up. He said they were his boots. Off the plane, interrogation, and the plane left two-and-a-half hours late."

And the laughs round the Rumson camp-fire keep coming with Elephant Dick. "When his bulldog died, he froze the body in a cryogenic chamber at his lab and brought it to the Hash lashed to a skateboard and pulling it on a leash." But readers will be spared details of his 'Perpetual Solo Butt Chug'[Boo! Hiss! We want our money back! –ed.].

Rumson bid for the Inter-Americas every time, with brilliantly prepared and highly amusing presentations, but have never won (and likely never will according to some). Chemical Mike feels they *might* win it one day … but then forget!

Kanaga sums it up: "R*nning with Rumson is like being in a David Lynch movie. It all looks harmless enough, until something happens."

Unbridled Hedonism.
While not a kennel, the ultimate, extreme, debauched Hashing fun – outside of Rumson – can be found at Camp Hedon, an annual camp-out on Memorial Day.

According to Head Nurse, Atlanta's 200th (Year Zero) is what got this started. "It was in March and cold, but they had so much fun that Erection Master decided to have a camp-out the next year on Memorial Day, 1985. It was training for Inter-Am, that's the year Atlanta hosted it."

The master of ceremony is Erection Master, who lords over the weekend of trails on his property (somewhere in Atlanta), and has developed cult status over the years.

"He is known for getting around the party in various ways," say Head Nurse. "He has mounted a full-sized lawn umbrella on his ride-on lawn mower and travelled place to place on it. He has also been carried in his hammock with a sun-shade over it to a better site for watching Izzy Dizzy. The king in his domain. His newest addition is his Bimbo-mobile. It's a four-person golf cart with a flat bed. This thing can probably hold 10 to 12 easy. He wants to fill it with topless babes and ride around the property. I'm sure he won't have a problem getting volunteers for the ride."

About 200 sweaty, smelly drunks are usually in attendance for the three-day camp-out. In the past, they've had a number of virgins and weak-hearted Hashers check out after the first night because they were horrified at the depravity, which comes free of charge with the registration fee.

One of the main attractions of the weekend is the Hedon Olympics, also known as Izzy Dizzy, " a drunken, dizzy, muddy r*nning challenge of teams". Six members in each team r*n across the "yard" for about 75 yards after drinking a full beer (well, that plus all the other hecta-litres already down your throat in the course of the weekend), spin around a baseball bat 10 times and then r*n back. The aim is to do all of these things without falling down, r*nning off course, or barfing. Many Camp Hedon survivors come back home with a new name, acquired in dubious and inescapable circumstances which are commonplace over the weekend. Just ask Face Plant Puke Princess!

Bitchin' and Barkin'.

Ed, a bus driver in Austin, Texas, for the Inter-Americas was driving the boisterous hounds to a r*n one day, when his mobile phone rang. "Man, I'm doing this Hashers weekend," the Vietnam veteran told his friend on the other end of the line. "To say these guys are wild is like saying a jalapeno is just another tasty pepper!"

And many would echo the sentiment that the Americans are indeed the wildest, loudest, roughest, toughest Hashers in the known universe. And that Hashing in America is, well, somehow different. "I know what you mean about Americans but it's not a thing I can quantify," says Gunga Dick, possibly the first American Hasher, who has been an expatriate for most of his life before settling in England.

She Mussel Bitch, GM of Austin says: "American Hash culture tends to focus on things like nudity and being really drunk and disgusting … I guess because those are the things that aren't really accepted here. It's not good or bad, just different."

In recent research by Public Agenda, 79 per cent of American adults said a lack of respect and courtesy in American society was a serious problem. Sixty-one per cent believe things have got worse in recent years. Many people admitted to rude behaviour themselves. More than a third said they used foul language in public.

Pearl Necklace from New York agrees: "Sometimes, things are so rude they're ridiculous," she says, adding that she's not offended. "You don't have to do it, but you've got to be prepared to see stuff on the Hash that you wouldn't ordinarily see," says Hasher Humper from White House H3. Does any of this sort of thing offend Womb With a View, a Harriette from Houston? "No, *I'm* usually the one they're talking about the next morning," she says, laughing. She had moved to Houston and was thinking of moving back to Dallas "until I met the Hash". A boyfriend had invited her to a Hashing away weekend with his 'r*nning club' … she turned up sceptically but ended up enjoying it immensely.

"I find US Hashers strange," says Kojak who has lived and Hashed extensively in Asia and Africa and is now back in Florida. "All this nakedness and debauchery – not that it bothers me – gets a bit much sometimes, especially if it's week after week," says the one-time Thailand Dirt Roader. The Great Kahuna, a Hashman of similar vintage agrees: "In the States nudity's become a big thing on Hash – not that I think it adds a whole lot, personally. Down in Trinidad public nudity is not something that's widely accepted so they were really worried about telling people how to do that, because they don't really approve of nudity in Trinidad … and everyone had a great time without that."

As an example of institutional nudism, a 'No Tan Lines' Hash was held as part of a bigger 'Bare as You Dare' festival in Decatur, Texas. Also the Camp Hedon weekend is legendary for its Bacchanalian romps. Spokane H3, Washington, take advantage of a naked fun r*n in their area each year in which about 80 Hashers take part. And South Bay H3, California, used to pride itself on its naked women and hot tub parties.

Doug 'Psycho' Stevens from Little Rock H3 was a doctor of psychology. "He couldn't help but analyse the Hash chapters he met," says Blowjob. "He said Hash kennels could be divided into three types: r*nning clubs, mating clubs, and bonding clubs. The r*nning clubs seemed more interested in competition and showing off how far and how fast they can r*n. The mating clubs are usually young, and are mostly interested in competing for bedding each other down. Needless to say, there is usually a lot of in-squabbling in these Hashes. As an older Hash, the Little Rock Hash is a bonding Hash. Although we do have some younger Hashers, the average age is probably over 40, and although most are divorced or unmarried, there is very little competition for males or females. People mostly just want to r*n and party with their friends."

For all that, Ear of the Sperm, a Harriette from Columbus, Ohio, says: "No matter what Hash you go to you know what kind of people to expect – it's not a surprise. Although there *is* a lot of surprise at the Hash!"

"If you're talking to a Hasher, you don't need to explain your addiction," says Himalaya of Hockessin H3 about the mystique of Hashing. "What is wonderful about it, and what is something of a unique Hash phenomenon, is the total, unquestioning acceptance that Hashers have for each other … the degree of harmony that seems to have become one of the major characteristics of our remarkably inclusive society. One of the really delightful things about Hashing is the chance it affords us to react to the smothering effect of political and social 'correctness'. To be a rebel. To leave, temporarily, our sheltered structures and directed work-a-day lives that are so filled with expectations and responsibilities."

Mitey Tite of Baltimore-Annapolis H3[13] agrees. "When you think about it, Hashing does embody the best of the human spirit. It exists all over the world because it stands for a free way of life and rejects narrow-minded beliefs that lead to hatred. Yes, it seems trivial to say we are men and women who drink beer and r*n, sing silly songs, and laugh about things that endear us to each other. But we are also brothers and sisters in the Hash. We r*n, drink and laugh with anyone, from any place in the world, who wants to share the camaraderie of the trail and the humour of the circle regardless of nationality or religion."

This becomes particularly apposite in the wake of September 11. "We'll win because we're free to Hash!" said Flying Booger[41] of the events that struck at the very heart of American society. "I hope that doesn't sound trivial to you. The Hash embodies the freedoms we cherish. Think about it. Would the Taliban allow Hashing? Is there a Hash in the Sudan? In North Korea? Have you noticed all the people wearing red, white, and blue lapel ribbons? Wear your On On Feet, Hashers!"

So how does Hashing fit into American society? Sociologically, most Americans consider themselves middle class. "Middle class implies that they work for a living and do not depend on either welfare or inherited millions," according to Calhoun, Light and Keller[100]. As sociologists, though, they're not happy with everyone being content with who they are and where they're at, so of course they break the middle class down into five distinct groups based on wealth (ie, what people own), income (how much they earn from outside sources) and occupational characteristics (how much esteem or approval people garner from their occupation). These wankers rate sociologists as one of the high-ranking occupations so you know they're immediately talking through their r*nning shorts and should never be allowed anywhere near a Hash site.

Hasher Humper embraces the egalitarianism of the Hash. "Nobody cares what you do and who you are – you could be on welfare or a rocket scientist. Eventually it might come out, but it's not all like business cards and networking." Two people who definitely don't pull out their business cards on the Hash are Golden Eagle and her husband Hunka Hunka Burning Shit from Las Vegas H3. "We're both teachers so all day you've got to mind your Ps and Qs," she explained as her attraction to the Hash as an outlet. She once did a Red Dress r*n in Vegas itself. "God, I hope my students don't recognise me," she remembers feeling at the time. Interestingly the Vegas kennel r*ns twice a week to cater for the many hospitality and shift workers who don't work a normal Monday-to-Friday nine-to-five job.

Comparing Hashing Stateside to elsewhere, Flying Booger weighs in with his two cents worth: "I've noticed that most of the British/Aussie/Kiwi expat Hashers I've met around the Pacific Rim are far more conservative in their behaviour than American Hashers." LCB also picked up on the difference: " Hashing in the US and Hashing in Asia are very different … over there it always seems to end at a whorehouse whereas here we try and pick up the loose women before the end of the Down Downs," he says, laughing. He gives an example of when he guested in Malacca, Malaysia, and the guys kept on trying to line him up with a local prostitute. But for Birdman from Colorado, his overseas experiences were different: "I enjoyed Malaysia the most … the back to basics thing is often the best … a nice r*n out in the jungle, a meal out in the middle of nowhere, and drinking with the Chinese and you can't understand a word they're saying!"

An observation many would make about America is that, with the exception of die-hard traditional chapters such as DC Men's, Rumson and Puget Sound, the chapters are all mixed, with a strong social emphasis and party culture. "It's a dating club ... a social club," says LCB of the Hash. "The self-selection is good – if a girl doesn't like a bit of nudity and profanity she wouldn't be there."

As a dating or mating club, the Hash should fare well. The Social Issues Research Centre in Britain has concluded that "a person looking to flirt is better off avoiding high-fliers and should seek out clubs full of happy, sociable under-achievers."[105] Hashmen pursuing this cupid-like course should take particular note of another study, of American women this time, who were asked which three magical words they would most like to hear from a male partner. "You've lost weight" was the most popular response!

"Most of the Hashers I know are losers," says Rumson's Mr Jackson. "They have no friends, never get fucked, and think: If I have no friends in the real world maybe I can have friends here." One of the big benefits he sees in men-only chapters is that it's a lot easier to get out of the house on a Saturday "to r*n with your mates than with a bunch of bimbos". For the record, he's married with "a lovely wife". But the tough man obviously doesn't wear the Hash shorts at home. "I get four sleepovers a year to attend Hash events," he admits.

Groper of Spokane says: "There is a friction or resentment towards men-only chapters," citing Puget Sound Men's as an example. "It's tradition more than anything," says Gympy, visiting Inter-Americas from Japan. "It's Monday night, it's men only."

Interestingly, in the American context, one Hasher made a comment in passing about men-only Hash being "gay Hash". Funnily enough, though, the only blatant transgressions of Rule #6 seem to come from mixed kennels. High Beams, a Texan blonde says: "They say that Austin Harriettes are only two beers away from being lesbians. I usually stop at one-and-a-half," she jokes. Also, at the glittering Miss Inter-Am contest in Austin, one of the contestants, Cream of Meat, was noticeably, well, different. "*She* had a dick at the last Inter-Am," explained a bystander, helpfully.

For all that, though, American Hashing generally has more testosterone on show than any other continent. Prof Graeme Turner of Monash University in Melbourne, Australia, made an observation which might explain this phenomenon partially: "The American series of Big Brother was driven by conflict and people taking each other apart. In Australia the same experiment produced people who acted as if they belonged in a family."[105] Another more plausible reason might be that the Hashes are younger and fitter, and peopled in many kennels with rank-and-file military types and commandos.

"Over the Hump H3 is full of marines," says Captain Titanic. "They're young and stupid and set trails that I consider dangerous – like a trail across a dam wall which is slick with algae ... I just won't do it. I've also seen every tunnel on the I-95 from Washington to Richmond," he complains. That kennel also r*ns twice a week, every week.

LCB is a good example of how military guys get recruited into the Hashing ranks. He started Hashing when with the military in Hawaii. "Guys stationed in Germany and Korea get exposed to Hashing and bring it back with them," he explains. One such person is Long & Hard from Fort Eustis, who highlights the competitive difference. "The trails I ran in Korea were a combination of live and dead hare trails, that is, the hares left with a 15-minute head start, but it was OK to pre-set certain parts of the trail."[42] He found Fort Eustis a bit of a rude shock. "It was a three-minute head start for a normal pack of about 20. You got an extra 30 [seconds] for every five people over 20 that were at the Hash."

And it's not just limited to military kennels or the USA. Pure Genius, whose sister winkle has Hashed in Thailand, Burma and now Canada, guested on a r*n with Vancouver. "They were very young," says the English Harriette, "and they took the r*nning part very seriously and it wasn't quite the same piss-up."

Still, there's no avoiding it. Hashing in America started with the military, and with 1.3 million actively serving in the US Armed Forces, and a further 1.3 million reserves, that's a big potential recruiting pool. But, again, is the spontaneous disorganised nature of the Hash paradoxical given the amount of military personnel (past and present) in it? "Perhaps there's a direct connection ... one that we have experienced but don't recognise," says Captain Zero.

Strangely, and ironically given the gregarious party culture of the US, the legal drinking age is 21. At 18 you can vote for your President and go and fight, and even die, for your country, but you're deemed too young to drink beer.

On the matter of recruitment and replenishing the Hashing ranks, Lofty from Perth – whose partner is Yo Adrian from Little Rock – believes the Americans have been smart. "They're expanding themselves to accommodate the younger set. In Australia, the young guns of yesterday are no longer young, and we don't have new young guns coming through. We've got a problem with ageing ... because we're so traditionalist. This is not Hashing as *I* know it over here," he said surveying a hotel pool full of pumped young things in Austin, Texas. "But it's fun!"

"These days you're surrounded by 25-year-olds," says long-time White House Hasher, Spinal Tap, "and they just wanna mix with other 25-year-olds. When you start a song they just scowl at you," he says.

Martha Fucking Stewart explains why San Diego is like the Bandung of America when it comes to the avid Hashing population: "Check the weather and it will usually be 70 degrees [Fahrenheit] and sunny. It's impossible to stay indoors. Then add all the military bases in the area and the former military people who stayed. Then add the colleges. There are about 13 local Hashes that cover every day of the week, except Thursday. Unless there's a full moon. When the monthly Porter's Pub Hashes on Tuesday and the Full Moon is on Thursday, we have something called Get a Life Week. During Get a Life Week you can Hash 13 days in a row!" He talks of so much cross-over between kennels that people just talk of 'San Diego' usually instead of specific kennels, and kennels which r*n the same night will often share a trail.

Some kennels face the opposite problem. "It seems impossible to get more than one or two undergraduates to r*n with us – they are much too serious," says Geezer of Princeton of the new generation in his area. Still, it's good to hear of some recruitment based on good old-fashioned values, such as Birdman from Colorado. "I used to r*n with Houston Orienteering who taught meaningful skills and values such as teambuilding and so on. They couldn't understand that I would always come in first or second and then get out the beer. Not a good example for our youth. Then this guy pulled me aside and said 'You'd like Hashing'. I've since notched up over 800 r*ns in 15 countries including Costa Rica, Germany, Malaysia and Mongolia."

And anyone fearing that Hashing might be a single-generation event should be heartened by Dark Tanyon's tale, which has a bit of a twist. He has been Hashing since 1985 and has introduced his *parents* to the Hash. "Dad's now like 80 years old," he says. "They just like hanging out with the younger folks because all their friends are like … [He imitates an old man creaking down the road with a stooped back]. They have Hashed KL, Bali, China and a few other places," he says proudly.

But Cock Pit from Albuquerque doesn't have quite the same wavelength with his parents: "My parents think I'm a freak, an alcoholic. 'You're going *where* to drink beer this time???' Then I tell 'em there'll be people from England, Singapore…," he laughs.

For all the success of infesting the New World with the dreaded Hash bacteria, South America has proved to be a more resistant host. Like France and Ireland, Hashing has taken root but never really flowered. South Americans are a passionate lot, especially about sport. This was best demonstrated by El Salvador and Honduras literally going to war over their World Cup Soccer qualifying games in 1969. No one remembers the final game's score – but, in the end, 150 cars were burnt, 6,000 people were killed, and their respective air forces bombed the shit out of each others' strategic targets for the next 100 hours. That, folks, is passion! Now, if we can just channel that energy into a bit of a r*n and a circle …

"We diminished in participation when the Americans left Panama, but now we are growing back and have almost caught up with our previous levels of participation," says Rompy of Panama. "We are a bit short of expats who are participating right now. We have an Australian, a couple of Americans, a Dutch, and some Colombians. The Hash is not wildly popular, but there are no barriers *per se* – we just have a bunch of lazy asses."

Prego of Mexico City H3 uses a bit of velvet lining to cushion his glove: "Mexicans are not of a volunteer spirit. They just won't volunteer for the most part, to expose themselves or their money to hare a Hash. That is why we have had to cut down on the number of r*ns from every other Saturday to only one Saturday afternoon a month – lack of hares. So, it's always the same ones doing the work organising and haring. Which also stops the flow of new things and freshness to the group. This Hash is very, very social and love to party yet low in the 'r*nning' department. It's almost all walkers and wimps." The pack usually consists of around 40, split evenly between locals and expats, a good amount of whom are Diplomatic Corps on two-year postings. "This is a very Catholic and family-oriented country and that makes Hashing not for everyone. The biggest turnover is in the new boot department. Many come once or twice thinking that it's a way to practise English or meet a foreign partner, get disillusioned, and then don't return. This pushes the pack to usually be a very easy and subdued group. Rarely is there any nudity or sexual behaviour." [Well, cross that off my list then –ed.]

Bermuda Shorts is a Costa Rican national who's been Hashing more than 15 years. "On average we have say 35 to 40 r*nners, with the mix about 50/50 expats and Costa Ricans." He was incredulous when told about men-only Hashes in Asia and Australia. "So macho!" he says, but says that format wouldn't work or appeal in South and Central America. "We like to have the mixed one," he says, winking.

Chile is, as her name suggests, from Chile. Currently the GM of the Philadelphia H3 she had never Hashed in South America before moving to the States in '91. "I met a Hasher who introduced me to it," she said. She thought they would be uptight as a group, but her first impression was that she loved it. "Very close to my culture," she says. "Warm, open, laid-back, humorous. They tell each other jokes and really nasty stuff and people take it for what it is – fun." One thing she has noticed is that people are treated equally, a Hasher is a Hasher. "You can find valuable human beings and develop good friendships from there." But what of Hashing in Chile? "I'd *heard* of it in Chile, but with family commitments and friends, my time was so little so I never did it. It seems to be more of a family thing there," she thinks. "The drinking and socialising wouldn't be a problem, but geographically it costs people a lot more money to get around (from there) to Inter-events. Also, people don't get visas easily, especially to USA, Canada and Europe. If people don't travel much, they're happy just to go to Brazil or Mexico where they won't be denied," she says, dashing hopes of a flood of Latina Harriettes on the worldwide market.

Spanish Fly is a Venezuelan-born Harriette, now living in England, who has been Hashing for about two years. "We knew about the Hash living in Caracas from this person with the Foreign Office. She was a very conservative, church-going type. A good friend helped her settle in. Every Sunday she had something to do – and what she did was this thing called the Hash. But everybody that we ran into that did that was British. So I associated it with being a British expat thing." So she never ran in Venezuela herself? "No, never, because that was something British expats did. I didn't know it was an international thing ... so when I came here [Britain] it was an Australian friend of mine who mentioned the Hash and I said 'Well I've heard of that but I was surprised that it happened *here* because I thought it was only expats, so then I thought it's expat returnees that are kind of bonding over that experience they've had overseas. I started because it was in my neighbourhood." Have her friends back home got into Hashing now? "I told them about it very reluctantly, and I'm really not sure what they think about it. Because their impression is much the same – they never ran and to them it's a bunch of beer-swilling Brits that go from one place to another. They appreciate a social, and they're familiar with the expat community…" She doesn't think it has anything to do with feelings of Catholic guilt. "Not at all," she says, adding that her parents do a lot of entertaining of the expat community themselves. "They're just not too sure what it's all about, and I don't know what else they've heard about it quite honestly that they didn't share with me when I was younger. So when I say I went on a Hash r*n they know I'm having fun but they're kind of a little bit … you wouldn't catch them on it." So how to expand the Hash in South America? "If I was to pick up in Caracas I suspect it's still very much expat, and very much British. Maybe there are Americans in it, I really don't know. But the Venezuelans? Culturally, women and drink is quite socially unacceptable for women to be considered equal in terms of alcohol consumption and even, in some cases, in terms of physical activity. My friends that I grew up with, OK we're all outdoorsy, but the guys are always stronger, more macho…" She feels it is a patriarchal society. "The whole macho side of drinking – ladies don't do that." So in that case, wouldn't the combination of physical exertion and drinking suit the South American *men* well then? "There's the drinking side, then there's all the other stuff that goes on … the crudeness and all that which, I have to say, is offensive. I'm open-minded, it cracks me up, but it'll take many years if, and ever, I get to the state I'm not prudish. In Latin America, guys behaving that way in front of ladies … it would be unlikely that a mixed Hash – which the expats do – would probably take off. They might think crude thoughts and do all that, but they won't necessarily voice them. And they probably won't fart in front of each other either after a certain age," she laughs. "It would be slightly different – the guys would drink rum, probably get quite drunk, loud, talk a lot of politics, some sex I'm guessing … I mean I'm not a man and I'm not part of their private conversations so I don't know how crude they get, but I suspect it's not that crude in the educated parts of the Latin society. And a single-sex Hash for ladies, r*nning and doing their thing with maybe juice and some wine … would probably work."

Bolivia and La Paz are two places where the Hash attracts good numbers, with expats in the minority. "La Paz is down on numbers as the city is so small with not much of an expat core," says Stool Sample. "Lima has a big group (usually 50 to 70), but oddly mostly Peruvians without much knowledge of the world order of doing things. But, the group have fun."

The problems in Brazil, according to Konkorde, are different. "I would say that Brazilians don't like to get dirty and are a bit more reserved when it comes to 'lowering' their status on the Hash – must be the macho streak." Having Hashed for over a decade in Indonesia, he points out that the culture in Brazil is very different. "There is far more leisure activity here so people have planned their Saturday afternoons for soccer or the day at the beach."

Perhaps Hashing would take off in South America if all these places were like the tiny island of Montserrat, near Antigua in the Caribbean. "There's not a lot to do on the island, that's one of the reasons the Hash has gained popularity quickly. We don't even have an airport, having to rely on a ferry and occasional helicopter to get to the nearest island," says Papa Smurf who did his Hashing in Poland before.

Spread 'em!

The kill-joy attitude of law enforcement officers, park rangers and do-gooders in the community has often rained on the Hash's parade in the so-called Land of the Free. Mostly it's benign, but every so often seems a little heavy-handed and out of proportion to the nature of the behaviour and the perceived problem.

At Fort Eustis, Virginia, in the early stages Hashmen had to be careful about drinking in public. Not that this put them off completely. "We had clip-on covers indicating that we were drinking cola!" says Mountain Rescue, smugly. "No overdoing the beer consumption, but barbecues crept into the equation," he says of the early Eighties. Today in the area of the peninsula which includes Hampton, Newport News, Williamsburg and York County, Preparation H feels they don't have a continuing problem with police. "But we do seem to be on the bad side of the park rangers at Newport News park. Seems they don't like us drinking beer in their park, and they *really* don't like us r*nning around in the woods after dark. The last time I laid trail into the park (in the daylight), several of them roared up in their vehicles and threatened to haul us off to jail. It took a few moments to ferret out the root of the problem. We continue to r*n freely in the more remote areas of the park, but we limit our presence in the picnic areas and particularly in the campground."

Following September 11 and the anthrax scares, Fort Eustis tried to appease the authorities and the local community by laying trail with substances other than flour. "We tried birdseed (hard to see), cheese puffs (birds ate them as fast as we laid them), popcorn (same bird problem), and breakfast cereals (some hard to see, some the birds and squirrels ate)," he says. "One of our major backsliders, Works for Sex, is still employed by the Hampton police department. We r*n in Hampton on Tuesdays and when he'd get a call he'd call our hotline to see where we were r*nning. If we were in the area of the call, he'd explain to the caller just what it was we were spreading about. The Saturday r*ns we were able to move out of the more densely populated areas and circumvent the problem."

When Hashing came to Washington, DC, in 1972, it was easy to be clandestine due to small pack sizes. "Our numbers were sufficiently small at the beginning and we could safely congregate for our On Ons by the roadside or in state parks with little risk of attracting police attention," recalls Tumbling Bill. In fact, the pack at that stage could usually "retreat into a medium-size station wagon. It took about two years for us to mature to the extent that our numbers were such that public drinking immediately attracted hostile attention from the state troopers, and basements became the regular On On rendezvous."

"We don't really have very many problems with police," says Duckjob from White House, of the situation today. "Unless we pick a bad spot for the circle and get complaints from residents. Even though DC has open container laws (no drinking in public), if the police do show up, they usually give us a few minutes to finish up the circle and clean up after ourselves."

At Little Rock, a guest reports he was enjoying the On On. Next thing a police car pulled up with lights flashing, and the tannoy blaring, "People of the Hash … put your drugs down and hands in the air!" He immediately soiled his Hash shorts, turning to see the cause of the commotion. They repeated the message, sternly. However, it all turned out well – the local cop was a Hasher!

In New York (Westchester), the problems are with residents rather than the law. A r*n in Croton featured a quick access to the power line and surrounding woods through a residential backyard. "In response to the irate landowner's interrogation, all r*nners referred him to the guy at the back. When the last hound panted up he was adamant that the organiser was way up in front," remembers Ian Cumming[74]. "There came a later time in North Salem when a particularly vociferous horn-blowing pack took off up a residential lane on a Sunday afternoon. A home-owner, disturbed from his post-prandial nap, or crap, came out to the garden gate and yelled: "What's the matter with you bastards – if you have to communicate between the front and the back, why don't you use walkie-talkies like everybody else!'" says Cumming.

Princeton seems to be never far from a scrap with the law, for reasons usually of their own making. A Joy to His Mother talks about Hard Core V, an annual ball-breaker event, held in Rocky Hill, New Jersey[74]: "Instead of following the unobtrusive trail through the tunnel, about 4,000 Hashers decided to attract the attention of The Man by going in the front gate of the quarry, despite the prominent sign reading 'Closed on Thanksgiving'. They had apparently never heard of a quarry being closed on Thanksgiving before so, with tears in their eyes, they climbed right over the barbed wire fence, leaving behind their VW Microbus with all of the trash in it. Not five minutes after, the Bad Guys showed up. While Wacko distracted them, I sauntered down the road, on trail, and zipped into the quarry." Looking back now, he can afford to laugh about it, but it wasn't so funny at the time. "I want to tell you about the town of Rocky Hill, where this happened. They've got three stop signs, two police officers, and one police car, but when we got to the 'Scene of the Crime', there were five police officers and three police cars, bein' the biggest crime of the last 50 years, and everybody wanted to get in the newspaper story about it. And they was usin' up all kinds of cop equipment that they had hangin' around the police station. They was takin' plaster tyre tracks, footprints, dog-smellin' prints, and they took 27 8x10 colour glossy photographs with circles and arrows and a paragraph on the back of each one explaining what each one was, to be used as evidence against us. Took pictures of the approach, the getaway, the north-west corner, the south-west corner, and that's not to mention the aerial photography." About half a dozen managed to make a break for it before the cops arrived and finished the trail, but the day was already over and it fizzled out. "It was I who was abandoned by the entire Hash pack," says Wacko, "as I was tracked down like a dog by the shotgun-wielding posse of two at the quarry (they didn't catch me) – suffice it to say they still throw darts at the photo they took of me."

Sometimes they r*n into so much legal shiggy they have to dedicate a name to that year. 1995 is the year they called 'YOMAMA' – The Year of Many Angry and Malicious Assholes. It started off on a bad footing on the very first r*n of the year when "Farmer Brown and the Ratchild" blazed away at them across a cornfield, fortunately missing the pack. The very next week, Wacko was apprehended in his van on the way to the start. He subsequently got to do community service for his sins. "Cablecop, Ctec's finest security patrol" then swung into action on a hapless hound, 242, who was inexplicably in a dumpster yelling, "Where's the beer? Where's the beer?" A few r*ns later saw the appearance of "Fred and Frederika the Huns, staunch defenders of the Wilderness Aryan Nation, and of Property Rights in general". A large contingent of New Jersey coppers turned up and broke up the *apres*. Then it was the turn of "Clem and his pit bull", as well as three squad cars chock full of New Jersey's finest. A few r*ns later, enter "Red Shirt, a foul-mouthed homeowner in Ewing Township", who ambitiously and optimistically ordered the Hash to wait quietly while he summoned the SWAT squad from Ewing Cop Central. "Ole Red gets the all time award for worst language ever heard on a PH3 r*n." It wasn't too long after this encounter that they found themselves "sensitively interacting with an Ecovigilante" at the Audubon Center. "He did a fine job of educating us as to the evils of beer". One of their last r*ns of what had, admittedly, been a very long year, had them shooed away from the start by "Jackbooted Thug Guards at the NJ Home for the Terminally Befuddled", and then chased by an incensed homeowner in a van as the pack crossed a stream close to his border.

They are now a little more prepared to deal with such humourless wankers in an organised and systematic manner. "We have a longstanding tradition in Princeton of silencing irate homeowners by informing them that 'Mr Barker said it was okay (to trespass)'," says Wacko. "This originates from an apocryphal event when our GM's son, Son of Geezer, claimed that a barking dog had given us permission to r*n through someone's yard."

"We finally had an opportunity to invoke Mr Barker's name legitimately when we followed a trail that finished in the Frick Chemistry Laboratory at Princeton," says Ouipee. "We passed the office, or maybe closet, of 'M. Barker, Facilities', en route to the On-In at the bottom of a stairwell. Morons and drunkards that we are, no one was sensible enough to tell the security guard who busted us, well into the second case of beer, that 'Mr Barker said it was okay'."

Carolina H3 had finished their r*n one day when a policeman pulled up to enquire what they were doing. "Seems one of the local old ladies had made a call about some kind of 'controlled substance' that was laying all over the streets of her neighbourhood," said Nabob. When they told him it was flour, the policeman laughed uncontrollably. He relayed this to the old lady, who still insisted the law enforcer do an on-the-spot 'field test' of the substance with hysterical results. This was before anthrax scares took powdery substances to a whole new level of perceived threat.

In the Boynton Beach area, the hare was laying his flour trail, which apparently "frightened several families in the park enough to notify the Sheriff's Office of the suspicious substance" according to a policeman at the scene[102]. Soon enough, the Fire Rescue department was scrambled and begun testing for traces of anthrax. Numerous units of police cars and a police helicopter followed the trail to find out who was responsible. More than two hours later they had their answer, much to the policemen's frustration.

In Lake Oswego, a month after September 11, a similar incident occurred, a motorist spotting the suspicious trail which ran slap-bang through the area's business district. People were told to stay at home, or in their offices. A section of Highway 43 was closed for a couple of hours while tests were conducted on the trail, and traffic re-routed.

Annapolis H3 generally report a "high frequency of r*n-ins with police, security guards and irate property owners." Amazon.cum, from Baltimore-Annapolis H3, says: "After the anthrax panic we were forced to start using chalk in all populated areas. So I was setting trail and part of the trail ran in front of the police station. Naturally I used chalk. Unfortunately, I attracted some attention from a cop who then followed me into the woods to find out what I was doing. When he caught up to me, I was at the bottom of a large, very steep cliff-face heading deep into the woods and he was at the top, telling me that was city property and I shouldn't be there. I talked him into letting me 'r*n through' to the other side and he agreed. However, when he turned round to walk out of the woods, he spotted some fresh clumps of anthrax-looking flour, and got hysterical. He r*ns back to the station and puts out an APB [All Points Bulletin] for me, though I was long gone by that time. Then the quarantines go up, the HazMat team is deployed and the FBI and bomb squad is called. By the time my Hash starts at 7pm, almost every Hasher who was able to make it to that point was stopped and questioned about a 'tall, gangly female in r*nning clothes throwing down a white powdery substance in the forest.' No, they never caught me."

That group has also had citations to appear in court from rangers on two violations: Failure to obtain a group permit and littering. "The littering charge was because of the flour used to mark the trail."

The drink driving regulations in Dallas in the late Eighties began to make Hashers paranoid to the point where it was suggested that beer stops were limited to one per r*n. They also reiterated – in the best arse-covering litigation-fearing way – that Down Downs were completely optional. As an alternative to a Down Down, miscreants could opt for the 'shampoo' route instead, ie, pouring the beer over their head.

In Philadelphia, a major Republican presidential convention was being held, so of course a Red Dress r*n was set around the very building in which the convention was being held. The Hash was accompanied by motorcycle police the whole way – paranoid, agitated, and spoiling for a fight. The back-sweeper was marking the checks on his own when he got arrested and told that as a security precaution no one was to be released until Saturday. It was then only Tuesday. He's now suing the city, with the help of three lawyers in his Philly kennel.

Big Gulp of Dallas/Fort Worth recalls: "Some time in the early Nineties for a Mardi Gras celebration Hash, one of the two hares happened to be in the military (and was sporting quite a short haircut) and the other was a bit older and balding. The trail was laid in the south side ('bad part') of town, and the locals called the police saying skin heads/white supremacists were making marks with a white powdery substance which was obviously a hate crime. It made the front page of the Metro section of the Sunday Dallas Morning News (and the retraction article the next day made something like page 17)."

Other than that, they report not much trouble with the authorities. Except for their On the Rag women's kennel, on which they occasionally let the guys r*n with them, provided the guys wear a dress. "During this Hash, one Hasher decided to moon the Dallas Area Rapid Transit (DART) light rail train," says Big Gulp. "There was a transit cop on the train and he found the circle and easily identified the guy in a red dress and matching bonnet and took him to the local jail. (He didn't even let the guy change his clothes.) At first the police at the station thought it was the neighbouring station playing a prank on them, but finally processed him. They put him in a cell until his girlfriend showed up to bail him out. There was a regular resident of the front cell, and the police asked the regular if he wanted a roommate or should he to go to general lockup. He took one look at the Hasher in a red dress, grabbed his blanket and said, 'general lockup'."

Tampon Drizzle from Minneapolis feels they have good relations with the cops in the area. "Most of our group is over 30, so when they see us drinking in the park, they usually don't bother to stop like they might with younger people. The times they have, we've just been asked what we're doing, and most cops seem to like the idea," he says.

Shiggy Bob concurs: "There are no military bases here, so we are an old, out-of-shape, middle-class type Hash who rarely do anything stupid enough to r*n afoul of the law. I have been stopped and questioned twice on the same trail by police from two separate municipalities assuming I was dropping arsenic on the ground to poison pets, but apparently I check out OK."

Portland H3 once (OK, often) earned the ire of the law. But back in the summer of '88 they had a memorable full moon r*n which turned into a r*n-in with the authorities. Down Downs were being held around a makeshift campfire made of road flares. This became a raging bonfire in a suburban area, with shops and a bar nearby. Soon enough, the local police turned up and ordered them to put out the fire hazard. They started to wrap things up in the traditional manner – with a version of Swing Low. Halfway through, a second police car turned up. Plus a whole lot of curious onlookers from the neighbourhood and bar. Next thing, sirens blaring … and two fire trucks and a paramedic vehicle come screeching to a halt. They managed to complete the whole song before they were seen off the premises.

Ranger Dick from Maryland wasn't so lucky: "I was setting the Wide Spot in the Dirt Road Hash about four years ago. I showed up to set trail around 5pm. As it was February it was already dark and about 25 degrees Fahrenheit. Off I go with about 10 pounds of flour (4kg for you metric folks) and two beers. Somehow, I miss a turn and end up stuck on the edge of a cliff, so finished setting trail around 7.30pm, and there's one injured Hasher milling around waiting for me to return so he can drink. I put my gear in the boot, pop a beer for both of us, and start getting ready for the wankers to arrive. Suddenly there are lights everywhere and a siren. 'Put your hands on your head. Put the beer down', the voice says. A park ranger comes up to us and asks for identification. He looks at my comrade's, then looks at mine. A smile comes to his face. 'Oh, Mr Zipper, we meet again', he said. Apparently this was the park ranger who had attempted to fine me two years previous. Fortunately for me I wasn't on parkland at that time. Unfortunately for me I was on parkland now. 'Is this some sort of club?' he asked. I stub the ground thinking to myself. 'I really would like to answer you, but I can't,' I said. He is less than pleased at my reply. He tells me and my friend to sit on the frozen ground. Finally after about 30 minutes the pack comes in. They are wondering what is happening. The park ranger addresses the pack: 'Mr Zipper here has a problem with authority'. The pack roars with laughter. They've known me and my Napoleonic tendencies for quite some time. Mr Park Ranger turns crimson. He is furious. 'Is this some sort of club?' he asks. The pack reacts exactly as I did. Mr Park Ranger now goes into convulsions. 'Do you people think you can r*n on public and private land whenever you want?' Silly rabbit. He makes me pour out the beer and fines me $50 for being on parkland after dark (I couldn't read the sign that said I wasn't allowed on parkland after dark … 'cause it was dark!) and $50 for having alcohol on parkland. We went to a local bar and got pissed."

Park rangers featured again during Inter-Am 1985. The pack was taken on a hilly trail through Red Top Mountain State Park on a hot day. Halfway along the trail, a drink check was held beside a beautiful lake. Of course the Hashers couldn't resist a refreshing dip so it was 'one in, all in'. Shortly afterwards, a park ranger comes zooming up in his boat to cut short the fun. It was apparently illegal to swim in the lake. After supervising the Hashers' retreat onto dry land, he was rewarded with a group mooning as the pack headed back on trail.

Rosie Lickety Split tells of a time when on the Emerald Coast H3 in Florida, they were surrounded by police and military and videotaped. 'We've been watching you for 30 minutes' they barked in warning. "They suspected us of being some sort of occult/KKK type of thing before finding out we were harmless," says Rosie.

A different type of authority comes into play in Utah – a moral authority. Salt Lake City H3 say they experience no bother or interference from the Mormons who are headquartered there. "It's a big city, and the Hash doesn't cause that much attention," says High Beams [Why not? –ed.]. Besides, they invariably r*n on private property or are at somebody's home for the On On, or otherwise away from the madding crowds. The legal drinking age is the standard 21, but the state has some curve-balls that come with it. In hotels and restaurants, alcohol may be served with food after midday [Quick, let's all adjust our watches –ed.]. But you can't ask for 'alcohol' … you quietly ask for the 'beverage' list. And – this'll kill it for Hashers – you're only allowed one drink at a time, meaning you can't order some wine if you haven't finished your beer yet. Bars are referred to as 'private clubs', and you obtain 'temporary membership' at the door for a few bucks.

A chapter on law and disorder wouldn't be complete without a story from those low-down nasties at Rumson. Mr Jackson takes up the story: "We came upon a frozen dead horse in a barren area during our Saturday morning Hash. It had probably been dumped there to avoid paying for a legal disposal. We had our Hash and tavern visit, and I didn't give it another thought. Kanaga asked me to help him cut down a tree so we went to his house. In the meantime, the worst elements of a bad Hash got a truck and returned to get the horse. The plan was to dump it on Kanaga's driveway. When they approached his place they saw us both and retreated to decide what to do next. Since they saw me there, they decided to go to my place instead. In the interim I returned home and hit the shower. The deed was done then. As I came downstairs, my wife, mother-in-law and kids were looking out the window, saying 'What's that in the driveway?' I knew. There was some hysteria in the family. My wife is the most low-key woman you can imagine, but she freaked out. Calls to my Hash friends met with claims of ignorance. I called rendering services to learn that it would cost hundreds of dollars to dispose of the horse legally. I then called the prime suspects and told them that I would have to call the police, because the horse had now been discovered by the neighbours. It was a dumb and un-Hashlike thing to do, but I was under a lot of pressure. I called the Rumson police and told them about the horse, saying I did not know how it got there. Rumson is a small, affluent town and the police are your friends and want to avoid scandal. The Chief himself showed up with another cop. Rumson police are not trained in animal ways. They check it out and the other cop pointed up the hill and speculated that it had to be r*nning and died here – the horse was frozen solid and it's eyes were cavities! The Chief called the city sanitation guys and told them to send over a truck and a couple of guys to get rid of it, then the police leave. The truck arrives and, after some discussion, they decide that even if they could get it in the truck they would have no legal way to dispose of it. They leave, the cops return, and tell me it's my problem and I need to solve it fast. Everyone in my family is in tears when I get a call from one of the more sensible Hashers [Oxymoron? –ed.] who tells me he'll round up some of the guys with a truck and come over. I also made a few calls.

"Now it is snowing, and the truck and the Hashers, many with wives and girlfriends, arrive. There is singing and drinking around the carcass. One of the more resourceful Hashers cut down some small trees from my woodlot and, after roping the horse, we were able to pull it on to the pickup, feet in the air. It is dark and snowing heavily. Three of us get in the truck and decide to return it to the general area where we found it. That plan went awry because we lost our way in the snow. We went to Plan B, which was to back up into the woods on a country road, tie the ropes on the horse to a tree and drive off. We did, and I thought that was the end of it. Not so! On Tuesday I get a call at work from one of the Hashers. The local newspaper had an article about a dead horse that was found with ropes and signs of animal torture. The State police gave a number if anyone had any information. There was a quote from the police that said 'Must have been some sick puppy to do this'. At that time, I had a very responsible position with Bell Telephone Laboratories. I was scared shitless. I called my lawyer to give him notice, because I was certain that the Rumson police would see the article and make the connection. Tuesday, Wednesday, Thursday, Friday, nothing. I am beginning to have hope. Saturday morning Kanaga picks me up for the Hash, starting at the Little Silver train station. We pull into the parking lot and there is a police car and the Rumson Hashers pointing at me, saying 'That's him, officer'. I don't buy it, it's got to be a set-up. The cop comes over and asks my name and claims he has a warrant for my arrest and has to take me to the state police barracks. I think he's bullshitting me so I say 'Let's go!' and jump in the front seat of his car. Called his bluff, I think, except he gets in and drives away accompanied by waves and catcalls from my friends. We drive a couple of miles and I'm beginning to worry – the guy's in uniform in a cop car. That's a risky prank. As I'm beginning to plan my one call to my lawyer, the cop starts to laugh. I breathe a sigh of relief and he drives me back. The statute of limitations has passed."

Given all of these r*n-ins with the law, isn't this contra to the notion of America as the much-vaunted 'Land of the Free'? Likk'mm, an American expatriate who has been living in Switzerland for the past 20 years, says: "America is not the Land of the Free, it's the land of the unlimited opportunities." [Opportunities to get busted, it seems –ed.]

Across the border in Canada, things seem a bit more relaxed with the powers that be. However, they did have one incident in Calgary: "In 1996, the Fire Department's hazardous materials unit was called in to clean up a 'mysterious white powder at the base of several telephone poles'," says King Shit. "It would've made the national news if a Calgary Hasher wasn't working at the [TV] station." Unwarranted publicity was thus narrowly averted.

And in Alaska, Backdoor Dwarf and the Frozen Chosen H3 had a rather comical r*n-in with the law. "It was the coldest I have ever Hashed at minus 22 Fahrenheit," says Backdoor Dwarf. "A group of us from my Mother Hash, Osan Bulgogi H3, were in North Pole ,AK, near Fairbanks, decided we were there and there was no Hash, so we started the Frozen Chosen. As we were laying the trail me and my co-hare, Sexy For 8 Seconds, were stopped by the North Pole police and asked what the hell we were doing. We kindly told the police that we were a drinking club with a r*nning problem and he looked at us and said: "Boys you must be nuts, 'cause the *locals* don't even go out when it gets this cold."

However, as we skip down to South and Central America, the heat gets turned up in more ways than one. In Peru, a series of bomb attacks were

launched in Lima in 1993 by the Shining Path movement, killing 40. In 1995, Peru sent troops into Ecuador, leading to a short conflict. Sixty thousand land mines remain as a legacy in the demilitarised zone. In December 1996, terrorists of the Tupac Maru seized hostages in a building owned by the Japanese embassy. With so many diplomatic personnel and other foreign expatriates in the Lima H3, it was not surprising that one of their members, Lost Child, was among the hostages. He was eventually freed; the terrorists were eventually buried.

In Panama they have things a lot easier. "Every now and then, specially when we r*n at parks, we have close encounters with our police," says Rompy. "They usually let us go easy. Drinking is a national sport down here."

In Mexico, they seem more influenced by the American state troopers. "Once you leave the city itself then you're okay," says Prego. "Especially since, like in most places, beer drinking in public areas is frowned upon by the cops. There are many parks and areas where you are not bothered as much, but we're always looking for some place new or out of the ordinary path."

Brazil's finest are largely apathetic to the Hash's antics too. "Police don't seem to care, but we upset a landowner last r*n when his stewards phoned him after seeing a crazy bunch r*nning through his land. We apologised and calmed him down – he later gave us permission to r*n anytime," says Konkorde. There was one incident years ago when the trigger-happy military got excited when there was a sacrilegious 'check' discovered at the base of the hallowed national flag in town. Fortunately, it came to nothing.

Even the idyllic Caribbean island of Montserrat is not exempt from the long rubber-gloved hand of the law. In the period of the 2001 anthrax scares they felt the full weight of the Royal Montserrat Police Force upon them. Papa Smurf takes up the story: "It was bucketing down on the day and one of the hares had to relay, with flour, the road part of the trail from the car (an offence in itself). A full three days later the police turned up at his office and escorted him [the Hasher soon to be known as Anthrax] down to the station. This was pretty embarrassing. It transpired that someone had seen him distributing a 'white substance' from his vehicle. This was assumed to be the deadly substance and had been so reported to the police. It was only when he volunteered the Commissioner of Police (Hashman 'Cedric McElder') as a witness, that the police relented somewhat. However, the Commissioner had since left the island on duty so could not corroborate his story in person. The police took the hare back to his house where he had to physically produce the flour in question. This was then taken by rubber-gloved constables away for verification. Finally, they realised that they were rather overdoing it and released him."

But all of this is child's play for Salvador H3 in El Salvador, probably the most oppressed kennel in the world. Having been established in 1984 by Peter Groenendyk, who had Hashed in Costa Rica, he set about getting El Salvador 'On'. But the ongoing civil war, coups, earthquakes and fear of terrorism against the Hashers conspired to keep the Hashers' heads down. The biggest break in proceedings came in June 1985 when there was a massacre at San Benito in the city's Zone Rosa, aimed at sending a clear and deliberate message about foreigners and foreign intervention in the country. The Hashers were clearly in their sights, too, so sensibly decided to suspend operations. It was restarted again by Groenendyk in September 1987. It took almost four years for them to reach r*n number 50, that milestone coming up in May 1988. Soon after, in 1989, safety concerns forced the club to shut down one more time. The SHHH was notorious at that time for having the "fastest and sneakiest" Hashers in the world. "Try r*nning looking for clues while dodging bullets and avoiding snipers."

In 1993, Olivier 'Black Peter' Van Lieshout decided to re-establish it, calling the kennel the 'Born Again Salvadoran Hash'. This manifestation died less than two years later. The current SHHH was re-founded in 1998 by Jeff 'Grapes of Wrath' Jacobson and has managed to notch up a comparatively respectable 60 r*ns in just two years. So things are looking up!

Every Dog Has Its Daydream.

Ian Cumming.
First r*n KL H3 1959
Founded Singapore H3 1962
Co-founded New York H3 1978

How did you get yourself into this lot?
IC: Dave Scourse was the stage manager of an amateur production being put on at the Victoria Theatre in KL. My wife, Jane, and I were part of the cast. During rehearsals the theatre was hot, humid and stuffy, the fans not r*nning to save electricity. We persuaded the bar-keep at the theatre foyer to open up at rehearsal time, and the simple call of 'Ah Fatt!' brought him r*nning with a two cold Anchors, one for Dave, and one for me. Later in the evening we would sit in the dark foyer and finish the case. After a few such episodes, Dave said: 'The way you drink beer leads me to believe you'd make a good harrier.' After some discussion, a great deal of disbelief on my part, and my wife saying that if I didn't believe Dave, I could at least drive out on Monday and see for myself, I did, and I've been Hashing ever since.

And what are your best Hashing memories?
IC: InterHashing has, for me, provided the most exciting and memorable experiences. The most outstanding example was the Philadelphia event in 1987. Those who attended, whenever we meet again, refrain from boring other folk with exchanging our mutual joy of recollection – one glance is all it takes to bring back incredible memories. My son, then 19 (legally drinking in those days) was talked into coming with us, even though the four-day weekend cost of $100 would not be discounted because he had to get back to school after the second day. He woke me up early on Sunday morning, his bag packed and his train ticket in his hand, to say 'Dad, that was the best $100 dollars I spent in my whole life!'

Any traumatic moments on trail you'd rather not remember?

IC: By far the most embarrassing experience I had was at the Mother Hash 50th anniversary. I was staying with Dave Scourse. As a special treat on the second day he had the cook prepare a *laksa*, redolent with prawn paste, fish balls and lots of coconut grease. In my greed I took a large second helping with extra hot sauce, and we hurried off to get the bus to the r*n. We had not progressed much into the trail – conveniently marked with special three-inch squares of paper, proudly printed with a Hash logo – when the *laksa* went to work. By some trick of fortune I found myself out ahead of the pack. I gathered a handful of trail markers over 100 yards, and retired behind an oil palm to take my ease. To my chagrin the pack soon enveloped my hiding place, and a young KL lady poked her head around the tree and inquired if I knew where the trail went. 'Oh yes!' I said, 'I know where it went – just give me another minute, and I'll show you where.'

Is there a difference in British v. American culture in how it applies to Hashing?

IC: Your question suggests that since Americans are not Brits there may be a cultural difference to resist some of the foibles of the Hash. On the contrary, the natives here are very familiar with the rugby ethic, nearly all colleges field a rugby team, most of them also feature a women's rugby club. Hashing in the States is as natural as it might have been in any other country; that it thrives, and develops, and retro-develops back to what the average Hash does anywhere.

How has Hashing changed over the years?

IC: We haven't learned a goddam thing!

What do you make of 'new' traditions in the Hash?

IC: Being present at so many new Hashes has been an interesting experience, since every founder had inherited different versions of how a Hash should r*n, and it took some discipline on our part not to try to pattern in the way we do things, still very close to the Mother Hash and Singapore, with no circles, no Hash names, no RA, but well supported singing at every opportunity. Sure, we have indescribable debates over the internet, some demanding a World Hash Police Force to make rules, to determine how many r*ns you must make before you are given a Hash name, the procedures for appealing a Hash name, the requirements for changing a Hash name in a new Hash; whether the r*ns should be live, or laid with due consideration for the r*n being for the pack, not an ego trip for the hare. But in due course some ancient Hasher will get on the wire and resolve the debate with a few solemn obscenities.

What's the main thing you got from Hashing?

IC: Integrity – bringing into my career (money-making life) the same principles I pursue in my leisure time. I learned a lot more about people, leadership, and how better to relax, forgive, and tolerate ugly distorted environments and individuals than I could have coped with before. To quote a non-Hasher, Jane my wife, who – having been brought up in a society where rugby players and Hashers, then a male society, were an accepted but not appreciated part of her life – was heard to mention over the telephone recently 'No, no! You don't understand the Hash. They have a far greater success rate than AA or the Episcopal Church. At least 90 per cent of them get total satisfaction of their problems every Monday night. In the church, we have a turnaround rate of less than 45 per cent.' At a later time, she mentioned the problems of dealing with what she described as the replacement of the old-fashioned extended family with the Hash. Unfortunately, when she attempted to introduce the Bishop into the merits of r*nning the church the same way the Hash operated, he got upset at the mention of the lack of need for bishops.

So what does the future hold for Hashing?

IC: In an informal discussion I learned from Bill Panton that the growth rate of the Hash, worldwide, exceeded the world birth rate by a considerable sum, and that the graphs would cross in this decade. I urge you to consider the consequences of this. Since everyone in the world will Hash, wars as we know them will be impossible, for which Hasher is going to take up arms against another unless there is an extreme shortage of suds. There will be no end of InterHashes taking place; start buying shares in breweries, hotels and airlines now, get in on the ground floor. It will also signal the end of democratic elections – all communities will be r*n by GMs. It behooves us to select these with care, for they will determine the identity of the Supreme GM of the world in due course. We don't want any Bin Ladens on the short list.

Keith Kanaga.

First r*n Kuala Lumpur H3 1972
Founder Rumson H3, Brooklyn H3, Queens H3
Member New York City H3, New Amsterdam Winter Wednesday H3, New Amsterdam Summer Sunday H3

Who are you going to blame for getting you into this mess, and how'd you find it?

KK: I was working for Chase Manhattan Bank at the time, and a competitor from Citibank, whom I met at the Royal Selangor Club pool, kindly invited me to attend, then tried to kill me in the jungle. I thought I was going to die.

And your best Hashing memory?

KK: Probably the time when four of us were trapped by a snake on a rubber plantation. We thought it was a cobra; luckily it turned out to be a python, and rather sleepy.

And what about your worst?

KK: When I fell in the underground vat of pig shit.

You've done half your Hashing in tropical jungle and half in the concrete jungle. How do you compare them?

KK: City hashes, such as New York City, Wellington (when they're in town), and the like require a different style. The noise, and the fact that buildings can block the call of 'On! On!', make it more challenging mentally. There is the compensating factor that even if you're well and truly separated from the pack, you're never really lost. And you can always carry taxi money with you. Rural Hashes favour the athletic a bit more.

How has Hashing changed?
KK: Beer's more dear. I've noticed some Hashes have a well-developed 'circle' culture. Kimchee Bob in Seoul was my favourite. He could keep a circle going for hours. His talent is pretty rare. Other Hashes are more laid back. As I've gotten older, I've come to appreciate the more leisurely Hashes, such as South Side H3 in Hong Kong, or Queens H3 in New York. My all-time favourite is Rumson H3, which I reckon is probably the best Hash in the Western World.

What's the main thing you've gotten from Hashing over the years?
KK: The odd mug and a sore butt.

Does InterHash belong in Asia or worldwide?
KK: I'm in favour of any place stupid enough to have us.

Kit Lee 'The Great Kahuna' Mognett.
First r*n Singapore H3 ("early Seventies")
Member Houston H3

How did you first hear about the Hash?
TGK: I had a friend that was r*nning in the Hash in Singapore. I was only 25 years old back in those days so … it was a lot of fun. The thing that got me hooked on the Hash over there was the singing – I just loved the singing … they really sang a lot, after the r*ns they used to go out to restaurants and sit around and sing until two or three o'clock in the morning and have a big ole time

Were you hooked after your first r*n?
TGK: Oh, yes, definitely. I knew I was a Hasher right from the start.

What's the thing that you've got from your 30 years of Hashing?
TGK: I think the main thing I like about Hashing is the fellowship, the camaraderie you have, you've got friends all over the world. My knees are bad now so I can't r*n any more so I'm limited in what I can do so the trails aren't that important to me. I enjoy a good trail, but by the same token I enjoy the social aspects of Hashing probably more than the physical aspects.

Could you have got the same kind of fellowship elsewhere?
TGK: Not the same kind, I don't think. Hashing's sort of a unique group of people … to say they're not average is, I guess, an understatement. Most Hashers have some sort of extrovert tendency of some kind, that's one reason they like to Hash because they can just go out there and be crazy, do whatever they wanna do … a safety valve, if you will, for a lot of people to go out and get rid of all their inhibitions, and their frustrations. The pressure that builds up during the week, you go and r*n a Hash all of a sudden that fades away.

What's your best Hashing memory from around the world?
TGK: Oh gosh, so many great memories. Trinidad/Tobago for the Americas was wonderful … well organised, good places to stay, the venue was good, the r*ns were superb, parties afterward were good, food was abundant – very good local

food not just standard fare, the bands were good, good facilities. They bussed us over the mountains to Maracas Beach. At the government beach house there, they had a full cordon of security around us. We didn't have to worry about any locals coming to crash the party and that sort of thing. That's the type of thing I like.

What's your worst Hashing memory?

TGK: I remember one time in Singapore – first time I ever got lost – it gets dark early and they used to lay the trail with chopped-up paper. When it starts getting dark in the jungle, all the bark starts getting luminescent so it all looks like newspaper, so you have to get on your hands and knees and feel your way out of the place. We used to get a group of us together when it got dark so we could do that and not worry about the cobras and things like that. The other thing that saves you is Singapore is an island, so if you go far enough in one direction you're gonna hit a road somewhere (laughs). That's some of my formative training – always carry some money with you so you've got cab fare … and get out of the jungle before it gets dark.

How have you found Hashing in different parts of the States?

TGK: It varies widely, depending on where you're at. The Hash, your local area, has a flavour of its own usually. Even here in the US, regions of the US have different flavours of how they Hash. The West Coast Hashes and the East Coast Hashes are entirely different to the way they are here in the Texas area. Like California, they tend to be a bit more on the upper scale, a little bit snooty almost – they're a fun group. Washington is not so wild and crazy as we are on the coast down here. Then you have a basic area, say, Texas that pride themselves on hospitality and this kind of stuff, while the East Coast and the northern part they're not that big on that kind of stuff – they're not real friendly to you if you're a stranger. A little bit of that comes into the Hash.

What about Hashing outside of the US?

TGK: I like the overseas Hashing better than the US Hashing, personally. I think it's more down to the essentials, the basics, here it's got to the point where it's started to be almost competitive … 'Let's see if we can have the longest trail, the furthest, the hardest … that to me is not really part of Hash … that's yuppie r*nning.

Was it more a gentleman's club back then?

TGK: It was to some extent – a set of standards that were just unspoken, certain things that you just didn't transgress. Here it's got to the point where all the younger kids are 'I've got to prove to this guy that I'm better', it's turned into a macho thing for a lot of places and I don't like that aspect of it.

I kind of enjoy all-men's Hash to some extent because you can pretty much do what you want and not worry about offending anybody. In fact I was really worried first time I came to a Hash in Houston in 1980 and went on a r*n – I wasn't sure what I was going to do with women, I had to be on my good behaviour and be nice. And we got on the trail out there, which they messed up real bad, and we're standing around, and this little girl about 4'2" beside me screams out: 'WHO LAID THE FUCKIN' TRAIL?' And I said OK, I guess I'm OK'.

How is political correctness affecting the Hash?
TGK: I think that part of the reason is that there are some people that don't wanna be overly regulated ... they wanna be able to let their hair down, have a good time, not worry about being politically correct, pretty much say what they feel like saying. If you don't like what they're saying you just walk away and go talk to somebody else. If you come to Hash and get offended easily, you shouldn't be here. That's the way Hash is. It's a place where I can say and do things I wouldn't do in normal society and it's not frowned upon. The nice thing about the Hash, it is dynamic, it does change. If you don't like what's going on at the Hash in a year or two it'll change ... it goes through cycles. It's about who's involved with the management of it at the time, you get good mismanagement you get bad mismanagement like everything else. Give it some time and it'll clear itself out.

Any views on InterHash venues?
TGK: I think holding it outside of Asia is a good thing ... the only thing that's good about Asia, like India, is those countries most probably are Third World countries and you can do a lot more with your dollars over there, put a lot more lavish things on. Places like the US you pay top dollar for everything. I think a European InterHash would be nice, I wouldn't mind to see us have a big Hash in somewhere like Hawaii...

Ralph Wadsworth.
First r*n Kuala Lumpur H3 1960
Founder member Washington DC H3

How did you first hear about the Hash?
RW: From a squash-playing buddy in KL who was a member.
So you obviously enjoyed your first gallop?
RW: First impressions of the Mother Hash were very positive. It was fun, a good way to keep fit for other sports and a few beers after the r*n seemed very civilised! I was a member of KL Mother Hash from 1960 to 1965, On Sec in 1963.
You've been Hashing since before I was born! How many r*ns in total?
RW: R*ns in KL approximately 200 which, with 1,050 r*ns with Washington DC Hash from inception to present, brings the total to 1,250. I was one of the original group of five who attended the inaugural DC r*n on May 27 1972.
Where and when was the most fun had?
RW: Far too many to list! Let me single out the second InterHash (KL 1980) where I celebrated my 50th birthday.
And any downsides where you wanted to give Hashing away?
RW: Not many, fortunately, although the On On and/or On On On and a few beers tend to quickly dissipate any negative experiences.
And do you have a favourite Hashing locale?
RW: Inevitably, I favour Malaysia, with its mix of rubber and oil plantations, secondary and primary jungle, tin tailings, etc. Or countries with similar terrain.

You must have witnessed some incredible changes over the years in the Hash?

RW: In some Hashes, elaborate and lengthy circles at the On Ons are an established part of the ritual, which I do not recall, as they say, 'in my younger days'. The size of a Hash can change the dynamics adversely, in my opinion. I recall r*nning with the Jakarta Hash in the 1980s and the pack was almost 120. This results in a breakdown into sub-groups with less interaction across the Hash in question. If the membership is fluid and constantly changing, size probably does not matter. It does become relevant, however, if a Hash is hoping to create a core, longstanding membership.

Speaking of longstanding, what have you derived from your 42 years (so far) of Hashing?

RW: Camaraderie and friendship, fun, exercise and fitness, and meeting a very interesting cross-section of people from all walks of life.

That sounds a lot more interesting than the hopeless bunch I r*n with! How do you think the Hash will change forthwith?

RW: Whatever is said, Hashing will take its own course. Hashes come and go but steady growth has, I understand, been the norm for the last few years, without any strategy, eg, publicity, etc.

You were at the second-ever InterHash in KL. What are your thoughts on InterHash in Asia versus the rest of the world?

RW: In a worldwide organisation, InterHash clearly has a place worldwide. However, as an old Malaysian hand I feel that perhaps one in four, or one in six, InterHashes should be held outside Asia (bids permitting, of course!). My view is governed partly by sentiment, and partly by economics – eg, the cost of an Inter-Hash outside Asia may be prohibitive to Malaysian, Thai and Indonesian nationals.

Ray 'Grease Monkey' Bennett.

First r*n Okinawa H3 1983
Founder BMT H3, Okinawa 1987
Member Over the Hump H3, Mt Vernon H3, DC Full Moon H3

What were you thinking to get caught up with this lot?

GM: My wife went to the Hash for approximately three months before she talked me into going. My first impression before I did a trail was (referring to my spouse) 'You're crazy – r*nning through the jungle when there are roads and sidewalks to r*n on!'

And how'd you get your handle?

GM: My spouse's name was Jungle Jane (she got lost in a very, very small jungle). Playing off the jungle theme, Hash nominations were Tarzan, Cheta, Baboon, Greased Vine – however, because I was in maintenance the name Grease Monkey fell into place.

And how many trails have you done since then?

GM: I have approximately 1,860 trails – give or take 10 or 20. Have hared over 500 trails. Since 1983 I have taken one week off from Hashing – was in ICU!

[Piss poor excuse –ed.] ICU was necessary to fill me back up with some fresh young blood. Had internal bleeding from a Sunday (still made that Hash) until a Wednesday morning before passing out at the emergency room – knew something was wrong but I'm no doctor!

Any or many good memories?

GM: Number one on my list is when the Over the Hump crew provided t-shirts (with my picture on it) for my 1,000 OTH4 trail – I did not know about the shirts until the finish when everyone was walking around with the t-shirt on – it was dark and I had hared the trail – one hell of a surprise. Hundreds of enjoyable trails and good times. Some of the most memorable ones are the Hash-a-Thons (four trails in one day – one after the other – started this annual event on Okinawa in 1988/89). The pig trough trail between north and southbound lanes of Hwy # 95 hared by Sex Cadet. Hashing in snow with coloured flour is always fun!

Any bad moments in between?

GM: Going to my first OTH trail in 1991 and not being able to r*n – I was just starting to recover from a ruptured L5 – ended up walking/haring for 15 minutes. Also hared on crutches after stepping on a nail while scouting trail (was hard to get the board off the bottom of my foot because the nail was bent and stuck on the top of my foot between the knuckles).

What have you got from your years of Hashing?

GM: My sanity (even if it is only half a mind, it is mine), and a feeling of belonging – something to do to get away from whatever it is that I want to get away from!

How could or should the Hash evolve?

GM: Hashing is not a controlled organisation. It should never be – and the more informal the better! If left alone, each Hash takes on its own personality and evolves, and wankers come and wankers go. I have seen three Hashes grow from small groups to significant Hashes. Once again, each Hash must adapt to the terrain it uses for trails and likewise to the local conditions – Hashing on private property in Hawaii can get wankers shot. R*nning through a shopping centre in Maryland can get pack members locked up, etc – a Hash must adapt to survive and evolve.

Marty 'Garfield' Hanratty.

First r*n Seoul H3 1975
Member Night R*nners of Bengal, Bangladesh; Jakarta H3; White House H3; Addis Ababa H3, Ethiopia; Harare H3, Zimbabwe; DCH3

How'd you get into this august society, Garfield?

G: I was working for Michigan State in Korea and a couple of guys in the office used to r*n with this crazy organisation called the Hash. They kept inviting me out and I said 'Look, I don't r*n' so they finally said 'We're gonna be the hares, you've gotta come out' so I went on a r*n with them ... so these guys they laid a trail straight through a Buddhist monastery. The Buddhists came out and said 'There's a Negro throwing trash in our monastery', cleaned it all up, along comes the pack – no trail! So we all went to a bar on Hooker Hill, had about two hours there. It was pretty good – no r*n, all this piss, and these guys come by with all the beer, so we set up the cooker in the street and we had a meal and drank the rest of the beer. So I thought this is a pretty good group of guys!

Any idea how many r*ns you've done?

G: No, I've tried to add it up. Over a thousand, but that's only the ones you r*n with the clubs that you ran on, not at an InterHash or something like that.

Is Hashing still an eccentric expatriate thing?

G: I think it's changed as Hashers have got more and more involved. The Addis Hash is 80 per cent Ethiopian … really great looking women, too, I must say. Harare Hash is about half expat/ half locals, and all the ones in the US – especially the ones in Washington – probably ten per cent will be expats and the rest will be locals, US Hashers. You have things like Bandung Number Two, where you've got 800 Chinese.

So that's a good thing for its stability and longevity…

G: I think so. The real problem for the Hash is that they've lost a lot of the traditions. You can see that when you come into the States … everybody and their brother is starting a Hash up and there's not a great deal of uniformity in terms of traditions, the circles, they add onto it, you lose some of those traditions and you have new ones that are generated. Which is good, it changes the character of the Hash.

What's the main thing you get or got from your years of Hashing?

G: Some of my best mates in the world. The Hash has allowed us to come together, go out on the piss and shoot the shit and get caught up on each other's lives. And there's four or five guys that if anything happens – they have a place in my home, no problem at all.

What's the best Hash memory you have?

G: Oh, Christ, that's a hard one. Probably the best was when we organised a Java Hash Dash from Bali InterHash up to Jakarta and it stopped off in Semerang, Jogjakarta, Bandung, Surabaya, and we had the brewery VIP bus, so we'd call into town and before we get in the brewery truck would come out, replace the kegs, put on the tinnies and it was a piss-up! It had a bathroom and a bar on the thing. We did the trip in a week and we were absolutely shit-faced the whole week. I remember we got into Jakarta and did a r*n in Jakarta and, for some reason, I decided I was going to take a piss outside the bus, and I'm walking down the aisle of the bus – we had barfed in the bus, people had shat in the bus, pissed in the bus – next thing I trip over something and I fall and I'm laying right on top of these two people that are rooting in the aisle. They had *everything* on this fucking bus!

My leaver's r*n down in Jakarta we had on a beach and this park was famous for all the old hookers that went down there, so I went down, we laid the trail and I hired 20 of them. So we're having a circle, and the beer's flowing really well, the circle's going great and these women come up and start grabbing people's asses and their balls and everything … they were old, really old, and these guys were like 'Fuck, get the hell out of here, Jesus Christ!'

How does Hashing differ between countries or continents?
G: Well, in South East Asia you've got your driver and you go out to the Hash, then you do the Hash, have a long circle that's put on by the brewery, the driver takes you on to the restaurant, you have a feed, more beer, driver takes you down to the whorehouse, it's much more freer. The real difference is between mixed and male Hashes. Male Hashes there's a lot more camaraderie … as soon as a woman walks in the circle, it changes the whole tenor of the Hash. Everybody's gotten their dick in their hand and is trying to get laid.

How has Hashing and Hashers changed over the years?
G: Well, I think it's got a lot more complicated … you've got 4,000 people showing up for InterHash. That gets complicated, and it takes a couple of years to put it together. What's actually amazing to me is that people who are volunteers – they never get paid – do these things. You know, take two years out of their life, and a hell of a lot of work and put on a piss-up for 4,000 people.

Are we being still true to the aims of the Hash?
G: Well, yeah – piss-up for a bunch of drunks … it hasn't changed!

InterHash – remain in Asia or elsewhere?
G: I think it should be held where people want it to be. And if the guys in the United States wanna put it on, fine. A couple of years ago people were saying 'Jesus Christ, if it goes to the United States it'll never get out of the United States, and I think that's the stupidest thing because basically Hashers are after good value for money, and it's extremely difficult in places like the UK or the United States to put on good value for money. They cost a lot of money to travel in. That's why you have a lot of them in South East Asia where it is cheap, and you have all the other *hors d'ouevres* available on request.

The world is moving more towards political correctness and social restraint, how is the Hash facing this?
G: I've r*n Hashes with bank presidents and ambassadors and army generals and KGB colonels, and I think a lot of times guys want a day away from the job just to forget about it and to be kids again. The piss-up at the rugby club. And that's what the Hash really is. So they go out, and get pissed up, and have a great time, get a little exercise … that's the reason why it makes no difference how complicated or how political the world gets.

I remember when I was the GM in Ethiopia … here I am, a white guy, and I've got two black women arguing because a Zimbabwean called an Ethiopian 'black'. She said 'I'm not black, I'm Ethiopian,' and they get into a god-dammed fistfight. I am between them, and I'm trying to say 'What the fuck are you doing? You're both black, for Christ sakes!' But I had to give the Hash a little lecture about there's no sexism, there's no racism … there's *Hashers*, that's it. And anybody that doesn't want to abide by that, get your ass out of here – it's just not for you. And the Hash isn't for everybody.

Have you seen a lot of that in action?
G: People come along, first-time Hashers, and they'll do one r*n and that'll be it … a lot of self-selection. I used to take care of some trails in the Appalachian trail in the eastern part of the United States and every summer the White House

Hash would go out there and do some trail work, have a r*n and a big piss-up in the woods. There was one guy who was a Dutch marine, got pissed on Saturday, went into a girl's tent and wouldn't leave. I had to say to him, 'I'm terribly sorry but that behaviour's not acceptable on the Hash. If you make someone feel threatened, we're not here to worry about shit like that, we're here to have fun and you're not welcome' and kicked his ass off the Hash.

Rick 'SmegmaBalls' Perkins.

First r*n Phoenix H3 1988
Founder Iguana H3 Travelling Hash; Guadalajara H3, Mexico
Member White House H3; Pentagon H3; Mt Vernon H3; Washington DC Hares and Harriettes; Arlington H3; Washington DC Pick Up H3; Austin H3

You must really be popular with the Harriettes with a name like that.
SB: I don't like my Hash name; never have. I have/had the reputation of a womaniser and recruiter of new boots to the Hash. I could always recruit an Alouette in a local bar. Anyway, I really don't know why I am called SmegmaBalls … most Harriettes enjoy my balls very much, thank you.
So how'd you get tangled up in this web, anyway?
SB: I was introduced to the Hash by Charlie 'Captain Crash' Cobb who was a pilot. I met him in Phoenix at a weekly Happy Hour of Texans. Before I met him at the Hash, he was an arrogant asshole and then one day he told me that there was a r*nning club and I should come out to it. He told me absolutely no details about following the marks, or singing, and drinking and so forth. I was on my own, out in the desert near the foothills. I don't recall any trail instructions, but it was a great trail. At the end the group started singing Father Abraham (led by Captain Crash) and at that point I snuck away to my car and left. My impression was that this was possibly a group of gay guys and I wasn't quite sure what would happen to me if I stayed.
So what changed your mind about that 'arrogant asshole'?
SB: Captain Crash (aka Pussy Hound) later became my idol. He was magical with the women, had a fantastic carefree attitude, jetted all over flying Boeing 747s, and he Hashed in places like Tokyo Ladies Hash and the Moscow Hash. The most amazing thing was that in May of 1992, Captain Crash died in a crash of his private airplane. It was incredible that he would die 'by his Hash name', and the Phoenix Hashers loved him so much. Even today, we have the Annual Captain Crash Memorial Hash in Phoenix, which usually visits the crash site, leaves flowers and such. After Captain Crash died, I felt like it was up to me to carry on his spirit. RIP Captain Crash!
What have been your most memorable Hashing moments?
SB: The Iguana Hash in Honolulu was very memorable. This is the Travelling Hash that Hashes in a different city each r*n … usually they are long-weekend Hashes. The Friday night in Honolulu ran us through the hills above Waikiki Beach, along the coastline, and ended up at Diamond Point, where the waves were crashing in, and a huge full moon was rising. The next day the trail was

on the west side of the island, the trail met up with the only train on the island (they pulled it out of mothballs just for the Hash!). We rode it for a few miles and at each road intersection all of the Hashers mooned the cars that were stopped for the train. Talk about a captive audience! At the circle our Religious Adviser, Two Guys Fucking, had about a *dozen* couples climb up on the picnic tables, and we had simultaneous Butt Chugs ... probably should be listed in some book of records.

And your worst Hash-related moments?

SB: The Hash is voluntary so if you don't like something about it, you can easily find your way home. But besides getting lost on trail in the darkness of night while visiting New York City H3 once, the deaths of Captain Crash and Dave 'Wrong Way' Arnold seemed senseless and before their time. I only wonder if the free-spirited nature of the Hash causes us to sometimes act without thinking thoroughly.

I should hope so. Any changes in store for Hashing?

SB: I don't see any big changes in Hashing. One thing notable is the lack of some minorities in the Hash. I have seen many Asians, Middle Easterners, Europeans, Australians and North Americans involved in the Hash. But, North American blacks have not jumped into the fray. I'm not sure why.

So where does Hashing go from here?

SB: I think Hashing is in a constant state of de-evolution. There is no hope for a higher level.

Rick 'Chapa Chatty' Chatham.
First r*n San Jose H3, Costa Rica 1983

That's nearly 20 years of Hashing South America. How did you get into it and how many r*ns on the board now?

CC: I was invited by a friend who said 'You may be as crazy as these guys'. He was right. Done about 600 r*ns in total now.

And what are the best moments out of that lot?

CC: Hard to pick, prefer more intimate gatherings of less than 50 Hashers, although Inter-Am is great fun – my favourites being Costa Rica, Calgary, Trinidad & Tobago. InterHash seems a bit much. Nice to get everyone together at least once – on the other hand 6,000 Hashers in one location seems pretty ridiculous. I've got a suggestion: Years ago I met some members of the Iguana Hash, a nomadic bunch who, rather than loiter, decided to move around geographically. Perhaps we can extrapolate that concept on the global stage?

And your worst moments out of that lot?

CC: Again, too many debacles to pick one, although perhaps the truth may be evident in bodily scars: Hip contusion ('84), torn anterior cruciate ligament ('88), hernia ('89), broken ankle ('90), etc.

What makes Costa Rica so Hashable?

CC: Costa Rica is exceptional Hashing country with varied terrain, steep slopes, primo forest, lots of creeks, coffee fields and banana plantations.

How has Hashing changed over the years?
CC: It's grown like hell, but currently in the doldrums. Stateside elitist thinking, not enough support of Hash traditions on her dickey di-do.

What's the main thing you've got from Hashing over the years?
CC: Lifelong friends, aforementioned scars.

How did you get your Hash name?
CC: Chapa is the Spanish word for beer cap, idiot, veneer. Chatty goes back to the college days."

Dave 'Captain Zero' Cummings.
First r*n San Francisco H3 1986
Member San Diego H3

How did a straight-backed military guy like you get involved in this shambles?
CZ: I first heard about the Hash from a military associate. Initially, since I already ran three to four days a week with the military folks, I didn't pursue Hashing. But once I went to my first Hash, I knew I would be a lifelong Hasher. The miles were not a chore – indeed, it was a fun time with fun and interesting people.

And you're still going strong well over 60?
CZ: I presently r*n three or four of the many Hashes in San Diego County. I presently have 625-plus r*ns with SDH3, and hundreds more with the other Hash groups here. I'm a member of all the 13 San Diego Hash clubs, except the bike Hash. In total, I probably have somewhere between 1,500 and 2,000 r*ns.

So why the handle?
CZ: I was named by San Francisco after we ran up a hill (indeed, San Francisco has a few hills) in the rain to 'moon' the Russian Consulate. Someone overheard me saying something stupid like 'This is supposed to be fun???' which they thought was a 'zero' statement, so they demoted me from being an active duty Lieutenant-Colonel. Someone also said that there was a cartoon character by that name someplace.

What was your most enjoyable Hash so far?
CZ: Playboy Television decided to do a story about 'Dave Cummings' turning 62 [He's the world's oldest porn star –ed.], doing a couple of porn girls for Knee Pad Nymphos, Vol 4 for his birthday, and doing an evening Hash r*n with the California Larrikin H3. The porn shoot went well, with Playboy filming me 'doing' two girls, then a Playboy limo trip to the Social Security office for me to pick up my old age retirement application forms (the girls were 'doing' me during the ride to/from the office), followed by a return to my condo where I 'did' a Playboy model they brought down as my birthday present, and culminating by Playboy filming that night's H3 r*n and On In where the Playboy model flashed her tits in the circle. Playboy's crew and on-camera personalities became instant Hash fans!

Ho hum. What about your worst trail?
CZ: When I slipped and rolled into poison oak on trail two days before a major porn shoot, and got a severe case of poison oak and had to cancel out of two weeks worth of porn bookings. As a result of that, I now shortcut around poison oak, sometimes not even venturing onto trail that might even have a possibility of the dreaded plant being on/near trail!
How would you compare different places you've Hashed in?
CZ: Hashing in the Arizona desert environment (as well as in Saudi Arabia) differed significantly from San Francisco and San Diego but, even though the terrain was different, the fun of Hashing was the same – nice people, good and plentiful beer, and wild fun! Fortunately, other Hashers treat me like a Hasher, not a porn star. Hashing is my escape back to reality and fun – no pressures of Hollywood.

Larry 'Stray Dog' McDowell.
First r*n Okinawa H3 1982
Founder Namsan H3, Korea; Huachuca H3, Arizona; Ozark H3 and Rolla H3, Missouri; Augusta H3, Georgia; Mannheim H3, German Bashers, German Full Moon H3, Germany; Huntsville Redstone H3; and Global Trash Hash
Member Columbia H3; Belleville-St Louis H3; Worms H3 and Heidelberg H3, Germany; Magic City H3; Orlando H3; Orlando N2BCWTO H3; Mosquito County H3; and Rocket Shitty H3

How did you hear of the Hash and what were your first impressions of it?
SD: My company commander kept talking about it until I finally went (I was under the impression you had to get into shape for it). The first trail was a long, poorly marked affair that had me hooked on Hashing for life.
And how does a Hash hound become a Stray Dog?
SD: I short-cut (some refer to it as 'ranging') four of my first six Hashes, usually coming in late, in an effort to catch the hare. As I came in late to the Down Down for my naming, the Japanese insult '*Nora Inu*' (Stray Dog) was bestowed upon me. Most Hashers who have ever Hashed with me agree that it fits.
And which was the best of times on the 1,000 r*ns you've done?
SD: My most enjoyable r*n was a half-marathon in length up and down a mountain three times between Weinheim and near Heidelberg, Germany. It was the 'Super Hasher' (ball-buster) trail for EuroHash III and included nine beer stops (some pubs) as well as some of the most beautiful trails in the world. It was live hare and I was not caught. For *good time*, I would say it was the German Halloween Hash we held in Germany. It began by a *strassebahn* (streetcar) trip, where even the Germans tried to pick up and sing our dirty lyrics, the costumes were outrageous, the Hash company friendly, the trail through a quaint village (the pubs and beer along the way the best in the world) then up a mountain to the castle dungeon.
    I have been to outrageous events including haring and participating in nude

r*ns, nude volleyball, several Red Dress Hashes, etc, but I never enjoyed myself as much as in some of the inter-Hashes we held in Germany.

And your worst Hashing moment or r*n?

SD: I would say the most difficult Hash r*n (maybe not worst, as it tends to improve with age) was the Houston 1,000th. The last r*nner crawled in at five and a half hours, most of the trail was swamp or mud over your ankles or higher due to weeks of rain. At many points, trail had washed away, leaving us ranging for up to a half mile to find a mark. Yeah, it is a trail I will never forget.

Compare Hashing in the different places you've Hashed.

SD: Due to the friendliness of the people (the least territorial of any location I have been), Okinawa is probably the most Hash-friendly location to lay a trail. Korea had a sense of anxiety – we learned quick not to use whistles (cops would chase us) or go into certain areas (shotguns would blast). The most friendly place to tolerate Hash behaviour, and even join in, would be Germany – as well as having beautiful trails and the best beer on earth.

Has the Hash changed at all?

SD: When I first started Hashing, I was most impressed by the fact that you could visit a Hash anywhere in the world (yes, even in the US) and be treated like a long-lost relative. Maybe because a few Hashers abused this hospitality over the years, or maybe because a creeping fraternity/'in-crowd' facet came into the Hash, it has marred the original friendliness. Don't get me wrong, there are still a lot of friendly Hashes out there, I'd say the great majority of them, but I do worry about the thieving and unfriendliness of a few Hashers messing up the tradition. I remember when Hashes could proudly display their banners and flags at an inter-Hash without worry about them being molested. Now everyone fears even showing up at r*ns with flags in their hands. That's a real shame.

What's the main thing you've got from Hashing over the years?

SD: It's a great stress releaser and, in most of the world, a friendly place to be. Like I said in the Bible, it is a gathering of kindred spirits who will not judge you by anything more than your sense of humour [That's me done for then –ed.]. To some of us more religious Hashers, it is not just a sport or social activity, but a way of life.

Where does InterHash belong?

SD: When you consider the Americas have almost a third of the Hashes in the world, and Europe and Africa also have significant Hash activity, it is unfair to keep the 'world event' in one area. Remember, to Americans, Cyprus was still in Asia in terms of borderline location and cost of getting there. So, yeah, it is time it toured Europe and the Americas, making a stop in Africa at some point as well.

How could/should Hash evolve from here?

SD: I am a little concerned about groups who call themselves Hashes, but over half of their gatherings do not include a trail, but pub gatherings and power-drinking. There should be a balance between the trail and social activity in the 'perfect Hash' (if there is such a thing). Other than those problems, and those are minor points when you consider most Hashes in the world, I think the Hash is perfect as it is.

Barbara 'She Mussel Bitch' Glaser.
First r*n Austin H3 1989
Co-founder Warrior H3; Austin on the Rag H3; Hyde Park Hump Day; Stan-Nats H3

How many trails under your belt so far?
SMB: I have 500 Hashes in Austin, but I couldn't even estimate how many around the world … thousands!

How did you hear of the Hash and your first impressions of it?
SMB: I found out about it from a co-worker in Austin. He worked on me for about a year before I went. First impressions were good!

You are the Grand Bitch of Austin, but how'd you get that handle?
SMB: I built a jail of mussel clams at a lake outside of Austin while camping … we weren't quite ourselves. We set them free at the end of the weekend!

What's your best time ever had on the Hash?
SMB: My most enjoyable Hash trip was 1992 to InterHash in Phuket, Thailand, with the prelude being in Kuala Lumpur – I had never seen anything like it! I Hashed every day for two weeks, awesome trails, and when I got home I had learned so many songs from the Marlborough H3 (Kiwis) as well as others that I couldn't stop singing! It was so hard to explain to everyone back here what it was like to meet great people from all over the world all at once. Everyone at home said I was a 'changed woman' when I returned. Cyprus in 1996 was also a great InterHash – met my husband there and didn't even know it.

And your worst Hashing moment?
SMB: Having to throw everyone out of the suite at 4.30am in Austin at Inter-Am 2001 – I was quoted as saying 'I hate you fuckers! I quit the Hash!'.

How does Hashing in the US compare to your worldwide experiences?
SMB: Hashing in US is varied, but overall has a different feel than Hashing overseas – not very accepted in the general public. UK/Europe definitely has a lot of wit and humour and the pub is a major factor. India/Asia are much more terrain-oriented and a bit more conservative with the nudity, etc. Kiwis/Aussies – kind of a melting pot of all – lots of wit, varied trails and clubs, and very widely accepted.

What's the main thing you've got from Hashing over the years?
SMB: Fortunately no social diseases! The camaraderie and friends that I have made are priceless. There's nothing better than going to any city in the world and having a group of friends to look after you.

Does InterHash belong in Asia or worldwide?
SMB: Anywhere but the US, mainly due to our favourite pastime … lawsuits. After IAH 2001 we realised how much you have to spend on insurance, etc just to not worry about lawsuits – pathetic really.

And where should Hashing go from here?
SMB: I think it needs to actually regress a bit and be not such a business/money-making industry – get back to what it was about originally – Hashing.

Paul 'Flying Booger' Woodford.
First r*n Tampa H3 1988
Founder Pima County Traditional H3 2000
Founding member Hawaii Full Moon H3
Member Okinawa H3, Japan; Honolulu H3 and Aloha H3, Hawaii; Las Vegas
Resur-Erection H3; jHavelina H3 and Mr Happy's Larrikins H3, Arizona

Tell us about your first r*n and the trails since then.
FB: My first Hash was, coincidentally, the inaugural Hash of the Tampa H3. I
first heard of the Hash about a year before my first trail in Tampa. I was r*nning
in a park in San Diego, California, where another r*nner told me about it. I
forgot about it until I was invited to join Tampa H3. At my first trail I remember
feeling quite intimidated by all the fit-looking r*nners who showed up. But
once trail started and I realised it was all in fun, I was in my element. I couldn't
wait for my next Hash trail, and I feel the same enthusiasm and excitement all
these years later. I've Hashed at least once a week ever since. Doing the math,
and including three years in Honolulu where I Hashed twice each week, I
count close to 900 Hashes. How disappointing … I would have guessed I'd
Hashed easily 1,000 times, but the calculator says otherwise. I'd better start
Hashing twice a week again!

Tell us about the best Hashing times ever had.
FB: My absolute favourite experiences have been the road trips – looking up
Hashes and Hashers when travelling, especially overseas. Dribble Dick taking
me to the Hong Kong Hash; meeting Ian Cumming and Magic in New Zealand,
talking about Hash genealogy with Bill Panton in Tasmania, a r*n in the Korean
DMZ with Seoul H3 and a drunken car ride to a whorehouse afterward … these
are memories I'll always cherish. The time I found myself bare-naked with six
Harriettes in a hot tub in Flagstaff, Arizona. The time Black Widow painted my
ass for an Iguana H3 photo session … picnicking in Golden Gate Park with San
Francisco H3 after the Bay to Breakers r*n … talking shit with Hash Potato …
damn, now I'm all thirsty for a beer!

Ever had a bad moment on the Hash?
FB: I've had only a couple of bad experiences, and they had to do with realising
Hashers are, after all, normal people, capable of thoughtless and even bad
behaviour. A dear friend – Diane 'Chikara' Goodman (now Hashing in Sicily)
once opened her house to the Okinawa Hash. Someone took her wallet and all
her money, and someone else nicked most of the hard liquor from her cabinet.
Once in Honolulu several Hashers failed to come in from a particularly
treacherous night trail (no moonlight, thick jungle shiggy, lots of cliffs). The
hares, instead of retracing trail to locate the missing members, hightailed it out
of there and left it up to the pack. One or two Hashers who'd always stiff the
rest of us on the bill at on-afters. We like to think Hashers are better than they
really are.

How did your Hash handle come about?

FB: Okinawa H3 held their annual general meeting – a posh affair at a military officers club, the pack dressed for the occasion. Halfway through the speeches and presentations I became bored, so I hung a spoon on the end of my nose as a signal to the MC to speed things up – an air force tradition, but one the majority of Okinawa Hashers apparently did not share. They noticed the spoon but didn't know why I was wearing it. A week later they named me Flying Booger. 'Flying' because I was the sole US Air Force fighter pilot in the Okinawa H3 at the time; 'Booger' for having hung the spoon on my nose – they wouldn't believe it stayed there all by itself, and insisted I must have used a natural adhesive.

How has Hashing/Hashers changed over the years?

FB: It's getting too damn big, too damn popular, too damn organised, and too well known. Here in the States, if we had to ask permission for what we routinely do, the answer would be 'no'. I suspect the same would be true in Europe, Australia, etc. Hashing is essentially an underground activity, and I say it's time we quit seeking out publicity and take it back underground. Whenever there's a major magazine article about Hashing, newbies start coming to the Hash for all the wrong reasons – they think it's a sex club with a r*nning problem! We don't need publicity to attract new members. Like-minded people have always managed to discover the Hash, just as you and I did.

What's the main thing you've got from Hashing?

FB: Lasting friendships around the country and the world. Enormous gratification from being able to help travelling Hashers find kennels and events (I edit one of the international Hashing internet sites). Confidence in speaking and generally holding my own in public (being RA or GM to a pack of drunken louts will make a leader out of anyone). The intimate knowledge and understanding of one's physical and cultural surroundings one can only get from Hashing through every nook and cranny of every neighbourhood, forest, swamp, junkyard, industrial park, graveyard, ghetto, or open field within a 100-mile radius of home.

Does InterHash belong in Asia or elsewhere?

FB: Asia, broadly defined so as to include Oceania. It's probably inevitable that InterHash will start to tour the world now that Hashing's so popular, but I've always felt that if I wanted to Hash in Europe there's EuroHash or UK Nash Hash, and so on for the Americas, Africa, wherever. InterHash will always be an Asia event to me. I think KL ought to get it automatically once a decade.

How could/should Hash evolve from here?

FB: More Hashers are travelling and getting exposed to different types of Hashing and Hashers. As they gain experience they'll find a style of Hashing they like, and then I predict they'll start small breakaway Hash kennels. I see larger clubs giving birth to smaller, more specialised ones. Here in Tucson three years ago, I founded a men-only Hash modelled after the original 1938 Kuala Lumpur group. No money, no rules, no names, no 'traditions'. Just a good trail with good mates, and we're keeping the membership under 20 so it doesn't get out of hand. Oh, I almost forgot – we're all over 40 years of age. My goodness, that sounds like rules, doesn't it? I hope the Hash never evolves into a mainstream activity. I hope it keeps its underground ethos and flavour, and I hope Hashers always feel like they're doing something John Q. Public would disapprove of or at least never understand. I think this is the nub of it, the reason Hashers are so much more enthusiastic about Hashing than churchgoers are about churchgoing, than barbershop quartet members are about singing, than Masons are about Freemasonry, than ruggers are about rugby, even.

Bill 'Atame' Small.
First r*n Guangzhou H3, China 1988
Member Madrid H3; Buenos Aires H3

What's your pitiful excuse?
A: What else is there to do in China? My first thought was why do I have to torture my body before I can drink a beer? I've now done 500 r*ns in total.
And what does Atame mean, pray tell?
A: I was named by Madrid H3 – it's a Spanish film name – tie me up – about bondage, because I turned up really late for the Hash straight from the office in my tie.
Any particularly memorable Hashing moments?
A: Guangzhou 200th, Madrid 1,000th, the Survivors Hash in Guangzhou the weekend after Tiananmen Square with champagne Down Downs, the recent Escrache Hash in Buenos Aires where Hashers demonstrated loudly at checks outside the banks.
And which r*n would you like to expunge from your memory banks?
A: Setting a summer Hash in hot and humid Guangzhou, while still suffering from flu, and collapsing with dehydration. Luckily I was rescued by the Chinese.
How have Hashers changed over the years?
A: They've got younger – I certainly haven't got older! I don't think it's necessary to try to force evolution. At its roots, each kennel should r*n their Hash according to what the majority enjoy, respecting a minimum of Hash principles such as setting a trail, having Down Downs, drinking beer etc. Humour and humility are essential attributes everywhere if you are going to be a long-time Hasher.

A round-up of hounds in the Americas *would* be complete without mention of the following characters, but we're going to give these Half Minds 15 seconds of fame anyway:

Dick the Boy Wonder from Texas is allergic to yeast, therefore cannot drink beer. Instead, he carries a common household plastic bucket on r*ns with him. Not just any old bucket – this one has an assortment of white spirits, mixers, ice … and even sliced lemons. Hashing doesn't get more civilised than that. "I get post-Hash depression which lasts at least until Happy Hour the following Friday," says the Hasher well-known for his epic bus-tour piss-ups.

John Wayne Bobbit, the guy who became famous when his penis was cut off by his wife, is a Hasher with Las Vegas H3. To prove that everything was in working order after the reattachment surgery, he made a porno video. His Hash name is 'Stitch In Time', but surely no one would dare call him a Short-Cutting Bastard!

Kay Hire is based at the Johnson Space Center and served as a Mission Specialist on a 16-day Space Shuttle flight in 1998. She r*ns in Houston and once visited Bahrain H3, too. Dan 'Rear Entry' Tani is another Hashing astronaut, going on a Shuttle mission to the International Space Station, where he walked outside the vehicle, in December 2001.

Yo, Mo Fo!

This list of hounds' names, some of which might make even Mike Tyson blush, reads more like an anatomy textbook and proves the Americans are masters of the *single* entendre, and will not let the truth stand in the way of a good story.

¼ Barrel, Dayton: "I brought ½ of a keg (ie, ¼ barrel) of Samuel Adams Lager which r*ns for $115/keg to my first Hash. The Hash was impressed a virgin would bring such a fine beer. They also say I'm built like a 1/4 Barrel."

2 Angry Inches, San Diego: "They tried to name me for my 100-ton US Coast Guard licence. **He Likes 'em Big** and **Tons of Fun** were a couple options. Perhaps someone just saw the jury movie 12 Angry Men and things went from there."

2x4, Howlin' H3: His surname's Beam.

8 Yellow Snow, Long Beach H3: "I was in the USAF for eight years, I'm quiet until I drink about eight beers, and I skied and fell face-first into a patch of snow I had just pissed into. That's not true, but it impresses the Harriettes and they bring me beer at the Hash (also a lie)."

Aids Carrier, Carolina Trash: "I wear hearing aids. I also work on an ambulance and sometimes carry Aids patients."

Alias: "I've had so many Hash names from so many places, eventually they just said 'Fuck it, we're calling you Alias'."

All Hands on Dick: "Sails as a hobby. Her friend Richard brought her to the Hash."

All Head and No Shaft, Houston: "Er, golf clubs."

All the Way There: "Married to **Only Half There**. She was six months pregnant at her first Hash. Son is **Are We There Yet**, pushed in baby-jogger."

Alphabet, Calgary H3: His real name is Zbigniew Wladyslaw Danielewicz. *Really*!

Amkneesia, White House H3: "During a Hash party, broke her knee cap. Was so drunk she doesn't remember how it happened."

An How's Her Bush, ex-Honolulu, now Austin: "A play on Anhauser Busch brewery."

Anal Recreation: "I am pretty organised about everything, including my Hashing, so when I brought along a guest to the r*n she said I was 'anal' so they figured I was anal about everything including my recreation."

Anal-Lytical, Ann Arbor H3: "During my 'virgin' months, I could never stay on trail because all the markings seemed awfully sloppy to me. So when I laid my trail, I actually had arrows that precisely pointed to where the next trail marking was … and, while I thought that tying together logs for the water crossings was a nice touch, everyone else thought it kinda compulsive."

Another Fucking Lawyer, North County H3: Exactly that.

Anthrax, Montserrat H3: "RMPF have a file on him as thick as the Hash Hymn Book. Perpetually in trouble."

Asshole on Wheels: "Lawyer who likes bikes."

Attila the Cunt, Fort Eustis H3: "She was riding to a Hash one day with **Tinky Winky** and her husband, **Neandersmall**. They were discussing possible names for her and she said something like 'They'll probably name me something stupid like Attila the Cunt'. So we did!"

Ankle Fester, Fort Eustis H3: "Got his name when the Addams Family was popular – he looks a bit like Uncle Fester with hair. Then he'd hurt his ankle …"

Backdoor Dwarf, ex-Korea, Alaska, Phoenix H3: "At my going away party from Shaw AFB I was thrown through the back door of my trailer. Doc, being my nickname since I don't know when, brought out the Dwarf part."

Bald Headed Fucking Cunt, Huw Jorgen Memorial H3: "He was called **Banshee** and wanted to be renamed."

Battery-Operated Buddy: "I prefer batteries to Hashers, but I'm out of batteries right now!"

Bee In the Bush, Fort Eustis H3: "I was stung on trail by a hornet. You can imagine where!"

Big Gulp: "Went missing on trail, sweepers found her holed up at a 7-11."

Black Hole, Monterey Bay: "He's a chimney sweep."

Blown Offshore, Blue Heron H3: "Many years at sea."

Body Fluid Hazard, Sin City H3: "Guy's legs were bleeding profusely after r*nning through the shiggy."

Booby Prize, Magic City H3: "Had big boobs, then lost 70lb and now they're gone … no more prize until the doctor puts some more in."

Broken Trojan: "Reputedly the best-endowed man at Inter-Am '97."

Buffy the Campfire Slayer, Mosquito County: "Because he pissed on the bonfire, and went r*nning at a nudist camp."

Bullshit, Montserrat H3: "His wife is **Cowpat**."

Burning Bush, San Diego: "Another fun redhead."

Burnt Sox, Mt Vernon H3: "I put my socks in the oven to dry and…"

Bush Wacker, Zone H3: His wife is **Tally Wacker**, his son is **Weed Wacker**.

Candy Wrapper: "'Cause she hangs out with **Nose Candy**."

Cannabis Licked Her, San Diego: "I responded to the question 'What do you like to do with your mouth?' My response was 'Smoke Mother Nature with my lips leading to applying a wicked pleasure-giving tongue to a willing Harriette'."

Captain Crash, Seattle H3: "Named for her great falls."

Chap Dick, Magic City: His partner is **Chap Lips**.

Cheap Weenie, Bakersfield: "Always tries to get away without paying. His wife is **Cheap Date**."

Chemical Whorefare, Eerie H3: "We were camping and all the guys were naked and farting, and I was in the middle, fully clothed and smiling with these eight boys around me."

Chew Chew Man, New Orleans: "I ran with an engineer's cap which inspired Choo Choo, but the Harriette I was dating changed it to Chew Chew. Go figure!"

Chunky Monkey, Wolf Pack: "Blew chunks on **Cheeky Monkey's** car."

Classy Chassis, White House H3: "Was a six-foot beauty that had a body men often die for. In addition she drove a classic Ford Mustang."

Cocker, OTR H3: Her surname is Spanihel.

Comes With Chicks, Cleveland: "He always shows up with broads, and we give him a Down Down if he doesn't."

Coppertone Bone, San Diego H3: "As a naturist, whenever I go to the beach, lie on my deck, or travel about on a warm and sunny vacation, I prefer *au naturel*. When queried why I wasn't afraid of burning it, I told them I was careful to always put suntan lotion on it."

Cox Stroker: "In college I was involved in rowing, and was coxing the fours…"

Crash and Burn, Ann Arbor H3: "I am physically impaired so I fall a lot."

Crotchduster, Charlotte H3: "He was a cropduster pilot at that time, so I am his **Cockpit**."

Cum Fuck Me, San Diego: "The sexiest Harriette."

Cums Anally, Little Rock H3: "Named because he used to only show up at the Hash once a year."

Cunt for Red October, San Diego H3: "A gorgeous redhead, US Naval Academy/Annapolis grad."

Cuntinental Breakfast, Waukesha H3: "My original name was **Cuntinental Divide**, because I worked at a wilderness outfitter. Then on a Hash road trip, we passed a motel sign that said 'Free Continental Breakfast', and everyone turned to look at me. I said 'I may be easy but I'm not free'."

Damian the AntiChrist, Dallas/Fort Worth H3: Real name – Andy Crist.

Damn Near Redneck, San Diego: "Otherwise known as **DNR**. Got his name because of recent open-heart surgery and because he was from the south. DNR is an acronym for 'Do Not Resuscitate'. It's used when someone is on terminal life-support and the family decides to 'let them go'."

Dancing Dick, LA H3: Son of **Lap Dancer** and **Chapped Dick**.

Dark Tanyon: "He was the Fourth Musketeer. As I was introduced by **The Three Musketeers**, it was a natural."

Dead Pussy, Pittsburg H3: "When he was a virgin hare he laid a trail through a dark railroad tunnel and over a dead cat."

Deep Cavity, Tampa Bay: "A dental assistant."

Deep Doo Doo, Magic City: "I r*n a dealer's tag on my car to avoid paying taxes, and basically I am always in or starting some shit."

Defloured, Wisconsin: "First time I ran the Hash everyone kept blabbering about looking for the flower. I saw no 'flour'. Figured they meant 'flower' so spent the whole time looking for flowers..."

Dick Long and Prosper, Columbus H5: "I was smart enough to postpone my naming until the Halloween Hash in Orlando where I was dressed as Mr Spock. I was counting on **Mr Cock**, but almost ended up with **Captain's Log**."

Dick on a Tit: "Infant son of **Dickup Truck** and **Tits Up**."

Dick Van Wrinkle: "My last name sounds like Dick Skin, and I fell asleep on my girlfriend one night."

Dinged Up Dick, California: Wife is **Ofeelya** and son – named hours after being born – **Feel My Dick**!

Dinky, Zonie H3: Double Income No Kids Yet ... also quite small.

Divine Bovine, Fort Eustis: "She rides a mechanical bull well..." Got pregnant and significant other became **Cow Poker**.

DOH!, Richmond: "DOH! was given a temporary name of **On-On Doh** since his nerd name is Ananda. When he got his permanent name, he told us that his favourite movie is Harold and Maude, so he was named **Does Old Hags**, or DOH!"

Don't Have One Yet, Las Vegas H3: "This guy went without a name for so long we named him this."

Dr Crotch Rot, Atlanta: "Dermatologist specialising in genital diseases."

Dr Sewage, Montserrat H3: "Interested in cycling and recycling."

Dr Strangeglove, Fort Eustis H3: "Works in health care. While I haven't verified he has anything to do with examinations of the prostate, he's certainly been accused of performing them."

Dreary the Hugging Man, Calgary H3: "I always r*n dead fucking last ... and I hug people a lot."

Driving Miss Daisy, Bitburg H3: "**Hooter Hunter** was without a vehicle for quite some time and relied on me to transport him to the Hash every Saturday. I drive the speed limit and obey all the traffic signs. One day on the way to the Hash he said 'You drive so slow you could drive Miss Daisy'."

Dudley J Noswell, Mud Hen H3: "The first Hash I went to, introductions around the circle were made so I said my name was Studley J. Hungwell – kiss on the first date, drop my pants on the second."

Dumb Shit, Magic City: "Followed lime on the railroad tracks and led the pack five miles down before he noticed it was not flour."

Ear of the Sperm, Columbus H5: "I turned my head at the wrong time ... no, just joking ... it's the sperm cell-shaped earrings."

ElectroCock Therapy, San Diego Full Moon: "She is a psychiatric nurse who does (or once did) give electric shock therapies."

Episiotomy: "At Inter-Am '97 he ran into a tree on trail and opened a huge gash in his head that was stitched shut by the only doctor available – a gynaecologist!"

Erection, Montserrat H3: "Known for his blue prints and Chinese swear words."

Every Sperm Is Sacred, Gainesville: "He worked at the university and was a real moraliser. After a few beers he'd get into this real sermon of fire and brimstone stuff. I don't think he Hashes anymore."

Extra Extra, Bakersfield: "A newspaper ad made her come to the Hash."

Face Plant Puke Princess: "I was named after the Hedon weekend … it pretty much sums it up."

Famous Anus: "He mooned the naming committee."

Fish Lips, Long Beach H3: "She was asked what she wanted her name to be and she said (with a mouthful of food and an accent), 'I'm Speechless'. Translation: 'I'm Fishlips'."

Flatliner, Bakersfield: "Anaesthetist."

Flying Booger: Wife is **Pick 'n' Flick**, daughter **Green Flagger**, son **Nose Candy**.

For Sale or Rent, DC: "On trail once I stopped outside a real estate agents' window and was looking at the property listings."

Forest Gulp, ex-Okinawa, Memphis: "I have a drinking problem … I don't have an uvula in my throat so the beer goes straight down my throat and blows out through my nose!" [Do you have a younger sister? –ed.]

Free Meat, Austin: "I wish there was a kinky or slutty story, but I got it when I was a virgin hare and serving up this meat, and two people were saying 'You got any vegetarian stuff?' and I'm like 'C'mon, it's free meat!'"

French Toasted: "He got so drunk on a Hash pub crawl he started speaking French to the exclusion of his native English."

Fried Green Tits: "She works in a cardiac ward and once forgot to put gel on the fibrillator, so when she did the whole 'Clear!' thing, she burnt two big squares on the guy's chest!"

Friendly Thighs, Florida: "I'm a flight attendant for United Airlines, the Friendly Skies."

Fuck 'em Dano, White House H3: "Named after the Hawaii Five-O line, 'Book 'em Dan-o', mainly because his nerd name is Dan."

Fucking Einstein, East Bay: "When asked a difficult question, replied 'Who do you think I am…?'"

Fucks Every Way But Up, Dayton H3: "Nice built Harriette and her name is self-explanatory."

Fucks Like an Egyptian, Little Rock H3: "Was named after his wife, **Little Egypt,** a professional Middle Eastern dancer."

Fuggin Crazy, Seattle H3: "For r*nning marathons and ultras on the same weekend."

Fukarwe, Seattle H3: "For his ability to get lost."

Garfield, ex-Seoul, Washington DC: "I used to r*n dive trips out to the islands, and on Sunday afternoon after two nights on the piss I'd usually curl up in the captain's cabin or in the wheelhouse and have a snooze, and I've always been a little fat fucker. When I got back to the States I got a name **Moby Whale, the Great White Dick** – but when I went back overseas I started using Garfield again."

Got Milk?, Fort Eustis H3: "They're really pretty nice!" says her proud husband.

Great Balls of Flour, Charlotte H3: "She set trail with a tennis ball dipped in flour!"

Great Buns of Fire, San Antonio: "Nude fire sitting."

Grunt, Pine Lake H3: Partner's name is **Groan**.

Had a Madam, ex-Yongsan, White House H3: "I was dating a Korean woman who worked as a madam (term used to describe a nightclub hostess and a woman who ran house of ill repute). Often they were the same thing. In my case they were not, only nobody believed me."

Hairy Foul Balls, Bakersfield: Hirsute baseball pitcher. His wife is **Foul Territory**.

Hamburger Helper, San Diego: "R*nning through a campground along the coast, when we came upon a cow that had escaped from the gay rodeo at the Del Mar Fairgrounds…"

Have Shit Will Travel, Viva Las Vegas: "Fertiliser salesman with large territory."

Hawking Up Pigeon Shit, San Diego Full Moon: "Is a recent rename of Pigeon Shit. He decided he wanted a new name and we didn't want to change his name too much as too many already knew him as just **Pigeon Shit**."

HIV+: "I'm a noisy bastard so they wanted a name that would shut me up. People are always asking me, but I'm glad I got this name – it was that or **Cinderella**."

Hoosier Daddy, Orlando: "From Indiana. Works for child support."

Hostitute, Big Hump H3: "I was a Las Vegas 'cocktail server' and in the hospitality industry for a long time…"

Hot Steaming Bush, Houston: "Squatted to pee in the bushes. When I got up the ground and the bush I peed on were steaming."

Houston We Have a Problem and **Austintacious**, Texas: These two American guys were actually adopted and named by the Newcastle H3, Australia. They were just on holiday in Darwin when they bumped into the Newcastle Hash, who were in town for the Aussie Nash Hash, and roped them in. Houston turned up for his virgin r*n the next day in full denim Wrangler jean outfit, stetson hat and leather shoes in 35 degree Celsius heat, wading through knee-deep mud and shiggy. They were both instant legends."

Huh?: "Administers hearing tests."

Human Resources, ex-Pensacola, Orlando: "Apply within! Because of my large, er, endowments, which they called Human Resources."

Hung Like a Fish, Little Rock H3: "He always tries to avoid getting wet on Hash r*ns."

Hung Like a Gerbil: "I go by the nickname Bear and had decided that was far too masculine a name. When they said a gerbil was a smaller furry animal I replied 'What, hung like a gerbil?' That fifth pint of Bristols had done the damage."

I B Dick: "**Bitchy Beaver** kept on going round saying 'I love dick, I love dick', and everyone was saying 'Who's Dick?' So when I turned up on the Hash she points to me and says '*That's* Dick!'"

I Blow Silver, San Diego: "At the time I started Hashing I was really into horses, playing polo, almost ready to buy a horse of my own. A derivative of Hi Ho Silver!"

Imelda Whistle Tits, ex-Philippines, Tidewater H3: "Decided to let my love jugs blow in the breeze without restraints. Imelda was the name of my maid in The Philippines."

In Deep, Tidewater H3: "Myself, wife and son took over as 'beverage people'. My wife became **Beverage Wench**, son is **Water Boy**."

It's Show Time, Dallas/Fort Worth: "Mooned a freight train and when the work train came by with all their spotlights on, she flashed them!"

Joe Nose-Pick, San Jose H3: "Joe Nose-Pick comes from '*Jo no spika engleesh*', Jorge's frequent response to visitors at Inter-Am #1."

John Handcock, Mt Vernon H3: "Refused to sign Hash log book for first 10 or so r*ns in a futile effort to avoid being named. John Hancock was the most prominent signatory of the American Declaration of Independence."

Joy to His Mother, Princeton H3: "You've probably heard the song, which ends 'He may be a joy to his mother/But he's a pain in the asshole to me'. My name involved my mother, an email message, and Hashing scoundrel Rambo."

Jurisdickhead, Mud Hen H3: "A retired cop and now a lawyer."

Kiddie Licker, Vancouver: "They were going to call me **Clitty Licker** but there was someone called that already, so they wanted to make it more disgusting. It's got nothing to do with anything I've done!"

Kimo-I-Wanna-Lei-Ya: "A Hasher of Hawaiian descent whose first name is Kimo."

L.O.U.S.E.: "Lousy Obnoxious Underhanded Sack of Excrement!"

Laa Laa, Fort Eustis/Tidewater H3: "My favourite colour's yellow. When they asked me what I *didn't* want to be named I said 'Anything that doesn't have to do with **Tinky Winky** (another Hasher). So of course they named me after the yellow TeleTubbie…"

Lady Bugger: "Plays on an adult soccer team called the Lady Bugs."

Lay Down and Shut Up, Jacksonville Beach: "His wife **Bite My Ass** is so obnoxious and verbal, the only way he'd get any is by commanding 'Lay down and shut up'."

Leaky Tampon, White House: "Stepped on a ketchup package which splattered on his shoes."

Lei Over: "Single babe, works for an airline."

Leisure Suit Larry, Washington DC: "One of the real early X-rated video games was called Leisure Suit Larry in the Land of the Lounge Lizards, about this horny guy going after all these women."

Licker Kicker, Orlando: "Caught my hubby eating cooter and it wasn't mine so … I beat him up."

Lickum Stickum, Sacramento H3: "I work for the Post Office."

Little Richard, Tidewater/Fort Eustis H3: "When asked what name he wanted, he answered '**Enormous Dick**'."

Little Weed, Montserrat H3: Narcotics expert.

Long Cutting Bastard, Gypsies in the Palace H3: "I was front r*nning once and mistook these blobs of paint for the trail and ended up taking the pack on a way longer trail."

Long Dong Sliver, White House H3: "He is about 5'4" and built like a fire plug but always bragged of his large member and prowess in the land of the little furry thing. He was one of those rape and pillage guys that wanted to tell you about it all the time. So to shut him up we christened him this."

Louisiana Reptile Fancier, Princeton H3: "A Princeton University professor from Louisiana – his frequent post-Hash lectures on snakes earned him the name."

Luft Schwein, Orange County: "I did the airline ticketing and Zulu knew my computer password was 'piglover'. When we started Hashing, he remembered that. Mighty Byte and Batta added the German flavour."

Martha Fucking Stewart, San Diego: "I had a friend and her family from Philadelphia – from where I had just moved – come visit me in San Diego. I was staying with a Harriette named Icebox who had a beautiful patio looking over the houses below, and the mountains behind. I decided to barbecue for my friends and used Icebox's dishes, stemware, placemats and cloth napkins. During dinner my friend exclaimed 'Jesus, John, you moved to San Diego and turned into Martha-fucking-Stewart.'"

Master Bates Twice, Ozark H3: "His surname is Bates so we called him **Master Bates.** He demanded a rename so we called him Master Bates Twice."

Math, ex-Huachuca, Alaska Midnight H3: Became **El Zero** after moving from Huachuca, Arizona to Alaska.

McTaco, East Bay: Real name is Jose Hanagan.

Mellow Foreskin Cheese, ex-Washington DC: "I am from Wisconsin, so my GM referred to me as a cheese-head, but apparently Mellow Foreskin Cheese is a line from a British drinking song."

Mental Floss, Fort Eustis H3: "I work in a mental hospital and … you'd have to see the rest."[Prepared to look into it –ed.]

Micki Mouse, Seattle H3: "Not for her big ears, but she's quiet as a mouse."

Micro-soft.cum, Harrisburg-Hershey H3: "Computer network administrator."

Missing Link, Orlando: "I wear size 10 4E width shoes and I used to have only one eye brow. Someone said 'He looks like a damn caveman!'"

Mistress Viagra: "I'm a chemist!"

Moan 'n Fucker, LA H3: Her real name is Ramona Tucker.

Mommy Rearest, Ann Arbor H3: "I have five children (Mommy). The first time that I Hashed, I mooned the expressway while r*nning over an overpass (Rearest). The first Hasher in my family was my mother – she introduced her daughters to the Hash. This is how she got her name, **Beaver Cleaver.** My sister, **Snatch to Match**, is a hairdresser. She changes her hair colour often and, yes, all hair matches. I have a brother, **Suck Queen**, that was a vacuum cleaner salesman."

Monsterbater, Waukesha H3: "From doing a hands-in-the-pants dance to a B52 song, There's a Monster in My Pants."

Mother Inferior, Ann Arbor H3: "On a weekend Hash two friends and I dressed up as nuns. A pregnant nun, a drunk nun, and me – the Mother Superior. We shortcut the trail and were standing on the steps of a Catholic church and, as the pack came over a hill and into view, we mooned them! The Catholic Hashers were especially moved by the experience."

Mother Theresa, Orlando: "There were several others named on the same day and they'd r*n out of names. I had previously Hashed in a very religious area and, after rejecting a bunch of names, someone yelled out 'Well, who is he then – Mother Theresa?'"

Mr Microbone, Fort Eustis H3: "Works for the TV cable company and does karaoke on the side. It was a natural progression since he keeps his hair cut close to his skull."

Trailer Trash, Fort Eustis H3: "I used to have a pop-up camping trailer. When **Cinderfella** and **Rack 'n' Sack** got married they had a Hash reception at **Tinky Winky**'s house. A virgin that day, Matt drank in abundance and we put him to bed in the trailer. I went home for the evening, and when I returned the next day for the trailer I found the door broken beyond repair. It seems Matt awoke early with a very full bladder, and unable to discern in the darkness how to open the door, he simply burst through it, 'trashing' my trailer."

Neandersmall, Fort Eustis H3: "A short fellow, close to five feet. With his long greying hair and beard, he looks somewhat like Jerry Garcia, and he acts like he belongs to the era. At the circle I chose him to lead Father Abraham – his movements were somewhat mechanical, a bit like the dinosaurs in the older movies."

Nabob, Carolina H3: "Nabob is the Indian word for someone who's made their fortune overseas. I was in the forces in Asia for many years."

Never Ben Layden, San Diego: "An Arab American."

Nice Cum, LA H3: Daughter of **Nice Pussy** and **Cums When He Can**.

Noody Blews, Wolfpack: "Has a picture in his dorm room of his wife wearing his Air Force Service dress coat and nothing else on."

Northern Exposure, Anchorage: "I usually take a piss on trail, and since I Hash in Alaska…"

Nutless Sac, Gypsies in the Palace H3: "I had a motorcycle accident and ended up with all these plates and screws in my leg. When they were finally taken out, I took all the pieces along in a plastic bag to show the Hash – it had bits of metal, screws, bolts, everything … except nuts."

Nuts 'n' Honey, Boise: "Got caught trying to pull a stinger out of **Quinton's** crotch area…"

Occupied: "Male flight attendant. Self-proclaimed Mile High Club member."[Wanking doesn't count! –ed.]

On Golden Pond, Wolf Pack: "Was so drunk, she passed out in a puddle of her own piss."

Oozing Syphilitic Dick-ta-phone, Rhode Island H3: "He was originally anointed as **Dick-ta-phone**, and the lad felt that the handle was not sufficiently cute or 'cool'. So he was promptly renamed."

Pane in the Glass, Monterey Bay: "Broke a window at a Hash event."

Parrot Head: "I'm a big Jimmy Buffet fan."

Pay Per View, Washington DC: "Something to do with a sports broadcasting van and a bunch of keen voyeurs outside watching the 'action' inside the van."

Pecker Wrecker, Charleston: "She used to wear braces."

Penis Fly Trap, Bakersfield: "Commented about the cobwebs on her boyfriend's bedroom ceiling."

Pillsbury Blow Boy, Long Beach H3: "When I first moved to Long Beach and started r*nning, I would bring fresh-baked bread every week as a get-to-know people better thing."

Piss in Boots, Miller Hill: "Got really fucked up and damn near pissed in my room-mate's boots." Wife is **Golden Shower**.

Polly Ringbald, Chicago: "Polly is from my work with parrots. The rest? Well, I need a hot-tub and some beer before I will reveal the rest." [See you in the hot tub with Mental Floss –ed.]

Polly Wanna Cocker: "I have a pet cockatiel who, believe it or not, masturbated on my hand watching Dawson's Creek. Now he does it regularly."

Pound Puppy: "Was **Deputy Dog** until my car got towed to the impound lot during an après. My offer to sell the name to whomever comes up with the $85 still stands."

Pubic Perm, San Francisco: "Caught r*nning into a beauty salon during a Hash, to use the bathroom she claims."

Public Dick, Monterey Bay: "She is a detective with the navy."

Pulleeze Babee, Ann Arbor H3: "We met in October of '95 and for a first date I took her on an Octobermess Hash weekend. When I would ask for favours I would get on my knees, wrap my arms around her and go 'Please baby, please baby, please baby'. So my wife got this name."

Pusseye Galore, Spokane H3: "We were on this r*n and this old guy's kind of flirting with her. He says 'I'll keep an eye out for you'. With that he removes his glass eyeball and hands it to her. She immediately gets it, and inserts it between her legs for all to see, like cyclops staring out at us. Photos are taken, and the r*n's about to start, so she hands the eye back to him, he washes it with beer and sticks it back in his head."

Pussy Gourmet: "I had this cat which I'd feed the best stuff to…"

R*nning Bare, Emerald Coast: "After my very first r*n I ended up sleeping naked on the lawn outside my house … no clothes, plus I'd lost my keys, my car, everything. The security guard said 'I'd better let you in, Sir'. Turns out my stuff was all safely locked inside the beer wagon."

Rambo on One, Seattle H3: "Calls 'On! On!' with just one mark."

Random Balls, Tallahassee Area: "Did work for the Florida Lottery."

Rear Buccaneer, ex-Seoul, Florida: "I used to fly a Learjet so they said 'You like the name **Lear Buccaneer?** Well, you can't have it because you're *Rear* Buccaneer!'"

Roach Motel, White House H3: "Whenever she brings a virgin to the Hash they are never seen again. Take-off on old US ad campaign for an adhesive insecticide with the slogan 'Roaches check in but they don't check out'."

Rosie Lickety Split, Ex-Korea, now Florida: "Named after Rosie, the lady who took the subway in the Boston Marathon and 'Split' from doing one too many splits at an office party and getting bruised."

Rum Titty Bum, Montserrat H3: "He's an engineer and there's a song about engineers …"

Rumpled Foreskin, Orange County: "I'm a swimmer, water polo player, lifeguard and swim coach…"

San Quentin Cream Puff, Houston: "San Quentin is the name of a large and infamous federal prison. His *first* ever Hash event was a weekend campout on the beach – Friday night people were just hanging out and drinking. As the hours grew late and the singing grew loud and people started getting naked, apparently somebody called the cops – Cream Puff suddenly found himself pinned to the beach, naked, by a police car's headlights. All the other Hashers magically melted into the dunes. He was arrested for public drunkenness and indecent exposure. He spent the night (still naked, I believe) in the county jail, before some Hashers came along the next day to bail him out so that he wouldn't miss his first Hash." *[Footnote: later acquitted after spirited defence by a Hash legal eagle.]*

Scratch 'n' Sniff, Richmond: "Ran naked through poison ivy one time."

Scrubbing Chubbies, LA H3: "I have three kids. My oldest boy of three years old likes to take baths, gets a little too excited with the soap and pops a little chubby."

Scum Sucking Fecal Philiac, Sin City H3: "Installs flow-meters in sewers and used to sleep after a few brews."

Seaman Swallower, Tampa Bay: "Dated a navy boy."

See More Buns, San Diego: "I got my name from Hash Harlot who saw me moon the finish line at the Honolulu Marathon one year."

See Spot Fuck: "I was dog-sitting a very friendly male Labrador for a co-worker. I had the house to myself and didn't bother to close the bathroom door when I showered. He was very 'happy'."

Shallow Entry, Charleston: "She once fell in a pond that wasn't deep enough."

Shit Eating Grin, Boston: "At San Fran's '94 'Green Shit With Nuts' r*n, I took the liberty of smearing chocolate all over my face…"

Shoots Blanks, White House H3: "Marine artillery reservist. Was activated and sent to Okinawa for Desert Storm but was never invited to the Gulf."

Shrimp Pimp, Tallahassee Area: "Works for the State of Florida, promoting seafood."

Slam Dunk, Orlando H3: "She dived head first into shallow water at an On On and broke her back. Then she was 'taken into temporary custody' by the police during the Miss Inter-Americas '89. She won, but earned herself the new nickname of **Slammer Dunk**."

Sleeps Around: "I have narcolepsy (yaaaaawn)."

Slug Flicker, Seattle H3: "For protecting novice campers from killer slugs."

Snatch Key Kid, White House H3: "At one Hash, she realised she had lost her key and she enlisted several Hashers to help her find it. She wasn't having any luck, but when she went to the bathroom, she discovered that her key was in the crotch of her shorts. She is tiny and looks very young."

Spermivore, Richmond: "She loves meat, and she gave a BJ in the shower."

Steaming Eruption, Montserrat H3: "Gets excited when his hot rocks reach the sea."

Stick Your Finger in It, Atlanta H3: "It was during Lent, and **Toilet Seat** gives up booze every year for Lent. So he had to do a Coke Down Down for giving up booze. The Coke was warm and all head, so I walked into the middle of the circle (I was a new-boot, I didn't realise that was inappropriate) to tell TS that if he stuck his finger in it, all the bubbles would go away…"

Stool Sample, Lima H3: "Socialising during a Down Down at the apartment of **SaltPeter** I noticed some mangy dogs that came up from the yard to the roof apartment begging for scraps; they looked bad. My thinking out loud 'I wonder what you'd find if you got a stool sample from one of those mutts' led shortly thereafter to the handle. Pissed me off, which of course guaranteed it stuck. I was thinking more along the lines of **Lady Killer**, or **Superman** … you know, something appropriately modest, yet accurately descriptive."

Struck from Behind, Houston: "There was a three-pound mosquito on my back, and this guy came along and splattered it."

Sympathy Fuck, San Antonio H3: "Many moons ago, when I wasn't dating much, it was **Ain't Gonna Get None**, but they found out about a certain incident …"

Tampon Drizzle, Minneapolis: "Sometime on trail, I knelt down on some thorns or stones or something. I didn't notice it until we got to the end, and my sweatpants, which had a ripped knee to begin with, were soaked in blood from the tear at the knee down."

Teddy, Montserrat H3: "Keeps **Polished Balls** interested with her selection of undergarments."

The Ass-o-Rockamundo, Little Rock H3: " He's a sports writer and wrote an article about the horses entered in the Arkansas Derby. He zeroed in on one horse named Rockamundo, and told his readers that this horse had never won a race and was so bad it shouldn't be allowed on the track with other horses for fear they would r*n over him. The next day Rockamundo won at 99-1 odds." [He probably had money on it! –ed.]

The Decorated Asshole, Ann Arbor/Motown H3: "My name was a combination of things … service recognition, and tattoos on my ass, one of which is the On On foot."

Topless Pussy, Magic City: Showed up to a r*n in a Jaguar convertible with the top down."

Topographical Panties, Onslow County H3: "I have a real fetish for tight clothes. Not being a big r*nner, I tend to have a lot of aerobic gear, so I usually wear spandex bike shorts and r*nning bras to the Hash. I also wear very tight pants, skirts, dresses, etc to other Hash frequented venues and events…"

Upchuck, Las Vegas H3: "I'm in the tooling and die-making business."

Van Go, San Diego H3: His surname is Painter.

Vitamin D Cup, Little Rock H3: "After a r*n she had wet spots around the nipples of her ample breasts."

Wandering Menstrual, San Diego: "A Harriette often playing a flute."

Wax on Whacks off (WoWo), White House H3: "He has his back waxed to remove body hair. The Hash thought that was a bit vain and decided to modify the line from the Karate Kid to imply that he beat off a lot. There is also a hand gesture that goes with his name, a circular waxing motion with the left hand and a beating off motion with the right hand."

Wet Dreams, ex-Calgary now Vancouver: "She woke up sweating one night … she had a dream about being swept downstream on a Hash river crossing."

Wet Toe Job: "I took a pogo stick to my first r*n because it was so wet, so they called me **Wet Job** (which is code for an assassination). Later, I injured my toe so became Wet Toe Job."

White Trash, ex-Caribbean: "Our Caribbean GM just came up to me and said 'You're looking like some kind of white trash, mon,' and it stuck."

Whiz Kid: Was caught peeing on a dumpster.

Who Said Head?, San Diego: "A pretty, cute, fun head-hunter."

Wipe Her Ass, ex-Jakarta, Texas: "As I'm from Texas they named me after the saying about big raw steaks … 'Cut off its horns and wipe its ass'."

Womb With a View, Houston: "I fell asleep naked in the tent one night and apparently gave them a good view … I was 'gang viewed'!"

Yard Dog, Seattle H3: "For his way with the opposite sex."

Zam-Bone-Me, BVD H3: "A female Hasher who sat on the ice as we threw out potential names. About five or 10 minutes into the naming we noticed her sliding back and forth on the iceblock and enjoying every minute of it – moaning with pleasure the entire time. So we named her after the ice skating rink Zambony machine."

And in our continuing series of wankers who were to busy getting pissed and optimistically trying to get laid to check their emails, a further list of anatomical, gynaecological and illogical offerings which might have a hint of humour behind them, but we doubt it:

A Maze'n Nuts, Able Bodied Reporter, Anal Enamel, Anal Vice, Any Ole Will Do, Any Orifice Will Do, Armadildo Dundee, Arsephault, Pussy Whipp'd, Art Dicko, Ass Gasket, Assholiness, Ass-on-Tap, Babawa Wawa, Babe the Blew Spand-Ox, Baboobs, Bang-a-Beast, Basket Boom Boom, Beat'er Butt, Beenerschnitzel, Big Bird Turd, Bitch Set Me Up, Bondo Jovi, Bovine Enema, But My Balls Are Hairy, Cave Person, Certified Porn Actress (CPA), Charm My Snake, Chucking Sparrow, Church Buster, Circuitcision, Cock O'dial Done Me, Conerub the Ballearian, Corpus Delectable, Cream De Mented, Creamy Butt Cheeks, Crusty Beaver, Cum of a Cum of a Sailor, Cums When He's Gone, Cuntsicle, Daily Swallow, Delay Llama, Ding Crosby, Doofus White Boy, Dozy Cunt, Dr Greenjeans, Dr Who-Gas, Dumber than a Redneck, E=Mcscrewed, El Passout, English as a Second Language, Esprit de Corpse, Everlasting

Gobstopper, Fairy Manilow, Fashion Plate, Fellatio Domingo, Flash Gonad, Flavour of the Month, Floundering Assplant, Fuck You I'm Leaving!, Gang Banker, Gerbil Entry, Gooey Blow, Goosed to Fulfilment, H Toad, esq., Herman of Hollywood, Hopeless Road Trash, Hump Me Dump Me, Hung Chow, Hung Daddy Tutu, Hyena Butt, I Do Testicles, Imitation Hot Sausage, Impotent Slug, Joe Fuzzroots, Kangaklit, King Tuk Tuk, Lacksadicksical, Legionnaires Disease, Lick Me I'm Salty, Likes 'em Tight, Limping Turtle, Little Dead Birds Covered With Oil, Loo Tenant, Looseal Bald, Lost Her Pussy, Lucille Queens Flasher, Made Marion of Sure Wood for US, Make Me an Offer, Maliniki Hui, Mamma Get Off Me, Marquis de Shiggy, McMuff Diver, Mean Uncle Buck, Meisterbator, Melt in Your Mouth, Midget Molester, Minor Minor Minor Tom the Army Guy, Missionary Position, Monkey Wench, Motel Sex, Mother Chalker, Mother Gerbil, Mr Peeeeeeeenut, Mr Potato Head, Muffstasche, Muscle Twat, My Lips Are Seals, Grouchy Tiger Hidden Tampon, Natural Born Lesbian, No Duchie No Nookie, Not Tonight, O'less Dick, Pablo Picasshole, Pablo the Goat, Paddle Me Silly, Paddy No'toole, Pay Per Screw, Penile Anchor, Phallus Nerfus, Pickin''n' Grinnin', Pigs in Spaaaaaaaace, Piss Whistle, Popacrotchi, Porn Piglet, Porno Flick, Postage Paid, Potato Mashing PBR Balls, Pound 69, Price of Turds, Prince Variant, Princess Jism, Probing Sex Knave, Proud Mary Keep on Spankin', Pull My Finger, Puta-Fatz, PV=nRT, Rabbi Doolittle, Rectum R*nner, Red Hot Anal Pepper, Red Hot Chili Pecker, Rev Poon Tang, Revirgination, Road Jaundice, Rodent Felcher, S&M&M&M Man, Sanitary Not, Saran Crap, Sauercrotch, ScabAss Rising, Seeester, Self-Executing Officer, Senator Diggler, Shit Fish, Shit on a Shingle, Side Saddle, Singing Menstrual, Sir Walter Raleigh, Smel Gibson, Smoking Wiener, Son of a Ditch, Spanking Ryans Privates, Sperm Burp, Spinning Fuck My Sister, Squid Humper, Stickman Horse's Ass #1, Stool Diver, Strap on Tool, Stupid Guide Dog, Suck and Swallow Her Saggy Behind, Sux2Bme, Testosternot, The Euclidean Hasher, The Gerbils are Sick And Dying, The Greenwich Grabber, The Other Woman, The Raj of Singapore, The Singing Nun, Throat Deep, Throatwarbler Mangrove, Through My Felching Straw, Thump Thump, Triple Tongue, Trojan Whore, Tropical Repression, Tuk Tuk, TV Hair, Vax Headroom, Virtually Hung, Wandering Woo Woo, Wankee Doodle, Was Hung Lo, Wax My Ass, Weeny Wanker Weevil Knievel, Whipped Von Nipple, Whore Durve, Whorenado Alley, www (nicehtml), Yak-O-Ono, Zero the Gay Blade, Zippy the Cyberpimp, Zippy's Doo Dah.

Anecdotes from the Americas.

The Urban Iditarod is an annual event based on the Alaskan race where 60-dog sled teams race across the frozen tundra. This is slightly different in that the four 'dogs' are humans and roped-up to pull a shopping cart through the busiest touristy areas of San Francisco, such as Fisherman's Wharf. Apart from liberal drinks stops for the thirsty hounds, "barking is encouraged" say the disorganisers. Police don't stop the traffic, adding to the chaos and disorder of the day. More than 35 teams (240 hounds in total) fronted for the seventh event. Of the Urban Iditarod, the San Francisco Examiner once wrote: "So odd it demands the question – who let *these* dogs out?" while the Stanford Business Magazine referred to it as "free of any redeeming social value whatsoever"[Guess they haven't registered a team for next time? –ed.]. A Hash is r*n in conjunction with this event, with San Francisco East Bay H3 and San Diablo H3 being the key participants. "We short-cut a lot of the first part of the r*n to the beer check, but were still out over three hours and probably did about 13 plus miles," remembers Debriefed of one classic fiasco.

A r*n set by Honolulu H3 had a trail going through the local Macy's department store, and up an escalator. The check was to be found in the ladies' lingerie department (where all good Hashmen should check regularly any way!). The dozing security guards were then alerted to this strange behaviour and hit the button to close the automatic security doors. By this time, all the pack had bolted clear. Unfortunately one Hasher had bought his son and dog along, and they were still on the *inside* of the doors. With cap in hand, and amid profuse apology and embarrassment, the Hash father returned to claim his son and dog.

The Cleveland Press ran a story about an unidentified Hasher in 1987 who had gone to a gas station to use their public toilets. Unknown to him, a station attendant had earlier poured leftover paint and thinners down the toilet bowl. The Hasher, now comfortably seated and doing his business, lit a cigarette and threw the match down into the toilet. The man "suffered first and second-degree burns of his genital area after the toilet he was sitting in … exploded". [Anyone going to own up? –ed.]

At the Inter-Am in Trinidad, they had a r*n up a mountain in beautiful countryside. "I was an FRB and came to this waterfall, about two storeys high," says Yo Adrian. "At the bottom was a guy with some inflatable inner-tubes calling out for me to jump, which I did, landing in a small pool, then down a fast-flowing chute, before r*nning down through the stream all the way to the end. My husband [Lofty] was not so lucky … he was stuck in this swirling eddy after he jumped down, and then one after one other members of the pack were jumping and landing on him pushing further under, time and time again. He's been a professional diver with the navy for 20 years and he reckons he's never been so close to death."

They occasionally lose hounds on the Boston H3, but they once managed to lose a hare! The pack turned up for the r*n, and spent a good time searching for the trail which then took them on a gruelling and disorientating 90-minute trail. They found the beer but, alas, no hare. Turns out by the time he'd returned from laying the trail, the pack had headed off – so he set off in pursuit losing his way on his own trail. The pack were well into the beers 45 minutes after the r*n when he finally made it back.

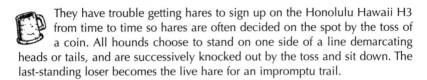

They have trouble getting hares to sign up on the Honolulu Hawaii H3 from time to time so hares are often decided on the spot by the toss of a coin. All hounds choose to stand on one side of a line demarcating heads or tails, and are successively knocked out by the toss and sit down. The last-standing loser becomes the live hare for an impromptu trail.

Long Beach H3 had a Blue Stain Dress r*n (instead of the traditional Red Dress r*n) at the time of the Monica Lewinsky affair.

Orlando Hashers used to r*n each r*n in any kind of wild costume of their choosing … plus mandatory Mickey Mouse ears. This guaranteed them wanted (and sometimes unwanted) attention when they attended Inter and/or Nash Hash events. They bestow an FRB award on the front r*nner each week. That person must wear an orange dog leash hooked to their waist at the next r*n – that way anyone behind them can give them a yank and slow them down or otherwise plain annoy them.

In one Texas kennel, they have regular naked fire-jumping as part of the circle.

Palm Beach H3 had an 84-year-old lady r*n together with her two daughters – both of them over 50!

Annapolis H3 uses a hospital specimen collection flask for their Down Downs.

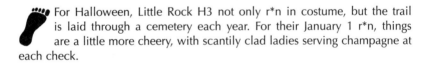

For Halloween, Little Rock H3 not only r*n in costume, but the trail is laid through a cemetery each year. For their January 1 r*n, things are a little more cheery, with scantily clad ladies serving champagne at each check.

Washington DC Hash House Harriettes, after nine years, changed their name by adding 'and Harriers' as a suffix. Mostly the added 'H' is for the female component. Is this the first inversely-sexist kennel in the world to do it the other way round?

Mexico City H3 has been known to hand out copper goat-bells at special occasion r*ns, guaranteeing an almighty clang as the pack thunders past en masse.

At Great Falls H3, Virginia you don't get named until your 100th r*n. Then you get a two-litre silver mug engraved with your name, and a Down Down of course. But the two-litre Down Downs continue each week until the next 'victim' reaches their 100th r*n and you're off the hook.

 Chapter 13 H3 in California r*ns only on the 13th of each month, regardless of what day that is.

 Colorado Full Moon have a Halloween r*n where you have to r*n dressed as your Hash name [Let's hope Mellow Foreskin Cheese never shows up for that! –ed.].

 Minneapolis Full Moon H3 not only Hash on the day of the full moon itself, but at the precise time of the full lunar phase. The whole pack then stares down the moon with a full moon of its own.

 In Orange County they have an annual 'Betty Ford Rehab' r*n. Past years have seen Half Minds turn up dressed as Liberace, Frank Sinatra, baseballer Micky Mantle, and a recent favourite, Harry Connick Jr.

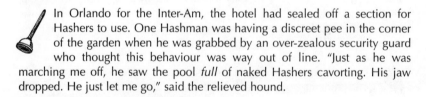 At Cleveland H4, each r*n has a theme, nominated by the hares. "One time we had 'scissors' as the theme, and only one guy managed to poke himself in the eye," says Grandslammer.

In Orlando for the Inter-Am, the hotel had sealed off a section for Hashers to use. One Hashman was having a discreet pee in the corner of the garden when he was grabbed by an over-zealous security guard who thought this behaviour was way out of line. "Just as he was marching me off, he saw the pool *full* of naked Hashers cavorting. His jaw dropped. He just let me go," said the relieved hound.

 At that same Inter-Am, two guys parachuted into the middle of the circle. Both were Hashers. Both were naked.

 Jerry's Kid, a Marine, was not deterred by something so trivial as a broken leg so, despite being in a cast, he rode the trail on his bike. "I got lost and ended up deep in this swamp, carrying my bike above my head," he says. "If it wasn't for my Hash whistle I'd still be out there," he laughs.

 Terra Porcus Lux H3 in Punxsutawney, Pa, has a Ground Hog Day r*n each year, to tie in with the prediction made famous by the Bill Murray movie of whether spring is here or not yet. They make a whole weekend camp out of it. "We basically stand around a campfire all night with only a break to r*n trail and then the survivors can go see Punxsutawney Phil's weather prediction," says Beaver Bam Bam Balls[57]. For this they brave snow and ice in the forest, with the start of the r*n being at the promisingly named Gobblers Knob.

 In April '87 Houston hosted a Doomsday Hash, for which Hashers were encouraged to sell all their possessions, send 'Up U' letters to the IRS and head to the ultimate date with Doomsday destiny. Thirty Half Minds fronted for the r*n, but didn't have the guts to follow instructions to the letter.

"One of my favourite one-liners was when a reporter asked us what we do during hunting season and Wrong Way replied, 'We take off our antlers'," says Wacko of Princeton.

A classic cock-up (or spontaneous joint r*n) happened in Virginia once when Washington DC H3 had laid a trail and – unknown to each other – so had Great Falls H3, in exactly the same area. The first they knew about it, the two packs rounded a corner and came face to face with each other. Much confusion and abuse ensued.

A hare from Sieta Cuerveza H3 in Florida was laying a trail for a town r*n when he came across the body of a homeless guy lying under a bridge, and they had the Florida Law Enforcement investigation team there, rather inconsiderately spoiling his meticulously pre-planned trail route. A slight detour was built into the trail to avoid the stiff. Rumson also came across a stiff on trail … some bloke had gone into the woods and hung himself from a tree.

On an Orlando City r*n, a Hasher broke his ankle rather seriously. His quick-thinking colleagues found a nearby abandoned shopping trolley, loaded him in, and pushed him as fast as they could, whizzing by Universal Studios to the end of the trail. Talk about a basket-case!

Gypsies in the Palace once did a pub r*n, with the trail marked by bar napkins which were indelicately stuck to walls around the city to mark the trail. All was going well until the hare decided it was all too hard, and was last seen in the back of a cab throwing napkins out of the window. Needless to say, half the pack was lost. But they didn't know which half!

Pelvic Congestion H3 in Houston r*ns on the 28th of each month "because it's that time of the month again and there's fuck-all else to do!" These men-only trails are described as "it's long and it's hard, and no woman could take the whole thing". The Harriettes' equivalent, the On the Rag H3, r*ns the same nights.

San Diego Mission Harriettes have an annual leather r*n for which the correct attire is "pants, skirts, strange-looking-used-for-bizarre-sex-acts kinda things, thongs, etc."

 Antarctica H3 once made a spoof bid for Inter-Am, showing tantalising films of penguins, and people freezing their arses off. Needless to say, they didn't get it, but will probably get it before Rumson ever does. Trinidad Inter-Am was also the time that Aviemore (a winter resort in Scotland) very nearly got the vote to host the next Inter-Am, says Scot, Haggissimo. "It was rumoured that Pittsburgh would be the venue unless somebody came up with an alternative. Well that was when Olymprick convinced 2AM and yours truly that we should put in a bid. The news spread like lightning and there was more than just the odd Hasher that was prepared to vote for us. The only reason Inter-Americas never ended up in Aviemore was that Olymprick and I missed the meeting since we'd ended up back at the Hilton Hotel trying to secure the Norwegian vote." They were woken later in the morning by the sound of the hotel maid screaming. "Olymprick and I were both totally legless and lying naked together on the bed … talk about a sight for sore eyes!"

 At the Atlanta Hash, after you r*n five r*ns with them you get your own free AtlantaHash.com email address.

The Nuclear Meltdown Hash – which r*ns in the shadows of the notorious Three Mile Island nuclear facility – always has an alcoholic 'nuclear waste' bright green drink on trail.

At DC's first Red Dress r*n in '94 the trail went into DC via the Memorial Bridge after a rousing Father Abraham on both sides of the major thoroughfare, Wilson Boulevarde. A trek around the Washington Monument was followed by a beer stop along the Potomac (where the pack formed a giant red arrow directing planes to the National Airport). Then the trail led to a Metro ride back to Arlington. Stained Sheets from Mount Vernon H3 jumped the turnstiles at the Metro station after losing his fare card and copped a $40 ticket from the Metro Police for his sins. The r*n was determined a success, and the Red Dress movement is now alive and well in DC. But it could've been a disaster: During scouting of the trail the hares planned on using a particular Metro stop as an egress from the trail to ensure they were one Metro train ahead of the pack. What they didn't know was that particular Metro stop is closed on Saturdays, so the hares were forced to use a different Metro stop. The confusion had our hapless hares get on the train going the *wrong* direction. Which in turn led them to being on the *same* Metro train that the pack was about to board. In their finest red dresses they hid behind some confused and nervous non-Hashers at the very front of the train, until it reached the Rosslyn stop where they exited and ran un-caught to the On On.

The fifth New York (Westchester) H3 AGM expected a promised busload of New York City Hashers, but they never showed up. Instead, Lee Carlson, founder and JM of NYCH3 arrived late, missed the briefing and rapidly disappeared into the snowdrifts of Outer Westchester. Someone had seen him on the trail and his car was at the start, but they never noticed his absence. The temperature then dropped from 45° to 10° F in the space of a couple of hours. "A heroic rescue operation was mounted involving the police in two states, and stoic volunteers with extra rations of beer were deputised and despatched." It turns out that Carlson was lurking 50 yards away waiting to see if he was really missed. "For the next 10 years all subsequent AGMs were subtitled 'Lee Carlson Memorial R*n' just to ensure that he would never attend," says Ian Cumming[74].

At Inter-Am in Philadelphia Garbage Man was named America's most obnoxious Hasher. He carried a confederate flag through the hotel and carried a battery-powered horn that played Dixie all the time. One night they stole his horn and took it to the parking lot where they drove back and forth over it until it was flat as a pancake.

Conversation at the second Alberta Intercourse:
Hotel owner: "You folks are much rowdier than the last group we had here."
King Shit: "Who was that?"
Hotel owner: "The Hell's Angels!"

In 1987, Armadildo Dundee introduced the Pooper Bowl Hashit to the Houston H4. At that stage it was a modest portable bedpan found in the bushes. Now it's a full-on sit-down affair with beer taps, toilet roll holder, huge steer horns, wheels, etc. and still it gets embellishments added each year. The recipient assumes the position on the throne and is then doused with all manner of foodstuffs including spaghetti, sauce, tinned fruit, and so on. One year a whole real plucked duck was placed crown-like on the sinning Harriette's head. Then there's the Down Down, drunk while lying prone under the toilet bowl. "And the Hash thought this was good."

Dick Tracy from Eerie H3 laid the shiggy trail from hell as part of the 'Can-Am thank you ma'am' pre-InterAm bus tour in 1999. "If you just threw old socks in the bin, get these back for the r*n," was the ominous warning from the hare, according to Higgins. A short ride later, the coach stopped along a countryside road next to what looked like wild vegetation after stormy rain. "Knee-deep muddy water is not a very encouraging sign at the start of a trail, and it was getting worse every step," says Higgins. "I almost lost one of my shoes which was sucked by the mud within the first 10 metres, and a couple of minutes later we were waist-deep into it. Without exaggeration, I think at least 80 per cent of the 'trail' was like that."

After half an hour, with no firm land in sight, Dick Tracy was almost lynched when he asked if they were ready for a beer stop. Naturally, they were, but out here??? There couldn't be beer for miles in any direction.

"A short moment before being drowned by the irate Hashers, Dick Tracy pulled a beer crate from under his feet. Not only was it a relieving sight of civilisation among this wilderness, we were also amazed he had been able to bring it all this way while laying the trail." All was momentarily forgiven. Until they had to forge on with the rest of the trail, battling wasp stings which got the pack moving at competitive speeds back to the bus. That night they drank all-night for a fixed fee as increasingly attractive 'beer wenches' cruised the room topping up the Hashers' mugs. All was now definitely forgiven.

Haggissimo recalls the Inter-Am in Trinidad: "I forget the name of the pub that the Hash frequented, but on the first night we rocked into it the place was full of local, er, 'ladies'. The whole place was packed and, since it was a hot sweaty summer night, most of the blokes were only wearing Hash r*nning shorts. Now they're very good for r*nning but they certainly weren't any good at concealing what 'popped up' once dem ladies started their local 'suggestive' dancing. What a sight – about 50 odd drunken Hashmen in an obviously erect state."

"I was a hare for the Inter-Am circa 1988 in San Diego," says Inuendo. "When my co-hares met at the r*n start we were advised that the flour for our trail was stolen out of our co-hare's pick up truck. Since one of the hares, Bambi, had flour, but her part of the trail wasn't until later, we took her flour and had her look for flour once the r*n began. The other hare, Power Lips, went door-to-door in a residential neighbourhood in an attempt to get flour. She eventually got some flour, but the delays caused the pack to catch her and 'pants her' for being caught. As if that little prank wasn't bad enough, I had pre-stashed a cooler full of goodies on the top of this nice scenic hilltop which provided views of the San Diego Harbor as well as the ocean. While re-stashing the cooler in the bushes so that it wouldn't be discovered, and stolen, I gave it one nudge too much and watched in both horror and wet-my-pants-laughter as all the goodies rolled to the bottom of the canyon."

"I went to the Mardi Gras Hash in 1993," says Blue Lugs, an Irish Hasher from Koh Samui, Thailand. "You'd be on a street corner and someone would set up a huge bowl of crawfish, then a U-Haul truck would pull up and this guy in a clown suit got out, opened up the trailer and there'd be three beer taps inside. Guys would stand around getting pissed and showing their dicks and no one took any notice. I mean you're surrounded by things like this nun sitting on a balcony with a beer, a cigarette in the other hand, fishnet stockings, and a hand grenade under the chair. I survived on a diet of Bloody Mary's and jalapeno peppers for four days. It was a good Hash!"

In Washington DC in 1989 a r*n was set through some fields leading to a disused rail cutting. At the disused railway track (minus many rails and sleepers by this stage, such was its state of disrepair), the trail followed the track along for a few hundred yards before disappearing into the old tunnel. The pack was well bunched together. On In! They ran confidently into the blackness of the tunnel, knowing the Hares wouldn't endanger them at all. What they didn't know is that there was a curve in the tunnel – a perfect place for the hares to rig up a 'train' headlight and powerful speaker system. As the Hashers rounded the curve, the prank was activated. Hashers heard the moaning train whistle, saw the train light, and scrambled in every direction for their lives, screaming, trying to scale the crumbling walls. "The pack shat themselves!" said one witness. Slowly, it dawned on them. The light wasn't moving. There were not even any rails for Christ's sake. There was no train. There hadn't been a train on this track for 50 years. Hares 1 – Hounds 0.

More on our website: If you really feel the need to see the Houston Pooper Bowl, and the Rumson rat mascot, plus other glorious moments of Hashit in full colour, go to *www.hash-onon.com*. You'll also find the unedited transcripts of our notes from Major Francis Arnold, Garfield, The Great Kahuna and Ian Cumming.

A R*n In Your Stockings.

The real story of the
Red Dress R*n phenomena.

America's biggest contribution to the Hashing world is arguably the Red Dress R*n. It has become a significant Hash movement in its own right, and thousands upon thousands of Hashers have participated without perhaps knowing where it all started, how it came about, and what they were really celebrating in the first place. Most Hashmen don't care … it gives them a legitimate excuse to do on public streets what they've been doing in private all these years anyway.

The Lady in Red (whose real name and location are known to the author – "You were the one that found me" – but are suppressed by request) tells her side of the story:

"Way back in 1985 a friend that I'd known since high school days, convinced me to come to Long Beach, California, for 'a visit, some beers and to meet a few friends'. So I grabbed a flight from Phoenix, Arizona, a toothbrush and not much more, and headed over to visit." Arriving late in the afternoon, she was met by her friend, 3M, and they stopped for something to drink on the way from the airport.

"He explained over the last of our beers about the double life he was leading, one as the upstanding business individual … and the other as 3M, the Hasher. 'Please come with me on a r*n tonight. You'll see, you'll understand. Oh, and there'll be beer'." She hadn't r*n since school days, and reluctantly agreed, heading to the Long Beach Hash meeting point. "As I got out of his truck I looked around. They looked like a mismatched group out for a field trip to the zoo. [3M] yelled out to the group: 'Listen up! I've got a virgin here that we need to make into a new recruit so make her feel the Hasher welcome!' I'm outgoing and trusted [3M] fully but this, I didn't know about. I was far from home with no ID or means to leave by … and this motley crew was now descending on me! Here I stood in nothing but a summer dress (red with buttons all the way down the front), four-inch red heels, and a red ribbon tying back my blonde curls. I felt, to say the least, like a lamb before Easter!" she says.

With that, 3M called out to the pack: "The damsel needs proper attire!" and they responded immediately. "Suddenly all sorts of shirts, shorts and shoes were being flung in my direction! I quickly sorted through the pile and found a pair of shorts that I slipped on and stuffed the dress into and, flipping off my shoes, wiggled into a pair of sneakers."

Next, she was made to report to the On Sec – "a semi-official looking person (he had a clipboard)" – who told her to fill out the parts about her real name and next of kin information. "My hand began to sweat, my heart to pound, and my mouth became dry. What was I getting myself into? Some strange cult? Becoming a human sacrifice? As I was pondering the papers and the scene before me, a guy with horns on his head and a bugle round his neck asked me if I'd met the hares (talking rabbits???) yet. The guy with the clipboard reappeared, took my scribbled release-from-harm forms, gave me a whistle (in case I got lost) and a huge chunk of chalk."

3M came over and reassured her she was going to love it, dazed and a tad confused as she was. "I took a deep breath, reminded myself that I always believed that life was to be an adventure and that I will try anything once (twice if it doesn't kill me the first time) and joined a group stretching to warm up and pretended that I knew what I was doing."

The r*n itself was *supposed* to be a fairly flat three miler. "Soon after the hare hopped off and I was left in a cloud of dust as everyone disappeared, I began wishing I'd thought this through a bit more. I did get lost a bit but a woman hanging out of a second-storey tenement building pointed out that 'my lily white ass looked like it don't belong around here' and that I should catch up to 'those crazy other folk r*nning four blocks down'. I also remember, while in the same very bad side of town, hearing a bugle blowing and, thinking the group was inside, burst through the door of a stranger's house and yelled 'Where the hell's the beer?' only to find a small child who'd been practising the trumpet standing next to a huge angry black man that explained – as I was offering to apologise – that he didn't allow beer, foul language or scantily clad strangers in his house!"

By now, five miles had already been completed, leaving a one mile r*n in to home. "I finally crawled my way down the beach to the end to join the group that had arrived well before me, and included a five-year-old child and a senior citizen who was recovering from a heart triple bypass surgery. I survived! Then I drank my first Down Down at record-setting speed and demanded a refill that went down just as fast. And as I started my third tankard, debated about if I was going to hit or hug 3M."

So far, it sounds like many a virgin's experience. But then things moved up a notch. The On On moved to a bar at TGI Fridays, where more imbibing went on, pub songs were sung, and a few limericks were learnt. "And taught a few too!" says Lady in Red. The Hash was then thrown out of the bar, despite having ordered food which hadn't yet arrived. Fuzzy Navel and Pokey were there, having spent the afternoon with Luft Schwein, an Orange County Harriette, as were Deep Throat and Strawberry Shortcake from San Diego.

"I believe it was Sandpiper and Gigo who approached me about the Hash buying the beer and moving things back over to my apartment," says Luft Schwein, now in the Middle East, admitting that they didn't realise history was in the making. That, coupled with excess libation, makes some specifics of what transpired that night at her Garden Grove apartment on Blackbird Lane a little difficult to recall.

This night coincided with the opening ceremony of the Calgary Winter Olympics and plenty of parties were going on at the time. Being winter, the apartment's steaming hot tub was a big drawcard. "Everyone in the know of such events had brought a bathing suit or at least had underwear. Since not one of the guys had a bathing suit or shirt to share – or just wanted to test how interesting things could get with only one other female present – all watched to see how I would handle the situation. I looked over at 3M who smiled back knowing I would somehow end up putting the Hashers on the spot. I told them 'No problem!' and slipped the shoes and shorts off and jumped into a hot tub full of only guys, with *only* the famous red dress on," says Lady in Red. "Underwear is not too important to me." One of the Hashers in the tub was Zulu Boy. "We spent the night hot tubbing and, since I hadn't eaten in eight hours, I demanded food. We ate chips as they floated by on a plastic lid from a garbage can."

"She apparently was flirting with the many male Hashers in the tub and Zulu decided to do something about it," says Luft Schwein. "He picked her up over his shoulder (she was still wearing her red dress) and carried her off to my bedroom!"

The party carried on well into the evening, with several sleeping overnight. "I do know that Fuzzy and I were among the ones who slept in the living room and for some reason Toilet Seat got to sleep in my bed and claims he got crabs. So the synopsis is: 3M brought the girl, Zulu had the girl, and Toilet Seat got the crabs!"

The Lady in Red enjoyed her first Hash so much she begged 3M to take her on more Hash r*ns that very weekend. "The last, he dragged me from after protest in order to get me to the airport on time! During that weekend I was deemed by three Hash groups as The Lady in Red and was hooked," she says. Unsurprisingly, it didn't end there.

"We thought it was fitting to honour all slutty women who wear red dresses," says Goulash of San Diego H3 (latterly with New Orleans H3), which decided to commemorate that eventful evening the previous year. "Thence the Red Dress R*n."

"Slutty? Please! As Jessica Rabbit said in Roger Rabbit: 'I'm just drawn that way!'" responds The Lady In Red, who was married "in name only" at the time of her first r*n.

"The following year, I had moved to Houston where the Long Beach Hashers tracked me down, sent tickets and demanded I attend the first annual Lady in Red R*n held in my honour," The Lady in Red remembers. Goulash takes up the story about that first Red Dress r*n in 1986: "It is true that on the morning of the Red Dress r*n I called B100 radio and requested Lady in Red as a reminder to Hashers to wear their red dresses," she says. "They actually spoke with me live on the radio about the Hash! It was a great free advertisement." Still, the disorganisers wondered if anyone else would really buy into this madcap scheme. "Before the r*n we drank champagne and wondered if Hashers would wear red dresses. We were elated – and a little tipsy from the champagne! – to see the ocean of red dresses."

Half Minds who attended the first Red Dress r*n in full regalia included Deep Throat and Mr Spock of SDH3 (who both wore a sarong), Walking Small of OCH3 and his bride Peter Meter, Angelfish, Bambi, Mary Poppins and

Manhandler of SDH3, Dark Tanyan of Long Beach H3, "and host of other names that I can't seem to recall," says Goulash. Californian TV and press turned out in force, too, to witness this sartorial spectacle.

"The original hares were myself, Bumps, and PrimaDonna," says Goulash. "I believe it was opening day at the races in Del Mar or else something big was happening at the Del Mar racetrack that night. We started the r*n at a park in Solana Beach very close to the racetrack. The Hash was a live hare r*n. There were over 100 Hashers and we were worried that we'd get caught because there were some real fast Hashers chasing us. The beer check was at the top of a sandstone cliff which offered a panoramic view of the ocean and the surrounding areas. Very expensive homes are and were located in the area of the beer check. The people who were waiting to get into the Del Mar racetrack on Friday night were entertained by the sea of red climbing up the sandstone cliffs. At the top of the cliffs was the limousine and our limo driver provided the beer to all those who climbed the cliffs."

The Hash covered about five miles and ended in a fellow Hasher's condo clubhouse. "However, we ran like the devil, had a lot of excellent checks and fences, and never got caught," says hare Goulash, who remembers Walking Small complaining about how much money he had spent on his hosiery to only have them last one r*n.

"*The* woman showed up to the r*n," says Goulash referring to The Lady in Red, "and she was awarded a cock whistle for Any Cock Will Do, a bouquet of flowers – handpicked by me – and a $1.99 bottle of cheap red wine. She was simply delighted! There was a giant Jacuzzi that accommodated a good 50 or more Hashers, and she 'Allouetted' in the same red dress and bra. I got a thank you note from her for the wonderful honour and great time she had in San Diego," remembers Goulash, who says it was decided there and then to make it an annual event.

"I was, and still am, overwhelmed at the notoriety and response!" says The Lady in Red. "In my acceptance speech at the crowning ceremony after the first annual Lady in Red r*n, I suggested the one thing that would make me most pleased for the annual event. That was to see a portion of the proceeds to go to worthwhile charities so as to benefit others and to help build a bit of a positive image for Hashers … if that were ever really possible!"

"As for the story about me and the hot tub, I didn't know it too became part of history until one of my sons came home from a bar and told a limerick about a lady in red in a hot tub! I smiled and told him that I knew her," says The Lady in Red, mother of three, the youngest of whom is now 21.

She still Hashes – albeit anonymously – when time permits, the city she's in appeals, and the mood strikes. "Now, every time I see a Lady in Red R*n on the calendar and read of a charity it is for, I can't help but smile and think maybe it's time to take the red dress and shoes out of the closet and attend as *The* Lady in Red!"

A Wag of the Tale.

In a quiet residential street in Hobart, Tasmania, your humble scribe rings the bell on the front door marked '16' and waits. In time, an elderly lady in gardening attire appears at the side. "No one ever uses that door," says Marjorie Kennedy. "Come round the side." At the side door, a smiling John Kennedy extends a warm welcome. "We keep the front door for the Mormons," he says. As he turns, it is with difficulty. He talks of having a hip-replacement operation. He is now 85 years old, but mentally still very astute and a gentleman of great humour.

In true English style, he puts the kettle on. "Coffee?" he offers, surprisingly, for the true Englishman would offer you tea. Then he reaches for a large bottle of Irish whiskey and pours a generous dollop – then a tiny splash more for good effect – into each mug.

We adjourn to his lounge room, a cosy area with deep padded chairs, and walled by books on two sides. Subjects include speaking Malay, the Tasmanian bush, his good friend Cecil Lee's Fall of the Raj, and sailing books. Outside, a beautiful spring day keeps his wife – whose father was Director of Forestry in Malaya – occupied in the garden. Kennedy left Malaya to join the Royal Air Force in 1941. In 1950, he and his family moved to Tasmania. They've been married "61 or 62 years" as of time of writing.

Unbeknown to anyone in Hashing circles, he had been quietly getting on with his life here for the past half century. Kennedy admits that in the intervening 60 years since he last did a Hash trail, his thoughts had never gone back to the Hash. "I always had other things to do. I built myself a boat when I first came out here, went on doing a bit of flying instruction, and so on. I refereed rugby for a while." It was only around 1996 when it was announced that Hobart was bidding to stage InterHash 2000 that he contacted the organisers to wish them well, and stated that he was in fact on that first r*n in Kuala Lumpur. Modestly, he says he feels like "a bit of a fraud" being interviewed about the Hash, but he is a living treasure.

So what was his reaction when he heard of the Hash again after so long? "It brought back memories of how it started. I was very surprised that it had expanded so much and developed. I don't think anyone ever thought it would develop into what it became." From his observations of the InterHash revelry – and his participation taking a boatload of Hashers across to Southport – does he feel it's true to the aims of the founders? "I don't think anyone was thinking that far ahead, but these traditions evolve and get fortified when people go on these InterHashes. I liked it very much. It's obviously a good idea. It's certainly not racist, and uninhibited, and generally people enjoying themselves in a very pleasant harmless way. I thought it was terrific … enjoyed it very much."

Could Kennedy equate the 4,000-strong Cascade-swilling, bugle-blowing, ice-sitting, red dress-wearing crowd to their little group having a couple of Tiger Beers in the tin tailings of Malaya? "It was like the difference between a hamlet and New York," he says, laughing. "The village sports and the Olympic Games."

The pendulum had came full swing. Or, as Cecil Lee once said: "How G would laugh if he knew what had happened!"[76]

– The End. Now sod off! –

Bibliography and Webliography.

The following sources have been shamelessly plundered in the name of research. Numbers refer to corresponding sources quotes used in the text.

1.   10 Times The Cost Of A Haircut – Will LB Bogarde
2.   A Short History of South East Asia – Peter Church
3.   A Walk in The Woods – Bill Bryson
4.   Aarhuis H3 website
5.   Almancil H3 website
6.   Asia Pacific Breweries website
7.   Assuncion H3 website
8.   Auckland H3 '94 magazine
8A.   Aussie Nash Hash magazine 2001
9.   Australian Women's Weekly Dec 2001.
10.   Backdoordwarf's Homepage
11.   Bahrain H3 website
12.   Baldrick's Hasher.net website
13.   Baltimore-Annapolis H3 website
14.   Barnes H3 website
15.   Benghazi H3 3rd Anniversary newsletter
16.   Bicester H3 website
17.   Bill Panton's Hash genealogy chart
18.   Black September to Desert Storm – Claude Salhani
19.   Britain's Small Wars website – Martin Spirit and James Paul
20.   Brunei Hen House Harriers website.
21.   Brussels Manneke Piss H3 website
22.   Budhapest H3 website
23.   Cambridge H3 magazine
24.   Cairo H3 800th 1995
25.   Cairo H3 website
26.   Calgary H3 website
27.   Canberra H3 website
28.   Cecil Lee – personal written account –1958
29.   Twentieth Century Day by Day – A Dorling Kindersley book
30.   Chittagong H3 500th 1994
31.   Costa Rica magazine January 1985
32.   Dallas/Fort Worth H3 website
33.   Dateline Singapore: 150 Years of the Straits Times – CM Turnbull
34.   Dave Cummings website – Captain Zero

35.   DC Red Dress Hash website
36.   Down Under – Bill Bryson
37.   Drake H3 website
38.   Durban H3 1,500th magazine
39.   Espresso With the Headhunters – John Wassner
40.   Expats – Christopher Dickey
41.   Flying Booger's website
42.   Fort Eustis H3 website
43.   Gazeteer of the World – Collins
44.   Glasgow H3 website
45.   Half a Mind – Alice 'Mad Rushin' Johnson
46.   Hamersley H3 website
47.   Hardy's H3 website
48.   Harrier International Magazine
49.   Hash Founder H3 website
50.   Hong Kong H3 1970/71 magazine
50A.   Hong Kong H3 1979/80 magazine
51.   Hong Kong H3 website
52.   Hotel Honolulu – Paul Theroux
53.   Houston H4 website
54.   Hunter H3website.
55.   Iguana H3 website
56.   Inter-Africa Hash program 2001
57.   InterHashional News
58.   Ipoh H3 21st year 1985
59.   Jakarta H3 Yearbook 1985/86
59A.   Jakarta H3 Yearbook 1972/73
60.   KL H3 50th Anniversary Souvenir program 1988
61.   KL H3 3000th magazine.
62.   Kuwait H3 100th 1986
63.   Likk'mm's Swiss Hash website
64.   London City H3 website
65.   Montserrat H3 website
66.   Muscat 1,000th 1995
67.   Muscat 500th 1986
68.   Muscat H3 website
69.   Nairobi H3 website
70.   Naked Island – Russell Braddon
71.   Nancy Wake – Peter FitzSimons
72.   Neptunus' Hash Handle website
73.   New Universal Encyclopedia
74.   New York (Westchester) H3 website.
75.   Notes From a Small Island – Bill Bryson
76.   On! On! 50th Anniversary Tribute – Tim 'Magic' Hughes
77.   Original H3, Nairobi, website

78. Pan-Asia program 2001
80. Perth H3 1,000th magazine 1989
82. Port Moresby H3 150th Run magazine
83. Port Moresby H3 400th Run magazine
84. Princeton H3 website
85. Pristina H3 website
86. Prof's UK Hash website
87. Rome H3 website
88. Royal Milan & Bordighera H3 website
89. San Diego Mission Harriettes website
90. SBS World Guide – Ninth edition
91. Silver Kris magazine – Singapore Airlines
92. Singapore 1,000th magazine 1980
93. Singapore 2,000th magazine 1999
94. Singapore Bike Hash website
95. Singapore Chronicles – Singapore Tatler
96. Singapore H3 30th Anniversary magazine
98. Singapore Hash House Harriettes website
99. Sydney Morning Herald /Cox News
100. Sociology – 7th edition – Craig Calhoun, Donald Light, Suzanne Keller
101. Sunset on the Raj: Fall of Singapore 1942 – Cecil Lee
102. Stray Dog's Global Trash website
103. Surrey H3 20 Years magazine 1995
104. Surrey H3 website
105. Sydney Morning Herald
105A. Sun Herald – October 21, 2001
106. Tahiti – David Howarth
107. Tales from the South China Seas – Charles Allen
108. Tanamera – Noel Barber
109. Tehran H3 magazine 1976/77
110. The Africans – David Lamb
111. The Daily Mail, England, August 29 2001
112. The Natives Were Friendly – Noel Barber
113. The New Standard Encyclopedia
114. The Soccer War – Ryszard Kapuscinski
115. The South African Way Through Europe – Dirk De Villiers
117. The Sydney Morning Herald – October 27-28 2001
118. The War of the Running Dogs – Noel Barber
119. Time.com website
120. Tracy: The Storm That Wiped Out Darwin on Christmas Day 1974 – Gary McKay
122. Washington DC H3 1,000th 1991
123. Hobart Wilderness InterHash magazine 2000
124. Zagreb H3 website

About the Half Mind
Who Wasted His Time On This Book.

Stu 'The Colonel' Lloyd is a tabloid hack. His work has not – and likely never will – grace the pages of salubrious and cerebral publications such as National Geographic, Wall Street Journal, and Mad Magazine. A nomad, he has spent a third of his life in Africa, a third in Asia and a third in Australia. He can't account for the rest of his time. He started Hashing in Hong Kong, then with Singapore Lion City and 'Father' Hashes. Now on a Monday night he can be found right at the back of the Sydney Posh H3 pack. He has Hashed on every continent except Antarctica. Arguably his biggest claim to fame is taking seventh place in the 2002 Australian Potato Carrying Championships (50kg around a racetrack). Harriettes might be interested to know his shoe size: 10EEEE.

If you've got nice things to say, you can contact The Colonel at **hhhareofthedog@hotmail.com** . For complaints or refunds please dial 1-800-WHOGIVESASHIT

HARE OF THE DOG WEBSITE
www.hash-onon.com

For a whole bunch more Hashit from around the world, check out our site… links to major Hash resources, full warts-and-all unedited transcriptions from some of the dogs of note we interviewed, more tips from Hammer on Hashing in extreme climates, Hashers talking about the terrain in their area (and other exotic places they've Hashed in), unloved items salvaged from the cutting-room floor, and a whole lot less …

All of which is just a front to get you to order more copies of the book for yourself or friends directly from our site! (Extra-special deals for bulk buys for your kennel.)

If you have Hashtorical or hysterical photos, stories, or information to add to our collection and knowledge, feel free to submit them. Who knows, we may be mad enough to do this again one day.

Missionaries, mercenaries, misfits and misadventurers in the Middle East and Africa.

Chock-full of anecdotes and interviews with expats, colonials, foreign residents and contractors who've spent time on the Dark Continent and/or the Arabian Peninsula.

The faces and places, highs and lows, trials and tribulations, fights and flights. The best and worst sides of life in this region from the bizarre to the bazaar. Editor now looking for contributions of good yarns and interesting characters to interview.

See www.hardshipposting.com for details, or email The Editor at **WildLifeEditor@hotmail.com**

A new book to be compiled and edited by Stu Lloyd – due for publication late 2003.

Published by Captions of Industry.
ISBN: 0-9578332-8-8

A SPECIAL OFFER FOR SCOTTISH HASHERS*

Captions, publishers of exclusive lifestyle publications to the gentry, are offering a **10% discount** off all our publications to Hashers. Simply type in **HHH** on our website order form where it says 'Discount Code' and you'll be in business.

There's only one condition ... you must promise to keep this a secret - we don't want to be giving the shop away to just any Jock, Dick and Harry.

* Actually, you don't have to be Scottish - any deep-pocketed, short-armed, tight-fisted Half Mind will do.